The Moorad Choudhry Finance Series

Analysing & Interpreting the Yield Curve

The Global Repo Markets: Instruments & Applications

Fixed Income Markets: Instruments, Applications, Mathematics

Structured Credit Products: Credit Derivatives & Synthetic Securitisation

The Money Markets Handbook: A Practitioner's Guide

Published in 2006 by John Wiley & Sons (Asia) Pte Ltd
2 Clementi Loop, #02-01, Singapore 129809

The views, thoughts and opinions expressed in this book are those of the author in his individual capacity and should not in any way be attributed to KBC Financial Products or KBC Bank N.V., or to Moorad Choudhry as a representative, director, or employee of KBC Financial Products or KBC Bank N.V.

Whilst every effort has been made to ensure accuracy, no responsibility for loss occasioned to any person acting or refraining from action as a result of any material in this book can be accepted by the author, publisher or any named person or corporate entity.

No part of this book constitutes investment advice and no part of this book should be construed as such. Neither the author nor the publishers or any named individual or entity is soliciting any action, response or trade in response to anything written in this book.

The material in this book is based on information that is considered reliable, but neither the author nor the publishers warrant that it is accurate or complete, and it should not be relied on as such. Opinions expressed are current opinions only and are subject to change. The author and publishers are not soliciting any action based upon this material. Moorad Choudhry and any named person or entity may or may not have a position in any capital-market instrument described in this book, at the time of writing or subsequently. Any such position is subject to change at any time and for any reason.

Other Wiley Editorial Offices

John Wiley & Sons, Inc., 111 River Street, Hoboken, NJ 07030, USA
John Wiley & Sons Ltd, The Atrium, Southern Gate, Chichester PO19, BSQ, England
John Wiley & Sons (Canada) Ltd, 5353 Dundas Street West, Suite 400, Toronto, Ontario M9B 6H8 Canada
John Wiley & Sons Australia Ltd, 42 McDougall Street, Milton, Queensland 4064, Australia
Wiley-VCH, Boschstrasse 12, D-69469, Weinheim, Germany

Library of Congress Cataloging-in-Publication Data
ISBN-13 978-0-470-82177-0
ISBN-10 0-470-82177-9

Typeset in 10.5/13 points, Times by Paul Lim
Printed in Singapore by Saik Wah Press Pte Ltd
10 9 8 7 6 5 4 3 2 1

the interest rate charged by the bank may be comparatively high for all but the highest quality companies. We say comparatively, because there is often a cheaper way for corporates to borrow money: by tapping the bond markets. An issue of bonds will fix the rate of interest payable by the company for a long-term period, and the chief characteristic of bonds – that they are *tradeable* – makes investors more willing to lend funds to a company.

Bond markets play a vital and essential role in raising finance for both governments and corporations. In 2004 the market in dollar-denominated bonds alone was worth over $13.5 trillion, which gives some idea of its importance. The basic bond instrument, which is a loan of funds by the buyer to the issuer of the bond, in return for regular interest payments up to the termination date of the loan, is still the most commonly issued instrument in the debt markets. Nowadays there is a large variety of bond instruments, issued by a variety of institutions. An almost exclusively corporate instrument, the international bond or Eurobond, is a large and diverse market. In 2004 the size of the Eurobond market was over $2.3 trillion.

Corporate entities also raise funds in the money markets. Although viewed traditionally as the preserve of the interbank market, they are now a vital conduit for the issuing and investing of cash for non-bank institutions. For example, the commercial paper market is now frequently accessed directly by large corporations wishing to raise funds of anything from one month to twelve months maturity. Smaller corporations also tap this market, but via dealer banks who act as a sort of broker for them. For this reason, we also cover in this book that part of the money markets that are of relevance to corporate borrowers.

Organisation of the book

This book is organised into 21 chapters. The corporate debt markets are extremely diverse, and it is often in corporate markets that the latest and most exciting innovations are found. Some of the instruments used in the corporate markets demand their own particular type of analysis; to this end we review the pricing and analytics of callable bonds, asset-backed bonds and convertibles, among others. There is also a chapter on credit analysis.

For beginners we have chapters on bond basics, including bond mathematics and an introduction to the yield curve. The chapters then go on to cover some of the most recent developments including:

- hybrid securities, and securities such as index-linked bonds;

Acknowledgments

To Anuk who has lit the pathway of my struggle with her lamp-like joy…

Thanks to some top people who were there for me when I really needed it… 4th time lucky eh guys? It's really great to know you… so lets big it up for Rod Pienaar, Nick Procter, Mike Hellmuth, Mark Burgess, Harry Cross, Neil Lewis, ("the lads will always be behind you – see you at football tomorrow"), Mike Brand, Abukar Ali, Jason Feasey, Richard Pereira, Didier Joannas, Khurram Butt, Michael Nicoll, Jonathan Rossington, Stuart Medlen, Jaz Ghag, Ketul Tanna, Suleman Baig, Kevin Liu, John Key, Brian Eales and Mo Dualeh … top guys and legends all. Love and respect.

Tony Fulling, thanks for being a top man and for some legendary quotes from the football pitch … my particular favourites include one about me:

"He sussed that equation out long ago …",

and one about the incomparable Alan Fulling, who has inspired me on countless occasions during the last five years:

"There's the benefits of a fat backside …!"

Priceless!

Big thanks to Michael Beddow at JPMorgan Chase who organises the same game, your movement on the pitch is pure poetry!

Craig Wotherspoon has an interesting idea on the value of a perpetual zero-coupon bond … surely obvious, right? But is it always zero? What about on a company with a credit default swap written on it trading at 500 bps? Intriguing …!

Thanks to Maj Haque, Niall Considine and Serj Walia at KBC Financial Products for helping me to keep in touch with those parts of the markets I'm not directly involved in! It is a great pleasure to work with you, and also to add to your p&l with our latest funding rates ☺

Thanks to Chris Cooper at Martin Brokers for the euro rates screen … managed to get your name in this book ahead of those legendary faces in the market, Dan Cunningham and Gavin Allan at KBC Bank in London – a privilege and my pleasure to help you chaps retain the Kelvin Watson trophy for the second year running!

It's my privilege to know and work with some top money market guys, big thanks to CP gurus Eric Subliskey (that's the mighty Eric Subliskey) at

Special mention for the mighty Treasury Support team, fabulous professionals all ("if it moves we can settle it"), that'll be Matt, Mark, Brian, Heather, Majid and Leigh - thanks for looking after me guys. It's been emotional.

Finally, and as anyone who has worked for him will know, thanks to the main man, Carlo Georg. Respect. Nuff said …

Moorad Choudhry
Surrey, England
September 2005

I'm a thousand miles from nowhere,
Time don't matter to me,
Cos I'm a thousand miles from nowhere,
And there's no place I want to be…

I got heartaches in my pocket,
I got echoes in my head,
And all that I keep hearing,
Are the cruel, cruel things that you said…

I got bruises on my memory,
I got tear stains on my hands,
And in the mirror there's a vision,
Of what used to be a man…

— Dwight Yoakam
A Thousand Miles From Nowhere (Coal Dust Music) 1992

I don't ask for much, I only want trust.
– Ringo Starr
It Don't Come Easy (EMI Apple) 1971

There ain't nothing wrong with nostalgia.

– Phil Broadhurst, Somewhere in England...

I love a good [five-a-side football] tournament.

– Jonathan Rossington, July 2004

No-one should be expected to go off to school or to work, or to join the army, without someone to kiss him goodbye.

We all need someone to kiss us goodbye.

– Marcie to Peppermint Patty,
from *You're Our Kind of Dog, Snoopy*
Charles M Schulz (Coronet Books) 1978

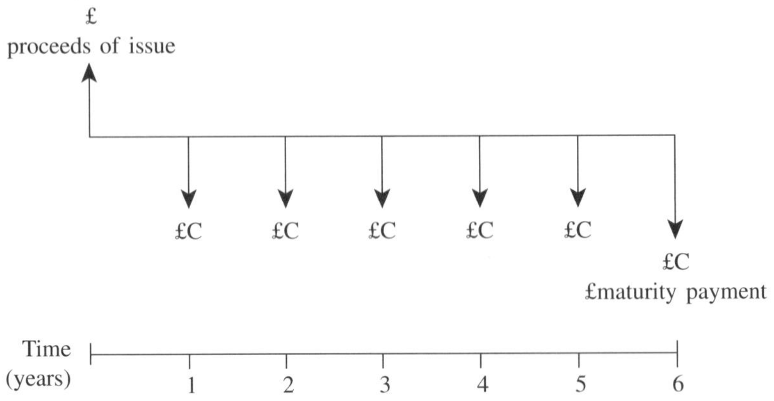

Figure 1.1 Cash flows associated with a six-year annual coupon bond

The upward-facing arrow represents the cash flow paid and the downward-facing arrows are the cash flows received by the bond investor. The cash flow diagram for a six-year bond that had a 5% fixed interest rate, known as a 5% *coupon*, would show interest payments of £5 per every £100 of bonds, with a final payment of £105 in the sixth year, representing the last coupon payment and the redemption payment. Again, the amount of funds raised per £100 of bonds depends on the price of the bond on the day it is first issued, and we will look further into this later. If our example bond paid its coupon on a semi-annual basis, the cash flows would be £2.50 every six months until the final redemption payment of £102.50.

Let us examine some of the key features of bonds.

Type of issuer

A primary distinguishing feature of a bond is its issuer. The nature of the issuer will affect the way the bond is viewed in the market. There are four issuers of bonds: sovereign governments and their agencies, local government authorities, supranational bodies such as the World Bank, and corporations. Within the corporate bond market there is a wide range of issuers, each with differing abilities to satisfy their contractual obligations to investors. The largest bond markets are those of sovereign borrowers, the government bond markets. The United Kingdom government issues *gilts*. In the United States, government bonds are known as *Treasury Notes* and *Treasury Bonds*, or simply *Treasuries*.

Currency

Bonds can be issued in virtually any currency. The largest volume of bonds in the global markets is denominated in US dollars; other major bond markets are denominated in euros, Japanese yen and sterling, and liquid markets also exist in Australian, New Zealand and Canadian dollars, Swiss francs and other major currencies. The currency of issue may impact on a bond's attractiveness and liquidity, which is why borrowers in developing countries often elect to issue in a currency other than their home currency, for example dollars, as this will make it easier to place the bond with investors. If a bond is aimed solely at a country's domestic investors it is more likely that the borrower will issue in the home currency.

Bond issuers

Issuers and participants

In most countries, government expenditure exceeds the level of government income received through taxation. This shortfall is made up by government borrowing and bonds are issued to finance the government's debt. The core of any domestic capital market is usually the government bond market, which also forms the benchmark for all other borrowing.

Gilts are identified by their coupon rate and year of maturity; they are also given names such as *Treasury* or *Exchequer*. There is no significance attached to any particular name – all gilts are equivalent irrespective of their name. If we are told that a stock has a closing price from the day before of 106.77, this means £106.77 of par value. (Remember that par is the lump sum paid at maturity.) This price might represent a *gross redemption yield* of 4.65%. If we pay £106.77 per £100 of stock today, we will receive £100 per £100 of stock on maturity. At first sight this appears to imply we will lose money; however, we also receive coupon payments every six months, which for this bond is £2.875 per £100 nominal of stock.

Government agencies also issue bonds. Such bonds are virtually as secure as government bonds. In the United States, agencies include the Federal National Mortgage Association. Local authorities issue bonds as part of financing for roads, schools, hospitals and other capital projects.

Corporate borrowers issue bonds both to raise finance for major projects and also to cover ongoing and operational expenses. Corporate finance is a mixture of debt and equity, and a specific capital project will often be financed as a mixture of both.

and pass the funds raised to this customer, is known as *origination*. Investment banks will also carry out a range of other functions for institutional customers, including export finance, corporate advisory and fund management. Other financial intermediaries will trade not on behalf of clients but for their own *book*. These include *arbitrageurs* and speculators. Usually such market participants form part of investment banks.

Investors

There is a large variety of players in the bond markets, each trading some or all of the different instruments available to suit their own purposes. We can group the main types of investors according to the time horizon of their investment activity.

Short-term institutional investors

These include banks and building societies, money market fund managers, central banks and the treasury desks of some types of corporates. Such bodies are driven by short-term investment views, often subject to close guidelines, and will be driven by the total return available on their investments. Banks will have an additional requirement to maintain *liquidity*, often in fulfilment of regulatory authority rules, by holding a proportion of their assets in the form of easily tradeable short-term instruments.

Long-term institutional investors

Typically these types of investors include pension funds and life assurance companies. Their investment horizon is long-term, reflecting the nature of their liabilities. Often they will seek to match these liabilities by holding long-dated bonds.

Mixed horizon institutional investors

This is possibly the largest category of investors and will include general insurance companies and most corporate bodies. Like banks and financial sector companies, they are also very active in the primary market, issuing bonds to finance their operations.

Market professionals

This category includes the banks and specialist financial intermediaries mentioned above, firms that one would not automatically classify as "investors" although they will also have an investment objective. Their time horizon will range from one day to the very long term. They include the proprietary trading desks of investment banks, as well as bond market-makers in securities houses and banks who are providing a service to their customers. Proprietary traders will actively position themselves in the market in order to gain trading profit; for example, in response to their view on where they think interest rate levels are headed. These participants will trade direct with other market professionals and investors, or via brokers. Market-makers or *traders* (also called *dealers* in the United States) are wholesalers in the bond markets; they make two-way prices in selected bonds. Firms will not necessarily be active market-makers in all types of bonds; smaller firms often specialise in certain sectors. In a two-way quote the *bid price* is the price at which the market-maker will buy stock, so it is the price the investor will receive when selling stock. The *offer price* or *ask price* is the price at which investors can buy stock from the market-maker. As one might expect the bid price is always higher than the offer price, and it is this *spread* that represents the theoretical profit to the market-maker. The bid-offer spread set by the market-maker is determined by several factors, including supply and demand, and liquidity considerations for that particular stock, the trader's view on market direction and *volatility*, as well as that of the stock itself and the presence of any market intelligence. A large bid–offer spread reflects low liquidity in the stock, as well as low demand.

Markets

Markets are that part of the financial system where capital market transactions, including the buying and selling of securities, takes place. A market can describe a traditional stock exchange, a physical trading floor where securities trading occurs. Many financial instruments are traded over the telephone or electronically over computer links; these markets are known as *over-the-counter* (OTC) markets. A distinction is made between financial instruments of up to one year's maturity and instruments of over one year's maturity. Short-term instruments make up the *money market* while all other instruments are deemed to be part of the *capital market*. There is also a distinction made between the *primary market* and the *secondary market*. A new issue of bonds made by an investment bank on behalf of its client is made in the primary market. Such an issue can be a *public* offer, in which anyone can apply to buy the bonds, or a *private* offer where the customers of the investment bank are offered the stock. The secondary market is the market in which existing bonds and shares are subsequently traded.

World bond markets

The origin of the spectacular increase in the size of global financial markets was the rise in oil prices in the early 1970s. Higher oil prices stimulated the development of a sophisticated international banking system, as they resulted in large capital inflows to developed country banks from the oil-producing countries. A significant proportion of these capital flows were placed in *Eurodollar* deposits in major banks. The growing trade deficit and level of public borrowing in the United States also contributed. The last twenty years has seen tremendous growth in capital markets' volumes and trading. As capital controls were eased and exchange rates moved from fixed to floating, domestic capital markets became internationalised. Growth was assisted by the rapid advance in information technology and the widespread use of financial engineering techniques. Today we would think nothing of dealing in virtually any liquid currency bond in financial centres around the world, often at the touch of a button. Global bond issues, underwritten by the subsidiaries of the same banks, are commonplace. The ease with which transactions can be undertaken has also contributed to a very competitive market in liquid currency assets.

The world bond market has increased in size more than fifteen times in the last thirty years. As at the end of 2004, outstanding volume stood at over $21 trillion.

Country	Nominal value ($ billion)	Percentage (rounded)
United States	5,490	48.5
Japan	2,980	26.3
Germany	1,236	10.9
France	513	4.5
Canada	335	3.0
United Kingdom	331	2.9
Netherlands	253	2.2
Australia	82	0.7
Denmark	72	0.6
Switzerland	37	0.3
Total	11,329	100.0

Table 1.1 Major government bond markets, December 2004
Source: IFC *World Statistics*, January 2005.

market in US Treasury securities is the largest bond market in the ike the government bond markets in the United Kingdom, Germany, nd other developed economies, it is also very liquid and transparent. l lists the major government bond markets in the world; the US nakes up nearly half of the total. The Japanese market is second in lowed by the German market. A large part of the government bond s concentrated therefore in just a few countries. Government bonds ed on major exchanges as well as OTC. Generally, OTC refers to hat are not carried out on an exchange but directly between the arties. Bonds are also listed on exchanges; for example, the NYSE 600 government issues listed on it at the end of 1998, with a total e of $2.6 billion.

corporate bond market varies in liquidity, depending on the currency of issuer of any particular bond. Outstanding volume as at the end as over $7.9 trillion. Corporate bonds are also traded on exchanges One of the most liquid corporate bond types is the *Eurobond*, n international bond issued and traded across national boundaries. anies finance their operations in a number of ways, from equity to debt such as bank overdrafts. It is often advantageous for to fix longer term finance, which is why bonds are so popular. also attractive as a means of raising finance because the interest n them to investors is tax deductible for the company. Dividends e not tax deductible. A corporate needs to get a reasonable mix sus equity in its funding, however, as a high level of interest ill be difficult to service in times of recession or general market For this reason the market views unfavourably companies that level of debt.

ventional bonds

on of bonds given earlier in this chapter referred to conventional *nilla* bonds. There are many variations on vanilla bonds and we ce a few of them here.

ate notes

arket is often referred to as the *fixed income* market, or the *fixed* ket in the United Kindom. Floating rate notes (FRNs) do not pon at all but instead link their interest payments to an e, such as the three-month bank lending rate. Bank interest rates will fluctuate constantly during the life of the bond and so an FRN's cash flows are not known with certainty. Usually, FRNs pay a fixed margin or *spread* over the specified reference rate; occasionally the spread is not fixed and such a bond is known as a *variable rate note*. Because FRNs pay coupons based on the three-month or six-month bank rate they trade essentially as money market instruments.

Index-linked bonds

An index-linked bond has its coupon and redemption payment, or possibly just either one of these, linked to a specified index. When governments issue index-linked bonds, the cash flows are linked to a price index such as consumer or commodity prices. Corporates have issued index-linked bonds that are connected to inflation or a stock market index.

Zero-coupon bonds

Certain bonds do not make any coupon payments at all and these are known as *zero-coupon bonds*. A zero-coupon bond or *strip* only has cash flow, the redemption payment, on maturity. If we assume that the maturity payment is, say, £100 per cent or *par*, the issue price will be at a discount to par. Such bonds are also known therefore as *discounted* bonds. The difference between the price paid on issue and the redemption payment is the interest realised by the bondholder. This has certain advantages for investors, the main one being that there are no coupon payments to be invested during the bond's life. Both governments and corporates issue zero-coupon bonds. Conventional coupon-bearing bonds can be *stripped* into a series of individual cash flows, which would then trade as separate zero-coupon bonds. This is a common practice in government bond markets such as Treasuries or gilts, where the borrowing authority does not actually issue strips, and they have to be created via the stripping process by market-makers.

Securitised bonds

There is a large market in bonds whose interest and principal liability payments are backed by an underlying cash flow from another asset. By securitising the asset, a borrower can provide an element of cash flow backing to investors. For instance, a mortgage bank can use the cash inflows it receives on its mortgage book as asset backing for an issue of bonds. Such an issue would be known as a mortgage-backed security (MBS). Because

bond, or "per cent". So, for example, if the all-in price of a US dollar denominated bond is quoted as "98.00", this means that for every $100 nominal of the bond a buyer would pay $98. The interest rate or discount rate used as part of the present value (price) calculation is the key to everything, as it reflects where the bond is trading in the market and how it is perceived by the market. All the determining factors that identify the bond – those discussed in this chapter and including the type of issuer, the maturity, the coupon and the currency – influence the interest rate at which a bond's cash flows are discounted, which will be roughly similar to the rate used for comparable bonds.

Since the price of a bond is equal to the present value of its cash flows, first we need to know the bond's cash flows before then determining the appropriate interest rate at which to discount the cash flows. We can then compute the price of the bond.

Bond cash flows

A vanilla bond's cash flows are the interest payments or coupons that are paid during the life of the bond, together with the final redemption payment. It is possible to determine the cash flows with certainty only for conventional bonds of a fixed maturity. So, for example, we do not know with certainty what the cash flows are for bonds that have embedded options and can be redeemed early. The coupon payments for conventional bonds are made annually, semi-annually or quarterly. Some bonds pay monthly interest.

Therefore a conventional bond of fixed redemption date is made up of an annuity (its coupon payments) and the maturity payment. If the coupon is paid semi-annually, this means exactly half the coupon is paid as interest every six months. Both gilts and US Treasuries pay semi-annual coupons. For example, the 5% 2012 gilt has the following cash flows:

$$\begin{aligned} \text{Semi-annual coupon} &= £100 \times 0.025 \\ &= £2.50 \\ \text{Redemption payment} &= £100 \end{aligned}$$

The bond was issued on 23 June 1999 and is redeemed on 7 March 2012, and pays coupon on 7 March and 7 September each year. So in 2002 the bond is made up of 20 cash flows of £2.50 and one of £100. The time between coupon payments for any bond is counted as one period, so there

$$P = C\,\frac{1 - \left[\dfrac{1}{(1+r)^N}\right]}{r}$$

or

$$P = \frac{C}{r}\left[1 - \frac{1}{(1+r)^N}\right]. \qquad (1.2)$$

The price of a bond that pays semi-annual coupons is given by the expression at (1.3), which is our earlier expression modified to allow for the twice-yearly discounting:

$$P = \frac{\frac{C}{2}}{(1+\frac{1}{2}r)} + \frac{\frac{C}{2}}{(1+\frac{1}{2}r)^2} + \frac{\frac{C}{2}}{(1+\frac{1}{2}r)^3} + \ldots + \frac{\frac{C}{2}}{(1+\frac{1}{2}r)^{2N}} + \frac{M}{(1+\frac{1}{2}r)^{2N}}$$

$$= \sum_{t=1}^{2T} \frac{\frac{C}{2}}{(1+\frac{1}{2}r)^N} + \frac{M}{(1+\frac{1}{2}r)^{2N}}$$

$$= \frac{C}{r}\left[1 - \frac{1}{\left[(1+\frac{1}{2}r)^{2N}\right]} + \frac{M}{(1+\frac{1}{2}r)^{2N}}\right]. \qquad (1.3)$$

Note how we set $2N$ as the power to which to raise the discount factor, as there are two interest payments every year for a bond that pays semi-annually. Therefore a more convenient function to use might be the number of interest periods in the life of the bond, as opposed to the number of years to maturity, which we could set as n, allowing us to alter the equation for a semi-annually paying bond as:

$$P = \frac{C}{r}\left[1 - \frac{1}{(1+\frac{1}{2}r)^n}\right] + \frac{M}{(1+\frac{1}{2}r)^n}. \qquad (1.4)$$

where the variables C, M, n and r are as before. Note that (1.5) assumes r for an annually paying bond and is adjusted to $r/2$ for a semi-annually paying bond.

EXAMPLE 1.1 Bond pricing calculations

In these examples we illustrate the long-hand price calculation, using both expressions for the calculation of the present value of the annuity stream of a bond's cash flows.

1.1(a)

Calculate the fair pricing of a UK gilt, the 9% Treasury 2008, which pays semi-annual coupons, with the following terms:

C = £9.00 per £100 nominal
M = £100
N = 10 years (i.e., the calculation is for value on 13 October 1998)
r = 4.98%

$$P = \frac{£9.00}{0.0498}\left[1 - \frac{1}{\left[1 + \frac{1}{2}(0.0498)\right]^{20}}\right] + \frac{£100}{\left[1 + \frac{1}{2}(0.0498)\right]^{20}}$$

$$= £70.2175 + £61.1463$$

$$= £131.3638$$

The fair price of the gilt is £131.3638, which is composed of the present value of the stream of coupon payments (£70.2175) and the present value of the return of the principal (£61.1463).

1.1(b)

What is the price of a 5% coupon sterling bond with precisely five years to maturity, with semi-annual coupon payments, if the yield required is 5.40%?

As the cash flows for this bond are 10 semi-annual coupons of £2.50 and a redemption payment of £100 in 10 six-month periods from now, the price of the bond can be obtained by solving the

$$P = 2.5\left[\frac{1 - \frac{1}{(1.03)^{10}}}{0.03}\right] + \frac{100}{(1.03)^{10}}$$

$$= £21.325507 + £74.409391$$

$$= £95.734898$$

As the required yield has risen, the discount rate used in the price calculation is now higher, and the result of the higher discount is a lower present value (price).

1.1(e)

Calculate the price of our sterling bond, still with five years to maturity but offering a yield of 5.10%.

$$P = 2.5\left[\frac{1 - \frac{1}{(1.0255)^{10}}}{0.0255}\right] + \frac{100}{(1.0255)^{10}}$$

$$= £21.823737 + £77.739788$$

$$= £99.563525$$

To satisfy the lower required yield of 5.10% the price of the bond has fallen to £99.56 per £100.

1.1(f)

Calculate the price of the 5% sterling bond one year later, with precisely four years lẹft to maturity and with the required yield still at the original 5.40%. This sets the terms in 2.1(a) unchanged, except now $n = 8$.

$$P = 2.5\left[\frac{1 - \frac{1}{(1.027)^{8}}}{0.027}\right] + \frac{100}{(1.027)^{8}}$$

African and Indian government bonds, quote prices in *ticks*, where the minimum increment is 1/32nd. One tick is therefore equal to 0.03125. A US Treasury might be priced at "98–05", which means "98 and 5 ticks". This is equal to 98 and 5/32nds, which is 98.15625.

EXAMPLE 1.2 Consideration

- What is the total consideration for £5 million nominal of a gilt, where the price is 114.50?

The price of the gilt is £114.50 per £100, so the consideration is:

$$1.145 \times 5{,}000{,}000 = £5{,}725{,}000$$

- What consideration is payable for $5 million nominal of a US Treasury, quoted at an all-in price of 99–16?

The US Treasury price is 99–16, which is equal to 99 and 16/32, or 99.50 per $100. The consideration is therefore:

$$0.9950 \times 5{,}000{,}000 = \$4{,}975{,}000$$

If the price of a bond is below par, the total consideration is below the nominal amount, whereas if it is priced above par the consideration will be above the nominal amount.

Clean and dirty bond prices

Accrued interest

Our discussion of bond pricing up to now has ignored coupon interest. All bonds (except zero-coupon bonds) accrue interest on a daily basis, and this is then paid out on the coupon date. The calculation of bond prices using present value analysis does not account for coupon interest or *accrued interest*. In all major bond markets the convention is to quote price as a *clean price*. This is the price of the bond as given by the net present value of its cash flows, but excluding coupon interest that has accrued on the bond since the last dividend payment. As all bonds accrue interest on a daily basis, even if a bond is held for only one day, interest will have been earned by the bondholder. However, we have referred already to a bond's *all-in* price, which is the price that is actually paid for the bond in the market. This is also known as the *dirty price* (or *gross price*), which is the clean price of a bond

without accrued interest are said to be trading *flat* or *clean*. By definition therefore,

$$\text{Clean price of a bond} = \text{Dirty price} - AI.$$

For bonds that are trading ex-dividend, the accrued coupon is negative and would be subtracted from the clean price. The calculation is given by (1.8) below.

$$AI = -C \times \frac{\text{Days to next coupon}}{\text{Day base}} \tag{1.8}$$

Certain classes of bonds, for example US Treasuries and Eurobonds, do not have an ex-dividend period and therefore trade cum dividend right up to the coupon date.

Accrual day count conventions

The accrued interest calculation for a bond is dependent on the day-count basis specified for the bond in question. We have already seen that when bonds are traded in the market the actual consideration that changes hands is made up of the clean price of the bond together with the accrued that has accumulated on the bond since the last coupon payment; these two components make up the dirty price of the bond. When calculating the accrued interest, the market will use the appropriate day-count convention for that bond. A particular market will apply one of five different methods to calculate accrued interest; these are:

actual/365	Accrued = Coupon × Days/365
actual/360	Accrued = Coupon × Days/360
actual/actual	Accrued = Coupon × Days/actual number of days in the interest period
30/360	See below
30E/360	See below

Figure 1.2 below shows the three-month period beginning 15 August 2003 in the UK market; we see that for a 30/360 day-count bond this is 93 days and also note that there is a public holiday in the UK market during this period.

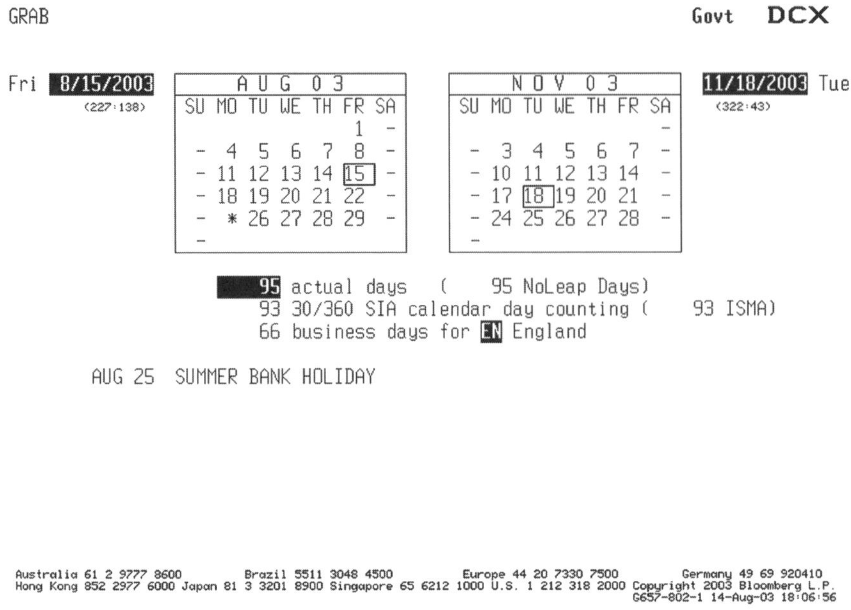

Figure 1.2 Bloomberg screen DCX
© Bloomberg L.P. Used with permission.

EXAMPLE 1.3 Accrual calculation for 7% Treasury 2008

This gilt has coupon dates of 7 June and 7 December each year. £100 nominal of the bond is traded for value on 27 August 1998. What is the accrued interest on the value date?

On the value date 81 days have passed since the last coupon date. Under the old system for gilts, act/365, the calculation was:

$$7 \times \frac{81}{365} = 1.55342.$$

see that it is not price changes that we are really interested in, but yields. It is a change in required yield that will drive a change in price.[1] So in the bond market we are concerned with examining the determinants of market yields.

The main quoted yield in any market is the government bond yield. This is the yield on a domestic market's government bonds. The required yield on these bonds is mainly a function of the central bank's *base rate* or *minimum lending rate*, set by the government or central bank. Other factors will also impact the yield, including the relative size of the public-sector budget deficit and national debt as a percentage of the national product (usually measured as gross domestic product or gross national product), the economic policies that are adopted, and of course supply and demand for government bonds themselves. A change in any of these factors can and does affect government bond prices. While it is common to view government bonds as the safest credit for investors, this really only applies to the largest developed country markets. Certain countries within the Organisation for Economic Co-operation and Development (OECD), for example, Greece, South Korea and Mexico, do not have their government debt given the highest possible rating by credit analysts.

Bonds issued by non-sovereign borrowers will be priced off government bonds, which means that the yields required on them will be at some level above their respective government bond yields, if they are domestic currency bonds. Bond yields are often quoted as a *yield spread* over the equivalent government bond. This is known as the *credit spread* on a bond. A change in the required credit spread for any bond will affect the bond's price. Credit spreads will fluctuate for a variety of reasons, including when there is a change in the way the borrower is perceived in the market (such as a poor set of financial results by a corporate), which will affect the rate at which the borrower can raise funds. Credit spreads can sometimes change because comparable bonds yield change, as well as due to supply and demand factors and liquidity factors.

Yield measurement

Bonds are generally traded on the basis of their prices, but because of the complicated patterns of cash flows that different bonds can have, they are

[1] We have observed how the price of a bond will gradually converge towards par as it approaches maturity, irrespective of the price it trades at during its life. However, this is an automatic process and a mechanical price change that is part of the properties of a bond. As such it need not concern us unduly.

coupon income as a proportion of the price paid for the bond, and to be accurate would have to assume that the bond was more like an annuity rather than a fixed-term instrument.

The current yield is useful as a "rough-and-ready" interest rate calculation; it is often used to estimate the cost of or profit from a short-term holding of a bond. For example, if other short-term interest rates such as the one-week or three-month rates are higher than the current yield, holding the bond is said to involve a *running cost*. This is also known as *negative carry* or *negative funding*. The term is used by bond traders and market-makers and *leveraged* investors. The *carry* on a bond is a useful measure for all market practitioners as it illustrates the cost of holding or funding a bond. The funding rate is the bondholder's short-term cost of funds. A private investor could also apply this to a short-term holding of bonds.

EXAMPLE 1.6 Running yield

A bond with a coupon of 6% is trading at a clean price of 97.89. What is the current yield of the bond?

$$rc = \frac{6.00}{97.89} \times 100$$

$$= 6.129\%$$

EXAMPLE 1.7 Current Yield

What is the current yield of a bond with 7% coupon and a clean price of 103.49?

$$rc = \frac{7}{103.49} \times 100$$

$$= 6.76\%$$

Note from examples 1.6 and 1.7 that the current yield of a bond will lie above the coupon rate if the price of the bond is below par, and vice-versa if the price is above par.

$$P = \sum_{n=1}^{N} \frac{C}{(1 + rm)^n} + \frac{M}{(1 + rm)^n} \tag{1.11}$$

Note that the expression at (1.11) has two variable parameters, the price *Pd* and yield *rm*. It cannot be rearranged to solve for yield *rm* explicitly and in fact the only way to solve for the yield is to use the process of numerical iteration. The process involves estimating a value for *rm* and calculating the price associated with the estimated yield. If the calculated price is higher than the price of the bond at the time, the yield estimate is lower than the actual yield, and so it must be adjusted until it converges to the level that corresponds with the bond price.[3] For YTM for a semi-annual coupon bond we have to adjust the formula to allow for the semi-annual payments. Equation (1.11) is modified as shown by (1.12), again assuming there are precisely six months to the next coupon payment.

$$P = \sum_{n=1}^{N} \frac{\frac{C}{2}}{\left[1 + \frac{1}{2}rm\right]^n} + \frac{M}{\left[1 + \frac{1}{2}rm\right]^n} \tag{1.12}$$

where *n* is now the number of interest periods in the life of the bond and therefore equal to the number of years to maturity multiplied by two.

All the YTM equations above use *rm* to discount a bond's cash flows back to the next coupon payment and then discount the value at that date back to the date of the calculation. In other words, *rm* is the internal rate of return that equates the value of the discounted cash flows on the bond to the current dirty price of the bond (at the current date). The internal rate of return is the discount rate that, if applied to all of the cash flows, will solve for a number that is equal to the dirty price of the bond (its present value). By assuming that this rate will be unchanged for the reinvestment of all the coupon cash flows, and that the instrument will be held to maturity, the IRR can then be seen as the yield to maturity. In effect, both measures are identical; the assumption of uniform reinvestment rate allows us to calculate the IRR as equivalent to the redemption yield. It is common for the IRR measure to be used by corporate financiers for project appraisal, while the redemption yield measure is used in bond markets. The solution to the equation for *rm* cannot be found analytically and has to be solved through numerical iteration; that is, by estimating the yield from two trial values for

[3] Bloomberg L.P. also uses the term yield-to-workout where "workout" refers to the maturity date for the bond.

EXAMPLE 1.8 Comparing the different yield measures

Assume a five-year bond with a coupon of 6% trading at a price of 97.89. Using the three common measures of return we would have:

Running yield = 6.129%
Simple yield = 6.560%
Redemption yield = 6.50%

Bond pricing and yield

The approach we have described is very much the traditional one. Academic texts express bond prices and yields in different terms, which we consider briefly now. The terminology is that used in leading texts, including Jarrow (1996), Neftci (1996), Baxter and Rennie (1996), and Hull (1997).

Consider a zero-coupon bond that has a maturity date at time T. The price of this bond today (at time t) is denoted by $P(t, T)$ and given by (1.13) below,

$$P(t,T) = \frac{1}{[r(t,T)]^{(T-t)}} \tag{1.13}$$

where $r(t, T)$ is the yield of the T-maturity bond at time t. Expression (1.13) above can be rewritten as follows, in terms of the bond yield.

$$r(t,T) = \left[\frac{1}{P(t,T)}\right]^{1/(T-t)} \tag{1.14}$$

This states that the yield on the zero-coupon bond is the percentage return earned in the period from the time the bond is held (t) to its maturity date T.

We can then derive an expression for the bond price in terms of a *forward rate*. The forward rate $rf(t, T)$ is the rate that applies at time t for the period $(T, T+1)$ and is given by (1.15) below,

$$rf(t,T) = \frac{P(t,T)}{P(t,T+1)} \tag{1.15}$$

and is the interest rate that is earned on a deposit over the time period $(T, T+1)$ that has been put on at time t. Expression (1.15) above may be used to obtain a formula for the price of a bond, given below.

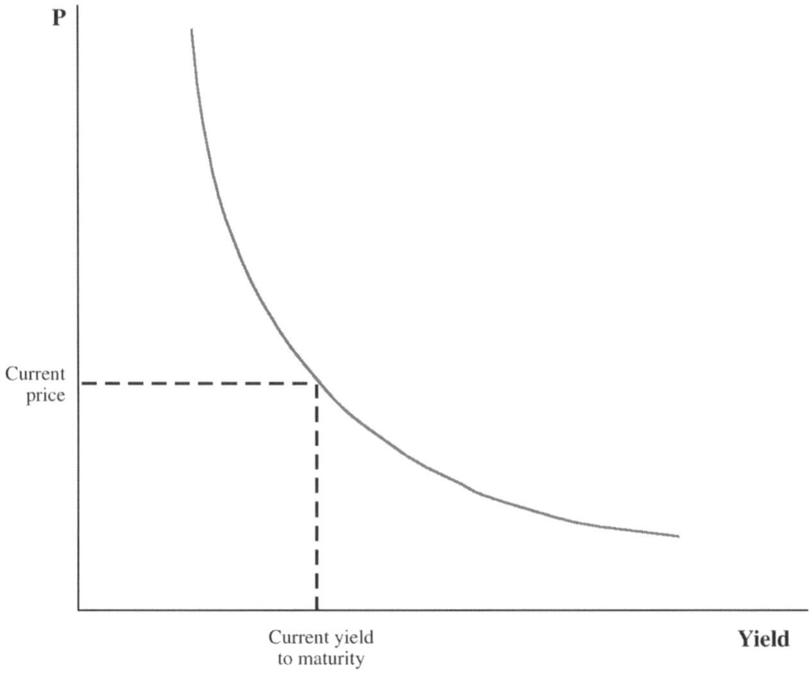

Figure 1.3 The bond price/yield relationship

The price of a bond will move for a variety of reasons, including the market-related ones noted here:

- when there is a change in the yield required by the market, either because of changes in the base rate or a perceived change in credit quality of the bond issuer (credit considerations do not affect developed country government bonds);
- when there is a change because as the bond is approaching maturity, its price moves gradually towards par;
- when there is a change in the market-required yield due to a change in the yield on comparable bonds.

Bond prices also move for liquidity reasons and normal supply and demand reasons, for example if there is a large amount of a particular bond on issue it is easier to trade the bond; also, if there is demand due to a large customer base for the bond. Liquidity is a general term used here to mean

yield changed. This is an important result. Let us consider the situation – if the required yield in the market for our 7% bond is fixed, investors will be happy to hold the bond. What if required yields subsequently rise above the 7% level? Bondholders will be unhappy as they are now being paid 7% when elsewhere in the market higher yields are available. The market price of the bond will therefore change so that the yield on the bond changes, to compensate bondholders. If the required yield for the bond changes to 8%, we see from Table 1.3 that the price has fallen from par to 96.00. If this did not happen bondholders would sell the 7% issue and buy a bond that was yielding 8%; the market price mechanism ensures that this does not happen. If the situation is reversed the price mechanism will again operate to equalise the yield on the bond with those prevalent in the marketplace. If required yields drop to 6% the bond price rises to 104.21, because bondholders would now be receiving 7% when yields available in the market are now only 6%. We can see then that when required yield in the market is equal to a bond's coupon, the bond price will be par; the price will move respectively above or below par if required yields are below or above the coupon rate.

If a bond is priced at below its par value it is said to be trading at a *discount*, while if it is trading above par value it is said to be trading at a *premium* to its par value.

When merchant banks issue bonds on behalf of borrowers, they will set a bond's coupon at the level that would make the bond price equal to par. This means that the bond coupon will be equal to the yield required by the market at the time of issue. The bond's price would then fluctuate as market yields changed, as we showed in Table 1.3. Investors generally prefer to pay par or just under par when they buy a new issue of bonds, which is why a merchant bank will set the coupon that equates the bond price to par or in a range between 99.00 and par. The reason behind this preference to pay no more than par is often purely cosmetic, since an issue price above par would simply indicate a coupon higher than the market rate. However, as many fund managers and investors buy a bond and hold it until maturity, one often finds this prejudice against paying over par for a new issue.

What will happen if market yields remain unchanged during the life of a bond from when it was issued? In this unlikely scenario the price of a conventional bond will remain unchanged at par. The price of any bond will ultimately equal its redemption value, which is par. Therefore a bond that is priced at a premium or a discount will gradually converge to par as it approaches maturity.

Duration, modified duration and convexity

Bonds pay a part of their total return during their lifetime, in the form of coupon interest, so that the term to maturity does not reflect the true period over which the bond's return is earned. Additionally, if we wish to gain an idea of the trading characteristics of a bond, and compare this to other bonds of, say, similar maturity, term to maturity is insufficient and so we need a more accurate measure. A plain vanilla coupon bond pays out a proportion of its return during the course of its life, in the form of coupon interest. If we were to analyse the properties of a bond, we would conclude quite quickly that its maturity gives us little indication of how much of its return is paid out during its life, or any idea of the timing or size of its cash flows, and hence its sensitivity to moves in market interest rates. For example, if comparing two bonds with the same maturity date but different coupons, the higher coupon bond provides a larger proportion of its return in the form of coupon income than does the lower coupon bond. The higher coupon bond provides its return at a faster rate; its value is theoretically therefore less subject to subsequent fluctuations in interest rates.

We may wish to calculate an average of the time to receipt of a bond's cash flows, and use this measure as a more realistic indication of maturity. However, cash flows during the life of a bond are not all equal in value, so a more accurate measure would be to take the average time to receipt of a bond's cash flows, but weighted in the form of the cash flows' present value. This is, in effect, *duration*. We can measure the speed of payment of a bond, and hence its price risk relative to other bonds of the same maturity by measuring the average maturity of the bond's cash flow stream. Bond analysts use duration to measure this property (it is sometimes known as *Macaulay's duration*, after its inventor, who first introduced it in 1938).[5] Duration is the weighted average time until the receipt of cash flows from a bond, where the weights are the present values of the cash flows, measured in years. At the time that he introduced the concept, Macaulay used the duration measure as an alternative for the length of time that a bond investment had remaining to maturity.

---

[5] Macaulay, F., *Some theoretical problems suggested by the movements of interest rates, bond yields and stock prices in the United States since 1865*, National Bureau of Economic Research, NY 1938. This remains a fascinating read and is available from Risk Classics publishing, under the title *Interest rates, bond yields and stock prices in the United States since 1856.*

Equation (1.21) is simplified using E notation as shown by (1.22).

$$D = \frac{\sum_{n=1}^{N} \frac{nC_n}{(1+r)^n}}{P} \qquad (1.22)$$

where C represents the bond cash flow at time n.

Example 1.10 calculates the Macaulay duration for a hypothetical bond, an 8% 2009 annual coupon bond.

EXAMPLE 1.10 Duration

Calculating the Macaulay duration for an 8% 2009 annual coupon bond:

Issued	30 September 1999
Maturity	30 September 2009
Price	102.497
Yield	7.634%

Period (*n*)	Cash flow	PV at current yield*	*n* × PV
1	8	7.43260	7.4326
2	8	6.90543	13.81086
3	8	6.41566	19.24698
4	8	5.96063	23.84252
5	8	5.53787	27.68935
6	8	5.14509	30.87054
7	8	4.78017	33.46119
8	8	4.44114	35.529096
9	8	4.12615	37.13535
10	108	51.75222	517.5222
	Total	102.49696	746.540686

*Calculated as $C/(1 + r)n$.

Macaulay duration = 746.540686/102.497 = 7.283539998 years.

Modified duration = 7.28354/1.07634 = 6.76695.

Table 1.4 Duration calculation for the 8% 2009 bond

payment. If we take the first derivative of (1.26) and then divide this by the current price of the bond P, the result is another expression for the modified duration formula, given at (1.27).

$$MD = \frac{\frac{C}{r^2}\left[1 - \frac{1}{(1+r)^n}\right] + \frac{n\left[M - \frac{C}{r}\right]}{(1+r)^{n+1}}}{P} \qquad (1.27)$$

We have already shown that modified duration and duration are related; to obtain the expression for Macaulay duration from (1.27) we multiply it by $(1 + r)$. This short-hand formula is demonstrated in Example 1.11 for a hypothetical bond, the annual coupon 8% 2009.

EXAMPLE 1.11 Modified duration

An 8% 2009 bond: using equation (1.27) for the modified duration calculation:

Coupon	8%, annual basis
Yield	7.634%
N	10
Price	102.497

Substituting the above terms into the equation we obtain:

$$MD = \frac{\frac{8}{(0.07634^2)}\left[1 - \frac{1}{(1.07634)^{10}}\right] + \frac{10\left[100 - \frac{8}{0.07634}\right]}{(1.07634)}}{102.497}$$

$$= 6.076695.$$

To obtain the Macaulay duration we multiply the modified duration by $(1 + r)$, in this case 1.07634, which gives us a value of 7.28354 years.

For an irredeemable bond, duration is given by:

$$D = \frac{1}{rc} \tag{1.28}$$

where $rc = (C/P_d)$ is the *running yield* (or *current yield*) of the bond. This follows from equation (1.22) as $N \rightarrow \infty$, recognising that for an irredeemable bond $r = rc$. Equation (1.28) provides the limiting value to duration. For bonds trading at or above par, duration increases with maturity and approaches this limit from below. For bonds trading at a discount to par, duration increases to a maximum at around 20 years and then declines towards the limit given by (1.28). So in general, duration increases with maturity, with an upper bound given by (1.28).

Properties of Macaulay duration

A bond's duration is always less than its maturity. This is because some weight is given to the cash flows in the early years of the bond's life, which brings forward the average time at which cash flows are received. In the case of a zero-coupon bond, there is no present value weighting of the cash flows, for the simple reason that there are no cash flows, and so duration for a zero-coupon bond is equal to its term to maturity. Duration varies with coupon, yield and maturity. The following three factors imply higher duration for a bond:

- the lower the coupon;
- the lower the yield;
- broadly, the longer the maturity.

Duration increases as coupon and yield decrease. As the coupon falls, more of the relative weight of the cash flows is transferred to the maturity date and this causes duration to rise. Because the coupon on index-linked bonds is generally much lower than on vanilla bonds, this means that the duration of index-linked bonds will be much higher than for vanilla bonds of the same maturity. As yield increases, the present values of all future cash flows fall, but the present values of the more distant cash flows fall relatively more than those of the nearer cash flows. This has the effect of increasing the relative weight given to nearer cash flows and hence of reducing duration.

The effect of the coupon frequency

Certain bonds such as Eurobonds pay coupon annually compared to, say, gilts, which pay semi-annual coupons. If we imagine that every coupon is divided into two parts, with one part paid a half-period earlier than the other, this will represent a shift in weight to the left, as part of the coupon is paid earlier. Thus, increasing the coupon frequency shortens duration, and of course decreasing coupon frequency has the effect of lengthening duration.

Duration as maturity approaches

Using our definition of duration we can see that initially it will decline slowly, and then at a more rapid pace as a bond approaches maturity.

Duration of a portfolio

Portfolio duration is a weighted average of the duration of the individual bonds. The weights are the present values of the bonds divided by the full price of the entire portfolio, and the resulting duration calculation is often referred to as a "market-weighted" duration. This approach is in effect the duration calculation for a single bond. Portfolio duration has the same application as duration for an individual bond, and can be used to structure an *immunised* portfolio.

Modified duration

Although it is common for newcomers to the market to think intuitively of duration much as Macaulay originally did, as a proxy measure for the time to maturity of a bond, such an interpretation is to miss the main point of duration, which is a measure of price volatility or interest rate risk.

Using the first term of a Taylor's expansion of the bond price function,[6] we can show the following relationship between price volatility and the duration measure, which is expressed as (1.29) below.

$$\Delta P = -\left[\frac{1}{(1+r)}\right] \times \text{Macaulay duration} \times \text{Change in yield} \qquad (1.29)$$

where r is the yield to maturity for an annual-paying bond (for a semi-annual coupon bond, we use $r/2$). If we combine the first two components of the right-hand side, we obtain the definition of modified duration. Equation (1.29) expresses the approximate percentage change in price as being equal

[6] For an accessible explanation of the Taylor expansion, see Butler, C., *Mastering Value-at-Risk*, FT Prentice Hall, 1998, pp. 112–14.

to the modified duration multiplied by the change in yield. We saw in the previous section how the formula for Macaulay duration could be modified to obtain the *modified duration* for a bond. There is a clear relationship between the two measures. From the Macaulay duration of a bond can be derived its modified duration, which gives a measure of the sensitivity of a bond's price to small changes in yield. As we have seen, the relationship between modified duration and duration is given by (1.30).

$$MD = \frac{D}{1 + r} \tag{1.30}$$

where *MD* is the modified duration in years. However, it also measures the approximate change in bond price for a 1% change in bond yield. For a bond that pays semi-annual coupons, the equation becomes:

$$MD = \frac{D}{1 + \frac{1}{2}r}. \tag{1.31}$$

This means that the following relationship holds between modified duration and bond prices:

$$\Delta P = MD \times \Delta r \times P. \tag{1.32}$$

In the UK markets the term *volatility* is sometimes used to refer to modified duration, but this is becoming increasingly uncommon in order to avoid confusion with the option markets' use of the same term, which there often refers to *implied volatility* and is something different.

EXAMPLE 1.12 USING MODIFIED DURATION

An 8% annual coupon bond is trading at par with a duration of 2.74 years. If yields rise from 8% to 8.50%, then the price of the bond will fall by:

$$\begin{aligned}\Delta P &= -\mathrm{D} \times \frac{\Delta r}{1 + r} \times P \\ &= -(2.74) \times \left(\frac{0.005}{1.080}\right) \times 100 \\ &= -£1.2685\end{aligned}$$

that is, the price of the bond will now be £98.7315.

The modified duration of a bond with a duration of 2.74 years and yield of 8% is obviously:

$$MD = \frac{2.74}{1.08}$$

which gives us *MD* equal to 2.537 years.

This tells us that for a 1% move in the YTM, the price of the bond will move (in the opposite direction) by 2.54%.

We can use modified duration to approximate bond prices for a given yield change. This is illustrated with the following equation:

$$\Delta P = -MD \times (\Delta r) \times P. \quad (1.33)$$

For a bond with a modified duration of 3.99, priced at par, an increase in yield of 1 basis point (100 basis = 1%) leads to a fall in the bond's price of:

$$\Delta P = (-3.24/100) \times (+0.01) \times 100.00$$

$$\Delta P = £0.0399\text{, or } 3.99 \text{ pence.}$$

In this case, 3.99 pence is the *basis point value* of the bond, which is the change in the bond price given a 1 basis point change in the bond's yield. The basis point value of a bond can be calculated using (1.34).

$$BPV = \frac{MD}{100} \times \frac{P}{100} \quad (1.34)$$

Basis point values are used in hedging bond positions. To hedge a bond position requires an opposite position to be taken in the hedging instrument. So if we are building long position in a 10-year bond, we may wish to sell short a similar 10-year bond as a hedge against it. Similarly, a short position in a bond will be hedged through a purchase of an equivalent amount of the hedging instrument. In fact, there are a variety of hedging instruments available, both on- and off-balance sheet. Once the hedge is put on, any loss in the primary position should in theory be offset by a gain in the hedge position, and vice-versa. The objective of a hedge is to ensure that the price change in the primary instrument is equal to the price change in the hedging instrument. If we are hedging a position with another bond, we use the basis point values (BPVs) of each bond to calculate the amount of the hedging instrument required. This is important because each bond will have different BPVs, so that to hedge a long position in say £1 million nominal of a 30-year bond does not mean we simply sell £1 million of another 30-year bond. This is because the BPVs of the two bonds will almost certainly be different. Also, there may not be another 30-year bond in that particular bond. What if we have to hedge with a 10-year bond? How much nominal of this bond would be required?

We need to know the ratio given at (1.35) to calculate the nominal hedge position.

$$\frac{BVP_p}{BVP_h} \tag{1.35}$$

where

BPVp is the basis point value of the primary bond (the position to be hedged)

BPVh is the basis point value of the hedging instrument.

The *hedge ratio* is used to calculate the size of the hedge position and is given at (1.36).

$$\frac{BVP_p}{BVP_h} \times \frac{\text{Change in yield for primary bond position}}{\text{Change in yield for hedge instrument}} \tag{1.36}$$

The second ratio in (1.36) is known as the *yield beta*.

Example 1.13 illustrates using the hedge ratio.

EXAMPLE 1.13 CALCULATING HEDGE SIZE USING BPV

A trader holds a long position of £1 million of the 8% 2019 bond. The modified duration of the bond is 11.14692 and its price is 129.87596. The BPV of this bond is therefore 0.14477. The trader decides, to protect against a rise in interest rates, to hedge the position using the 0% 2009 bond, which has a BPV of 0.05549. If we assume that the yield beta is 1, what nominal value of the zero-coupon bond must be sold in order to hedge the position?

The hedge ratio is:

$$\frac{0.14477}{0.05549} \times 1 = 2.60894$$

Therefore to hedge £1 million of the 20-year bond the trader shorts £2,608,940 of the zero-coupon bond. If we use the respective BPVs to see the net effect of a one basis point rise in yield, the loss on the long position is approximately equal to the gain in the hedge position.

EXAMPLE 1.14 THE NATURE OF THE MODIFIED DURATION APPROXIMATION

Table 1.5 shows the change in price for one of our hypothetical bonds, the 8% 2009, for a selection of yields. We see that for a 1 basis point change in yield, the change in price given by the dollar duration figure, while not completely accurate, is a reasonable estimation of the actual change in price. For a large move, however, say 200 basis points, the approximation is significantly in error and analysts would not use it. Notice also for our hypothetical bond how the dollar duration value, which is the suggested change in cash value resulting from the change in yields calculated from the modified duration measurement, underestimates the change in price resulting from a fall in yields but overestimates the price change for a rise in yields. This is a reflection of the price/yield relationship for this bond. Some bonds will have a more pronounced convex relationship between price and yield, and the modified duration calculation will underestimate the price change resulting from both a fall or a rise in yields.

Bond	8% 2009
Maturity (years)	10
Modified duration	6.76695
Price duration of basis point	0.06936
Yield	
6.00%	114.72017
6.50%	110.78325
7.00%	107.02358
7.50%	103.43204
7.99%	100.0671311
8.00%	**100.00000**
8.01%	99.932929
8.50%	96.71933
9.00%	93.58234
10.00%	87.71087

Yield change	**Price change**	**Estimate using price duration**
down 1 bp	0.06713	0.06936
up 1 bp	0.06707	0.06936
down 200 bp	14.72017	13.872
up 200 bp	12.28913	13.872

Table 1.5 Nature of the modified duration approximation

Convexity

Duration can be regarded as a first-order measure of interest rate risk: it measures the *slope* of the present value/yield profile. It is, however, only an approximation of the actual change in bond price given a small change in YTM. Similarly for modified duration, which describes the price sensitivity of a bond to small changes in yield. However, as Figure 1.4 below illustrates, the approximation is an underestimate of the actual price at the new yield. This is the weakness of the duration measure.

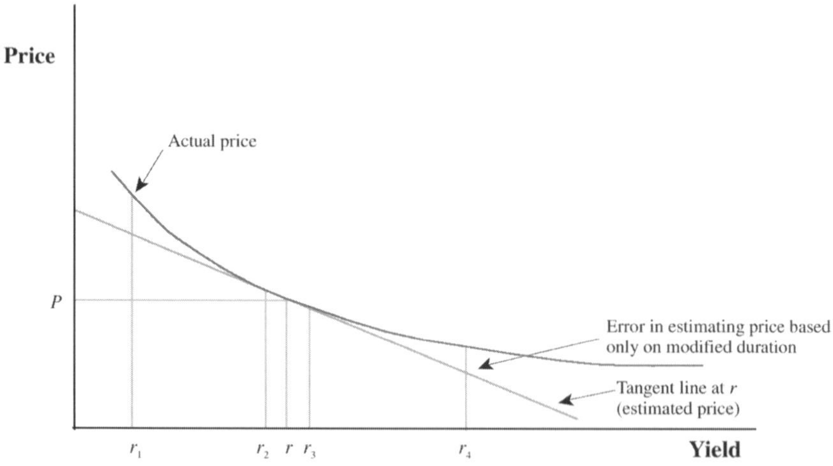

Figure 1.4 Approximation of the bond price change using modified duration. Reproduced with permission from Frank J Fabozzi 1997, *Fixed Income Mathematics*, McGraw-Hill, New York.

Convexity is a second-order measure of interest rate risk; it measures the *curvature* of the present value/yield profile. Convexity can be regarded as an indication of the error we make when using duration and modified duration, as it measures the degree to which the curvature of a bond's price/yield relationship diverges from the straight-line estimation. The convexity of a bond is positively related to the dispersion of its cash flows, thus other things being equal, if one bond's cash flows are more spread out in time than another's, then it will have a higher *dispersion* and hence a higher convexity. Convexity is also positively related to duration.

The second-order differential of the bond price equation with respect to the redemption yield r is:

$$\begin{aligned} \frac{\Delta P}{P} &= \frac{1}{P} + \frac{\Delta P}{\Delta r}(\Delta r) + \frac{1}{2P}\frac{\Delta^2 P}{\Delta r^2}(\Delta r2) \\ &= -MD\left(\Delta r + \frac{CV}{2}\right)(\Delta r)^2 \end{aligned} \qquad (1.37)$$

where CV is the convexity.

From equation (1.37), convexity is the rate at which price variation to yield changes with respect to yield. That is, it describes a bond's modified duration changes with respect to changes in yield. It can be approximated by expression (1.38).

$$CV = 10^8 \left(\frac{\Delta P'}{P} + \frac{\Delta P''}{P}\right) \tag{1.38}$$

where
$\Delta P'$ is the change in bond price if yield increases by 1 basis point (0.01)
$\Delta P''$ is the change in bond price if yield decreases by 1 basis point (0.01).

The unit of measurement for convexity using (1.38) is the number of interest periods. For annual coupon bonds this is equal to the number of years; for bonds paying coupon on a different frequency we use (1.39) to convert the convexity measure to years.

$$CV_{years} = \frac{CV}{C^2} \tag{1.39}$$

The convexity measure for a zero-coupon bond is given by (1.40).

$$CV = \frac{n(n+1)}{(1+r)^2} \tag{1.40}$$

Convexity is a second-order approximation of the change in price resulting from a change in yield. This is given by:

$$\Delta P = \frac{1}{2} \times CV \times (\Delta r)^2 . \tag{1.41}$$

The reason we multiply the convexity by $^1/_2$ to obtain the convexity adjustment is because the second term in the Taylor expansion contains the coefficient $^1/_2$. The convexity approximation is obtained from a Taylor expansion of the bond price formula. An illustration of Taylor expansion of the bond price/yield equation is given in Appendix 39.3 of my book *The Bond and Money Markets*. The formula is the same for a semi-annual coupon bond.

Note that the value for convexity given by the expressions above will always be positive; that is, the approximate price change due to convexity is positive for both yield increases and decreases.

Convexity is an attractive property for a bond to have. What level of premium will be attached to a bond's higher convexity? This is a function of the current yield levels in the market as well as market volatility. Remember that modified duration and convexity are functions of yield level, and that the effect of both is magnified at lower yield levels. As well as the relative level, investors will value convexity higher if the current market conditions are volatile. Remember that the cash effect of convexity is noticeable only for large moves in yield. If an investor expects market yields to move only by relatively small amounts, they will attach a lower value to convexity; and vice-versa for large movements in yield. Therefore the yield premium attached to a bond with higher convexity will vary according to market expectations of the future size of interest rate changes.

The convexity measure increases with the square of maturity, and it decreases with both coupon and yield. As the measure is a function of modified duration, index-linked bonds have greater convexity than conventional bonds. We discussed how the price/yield profile will be more convex for a bond of higher convexity, and that such a bond will outperform a bond of lower convexity whatever happens to market interest rates. High convexity is therefore a desirable property for bonds to have. In principle a more convex bond should fall in price less than a less convex one when yields rise, and rise in price more when yields fall. That is, convexity can be equated with the potential to outperform. Thus, other things being equal, the higher the convexity of a bond the more desirable it should, in principle, be to investors. In some cases investors may be prepared to accept a bond with a lower yield in order to gain convexity. We noted also that convexity is in principle of more value if uncertainty, and hence expected market volatility, is high, because the convexity effect of a bond is amplified for large changes in yield. The value of convexity is therefore greater in volatile market conditions.

For a conventional vanilla bond, convexity is almost always positive. Negative convexity resulting from a bond with a concave price/yield profile would not be an attractive property for a bondholder; the most common occurrence of negative convexity in the cash markets is with callable bonds.

Selected bibliography and references

Baxter, M. and Rennie, A. 1996, *Financial Calculus*, Cambridge University Press, Cambridge.

Bierwag, G.O. 1977, "Immunization, duration and the term structure of interest rates", *Journal of Financial and Quantitative Analysis*, Vol. 15, Issue 5, December, pp. 725–41.

Bierwag, G.O. 1978, "Measures of duration," *Economic Inquiry*, Vol. 16, Issue 4, October, pp. 497–507.

Burghardt, G. 1994, *The Treasury Bond Basis*, McGraw-Hill, New York.

Choudhry, M. 2001, *The Bond and Money Markets: Strategy, Trading, Analysis*, Butterworth-Heinemann, Oxford, Chapters 2–10 and 39.

Fabozzi, F. 1989, *Bond Markets, Analysis and Strategies*, Prentice Hall, New York, Chapter 2.

Garbade, K. 1996, *Fixed Income Analytics*, MIT Press, Cambridge, MA, Chapters 3, 4 and 12.

Hull, J. 1997, *Options, Futures and Other Derivatives*, 3rd edition, Prentice Hall, London.

Jarrow, R. 1996, *Modelling Fixed Income Securities and Interest Rate Options*, McGraw-Hill, New York.

Macaulay, F. 1999, *The Movements of Interest Rates, Bond Yields and Stock Prices in the United States Since 1856*, RISK Classics Library, London.

Neftci, S. 1996, *Mathematics of Financial Derivatives*, Academic Press, San Francisco.

Stafford Johnson, R. 2004, *Bond Evaluation, Selection and Management*, Blackwell Publishing, Oxford.

Steiner, R. 1998, *Mastering Financial Calculations*, FT Pitman, London.

The long-term government bond yield is the single most important financial variable in any market economy, setting the tone for equity and house prices, governing business investment decisions and establishing the discount rate for pension liabilities and insurance policies.

– Anatole Kaletsky, "Economic View",
The Times, 22 February 2005

CHAPTER

2

The Yield Curve

The main measure of return associated with holding bonds is the *yield to maturity* (YTM) or *gross redemption yield*. In developed markets, as well as a fair number of developing ones, there is usually a large number of bonds trading at one time, at different yields and with varying terms to maturity. Investors and traders frequently examine the relationship between the yields on bonds that are in the same class; plotting yields of bonds that differ only in their term to maturity produces what is known as a *yield curve*. The yield curve is an important indicator and knowledge source of the state of a debt capital market. It is sometimes referred to as the *term structure of interest rates*, but strictly speaking this is not correct, as this term should be reserved for the zero-coupon yield curve only. We shall examine this in detail later.

Much of the analysis and pricing activity that takes place in the bond markets revolves around the yield curve. The yield curve describes the relationship between a particular redemption yield and a bond's maturity. Plotting the yields of bonds along the maturity term structure will give us our yield curve. It is very important that only bonds from the same class of issuer or with the same degree of liquidity are used when plotting the yield curve; for example, a curve may be constructed for UK gilts or for AA-rated sterling Eurobonds, but not a mixture of both, because gilts and Eurobonds are bonds from different class issuers. The primary yield curve in any domestic capital market is the government bond yield curve, so for example in the US market it is the US Treasury yield curve. With the advent of the euro currency in 12 countries of the European Union, in theory any euro-currency government bond can be used to plot a default-free euro yield curve. In practice only bonds from the same government are used, as for various reasons different country bonds within euroland trade at different yields. Outside the government bond markets yield curves are plotted for Eurobonds, money market instruments, off-balance sheet instruments; in fact, virtually all debt market instruments. So it is always important to remember to compare like-for-like when analysing yield curves across markets.

In this chapter we will consider the YTM yield curve as well as other types of yield curve that may be constructed. Later in this chapter we will consider how to derive spot and forward yields from a current redemption yield curve.

Using the yield curve

Let us first consider the main uses of the yield curve. All participants in the debt capital markets have an interest in the current shape and level of the yield curve, as well as what this information implies for the future. The main uses are summarised below.

Setting the yield for all debt market instrument

The yield curve essentially fixes the cost of money over the maturity term structure. The yields of government bonds from the shortest maturity instrument to the longest set the benchmark for yields for all other debt instruments in the market, around which all debt instruments are analysed. Issuers of debt (and their underwriting banks) therefore use the yield curve to price bonds and all other debt instruments. Generally, the zero-coupon yield curve is used to price new issue securities, rather than the redemption yield curve.

Acting as an indicator of future yield levels

As we discuss later in this chapter, the yield curve assumes certain shapes in response to market expectations of future interest rates. Bond market participants analyse the present shape of the yield curve in an effort to determine the implications regarding the future direction of market interest rates. This is perhaps one of the most important functions of the yield curve, and it is as much an art as a science. The yield curve is scrutinised for its information content, not just by bond traders and fund managers, but also by corporate financiers as part of project appraisal. Central banks and government treasury departments also analyse the yield curve for its information content, not just regarding forward interest rates but also with regard to expected inflation levels.

Measuring and comparing returns across the maturity spectrum

Portfolio managers use the yield curve to assess the relative value of investments across the maturity spectrum. The yield curve indicates the returns that are available at different maturity points and is therefore very important to fixed-income fund managers, who can use it to assess which point of the curve offers the best return relative to other points.

Indicating relative value between different bonds of similar maturity

The yield curve can be analysed to indicate which bonds are cheap or dear to the curve. Placing bonds relative to the zero-coupon yield curve helps to highlight which bonds should be bought or sold either outright or as part of a bond spread trade.

Pricing interest rate derivative securities

The price of derivative securities revolves around the yield curve. At the short-end, products such as Forward Rate Agreements are priced off the futures curve, but futures rates reflect the market's view on forward three-month cash deposit rates. At the longer end, interest rate swaps are priced off the yield curve, while hybrid instruments that incorporate an option feature such as convertibles and callable bonds also reflect current yield curve levels. The "risk-free" interest rate, which is one of the parameters used in option pricing, is the Treasury bill rate or short-term government repo rate, both constituents of the money market yield curve.

Yield-to-maturity (YTM) yield curve

The most commonly occurring yield curve is the YTM yield curve. The equation used to calculate the yield to maturity was shown in Chapter 1 (1.1). The curve itself is constructed by plotting the YTM against the term to maturity for a group of bonds of the same class. Three different examples are shown at Figure 2.1. Bonds used in constructing the curve will only rarely have an exact number of whole years to redemption; however, it is often common to see yields plotted against whole years on the *x*-axis. This is because once a bond is designated the *benchmark* for that term, its yield is taken to be the representative yield. For example, the then 10-year benchmark bond in the UK gilt market, the 5% Treasury 2012, maintained its benchmark status throughout 2002 and into 2003, even as its term to maturity fell below ten years. The YTM yield curve is the most commonly observed curve simply because YTM is the most frequent measure of return used. The business sections of daily newspapers, where they quote bond yields at all, usually quote bond yields to maturity.

As we might expect, given the source data from which it is constructed, the YTM yield curve contains some inaccuracies. We have already come across the main weakness of the YTM measure, which is the assumption of a constant rate for coupon reinvestment during the bond's life at the redemption yield level. Since market rates will fluctuate over time, it will not be possible to achieve this (a feature known as *reinvestment risk*). Only zero-coupon bondholders avoid reinvestment risk as no coupon is paid during the life of a zero-coupon bond.

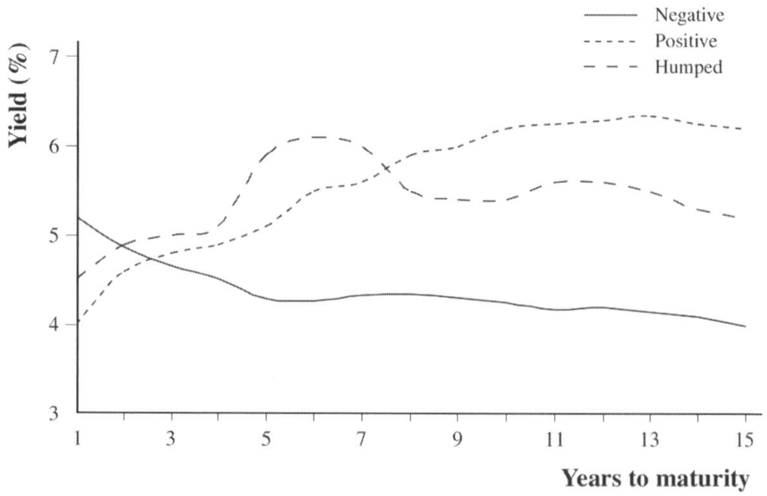

Figure 2.1 YTM yield curves

The YTM yield curve does not distinguish between different payment patterns that may result from bonds with different coupons; that is, the fact that low-coupon bonds pay a higher portion of their cash flows at a later date than high-coupon bonds of the same maturity. The curve also assumes an even cash flow pattern for all bonds. Therefore in this case cash flows are not discounted at the appropriate rate for the bonds in the group being used to construct the curve. To get around this, bond analysts may sometimes construct a *coupon yield curve,* which plots YTM against term to maturity for a group of bonds with the same coupon. This may be useful when a group of bonds contains some with very high coupons; high coupon bonds often trade "cheap to the curve", that is they have higher yields, than corresponding bonds of the same maturity but lower coupon. This is usually because of reinvestment risk and, in some markets (including the United Kingdom), for tax reasons.

For the reasons we have discussed the market often uses other types of yield curve for analysis when the YTM yield curve is deemed unsuitable.

That there are a number of yield curves that can be plotted, each relevant to its own market, can be seen from Figure 2.2 below, which shows the curves that can be selected for the US dollar market, from screen IYC on Bloomberg. We see that curves can be selected for US Treasuries, US dollar swaps, strips, agency securities, and so on. Figure 2.3 below shows the curves for Treasuries, interest-rate swaps and strips as at August 2003.

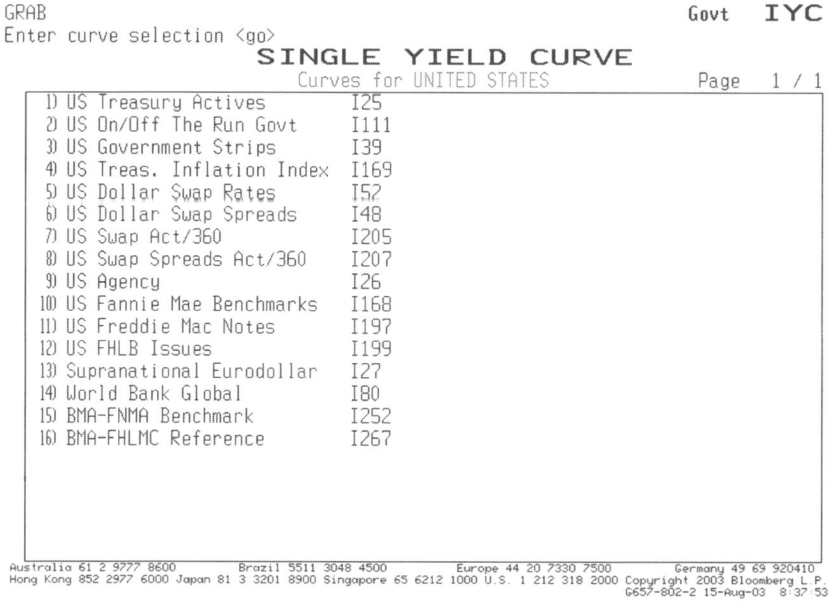

Figure 2.2 US menu page from screen IYC on Bloomberg
© Bloomberg L.P. Used with permission.

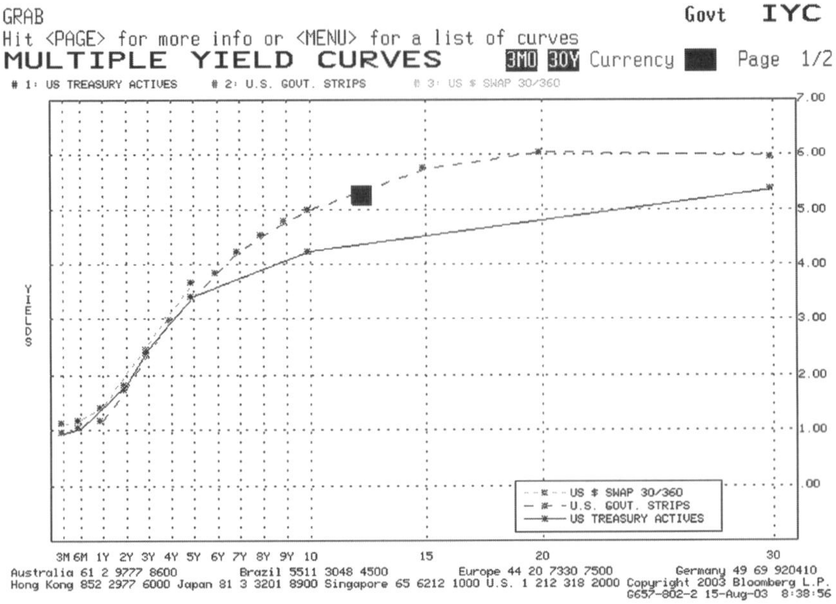

Figure 2.3 US yield curves, August 2003
© Bloomberg L.P. Used with permission.

We discuss next the various types of curve that can be plotted.

The coupon yield curve

The *coupon yield curve* is a plot of the YTM against term to maturity for a group of bonds with the same coupon. If we were to construct such a curve we would see that in general high-coupon bonds trade at a discount (have higher yields) relative to low-coupon bonds, because of reinvestment risk and for tax reasons (in the United Kingdom, for example, on gilts the coupon is taxed as income tax, while any capital gain is exempt from capital gains tax; even in jurisdictions where capital gain on bonds is taxable, this can often be deferred whereas income tax cannot). It is frequently the case that yields vary considerably with coupons for the same term to maturity, and with term to maturity for different coupons. Put another way, usually we observe different coupon curves not only at different levels but also with different shapes. Distortions arise in the YTM curve if no allowance is made for coupon differences. For this reason bond analysts frequently draw a line of "best fit" through a plot of redemption yields, because the coupon effect in a group of bonds will produce a curve with humps and troughs. Figure 2.4 shows a hypothetical set of coupon yield curves. However, since in any group of bonds it is unusual to observe bonds with the same coupon along the entire term structure this type of curve is relatively rare.

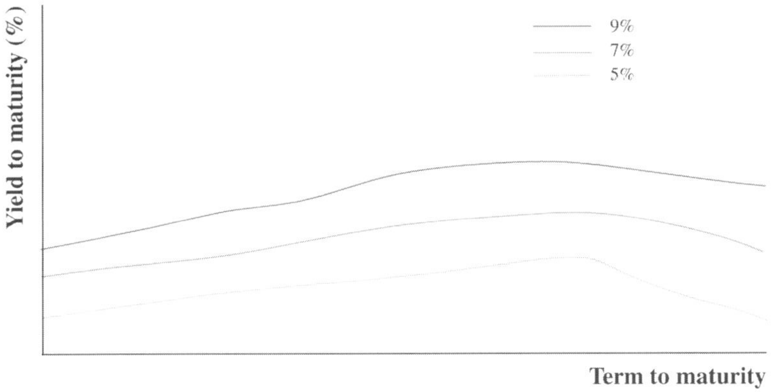

Figure 2.4 Coupon yield curves

The par yield curve

The *par yield curve* is not usually encountered in secondary market trading; however, it is often constructed for use by corporate financiers and others in the new issues or *primary* market. The par yield curve plots YTM against term to maturity for current bonds trading at par.[1] The par yield is therefore equal to the coupon rate for bonds priced at par or near to par, as the YTM for bonds priced exactly at par is equal to the coupon rate. Those involved in the primary market will use a par yield curve to determine the required coupon for a new bond that is to be issued at par. This is because investors prefer not to pay over par for a new-issue bond, so the bond requires a coupon that will result in a price at or slightly below par.

The par yield curve can be derived directly from bond yields when bonds are trading at or near par. If bonds in the market are trading

[1] Par price for a bond is almost invariably 100%. Certain bonds have par defined as 1000 per 1000 nominal of paper.

substantially away from par then the resulting curve will be distorted. It is then necessary to derive it by iteration from the spot yield curve. As we would observe at almost any time, it is rare to encounter bonds trading at par for any particular maturity. The market therefore uses actual non-par vanilla bond yield curves to derive *zero-coupon yield curves* and then constructs hypothetical par yields that would be observed were there any par bonds being traded.

The zero-coupon (or spot) yield curve

The *zero-coupon* (or *spot*) *yield curve* plots zero-coupon yields (or spot yields) against term to maturity. A zero-coupon yield is the yield prevailing on a bond that has no coupons. In the first instance if there is a liquid zero-coupon bond market we can plot the yields from these bonds if we wish to construct this curve. However, it is not necessary to have a set of zero-coupon bonds in order to construct the curve, as we can derive it from a coupon or par yield curve; in fact, in many markets where no zero-coupon bonds are traded, a spot yield curve is derived from the conventional YTM yield curve. This is of course a *theoretical* zero-coupon (spot) yield curve, as opposed to the *market* or *observed* spot curve that can be constructed using the yields of actual zero-coupon bonds trading in the market.[2]

Basic concepts

Spot yields must comply with equation (2.1). This equation assumes annual coupon payments and that the calculation is carried out on a coupon date so that accrued interest is zero.

$$
\begin{aligned}
P_d &= \sum_{n=1}^{N} \frac{C}{(1 + rs_n)^n} + \frac{M}{(1 + rs_N)^N} \\
&= \sum_{n=1}^{N} C \times df_n + M \times df_N
\end{aligned}
\tag{2.1}
$$

where

rs_n is the spot or zero-coupon yield on a bond with n years to maturity

df is the corresponding *discount factor*.

---

[2] It is common to see the terms spot rate and zero-coupon rate used synonymously. However, the spot rate is a theoretical construct and cannot be observed in the market. The definition of the spot rate, which is the rate of return on a single cash flow that has been dealt today and is received at some point in the future, comes very close to that of the yield on a zero-coupon bond, which can be observed directly in the market. Zero-coupon rates can therefore be taken to be spot rates in practice, which is why the terms are frequently used interchangeably.

In (2.1) rs_1 would be the current one-year spot yield, rs_2 the current two-year spot yield, and so on. Theoretically the spot yield for a particular term to maturity is the same as the yield on a zero-coupon bond of the same maturity, which is why spot yields are also known as zero-coupon yields.

This last is an important result, as spot yields can be derived from redemption yields that have been observed in the market.

As with the yield to redemption yield curve, the spot yield curve is commonly used in the market. It is viewed as the true term structure of interest rates because there is no reinvestment risk involved; the stated yield is equal to the actual annual return. That is, the yield on a zero-coupon bond of n years maturity is regarded as the true n-year interest rate. Because the observed government bond redemption yield curve is not considered to be the true interest rate, analysts often construct a theoretical spot yield curve. Essentially, this is done by breaking down each coupon bond being observed into its constituent cash flows, which become a series of individual zero-coupon bonds. For example, £100 nominal of a 5% two-year bond (paying annual coupons) is considered equivalent to £5 nominal of a one-year zero-coupon bond and £105 nominal of a two-year zero-coupon bond.

Let us assume that in the market there are 30 bonds all paying annual coupons. The first bond has a maturity of one year, the second bond of two years, and so on out to thirty years. We know the price of each of these bonds, and we wish to determine what the prices imply about the market's estimate of future interest rates. We naturally expect interest rates to vary over time, but that all payments being made on the same date are valued using the same rate. For the one-year bond we know its current price and the amount of the payment (comprised of one coupon payment and the redemption proceeds) we will receive at the end of the year; therefore we can calculate the interest rate for the first year: assume the one-year bond has a coupon of 5%. If the bond is priced at par and we invest £100 today we will receive £105 in one year's time, hence the rate of interest is apparent and is 5%. For the two-year bond we use this interest rate to calculate the future value of its current price in one year's time: *this is how much we would receive if we had invested the same amount in the one-year bond.* However, the two-year bond pays a coupon at the end of the first year; if we subtract this amount from the future value of the current price, the net amount is what we should be giving up in one year in return for the one remaining payment. From these numbers we can calculate the interest rate in year two.

Assume that the two-year bond pays a coupon of 6% and is priced at 99.00. If the 99.00 were invested at the rate we calculated for the one-year bond (5%), it would accumulate £103.95 in one year, made up of the £99 investment and interest of £4.95. On the payment date in one year's time, the one-year bond matures and the two-year bond pays a coupon of 6%. If everyone expected that at this time the two-year bond would be priced at more than 97.95 (which is 103.95 minus 6.00), then no investor would buy the one-year bond, since it would be more advantageous to buy the two-year bond and sell it after one year for a greater return. Similarly, if the price was less than 97.95 no investor would buy the two-year bond, as it would be cheaper to buy the shorter bond and then buy the longer dated bond with the proceeds received when the one-year bond matures. Therefore the two-year bond must be priced at exactly 97.95 in 12 months' time. For this £97.95 to grow to £106.00 (the maturity proceeds from the two-year bond, comprising the redemption payment and coupon interest), the interest rate in year two must be 8.20%. We can check this by using the present value formula covered earlier. At these two interest rates, the two bonds are said to be in equilibrium.

This is an important result and shows that (in theory) there can be no arbitrage opportunity along the yield curve; using interest rates available today the return from buying the two-year bond must equal the return from buying the one-year bond and rolling over the proceeds (or *reinvesting*) for another year. This is the known as the *break-even principle*, a law of no-arbitrage.

Using the price and coupon of the three-year bond we can calculate the interest rate in year three in precisely the same way. Using each of the bonds in turn, we can link together the *implied one-year rates* for each year up to the maturity of the longest dated bond. The process is known as *boot-strapping*. The "average" of the rates over a given period is the spot yield for that term: in the example given above, the rate in year one is 5% and in year two it is 8.20%. An investment of £100 at these rates would grow to £113.61. This gives a total percentage increase of 13.61% over two years, or 6.588% per annum (the average rate is not obtained by simply dividing 13.61 by 2, but – using our present value relationship again – by calculating the square root of "1 plus the interest rate" and then subtracting 1 from this number). Thus, the one-year yield is 5% and the two-year yield is 8.20%.

In real-world markets it is not necessarily as straightforward as this; for instance, on some dates there may be several bonds maturing, with different coupons, and on some dates there may be no bonds maturing. It is most unlikely that there will be a regular spacing of bond redemptions exactly one year apart. For this reason it is common for analysts to use a software model to calculate the set of implied spot rates which best fits the market prices of the bonds that do exist in the market. For instance, if there are several one-year bonds, each of their prices may imply a slightly different rate of interest. We choose the rate which gives the smallest average price error. In practice all bonds are used to find the rate in year one, all bonds with a term longer than one year are used to calculate the rate in year two, and so on. The zero-coupon curve can also be calculated directly from the coupon yield curve using a method similar to that described above; in this case the bonds would be priced at par and their coupons set to the par yield values.

The zero-coupon yield curve is ideal to use when deriving implied forward rates, which we consider next, and defining the term structure of interest rates. It is also the best curve to use when determining the *relative value*, whether cheap or dear, of bonds trading in the market, and when pricing new issues, irrespective of their coupons. However, it is not an absolutely accurate indicator of average market yields because most bonds are not zero-coupon bonds.

Zero-coupon discount factors

Having introduced the concept of the zero-coupon curve in the previous paragraph, we can illustrate more formally the mathematics involved. When deriving spot yields from redemption yields, we view conventional bonds as being made up of an *annuity*, which is the stream of fixed coupon payments, and a zero-coupon bond, which is the redemption payment on maturity. To derive the rates we can use (2.1), setting $P_d = M = 100$ and $C = rm_N$ as shown in (2.2) below. This has the coupon bonds trading at par, so that the coupon is equal to the yield.

$$\begin{aligned} 100 &= rm_N \times \sum_{n=1}^{N} df_n + 100 \times df_n \\ &= rm_N \times A_N + 100 \times df_N \end{aligned} \tag{2.2}$$

where rm_N is the par yield for a term to maturity of N years, where df_n the discount factor is the fair price of a zero-coupon bond with a par value of £1 and a term to maturity of N years, and where

$$A_N = \sum_{n=1}^{N} df_n = A_{N-1} + df_N \tag{2.3}$$

is the fair price of an annuity of £1 per year for N years (with A_0 by convention). Substituting (2.3) into (2.2) and rearranging will give us the expression below for the N-year discount factor, shown at (2.4):

$$df_N = \frac{1 - rm_N \times A_{N-1}}{1 + rm_N}. \tag{2.4}$$

If we assume one-year, two-year and three-year redemption yields for bonds priced at par to be 5%, 5.25% and 5.75% respectively, we will obtain the following solutions for the discount factors:

$$df_1 = \frac{1}{1 + 0.05} = 0.95238$$

$$df_2 = \frac{1 - (0.0525)(0.95238)}{1 + 0.0525} = 0.90261$$

$$df_3 = \frac{1 - (0.0575)(0.95238 + 0.90261)}{1 + 0.0575} = 0.84476.$$

We can confirm that these are the correct discount factors by substituting them back into equation (2.2); this gives us the following results for the one-year, two-year and three-year par value bonds (with coupons of 5%, 5.25% and 5.75% respectively):

$$100 = 105 \times 0.95238$$
$$100 = 5.25 \times 0.95238 + 105.25 \times 0.90261$$
$$100 = 5.75 \times 0.95238 + 5.75 \times 0.90261 + 105.75 \times 0.84476.$$

Now that we have found the correct discount factors it is relatively straightforward to calculate the spot yields using equation (2.1), and this is shown below:

$$df_1 = \frac{1}{(1 + rs_1)} = 0.95238 \text{ which gives } rs_1 = 5.0\%$$

$$df_2 = \frac{1}{(1 + rs_2)} = 0.90261 \text{ which gives } rs_2 = 5.269\%$$

$$df_3 = \frac{1}{(1 + rs_3)} = 0.84476 \text{ which gives } rs_3 = 5.778\%.$$

Equation (2.1) discounts the n-year cash flow (comprising the coupon payment and/or principal repayment) by the corresponding n-year spot yield. In other words, rs_n is the *time-weighted rate of return* on an n-year bond. Thus as we said in the previous section the spot yield curve is the correct method for pricing or valuing any cash flow, including an irregular cash flow, because it uses the appropriate discount factors. That is, it matches each cash flow to the discount rate that applies to the time period in which the cash flow is paid. Compare this to the approach for the YTM procedure discussed earlier, which discounts all cash flows by the same yield to maturity. This illustrates neatly why the N-period zero-coupon interest rate is the true interest rate for an N-year bond.

The expressions above are solved algebraically in the conventional manner, although those wishing to use a spreadsheet application such as Microsoft Excel® can input the constituents of each equation into individual cells and solve using the "Tools" and "Goal Seek" functions.

EXAMPLE 2.1 Zero-coupon yields

Consider the following zero-coupon market rates:

One-year (1y)	5.000%
2y	5.271%
3y	5.598%
4y	6.675%
5y	7.213%

Calculate the zero-coupon discount factors and the prices and yields of:
(a) a 6% two-year bond;
(b) a 7% five-year bond.
Assume both are annual coupon bonds.

The zero-coupon discount factors are:

1y: $1/1.05 = 0.95238095$
2y: $1/(1.05271)^2 = 0.90236554$
3y: $1/(1.05598)^3 = 0.84924485$
4y: $1/(1.06675)^4 = 0.77223484$
5y: $1/(1.07213)^5 = 0.70593182$

The price of the 6% two-year bond is then calculated in the normal fashion using present values of the cash flows:

$$(6 \times 0.95238095) \times (106 \times 0.90236554) = 101.365.$$

The YTM is 5.263%, obtained using the iterative method, with a spreadsheet function such as Microsoft Excel® "Goal Seek" or a Hewlett Packard (HP) calculator.

The price of the 7% five-year bond is:

$$(7 \times 0.95238095) + (7 \times 0.90236554) + (7 \times 0.84924485) + (7 \times 0.77223484) + (107 \times 0.70593182) = 99.869$$

The yield to maturity is 7.032%.

FORMULA SUMMARY

Example 2.1 illustrates that if the zero-coupon discount factor for n years is df_n and the par yield for N years is rp, then the expression at (2.5) is always true.

$$(rp \times df_1) + (rp \times df_2) + \ldots + (rp \times df_N) + (1 \times df_N) = 1$$

$$rp \times (df_1 + df_2 + \ldots + df_N) = 1 - df_N \qquad (2.5)$$

$$rp = \frac{1 - df_N}{\sum_{n=1}^{N} df_N}$$

Using spot rates in bond analysis

The convention in the markets is to quote the yield on a non-government bond as a certain *spread* over the yield on the equivalent maturity government bond, usually using gross redemption yields. Traders and investment managers will assess the relative merits of holding the non-government bond based on the risk associated with the bond's issuer and the magnitude of its yield spread. For example, in the United Kingdom at the beginning of 2003 companies such as National Grid, Severn Trent Water, Abbey National plc and Tesco plc issued sterling-denominated bonds, all of which paid a certain spread over the equivalent gilt bond.[3] Figure 2.5 shows the average yield spreads of corporate bonds over gilts in the UK market through 2001/2002.

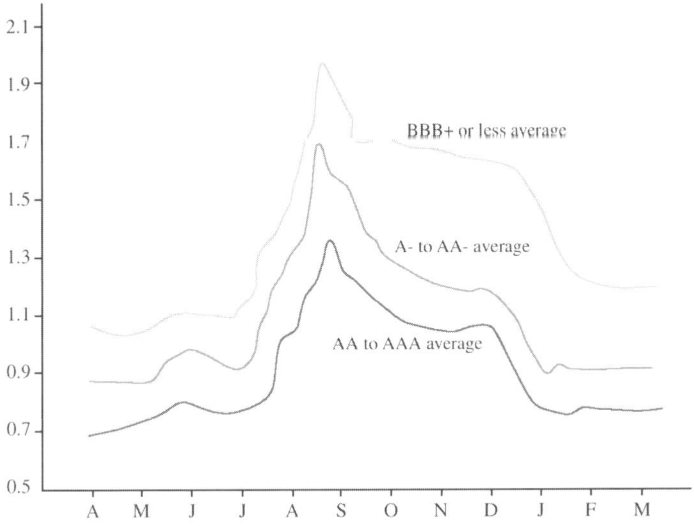

Figure 2.5 Average yield spreads of UK corporate bonds versus gilts, 2001/2002
Source: Bank of England.

Traditionally, investors will compare the redemption yield of the bond they are analysing with the redemption yield of the equivalent government bond. Just as with the redemption yield measure, however, there is a flaw with this measure, in that the spread quoted is not really comparing like-for-like, as the yields do not reflect the true term structure given by the spot rate curve. There is an additional flaw if the cash flow stream of the two bonds do not match, which in practice they will do only rarely.

Therefore the correct method for assessing the yield spread of a corporate bond is to replicate its cash flows with those of a government bond, which can be done in theory by matching the cash flows of the corporate bond with a package of government zero-coupon bonds of the

[3] The spread is, of course, not fixed and fluctuates with market conditions and supply and demand.

same nominal value. If no zero-coupon bond market exists, the cash flows can be matched synthetically by valuing a coupon bond's cash flows on a zero-coupon basis. The corporate bond's price is of course the sum of the present value of all its cash flows, which should be valued at the spot rates in place for each cash flow's maturity. It is the yield spread of each individual cash flow over the equivalent maturity government spot rate that is then taken to be the true yield spread.

This measure is known in US markets as the *zero-volatility spread* or *static spread*, and it is a measure of the spread that would be realised over the government spot rate yield curve if the corporate bond were to be held to maturity. It is therefore a different measure to the traditional spread, as it is not taken over one point on the (redemption yield) curve but over the whole term to maturity. The zero-volatility spread is that spread which equates the present value of the corporate bond's cash flows to its price, where the discount rates are each relevant government spot rate. The spread is found through an iterative process, and it is a more realistic yield spread measure than the traditional one.

The forward yield curve

Forward yields

Most transactions in the market are for immediate delivery, which is known as the *cash* market, although some markets also use the expression *spot* market, which is more common in foreign exchange. Cash market transactions are settled straight away, with the purchaser of a bond being entitled to interest from the settlement date onwards.[4] There is a large market in *forward* transactions, which are trades carried out today for a forward settlement date. For financial transactions that are forward transactions, the parties to the trade agree today to exchange a security for cash at a future date, but at a price agreed today. So the *forward rate* applicable to a bond is the spot bond yield as at the forward date. That is, it is the yield of a zero-coupon bond that is purchased for settlement at the forward date. It is derived today, using data from a present-day yield curve, so it is not correct to consider forward rates to be a prediction of the spot rates as at the forward date.

---

[4] We refer to "immediate" settlement, although of course there is a delay between trade date and settlement date, which can be anything from one day to seven days, or even longer in some markets. The most common settlement period is known as "spot" and is two business days.

Forward rates can be derived from spot interest rates. Such rates are then known as *implied* forward rates, since they are implied by the current range of spot interest rates. The *forward* (or *forward–forward*) *yield curve* is a plot of forward rates against term to maturity. Forward rates satisfy expression (2.6):

$$P_d = \frac{C}{(1 + {}_0rf_1)} + \frac{C}{(1 + {}_0rf_1)(1 + {}_0rf_2)} + \ldots + \frac{M}{(1 + {}_0rf_1) \ldots (1 + {}_{N-1}rf_N)}$$

$$= \sum_{n=1}^{N} \frac{C}{\prod_{n-1}^{n}(1 + {}_{i-1}rf_i)} + \frac{M}{\prod_{n=1}^{N}(1 + {}_{i-1}rf_i)}. \qquad (2.6)$$

where ${}_{n-1}rf_n$ is the implicit forward rate (or forward–forward rate) on a one-year bond maturing in year N.

As a forward or forward–forward yield is implied from spot rates, the forward rate is a forward zero-coupon rate. Comparing (2.1) and (2.6) we see that the spot yield is the *geometric mean* of the forward rates, as shown below:

$$(1 + rs_n)^n = (1 + {}_0rf_1)(1 + {}_1rf_2) \ldots (1 + {}_{n-1}rf_n). \qquad (2.7)$$

This implies the following relationship between spot and forward rates:

$$(1 + {}_{n-1}rf_n) = \frac{(1 + rs_n)^n}{(1 + rs_{n-1})^{n-1}} = \frac{df_{n-1}}{df_n}. \qquad (2.8)$$

Using the spot yields we calculated in the earlier paragraph we can derive the implied forward rates from (2.8). For example, the two-year and three-year forward rates are given by:

$$(1 + {}_1rf_2) = \frac{(1 + 0.05269)^2}{(1 + 0.05)} = 5.539\%$$

$$(1 + {}_2rf_3) = \frac{(1 + 0.05778)^3}{(1 + 0.05269)^2} = 6.803\%.$$

Using our expression gives us ${}_0rf_1$ equal to 5%, ${}_1rf_2$ equal to 5.539% and ${}_2rf_3$ as 6.803%. This means, for example, that given current spot yields, which we calculated from the one-year, two-year and three-year bond redemption yields (which were priced at par), the market is expecting the yield on a bond with one year to mature in three years' time to be 6.803% (that is, the three-year one-period forward–forward rate is 6.803%).

The relationship between the par yields, spot yields and forward rates is shown in Table 2.1.

Year	Coupon yield (%)	Zero-coupon yield (%)	Forward rate (%)
1	5.000	5.000	5.000
2	5.250	5.269	5.539
3	5.750	5.778	6.803

Table 2.1 Coupon, spot and forward yields

Figure 2.6 highlights our results for all three yield curves graphically. This illustrates another important property of the relationship between the three curves, in that as the original coupon yield curve was positively sloping, so the spot and forward yield curves lie above it. The reasons behind this will be considered later in the chapter.

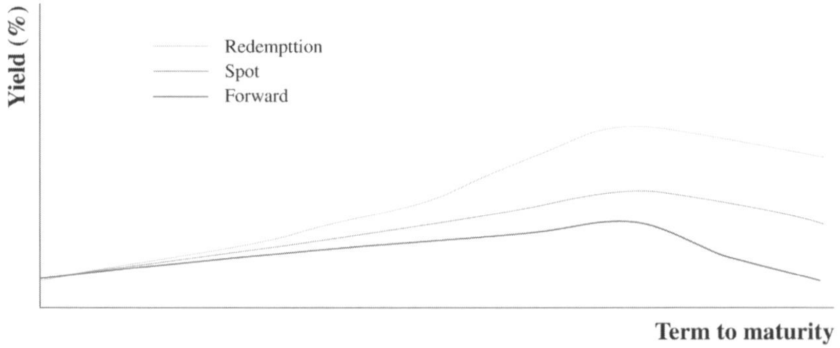

Figure 2.6 Redemption, spot and forward yield curves: traditional analysis

Let us now consider the following example. Suppose that a two-year bond with cash flows of £5.25 at the end of year one and £105.25 at the end of year two is trading at par, hence it has a redemption yield (indeed, a par yield) of 5.25% (this is the bond in Table 2.1 above). As we showed in the section on zero-coupon yields and the idea of the break-even principle, in order to be regarded as equivalent to this a pure zero-coupon bond or discount bond making a lump sum payment at the end of year two only (so with no cash flow at the end of year one) would require a rate of return of 5.269%, which is the spot yield. That is, for the same investment of £100 the maturity value would have to be £110.82 (this figure is obtained by multiplying 100 by $(1 + 0.05269)^2$).

This illustrates why the zero-coupon curve is important to corporate financiers involved in new bond issues. If we know the spot yields, then we can calculate the coupon required on a new three-year bond that is going to be issued at par in this interest rate environment by making the following calculation:

$$100 = \frac{C}{(1.05)} + \frac{C}{(1.05269)^2} + \frac{C + 100}{(1.05778)^3}\,.$$

This is solved in the conventional algebraic manner to give C equal to 5.75%.

The relationship between spot rates and forward rates was shown at (2.8). We can illustrate it as follows. If the spot yield is the *average return*, then the forward rate can be interpreted as the *marginal return*. If the marginal return between years two and three increases from 5.539% to 6.803%, then the average return increases from 5.269% up to the three-year spot yield of 5.778% as shown below:

$$[(1.05269)^2\,(1.06803)]^{1/3} - 1 = 0.05777868$$

or 5.778%, as shown in Table 2.1.

Formula Summary

The forward zero-coupon rate from interest period a to period b is given by (2.9).

$$ {}_a rf_b = \left[\frac{(1 + rs_b)^b}{(1 + rs_a)^a} \right]^{1/(b-a)} - 1 \qquad (2.9)$$

where rs_a and rs_b are the a and b period spot rates respectively.

The forward rate from interest period a to period $(a + 1)$ is given by (2.10):

$$_{a}rf_{a+1} = \frac{(1 + rs_{a+1})^{a+1}}{(1 + rs_{a})^{a}} - 1. \qquad (2.10)$$

Calculating spot rates from forward rates

The previous section showed the relationship between spot and forward rates. Just as we have derived forward rates from spot rates based on this mathematical relationship, it is possible to reverse this and calculate spot rates from forward rates. If we are presented with a forward yield curve, plotted from a set of one-period forward rates, we can use this to construct a spot yield curve. Equation (2.7) states the relationship between spot and forward rates, rearranged as (2.11) to solve for the spot rate:

$$rs_{n} = [(1 + {}_{1}rf_{1}) \times (1 + {}_{2}rf_{1}) \times (1 + {}_{3}rf_{1}) \times \ldots \times (1 + {}_{n}rf_{1})]^{1/n} - 1 \qquad (2.11)$$

where ${}_{1}rf_{1}$, ${}_{2}rf_{1}$, ${}_{3}rf_{1}$ are the one-period versus two-period, two-period versus three-period forward rates up to the $(n - 1)$ period versus n-period forward rates.

Remember to adjust (2.11) as necessary if dealing with forward rates relating to a deposit of a different interest period. If we are dealing with the current six-month spot rate and implied six-month forward rates, the relationship between these and the n-period spot rate is given by (2.11) in the same way as if we were dealing with the current one-year spot rate and implied one-year forward rates.

EXAMPLE 2.2(i) Spot rates

The one-year cash market yield is 5.00%. Market expectations have priced one-year rates in one year's time at 5.95% and in two years' time at 7.25%. What is the current three-year spot rate that would produce these forward rate views?

To calculate this we assume an investment strategy dealing today at forward rates, and calculate the return generated from this strategy. The return after a three-year period is given by the future value relationship, which in this case is 1.05 × 1.0595 × 1.0725 = 1.1931.

The three-year spot rate is then obtained by:

$$\left(\frac{1.1931}{1}\right)^{1/3} - 1 = 6.062\%.$$

2.2(ii)

Consider the following six-month implied forward rates, when the six-month spot rate is 4.0000%:

${}_1rf_1$	4.0000%
${}_2rf_1$	4.4516%
${}_3rf_1$	5.1532%
${}_4rf_1$	5.6586%
${}_5rf_1$	6.0947%
${}_6rf_1$	7.1129%

An investor is debating between purchasing a three-year zero-coupon bond at a price of £72.79481 per £100 nominal, or buying a six-month zero-coupon bond and then rolling over her investment every six months for the three-year term. If the investor was able to reinvest her proceeds every six months at the actual forward rates in place today, what would her proceeds be at the end of the three-year term? An investment of £72.79481 at the spot rate of 4% and then reinvested at the forward rates in our table over the next three years would yield a terminal value of:

$$72.79481 \times (1.04)(1.044516)(1.051532)(1.056586)(1.060947)(1.071129) = 100.$$

This merely reflects our spot and forward rates relationship, in that if all the forward rates are indeed realised, our investor's £72.79 will produce a terminal value that matches the investment in a three-year zero-coupon bond priced at the three-year spot rate. This illustrates the relationship between the three-year spot rate, the six-month spot rate and the implied six-month forward rates. So what is the three-year zero-coupon bond trading at? Using (2.11) the solution to this is given by:

$$rs_6 = [(1.04)(1.044516)(1.051532)(1.056586)(1.060947)(1.071129)]^{1/6} - 1 = 5.4346\%$$

which solves our three-year spot rate rs_6 as 5.4346%. Of course, we could have also solved for rs_6 using the conventional price/yield formula for zero-coupon bonds; however, the calculation above illustrates the relationship between spot and forward rates.

An important note on spot and forward rates

Forward rates that exist at any one time reflect everything that is known in the market *up to that point*. Certain market participants may believe that the forward rate curve is a forecast of the future spot rate curve. This is implied by the *unbiased expectations hypothesis* that we consider below. In fact there is no direct relationship between the forward rate curve and the spot rate curve; for an excellent analysis of this see Jarrow (1996). It is possible for example for the forward rate curve to be upward sloping at the same time that short-dated spot rates are expected to decline.

To view the forward rate curve as a predictor of rates is a misuse of it. The derivation of forward rates reflects all currently known market information. Assuming that all developed country markets are at least in a semi-strong form,[5] to preserve market equilibrium there can only be one set of forward rates from a given spot rate curve. However, this does not mean that such rates are a prediction because the instant after they have been calculated new market knowledge may become available that alters the market's view of future interest rates. This will cause the forward rate curve to change.

[5] See Fama (1970).

Forward rates are important because they are required to make prices today for dealing at a future date. For example, a bank's corporate customer may wish to fix today the interest rate payable on a loan that begins in one year from now; what rate does the bank quote? The forward rate is used by market-makers to quote prices for dealing today, and is the best *expectation* of future interest rates given everything that is known in the market up to now, but it is not a prediction of future spot rates. What would happen if a bank was privy to insider information; for example, it knew that central bank base rates would be changed very shortly? A bank in possession of such information (if we ignore the ethical implications) would not quote forward rates based on the spot rate curve, but would quote rates that reflected its insider knowledge.

Bond valuation using forward rates

That there is a relationship between spot rates and implied forward rates, although it is not necessarily a straightforward one, should tell us that, in theory, there is no difference in valuing a conventional bond with either spot rates or forward rates. The present value of a cash flow C received in period n using forward rates is given by (2.12):

$$PV_C = \frac{C}{(1 + rs_1)(1 + {}_1rf_1)(1 + {}_2rf_1) \ldots (1 + {}_nrf_1)}. \tag{2.12}$$

Therefore we use (2.12) to assemble the expression for valuing an N-period term bond using implied forward rates, with coupon C, given at (2.13). Note that we use the six-month or one-year spot rates and the six-month or one-year implied forward rates for the forward dates according to whether the bond pays annual or semi-annual coupons. Equation (2.13) assumes an exact number of interest periods to maturity.

$$P_d = \frac{C}{(1 + rs_1)} + \frac{C}{(1 + rs_1)(1 + {}_0rf_1)} + \frac{C}{(1 + rs_1)(1 + {}_1rf_1)(1 + {}_2rf_1)} + \ldots$$
$$+ \frac{C + M}{(1 + rs_1)(1 + {}_1rf_1)(1 + {}_2rf_1) \ldots (1 + {}_Nrf_1)} \tag{2.13}$$

Although bond analysts may use either spot or implied forward rates to present value cash flow streams, the final valuation will be the same regardless of whichever rates are used.

The annuity yield curve

Life assurance companies and other providers of personal pensions are users of the *annuity yield curve*, which is a plot of annuity yields against term to maturity. The *annuity yield* is the implied yield on an annuity where the annuity is valued using spot yields. In (2.2) above we decomposed a bond into an annuity and a zero-coupon discounted bond. We used the spot yield to price the discount bond component. Now we are concerned with the annuity or pure coupon component.

The value of the annuity component of a bond is given by (2.14):

$$A_N = \sum_{n=1}^{N} \frac{C}{(1 + rs_n)^n} = \sum_{n=1}^{N} C \times df_n \qquad (2.14)$$

$$= C \times A_N$$

where rs_n and df_n are the n-period spot rate and discount factor, as defined earlier, and A_N is the fair price of an N-year annuity of £1. However, A_N is also given by the standard formula (2.15):

$$A_N = \frac{1}{ra_N}\left[1 - \frac{1}{(1 + ra_N)^N}\right] \qquad (2.15)$$

where ra_N is the annuity yield on an N-year annuity.

Again using the same rates as before, consider a three-year bond with a coupon of 5.75%. To obtain the value of the annuity portion of the bond we would use (2.14) to give us:

$$A_3 = \frac{5.75}{1.05} + \frac{5.75}{(1.05269)^2} + \frac{5.75}{(1.05778)^3}$$

$$= 15.52.$$

This indicates a value for A_3 of £2.70, obtained by dividing 15.52 by 5.75. We can then use this value to solve for the annuity yield ra using (2.15) or using annuity tables; in this case the three-year annuity yield is 5.46%.

The relationship between the spot and annuity yield curves will depend on the level of market rates. With a positive-sloping spot yield curve, the annuity yield is below the end-of-period spot yield; with a negative-sloping spot yield curve, the annuity yield curve lies above it. With a low-coupon bond the present value will be dominated by the terminal payment and the annuity curve will lie close to the spot curve; with a high-coupon bond the two curves will be further apart.

Analysing and interpreting the yield curve

From observing yield curves in different markets at any time, we notice that a yield curve can adopt one of four basic shapes. These are:

- ***normal*** **or** ***conventional***: in which yields are at "average" levels and the curve slopes gently upwards as maturity increases;
- ***upward sloping*** **or** ***positive*** **or** ***rising***: in which yields are at historically low levels, with long rates substantially greater than short rates;
- ***downward sloping*** **or** ***inverted*** **or** ***negative***: in which yield levels are very high by historical standards, but long-term yields are significantly lower than short rates;
- ***humped***: where yields are high with the curve rising to a peak in the medium-term maturity area, and then sloping downwards at longer maturities.

Sometimes yield curves will incorporate a mixture of the above features.

A great deal of effort is expended by bond analysts and economists in analysing and interpreting yield curves. There is often a considerable information content associated with any curve at any time. For example, Figure 2.7 shows the UK gilt redemption yield curve at three different times in the ten years from June 1989 to June 1999. What does the shape of each curve tell us about the UK debt market, and the UK economy at each particular time?

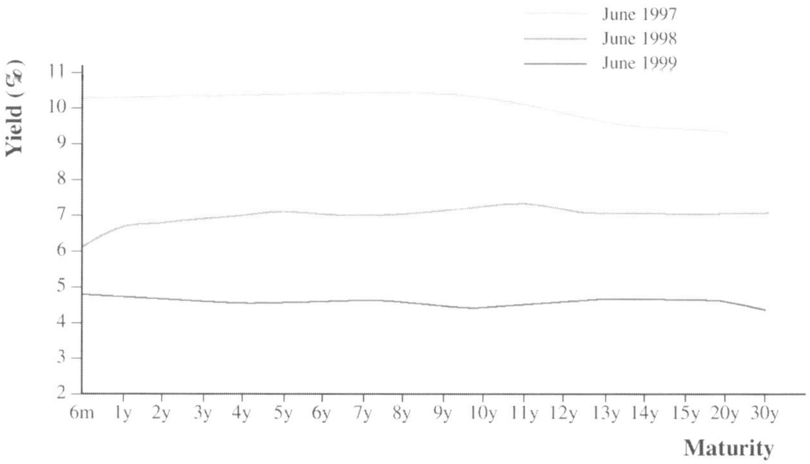

Figure 2.7 UK gilt redemption yield curves
Source: Bloomberg L.P. Used with permission.

In this section we will consider the various explanations that have been put forward to explain the shape of the yield curve at any one time. None of the theories can adequately explain everything about yield curves and the shapes they assume at any time, so generally observers seek to explain specific curves using a combination of the accepted theories. This subject is a large one; indeed, we could devote several books to it, so at this stage we will introduce the main ideas; readers wishing to read about this in further degree may consult the author's book *Advanced Fixed Income Analysis* (Butterworth-Heinemann 2004).

The existence of a yield curve itself indicates that there is a cost associated with funds of different maturities, otherwise we would observe a flat yield curve. The fact that we very rarely observe anything approaching a flat yield suggests that investors require different rates of return depending on the maturity of the instrument they are holding. In this section we review the main theories that have been put forward to explain the shape of the yield curve, which all have fairly long-dated antecedents.

An excellent account of the term structure is given in *Theory of Financial Decision Making* by Jonathan Ingersoll (1987), Chapter 18. In fact it is worth purchasing this book just for Chapter 18 alone. Another quality account of the term structure is by Shiller (1990). In the following section we provide an introductory review of the research on this subject to date.

The expectations hypothesis

The expectations hypothesis suggests that bondholders' expectations determine the course of future interest rates. There are two main competing versions of this hypothesis, the *local expectations hypothesis* and the *unbiased expectations hypothesis*. The *return-to-maturity expectations* hypothesis and *yield-to-maturity expectations* hypothesis are also quoted (see Ingersoll 1987). The local expectations hypothesis states that all bonds of the same class but differing in term to maturity will have the same expected holding period rate of return. This suggests that a six-month bond and a 20-year bond will produce the same rate of return, on average, over the stated holding period. So if we intend to hold a bond for six months, we will receive the same return no matter what specific bond we buy. The author feels that this theory is not always the case or relevant, despite being mathematically neat; however, it is worth spending a few moments discussing it and related points. Generally, holding period returns from longer dated bonds are on average higher than those from short-dated bonds. Intuitively we would expect this, with longer dated bonds offering higher returns to compensate for their higher price volatility (risk). The local expectations hypothesis would not agree with the conventional belief that investors, being risk averse, require higher returns as a reward for taking on higher risk; in addition, it does not provide any insight about the shape of the yield curve. An article by Cox, Ingersoll and Ross (1981) showed that the local expectations hypothesis best reflected equilibrium between spot and forward yields. This was demonstrated using a feature known as Jensen's inequality, which is described in Appendix 2.2 at the end of this chapter. Robert Jarrow (1996) states:

> … in an economic equilibrium, the returns on … similar maturity zero-coupon bonds cannot be too different. If they were too different, no investor would hold the bond with the smaller return. This difference could not persist in an economic equilibrium.
> (Jarrow 1996, p. 50)

This reflects economic logic, but in practice other factors can impact on holding period returns between bonds that do not have similar maturities. For instance, investors will have restrictions as to which bonds they can hold; for example, banks and building societies are required to hold short-dated bonds for liquidity purposes. In an environment of economic disequilibrium, these investors would still have to hold shorter dated bonds, even if the holding period return was lower.

So although it is economically neat to expect that the return on a long-dated bond is equivalent to rolling over a series of shorter dated bonds, it is often observed that longer term (default-free) returns exceed annualised short-term default-free returns. So an investor who continuously rolled over a series of short-dated zero-coupon bonds would most likely receive a lower return than if she had invested in a long-dated zero-coupon bond. Rubinstein (1999) gives an excellent, accessible explanation of why this should be so. The reason is that compared to the theoretical model, in reality future spot rates are not known with certainty. This means that short-dated zero-coupon bonds are more attractive to investors for two reasons; first, they are more appropriate instruments to use for hedging purposes, and second they are more liquid instruments, in that they may be more readily converted back into cash than long-dated instruments. With regard to hedging, consider an exposure to rising interest rates. If the yield curve shifts upwards at some point in the future, the price of long-dated bonds will fall by a greater amount. This is a negative result for holders of such bonds, whereas the investor in short-dated bonds will benefit from rolling over his funds at the (new) higher rates. With regard to the second issue, Rubinstein (1999) states:

> … it can be shown that in an economy with risk-averse individuals, uncertainty concerning the timing of aggregate consumption, the partial irreversibility of real investments (longer-term physical investments cannot be converted into investments with earlier payouts without sacrifice), [and] … real assets with shorter-term payouts will tend to have a "liquidity" advantage.
> (Rubinstein 1999, pp. 84–85)

Therefore the demand for short-term instruments is frequently higher, and hence short-term returns are often lower than long-term returns.

The *pure* or *unbiased expectations hypothesis* is more commonly encountered and states that current implied forward rates are unbiased estimators of future spot interest rates.[6] It assumes that investors act in a way that eliminates any advantage of holding instruments of a particular maturity. Therefore if we have a positive-sloping yield curve, the unbiased expectations hypothesis states that the market expects spot interest rates to rise. Equally, an inverted yield curve is an indication that spot rates are expected to fall. If short-term interest rates are expected to rise, then longer yields should be higher than shorter ones to reflect this. If this were not the case, investors would only buy the shorter dated bonds and roll over the investment when they matured. Likewise, if rates are expected to fall then longer yields should be lower than short yields. The unbiased expectations hypothesis states that the long-term interest rate is a geometric average of expected future short-term rates. This was in fact the theory that was used to derive the forward yield curve using (2.5) and (2.7) previously. This gives us:

$$(1 + rs_N)^N = (1 + rs_1)(1 + {}_1rf_2) \dots (1 + {}_{N-1}rf_N) \qquad (2.16)$$

or

$$(1 + rs_N)^N = (1 + rs_{N-1})^{N-1}(1 + {}_{N-1}rf_N) \qquad (2.17)$$

where rs_N is the spot yield on a N-year bond and ${}_{n-1}rf_n$ is the implied one-year rate n years ahead. For example, if the current one-year spot rate is rs_1 and the market is expecting the one-year rate in a year's time to be ${}_1rf_2$ =

6 For original discussion, see Lutz (1940) and Fisher (1986, although he formulated his ideas earlier).

5.539%, then the market is expecting a £100 investment in two one-year bonds to yield:

$$£100(1.05)(1.05539) = £110.82$$

after two years. To be equivalent to this an investment in a two-year bond has to yield the same amount, implying that the current two-year rate is rs_2 as shown below:

$$£100(1 + rs_2)^2 = £110.82$$

which gives us rs_2 equal to 5.27%, and gives us the correct future value as shown below:

$$£100(1.0527)^2 = £110.82.$$

This result must be so, to ensure no arbitrage opportunities exist in the market and in fact we showed as much earlier in the chapter when we considered forward rates. According to the unbiased expectations hypothesis therefore the forward rate ${}_0rf_2$ is an unbiased predictor of the spot rate ${}_2rs_1$ observed one period later; on average the forward rate should equal the subsequent spot rate. The hypothesis can be used to explain any shape in the yield curve.

A rising yield curve is therefore explained by investors expecting short-term interest rates to rise; that is, ${}_1rf_2 > rs_2$. A falling yield curve is explained by investors expecting short-term rates to be lower in the future. A humped yield curve is explained by investors expecting short-term interest rates to rise and long-term rates to fall. Expectations, or views on the future direction of the market, are a function mainly of the expected rate of inflation. If the market expects inflationary pressures in the future, the yield curve will be positively shaped, while if inflation expectations are inclined towards disinflation, then the yield curve will be negative. However, several empirical studies, including one by Fama (1976), have shown that forward rates are essentially biased predictors of future spot interest rates, and often over-estimate future levels of spot rates. The unbiased hypothesis has also been criticised for suggesting that investors can forecast (or have a view on) very long-dated spot interest rates, which might be considered slightly unrealistic. As yield curves in most developed country markets exist to a maturity of up to thirty years or longer, such criticisms may have some substance. Are investors able to forecast interest rates 10, 20 or 30 years into the future? Perhaps not, nevertheless this is indeed the information content of, say, a 30-year bond; since the yield on the bond is set by the market, it is valid to suggest that the market has a view on inflation and future interest rates for up to thirty years forward.

The expectations hypothesis is stated in more than one way; we have already encountered the local expectations hypothesis. Other versions include the *return-to-maturity* expectations hypothesis, which states that the total return from holding a zero-coupon bond to maturity will be equal to the total return that is generated by holding a short-term instrument and continuously rolling it over the same maturity period. A related version, the *yield-to-maturity* hypothesis, states that the periodic return from holding a zero-coupon bond will be equal to the return from rolling over a series of coupon bonds, but refers to the annualised return earned each year rather than the total return earned over the life of the bond. This assumption enables a zero-coupon yield curve to be derived from the redemption yields of coupon bonds. The unbiased expectations hypothesis of course states that forward rates are equal to the spot rates expected by the market in the future. The Cox, Ingersoll and Ross article suggests that only the local expectations hypothesis describes a model that is purely arbitrage-free, as under the other scenarios it would be possible to employ certain investment strategies that would produce returns in excess of what was implied by today's yields. Although it has been suggested[7] that the differences between the local and the unbiased hypotheses are not material, a model that describes such a scenario would not reflect investors' beliefs, which is why further research is ongoing in this area.

The unbiased expectations hypothesis does not by itself explain all the shapes of the yield curve or the information content contained within it, so it is often tied in with other explanations, including the liquidity preference theory. For a description on testing the unbiased expectations hypothesis, see Appendix 2.1.

Liquidity preference theory

Intuitively we might feel that longer maturity investments are more risky than shorter ones. An investor lending money for a five-year term will usually demand a higher rate of interest than if she were to lend the same customer money for a five-week term. This is because borrowers may not be able to repay the loan over the longer time period as they may for instance,

---

[7] For example, see Campbell (1986) and Livingstone (1990).

have gone bankrupt in that period. For this reason longer dated yields should be higher than short-dated yields, to recompense the lender for the higher risk exposure during the term of the loan.[8]

We can consider this theory in terms of inflation expectations as well. Where inflation is expected to remain roughly stable over time, the market would anticipate a positive yield curve. However, the expectations hypothesis cannot by itself explain this phenomenon, as under stable inflationary conditions one would expect a flat yield curve. The risk inherent in longer dated investments, or the *liquidity preference theory*, seeks to explain a positive-shaped curve. Generally, borrowers prefer to borrow over as long a term as possible, while lenders will wish to lend over as short a term as possible. Therefore, as we first stated, lenders have to be compensated for lending over the longer term; this compensation is considered a premium for a loss in *liquidity* for the lender. The premium is increased the further the investor lends across the term structure, so that the longest dated investments will, all else being equal, have the highest yield. So the liquidity preference theory states that the yield curve should almost always be upward sloping, reflecting bondholders' preference for the liquidity and lower risk of shorter dated bonds. An inverted yield curve could still be explained by the liquidity preference theory when it is combined with the unbiased expectations hypothesis. A *humped* yield curve might be viewed as a combination of an inverted yield curve together with a positive-sloping liquidity preference curve.

The difference between a yield curve explained by unbiased expectations and an actual observed yield curve is sometimes referred to as the *liquidity premium*. This refers to the fact that in some cases short-dated bonds are easier to transact in the market than long-term bonds. It is difficult to quantify the effect of the liquidity premium, which in any cases is not static and fluctuates over time. The liquidity premium is so-called because, in order to induce investors to hold longer dated securities, the yields on such securities must be higher than those available on short-dated securities, which are more liquid and may be converted into cash more easily. The liquidity premium is the compensation required for holding less liquid instruments. If longer dated securities then provide higher yields, as is suggested by the existence of the liquidity premium, they should generate on average higher total returns over an investment period. This is not consistent with the local expectations hypothesis. More formally we can write:

8 For original discussion, see Hicks (1946).

$$0 = L_1 < L_2 < L_3 < \ldots < L_n$$

$$\text{and } (L_2 - L_1) > (L_3 - L_2) > \ldots (L_n - L_{n-1})$$

where L is the premium for a bond with term to maturity of n years, which states that the premium increases as the term to maturity rises and that an otherwise flat yield curve will have a positively sloping curve, with the degree of slope steadily decreasing as we extend along the yield curve. This is consistent with observation of yield curves under "normal" conditions.

The expectations hypothesis assumes that forward rates are equal to the expected future spot rates; that is, as shown in (2.18):

$$_{n-1}rf_n = E(_{n-1}rs_n) \tag{2.18}$$

where $E()$ is the expectations operator for the current period. This assumption implies that the forward rate is an unbiased predictor of the future spot rate, as we suggested in the previous paragraph. Liquidity preference theory, on the other hand, recognises the possibility that the forward rate may contain an element of liquidity premium that declines over time as the period approaches, given by (2.19):

$$_{n-1}rf_n > E(_{n-1}rs_n). \tag{2.19}$$

If there was uncertainty in the market about the future direction of spot rates and hence where the forward rate should lie, (2.19) is adjusted to give the reverse inequality.

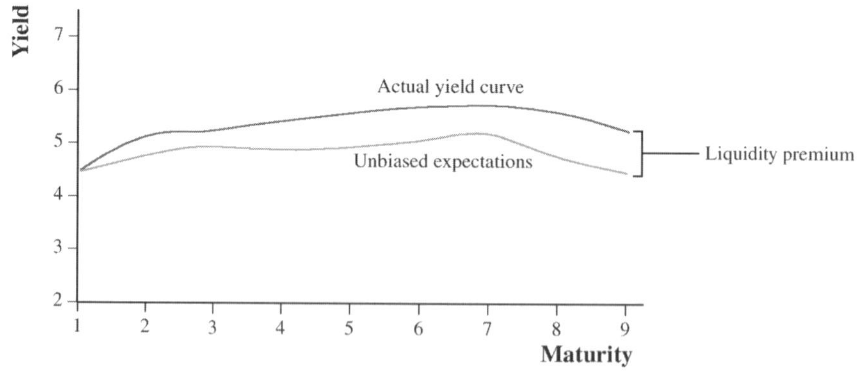

Figure 2.8 Yield curve explained by expectations hypothesis and liquidity preference

Money substitute hypothesis

A particular explanation of short-dated bond yield curves has been attempted by Kessel (1965). In the *money substitute* theory, short-dated bonds are regarded as substitutes for holding cash. Investors hold only short-dated market instruments because these are viewed as low or negligible risk. As a result the yields of short-dated bonds are depressed due to the increased demand and lie below longer dated bonds. Borrowers, on the other hand, prefer to issue debt for longer maturities, and on as few occasions as possible to minimise costs. Therefore the yields of longer dated paper are driven upwards due to a combination of increased supply and lower liquidity. In certain respects the money substitute theory is closely related to the liquidity preference theory, and by itself does not explain inverted or humped yield curves.

Segmentation hypothesis

The capital markets are made up of a wide variety of users, each with different requirements. Certain classes of investors will prefer dealing at the short-end of the yield curve, while others will concentrate on the longer end of the market. The *segmented markets* theory suggests that activity is concentrated in certain specific areas of the market, and that there are no inter-relationships between these parts of the market; the relative amounts of funds invested in each of the maturity spectrum causes differentials in supply and demand, which results in humps in the yield curve. That is, the shape of the yield curve is determined by supply and demand for certain specific maturity investments, each of which has no reference to any other part of the curve.

For example, banks and building societies concentrate a large part of their activity at the short end of the curve, the routine of daily cash management (part of *asset and liability management*) and for regulatory purposes (part of *liquidity* requirements). Fund managers such as pension funds and insurance companies are active at the long end of the market. Few institutional investors however have any preference for medium-dated bonds. This behaviour on the part of investors will lead to high prices (low yields) at both the short and long ends of the yield curve and lower prices (higher yields) in the middle of the term structure.

Since according to the segmented markets hypothesis a separate market exists for specific maturities along the term structure, interest rates for these maturities are set by supply and demand.[9] Where there is no demand for a

[9] See Culbertson (1957).

particular maturity, the yield will lie above other segments. Market participants do not hold bonds in any other area of the curve outside their area of interest[10] so that short-dated and long-dated bond yields exist independently of each other. The segmented markets theory is usually illustrated by reference to banks and life companies. Banks and building societies' Treasury desks hold their funds in short-dated instruments, usually no longer than five years in maturity. This is because of the nature of retail banking operations, with a large volume of instant access funds being deposited in banks, and also for regulatory purposes. Holding short-term, liquid bonds enables banks to meet any sudden or unexpected demand for funds from customers. The classic theory suggests that as banks invest their funds in short-dated bonds, the yields on these bonds are driven down. When they then liquidate part of their holding, perhaps to meet higher demand for loans, the yields are driven up and prices of the bonds fall. This affects the short end of the yield curve but not the long end.

The segmented markets theory can be used to explain any particular shape of the yield curve, although it fits best perhaps with positive-sloping curves. However, it cannot be used to interpret the yield curve whatever shape it may be, and therefore it offers no information content during analysis. By definition, the theory suggests that investors' bonds with different maturities are not perfect substitutes for each other. This is because different bonds would have different holding period returns, making them imperfect substitutes of one another.[11] As a result of bonds being imperfect substitutes, markets are segmented according to maturity.

The segmentations hypothesis is a reasonable explanation of certain features of a conventional positively sloping yield curve, but by itself it is not sufficient. There is no doubt that banks and building societies have a requirement to hold securities at the short end of the yield curve, as much for regulatory purposes as for yield considerations; however, other investors are probably more flexible and will place funds where value is deemed to exist. Nonetheless, the higher demand for benchmark securities does drive down yields along certain segments of the curve.

A slightly modified version of the market segmentation hypothesis is known as the *preferred habitat theory*. This suggests that different market participants have an interest in specified areas of the yield curve, but can be induced to hold bonds from other parts of the maturity spectrum if there is

[10] For example, retail and commercial banks hold bonds in the short dates, while life assurance companies hold long-dated bonds.

[11] See note 10.

sufficient incentive. Hence banks may at certain times hold longer dated bonds once the price of these bonds falls to a certain level, making the return on the bonds worth the risk involved in holding them. Similar considerations may persuade long-term investors to hold short-dated debt. So higher yields will be required to make bondholders shift out of their usual area of interest. This theory essentially recognises the flexibility that investors have, outside regulatory or legal requirements (such as the terms of an institutional fund's objectives), to invest in whatever part of the yield curve they identify value.

Humped yield curves

When plotting a yield curve of all the bonds in a certain class, it is common to observe humped yield curves. These usually occur for a variety of reasons. In line with the unbiased expectations hypothesis, humped curves will be observed when interest rates are expected to rise over the next several periods and then decline. On other occasions humped curves can result from skewed expectations of future interest rates. This is when the market believes that fairly constant future interest rates are likely, but also believes that there is a small probability for lower rates in the medium term. The other common explanation for humped curves is the preferred habitat theory.

The combined theory

The explanation for the shape of the yield curve at any time is more likely to be described by a combination of the pure expectations hypothesis and the liquidity preference theory, and possibly one or two other theories. Market analysts often combine the unbiased expectations hypothesis and the liquidity preference theory into an "eclectic" theory. The result is fairly consistent with any shape of yield curve, and is also a predictor of rising interest rates. In the combined theory the forward interest rate is equal to the expected future spot rate, together with a quantified liquidity premium. This is shown at (2.20):

$$ {}_0rf_i = E({}_{i-1}rs_1) + L_i \qquad (2.20) $$

where L_i is the liquidity premium for a term to maturity of i. The size of the liquidity premium is expected to increase with increasing maturity.[12] An illustration is given at Example 2.3.

[12] So that $L_i > L_{i-1}$.

EXAMPLE 2.3 **Positive yield curve with constant expected future interest rates**

Consider the interest rate structure in Table 2.2.

Period n	0	1	2	3	4	5
$E(rs)$		4.5%	4.5%	4.5%	4.5%	4.5%
Forward rate ${}_0rf_n$		5.0%	5.5%	6.0%	6.5%	7.5%
Spot rate rs_n	5.0%	5.3%	5.8%	6.2%	6.8%	7.0%

Table 2.2 Positive yield curve with constant expected future rates

The current term structure is positively-sloping since the spot rates increase with increasing maturity. However, the market expects future spot rates to be constant at 4.5%. The forward and spot rates are also shown; however, the forward rate is a function of the expected spot rate and the liquidity premium. This premium is equal to 0.50% for the first year, 1.0% in the second, and so on.

The combined theory is consistent with an inverted yield curve. This will apply even when the liquidity premium is increasing with maturity; for example, where the expected future spot interest rate is declining. Typically, this would be where there was a current term structure of falling yields along the term structure. The spot rates might be declining where the fall in the expected future spot rate exceeds the corresponding increase in the liquidity premium.

The flat yield curve

The conventional theories do not seek to explain a flat yield curve. Although it is rare to observe flat curves in a market, certainly for any length of time, at times they do emerge in response to peculiar economic circumstances. In the conventional thinking, a flat curve is not tenable because investors should in theory have no incentive to hold long-dated bonds over shorter dated bonds when there is no yield premium, so that as they sell off long-dated paper the yield at the long end should rise, producing an upward-sloping curve. In the previous circumstances of a flat curve, analysts have produced different explanations for their existence. In November 1988 the US Treasury yield curve was flat relative to the recent past; researchers contended that this was the result of the market's view that long-dated yields would fall as bond prices rallied upwards.[13] One recommendation is to buy longer maturities when the yield curve is flat, in anticipation of lower long-term interest rates, which is the direct opposite to the view that a flat curve is a signal to sell long bonds. In the case of the US market in 1988, long bond yields did in fact fall by approximately 2% in the following 12 months. This would seem to indicate that one's view of future long-term rates should be behind the decision to buy or sell long bonds, rather than the shape of the yield curve itself. A flat curve may well be more heavily influenced by supply and demand factors than anything else, with the majority opinion eventually winning out and forcing a change in the curve to a more conventional shape.

Yield curves as a function of the stochastic behaviour of interest rates

As a result of research into the behaviour of asset prices more recent explanations for the shape of the yield curve have sought to describe it as reflecting the behaviour of interest rates and the process that interest rates follow. These explanations are termed *stochastic processes*. A stochastic process is one where random phenomena evolve over time, and these may be asset prices, interest rates, returns on an investment portfolio, and so on. Under these explanations then, yield curves reflect the following:

- bond yields follow a stochastic process over time, and hence the yield curve reflects this;
- bond yields at any one time satisfy the no-arbitrage pricing rule for spot and forward rates.

The model of the term structure as being an arbitrage-free stochastic process evolved with option pricing theory and was described separately.[14] Such models sought to describe the term structure in terms of the short-term interest rate only, more recent models describe the whole term structure as part of a stochastic process.[15] This subject is key to yield curve modelling and is discussed further in Choudhry (2004).

---

13 See Levy (1999).

14 See Black and Scholes (1973) and Merton (1973).

15 For example, see Heath, Jarrow and Morton (1992).

Further views on the yield curve

In this and the previous chapter our discussion of present values, spot and forward interest rates assumed an economist's world of the *perfect market* (also sometimes called the *frictionless* financial market). Such a perfect capital market is characterised by:

- perfect information;
- no taxes;
- bullet maturity bonds;
- no transaction costs.

Of course, practice markets are not completely perfect. However, assuming perfect markets makes the discussion of spot and forward rates and the term structure easier to handle. When we analyse yield curves for their information content, we have to remember that the markets that they represent are not perfect, and that frequently we observe anomalies that are not explained by the conventional theories.

At any one time it is probably more realistic to suggest that a range of factors contributes to the yield curve being one particular shape. For instance, short-term interest rates are greatly influenced by the availability of funds in the money market. The slope of the yield curve (usually defined as the 10-year yield minus the three-month interest rate) is also a measure of the degree of tightness of government monetary policy. A low, upward-sloping curve is often thought to be a sign that an environment of cheap money, due to a more loose monetary policy, is to be followed by a period of higher inflation and higher bond yields. Equally, a high downward-sloping curve is taken to mean that a situation of tight credit, due to more strict monetary policy, will result in falling inflation and lower bond yields. Inverted yield curves have often preceded recessions; for instance, *The Economist* in an article from April 1998 remarked that in the United States every recession since 1955 bar one had been preceded by a negative yield curve. The analysis is the same: if investors expect a recession they also expect inflation to fall, so the yields on long-term bonds will fall relative to short-term bonds. So the conventional explanation for an inverted yield curve is that the markets and the investment community expect either a slow-down of the economy, or an outright recession.[16] In this case one would expect the monetary authorities to ease the money supply by reducing the base interest rate in the near future; hence, an inverted curve. At the same

[16] A recession is formally defined as two successive quarters of falling output in the domestic economy.

time, a reduction of short-term interest rates will affect short-dated bonds and these are sold off by investors, further raising their yield.

While the conventional explanation for negative yield curves is an expectation of economic slow-down, on occasion other factors will be involved. In the United Kingdom in the period July 1997–June 1999 the gilt yield curve was inverted.[17] There was no general view that the economy was heading for recession, however. In fact, the new Labour government led by Tony Blair inherited an economy believed to be in good health. Instead the explanation behind the inverted shape of the gilt yield curve focused on two other factors: first, the handing of responsibility for setting interest rates to the Monetary Policy Committee (MPC) of the Bank of England, and second, the expectation that the United Kingdom would over the medium term abandon sterling and join the euro currency. The yield curve in this time suggested that the market expected the MPC to be successful and keep inflation at a level around 2.5% over the long term (its target is actually a 1% range either side of 2.5%),[18] and also that sterling interest rates would need to come down over the medium term as part of *convergence* with interest rates in euroland. These are both medium-term expectations, however, and in the author's view not logical at the short-end of the yield curve. In fact, the term structure moved to a positive-sloped shape up to the 6–7 year area, before inverting out to the long-end of the curve, in June 1999. This is a more logical shape for the curve to assume, but it was short-lived and returned to being inverted after the two-year term.

There is therefore significant information content in the yield curve, and economists and bond analysts will consider the shape of the curve as part of their policymaking and investment advice. The shape of parts of the curve, whether the short-end or long-end, as well that of the entire curve, can serve as useful predictors of future market conditions. As part of an analysis it is also worthwhile considering the yield curves across several different markets and currencies. For instance, the interest rate swap curve, and its position relative to that of the government bond yield curve, is also regularly analysed for its information content. In developed country economies the swap market is invariably as liquid as the government bond market, if not more liquid, and so it is common to see the swap curve analysed when making predictions about, say, the future level of short-term interest rates.

---

17 Although the curve briefly went positively sloped out to 7–8 years in July 1999, it very quickly reverted to being inverted throughout the term structure, and remained so until certain restrictions on the need for institutional investors to hold long-dated gilts were lifted by the government in 2002.

18 From 2004 the Bank of England adopted the European Unions' harmonised Consumer Price Index (CPI) inflation measure, and its target rate for CPI is now 2%.

Government policy will influence the shape and level of the yield curve, including policy on public-sector borrowing, debt management and open-market operations. The market's perception of the size of public-sector debt will influence bond yields; for instance, an increase in the level of debt can lead to an increase in bond yields across the maturity range. Open-market operations, which refer to the daily operation by the Bank of England to control the level of the money supply (to which end the Bank purchases short-term bills and also engages in repo dealing), can have a number of effects. In the short-term it can tilt the yield curve both upwards and downwards; longer term, changes in the level of the base rate will affect yield levels. An anticipated rise in base rates can lead to a drop in prices for short-term bonds, whose yields will be expected to rise – this can lead to a temporary inverted curve. Finally, debt management policy will influence the yield curve. (In the United Kingdom this is now the responsibility of the Debt Management Office.) Much government debt is rolled over as it matures, but the maturity of the replacement debt can have a significant influence on the yield curve in the form of humps in the market segment in which the debt is placed, if the debt is priced by the market at a relatively low price and hence high yield.

Interpreting the yield curve

We illustrate some of the points we have raised here using yield curves from the United Kingdom gilt market during the 1990s. It is of course easier to analyse them for their information content in hindsight than it might have been at the time, but these observations help illustrate the general conclusions that might be made.

To begin, consider the observed yield curves for January and June 1990 in Figures 2.9 and 2.10.[19]

[19] All government yield curves shown are fitted par yield curves, using the Bank of England's internal model (see Mastronikola (1991) and Anderson and Sleath (1999)), except where indicated. Source data is the Bank of England. The other curve is the interest rate swap curve, also called the Libor curve, for sterling swaps. In practice, interest rate swaps are priced off the government yield curve, and reflect the market's view of interbank credit risk, as the swap rate is payable by a bank (or corporate) viewed as having an element of credit risk. All swap curves are drawn using interest data from Bloomberg.

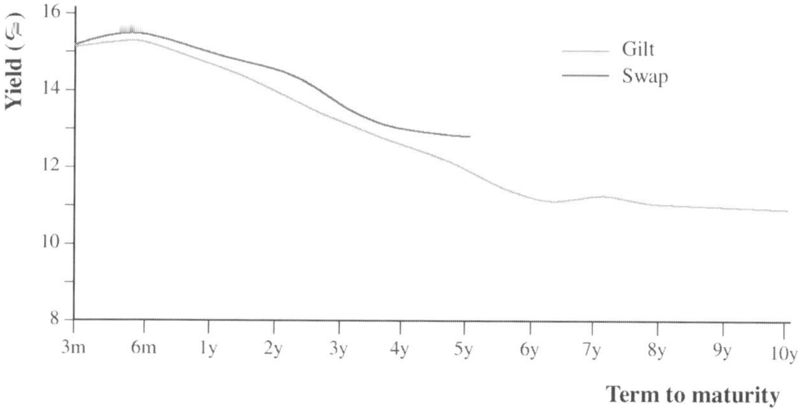

Figure 2.9 January 1990

The yield curve for the first date suggests declining short-term rates and this is indicated by the yield curve for June 1990. The prediction is approximately accurate.

That the yield curves were inverted is not surprising given that the UK economy was shortly to enter an economic recession; however, at that date – January 1990 – it had not yet begun. The evidence of GDP output data is that the recession took place during 1990–91. The markets were therefore expecting some loosening of monetary policy given the economic slowdown during 1989. There was an additional anomaly in that during 1988 the government had been paying off public-sector debt, leading some commentators to suggest that gilt supply would be reduced in coming years. This may have contributed to the depressed yields at the long end in January 1990 but almost certainly had less influence in June 1990, when the recession was underway.

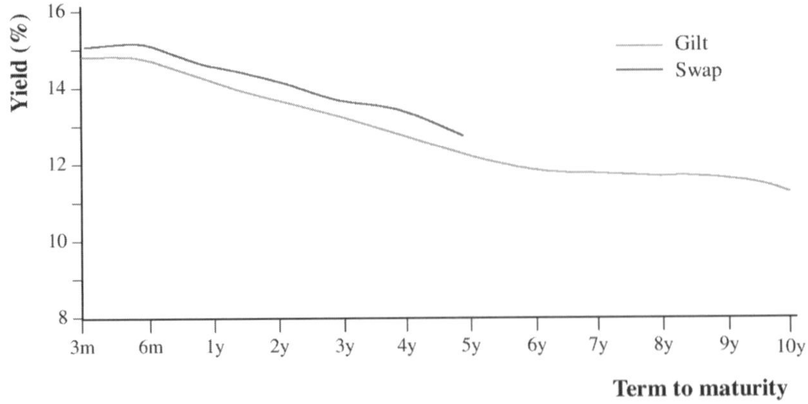

Figure 2.10 June 1990

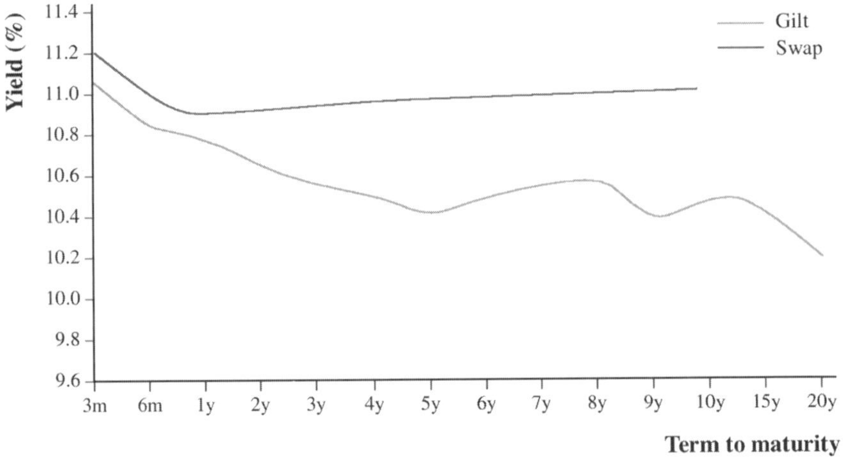

Figure 2.11 June 1991

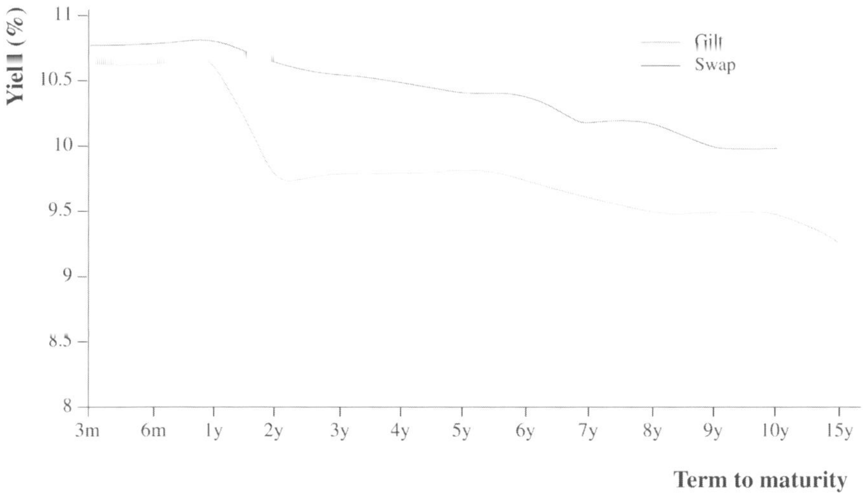

Figure 2.12 January 1992

Consider the same curves for June 1991 and January 1992, shown as Figures 2.11 and 2.12 respectively. In this case the money market has priced swaps to give a different shape yield curve; does this mean that the money market has a different view of forward rates to government bond investors? Observing the yield curves for January 1992 suggests not: the divergence in the swap curve reflects credit considerations that price long maturity corporate rates at increasing yield spreads. This is common during recessions, and indeed the curves reflect recession conditions in the UK economy at the time, as predicted by the yield curves during 1990. Another indicator is the continuation of the wide swap spread as the term to maturity increases to ten years, rather than the conventional mirroring of the government curve. Note also that the short-term segment of the swap curve in June 1991 (Figure 2.11) matches the government yield curve, indicating that the market agreed with the short-term forward rate prediction of the government curve.

During 1992, as the UK economy came out of recession, the government yield curve changed from inverted to steadily positive, while the swap curve mirrored the shape of the government curve. The swap spread itself has declined, to no more than 10 basis points at the short end. This was most pronounced shortly after sterling fell out of the European Union's exchange rate mechanism. Shown in Figure 2.13 are the curves for November 1992.

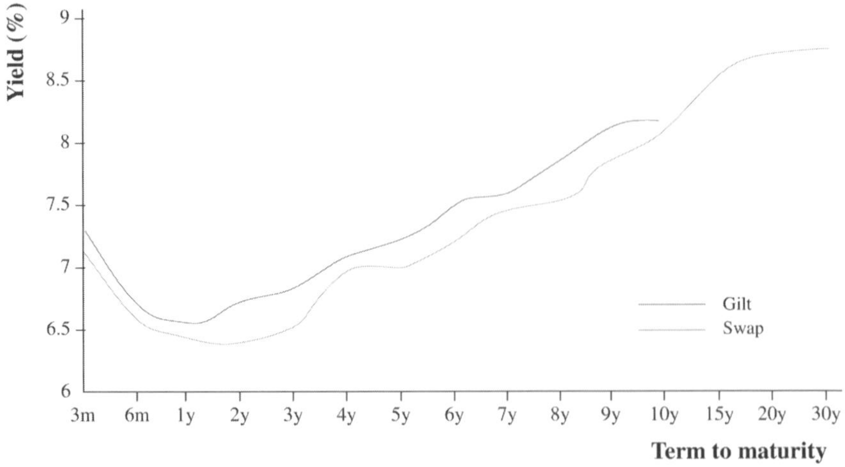

Figure 2.13 5 November 1992

Both yield curves had reverted to being purely positively-sloping by January 1993.

The illustrations used are examples where government yield curves were shown to be accurate predictors of the short-term rates that followed, more so than the swap curve. This is to be expected: the government or *benchmark* yield curve is the cornerstone of the debt markets, and is used by the market to price all other debt instruments, including interest rate swaps. This reflects both the liquidity of the government market and its risk-free status.

Fitting the yield curve

When graphing a yield curve, we plot a series of discrete points of yield against maturity. Similarly, for the term structure of interest rates, we plot spot rates for a fixed time period against that time period. The yield curve itself however is a smooth curve drawn through these points. Therefore we require a method that allows us to fit the curve as accurately as possible, known as *yield curve modelling* or *estimating the term structure*. There are several ways to model a yield curve, which we introduce in this section. The subject is covered in greater depth in the author's book *Fixed Income Markets* (John Wiley & Sons, Singapore 2004).

Ideally, the fitted yield curve should be a continuous function, with no gaps in the curve, while passing through the observed yield vertices. The curve also needs to be "smooth", as kinks in it will produce sudden sharp jumps in derived forward rates. We have stated how it is possible to calculate a set of discrete discount factors or a continuous discount function. It has been shown that the discount function, par yield curve, spot rate yield curve and forward rate curve are all related mathematically, such that if one knows any one of these, the other three can be derived. In practice, in many markets it is not possible usually to observe the curves directly, hence they need to be derived from coupon bond prices and yields. In attempting to model a yield curve from bond yields we need to consider the two fundamental issues introduced above. First is the problem of gaps in the maturity spectrum, as in reality there will not be a bond maturing at regular intervals along the complete term structure. For example, in the UK gilt market, currently there is no bond at all maturing between 2017 and 2021, or between 2021 and 2028. Second, as we have seen the term structure is formally defined in terms of spot or zero-coupon interest rates, but in many markets there is no actual zero-coupon bond market. In such cases spot rates cannot be inferred directly but must be implied from coupon bonds. Where zero-coupon bonds are traded, for example in the US and UK government bond markets, we are able to observe zero-coupon yields directly in the market.

Further problems in fitting the curve arise from these two issues. How is the gap in maturities to be tackled? Analysts need to choose between "smoothness" and "responsiveness" of the curve estimate. Most models opt for a smooth fitting; however, enough flexibility should be retained to allow for true movements in the term structure where indicated by the data. Should the yield curve be estimated from the discount function or, say, the par yield curve? There are other practical factors to consider as well, such as the effect of withholding tax on coupons, and the size of bond coupons themselves. We will consider the issues connected with estimating the yield curve in a later chapter; at this point we confine ourselves to introducing the main methods.

Interpolation

The simplest method that is employed to fit a curve is *linear interpolation*, which involves drawing a straight line joining each pair of yield vertices. To calculate the yield for one vertex we use (2.21):

$$rm_t = rm_i + \frac{t - n_i}{n_{i+1} - n_i} \times (rm_{i+1} - rm_i) \tag{2.21}$$

where rm_t is the yield being estimated and n is the number of years to maturity for yields that are observed. For example, consider the following redemption yields:

1 month:	4.00%
2 years:	5.00%
4 years:	6.50%
10 years:	6.75%

If we wish to estimate the six-year yield we calculate it using (2.21), which is:

$$rm_{6y} = 6.50\% + \frac{6-4}{10-6} \times 6.75\% - 6.5\%$$

$$= 6.5833\%.$$

The limitations of using linear interpolation are that first the curve can have sharp angles at the vertices where two straight lines meet, resulting in unreasonable jumps in the derived forward rates. Second, and more fundamentally being a straight-line method, it assumes that the yield between two vertices should automatically be rising (in a positive yield curve environment) or falling. This assumption can lead to gross inaccuracies in the fitted curve.

Another approach is to use *logarithmic interpolation*, which involves applying linear interpolation to the natural logarithms of the corresponding discount factors. Therefore given any two discount factors we can calculate an intermediate discount factor using (2.22):

$$ln(df_t) = ln(df_{n_i}) + \frac{t - n_i}{n_{i-1} - n_i} \times [ln(df_{n_i+1}) - ln(df_{n_i})]. \qquad (2.22)$$

To calculate the six-year yield from the same yield structure above, we use the following procedure:

- calculate the discount factors for years four and 10 and then take the natural logarithms of these discount factors;
- perform a linear interpolation on these logarithms;
- take the anti-log of the result, to get the implied interpolated discount factor;
- calculate the implied yield in this discount factor.

Using (2.22) we obtain a six-year yield of 6.6388%. The logarithmic interpolation method reduces the sharpness of angles on the curve and so makes it smoother, but it retains the other drawbacks of the linear interpolation method.

Polynomial models[20]

The most straightforward method for estimating the yield curve involves fitting a single polynomial in time. For example, a model might use an F-order polynomial, illustrated with (2.23):

$$rm_i = \alpha + \beta_1 n_i + \beta_2 N_i^2 + \ldots + \beta_F N_i^F + u_i \tag{2.23}$$

where

rm_i is the yield to maturity of the i-th bond
N_i is the term to maturity of the i-th bond
α, β_i are coefficients of the polynomial
u_i is the residual error on the i-th bond.

To determine the coefficients of the polynomial we minimise the sum of the squared residual errors, given by:

$$\sum_i^T u_i^2 \tag{2.24}$$

where T is the number of bonds used. This is represented graphically in Figure 2.14.

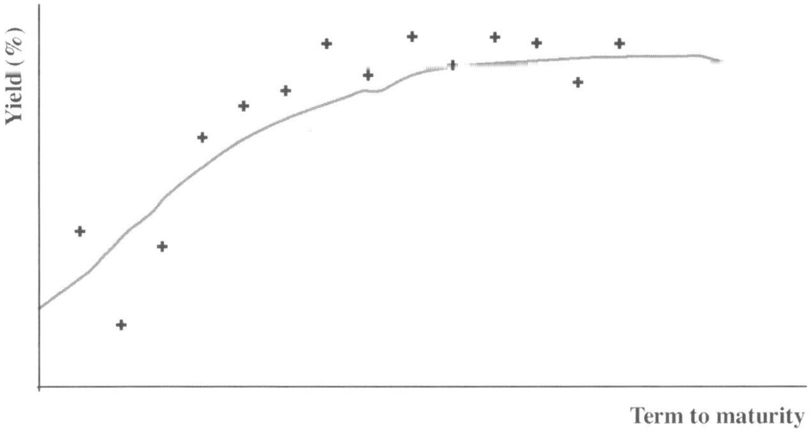

Figure 2.14 Polynomial curve fitting

[20] These are standard econometric techniques. For an excellent account see Campbell et al. (1997).

The type of curve that results is a function of the order of the polynomial F. If F is too large the curve will not be smooth but will be in effect too "responsive", such that the curve runs through every point, known as being "over-fitted". The extreme of this is given when $F = T - 1$. If F is too small the curve will be an over-estimation.

The method described above has been supplanted by a more complex method, which fits different polynomials over different but overlapping terms to maturity. The fitted curves are then spliced together to produce a single smooth curve over the entire term structure. This is known as a *spline* curve and is the one most commonly encountered in the markets. For an accessible introduction to spline techniques see James and Webber (2000) and Choudhry et al. (2001).

The limitation of the polynomial method is that a blip in the observed series of vertices, for instance a vertex which is out of line with others in the series, produces a "wobbled" shape, causing wild oscillations in the corresponding forward yields. This can result in the calculation of negative long-dated forward rates.

Cubic splines

The cubic spline method involves connecting each pair of yield vertices by fitting a unique cubic equation between them. This results in a yield curve where the whole curve is represented by a chain of cubic equations, instead of a single polynomial. This technique adds some "stiffness" to the yield curve, while at the same time preserving its smoothness.[21]

Using the same example as before, we wish to fit the yield curve from 0 to 10 years.

There are four observed vertices, so we require three cubic equations, $rm(_{i,t})$, each one connecting two adjacent vertices n_i and n_{i+1} as follows:

$$rm_{(0,t)} = a_0 n_3 + b_0 n_2 + c_0 n + d_0, \text{ which connects vertex } n_0 \text{ with } n_1$$
$$rm_{(1,t)} = a_1 n_3 + b_1 n_2 + c_1 n + d_1, \text{ which connects vertex } n_1 \text{ with } n_2$$
$$rm_{(2,t)} = a_2 n_3 + b_2 n_2 + c_2 n + d_2, \text{ which connects vertex } n_2 \text{ with } n_3$$

where a, b, c, and d are unknowns. The equations each contain four unknowns (the coefficients a to d), and there are three equations so we require twelve conditions in all to solve the system. The cubic spline method imposes certain conditions on the curves which makes it possible to solve the system. The solution for this set is summarised in Appendix 2.3.

[21] In case you're wondering, a spline is a tool used by a carpenter to draw smooth curves.

The three cubic equations for the data in this example are:

$rm_{(0,t)} = 0.022 \times n^3 + 0.413 \times n + 4.000$ for vertices $n_0 - n_1$
$rm_{(1,t)} = -0.047 \times n^3 + 0.411 \times n^2 - 0.410 \times n + 4.548$ for vertices $n_1 - n_2$
$rm_{(2,t)} = 0.008 \times n^3 - 0.249 \times n^2 + 2.230 \times n + 1.029$ for vertices $n_2 - n_3$.

Using a cubic spline produces a smoother curve for both the spot rates and the forward rates, while the derived forward curve will have fewer "kinks" in it.

To calculate the estimated yield for the six-year maturity we apply the third cubic equation, which spans the 4–10 year vertices, which is:

$$rm_{(2,t)} = 0.008 \times 6^3 - 0.249 \times 6^2 + 2.230 \times 6 + 1.029 = 7.173\%.$$

From Appendix 2.3 it is clear that simply to fit a 4-vertex spline requires the inversion of a fairly large matrix. In practice, more efficient mathematical techniques, known as basis splines or *B-splines,* are typically used when there are a larger number of observed yield vertices. This produces results that are very close to what we would obtain by simple matrix inversion.

Regression models

A variation on polynomial fitting is regression analysis. In this method bond prices are used as the dependent variable, with the coupon and maturity cash flows of the bonds being the independent variables. This is given by (2.25):

$$P_{di} = \beta_1 c_{1i} + \beta_1 c_{1i} + \ldots + \beta_N (C_{Ni} + M) + u_i \qquad (2.25)$$

where

P_{di} is the dirty price of the *i*-th bond
C_{Ni} is the coupon of the *i*-th bond in period *n*
β_N is the coefficient of the regression equation
u_i is the residual error in the *i*-th bond.

In fact, the coefficient in (2.25) is an estimate of the discount factor, as shown by (2.26) and can be used to generate the spot interest rate curve.

$$\beta_n = df_n = \frac{1}{(1 + rs_n)^n} \tag{2.26}$$

In the form shown, (2.25) cannot be estimated directly. This is because individual coupon payment dates will differ across different bonds, and in a semi-annual coupon market there will be more coupons than bonds available. In practice therefore the term structure is divided into specific dates, known as *grid points*, along the entire maturity term; coupon payments are then allocated between two grid points. The allocation between two points is done in such a way so that the present value of the coupon is not altered. This is shown in Figure 2.15.

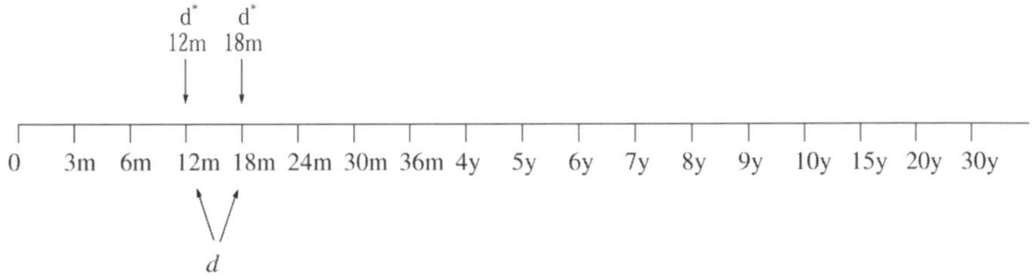

Figure 2.15 Grid point allocation in regression analysis

Note how there are more grid points at the short end of the term structure, with progressively fewer points as we reach the longer end. This is because the preponderance of the data is invariably at the shorter end of the curve, which makes yield curve fitting more difficult. At the long end however the shortage of data, due to the relative lack of issues, makes curve estimation more inaccurate.

The actual regression equation that is used in the analysis is given at (2.27) where d_{ni} represents the grid points.

$$P_{di} = \beta_1 d_{1i} + \beta_2 d_{2i} + \ldots + \beta_N (d_{Ni} + M) + u_i \tag{2.27}$$

The two methodologies described above are the most commonly encountered in the market. Generally, models used to estimate the term structure generally fall into two distinct categories: these being the ones that estimate the structure using the par yield curve and those that fit it using a discount function. This is examined in greater detail in Choudhury (2004).

Spot and forward rates in the market

Using spot rates

The concepts discussed in this chapter are important and form a core part of debt markets analysis. It may appear that the content is largely theoretical, especially since many markets do not trade zero-coupon instruments and so spot rates are therefore not observable in practice; however, the concept of the spot rate is an essential part of bond (and other instruments') pricing. In the first instance we are already aware that bond redemption yields do not reflect a true interest rate for that maturity, for which we use the spot rate. For relative value purposes, traders and portfolio managers frequently compare a bond's actual market price to its theoretical price, calculated using specific zero-coupon yields for each cash flow, and determine whether the bond is "cheap" or "dear". Even where there is some misalignment between the theoretical price of a bond and the actual price, the decision to buy or sell may be based on judgemental factors, since there is often no zero-coupon instrument against which to effect an arbitrage trade. In a market where no zero-coupon instruments are traded, the spot rates used in the analysis are theoretical and are not represented by actual market prices. Traders therefore often analyse bonds in terms of relative value against each other, and the redemption yield curve, rather than against their theoretical zero-coupon based price.

What considerations apply where a zero-coupon bond market exists alongside a conventional coupon-bond market? In such a case, in theory arbitrage trading is possible if a bond is priced above or below the price suggested by zero-coupon rates. For example, a bond priced above its theoretical price could be sold, and zero-coupon bonds that equated its cash flow stream could be purchased; the difference in price is the arbitrage profit. Or a bond trading below its theoretical price could be purchased and its coupons "stripped" and sold individually as zero-coupon bonds; the proceeds from the sale of the zero-coupon bonds would then exceed the purchase price of the coupon bond. In practice, often the existence of both markets equalises prices between both markets so that arbitrage is no longer possible, although opportunities will still occasionally present themselves.

Using forward rates

Newcomers to the markets frequently experience confusion when first confronted with forward rates. Do they represent the market's expectation of where interest rates will actually be when the forward date arrives? If forward rates are a predictor of future interest rates, exactly how good are they at making this prediction? Empirical evidence[22] suggests that in fact forward rates are not accurate predictors of future interest rates, frequently over-stating them by a considerable margin. If this is the case, should we attach any value or importance to forward rates?

The value of forward rates does not lie however in its track record as a market predictor, but moreover in its use as a hedging tool. As we illustrate in Example 2.4 the forward rate is calculated on the basis that if we are to price, say, a cash deposit with a forward starting date, but we wish to deal today, the return from the deposit will be exactly the same as if we invested for a start date today and rolled over the investment at the forward date. The forward rate allows us to lock in a dealing rate now. Once we have dealt today, it is irrelevant what the actual rate pertaining on the forward date is – we have already dealt. Therefore forward rates are often called *hedge* rates, as they allow us to lock in a dealing rate for a future period, thus removing uncertainty.

The existence of forward prices in the market also allows us to make an investment decision, based on our view compared to the market view. The forward rate implied by, say, government bond prices is in effect the market's view of future interest rates. If we happen not to agree with this view, we will deal accordingly. In effect we are comparing our view on future interest rates with that of the market, and making our investment decision based on this comparison.

EXAMPLE 2.4 Spot and forward rates calculation: Practical demonstration of boot-strapping from the par yield curve

Zero-coupon rates

As we have seen, zero-coupon (or spot), par and forward rates are linked. The term "zero-coupon" is a bond market term and describes a bond that has no coupons. The yield on a zero-coupon bond can be viewed as a true yield, if the paper is held to maturity as no reinvestment is involved and there are no interim cash flows vulnerable to a change in interest rates. Because zero-coupon rates can be derived from coupon rates, we can assume that:

[22] Including Fama (1976).

- zero-coupon rates can be derived at any time where there is a liquid government bond market;
- these zero-coupon rates can then be used as the benchmark term structure.

Where zero-coupon bonds are traded the yield on a zero-coupon bond of a particular maturity is the zero-coupon rate for that maturity. However, it is not necessary to have zero-coupon bonds in order to deduce zero-coupon rates. It is possible to calculate zero-coupon rates from a range of market rates and prices, including coupon bonds, interest-rate futures and currency deposits. The price of a zero-coupon bond of a particular maturity defines directly the value today of a cash flow due on the bond's redemption date, and indirectly the zero-coupon rate for that maturity. It is therefore that term to maturity's true interest rate.

Discount factors and the discount function

As we have seen already it is possible to determine a set of *discount factors* from market rates. A discount factor is the number in the range zero to one that can be used to obtain the present value of some future value. This is because:

$$PV = \frac{FV}{(1 + r)^n} \tag{2.28}$$

where

PV is the present value
FV is the future value
r is the required interest rate
n is the number of interest rate periods.

We know that:

$$PV_n = df_n \times FV_n \tag{2.29}$$

where

PV_n is the present value of the future cash flow occurring at time n
FV_n is the future cash flow occurring at time n
df_n is the discount factor for cash flows occurring at time n.

Discount factors can be calculated most easily from zero-coupon rates; equations (2.30) and (2.31) apply to zero-coupon rates for periods up to one year (which would be money market terms) and over one year (bond market maturities) respectively.

$$df_n = \frac{1}{(1 + rs_n T_n)} \tag{2.30}$$

$$df_n = \frac{1}{(1 + rs_n)^{T_n}} \tag{2.31}$$

where

df_n is the discount factor for cash flows occurring at time n
rs_n is the zero-coupon or spot rate for the period to time n
T_n is the time from the value date to time n, expressed in years and fractions of a year.

Individual zero-coupon rates allow discount factors to be calculated at specific points along the maturity spectrum. As cash flows may occur at any time in the future, and not necessarily at convenient times like in three months or one year, discount factors often need to be calculated for every possible date in the future. The complete set of discount factors is called the *discount function.*

Implied spot and forward rates[23]

In this section we describe how to obtain zero-coupon and forward interest rates from the yields available from coupon bonds, using a method known as *boot-strapping*. In a government bond market such as that for US Treasuries or UK gilts, the bonds are considered to be *default-free*. The rates from a government bond yield curve describe the risk-free rates of return available in the market *today,* however, they also *imply* (risk-free) rates of return for *future time periods.* These implied future rates, known as *implied forward rates*, or simply *forward rates,* can be derived from a given spot yield curve using boot-strapping. This term reflects the fact that each calculated spot rate is used to determine the next period spot rate, in successive steps.

[23] This section follows, with permission, the approach described in Windas (1993), Chapter 5.

Table 2.3 shows a hypothetical benchmark gilt yield curve for value as at 7 December 2000. The observed yields of the benchmark bonds that compose the curve are displayed in the last column. All rates are annualised and assume semi-annual compounding. The bonds all pay on the same coupon dates of 7 June and 7 December, and as the value date is a coupon date, there is no accrued interest on any of the bonds.[24] The *clean* and *dirty* prices for each bond are identical.

Bond	Term to maturity (years)	Coupon	Maturity date	Price	Yield to maturity
4% Treasury 2001	0.5	4%	7-Jun-01	100	4%
5% Treasury 2001	1	5%	7-Dec-01	100	5%
6% Treasury 2002	1.5	6%	7-Jun-02	100	6%
7% Treasury 2002	2	7%	7-Dec-02	100	7%
8% Treasury 2003	2.5	8%	7-Jun-03	100	8%
9% Treasury 2003	3	9%	7-Dec-03	100	9%

Table 2.3 Hypothetical UK government bond yields as at 7 December 2000

The gross redemption yield or YTM of a coupon bond describes the single rate that present-values the sum of all its future cash flows to its current price. It is essentially the *internal rate of return* of the set of cash flows that make up the bond. This yield measure suffers from a fundamental weakness in that each cash flow is present-valued at the same rate, an unrealistic assumption in anything other than a flat yield curve environment. So the yield to maturity is an *anticipated* measure of the return that can be expected from holding the bond from purchase until maturity. In practice it will only be achieved under the following conditions:

- the bond is purchased on issue;
- all the coupons paid throughout the bond's life are reinvested at the same YTM at which the bond was purchased;
- the bond is held until maturity.

[24] Benchmark gilts pay coupon on a semi-annual basis on 7 June and 7 December each year, so we've used these dates for our exercise.

In practice these conditions will not be fulfilled, and so the YTM of a bond is not a true interest rate for that bond's maturity period.

The bonds in Table 2.3 pay semi-annual coupons on 7 June and 7 December and have the same time period – six months – between 7 December 2000, their valuation date and 7 June 2001, their next coupon date. However, since each issue carries a different yield, the next six-month coupon payment for each bond is present-valued at a different rate. In other words, the six-month bond present-values its six-month coupon payment at its 4% YTM, the one-year at 5%, and so on. Because each of these issues uses a different rate to present-value a cash flow occurring at the same future point in time, it is unclear which of the rates should be regarded as the true interest rate or benchmark rate for the six-month period from 7 December 2000 to 7 June 2001. This problem is repeated for all other maturities.

For the purposes of valuation and analysis however, we require a set of true interest rates, and so these must be derived from the redemption yields that we can observe from the benchmark bonds trading in the market. These rates we designate as rs_i, where rs_i is the *implied spot rate* or *zero-coupon rate* for the term beginning on 7 December 2000 and ending at the end of period i.

We begin calculating implied spot rates by noting that the six-month bond contains only one future cash flow, the final coupon payment and the redemption payment on maturity. This means that it is in effect trading as a zero-coupon bond, as there is only one cash flow left for this bond, its final payment. Since this cash flow's present value, future value and maturity term are known, the unique interest rate that relates these quantities can be solved using the compound interest equation (2.32):

$$\begin{aligned} FV &= PV \times \left(1 + \frac{rs_i}{m}\right)^{(nm)} \\ rs_i &= m \times \left(\sqrt[(nm)]{\frac{FV}{PV}} - 1\right) \end{aligned} \qquad (2.32)$$

where

FV is the future value
PV is the present value
rs_i is the implied i-period spot rate
m is the number of interest periods per year
n is the number of years in the term.

The first rate to be solved is referred to as the implied six-month spot rate and is the true interest rate for the six-month term beginning on 2 January and ending on 2 July 2000.

Equation (2.32) relates a cash flow's present value and future value in terms of an associated interest rate, compounding convention and time period. Of course, if we rearrange it we may use it to solve for an implied spot rate. For the six-month bond the final cash flow on maturity is £102, comprised of the £2 coupon payment and the £100 (*par*) redemption amount. So we have for the first term, $i = 1$, $FV = £102$, $PV = £100$, $n = 0.5$ years and $m = 2$. This allows us to calculate the spot rate as follows:

$$rs_i = m \times (\sqrt[(nm)]{FV/PV} - 1)$$

$$rs_i = 2 \times (\sqrt[(0.5 \times 2)]{£102/£100} - 1)$$

$$rs_i = 0.04000$$

$$rs_i = 4.000\%.$$

Thus the implied six-month spot rate or zero-coupon rate is equal to 4%.[25] We now need to determine the implied one-year spot rate for the term from 7 December 2000 to 7 June 2001. We note that the one-year issue has a 5% coupon and contains two future cash flows: a £2.50 six-month coupon payment on 7 June 2001, and a £102.50 one-year coupon and principal payment on 7 December 2001. Since the first cash flow occurs on 7 June – six months from now – it must be present-valued at the 4% six-month spot rate established above. Once this present value is determined, it may be

[24] Of course, intuitively we could have concluded that the six-month spot rate was 4%, without the need to apply the arithmetic, as we had already assumed that the six-month bond was a quasi-zero-coupon bond.

subtracted from the £100 total present value (its current price) of the one-year issue to obtain the present value of the one-year coupon and cash flow. Again we then have a single cash flow with a known present value, future value and term. The rate that equates these quantities is the implied one-year spot rate. From equation (2.32) the present value of the six-month £2.50 coupon payment of the one-year benchmark bond, discounted at the implied six-month spot rate, is:

$$PV_{\text{6-mo cash flow, 1-yr bond}} = £2.50/(1 + 0.04/2)^{0.5\times 2}$$

$$= £2.45098.$$

The present value of the one-year £102.50 coupon and principal payment is found by subtracting the present value of the six-month cash flow, determined above, from the total present value (current price) of the issue:

$$PV_{\text{1-yr cash flow, 1-yr bond}} = £100 - £2.45098$$

$$= £97.54902.$$

The implied one-year spot rate is then determined by using the £97.54902 present value of the one-year cash flow determined above:

$$rs_2 = 2 \times \left(\sqrt[(1 \times 2)]{£102.50/£97.54902} - 1\right)$$

$$= 0.0501256$$

$$= 5.01256\%.$$

The implied 1.5-year spot rate is solved in the same way:

$$PV_{\text{6-mo cash flow, 1.5-yr bond}} = £3.00/(1 + 0.04/2)^{0.5\times 2}$$
$$= £2.94118$$

$$PV_{\text{1-yr cash flow, 1.5-yr bond}} = £3.00/(1 + 0.0501256/2)^{1\times2}$$
$$= £2.85509$$

$$PV_{\text{1.5-yr cash flow, 1.5-yr bond}} = £100 - £2.94118 - £2.85509$$
$$= £94.20373$$

$$rs_3 = 2 \times \left(\sqrt[(1.5 \times 2)]{£103/£94.20373} - 1\right)$$

$$= 0.0604071$$

$$= 6.04071\%.$$

Extending the same process for the two-year bond, we calculate the implied two-year spot rate rs_4 to be 7.0906%. The implied 2.5-year and three-year spot rates rs_5 and rs_6 are 8.1709% and 9.2879% respectively.

The interest rates rs_1, rs_2, rs_3, rs_4, rs_5 and rs_6 describe the true zero-coupon interest rates for the six-month, one-year, 1.5-year, two-year, 2.5-year and three-year terms that begin on 7 December 2000 and end on 7 June 2001, 7 December 2001, 7 June 2002, 7 December 2002, 7 June 2003 and 7 December 2003 respectively. They are also called *implied spot rates* because they have been calculated from redemption yields observed in the market from the benchmark government bonds that were listed in Table 2.3.

Note that the one-year, 1.5-year, two-year, 2.5-year and three-year implied spot rates are progressively greater than the corresponding redemption yields for these terms. This is an important result, and occurs whenever the yield curve is positively sloped. The reason for this is that the present values of a bond's shorter dated cash flows are discounted at rates that are lower than the bond's redemption yield; this generates higher present values that, when subtracted from the current price of the bond, produce a lower present value for the final cash flow. This lower present value implies a spot rate that is greater than the issue's yield. In an inverted yield curve environment we observe the opposite result; that is, implied rates that lie below the corresponding redemption yields. If the redemption yield curve is flat, the implied spot rates will be equal to the corresponding redemption yields.

The methodology we have described to construct theoretical spot rates from observed coupon bond yields is known as bootstrapping. This method, while useful, is in practice more complex. A number of problems may present themselves. For instance, within the group of bonds one is using to derive the spot curve, there may be more than one issue with the same maturity but trading at different yields. As we noted elsewhere, this may be due to differing coupon rates and their tax effects, or the presence of embedded option features such as call provisions. In addition, there may not be a current bond issue for every required maturity, so that a continuous curve cannot be calculated.

Calculating implied forward rates

Once we have calculated the spot or zero-coupon rates for the six-month, one-year, 1.5-year, two-year, 2.5-year and three-year terms, we can determine the rate of return that is implied by the yield curve for the sequence of six-month periods beginning on 7 December 2000, 7 June 2001, 7 December 2001, 7 June 2002 and 7 December 2002. These period rates are referred to as *implied forward rates* or *forward–forward rates* and we denote these as rf_i, where rf_i is the implied six-month forward interest rate today for the *i*th period.

Since the implied six-month zero-coupon rate (spot rate) describes the return for a term that coincides precisely with the first of the series of six-month periods, this rate describes the risk-free rate of return for the first six-month period. It is therefore equal to the first period spot rate. Thus we have $rf_1 = rs_1 = 4.0\%$, where rf_1 is the risk-free forward rate for the first six-month period beginning at period one. We show now how the risk-free rates for the second, third, fourth, fifth and sixth six-month periods, designated rf_2, rf_3, rf_4, rf_5 and rf_6 respectively may be solved from the implied spot rates.

The benchmark rate for the second semi-annual period rf_2 is referred to as the one-period forward six-month rate, because it goes into effect one six-month period from now ("one-period forward") and remains in effect for six months ("six-month rate"). It is therefore the six-month rate in six months' time, and is also referred to as the six-month forward–forward rate. This rate, in conjunction with the rate from the first period rf_1, must provide returns that match those generated by the implied one-year spot rate for the entire one-year term. In other words, £1 invested for six months from 7 December 2000 to 7 June 2001 at the first period's benchmark rate of 4% and then reinvested for another six months from 7 June 2001 to 7 December 2001 at the second period's (as yet unknown) implied *forward* rate must enjoy the same returns as £1 invested for one year from 7 December 2000 to 7 December 2001 at the implied one-year *spot* rate of 5.0125%. This reflects the law of no-arbitrage.

A moment's thought will convince us that this must be so. If this were not the case, we might observe an interest rate environment in which the return received by an investor over any given term would depend on whether an investment is made at the start period for the entire maturity term or over a succession of periods within the whole term and reinvested. If there were any discrepancies between the returns received from each approach, there would exist an unrealistic arbitrage opportunity, in which investments for a given term carrying a lower return might be sold short against the simultaneous purchase of investments for the same period carrying a higher return, thereby locking in a risk-free, cost-free profit. Therefore forward interest rates must be calculated so that they are *arbitrage-free*. Forward rates are not therefore a prediction of what spot interest rates are likely to be in the future, rather a mathematically derived set of interest rates that reflect the current spot term structure and the rules of no-arbitrage. Excellent mathematical explanations of the no-arbitrage property of interest-rate markets are contained in Ingersoll (1987), Jarrow (1996), and Shiller (1990) among others.

It is important to remember that our discussion centres on forward rates are calculated for dealing *today*. If one wishes to enter into a bargain for a forward date but writes the ticket today, we assume the principle of no-arbitrage pricing. If an actual strategy of investment for a shorter term followed by reinvestment at the actual *spot* rate (in place at the time) for the remainder of the term was followed, the final return would of course be different. We have no way of knowing what the actual result would be of dealing always at spot rates (or, if we did, we would not be here now!). But if we wish to deal today for a period that begins at a future date, there will be no difference if we follow a strategy of investing for the whole term or if we decide on reinvesting at a later date.

The existence of a no-arbitrage market of course makes it straightforward to calculate forward rates; we know that the return from an investment made over a period must equal the return made from investing in a shorter period and successively reinvesting to a matching term. If we know the return over the shorter period, we are left with only one unknown, the full-period forward rate, which is then easily calculated. Returning to our example then, having established the rate for the first six-month period, the rate for the second six-month period – the one-period forward six-month rate – is determined below.

The future value of £1 invested at rf_1, the period one forward rate, at the end of the first six-month period is calculated as follows:

$$
\begin{aligned}
FV_1 &= £1 \times \left(1 + \frac{rf_1}{2}\right)^{(0.5 \times 2)} \\
&= £1 \times \left(1 + \frac{0.04}{2}\right)^{1} \\
&= £1.02000.
\end{aligned}
$$

The future value of £1 at the end of the one-year term, invested at the implied benchmark one-year spot rate, is determined as follows:

$$
\begin{aligned}
FV_2 &= £1 \times \left(1 + \frac{rs_2}{2}\right)^{(1 \times 2)} \\
&= £1 \times \left(1 + \frac{0.0501256}{2}\right)^{2} \\
&= £1.050754.
\end{aligned}
$$

The implied benchmark one-period forward rate rf_2 is the rate that equates the value of FV_1 (£1.02) on 7 June 2001 to FV_2 (£1.050754) on 7 December 2001. From equation (2.32) we have:

$$rf_2 = 2 \times \left(\sqrt[(0.5\times 2)]{\frac{FV_2}{FV_1}} - 1\right)$$

$$= 2 \times \left(\frac{£1.050754}{£1.02} - 1\right)$$

$$= 0.060302$$
$$= 6.0302\%$$

In other words, £1 invested from 7 December to 7 June at 4% (the implied forward rate for the first period) and then reinvested from 7 June to 7 December 2001 at 6.0302% (the implied forward rate for the second period) would accumulate the same returns as £1 invested from 7 December 2000 to 7 December 2001 at 5.01256% (the implied one-year spot rate).

The rate for the third six-month period – the two-period forward six-month interest rate – may be calculated in the same way:

$$FV_2 = £1.050754$$

$$FV_3 = £1 \times (1 + rs_3/2)^{1.5\times 2}$$

$$= £1 \times (1 + 0.0604071/2)^3$$

$$= £1.093375$$

$$rf_3 = 2 \times \left(\sqrt[(0.5\times 2)]{\frac{FV_3}{FV_4}} - 1\right)$$

$$= 2 \times \left(\sqrt[1]{\frac{£1.093375}{£1.050754}} - 1\right)$$

$$= 0.081125$$
$$= 8.1125\%.$$

In the same way the three-period forward six-month rate rf_4 is calculated to be 10.27247%. The rest of the results are shown in Table 2.4. We say *one-period* forward rate because it is the forward rate that applies to the six-month period. The results of the implied spot (zero-coupon) and forward rate calculations along with the given redemption yield curve are illustrated graphically in Figure 2.16. The simple boot-strapping methodology can be applied using a spreadsheet for actual market redemption yields. However, in practice we will not have a set of bonds with exact and/or equal periods to maturity and coupons falling on the same date. Nor will they all be priced conveniently at par. In designing a spreadsheet spot rate calculator therefore, the coupon rate and maturity date is entered as standing data and usually interpolation is used when calculating the spot rates for bonds with uneven maturity dates. A spot curve model that uses this approach in conjunction with the boot-strapping method is available for downloading at:

http://www.yieldcurve.com

Market practitioners usually use discount factors to extract spot and forward rates from market prices. For an account of this method, see the chapter by Dr Didier Joannas in Choudhry *et al.* (2001).

Term to maturity	**Yield to maturity**	**Implied spot rate**	**Implied one-period forward rate**
0.5	4.0000%	4.0000%	4.0000%
1	5.0000%	5.0126%	6.0302%
1.5	6.0000%	6.0407%	8.1125%
2	7.0000%	7.0906%	10.2725%
2.5	8.0000%	8.1709%	12.2483%
3	9.0000%	9.2879%	14.5565%

Table 2.4 Implied spot and forward rates

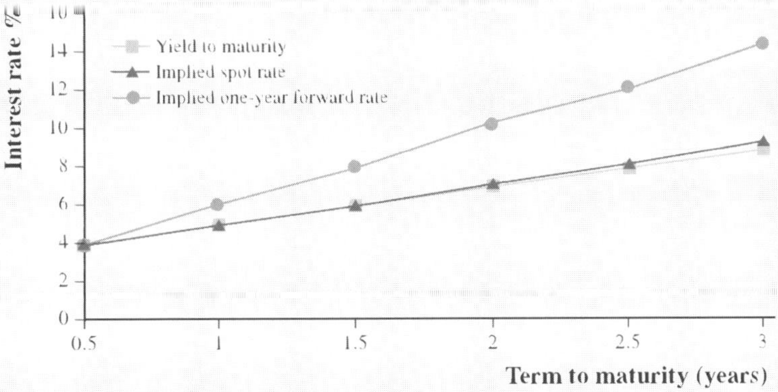

Figure 2.16 Par, spot and forward yield curves

CASE STUDY Deriving a discount function[26]

In this example we present a traditional boot-strapping technique for deriving a discount function for yield curve fitting purposes. This technique has been called "naïve" (for instance, see James and Webber 2000, p. 129) because it suffers from a number of drawbacks; for example, it results in an unrealistic forward rate curve, which means that it is unlikely to be used in practice. We review the drawbacks at the end of the case study.

Today is 14 July 2000. The following rates are observed in the market. We assume that the day-count basis for the cash instruments and swaps is act/365. Construct the money market discount function.

Money market rates	*Rate (%)*	*Expiry*	*Days*
One month (1m)	4 $^{1}/_{32}$	14/8/00	31
3m	4 $^{1}/_{4}$	16/10/00	94
6m	4 $^{1}/_{2}$	15/1/01	185

[26] In this illustration, the discount function is derived using interest rate data from two off-balance-sheet-derivative instruments, futures and swaps, as well as money market deposit rates. For readers unfamiliar with these products, futures and swaps are covered in Appendix B at the back of this book.

Future prices			
Sep-00	95.60	20/9/00	68
Dec-00	95.39	20/12/00	159
Mar-01	95.25	21/3/01	249
Jun-01	94.80	20/6/01	340
Swap rates			
One year (1y)	4.95	16/7/01	367
2y	5.125	15/7/02	731
3y	5.28	14/7/03	1095
4y	5.55	14/7/04	1461
5y	6.00	14/7/05	1826

Creating the discount function

Using the cash money market rates we can create discount factors up to a maturity of six months, using the expression at (2.33):

$$df = \frac{1}{(1 + r \times \frac{days}{365})}. \tag{2.33}$$

The resulting discount factors are shown below.

From	*To*	*Days*	*r%*	*df*
14/7/00	14/8/00	31	$4\ ^7/_{32}$	0.99642974
	16/10/00	94	$4\ ^1/_4$	0.98917329
	15/1/01	185	$4\ ^1/_2$	0.97770040

We can also calculate forward discount factors from the rates implied in the futures prices, which are shown below.

From	*To*	*Days*	*r%*	*df*
20/9/00	20/12/00	91	4.40	0.98914917
20/12/00	21/3/01	91	4.61	0.98863717
21/3/01	20/6/01	91	4.75	0.98829614
20/6/01	19/9/00	91	5.20	0.98720154

In order to convert these values into zero-coupon discount factors, we need to first derive a cash "stub" rate up to the expiry of the first futures contract. The most straightforward way to do this is by linear interpolation of the one-month and three-month rates, as shown in Figure 2.17 below.

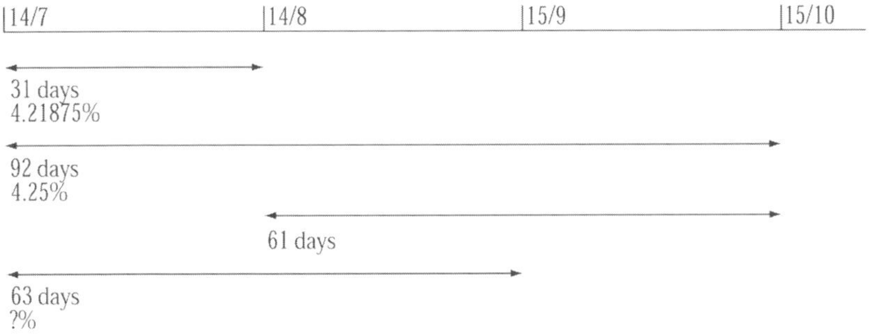

Figure 2.17 Linear interpolation of money market and futures rates

For instance, the calculation for the term marked is:

$$4.21875 + \left((4.25 - 4.21875) \times \tfrac{32}{61}\right) = 4.235143\%.$$

To convert this to a discount factor:

$$\frac{1}{1 + (0.04235143 \times \frac{63}{365})} = 0.99274308.$$

From the futures implied forward rates, the zero-coupon discount factors are calculated by successive multiplication of the individual discount factors. These are shown below.

From	*To*	*Days*	*df*
14/7/00	0/9/00	68	0.99172819
	20/12/00	159	0.98172542
	21/3/01	250	0.96992763
	20/6/01	341	0.960231459
	19/9/01	432	0.948925494

For the interest rate swap rates, to calculate discount factors for the relevant dates we use the boot-strapping technique.

1y swap

We assume a par swap, the present value is known to be 100, and as we know the future value as well, we are able to calculate the one-year zero-coupon rate as shown from the one-year swap rate:

$$df_1 = \frac{1}{1+r} = \frac{100}{104.95}$$

$$= 0.95283468.$$

2y swap

The coupon payment occurring at the end of period one can be discounted back using the one-year discount factor above, leaving a zero-coupon structure as before.

$$df_2 = \frac{100 - C \times df_1}{105.28}$$

$$= 0.95283468.$$

This gives df_2 equal to 0.91379405.

The same process can be employed for the three-, four- and five-year par swap rates to calculate the appropriate discount factors.

$$df_3 = \frac{100 - C \times (df_1 + df_2)}{105.28}.$$

This gives df_3, equal to 0.87875624. The discount factors for the four-year and five-year maturities, calculated in the same way, are 0.82899694 and 0.77835621 respectively.

The full discount function is given in Table 2.5 and illustrated graphically in Figure 2.18.

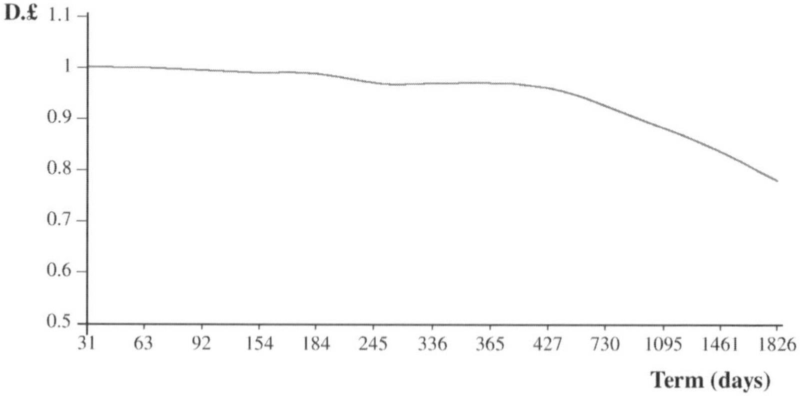

Figure 2.18 Discount function

From	To	Days	Zero coupon (%)	Discount factor	Source
14/07/2000	14/08/2000	31	4.21875	0.99642974	Money market
	20/09/2000	63	4.23500	0.99274308	Money market
	16/10/2000	94	4.25000	0.98917329	Money market
	20/12/2000	159	4.38000	0.98172542	Futures
	15/01/2001	185	4.50000	0.97777004	Money market
	21/03/2001	250	4.55000	0.96992763	Futures
	20/06/2001	341	4.73000	0.96023145	Futures
	16/07/2001	367	4.95000	0.95283468	Swap
	19/09/2001	432	5.01000	0.94892549	Futures
	15/07/2002	731	5.12500	0.91379405	Swap
	14/07/2003	1095	5.28000	0.87875624	Swap
	15/07/2004	1461	5.58000	0.82899694	Swap
	15/07/2005	1826	6.10000	0.77835621	Swap

Table 2.5 Discount factors

Critique of the traditional technique

The method used to derive the discount function in the case study used three different price sources to produce an integrated function and hence yield curve. However, there is no effective method by which the three separate curves, which are shown at Figure 2.19, can be integrated into one complete curve. The result is that a curve formed from the three separate curves will exhibit distinct kinks or steps at the points at which one data source is replaced by another data source.

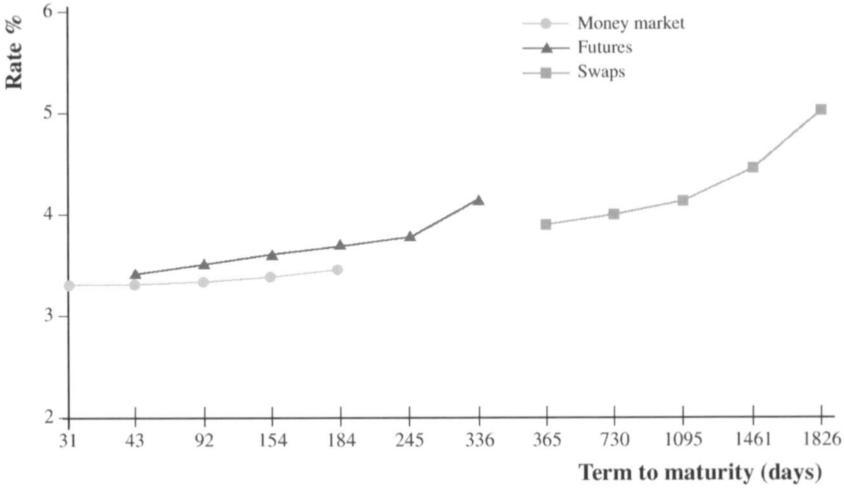

Figure 2.19 Comparison of money market curves

The money market and swap rates incorporate a credit risk premium, reflecting the fact that interbank market counterparties carry an element of default risk. This means that money market rates lie above government repo rates. Futures rates do not reflect default risk, as they are exchange-traded contracts and the exchange clearing house takes on counterparty risk for each transaction. However, futures rates are treated as one-point period rates, in effect making them equivalent to forward-rate agreement (FRA) rates. In practice, as the cash flow from FRAs is received as a discounted payoff at one point, whereas futures contract trades require a daily margin payment, a *convexity adjustment* is required to convert futures accurately to FRA rates. This adjustment is considered in Choudhry (2004).

Swap rates also incorporate an element of credit risk, although generally they are considered lower risk as they are off-balance-sheet instruments and no principal is at risk. As liquid swap rates are only available for set maturity points, linear interpolation is used to plot points in between available rates. This results in an unstable forward rate curve calculated from the spot rate curve (see James and Webber 2000), due to the interpolation effect. Nevertheless, market-makers in certain markets price intermediate-dated swaps based on this linear interpolation method. Another drawback is that the boot-strapping method uses near-maturity rates to build up the curve to far-maturity rates. One of the features of a spot curve derived in this way is that even small changes in short-term rates causes excessive changes in long-dated spot rates, and oscillations in the forward curve. Finally, money market rates beyond the "stub" period are not considered once the discount factor to the stub date is calculated, so their impact is not felt.

For these reasons the traditional technique, while still encountered in textbooks and training courses (including this one), is not used very often in the markets.

CASE STUDY Deriving the theoretical zero-coupon (spot) rate curve[27]

Here we construct a theoretical spot interest rate curve using the yields observed on coupon bonds. To illustrate the methodology, we will use a hypothetical set of bonds that are trading in a positive yield curve environment. The maturity, price and yield for ten bonds are shown in Table 2.6. The prices shown are for settlement on 1 March 1999, and all the bonds have precisely one, 1.5, two and so on years to maturity; that is, they mature on 1 March or 1 September of their maturity year. That means that the first bond has no intermediate coupon before it is redeemed, and we can assume it trades as a zero-coupon bond. All bonds have no accrued interest because the settlement date is a coupon date. Bonds pay semi-annual coupon.

Maturity date	Years to maturity	Coupon (%)	Yield to maturity	Price
1-Sep-99	0.5	5.0	6.00	99.5146
1-Mar-00	1.0	10.0	6.30	103.5322
1-Sep-00	1.5	7.0	6.40	100.8453
1-Mar-01	2.0	6.5	6.70	99.6314
1-Sep-01	2.5	8.0	6.90	102.4060
1-Mar-02	3.0	10.5	7.30	108.4838
1-Sep-02	3.5	9.0	7.60	104.2327
1-Mar-03	4.0	7.3	7.80	98.1408
1-Sep-03	4.5	7.5	7.95	98.3251
1-Mar-04	5.0	8.0	8.00	100.0000

Table 2.6 Set of hypothetical bonds

[27] This illustrates boot-strapping, as well as the principle behind stripping a coupon bond, and follows the approach described in Fabbozi (1993).

According to the principle of no-arbitrage pricing, the value of any bond should be equal to the value of the sum of all its cash flows, should these be stripped into a series of zero-coupon bonds whose last bond matures at the same time as the coupon bond. Consider the first bond in the table above. As it matures in precisely six months' time, it is effectively a zero-coupon bond; its yield of 6% is equal to the six-month spot rate. Given this spot rate we can derive the spot rate for a one-year zero-coupon gilt. The price of a one-year gilt strip must equal the present value of the two cash flows from the 10% one-year coupon gilt. If we use £100 as par, the cash flows from the one-year coupon bond are:

0.5 years $\quad 10\% \times £100 \times 0.5 = £5$

1.0 years $\quad 10\% \times £100 \times 0.5 = £5 + £100$ redemption payment.

The present value of the total cash flow is $\dfrac{5}{(1 + \frac{1}{2}r_1)} + \dfrac{105}{(1 + \frac{1}{2}r_2)^2}$

where
r_1 is the six-month theoretical spot rate
r_2 is the one-year theoretical spot rate.

Therefore the present value of the one-year coupon gilt is $4/(1.03) + 105/(1 + r_2)^2$. As the price of the one-year gilt is 103.5322, from Table 2.6 above, the following relationship must be true:

$$103.5322 = \frac{5}{(1.03)} + \frac{105}{(1 + \frac{1}{2}r_2)^2}.$$

Using this relationship we are now in a position to calculate the one-year theoretical spot rate as shown below:

$$103.5322 = 4.85437 + \frac{105}{(1 + \frac{1}{2}r_2)^2}$$

$$98.67783 = 105/(1 + \tfrac{1}{2}r_2)^2$$

$$(1 + \tfrac{1}{2}r_2)^2 = 105/98.67783 = 1.064069$$

$$(1 + \tfrac{1}{2}r_2) = \sqrt{1.064069}$$

$$\tfrac{1}{2}r_2 = 0.03154.$$

Therefore r_2 is 0.06308, or 6.308%, which is the theoretical one-year spot rate. Now that we have obtained the theoretical one-year spot rate, we are in a position to calculate the theoretical 1.5-year spot rate. The cash flow for the 7% 1.5-year coupon gilt shown in the table is:

0.5 years	7% × £100 × 0.5 = £3.5
1.0 years	7% × £100 × 0.5 = £3.5
1.5 years	7% × £100 × 0.5 = £3.5 + redemption payment (£100).

The present value of this stream of cash flows is:

$$\frac{3.5}{(1+\frac{1}{2}r)} + \frac{3.5}{(1+\frac{1}{2}r_2)^2} + \frac{103.5}{(1+\frac{1}{2}r_3)^3}$$

where r_3 is the 1.5-year theoretical spot rate. We have established that the six-month and one-year spot rates are 6% and 6.308% respectively, so that r_1 is 0.06 and r_2 is 0.06308. Therefore the present value of the 7% 1.5-year coupon bond is:

$$\frac{3.5}{(1.03)} + \frac{3.5}{(1.03154)^2} + \frac{103.5}{(1+\frac{1}{2}r_3)^3}.$$

From Table 2.6 the price of the 7% 1.5-year bond is 100.8453; therefore the following relationship must be true:

$$100.8543 = \frac{3.5}{(1.03)} + \frac{3.5}{(1.03154)^2} + \frac{103.5}{(1+\frac{1}{2}r_3)^3}.$$

This equation can then be solved to obtain r_3:

$$100.8453 = 3.39806 + 3.28924 + 103.5/(1+\tfrac{1}{2}r_3)^3$$

$$94.158 = 103.5/(1+\tfrac{1}{2}r_3)^3$$

$$(1+\tfrac{1}{2}r_3)^3 = 1.099216$$

$$\tfrac{1}{2}r_3 = 0.032035.$$

The theoretical 1.5-year spot rate bond equivalent yield is two times this result, which is 6.407%.

For readers to complete ...

Calculate the spot rates for the remaining terms in Table 2.6.

Mathematical relationship

The relationship used to derive a theoretical spot rate can be generalised, so that in order to calculate the theoretical spot rate for the *n*th six-month period, we use the following expression:

$$P_n = \frac{C/2}{(1 + \frac{1}{2}r)} + \frac{C/2}{(1 + \frac{1}{2}r_2)^2} + \frac{C/2}{(1 + \frac{1}{2}r_3)^3} + \ldots + \frac{C/2 + 100}{(1 + \frac{1}{2}r_n)^n}$$

where

P_n is the dirty price of the coupon bond with *n* periods to maturity

C is the annual coupon rate for the coupon bond

r_n is the theoretical *n*-year spot rate.

We can rewrite this expression as:

$$P_n = \frac{C}{2}\sum_{t=1}^{n-1} \frac{1}{(1 + \frac{1}{2}r_t)^t} + \frac{C/2 + 100}{(1 + \frac{1}{2}r_n)^n}$$

where r_t for $t = 1, 2, \ldots n - 1$ is the theoretical spot rates that are already known. This equation can be rearranged so that we may solve for r_n:

$$r_n = \left[\frac{C/2 + 100}{P_n - \frac{C}{2}\sum_{t=1}^{n-1} \frac{1}{(1 + \frac{1}{2}r_t)^t}}\right]^{1/n} - 1.$$

The methodology used here is the *boot-strapping* technique.

If we carry on the process for the bonds in Table 2.6 we obtain the results shown in Table 2.7.

Maturity date	Years to maturity	Yield to maturity (%)	Theoretical spot rate (%)
1-Sep-99	0.5	6.00	6.000
1-Mar-00	1.0	6.30	6.308
1-Sep-00	1.5	6.40	6.407
1-Mar-01	2.0	6.70	6.720
1-Sep-01	2.5	6.90	6.936
1-Mar-02	3.0	7.30	7.394
1-Sep-02	3.5	7.60	7.712
1-Mar-03	4.0	7.80	7.908
1-Sep-03	4.5	7.95	8.069
1-Mar-04	5.0	8.00	8.147

Table 2.7 Theoretical spot rates

Implied forward rates

We now use the theoretical spot rate curve to infer the market's expectations of future interest rates. Consider the following, where an investor with a one-year time horizon has the following two investment options:

- Option 1: Buy the one-year bond
- Option 2: Buy the six-month bond, and when it matures in six months buy another six-month bond.

The investor will be indifferent between the two alternatives if she produces the same yield at the end of the one-year period. The investor knows the spot rate on the six-month bond and the one-year bond, but does not know what yield will be available on a six-month bond purchased six months from now. The yield on a six-month bond six months from now is the *forward rate*. Given the spot rate for the six-month bond and the one-year bond spot yield, the forward rate on a six-month bond that will make the investor indifferent to the two alternatives can be derived from the spot curve, shown below.

By investing in a one-year zero-coupon bond, the investor will receive the maturity value at the end of one year. The redemption proceeds of the one-year zero-coupon bond is £105. The price (cost) of this bond is:

$$105/(1 + \tfrac{1}{2}r_2)^2$$

where r_2 is half the bond-equivalent yield of the theoretical one-year spot rate.

Suppose that the investor purchases a six-month gilt for P pounds. At the end of the six months the value of this investment would be:

$$P(1 + \tfrac{1}{2}r_1)$$

where r_1 is the bond-equivalent yield of the theoretical six-month spot rate.

Let f be the forward rate on a six-month bond available six months from now. The future value of this bond in one year from the £P invested is given by:

$$P(1 + \tfrac{1}{2}r_1)(1 + f).$$

How much would we need to invest to get £105 one year from now? This is found as follows:

$$P(1 + \tfrac{1}{2}r_1)(1 + f) = 105.$$

Solving this expression gives us:

$$P = \frac{105}{(1 + \frac{1}{2}r_1)(1 + f)}.$$

The investor is indifferent between the two methods if she receives £105 from both methods in one year's time. That is, the investor is indifferent if:

$$\frac{105}{(1 + \frac{1}{2}r_2)^2} = \frac{105}{(1 + \frac{1}{2}r_1)(1 + f)}.$$

Solving for f gives us

$$f = \frac{(1 + \frac{1}{2}r_2)^2}{(1 + \frac{1}{2}r_1)} - 1.$$

Therefore f gives us the bond-equivalent rate for the six-month forward rate. We can illustrate this by using the spot rates from Table 2.7:

Six-month bond spot rate = 6% $\Rightarrow {}^1\!/_2\, r_1 = 0.03$
One-year bond spot rate = 6.308% $\Rightarrow {}^1\!/_2\, r_2 = 0.03154$.

Substituting these vales into the equation gives us:

$$f = \frac{(1.03154)^2}{(1.03)} - 1 = 0.0330823.$$

We double this result to give the forward rate on a six-month bond as 6.6165%. As we use theoretical spot rates in its calculation, the resulting forward rate is called the *implied forward rate.*

We can use the same methodology to determine the implied forward rate six months from now for an investment period longer than six months. We can also look at forward rates that start more than six months from now.

We use the following notation for forward rates: ${}_nf_t$ = the forward rate n periods from now for t periods. We can use the following equation when calculating forward rates where the final maturity is one year or more from now:

$${}_nf_t = \left[\frac{(1 + \frac{1}{2}r_{n+1})^{n+t}}{(1 + \frac{1}{2}r_n)^n}\right]^{1/t} - 1$$

where r_n is the spot rate. The result ${}_nf_t$ gives us the implied forward rate on a bond-equivalent basis.

Readers may wish to complete the six-month forward rates in Table 2.8 below.

Maturity date	Years to maturity	Yield to maturity (%)	Theoretical spot rate (%)	Forward rate (%)
1-Sep-99	0.5	6.00	6.000	–
1-Mar-00	1.0	6.30	6.308	–
1-Sep-00	1.5	6.40	6.407	–
1-Mar-01	2.0	6.70	6.720	7.133%
1-Sep-01	2.5	6.90	6.936	–
1-Mar-02	3.0	7.30	7.394	8.755%
1-Sep-02	3.5	7.60	7.712	–
1-Mar-03	4.0	7.80	7.908	9.465%
1-Sep-03	4.5	7.95	8.069	–
1-Mar-04	5.0	8.00	8.147	9.108%

Table 2.8 Forward rates

Appendices

Appendix 2.1 Testing the unbiased expectations hypothesis

For empirical studies testing the unbiased expectations hypothesis see Kessel (1965) and Fama (1976). If we consider the expectations hypothesis to be true then the forward rate ${}_0rf_2$ should be an accurate predictor of the spot rate in period 2. Put another way, the mean of ${}_0rf_2$ should be equal to the mean of ${}_1rs_1$. In previous studies (Fama 1976) it has been shown that forward rates are in fact biased upwards in their estimates of future spot rates. That is, ${}_0rf_2$ is usually higher than the mean of ${}_1rs_1$. This bias tends to be magnified the further one moves along the term structure. We can test the unbiased expectations hypothesis by determining if the following condition holds:

$$ {}_1rs_1 = p + q\,({}_0rf_2). \tag{2.34} $$

In an environment where we upheld the expectations hypothesis, then p should be equal to zero and q equal to one. Outside of the very short end of the yield curve, there is no evidence that this is true. Another approach, adopted by Fama (1984), involved subtracting the current spot rate rs_1 from both sides of equation (2.35) and testing whether:

$$ {}_1rs_1 - {}_0rs_1 = p + q({}_0rf_2 - {}_0rs_1). \tag{2.35}$$

If the hypothesis were accurate, we would again have p equal to zero and q equal to one. This is because ${}_1rs_1 - {}_0rs_1$ is the change in the spot rate predicted by the hypothesis. The left-hand side of (2.35) is the actual change in the spot rate, which must equal the right-hand side of the equation if the hypothesis is true. Evidence from the earlier studies mentioned has suggested that q is a positive number less than one. This of course is not consistent with the unbiased expectations hypothesis. However, the studies indicate that the prediction of changes in future spot rates is linked to actual changes that occur. This suggests then that forward rates are indeed based on the market's view of future spot rates, but not in a completely unbiased manner.

An earlier study was conducted by Meiselman (1962), referred to as his error-learning model. According to this, if the unbiased expectations hypothesis is true, forward rates are not then completely accurate forecasts of future spot rates. The study tested whether (2.36) was true.

$$ {}_1rf_n - {}_0rf_n = p + q_1rs_1 - {}_0rf_2 \,. \tag{2.36}$$

If the hypothesis is true then p should be equal to zero and q should be positive. The error-learning model suggests a positive correlation between forward rates, but this would hold in an environment where the unbiased expectations hypothesis did not apply.

The empirical evidence suggests that the predictions of future spot rates reflected in forward rates is related to subsequent actual spot rates. So forward rates do include an element of market interest rate forecasts. However, this would indicate more a biased expectations theory, rather than the pure unbiased expectations hypothesis.

APPENDIX 2.2 Jensen's inequality and the shape of the yield curve

In Cox, Ingersoll and Ross (1981) an analysis on the shape of the term structure used a feature known as *Jensen's inequality* to illustrate that the expectations hypothesis was consistent with forward rates being an indicator of future spot rates. Jensen's inequality states that the expected value of the reciprocal of a variable is not identical to the reciprocal of the expected value of that variable. Following this, if the expected holding period returns on a set of bonds are all equal, the expected holding period returns on the bonds cannot then be equal over any other holding period. Applying this in practice, consider two zero-coupon bonds, a one-year bond with a yield of 11.11% and a two-year zero-coupon bond with a yield of 11.8034%. The prices of the bonds are as follows:

1 year: 90
2 year: 80.

Assume that the price of the two-year bond in one year's time can be either 86.89 or 90.89, with identical probability. At the end of year one, the total return generated by the two-year bond will be either (86.89/80) 8.6125% or (90.89/80) 13.6125%, while at this point the (now) one-year bond will offer a return of either (100/86.89) 15.089% or (100/90.89) 10.023%. The two possible prices have been set deliberately so as to ensure that the expected return over one year for the two-year bond is equal to the return available today on the one-year bond, which is 11.11% as we noted at the start. The return expected on the two-year bond is indeed the same (provided either of the two prices is available); that is [(0.5) × (86.89/80) + (0.5) × (90.89/80)], or 11.11%. Therefore it cannot also be true that the certain return over two years for the two-year bond is equal to the expected return for two years from rolling over the investment in the one-year bond. At the start of the period the two-year bond has a guaranteed return of [100/80] 25% over its lifetime. However, investing in the one-year bond and then reinvesting at the one-year period after the first year will produce a return that is higher than this, as shown:

$$11.11\% \times [(0.5) \times (100/86.89) + (0.5) \times (100/90.89)]$$

or 25.063%. Under this scenario, investors cannot expect equality of returns for all bonds over all investment horizons.

APPENDIX 2.3 Cubic spline interpolation

There are four observed vertices in the example quoted in the main text, which requires three cubic equations, $rm_{(i,t)}$, each one connecting two adjacent vertices, n_i and n_{i+1}, as follows:

$rm_{(0,t)} = a_0n^3 + b_0n^2 + c_0n + d_0$, connecting vertex n_0 with n_1

$rm_{(1,t)} = a_1n^3 + b_1n^2 + c_1n + d_1$, connecting vertex n_1 with n_2

$rm_{(2,t)} = a_2n^3 + b_2n^2 + c_2n + d_2$, connecting vertex n_2 with n_3

where *a, b, c* and *d* are unknowns. The three equations require twelve conditions in all. The cubic spline method imposes the following set of conditions on the curves:

Each cubic equation must pass through its own pair of vertices. Thus, for the first equation:

$$a_0n_0^3 + b_0n_0^2 + c_0n_0 + d_0 = 4.00$$

$$a_0n_1^3 + b_0n_1^2 + c_0n_1 + d_0 = 5.00.$$

For the second and third equations:

$$a_1n_1^3 + b_1n_1^2 + c_1n_1 + d_1 = 5.00$$

$$a_1n_2^3 + b_1n_2^2 + c_1n_2 + d_1 = 6.50$$

$$a_2n_2^3 + b_2n_2^2 + c_2n_2 + d_2 = 6.50$$

$$a_2n_3^3 + b_2n_3^2 + c_2n_3 + d_2 = 6.75.$$

The resulting yield curve should be smooth at the point where one cubic equation joins with the next one. This is achieved by requiring the slope and the convexity of adjacent equations to be equal at the point where they meet, ensuring a smooth rollover from one equation to the next. Mathematically, the first and second derivatives of all adjacent equations must be equal at the point where the equations meet.

Thus, at vertex n_1:
$3a_0n_1^2 + 2b_0n_1 + 1 = 3a_1n_1^2 + 2b_1n_1 + 1$ (the first derivative)

$6a_0n_1 + 2 = 6a_1n_1 + 2$ (the second derivative).

And at vertex n_2:
$3a_1n_2^2 + 2b_1n_2 + 1 = 3a_2n_2^2 + 2b_2n_2 + 1$ (the first derivative)

$6a_1T_2 + 2 = 6a_2T_2 + 2$ (the second derivative).

Finally, we may impose the condition that the splines tail off flat at the end vertices, or more formally we state mathematically that the second derivatives should be zero at the end points:
$6a_0n_0 + 2 = 0$ (first spline starts flat)

$6a_2n_3 + 2 = 0$ (second spline ends flat).

These constraints together give us a system of twelve equations from which we can solve for the 12 unknown coefficients. The solution is usually using matrices, where the equations are expressed in matrix form. This is shown below.

n_0^3	n_0^2	n_0	1	0	0	0	0	0	0	0	0		a_0		4
n_1^3	n_1^2	n_1	1	0	0	0	0	0	0	0	0		b_0		5
0	0	0	0	n_1^3	n_1^2	n_1	1	0	0	0	0		c_0		6.5
0	0	0	0	n_2^3	n_2^2	n_2	1	0	0	0	0		d_0		6.75
0	0	0	0	0	0	0	0	n_2^3	n_2^2	n_2	1		a_1		0
0	0	0	0	0	0	0	0	n_3^3	n_3^2	n_3	1	×	b_1	=	0
$3n_1^2$	$2n_1$	1	0	$-3n_1^2$	$-2n_1$	1	0	0	0	0	0		c_1		0
$6n_1$	2	0	0	$-6n_1$	-2	0	0	0	0	0	0		d_1		0
0	0	0	0	$3n_2^2$	$2n_2$	1	0	$-3n_2^2$	$-2n_1$	-1	0		a_2		0
0	0	0	0	$6n_2$	2	0	0	$-6n_2$	-2	0	0		b_2		0
$6n_0$	2	0	0	0	0	0	0	0	0	0	0		c_2		0
0	0	0	0	0	0	0	0	$6n_3$	2	0	0		d_2		0

Figure A2.1 Cubic spline interpolation matrix

In matrix notation we have:

$$n \times \text{Coefficients} = rm,$$

therefore the solution is:

$$\text{Coefficients} = n^{-1} \times rm.$$

Inverting the matrix n and then pre-multiplying rm with the resulting inverse, we obtain the array of required coefficients:

$$\text{Coefficients} = \{0.022, 0.000, 0.413, 4.000, -0.047, 0.411, -0.410, 4.548, 0.008, -0.249, 2.230, 1.029\}.$$

So the three cubic equations are specified as:

$$rm_{(0,t)} = 0.022 \times \mathrm{n}^3 + 0.413 \times n + 4.000 \text{ for vertices } n_0 - n_1$$

$$rm_{(1,t)} = -0.047 \times n^3 + 0.411 \times n^2 - 0.410 \times n + 4.548 \text{ for vertices } n_1 - n_2$$

$$rm_{(2,t)} = 0.008 \times n^3 - 0.249 \times n^2 + 2.230 \times n + 1.029 \text{ for vertices } n_2 - n_3.$$

Selected bibliography and references

Anderson, N. and Sleath, J. 1999, *Bank of England Quarterly Bulletin*, November.

Black, F. and Scholes, M. 1973, "The pricing of options and corporate liability", *Journal of Political Economy*, 81, May–June, pp. 637–59.

Campbell, J. 1986, "A defence of traditional hypotheses about the term structure of interest rates", *Journal of Finance*, March, pp. 183–93.

Campbell, J., Lo, A. and MacKinlay, A. 1997, *The Econometrics of Financial Markets*, Princeton UP, Chapters 10–11, Princeton.

Choudhry, M. 1998, "The information content of the United Kingdom gilt yield curve", unpublished MBA assignment, Henley Management College.

Choudhry, M., Joannas, D., Pereira, R. and Pienaar, R. 2001, *Capital Markets Instruments*, FT Prentice Hall, London.

Choudhry, M. 2004, *Advanced Fixed Income Analysis*, Elsevier, Oxford.

Choudhry, M. 2004, *Fixed Income Markets*, John Wiley & Sons, Singapore.

Cox, J., Ingersoll, J.E. and Ross, S.A. 1981, "A re-examination of traditional hypothesis about the term structure of interest rates", *Journal of Finance*, 36, Sept., pp. 769–99.

Culbertson, J.M. 1957, "The term structure of interest rates," *Quarterly Journal of Economics* 71, November 7, pp. 485–517.
The Economist, "Admiring those shapely curves", 4 April 1998, p. 117.
Fabozzi, F. 1993, *Bond Markets, Analysis and Strategies*, 2nd edition, Prentice Hall, New Jersey.
Fama, E.F. 1970, "Efficient Capital Markets: A Review of Theory and Empirical Work", *Journal of Finance*, Vol. 25, pp. 383-417.
Fama, E.F. 1976, "Forward rates as predictors of future spot interest rates", *Journal of Financial Economics*, Vol. 3, No. 4, Oct., pp. 361–77.
Fama, E.F. 1984, "The information in the term structure," *Journal of Financial Economics*, 13, Dec., pp. 509–28.
Fisher, I. 1986, "Appreciation of Interest", *Publications of the American Economic Association*, August, pp. 23–39.
Heath, D., Jarrow, R. and Morton, A. 1992, "Bond pricing and the term structure of interest rates", *Journal of Financial and Quantitative Analysis*, 25, pp. 419–40.
Hicks, J. 1946, *Value and Capital*, OUP, Oxford.
Ingersoll, J. 1987, *Theory of Financial Decision Making*, Rowman & Littlefield, Chapter 18, Savage, MA.
James, J. and Webber, N. 2000, *Interest Rate Modelling*, John Wiley & Sons, Chichester.
Jarrow, R. 1981, "Liquidity premiums and the expectations hypothesis", *Journal of Banking and Finance* 5(4), pp. 539–46.
Jarrow, R. 1996, *Modelling Fixed Income Securities and Interest Rate Options*, McGraw-Hill, New York.
Kessel, R.A. 1965, "The cyclical behaviour of the term structure of interest rates", *Essays in Applied Price Theory*, University of Chicago.
Levy, H. 1999, *Introduction to Investments*, 2nd edition, South-Western College Publishing, Cincinatti.
Livingstone, M. 1990, *Money and Capital Markets*, Prentice Hall, New Jersey, pp. 254–56
Lutz, F. 1940, "The structure of interest rates", *Quarterly Journal of Economics*, November, pp. 36–63.
Mastronikola, K. 1991, "Yield curves for gilt-edged stocks: A new model", *Bank of England Discussion Paper (Technical Series)*, No. 49.
McCulloch, J.H. 1975, "An estimate of the liquidity premium," *Journal of Political Economy*, 83, Jan.–Feb., pp. 95–119.
Merton, R. 1973, "Theory of rational option pricing", *Bell Journal of Economics and Management Science*, 4, Spring, pp. 141–83.
Meiselman, D. 1962, *The Term Structure of Interest Rates*, Prentice Hall, New Jersey.
Ryan, R. (ed.) 1997, *Yield Curve Dynamics*, Glenlake Publishing Company, Chicago.
Rubinstein, M. 1999, *Rubinstein on Derivatives*, RISK, London, pp. 84–5.
Shiller, R. 1990, "The term structure of interest rates", in Friedman, B. and Hahn, F. (eds), *Handbook of Monetary Economics*, North-Holland, Amsterdam, Chapter 13.
Windas, T. 1993, *An Introduction to Option-adjusted Spread Analysis*, Bloomberg Publishing, Princeton.

Knowledge isn't a zero-sum game, for a firm or industry. If Miller and Modigliani, Markowitz, Sharpe, Lintner and Treynor, Black, Scholes and Merton, or Ross had suppressed their discoveries, the world would be a poorer place, in both senses of the word ... Whenever possible, I believe we owe it to ourselves and the world to spread ideas.

– Professor Emanuel Derman
"For our eyes only?", *RISK*, August, 2004

CHAPTER

3

Review of Bond Market Instruments

The development of financial engineering techniques in banks around the world has resulted in a great variety of financial instruments being traded. The bond markets are no exception to this and there are a range of instruments in the debt market with special features. Analysis of such bonds requires a variation of the basic tools we considered in Chapter 1, which limited the discussion and analysis to conventional or plain vanilla bonds; that is, instruments with a fixed coupon and term to maturity. We will use this chapter to introduce in overview form some variations on the basic plain vanilla bond. This is to give readers some flavour of the other types of bonds that exist in the market, and which we will look at in greater detail later in this book.

Floating rate notes

Floating rate notes (FRNs) are bonds that have variable rates of interest; the coupon rate is linked to a specified index and changes periodically as the index changes. An FRN is usually issued with a coupon that pays a fixed spread over a reference index; for example, the coupon may be 50 basis points over the six-month interbank rate. An FRN whose spread over the reference rate is not fixed is known as a *variable rate note*. Since the value for the reference benchmark index is not known, it is not possible to calculate the redemption yield for an FRN. Additional features have been added to FRNs, including *floors* (the coupon cannot fall below a specified minimum rate), *caps* (the coupon cannot rise above a maximum rate) and *callability.* There also exist perpetual FRNs. As in other markets, borrowers frequently issue paper with specific or even esoteric terms in order to meet particular requirements or meet customer demand; for example, a US bank recently issued US dollar-denominated FRNs with interest payments indexed to the euribor rate, and another FRN with its day-count basis linked to a specified Libor range.

Generally, the reference interest rate for FRNs is the London interbank rate; the *offered* rate – that is, the rate at which a bank will lend funds to another bank is Libor. An FRN will pay interest at Libor plus a quoted margin (or spread). The interest rate is fixed for a three-month or six-month period and is re-set in line with the Libor *fixing* at the end of the interest period. Hence, at the coupon re-set date for a sterling FRN paying six-month Libor + 0.50%, if the Libor fix is 7.6875%, then the FRN will pay a coupon of 8.1875%. Interest therefore will accrue at a daily rate of £0.0224315.

On the coupon re-set date an FRN will be priced precisely at par. Between re-set dates it will trade very close to par because of the way in which the coupon is re-set. If market rates rise between re-set dates an FRN will trade slightly below par, similarly if rates fall the paper will trade slightly above. This makes FRNs very similar in behaviour to money market instruments traded on a yield basis, although of course FRNs have much longer maturities. Investors can opt to view FRNs as essentially money market instruments or as alternatives to conventional bonds. For this reason one can use two approaches in analysing FRNs. The first approach is known as the *margin method.* This calculates the difference between the return on an FRN and that on an equivalent money market security. There are two variations on this: simple margin and discounted margin.

The simple margin method is sometimes preferred because it does not require the forecasting of future interest rates and coupon values. *Simple margin* is defined as the average return on an FRN throughout its life compared with the reference interest rate. It has two components: a *quoted margin* either above or below the reference rate, and a capital gain or loss element which is calculated under the assumption that the difference between the current price of the FRN and the maturity value is spread evenly over the remaining life of the bond. Simple margin uses the expression at (3.1):

$$\text{Simple margin} = \frac{(M - P_d)}{(100 \times \text{T})} + M_q \qquad (3.1)$$

where

P_d is P + AI, the dirty price

M is the par value

T is the number of years from settlement date to maturity

M_q is the quoted margin.

A quoted margin that is positive reflects yield for an FRN that is offering a higher yield than the comparable money market security.

EXAMPLE 3.1 Simple margin

An FRN with a par value of £100, a quoted margin of 10 basis points over six-month Libor is currently trading at a clean price of 98.50. The previous Libor fixing was 5.375%. There are 90 days of accrued interest, 92 days until the next coupon payment and five years from the next coupon payment before maturity. Therefore we have:

$$P_d = 98.50 + \frac{90}{365} \times 5.375 = 99.825.$$

We obtain T as shown:

$$T = 10 + \frac{92}{365} = 10.252.$$

Inserting these results into (3.1) we have the following simple margin:

$$\text{Simple margin} = \frac{100 - 99.825}{100 \times 10.252} + 0.0010 = 0.00117$$

or 11.7 basis points.

At certain times the simple margin formula is adjusted to take into account any change in the reference rate since the last coupon re-set date. This is done by defining an adjusted price, which is either:

$$AP_d = P_d + (re + QM) \times \frac{N_{sc}}{365} \times 100 - \frac{C}{2} \times 100$$

or (3.2)

$$AP_d = P_d + (re + QM) \times \frac{N_{sc}}{365} \times P_d - \frac{C}{2} \times 100$$

where
AP_d is the adjusted dirty price
re is the current value of the reference interest rate (such as Libor)
C/2 is the next coupon payment (that is, *C* is the reference interest rate on the last coupon re-set date plus *QM)*
N_{sc} is the number of days between settlement and the next coupon date.

The upper equation in (3.2) above ignores the current yield effect: all payments are assumed to be received on the basis of par, and this understates the value of the coupon for FRNs trading below par and overstates the value when they are trading above par. The lower equation in (3.2) takes account of the current yield effect.

The adjusted price AP_d replaces the current price P_d in (3.1) to give an *adjusted simple margin*. The simple margin method has the disadvantage of amortising the discount or premium on the FRN in a straight line over the remaining life of the bond rather than at a constantly compounded rate. The discounted margin method uses the latter approach. The distinction between simple margin and discounted margin is exactly the same as that between simple YTM and YTM. The discounted margin method does have a disadvantage in that it requires a forecast of the reference interest rate over the remaining life of the bond.

The discounted margin is the solution to equation (3.3) shown below, given for an FRN that pays semi-annual coupons.

$$P_d = \left[\frac{1}{(1 + {}^1\!/_2(r + DM))^{days/years}}\right] \times \left[\frac{C}{2} + \sum_{t=1}^{N-1} \frac{(re^* + QM) \times 100/2}{(1 + {}^1\!/_2(r + DM))^t} + \frac{M}{(1 + {}^1\!/_2(r + DM))^{N-1}}\right] \tag{3.3}$$

where
DM is the discounted margin
*re** is the assumed (or forecast) value of the reference rate over the remaining life of the bond
QM is the quoted margin
N is the number of coupon payments before redemption.

Equation (3.3) may be stated in terms of discount factors instead of the reference rate. This version is given in Appendix 3.1. The *yield to maturity spread* method of evaluating FRNs is designed to allow direct comparison between FRNs and fixed-rate bonds. The YTM on the FRN (rmf) is calculated using (3.3) with both ($re + DM$) and ($re^* + DM$) replaced with rmf. The YTM on a reference bond (rmb) is calculated using the basic equation shown in Chapter 1. The *yield to maturity spread* is defined as:

$$rmf - rmb.$$

If this is positive the FRN offers a higher yield than the reference bond.

Table 3.1 shows an extract from the screen of a market-maker in sterling FRNs as at May 1997. The screen shows bonds at the price they are offered to investors, as well as the discount margin in basis points and the credit rating for the bond. The "amount" is the amount of paper that the bank had to offer at that time.

Name	**Maturity**	**Price**	**d/m**	**Amount (£m)**	**Rating**	**Notes**
Bradford & Bingley	Oct-99	100.00	6.5	4	A1	
Bradford & Bingley	Mar-01	100.14	7.5	3		
Bradford & Bingley	Nov-01	99.89	8.1	4.9	A2	
Britannia BS	Jan-00	100.12	6	3		
Britannia BS	Feb-01	99.89	8.7	1.5		
Bankers Trust	Feb-02	99.78	11.8	5		
Irish Permanent	Oct-98	100.37	4	10	A2	
Nationwide	Aug-01	99.78	5.7	5	A1	Callable Aug-00 at 99.93
Midland	Mar-02	99.97	0.5	5		
Midland	May-01	99.65	20	8		Sub-ordinated issue
Woolwich	Mar-99	100.14	6.1	0.930	A1	
Woolwich	Mar-01	99.87	6.8	0.600		
Royal Bank of Scotland	Jan-04	99.93	3.5	10	AA3/AA-	
Royal Bank of Scotland	Jun-05	100.05	36.5	4.5		Sub-ordinated issue; callable after Jun-00

Table 3.1 Author's FRN Offer page as at July 1997

In addition to plain vanilla FRNs, some of the other types of floating-rate bonds that have traded in the market are:

- *Collared FRNs*: these offer caps and floors on an instrument, thus establishing a maximum and minimum coupon on the deal. Effectively these securities contain two embedded options, the issuer buying a cap and selling a floor to the investor.
- *Step-up recovery FRNs*: where coupons are fixed against comparable longer maturity bonds, thus providing investors with the opportunity to maintain exposure to short-term assets while capitalising on a positive-sloping yield curve.
- *Corridor FRNs*: these were introduced to capitalise on expectations of comparative interest rate inactivity. A high-risk/high-reward instrument, it offers investors a very substantial uplift over a chosen reference rate. But rates have to remain within a relatively narrow corridor if the interest payment is not to be forfeited entirely.

Yield calculation using Bloomberg pages

The main page used on Bloomberg to calculate bond yields is YA, which is also suitable for FRN securities. Figure 3.1 shows page YA used for the Ford Motor Credit FRN maturing in June 2005.

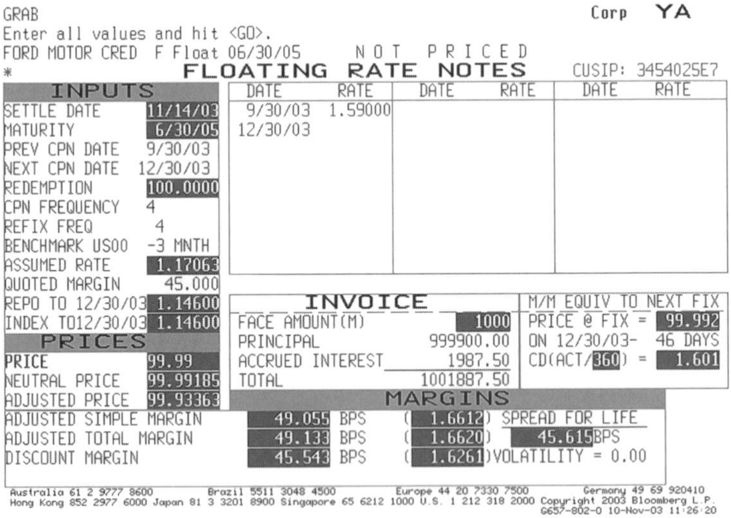

Figure 3.1 Ford Motor Credit June 2005 floating-rate bond yield analysis on Bloomberg page YA, 10 November 2003
©Bloomberg L.P. Used with permission.

The relevant fields for FRNs are as follows:

- refix freq: the number of times that the coupon is re-set each year; this is a static data field;
- benchmark: the reference index or security to which the bond is linked, of which the most common is Libor; this is a static data field;
- assumed rate: the assumed average rate of the benchmark for all future rate re-fixes. This rate is based on the current level of the reference benchmark, and is the assumed rate used to calculate the present values of the cash flows, to determine the discount margin for the security;
- quoted margin: the basis point spread above the benchmark reference rate; in the example at Figure 3.1, the spread is 45 basis points above three-month Libor for the Ford Motor Credit FRN. Unless the bond is a variable rate note, this is a static data field;
- repo to: the next rate refix date and the assumed repo funding rate for the period from settlement to the next refix. The rate is specified by the user, and is the funding rate used to calculate the adjusted price;
- index to: the assumed benchmark rate for the period from settlement to the next coupon date. It is used to calculate present value of the current coupon in discounted margin calculation. Where the period between the settlement date and the next coupon is less than the bond's refix frequency, the rate assumed may not be appropriate to use for the discounted margin calculation, so the user may select a more suitable rate in this field.

For FRNs that have a cap, floor or collar on their interest yield, the user must adjust the assumed rate, entering the relevant rate that results from imposition of the cap or floor.

The YA page calculates three prices for FRNs. The price used can be that resulting either from treating the bond as a conventional bond or as a money market instrument. The price fields are:

- price: this is the current market price, specified by the user. It defaults using the price link that is set for the particular Bloomberg terminal;
- neutral price: the price that results in the same discount margin as calculated to the next coupon date and not the settlement date. This is used to determine value if trading the bond after the next coupon date, so this is in effect the next coupon forward trade price;

- adjusted price: the fair value or break-even price of the bond to the next coupon refix date; it is used when funding the bond to this date in the repo market. For a fixed-rate bond this function is carried out by COC (cost-of-carry) on the same YA page;
- price @ fix: the price of the bond on the coupon refix date;
- on: the number of days between the settlement date to the next coupon date; a static field;
- CD (Act/xxx): the day-count basis used for the bond, which defaults to its normal market convention. In Figure 3.1 this is Act/365, the sterling money market day-count basis.

Yields on FRNs are usually expressed as a margin spread over the reference rate. Page YA calculates the following margins, as basis points and as effective yield:

- adjusted simple margin: referred to as ASM, the simple margin comprised of the quoted spread over the reference rate together with the difference between the adjusted bond price and par. The combined spread is amortised over the bond's term to maturity;
- adjusted total margin: the ASM plus the interest earned from investing any surplus gain if the difference between par and the adjusted price is below par. The assumed interest rate is used to calculate the gain;
- discount margin: the margin spread, when compared against the base reference index rate, that results in the present value of the cash flows being equal to the dirty bond price. The discount rate is the assumed rate plus the discount margin itself. In other words this is the equivalent "yield-to-maturity" of the note;
- spread for life: the spread above or below the reference rate (quoted margin) and any capital gain resulting from convergence of the bond price to par of maturity. The latter will be negative if the current price is above par; it is calculated as a percentage gain and discounted over the term to maturity;
- volatility: the relative change in the discount margin for a 100 basis points change in the assumed interest rate.

Inverse/Reverse floating-rate bonds

Introduction

The coupon rate for some FRNs is set so that it does not change in the same direction as the reference interest rate, but rather in the opposite direction to the change in the reference rate. This means that if the reference rate increases from its level at the previous coupon re-set date, the coupon rate on the bond will decline. These bonds are known as *inverse floating-rate notes*. Generally, the coupon is calculated as a fixed rate, less a floating reference rate, implying that the product has an interest rate cap equal to the fixed rate element. Inverse FRNs originated in the US municipal and mortgage-backed bond markets. One of the first examples was a combined vanilla and inverse *collateralised mortgage obligation* FRN issued by Lehman Brothers in 1986, created by converting an existing fixed-rate bond issue into the combined FRN structure. They are common in the US corporate, municipal and collateralised mortgage obligation markets. The combined structure typically has an FRN with a coupon re-set at a specified margin to an index such as Libor or (in the US market) the Federal Home Loan Cost of Funds Index or COFI. The coupon of the associated inverse FRN moves inversely with the specified index. Vanilla and inverse FRNs combination structures usually have caps and floors that set the maximum and minimum coupon payable on both bonds. The cap and floor may be explicit, in the form a specified maximum rate payable, or implicit, for example, setting a floor equal to the margin if the index rate fell below, say, 1%. Caps and floors may be fixed throughout the life of the bond or may be altered during its life. The inverse floater is sometimes issued with a set level from which the reference rate is subtracted; for example, it may pay a rate of 10% – Libor. In some cases a *multiplier* is used; for example, an inverse FRN paying a coupon of 20% – (2 × Libor) has a multiplier of two.

£200m 10% bond, five-year maturity
Used to create:
    100m FRN coupon set as Libor + 25 basis points, cap 9%
    100m inverse FRN coupon set as 9.75 – Libor, floor 1%

Libor	FRN coupon	Inverse FRN coupon	Total coupon
0.00	0.25	9.75	10
1.00	1.25	8.75	10
2.00	2.25	7.75	10
3.00	3.25	6.75	10
4.00	4.25	5.75	10
5.00	5.25	4.75	10
6.00	6.25	3.75	10
7.00	7.25	2.75	10
8.00	8.25	1.75	10
9.00	9.00	1.00	10
10.00	9.00	1.00	10
12.00	9.00	1.00	10
15.00	9.00	1.00	10

Table 3.2 Creation of FRN and inverse FRN from conventional coupon bond

Where a combined structure has been created from an existing fixed coupon bond, the nominal amounts of the two new FRNs will add to the total size of the original issue. The sum of interest paid on the vanilla and inverse FRNs will also equal the coupon paid on the source bond. If a multiplier is used for the inverse FRN, its nominal size will need to be less than that of the vanilla FRN, in order to keep the combined interest payable at the same level as the original bond's coupon. The original conventional bond from which the floating rate and inverse floater bonds are created is called the *collateral*.

Table 3.2 illustrates an hypothetical example for a combined vanilla and inverse FRN from a conventional 10% coupon bond. The two FRNs have their coupon set in line with Libor; the vanilla FRN coupon is fixed at Libor plus 25 basis points, with a cap at 9%, while the inverse FRN coupon is set as 9.75 – Libor. It has a floor of 1%. There is no multiplier so therefore the two bonds have equal nominal values.

Modified duration[1]

As we noted above an inverse floater is a security whose coupon rate changes inversely with the change in the specified reference rate. In many

[1] Duration and modified duration are reviewed in Chapter 1.

cases inverse floating-rate bonds are created from conventional bonds. The duration of such an inverse floater is a multiple of the duration of the collateral bond from which it was created. To illustrate this, consider a 25-year conventional bond with a market value of £100 million that is split into a floating-rate bond and an inverse floater security, which have market values of £80 million and £20 million respectively. Assume that the conventional bond has a modified duration of 9.50; for a 1% change in yield, the value of this bond will change by approximately 9.5% or £9.5 million. Therefore, the two securities created by splitting the collateral bond must also change in value by a total of £9.5 million for the same change in rates. As we saw in Chapter 1, both the duration and the modified duration of an FRN are relatively small, due to the nature of the coupon re-set making the bond more of a money market security (that is, a semi-annually paying FRN has an interest rate sensitivity similar to a six-month instrument). This means that the change in value of the new portfolio must come virtually entirely from the inverse floater bond. In our example, the modified duration of this bond must be 47.50. A modified duration of 47.50 means that there will be a 47.5% change in the value of the inverse floater for a 1% change in interest rates, a change in value of £9.5 million. Inverse floater securities have the highest modified duration measures of any instrument in the bond markets.

From the example given we see that the modified duration of the inverse floater bond is higher than the number of years to maturity of the collateral bond. This is an unexpected result for those who are more familiar with the duration measure referring to years, as originally defined by Macaulay, as the inverse floater bond has a duration higher than the bond from which it was created.

The general expression for the modified duration, *MD*, of an inverse floating rate security is given by (3.4), which assumes that the modified duration for the FRN is close to zero.

$$MD_{inverse} = (1 + l)(MD_{collateral}) \times \frac{P_{collateral}}{P_{inverse}} \tag{3.4}$$

where l is the leverage level of the inverse floating-rate security.

Introduction to asset-backed bonds

Introduction

There is a large group of bond instruments that trade under the overall heading of *asset-backed bonds*. These are bundled securities, so called because they are marketable instruments that result from the bundling or packaging together of a set of non-marketable assets. This process is known as *securitisation*, when an institution's assets or cash flow receivables are removed from its balance sheet and packaged together as one large loan, and then "sold" on to an investor, or series of investors, who then receive the interest payments due on the assets until they are redeemed. The purchasers of the securitised assets often have no recourse to the original borrowers; in fact, the original borrowers are not usually involved in the transaction or any of its processes. In this section we provide a brief overview of asset-backed bonds.

Securitisation was introduced in the US market and this market remains the largest for asset-backed bonds. The earliest examples of such bonds were in the US mortgage market, where residential mortgage loans made by a *thrift* (building society) were packaged together and sold on to investors who received the interest and principal payments made by the borrowers of the original loans. The process benefited the original lender in a number of ways. One key benefit was that removing assets from the balance sheet reduced risk exposure for the bank and enhanced its liquidity position.

The effect of these benefits are increased with the maturity of the original loans. For example, in the case of mortgage loans, the term to maturity can be up to 25 years, perhaps longer. The bulk of these loans are financed out of deposits that can be withdrawn on demand, or at relatively short notice. In addition, it is often the case that as a result of securitisation, the packaged loans are funded at a lower rate than that charged by the original lending institution. This implies that the bundled loans can be sold off at a higher value than the level at which the lending institution valued them. Put another way, securities loans add value to the loan book and it is the original lender that receives this value. Another benefit is that as a result of securitisation, the total funding available to the lending institution may well increase due to its access to capital markets; in other words, the firm becomes less dependent on its traditional deposit base. And finally, by reducing the level of debt on the lending institution's balance sheet, it will improve the firm's gearing ratio.[2]

The main advantage to the investor of securitisation is that it offers a marketable asset-backed instrument to invest in. Often the instrument offers two levels of protection: the original assets and credit enhancement. The original assets will provide good security if they are well-diversified and equivalent in terms of quality, terms and conditions (for example, the

[2] Gearing is a firm's debt-to-equity ratio.

repayment structure and maturity of assets). A diversified asset base reduces the risk of a single drastic failure, while homogeneous assets make it more straightforward to analyse the loan base. If there is little or no liquidity in the original loans (no secondary market), then investors will often require *credit enhancement* in the form of an insurance contract, letters of credit, subordination of a second tranche which absorbs losses first,[3] over-collateralisation or a reserve fund, for the instrument to be sold at a price acceptable to the original lender. Ironically, by implementing one or more of the protection features described, securitisation provides a better credit risk for the investor than the loans represented to the original lender.

Securitisation began in the US housing market in 1970 after the Government National Mortgage Association (GNMA or "Ginnie Mae") began issuing *mortgage pass-through certificates*. A pass-through is a security representing ownership in a pool of mortgages. The mortgages themselves were sold through a grantor trust and the certificates sold in the capital markets. As with standard mortgages the interest and amortised principal were paid monthly. Later on, *mortgage-backed bonds* were issued with semi-annual payments and maturities of up to 15 years, which were terms familiar to domestic bondholders. In 1983 *collateralised mortgage obligations* were issued, the collateral provided by mortgages issued by the Federal Home Loans Mortgage Corporation. Being government agencies, the bonds that they issue are guaranteed and as such carry little additional risk compared to US Treasury securities. They can therefore be priced on the same basis as Treasuries. However, they present an additional type of risk, that of *prepayment risk*. This is the risk that mortgages will be paid off early, ahead of their term, a risk that increases when mortgages have been taken out at high fixed interest rates and rates have subsequently fallen. The existence of this risk therefore dictates that these bonds pay a higher return than corresponding Treasury bonds. The term *average life* is used to describe the years to maturity for asset-backed bonds that have an element of prepayment risk about them, and is obviously an estimate used by bond analysts.

Securitisation was introduced in the UK market in 1985. A number of institutions were established for the purpose of securitising mortgages and other assets such as car loans and credit card debt. These included National Home Loans Corporation, Mortgage Funding Corporation and First Mortgage Securities.

---

[3] A second tranche of bonds that is junior to the first, so it would absorb any losses first.

Credit rating

In the sterling market all public mortgage-backed and asset-backed securities (MBS/ABS) are explicitly rated by one or both of two of the largest credit-rating agenices, Moody's and Standard & Poor's. In structured financing it is normal for the rating of the paper to be investment grade, with most issues at launch being rated Aaa and/or AAA. We briefly touch here the issues involved in rating such paper, a detailed look appears later. The rating of the issue is derived from a combination of factors. As it cannot generally be expected that investors will be sufficiently protected by the performance of the collateral alone, the rating agencies look to minimise the risk of principal default and ensure timely payment of interest coupons by requiring additional credit enhancement. The percentage of additional enhancement is determined by analysing the "riskiness" of the collateral under a range of stress-tested environments that seek to quantify the effect of various interest rate, foreclosure and loss scenarios, which are largely based on the expected performance of the collateral base in a recession. Much of the analysis is based on performance in the US markets, and the rating agencies try to establish criteria for each market and collateral type that is rated. The amount of enhancement required depends on the rating required at launch; for instance, less is required for a lower rated issue. In many cases issues will be backed by a larger nominal value of collateral; for example, an issue size of £100 million is formed out of assets composed of, say, £110 million or a higher amount.

Enhancement levels are also determined by the agencies reviewing the legal risks in the transaction. The legal analysis examines the competing rights and interests in the assets, including those of the bondholders and various third parties. Mortgage-backed securities (MBS) and asset-backed securities (ABS) are typically issued out of low capitalised "special purpose vehicle" companies (SPV), established solely for the purpose of issuing the securities. The rating agencies need to be assured that there is no risk to the bondholders in the event of the originator, that is the seller of the assets to the SPV, becoming insolvent, and to be certain that a receiver or administrator cannot seize the assets or obtain rights to the SPV's cash flows. In addition, the agencies need to be satisfied that the SPV will be able to meet its obligations to its investors in circumstances where the service body (the entity responsible for administering the collateral, usually the originator) becomes insolvent. Consequently, significant emphasis is placed on ensuring that all primary and supporting documentation preserves the rights of investors in the security. An independent trustee is appointed to represent the interests of investors. Providing trustee services results in valuable fee-based income for banks.

A change in rating for an ABS or MBS issue may occur due to deterioration in performance of the collateral, heavy utilisation of credit enhancement, or downgrade of a supporting rating; for example, an insurance company that was underwriting insurance on the pool of the assets.

Credit enhancement

Credit support enhancement for ABS and MBS issues is usually by either of the following methods.

- *Pool insurance*: an insurance policy provided by a composite insurance company to cover the risk of principal loss in the collateral pool. The claims paying rating of the insurance company is important in determining the overall rating of the issue. In many cases in the past the rating of the insurance company at launch proved to be insufficient to achieve the desired rating and a reinsurance policy was entered into with a higher rated company in order to achieve the desired rating.
- *Senior/Junior note classes*: credit enhancement is provided by subordinating a class of notes ("class B" notes) to the senior class notes ("class A" notes). The class B note's right to its proportional share of cash flows is subordinated to the rights of the senior noteholders. Class B notes do not receive payments of principal until certain rating agency requirements have been met, specifically satisfactory performance of the collateral pool over a predetermined period, or in many cases until all of the senior note classes have been redeemed in full.
- *Margin step-up*: a number of ABS issues incorporate a step-up feature in the coupon structure, which typically coincides with a call date. Although the issuer is usually under no obligation to redeem the notes at this point, the step-up feature is an added incentive for investors, to convince them from the outset that the economic cost of paying a higher coupon would be unacceptable and that the issuer will seek to refinance by exercising its call option.
- *Substitution*: this feature enables the issuer to utilise principal cash flows from redemptions to purchase new collateral from the originator. This has the effect of lengthening the effective life of the transaction as the principal would otherwise have been used to

redeem the notes. The issuer is usually under no obligation to substitute and it is an option granted by the investor.

Redemption mechanism

ABS and MBS issue terms usually incorporate one of two main methods through which the redeeming principal can be passed back to investors.

- *Drawing by lot*: the available principal from the relevant interest period is repaid to investors by the international clearing agencies Euroclear and Clearstream drawing notes, at random, for cancellation. Notes will therefore trade at their nominal value.
- *Pro rata*: the available principal for the interest period is distributed among all investors, dependent upon their holding in the security. A *pool factor* is calculated, which is the remaining principal balance of the note expressed as a factor of one. For instance, if the pool factor is 0.62557, this means that for each note of £10,000 nominal, £3,744.30 of principal has been repaid to date. A pool factor value is useful to investors since early repayment of, say, mortgages reduces the level of asset backing available for an issue, the outstanding value of such an issue is reduced on a pro-rata basis, like early redemption, by a set percentage so that the remaining amount outstanding is adequately securitised.

Additional features

Some ABS structures will incorporate a *call option* feature. In some cases the terms of the issue prevent a call being exercised until a certain percentage of the issue remains outstanding, usually 10%, and a certain date has been passed.

It is common for ABS issues to have an *average life* quoted for them. This says that based on the most recent principal balance for the security, it is assumed that a redemption rate is applied such that the resultant average life equals the number of months left from the last interest payment date until 50% of the principal balance remains. Some issuers will announce the expected average life of their paper, and yield calculations are based on this average life.

Callable bonds

A callable bond is one that allows the issue to *call* the issue before its stated maturity date; that is, redeem the bond early. This provision is sometimes referred to as a *call feature* and is widely used by corporate and local authority issuers of debt. A bond with a call provision carries two disadvantages for the bondholder. First an issuer will call a bond when the market interest rates are lower than the issue's coupon rate; for example, if the coupon on a callable bond is 10% and market interest rates are 8%, it will be advantageous for the issuer to call the 10% issue and refinance it with an 8% issue. The investor is faced with reinvesting the monies received as a result of the call at a lower interest rate. Thus callable bonds present investors with a higher level of reinvestment risk. Second, the potential for the price of a callable bond to appreciate in a falling interest rate environment is less than that of a conventional bond. This is because the price of a callable bond will remain at or near its call price (the price above which it is economical for the issuer to redeem the bond) rather than rise to the higher price that would result for an otherwise comparable non-callable bond. Because callable bonds carry such disadvantages for the investor, the market also requires them to offer sufficient compensation for bondholders, in the form of a higher yield compared to conventional bonds. The higher yield on callable bonds is the price they pay in return for asking investors to bear the associated call risk.

The *call price* for a callable bond is the price paid to bondholders when the bond is called. It is usually par, but it may be above par or set at different levels for different times. The prices and times at which a bond can be called are set out in the issue terms and form part of the *call schedule*. The most common reason why a bond is called is because the issuer can refinance borrowing requirements at a lower interest rate; for example, because it has achieved an improved credit rating. When lower borrowing costs are available an issuer will call an existing issue and replace it with a bond carrying a lower coupon. Another reason why a bond may be called is when the issuer can re-fund existing debt at a lower rate; in this case, following a drop in interest rates the current issue is called and replaced, again with a bond paying a lower coupon.

Investors in a callable bond are aware of the call feature attached to the bond, and the potential downside of holding the bond. For this reason, investors require a higher yield from holding callable bonds compared to non-callable bonds of similar maturity issued by the same or similar issuers. There is often a period of *call protection* built into the bond's terms, during which the bond may not be called. If we assume an efficient market mechanism, bondholders will have the same information about the market as the bond issuer, and the premium required by them when compared to the return from holding a non-callable bond is known at the time of issue of the callable bond. In an efficient market therefore there is no advantage to a borrower in issuing a callable bond compared to a non-callable one, since the advantages of the call feature are balanced by the higher funding cost associated with incorporating a call feature.

In certain cases, callable bonds are issued with a period of *call protection* included in the terms. This is a period during which the bond cannot be called; for example, a callable bond with a 10-year term to maturity that is not callable for the first five years of its life. Call protection is often provided by the issuer as an added incentive to investors to buy the bond.

Analysis

For callable bonds the market calculates a YTM in the normal fashion but also calculates a *yield to call* for the bond. The yield to call is calculated on the assumption that the bond will be called at the first call date. The procedure is the same as for the normal yield calculation; that is, to determine the market interest rate of return that will equate the present value of all the cash flows to the current price. For yield to call the cash flows are those to the first call date. The normal practice for a bond trading above par is to calculate the YTM and the yield to call and take the lower value as the bond's yield. In fact bond investors and analysts will usually calculate the yield to the first call date and also the yield to all possible call dates, and then use the lowest of these values as the bond's yield. Bloomberg analysis refers to this value as the *yield to worst*. This yield calculation suffers from the same problems as YTM, in that the figure computed assumes reinvestment of coupon at the same rate, and that bondholders will hold the bond to maturity. Yield to call also assumes that the issuer will call the bond on the assumed call date.

The price/yield relationship for a conventional bond is convex. For a bond with an option feature, such as a callable bond, the relationship differs at a certain yield point, such that the bond is said to then display *negative convexity*.

Constituents of a callable bond

The best way to analyse a callable bond is to consider it as one for which the bondholder has sold the issuer an option that allows the issuer to redeem the bond, at her discretion, from the first call date until maturity. The bondholder has effectively entered into two separate transactions: first, the purchase of a non-callable bond from the issuer at a price, and second, the sale to the issuer of a *call option* for which she receives a price (it is a call option as the issuer has the right, but not the obligation, to buy back the bond from the bondholder at a call date(s), which is in effect the expiry date(s) of the option). The position of the bondholder is therefore:

Long position in callable bond = Long position in non-callable bond + short position in call option.

The price of the callable bond is therefore equal to the net position of the two component parts.

Price of callable bond = Price of non-callable bond − price of call option

If you think about it, the bondholder has sold the issuer a call option, therefore the "proceeds" of this sale are subtracted from the price of the hypothetical non-callable bond. This is shown in Figure 3.2; at point *r* the price of the non-callable bond and the callable bond is the price of the call option on the bond.

As most callable bonds have a set of dates on which they can be called, or even a time period during which the bond can be called at any time after a requisite notice period, the bondholder can be said to have sold not one call option on the bond, but a strip of options. The underlying asset for these call options is the set of cash flows that are not paid if the issuer exercises the call.

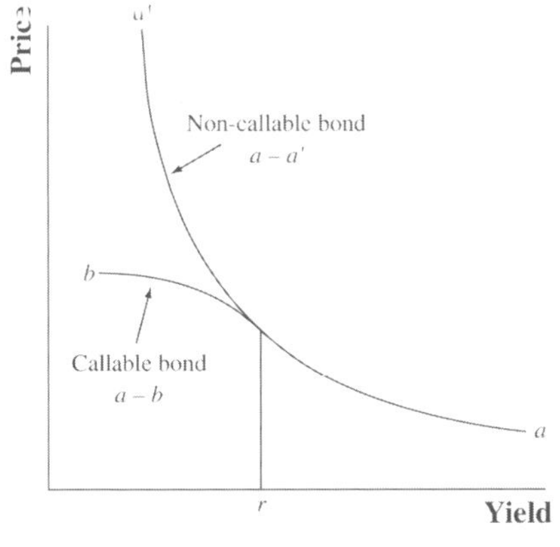

Figure 3.2 Price/yield relationship for callable bond.
Reproduced with permission from Frank J Fabozzi 1997, *Fixed Income Mathematics*, McGraw Hill, New York.

Constituents of a putable bond

The analysis we have applied to callable bonds can be repeated for bonds that have an embedded *put* feature. With a putable bond the bondholder has the right to sell the bond back to the issuer at a designated price and time. Again a putable bond can be viewed as representing two separate transactions; first the bondholder buys a non-putable bond; second, the investor buys an option from the issuer that allows her to sell the bond to the issuer. This type of option is called a *put option*. The price of the putable bond is therefore:

Price of putable bond = Price of non-putable bond + Price of put option.

Refunding

The term refunding is used to describe the process when a borrower calls an existing bond issue and replaces it with a new lower coupon bond issue. This is at the discretion of the issuer. A company that has borrowed funds via a callable bond will want to be aware of the best time at which to call the issue. The primary issues are if there is any net gain to be had from an immediate refinancing, and what the appropriate replacement bond should be.

On issue the yield of the callable yield will lie above a non-callable bond of the same maturity; this reflects the call premium benefit to the bondholder. At any point during the bond's life, market interest rates may fall far enough below the coupon level such that it becomes attractive to the issuer to call in the bonds (before the stated maturity date) and replace the borrowing. The first issue for the borrower is what type of bond should be used to replace the called debt. If the replacement bond is non-callable and has the same maturity date as the original issue, it would have to offer the same yield as the existing issue in order to be attractive to investors. However, the lower general level of interest rates may result in the issuer needing to offer a spread over, say, the government yield level that is lower than the spread offered on the original issue.

Borrowers also need to consider the timing of the refinancing and whether it is advantageous to delay calling the issue until a later date. However, this is a judgement call based on the corporate treasurer's view of market interest rates. The decision to refinance after a material change in the general level of interest rates is an important one. If interest rates have fallen sufficiently an issuing company has an opportunity to refinance at a new (lower) borrowing rate, and this will be at the expense of the existing bondholders. Thus the existence of a call option provision as part of the bond's terms is an advantage to the borrower, and this option needs to be exercised in order for the borrower to gain from any fall in the level of interest rates.

Advance refunding

It is common for corporate borrowers to issue callable bonds that include a period of call protection. If there is a significant fall in interest rates during the period of this call protection, the borrower may consider an *advance refunding*. This is where the borrower offers to buy call-protected bonds at a price above the call price; when this happens bondholders are not obliged to respond to the call but may be tempted to do so because the terms of the call are attractive, while still enabling the borrower to achieve a funding gain.

EXAMPLE 3.2 Callable bond

A callable bond with a coupon of 8% has two years remaining on its call protection provision. The call price is £110 once the bond becomes callable. Market interest rates are now at 5%. The firm may wish to refund immediately, rather than wait for two years and refund at an as yet unknown rate, providing it can offer a call price attractive enough to the bondholders while retaining an element of funding benefit for itself.

The fair value of the bond is the present value of the £8 coupon for the next two years together with the present value of the call price two years from now. This is given at (3.5):

$$P = \frac{8}{(1+r)} + \frac{8}{(1+r)^2} + \frac{110}{(1+r)^2}. \qquad (3.5)$$

At a discount rate of 5% the price of the bond is 114.6485. If it wishes to advance refund, the issuer will have to set a call price above this level in order to induce to bondholders to sell their bonds. However, this allows it to gain a refunding advantage immediately instead of having to wait two years. Any funding gain must take into account the transaction costs associated with calling back the bonds and issuing new debt.

Sinking funds

In certain domestic markets, including the UK and US markets, corporate bonds are issued with a *sinking fund* attached. This requires the borrower to redeem a part of the bond issue at regular intervals during the bond's life. An example of a sinking fund provision is illustrated in Figure 3.3.

£200 million 20-year bond issue

	Year										
Time periods	0 ...	10	11	12	13	14	15	16	17	18	19	20
Sinking fund payments as 5% of outstanding nominal (£m)		10	9.5	9.025	8.57375	8.14506	7.73781	7.35092	6.98337	6.63420	6.30249	
Final principal												119.7474

Figure 3.3 Bond sinking fund payments

In the example in Figure 3.3 a bond with a twenty-year maturity and a total issue size of £200 million has 5% of its outstanding issue size redeemed each year after ten years have elapsed, leaving £119.75 million to be paid back on maturity. At each anniversary of the sinking fund dates the borrowing firm can either purchase the required number of bonds in the open market or call the same number of bonds. The exact procedure will be set out in the bond issue terms, and the firm will elect the cheapest option.

The main reason why an issuer will include a sinking fund provision is to provide comfort to potential investors. A sinking fund will indicate a lower level of risk of default, since the availability of funds to repay a set proportion of the debt indicates a healthy cash flow state. However, if the sinking fund is sourced from external funds this may not actually be the case. Nevertheless, in theory a sinking fund signals favourable future prospects for the borrowing company, so as a result the yield required by investors from holding the bond consequently is lower.

Analysing call provisions

Callable bonds are very popular in corporate debt markets, significantly so in the United States. A study by Kish and Livingston (1992) found that approximately 80% of corporate debt in the US market in the second half of the 1980s was issued with call provisions attached. It is often observed that only issuers whose paper is highly sought after by investors raise funds without the existence of any call provision, and consequently at a lower yield.

In an economist's perfect market the increased yield available on a callable bond together with any period of call protection should take into account the probability of the call option being exercised. In theory therefore there should be no advantage either way to issuing a bond with a call provision attached. In practice however corporate issuers continue to issue a large volume of debt incorporating call features. Previous studies including the one by Kish and Livingston have attempted to explain this phenomenon. These are summarised below.

- *Corporate management superior knowledge on direction of interest rates.* While an above-average forecasting ability on the direction of interest rates would indeed be a valuable skill, and would be advantageous to the issuers of callable bonds, it is highly unlikely that corporate managers possess such a skill. In any case the investors who purchase callable debt carry out their own market analysis and one would not expect their forecasting ability to be any poorer than that of corporate borrowers.
- *The risk-averse nature of borrowers and lenders.* This premise suggests that borrowers do not favour locking in to high interest rates for anything more than short periods of time, while lenders wish to avoid large downward fluctuations in bond prices, and do not attach great value to the call feature. Again this is unrealistic with regard to the lender's position, since the conventional preference for lenders is to lock in a fixed return over the complete term of a bond's life.
- *Corporate management knowledge of the firm's prospects.* In this analysis the suggestion is that managers possess superior knowledge of their firms' prospects over that of investors, who view the firm in less favourable light and therefore demand a higher yield on the debt. The managers expect the firm's circumstances to improve and refinance the borrowing at a better rate when this occurs. However, this analysis does not explain why even well-rated firms issue callable bonds, or why firms issue both callable and non-callable debt.

Whatever the primary rationale behind the issue of callable debt, investors are frequently interested in increasing the yields on their investments and callable bonds provide one of the ways of achieving this. Therefore it is advantageous to both investors and borrowers for corporates to issue some callable debt as part of their overall funding requirement.

Index-linked bonds

Inflation-indexed bonds and derivatives

In certain countries there is a market in bonds whose return, both coupon and final redemption payment, is linked to the consumer price index. Investors' experience with inflation-indexed bonds differs across countries, as they were introduced at different times, and as a result the exact design of *index-linked bonds* varies across the different markets. For instance, some index-linked bonds link both coupon and maturity payments to a specified index; in other markets only the coupon payment is index-linked. Generally, the most liquid market available will be the government bond market in index-linked instruments. Index-linked bonds are generally issued by governments, but corporate borrowers have also issued such bonds, necessitating their inclusion in this book.

The structure of index-linked bond markets across the world differs in various ways, including those noted below. Appendix 3.2 at the end of this chapter lists those countries that currently issue public-sector indexed securities.

Introduction and basic concepts

There are a number of reasons why investors and issuers alike are interested in inflation-indexed bonds. Investors will be interested in holding inflation-linked bonds whenever they have a fear that long-term inflation levels will be such that the real value of their investments will be significantly eroded. At times like these, issuers, both governments and corporates alike, may not be able to place long-dated paper unless they link the bond's return to inflation.

We look first at some of the factors involved in security design.

Choice of index. In principle, bonds can be indexed to any number of variables, including various price indices, earnings, output, specific commodities or foreign currencies. Although ideally the chosen index would reflect the hedging requirements of both parties, these may not coincide. For instance, the overwhelming choice of retail investors is for indexation to consumer prices, whereas pension funds prefer linking to earnings levels, to offset earnings-linked pension liabilities. In practice most bonds have been linked to an index of consumer prices such as the UK Retail Price Index, since this is usually widely circulated and well understood, and issued on a regular basis.

Indexation lags. In order to provide practically precise protection against inflation, interest payments for a given period would need to be corrected for actual inflation over the same period. However, for two important reasons, there are unavoidable lags between the movements in the price index and the adjustment to the bond cash flows as they are paid. This reduces the inflation-proofing properties of indexed bonds. Deacon and Derry (1998) state two reasons why indexation lags are necessary. First, inflation statistics can only be calculated and published with a delay. The data for one month is usually known well into the next month, and there may be delays in publication. This calls for a lag of at least one month. Second, in some markets the size of the next coupon payment must be known before the start of the coupon period in order to calculate the accrued interest; this leads to a delay equal to the length of time between coupon payments.[4]

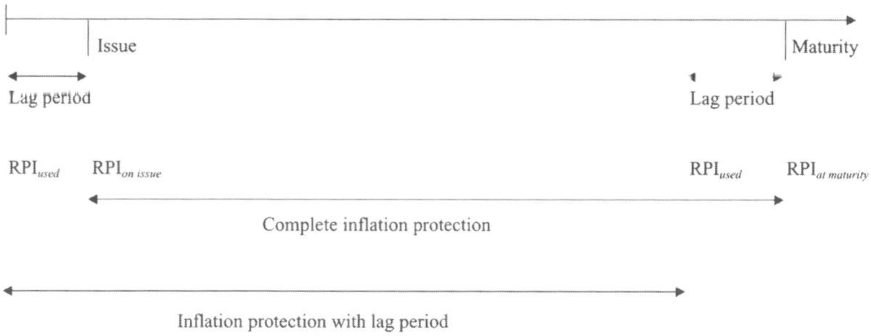

Figure 3.1 The indexation lag

[4] The same source cites various methods by which the period of the lag may be minimised; for example, the accrued interest calculation for Canadian Real Return Bonds is based on cumulative movements in the consumer prices index, which run from the last coupon date. This obviates the need to know with certainty the nominal value of the next coupon, unlike the arrangement for UK index-linked gilts (see Deacon and Derry (1998), pp. 30–1).

Coupon frequency. Index-linked bonds often pay interest on a semi-annual basis, but long-dated investors such as fund managers whose liabilities may well include inflation-indexed annuities are also, at least in theory, interested in indexed bonds that pay on a quarterly or even monthly basis.

Indexing the cash flows. There are four basic methods of linking the cash flows from a bond to an inflation index. These are:

- Interest-indexed bonds: these pay a fixed real coupon and an indexation of the fixed principal every period; the principal repayment at maturity is not adjusted. In this case all the inflation adjustment is fully paid out as it occurs and does not accrue on the principal. These type of bonds have been issued in Australia, although the most recent issue was in 1987.
- Capital-indexed bonds: the coupon rate is specified in real terms. Interest payments equal the coupon rate multiplied by the inflation-adjusted principal amount. At maturity the principal repayment is the product of the nominal value of the bond multiplied by the cumulative change in the index. Compared with interest-indexed bonds of similar maturity, these bonds have higher duration and lower reinvestment risk. These type of bonds have been issued in Australia, Canada, New Zealand, the United Kingdom and the United States.
- Zero-coupon indexed bonds: as their name implies these pay no coupons but the principal repayment is scaled for inflation. These have the highest duration of all indexed bonds and have no reinvestment risk. These type of bonds have been issued in Sweden.
- Indexed-annuity bonds: the payments consist of a fixed annuity payment and a varying element to compensate for inflation. These bonds have the lowest duration and highest reinvestment risk of all index-linked bonds. They have been issued in Australia, although not by the central government.
- Current pay bond: as with interest indexed bonds, the principal cash flow on maturity is not adjusted for inflation. The difference with current pay bonds is that their term cash flows are a combination of an inflation-adjusted coupon and an indexed amount that is related to the principal. Thus in effect current pay bonds are an inflation-indexed floating-rate note. They have been issued in Turkey.

The choice of instrument will reflect the requirements of investors and issuers. Deacon and Derry (1998) cite duration, tax treatment and reinvestment risk as the principal factors that influence instrument design. Although duration for an indexed bond measures something slightly different to that for a conventional bond, being an indication of the bond price sensitivity due to changes in the real interest rate, as with a conventional bond it is higher for zero-coupon indexed bonds compared to coupon bonds. Indexed annuities will have the shortest duration. Longer duration instruments will (in theory) be demanded by investors that have long-dated hedging liabilities. Again, similarly to conventional bonds, investors holding indexed bonds are exposed to reinvestment risk, which means that the true yield earned by holding a bond to maturity cannot be determined when it is purchased, as the rate at which interim cash flows can be invested is not known. Hence, bonds that pay more of their return in the form of coupons are more exposed to this risk, which would be indexed annuities. Indexed zero-coupon bonds, like their conventional counterparts, do not expose investors to reinvestment risk. The tax regime in individual markets will also influence investor taste. For instance, some jurisdictions tax the capital gain on zero-coupon bonds as income, with a requirement that any tax liability be discharged as current income. This is unfavourable treatment as the capital is not available until maturity, which would reduce institutional investor demand for zero-coupon instruments.

It should be noted also that in three countries – namely, Canada, New Zealand and the United States – there exists a facility for investors to strip indexed bonds, thus enabling separate trading of coupon and principal cash flows.[5] Such an arrangement obviates the need for a specific issue of zero-coupon indexed securities, as the market can create them in response to investor demand.

Coupon stripping feature. Allowing market practitioners to strip indexed bonds enables them to create new inflation-linked products that are more specific to investors needs, such as indexed annuities or deferred payment indexed bonds. In markets which allow stripping of indexed government bonds, a strip is simply an individual uplifted cash flow. An exception to this is in New Zealand, where the cash flows are separated into three components: the principal, the principal inflation adjustment and the set of inflation-linked coupons (that is, an indexed annuity).

---

[5] In the United Kingdom the facility of "stripping" exists for conventional gilts but not index-linked gilts. The term originates in the US market, being an acronym for *S*eparate *T*rading of *R*egistered *I*nterest and *P*rincipal.

Index-linked bond yields

Calculating index-linked yields

Inflation-indexed bonds have either or both of their coupon and principal linked to a price index such as the retail price index (RPI), a commodity price index (for example, wheat) or a stock market index. In the United Kingdom the reference is to the RPI, whereas in other markets the price index is the consumer price index (CPI). If we wish to calculate the yield on such bonds it is necessary to make forecasts of the relevant index, which are then used in the yield calculation. In the United Kingdom, both the principal and coupons on UK index-linked government bonds are linked to the RPI and are therefore designed to give a constant *real* yield. Most of the index-linked stocks that have been issued by the UK government have coupons of 2 or $2^1/_2$%. This is because the return from an index-linked bond represents in theory *real* return, as the bond's cash flows rise in line with inflation. Historically, real rate of return on UK market debt stock over the long-term has been roughly $2^1/_2$%.

Indexed bonds differ in their make-up across markets. In some markets only the principal payment is linked, whereas other indexed bonds link only their coupon payments and not the redemption payment. In the case of the former, each coupon and the final principal are scaled up by the ratio of two values of the RPI. The main RPI measure is the one reported for eight months before the issue of the gilt, and is known as the *base RPI*. The base RPI is the denominator of the index measure. The numerator is the RPI measure for eight months prior to the month coupon payment, or eight months before the bond maturity date.

The coupon payment of an index-linked gilt is given by (3.6) below.

$$\text{Coupon payment} = (C/2) \times \frac{RPI_{c-8}}{RPI_0} \tag{3.6}$$

Equation (3.6) above shows the coupon divided by two before being scaled up, because index-linked gilts pay semi-annual coupons. The formula for calculating the size of the coupon payment for an annual-paying indexed bond is modified accordingly.

The principal repayment is given by (3.7) below.

$$\text{Coupon payment} = 100 \times \frac{RPI_{M-8}}{RPI_0} \tag{3.7}$$

where

C is the annual coupon payment

RPI_0 is the RPI value eight months prior to the issue of the bond (the base RPI)

RPI_{C-8} is the RPI value eight months prior to the month in which the coupon is paid

RPI_{M-8} is the RPI value eight months prior to the bond redemption.

Price indices are occasionally "re-based", which means that the index is set to a base level again. In the United Kingdom the RPI has been re-based twice, the last occasion being in January 1987, when it was set to 100 from the January 1974 value of 394.5.

EXAMPLE 3.3 Index-linked bond

An index-linked gilt with a coupon of 4.625% was issued in April 1988 and matured in April 1998. The base measure required for this bond is the RPI for August 1987, which was 102.1. The RPI for August 1997 was 158.5. We can use these values to calculate the actual cash amount of the final coupon payment and principal repayment in April 1998, as shown below:

$$\text{Coupon payment} = (4.625 \,/\, 2) \times (158.5 \,/\, 102.1) = £3.58992$$

$$\text{Principal repayment} = 100 \times (158.5 \,/\, 102.1) = £155.23996.$$

We can determine the accrued interest calculation for the last six-month coupon period (October 1987 to April 1998) by using the final coupon payment, given below.

The markets use two main yield measures for index-linked bonds, both of which are a form of YTM. These are the *money* (or *nominal*) *yield*, and the *real yield*.

In order to calculate a money yield for an indexed bond we require forecasts of all future cash flows from the bond. Since future cash flows from an index-linked bond are not known with certainty, we require a forecast of all the relevant future RPIs, which we then apply to all the cash flows. In fact the market convention is to take the latest available RPI and assume a constant inflation rate thereafter, usually $2^1/_2$% or 5%. By assuming a constant inflation rate we can set future RPI levels, which in turn allow us to calculate future cash flow values.

We obtain the forecast for the first relevant future RPI using (3.8):

$$RPI_1 = RPI_0 \times (1 + \tau)^{m/12} \tag{3.8}$$

where

RPI_1 is the forecast RPI level
RPI_0 is the latest available RPI
τ is the assumed future annual inflation rate
m is the number of months between.

Consider an indexed bond that pays coupons every June and December. For analysis we require the RPI forecast value for eight months prior to June and December, which will be for October and April. If we are now in February, we require a forecast for the RPI for the following April. This sets $m = 2$ in our equation at (3.8). We can then use (3.9) to forecast each subsequent relevant RPI required to set the bond's cash flows:

$$RPI_{j+1} = RPI_1 \times (1 + \tau)^{j/2} \tag{3.9}$$

where j is the number of semi-annual forecasts after RPI_1 (which was our forecast RPI for April). For example, if the February RPI was 163.7 and we assume an annual inflation rate of 2.5%, then we calculate the forecast for the RPI for the following April to be:

$$\begin{aligned} RPI_1 &= 163.7 \times (1.025)^{2/12} \\ &= 164.4 \end{aligned}$$

and for the following October it would be:

$$\begin{aligned} RPI_3 &= 164.4 \times (1.025) \\ &= 168.5. \end{aligned}$$

Once we have determined the forecast RPIs we can calculate the yield. Under the assumption that the analysis is carried out on a coupon date, so that accrued interest on the bond is zero, we can calculate the money yield (ri) by solving equation (3.10):

$$P_d = \frac{(C/2)(RPI_1/RPI_0)}{(1 + \frac{1}{2} ri)} + \frac{(C/2)(RPI_2/RPI_0)}{(1 + \frac{1}{2} ri)^2} + \ldots + \frac{([C/2]+M)(RPI_N/RPI_0)}{(1 + \frac{1}{2} ri)^N} \quad (3.10)$$

where
ri is the semi-annualised money YTM
N is the number of coupon payments (interest periods) up to maturity.

Equation (3.10) is for semi-annual paying indexed bonds such as index-linked gilts. The equation for annual coupon indexed bonds is given at (3.11):

$$P_d = \frac{C(RPI_1/RPI_0)}{(1 + ri)} + \frac{C(RPI_2/RPI_0)}{(1 + ri)^2} + \ldots + \frac{(C+M)(RPI_N/RPI_0)}{(1 + ri)^N}. \quad (3.10)$$

The real yield ry is related to the money yield through equation (3.11), as it applies to semi-annual coupon bonds, which was first described by Fisher in *Theory of Interest* (1930).

$$(1 + \tfrac{1}{2} ry) = (1 + \tfrac{1}{2} ri) / (1 + \tau)^{1/2} \quad (3.11)$$

To illustrate this, if the money yield is 5.5% and the forecast inflation rate is 2.5%, then the real yield is calculated using (3.11) as shown below.

$$ry = \left[\frac{[1 + \frac{1}{2}(0.055)]}{[1 + (0.025)^{1/2}]} - 1 \right] \times 2$$

$$= 0.0297 \text{ or } 2.97\% .$$

We can rearrange equation (3.9) and use (3.11) to solve for the real yield, shown at (3.12) and applicable to semi-annual coupon bonds. Again, we use (3.12) where the calculation is performed on a coupon date.

$$P_d = \frac{RPI_a}{RPI_0} \left[\frac{(C/2)(1+\tau)^{1/2}}{(1 + \frac{1}{2} ri)} + \frac{(C/2)(1+\tau)}{(1 + \frac{1}{2} ri)^2} + \ldots + \frac{([C/2] + M)(1+\tau)^{N/2}}{(1 + \frac{1}{2} ri)^N} \right]$$

$$= \frac{RPI_a}{RPI_0} \left[\frac{(C/2)}{(1 + \frac{1}{2} ry)} + \ldots + \frac{(C/2) + M}{(1 + \frac{1}{2} ry)^N} \right] \quad (3.12)$$

where

$$RPI_a = \frac{RPI_1}{(1 + \tau)^{1/2}} \ .$$

RPI_0 is the base index level as initially described. RPI_a / RPI_0 is the rate of inflation between the bond's issue date and the date the yield calculation is carried out.

It is best to think of the equations for money yield and real yield by thinking of which discount rate to employ when calculating a redemption yield for an indexed bond. Equation (3.10) can be viewed as showing that the money yield is the appropriate discount rate for discounting money or nominal cash flows. We then rearrange this equation as given in (3.11) to show that the real yield is the appropriate discount rate to use when discounting real cash flows.

Assessing yield for index-linked bonds

Index-linked bonds do not offer *complete* protection against a fall in real value of an investment. That is, the return from index-linked bonds including index-linked gilts is not in reality a guaranteed real return, in spite of the cash flows being linked to a price index such as the RPI. The reason for this is the lag in indexation, which for index-linked gilts is eight months. The time lag means that an indexed bond is not protected against inflation for the last interest period of its life, which for gilts is the last six months. Any inflation occurring during this final interest period will not be reflected in the bond's cash flows and will reduce the real value of the redemption payment and hence the real yield. This can be a worry for investors in high inflation environments. The only way to effectively eliminate inflation risk for bondholders is to reduce the time lag in indexation of payments to something like one or two months.

Bond analysts frequently compare the yields on index-linked bonds with those on conventional bonds, as this implies the market's expectation of inflation rates. To compare returns between index-linked bonds and conventional bonds, analysts calculate the *break-even inflation rate*. This is the inflation rate that makes the money yield on an index-linked bond equal to the redemption yield on a conventional bond of the same maturity. Roughly speaking, the difference between the yield on an indexed bond and a conventional bond of the same maturity is what the market expects inflation during the life of the bond to be; part of the higher yield available on the conventional bond is therefore the inflation *premium*. In August 1999 the redemption yield on the $5^3/_4$% Treasury 2009, the 10-year benchmark gilt, was 5.17%. The real yield on the $2^1/_2$% index-linked 2009 gilt, assuming a constant inflation rate of 3%, was 2.23%. Using (3.10) this gives us an implied break-even inflation rate of:

$$\tau = \left[\frac{[1 + {}^1/_2\,(0.0517)]}{[1 + {}^1/_2\,(0.0223)]} \right]^2 - 1$$

$$= 0.029287 \text{ or } 2.9\%.$$

If we accept that an advanced and liquid market such as the gilt market is of at least semi-strong form, if not strong form, then the inflation expectation in the market is built into these gilt yields. However, if this implied inflation rate understated what was expected by certain market participants, investors will start holding more of the index-linked bond rather than the conventional bond. This activity will then force the indexed yield down (or the conventional yield up). If investors had the opposite view and thought that the implied inflation rate overstated inflation expectations, they would hold the conventional bond. In our illustration above, the market is expecting long-term inflation to be at around 2.9% or less, and the higher yield of the $5^3/_4$% 2009 bond reflects this inflation expectation. A fund manager will take into account her view of inflation, among other factors, in deciding how much of the index-linked gilt to hold compared to the conventional gilt. It is often the case that investment managers hold indexed bonds in a portfolio against specific index-linked liabilities, such as pension contracts that increase their payouts in line with inflation each year.

The premium on the yield of the conventional bond over that of the index-linked bond is therefore compensation against inflation to investors holding it. Bondholders will choose to hold index-linked bonds instead of conventional bonds if they are worried by unexpected inflation. An individual's view on expected inflation will depend on several factors, including the current macroeconomic environment and the credibility of the monetary authorities, be they the central bank or the government. In certain countries such as the United Kingdom and New Zealand, the central bank has explicit inflation targets and investors may feel that over the long term these targets will be met. If the track record of the monetary authorities is proven, investors may feel further that inflation is no longer a significant issue. In these situations the case for holding index-linked bonds is weakened.

The real-yield level on indexed bonds in other markets is also a factor. As capital markets around the world have become closely integrated in the last twenty years, global capital mobility means that high inflation markets are shunned by investors. Therefore over time expected returns, certainly in developed and liquid markets, should be roughly equal, so that real yields are at similar levels around the world. If we accept this premise, we would then expect the real yield on index-linked bonds to be at approximately similar levels, whatever market they are traded in. For example, we would expect indexed bonds in the United Kingdom to be at a level near to that in, say, the US market. In fact in May 1999 long-dated index-linked gilts traded at just over 2% real yield, while long-dated indexed bonds in the United States were at the higher real yield level of 3.8%. This was viewed by analysts as reflecting that international capital was not as mobile as had previously been thought, and that productivity gains and technological progress in the US economy had boosted demand for capital there to such an extent that real yield had had to rise. However, there is no doubt that there is considerable information content in index-linked bonds, and analysts are always interested in the yield levels of these bonds compared to conventional bonds.

Inflation-indexed derivatives

Inflation-indexed derivatives, also known as inflation-linked derivatives *or inflation derivatives*, have become widely traded instruments in the capital markets in a relatively short space of time. They are traded generally by the same desks in investment banks that trade inflation-linked sovereign bonds, who use these instruments for hedging, as well as to meet the requirements of clients such as hedge funds, pension funds and corporates. They are a natural development of the inflation-linked bond market.

Inflation derivatives are an additional means by which market participants can have an exposure to inflation-linked cash flows. They can also improve market liquidity in inflation-linked products, as an earlier generation of derivatives did for interest rates and credit risk. As flexible OTC products, inflation derivatives offer advantages over cash products in certain circumstances. They provide:

- an ability to tailor cash flows to meet investors' requirements;
- a means by which inflation-linked exposures can be hedged;
- an instrument via which relative value positions can be put on across cash and synthetic markets;
- a building block for the structuring of more complex and hybrid products.

The inflation derivatives market in the United Kingdom was introduced after the introduction of the gilt repo market in 1996. In most gilt repo trades, index-linked (IL) gilts could be used as collateral; this mean that both IL and conventional gilts could be used as hedging tools against positions in inflation derivatives. In the euro area, IL derivatives were introduced later, but experienced significant growth during 2002–2003. The existence of a sovereign IL bond market can be thought of as a necessary precursor to the development of IL derivatives, and although there is no reason why this should be the case, up to now this has been the case. The reason for this is probably because such a cash market suggests that investors are aware of the attraction of IL products, and wish to invest in them. From a market in IL bonds develops a market in IL swaps, which are the most common IL derivatives. The IL bond market also provides a ready reference point from which IL derivatives can be priced.

Market instruments

We describe first some common inflation derivatives, before considering some uses for hedging and other purposes. We then consider IL derivatives pricing.

Inflation-linked bond swap

This is also known as a *synthetic index-linked bond*. It is a swap with the following two cash flow legs:

- pay (receive) the cash flows on a government IL bond;
- receive (pay) a fixed or floating cash flow.

This converts existing conventional fixed- or floating-rate investments into inflation-linked investments. An example of such a swap is given below.

IL bond swap

Nominal	€100,000,000
Start date	15 March 2004
Maturity term	15 March 2009
Bank receives	Six-month Euribor flat [+ spread], semi-annual, act/360
	or
	Fixed rate coupon $x\%$, annual 30/360

Bank pays Real coupon of $y\%$
$y \times [HICP(p - 3)/(HICP(s - 3))] \times$ day-count $\times$ notional
annual 30/360
On maturity:
Notional $\times$ max. $\{0\%, [HICP(m - 3) / HICP(s - 3) - 1]\}$

The symbols in the formulas above are:

p payment date
s start date
m maturity date
$HICP$ Harmonised Index of Consumer Prices.

The "minus 3" in the formula for HICP refers to a three-month lag for indexation, common in euro sovereign IL bond markets.

The swap is illustrated at Figure 3.5.

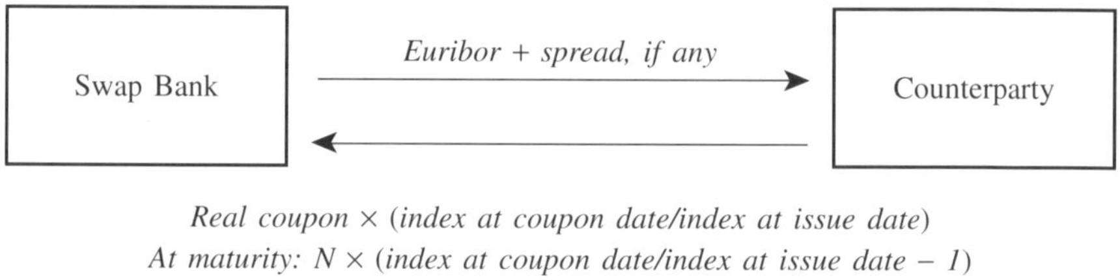

Figure 3.5 Synthetic index-linked bond

Year-on-year inflation swap

This swap is commonly used to hedge issues of IL bonds. The swap is comprised of:

- pay (receive) an index-linked coupon, which is a fixed rate component plus the annual rate of change in the underlying index;
- receive (pay) Euribor or Libor, plus a spread if necessary.

With these swaps, the index-linked leg is usually set at a floor of 0% for the annual change in the underlying index. This guarantees the investor a minimum return of the fixed rate coupon.

This swap is also known as a *pay-as-you-go swap*. It is shown at Figure 3.6.

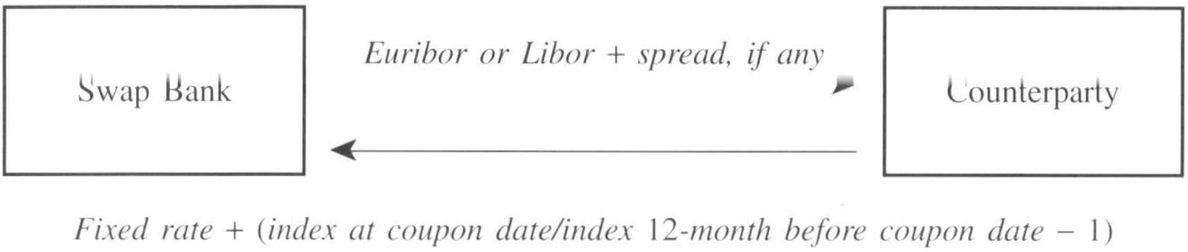

Figure 3.6 Year-on-year inflation swap

Tips swap

The Tips swap is based on the structure of US Tips securities. It pays a periodic fixed rate on an accreting notional amount, together with an additional one-off payment on maturity. This payout profile is identical to many government IL bonds. They are similar to synthetic IL bonds described above.

Tips swaps are commonly purchased by pension funds and other long-dated investors. They may prefer the added flexibility of the IL swap market compared to the cash IL bond market. Figure 3.7 shows the Tips swap.

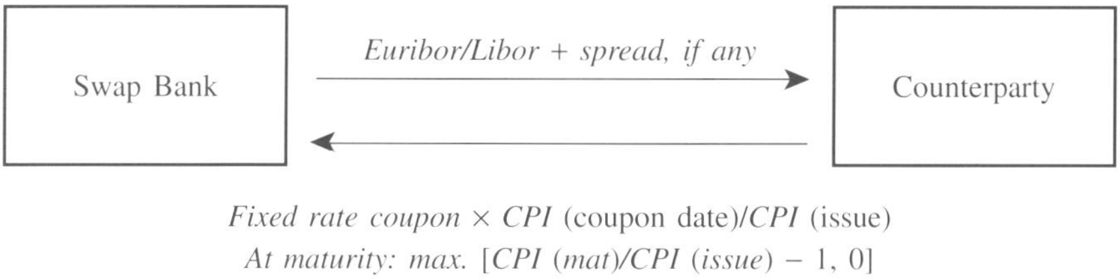

Figure 3.7 Illustration of a Tips swap

Break-even swap

This is also known as a zero-coupon inflation swap or zero-coupon swap. It allows the investor to hedge away a break-even exposure. Compared to IL swaps such as the synthetic bond swap, which hedge a real yield exposure, the break-even swap has both cash flow legs paying out on maturity. The legs are:

- the total return on the inflation index;
- a compounded fixed break-even rate.

This structure enables IL derivative market-makers to hedge their books. It is illustrated at Figure 3.8.

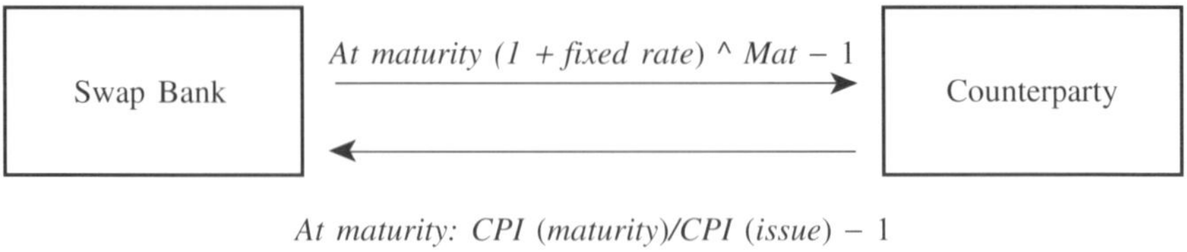

Figure 3.8 Break-even inflation swap

Real-annuity swap

A real-annuity swap is used to hedge inflation-linked cash flows where this applies for payments such as rental streams, lease payments, project finance cash flows, and so on. It enables market participants who pay or receive such payments to replace the uncertainty of the future level of these cash flows with a fixed rate of growth. The swap is written on the same notional amount for both legs, but payout profiles differ as follows:

- the index-linked leg of the swap compounds its payments with the rate of change of the index;
- the fixed leg of the swap compounds its payments at a pre-specified fixed rate.

These swaps are one of the most commonly traded. The fixed rate quoted for the swap provides a ready reference point against which to compare expected future rates of inflation. So, for instance, if a bank is quoting for a swap with a fixed rate of 3.00%, and an investor believes that inflation rates will not rise above 3.00% for the life of the swap, then it will receive "fixed" (here meaning a fixed rate of growth) and pay inflation-linked returns on the swap.

Appendices

Appendix 3.1 Floating rate note discount margin equation using discount factor

The discounted margin for FRNs redeemed on a normal coupon date is given by (3.13):

$$P \times \left(1 + \frac{re + DM}{100}B\right) = C + \sum_{n=1}^{n-1} \frac{(re_2 + QM)}{m} v^n + Mv^{n-1} \qquad (3.13)$$

where

DM is the required discounted margin %
P is the dirty price
re is the current market reference rate from the value date to the first coupon date
re_2 is the assumed market reference rate for subsequent coupon payments
B is the number of days from the value date to the next coupon date, as a fraction of the day-count base (360, 365 or 365/366 days)
C is the next coupon payment %
n is the number of future coupon payments
QM is the quoted margin %
m is the number of coupon payments per year adjusted for the assumed number of days in the year
M is the redemption value
v is the discount factor; that is, $v = 1/(1 + (re_2 + DM)/100h)$.

The left-hand side of (3.13) represents the cost of the bond adjusted using current reference rates to the next coupon date.

For perpetual or undated FRNs, Equation (3.13) is simplified as shown at (3.14):

$$P \times \left(1 + \frac{re + DM}{100} \times B\right) = C + 100\left(\frac{(re_2 + QM)}{re_2 + DM}\right) \qquad (3.14)$$

A gross redemption yield for an FRN can only be calculated if one assumes unchanged market reference rates during the remaining life of the bond, so that future coupon rates may be predicted. Under this restrictive assumption we may set an FRN redemption yield as (3.15) below.

$$P = \sum_{n=1}^{N} C_i \times v^{B+t_i} + M \times v^{B+tn} \qquad (3.15)$$

where

n is the number of coupon payments to redemption
t_i is the time in periods from the next to the ith coupon payment
v is the discount factor, that is, $v = 1/(1 + y/h)$
y is the required redemption yield compounded m times per year.

APPENDIX 3.2 Current issuers of public-sector indexed securities

Country	Date first issued	Index linking
Australia	1983	Consumer prices
	1991	Average weekly earnings
Austria	1953	Electricity prices
Brazil	1964–1990	Wholesale prices
	1991	General prices
Canada	1991	Consumer prices
Chile	1966	Consumer prices
Colombia	1967	Wholesale prices
	1995	Consumer prices
Czech Republic	1997	Consumer prices
Denmark	1982	Consumer prices
France	1956	Average value of French securities
Greece	1997	Consumer prices
Hungary	1995	Consumer prices
Iceland	1964–1980	Cost of Building Index
	1980–1994	Credit Terms Index
	1995	Consumer prices
Ireland	1983	Consumer prices
Italy	1983	Deflator of GDP at factor cost
Mexico	1989	Consumer prices
New Zealand	1977–1984	Consumer prices
	1995	Consumer prices
Norway	1982	Consumer prices
Poland	1992	Consumer prices
Sweden	1952	Consumer prices
	1994	Consumer prices
Turkey	1994–1997	Wholesale prices
	1997	Consumer prices
United Kingdom	1981	Consumer prices
United States	1997	Consumer prices

Table A3.1 Current issuers of public-sector inflation-indexed securities
Source: Deacon and Derry (1998). Used with permission of Prentice Hall Europe.

Selected bibliography and references

Anderson, N., Breedon, F., Deacon, M., Derry, A. and Murphy, J. 1996, *Estimating and Interpreting the Yield Curve*, John Wiley & Sons, Chichester.

Arak, M. and Kreicher, L. 1985, "The real rate of interest: Inferences from the new UK indexed gilts", *International Economic Review*, (26) 2, pp. 399–408

Bootle, R. 1991, *Index-linked Gilts: A Practical Investment Guide*, 2nd edition, Woodhead-Faulkner, Oxford.

Brown, P.J. 1998, *Bond Markets: Structures and Yield Calculations*, Glenlake Publishing Company, Chicago.

Brown, R. and Schaefer, S. 1994, "The term structure of real interest rates and the Cox, Ingersoll and Ross model", *Journal of Financial Economics*, 35:1, pp. 3–42.

Brynjolfsson, J. and Fabozzi, F. 1999, *Handbook of Inflation-indexed Bonds*, FJF Associates, New Hope, PA.

Deacon, M. and Derry, A. 1994, "Deriving estimates of inflation expectations from the prices of UK Government bonds", *Bank of England Working Paper*, no. 23, July.

Deacon, M. and Derry, A. 1998, *Inflation Indexed Securities*, Prentice Hall, London.

Fisher, I. 1930, *The Theory of Interest: As Determined by Impatience to Spend Income and Opportunity to Invest It*, 1954 reprint, Kelley & Millman, New York.

Foresi, S., Penati, A. and Pennacchi, G. 1997, "Reducing the cost of government debt: The role of index-linked bonds", in de Cecco, M., Pecchi, L. and Piga, G. (eds), *Public Debt: Index-Linked Bonds in Theory and Practice*, Edward Elgar, London.

James, J. and Webber, N. 2000, *Interest Rate Modelling*, John Wiley & Sons, Chichester.

Kish, R.J. and Livingston, M. 1992, "The determinants of the call feature on corporate bonds", *Journal of Banking and Finance*, 16, pp. 687–703.

Levy, H. 1999, *Introduction to Investments*, South-Western, Cincinatti.

Livingston, M. 1993, *Money and Capital Markets*, 2nd edition, New York Institute of Finance, New York.

Narayan, M.P. and Lim, S.P. 1989, "The call provision on corporate zero-coupon bonds", *Journal of Financial and Quantitative Analysis*, 24, March, pp. 91–103.

Waggoner, D. 1997, "Spline methods for extracting interest rate curves from coupon bond prices", *Federal Reserve Bank of Atlanta Working Paper*, 97–10.

Wojnilower, A. 1997, *Inflation-indexed Bonds: Promising the Moon*, Clipper Group, London.

It did fleetingly occur to me as we were running up to our aiming point and the flak around us was getting even heavier … to wonder what had possessed me to give up my safe and easy instructing job and put myself back into a place like this, with people trying very hard indeed to kill me. Of course, there is no real answer.

– Ken Rees, *Lie In the Dark and Listen*,
Grub Street Publishing 2004

CHAPTER 4

Hybrid Securities

In this chapter we describe in generic format some of the more exotic or structured notes that have been introduced into the fixed income market. The motivations behind the development and use of these products are varied, but include the desire for increased yield without additional credit risk, as well as the need to alter, transform or transfer risk exposure and risk-return profiles. Certain structured notes were also developed as hedging instruments. The instruments themselves have been issued by banks, corporate institutions and sovereign authorities. By using certain types of notes, investors can gain access to different markets, sometimes synthetically, that were previously not available to them. For instance, by purchasing a structured note an investor can take on board a position that reflects her views on a particular exchange rate and anticipated changes in the yield curve but in a different market. The investment instrument can be tailored to suit the investor's particular risk profile.

We describe a number of structured notes that are currently available to investors today, although often investors will seek particular features that suit their needs, and so there are invariably detailed variations in each note. We stress that this is only the tip of the iceberg, and many different types of notes are available; indeed, if any particular investor or issuer requirement has not been met, it is a relatively straightforward process whereby an investment bank can structure a note that meets one or both specific requirements.

Indexed amortising note

Description

Another type of hybrid note is the Indexed Amortising Note or IAN. They were introduced in the US domestic market in the early 1990s as the demand grew from investors in asset-backed notes known as collateralised mortgage obligations or CMOs. IANs are fixed-coupon unsecured notes issued with a nominal value that is not fixed. That is, the nominal amount may reduce in value ahead of the legal maturity according to the levels recorded by a specified reference index such as six-month Libor. If the reference remains static or its level decreases, the IAN value will amortise in nominal value. The legal maturity of IANs is short- to medium-term, with the five-year maturity being common. The notes have been issued by banks and corporates, although a large volume has been issued by US government agencies. The yield payable on IANs is typically at a premium above that of similar credit quality conventional debt. The amortisation schedule on an IAN is linked to the movement of the specified reference index, which is easily understood. This is considered an advantage to certain mortgage-backed notes, which amortise in accordance with less clearly defined patterns such as a *prepayment schedule*.

An issuer of IANs will arrange a hedge that makes the funding obtained more attractive; for example, a straight Libor-type exposure. This is most commonly arranged through a swap arrangement that mirrors the note structure. A diagrammatic representation is shown in Figure 4.1. In fact it is more common for the swap arrangement to involve a series of options on swaps. The coupon available on an IAN might be attractive to investors when the volatility on *swaptions* is high and there is a steep positively sloping yield curve; under such an environment the option-element of an IAN would confer greatest value.

Figure 4.1 IAN hedge arrangement

The terms of a hypothetical IAN issue are given in Table 4.1.

Issuer	Mortgage agency
Nominal value	$250,000,000
Legal maturity	6 years
Coupon	2-year Treasury plus 100 bps
Interest basis	Monthly
"Lock-out period"	Three years
Reference index	6-month Libor
6-m Libor fixing on issue	5.15%
Minimum level of note	20%

Average life sensitivity

Libor rate	Amortisation rate	Average life (years)
5.15%	100%	3
6.00%	100%	3
7.00%	21%	4.1
8.00%	7%	5.6
9.00%	0.00%	6

Table 4.1 Hypothetical IAN issue

Under the terms of issue of the note summarised in Table 4.1, the coupon payable is the current two-year government benchmark plus a fixed spread of 1%. The note has a legal maturity of six years; however, it will mature in three years if the six-month Libor rate is at a level of 6.00% or below two years from the date of issue. If the rate is above 6.00%, the maturity of the note will be extended. The "lock-out" of three years means that the note has a minimum life of three years, irrespective of what happens to Libor rates. Amortisation takes place if on subsequent rate-fixing dates after the lock-out period the Libor rate rises. The maximum maturity of the note is six years. If at any time there is less than 20% of the nominal value in issue, the note is cancelled in full.

Advantages to investors

The IAN structure offers advantages to investors under certain conditions. If the credit quality is acceptable, the notes offer a high yield over a relatively low term to maturity. The amortisation structure is easier to understand than that on mortgage-backed securities, which contain prepayment schedules that are based on assumptions that may not apply. This means that investors will know with certainty how the amortisation of the note will proceed, given the level of the reference index at any given time. The "lock-out" period of a note is usually set at a period that offers investor comfort, such as three years; during this time no amortisation can take place.

As with the other instruments described here, IANs can be tailored to meet individual investor requirements. The legal maturity and lock-out period are features that are most frequently subject to variation, with the yield premium decreasing as the lock-out period becomes closer to the formal maturity. The reference index can be a government benchmark or interbank rate such as the swap rate. However, the most common reference is the Libor rate.

Synthetic convertible note

Description

Synthetic convertible notes are fixed-coupon securities whose total return is linked to an external source such as the level of an equity index, or the price of a specific security. The fixed-coupon element is typically at a low level, and the investor has greater exposure to the performance of the external index. A common arrangement has the note redeeming at par, but redeemable at a greater amount if the performance of the reference index exceeds a stated minimum. However, the investor has the safety net of redemption at par. Another typical structure is a zero-coupon note, issued at par and redeemable at par, but redeemable at a higher level if a specified equity index performs above a pre-specified level.

Table 4.2 lists the terms of a hypothetical synthetic convertible note issue that is linked to the FTSE-100 equity index. This note will pay par on maturity, but if the level of the FTSE-100 has increased by more than 10% from the level on note issue, the note will be redeemed at par plus this amount. Note, however, that this is an investment suitable only for someone who is very bullish on the prospects for the FTSE-100. If this index does not raise by the minimum level, the investor will have received a coupon of 0.5%, which is roughly five percentage points below the level for two-year sterling at this time.

Nominal value	$50,000,000
Term to maturity	Two years
Issue date	17-Jun-99
Maturity date	17-Jun-01
Issue price	$100
Coupon	0.50%
Interest basis	Semi-annual
Redemption proceeds	Min. [100, Formula level]
Formula level	100 + [100 × (R(I) − (1.1 × R(II)) / R(II)]
Index	FTSE-100
R(I)	Index level on maturity
R(II)	Index level on issue
Hedge terms	
Issuer pays	Libor
Swap bank pays	Redemption proceeds in accordance with formula

Table 4.2 Terms of a synthetic convertible note issue

Investor benefits

Similarly to a convertible bond, a synthetic convertible note provides investors with a fixed coupon together with additional market upside potential if the level of the reference index performs above a certain level. Unlike the convertible, however, the payoff is in the form of cash.

The reference can be virtually any publicly quoted source, and notes have been issued whose payout is linked to the exchange rate of two currencies, the days on which Libor falls within a specified range, the performance of a selected basket of stocks (say "technology stocks"), and so on.

Interest differential notes

Interest differential notes or IDNs are hybrid securities which are aimed at investors who wish to put on a position that reflects their view on the interest rate differential between rates of two different currencies. Notes in the US market are usually denominated in US dollars, whereas Euro market notes have been issued in a wide range of global currencies.

There are a number of variations of IDNs. Notes may pay a variable coupon and a fixed redemption amount, or a fixed coupon and a redemption amount that is determined by the level or performance of an external reference index. IDNs have also been issued with payoff profiles that are linked to the differentials in interest rates of two specified currencies, or between one currency across different maturities.

Example of IDN

Here we discuss a five-year note that is linked to the differential between US dollar Libor and euro-libor.

Term to maturity	Five years
Coupon	[(2 × USD Libor) − (2 × EUR Libor) − 50%]
Current USD Libor	6.15%
Current EUR Libor	3.05%
Rate differential	2.65%
First coupon fix	5.70%
Current five-year benchmark	4.75%
Yield spread over benchmark	0.95%

Change in Libor spread (bps p.a.)	**Libor spread at rate reset**	**Spread over benchmark**
75	4.78%	2.34%
50	3.90%	1.88%
25	3.15%	1.21%
0	2.65%	0.95%
0	1.97%	0.56%
0	1.32%	0.34%
0	0.89%	0.12%
0	0.32%	–0.28%

Table 4.3 An IDN example

The return on this note is a function of the spread between the US dollar Libor rate and euro-libor. An increase in the spread results in a higher coupon payable on the note, while a narrowing of the spread results in a lower coupon payable. Such a structure will appeal to an investor who has a particular view on the USD and EUR yield curves. For instance, assume that the USD dollar curve is inverted and the euro curve is positively sloping. A position in an IDN (structured as above) on these two currencies allows an investor to avoid outright yield curve plays in each currency, and instead puts on a trade that reflects a view on the relative level of interest rates in each currency. An IDN in this environment would allow an investor to earn a high yield while taking a view that is different to the market consensus.

When analysing an IDN, an investor must regard the note to be the equivalent to a fixed-coupon bond together with a double indexation of an interest rate differential. The effect of this double indexation on the differential is to create two long positions in a five-year USD fixed-rate note and two short positions in a EUR fixed-rate note. The short position in the EUR note means that the EUR exchange-rate risk is removed and the investor has an exposure only to the EUR interest rate risk, which is the desired position.

The issuer of the note hedges the note with a swap structure as with other hybrid securities. The arrangement involves both USD and EUR interest rate swaps. The swap bank takes the opposite position in the swaps.

Table 4.3 also illustrates the return profiles possible under different interest rate scenarios. One possibility shows that the IDN provides a 95 basis point yield premium over the five-year government benchmark yield; however, this assumes rather unrealistically that the interest differential between the USD and EUR interest rates remains constant through to the final coupon setting date. More significantly though we see that the yield premium available on the note increases as the spread differential between the two rates increases. In a spread-tightening environment, the note offers a premium over the government yield as long as the tightening does not exceed 100 basis points each year.

Benefits to investors

IDN-type instruments allow investors to put on positions that reflect their view on foreign interest rate direction and/or levels, but without having to expose themselves to currency (exchange rate) risk at the same time. The notes may also be structured in a way that allows investors to take a view on any maturity point of the yield curve. For instance, the coupon may be set in accordance with the differential between the 10-year government benchmark yields of two specified countries. As another approach, investors can arrange combinations of different maturities in the same currency, which is a straight yield curve or relative value trade in a domestic or foreign currency.

The risk run by a noteholder is that the interest rate differential moves in the opposite direction to that sought, which reduces the coupon payable and may even result in a lower yield than that available on the benchmark bond.

Convertible Quanto Note

The index-linked Quanto Note is aimed at investors who wish to gain exposure to a company's equity, but do not wish to invest in assets denominated in the currency of that equity. For example, investors who wished to gain exposure to a Japanese company share, but who do not wish to hold Yen-denominated assets.

The note enables investors to gain from upside performance of the selected equity but with no associated foreign exchange risk. For added comfort, investors are protected against any downside performance of the underlying equity by means of the note structure, which sets a "bond floor" of a minimum stated return. This is similar to the bond floor in a convertible bond (see Chapter 8). Purchasing the note is equivalent to purchasing market volatility, in the expectation of higher volatility leading to higher equity prices, while retaining an element of downside market protection.

Figure 4.2 below illustrates the concept behind the note.

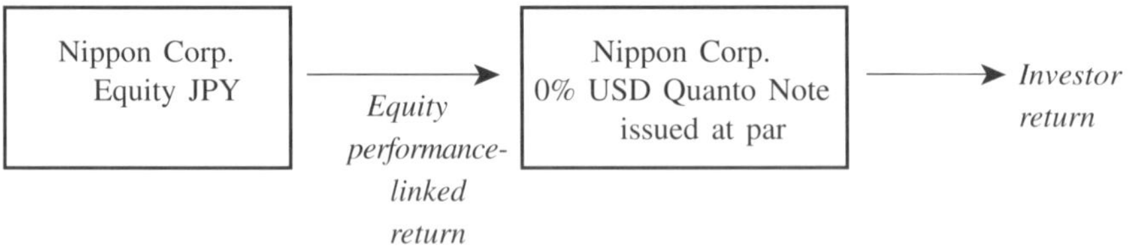

Figure 4.2 Convertible Quanto Note

Investors are in effect holding a long position in an option and hence will be exposed to volatility. However, the bond floor protects the investor from downside risk, irrespective of volatility.

Example 4.1 Japanese equity note

This note is a USD-denominated bond, issued at par, that pays investors a return, in USD, connected to the share-price performance of a Japanese corporate entity (denominated in ¥). If the underlying equity rises in price (above a specified level, the strike price), the proportionate increase in the share price is paid out on maturity to the note investor, as a percentage of par. At any time during its life, the price of the note will reflect (among other things) this increase in underlying share price.

The value of the note is comprised of two components: the intrinsic value and the option value. On first issue, an equity strike price is set on the note. This may be at the current underlying share price, or above it. As the underlying share price rise above the strike price, the note intrinsic value will increase proportionally with that of the equity. The option value is an additional value (the "premium") above the intrinsic value, and is composed of volatility, time value and the level of USD interest rates. These are standard option pricing parameters.

If the underlying equity falls in price, the investor is protected by the minimum value of the note, known as the "bond floor". This is the minimum price of the note at any one time; hence, if the equity price falls below a level at which the bond floor kicks in, there is no further downside price risk for the investor.

We can illustrate this with an hypothetical example. Consider the following terms for a USD Quanto Note:

Underlying	Nippon Corp equity (¥)
Strike	¥1,200
Spot	¥1,150
Note offer	100.00%
Parity	95.83%
Premium	4.35%
Life	3 years
US 3-year rates	3.68%
Bond floor	88.36%
Delta	0.50

The note is issued at par with a strike of ¥1,200.

Consider the following scenarios based on both upside and downside performance of the underlying equity.

If the shares rise to ¥1,700, a rise of 47.8%, the parity, or intrinsic value would be (1,700/1,200 × 100) or 141.66%. This is the minimum value of the note. Hence, a 47.8% gain in the shares has resulted in a minimum 41.66% gain in the note.

Should the underlying equity price fall below the strike price, the note is protected by the sponsor bank's credit and hence carries a bond floor, currently at 88.36%, accreting to par at maturity. This represents the downside protection for the investor. The option premium above this floor will still reflect the three option components, and because time value is always positive, the total value of the note will be above this bond floor up to maturity.

If the shares fell to ¥800, the parity would be 66.66%; however, the minimum value of the note would still be the bond floor of 88.36%. Therefore in this instance a fall of 30.4% in the shares has resulted in a maximum 11.6% decline in the note.

Investors are not exposed to any foreign exchange (FX) risk because they pay USD for the note, and receive returns in USD. However, one of the option value parameters is the level of interest rates, hence investors are exposed to USD interest rates. A call option written on an equity will rise in value if (all other parameters hold constant) there is a rise in interest rates, because the COC associated with the equity also rises. This sensitivity is carried over in the value of the note, because the secondary market price of the note is related to OTC options market.

A partial measure of the change in the price of an option with respect to a change in the price of the underlying equity is given by the *delta* of the option, which is:

$$\delta = \frac{\text{Change in note price}}{\text{Change in underlying price}}.$$

For convertible bonds, delta is defined in terms of the sensitivity of the bond's price to changes in its parity. The parity is given from the value of the underlying equity price. The value of this delta can be gauged from Figure 4.3, which illustrates an hypothetical parity and bond floor. The delta is seen from the relationship of the parity and note price.

In our example the delta is given as 0.5. So if the note's theoretical price moved from 100 to 100.5, while its parity changed from 95 to 96, the delta would be 0.5.

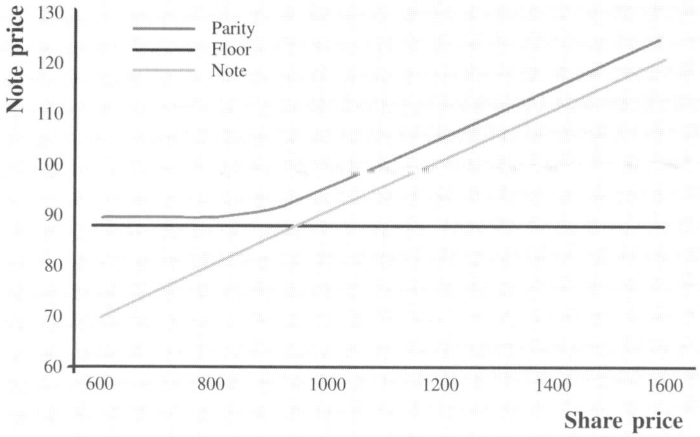

Figure 4.3 Parity and bond floor for a convertible bond

Brady bonds

Brady bonds are bonds that have been issued as part of a restructuring of a country's commercial bank loans and other debt. Existing creditors tender their loans in exchange for the new bonds, which are sovereign bonds. The name refers to Nicholas Brady, chairman of the US Federal Reserve at the time the bonds were first introduced. The Brady market is characterised by high yields and liquidity levels ranging from very liquid to illiquid. Many Brady bonds are large size issues and trade in a liquid market. Due to the features of a Brady bond, they are traded by investors taking a view on the country risk, the yield spread to Treasuries or the volatility level.

There are a number of different types of bonds in existence, for example collateralised and uncollateralised, fixed-rate and floating-rate and so on. Although most of the issues to date have been long-dated bonds, short-term Brady bonds have also been issued. The bonds are denominated in US dollars, therefore they yield a spread over Treasury bonds. This makes the bonds very interesting to trade, as the yield on them reflects both the country credit risk as well as the shape and expectation of the Treasury yield curve. At the end of 2000 there was over $160 billion of total such debt in existence.

Brady bond structure

Brady bonds were introduced in the wake of the Latin American debt crisis of 1982. As countries threatened to default it was realised that the global banking system could be in danger if there was large-scale default. Therefore the debt was renegotiated and repackaged as Brady bonds. The first step of the process is when the creditor banks negotiate with the debtor country to establish the level of borrowing that the country can realistically afford to service. This is sometimes undertaken in conjunction with the International Monetary Fund. The difference between the amount that the country can afford to service, and the actual level of its debt, is reconciled using one or more of the following:

- Discount bonds, where the principal amount is cut;
- Par bonds, where the debtor pays sub-market interest rates;
- a debt buy-back at an agreed discount rate.

There is an option available for creditors who do not wish to see the principal value of the loans reduced or receive below-market rates, in which case they must agree to lend additional funds in return for retaining the existing value of the obligation. Arrears in interest are usually rescheduled into a separate tradable bond.

The principal amount of par and discount bonds is fully collateralised using zero-coupon US Treasury bonds. This provides comfort to creditors that the obligations will ultimately be repaid. In many cases interest payments, usually for the first few years of the issue, are also collateralised on a rolling basis; that is when the collateral backing of a coupon payment is not used, it rolls forward to back the next coupon payment. This collateral arrangement therefore acts as a form of security for the investor in a Brady bond.

Types of Brady bond

The main type of Brady bond is the *collateralised fixed-rate par bond* or *par bond*. These bonds are received in exchange for debt that is tendered at the face value. They offer the debtor permanent interest rate relief and protection from fluctuations in interest rates. The bonds are long-dated, usually of 25 or 30 years maturity, and are conventional bullet bonds. The principal is collateralised with specially-issued zero-coupon US Treasury bonds which are held at the US Federal Reserve. There is also usually a rolling interest payment guarantee, collateralised by high-quality financial instruments rated at double-A or better, which cover 12-24 months of interest payments. In certain cases *value recovery rights* are attached to the bonds, which grant bondholders rights to payments under a formula linked to a commodity price index.

Collateralised floating-rate discount bonds or *discount bonds* are received in exchange for eligible debt at a discount to face value, which results in permanent debt relief for the debtor in the form of partial relief on the debt obligation. In return for this the creditor receives higher interest payments, usually Libor plus 13-15%. When Mexico and Argentina issued discount bonds the yield spread was 35%, while for Bulgaria and Poland the spread was 50%. Again the bonds are long-dated, 25 or 30 years and have a single bullet payment at maturity. The principal is collateralised with zero-coupon Treasury bonds, and there is usually a rolling interest guarantee. Value recovery rights have also been attached to discount bonds.

Another type of Brady bond is the *front-loaded interest reduction bond* or *Flirb*. These bonds are received in exchange for debt at face value. They pay below-market interest rates for the first few years of their life, which is a temporary interest relief for the debtor. The principal is not collateralised, although there may be a rolling interest guarantee. As there is no collateralisation the bonds have a shorter average life, and amortise after an initial grace period of up to nine years.

Debt conversion bonds or *new money bonds* are received in exchange for debt at face value. They are conditional upon the creditor providing additional new money equivalent to a certain percentage of the amount of the eligible debt. Neither the principal or the interest payments is collateralised, so the average lives of the bonds are shorter than par or discount bonds.

Interest arrears bonds are received in exchange for a creditor's claim on certain past due interest payments which have not been paid. There is no collateral backing for the bonds.[1] The bonds are known by a number of names, including *Interest due and unpaid* or IDU bonds, *past due interest bonds* (PDI), or *interest arrears bonds* (IAB).[2]

Relative value

Since Brady bonds are (in most cases) collateralised instruments, we require additional techniques when assessing their value, beyond the simple gross redemption yield measure. Essentially a par bond has three elements: the principal, which is collateralised by US Treasuries, the collateralised rolling interest guarantee, and the (risk-carrying) remaining bond cash flows. The

1 The exception to this was in the case of bonds issued by Costa Rica.

2 In the case of Russia the bonds are known as *interest arrears notes*.

yield on a collateralised bond will be lower than that of a non-collateralised bond because of the credit protection. The country-specific risk factor, which is in the form of the spread to the Treasury yield, should in theory apply to the risk-carrying cash flows only. This means that an investor will calculate the present value of both the principal and the collateralised interest payments and subtract this from the price of the bond. This "stripped" price is then used when calculating the YTM of the non-collateralised cash flows, and is known as the *stripped yield*. The stripped yield spread (as a spread to the Treasury bond) is viewed as the market's assessment of the sovereign risk. This approach enables the yields of collateralised and non-collateralised bonds to be compared. As we noted at the start of this section, the yield sensitivity of a Brady bond will reflect both the country credit risk and the Treasury yield curve. Separating a Brady bond's yield sensitivity to US interest rates and to credit risk is therefore of some importance for the market-maker. We consider this here.

For a US Treasury bond we are familiar with the price / yield formula, given here as 4.1.

$$P = \frac{C/2}{(1 + \frac{1}{2}r)} + \frac{C/2}{(1 + \frac{1}{2}r)^2} + \frac{C/2}{(1 + \frac{1}{2}r)^3} + \dots + \frac{C/2 + 100}{(1 + \frac{1}{2}r)^{2n}} \qquad (4.1)$$

The most common Brady bond is the Par bond, for which the principal is collateralised. Given this security backing, the redemption payment can be taken as risk-free, which means that in theory it should be discounted at the Treasury yield for that maturity, rather than at a yield spread to the Treasury. Therefore the price / yield equation can be given as 4.2,

$$P = \frac{C/2}{(1 + \frac{1}{2}[y + s])} + \frac{C/2}{(1 + \frac{1}{2}[y + s])^2} + \dots + \frac{C/2}{(1 + \frac{1}{2}[y + s])^{2n}} + \frac{100}{(1 + \frac{1}{2}rs)^{2n}} \qquad (4.2)$$

where

y is the corresponding US Treasury yield
s is the bond credit spread over the Treasury yield
rs is the Treasury zero-coupon yield.

The s is the stripped spread.

We apply the same analysis when calculating interest-rate sensitivity for a Brady bond. The duration of a par bond is given by 4.3.

$$D = \left[\begin{array}{l} \dfrac{C/2}{(1+\frac{1}{2}[y+s])} \cdot \dfrac{1}{2} + \dfrac{C/2}{(1+\frac{1}{2}[y+s])^2} \cdot \dfrac{2}{2} + \ldots \\ + \dfrac{C/2}{(1+\frac{1}{2}[y+s])^{2n}} \cdot n + \dfrac{100}{(1+\frac{1}{2}rs)^{2n}} \times n \times \dfrac{1+\frac{1}{2}[y+s]}{1+\frac{1}{2}rs} \end{array} \right] \Big/ P \quad (4.3)$$

The final term in the expression at (4.3) receives a greater weight, because it is risk-free and therefore is discounted less heavily. This is the correct analysis; what it means is that a change in the Treasury yield curve will have a significant impact on the bond yield, as it affects all the bond's cash flows. However a change in the credit risk should have a smaller impact, because as it impact only the coupon payments. This has the effect of raising the duration of a Par bond, compared to the duration calculation carried out using the conventional approach.

Using this analysis, the yield sensitivity of a Par bond, with respect to changes in the Treasury yield, is given by (4.4) below.

$$\frac{\Delta P/P}{\Delta y} = -\frac{D}{(1+\frac{1}{2}[y+s])}. \quad (4.4)$$

The credit risk sensitivity is a function of changes in the credit quality of the bond, and so it is not symmetrical with the bond's Treasury yield sensitivity. This is because the credit risk yield premium is only applicable to the bond's coupon payments, so the sensitivity measure will be lower. It is given by (4.5) below,

$$\frac{\Delta P/P}{\Delta s} = -\frac{D - A/P}{(1+\frac{1}{2}y+s)} \quad (4.5)$$

where

$$A = n \cdot 100 \cdot \frac{(1+\frac{1}{2}[y+s])}{(1+\frac{1}{2}rs)^{2n+1}}.$$

The presence of the *A/P* term has the effect of reducing the impact of a change in the yield premium on the price of the bond compared to a change in the Treasury yield.

Selected bibliography and references

Fabozzi, F. (ed.) 2005, *Handbook of Fixed Income Securities*, 7th edition, McGraw-Hill, New York.

When I was young I dreamed and dreamed about all the things that
I was gonna be,
A handsome pop star on the screen or captain, of the England team,
A brave explorer holding court,
Or a really famous astronaut...

Well they said, "Son, it could all be yours,
"You just work hard, and pay your dues,
"Don't be content with what you've got, there's always more that
you can want,
"Everybody's on the make, that's what made this country great!"

It's all I wanted in the end,
Was world domination and a whole lot of money to spend..!
Everything I touch, everything I see
Fame and fortune, immortality...
Well it's not much to ask, it's really not
Not much to ask,
Just the same as anybody else...

– New Model Army, *Great Expectations*
(Justin Sullivan/Stuart Morrow)
Abstract Records 1984

PART

II

Corporate Debt Markets

The market for corporate debt is large and diverse. In fact it is in the corporate markets that the most exciting innovations and the most exotic products are observed, as government markets are fairly plain vanilla in nature. In part II we review the most important instruments that form part of this market. There is also a chapter dealing with credit analysis.

The bonds described here are not exclusively corporate instruments; many sovereign governments, for example, issue Eurobonds. Not surprisingly, the quality of paper issued ranges from triple-A risk-free, such as World Bank bonds, to high-yield and un-rated bonds. Bonds that feature embedded options, such as callable bonds and convertibles, are now traded under a much more rigorous analytical regime than previously; most banks will use a binomial valuation model to price these bonds. This serves to illustrate that the corporate debt markets continuously benefit from the latest developments in financial engineering, and it is here that one will observe the latest structures and innovations.

It would be foolish to say we were not frightened when we went off on operations, but you always hope that you'll be the lucky ones, and I think that the main definition of courage is your ability to conquer your fear, or at least not to show it, and certainly not to let it dominate you.

— Ken Rees, *Lie In the Dark and Listen*,
Grub Street Publishing, 2004

CHAPTER

5

Corporate Debt Markets

In this and the next 11 chapters we review the corporate bond markets. The corporate markets cover a wide range of instruments and issuer currencies. There is a great variety of structures and products traded in the corporate markets, many of which easily could be the subject of separate books in their own right. All instruments serve the same primary purpose however – as an instrument of corporate finance. The exotic structures that exist have usually been introduced in order to attract new investors, or retain existing investors, in what is an extremely competitive market.

Generally, the term "corporate markets" is used to cover bonds issued by non-government borrowers. The bonds issued by regional governments and certain public-sector bodies, such as national power and telecommunications utilities, are usually included as "government" debt, as they almost always are covered by an explicit or implicit government guarantee. All other categories of borrower are therefore deemed to be "corporate" borrowers. The combined market is a large one, as we indicated in the previous chapter. Table 5.1 below shows non-government international bond issuance from 2004, split by currency. The majority of bonds are denominated in US dollars, euros and Japanese yen.

	US$	Sterling	Euro	Other	Total
2004	480	93	331	88	762
					Volumes are $ billion

Table 5.1 Non-government international bond issuance
Sources: CapitalData Bondware; Bank of England.

The euro, introduced in 11 countries of the European Union in January 1999, has already become a popular currency for corporate bond issuers. This is indicated in Figure 5.1, which shows that the volume of issues in the euro currency was already over twice that in the first eight months of the year compared to issue volumes for the eleven currencies separately during the whole of 1998. Corporate bond issues in sterling are detailed in Figure 5.2, split into maturity bands of short-, medium- and long-dated bond issues. Figure 5.3 shows USD corporate bond issuance split the same way.

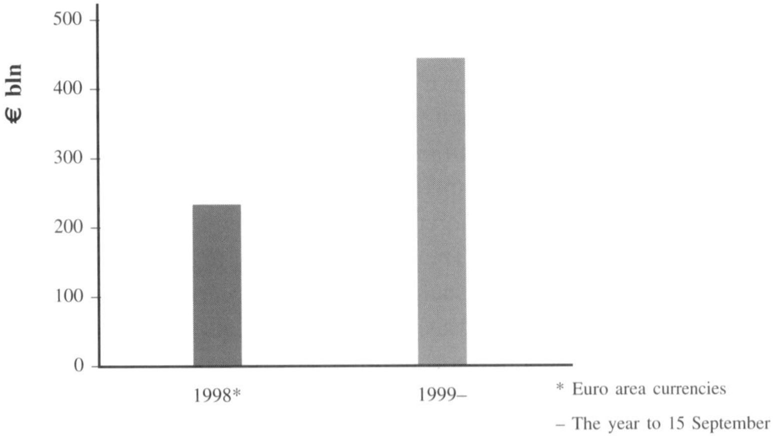

Figure 5.1 International bonds issued in euro
Source: *The Economist*.

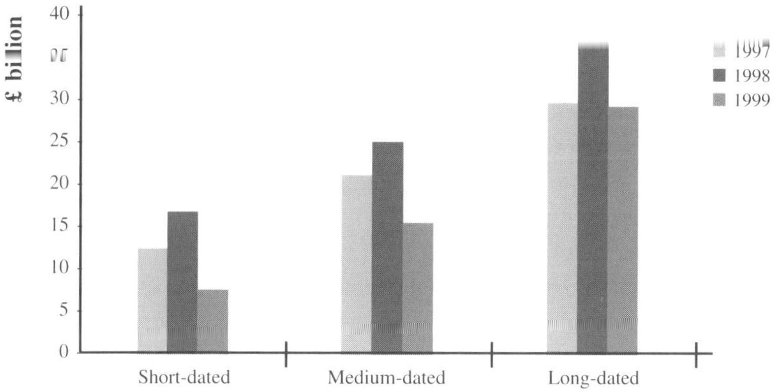

Figure 5.2 Sterling non-government bond issuance
Source: Bank of England.

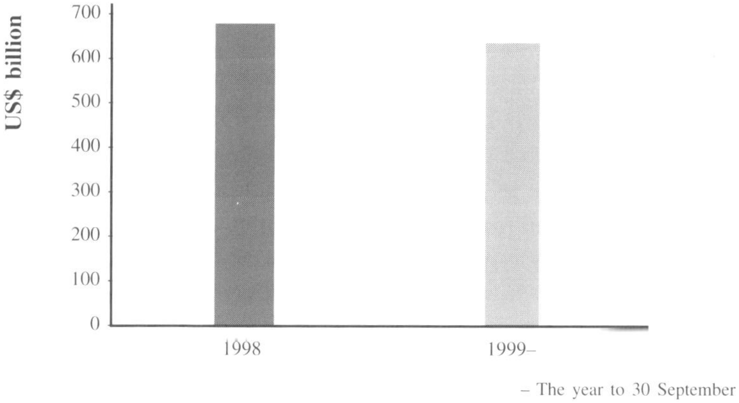

Figure 5.3 US dollar corporate bond issuance
Source: Bank of England.

Introduction

Corporate bonds are tradeable debt instruments issued by non-government borrowers. The majority of corporate bonds are plain vanilla instruments, paying a fixed coupon and with a fixed term to maturity. Corporate debt covers a wide range of instruments traded in the primary and secondary markets. Corporate issuers will use the debt capital markets to raise finance for short-, medium- and long-term requirements and projects. Corporate borrowers will raise both *secured* and *unsecured debt,* with the former type of borrowing secured on assets of the company. The ease with which a corporation can raise unsecured finance in the public market is a function of its *credit rating*. Often corporate bonds are classified by the type of issuer; for example, banks and financial services companies, utility companies and so on. Issuer classification is then broken down further; for example, utility companies will be subdivided into electricity companies, water companies and gas distribution companies.

Under the terms of any corporate bond issue, the borrower is obliged to pay the periodic interest on the loan, represented by the coupon rate, as well as repay the principal on maturity of the debt. If the borrower fails to pay interest on the loan as it is due, or to repay the principal on maturity, this is known as *default* and the borrower will be in breach of the terms of the issue. This is a serious event. In the event of default,[1] bondholders are entitled to enforce payment via the legal process and the courts. As providers of debt finance, bondholders rank higher than preferred and ordinary shareholders in the event of a winding-up of the company. Depending on the level of the *security* associated with the particular bond issue, bondholders may rank ahead of other creditors. The issue of the *credit risk* of a specific issuer is the key concern for corporate bond investors.

The yield on corporate bonds is set by the market and reflects the credit quality of the issuer of the paper, as well as the other considerations relevant to price setting such as level of liquidity, yield on similar bonds, supply and demand, and general market conditions. Yields are always at a *spread* above the similar maturity government bond. A well-received corporate bond will trade at a relatively low spread over the government yield curve. Although the common perception is that bonds are held by investors for their income, and are less price volatile than equities, this is an over-generalisation. Certain bonds are highly volatile, while others are held for their anticipated price appreciation.

Certain corporate issues are aimed at only the professional (institutional) market and have minimum denominations of $10,000 or £10,000. Generally, however, they are issued in denominations of $1,000 (or £1,000, €1,000 and so on). In the US domestic market the par value for corporate bonds is sometimes taken to be $1,000 instead of the more conventional $100. A market order to purchase "100 bonds" (or simply "100") would therefore mean $100,000 nominal of the bond. In other markets, though, the standard convention is followed of using 100 as the par value of the bond.

---

1 The term *technical default* is used to refer to non-payment or delay of a coupon as it becomes due, when the issuer is still otherwise financially solvent.

Basic provisions

The majority of corporate bonds are term bonds; that is, they will have a fixed term to maturity, at which point they must be redeemed by the borrower. Only companies of the highest quality can issue bonds of maturity much greater than 10 years at anything less than prohibitive cost; however, it is common to see long-dated bonds of up to 30 years maturity or longer issued by high-credit-quality companies. Let us look at some other relevant features.

Bond security

A corporate that is seeking lower cost debt, or that does not have a sufficiently high credit rating, may issue secured debt. As security the issuer will pledge either fixed assets such as land and buildings, or personal property. The security offered my be *fixed*, in which case a specific asset is tied to the loan, or *floating*, meaning that the general assets of the company are offered as security for the loan, but not any specific asset. A *mortgage debenture* gives bondholders a charge over the pledged assets, called a *lien* (a lien is a legal right to sell mortgaged property to satisfy unpaid obligations to creditors). Where companies do not own fixed assets or other real property they often offer as collateral the securities of other companies that they hold. A *debenture* bond is secured not by a specific pledge of property, but bondholders have a claim over company assets in general, often ahead of other creditors.

Provisions for paying off bonds

In some cases a corporate issue will have a call provision that gives the issuer the option to buy back all or part of the issue before maturity. The issuer will find a call option useful as it means that debt can be refinanced when market interest rates drop below the rate currently being paid, without having to wait until the bond's maturity. At the same time such a provision is disadvantageous to the bondholder, who will require a higher yield as compensation. Call provisions can take various forms. There may be a requirement for the issuer to redeem a predetermined amount of the issue at regular intervals. Such a provision is known as a *sinking fund* requirement. This type of provision for repayment of corporate debt may be designed to retire all of a bond issue by the maturity date, or it may be arranged to pay off only a part of the total by the end of the term. If only a part is paid off, the remaining balance is known as a *balloon maturity*. The purpose of a sinking fund is to reduce the credit risk attached to the bond. Investors will derive comfort from the fact that provisions have been made regarding the final redemption of the bond, and will be more willing to buy the bond. Clearly, this may be necessary for borrowers of lower credit quality.

In most cases the issuer will satisfy any sinking fund requirement by either making a cash payment of the face amount of the bonds to be redeemed to the bond trustee, who will call the bonds for repayment by drawing serial numbers randomly, or by delivering to the trustee bonds with a total face value equal to the amount that must be retired from bonds purchased in the open market. The sinking fund call price, as with callable bonds generally, is the par value of the bonds, although in a few cases there may be a set percentage of par that is redeemable.

These are only a sample of the features that can be attached to corporate bonds. We will consider them and certain others in the remainder of this chapter and in the following chapters.

Determinants of the development of a corporate market

Corporate bond markets generally develop after a functioning market in government securities has been established. A study by the International Monetary Fund[2] has found that six general areas of the debt markets, concerned with the infrastructure and regulation of the markets, are generally required to be in place before corporate markets can develop. Some of these six areas are described below.

Money markets

The IMF study found that an already established and liquid money market will facilitate the development of a corporate market. This is essentially because in order to develop a yield curve against which corporate debt can be priced, the short-end of the yield curve must be established first, as short-date rates form the cornerstone for longer dated benchmark interest rates (Schinasi states that the short-end "anchors" the rest of the yield curve). A liquid market in short-term instruments serves as a benchmark for corporate bonds that offer different levels of liquidity, credit quality and terms to maturity. A well-established money market, particularly a repo market, also enables market participants to finance both long and short positions in other bond instruments.

---

[2] Schinasi and Todd Smith (1998).

Regulatory infrastructure

A common observation is that regulatory policies have an influence in either encouraging or inhibiting the development of a corporate market. Generally, the essential prerequisite is that *supervision* provision should be well established in order to provide comfort to investors that the market is well policed. However, regulation should not be unnecessarily cumbersome or bureaucratic as this will drive business elsewhere. Overly strict financial regulations often result in the growth of "offshore" markets; witness the development of the Eurobond market in London and the growth of Singapore and Hong Kong as financial trading centres for the products of several Asian countries. Capital controls in the United States are said to have been the prime factor behind the development of the "Eurodollar" market, the offshore market in US dollars.[3] This is a topical issue; for instance, towards the end of 1999 the European Union, as part of an effort to harmonise tax policies across its member countries, debated the introduction of a withholding tax for cross-border investments. The UK government was resisting the implementation of such a tax, on the grounds that this would drive the Eurobond market away from London, with a consequent loss in trading income and employment opportunities. Excessive regulation and taxation policies are considered to be partly behind the slow growth of the money markets in countries such as France, Germany, Italy and Japan; for example, the *commercial paper* market in these countries has grown only slowly.[4] Taxation policies also impact the development of markets, and may serve to force debt issuance offshore. It is common for developed markets to allow gross payment of coupons to overseas investors, while corporate accounting policy often enables companies to offset the interest payable on debt against their income tax liability.

Investor base

Another ingredient that is believed to be important in the development of corporate debt markets is a professional and diversified investor base. In advanced economies it is institutional investors such as life companies and pension funds that are the largest investing firms. At the shorter end of the yield curve, banks and corporates are important investors. In the United

[3] The term "Eurodollar" originally referred to a deposit of US dollars outside the United States, originally in Europe. A Eurodollar deposit can of course be in any country outside of the United States, not just in Europe.

[4] See Alworth and Borio (1993).

States, money market mutual funds are also heavily invested in short-dated instruments. An institutional investor base will lead to a demand for corporate debt, which will facilitate the market's development.

Other areas cited by the IMF study (1998) include the concentration of market power among financial firms and the culture of corporate finance in the domestic market.

The primary market

The issue of corporate debt in the capital markets require a primary market mechanism. The first requirement is a collection of merchant banks or investment banks that possess the necessary expertise. Investment banks provide advisory services on corporate finance as well as *underwriting* services, which is a guarantee to place an entire bond issue into the market in return for a fee.[5] As part of the underwriting process the investment bank will either guarantee a minimum price for the bonds, or aim to place the paper at the best price available. The IMF study (1998) notes that investment banking expertise is something that is acquired over time. This is one reason why the major underwriting institutions in emerging economies are often branch offices of the major integrated global investment banks.

Small-size bond issues may be underwritten by a single bank. It is common however for larger issues, or issues that are aimed at a cross-border investor base, to be underwritten by a *syndicate* of investment banks. This is a group of banks that collectively underwrites a bond issue, with each syndicate member being responsible for placing a proportion of the issue. The bank that originally won the *mandate* to place the paper invites other banks to join the syndicate. This bank is known as the *lead underwriter, lead manager* or *book-runner*. An issue is brought to the market simultaneously by all syndicate members, usually via the *fixed price re-offer* mechanism. This is designed to guard against some syndicate members in an offering selling stock at a discount in the grey market, to attract investors, which would force the lead manager to buy the bonds back if it wished to support the price. Under the fixed price re-offer method, price undercutting is not possible as all banks are obliged not to sell their bonds below the initial offer price that has been set for the issue. The fixed price usually is in place up to the first settlement date, after which the bond is free to trade in the secondary market.

---

5 If the bank cannot sell an entire issue to its customers or other institutions in the market, it will take the remaining stock on to its own books. The fee payable by the borrower is compensation to the bank for taking on this underwriting risk.

A corporate debt issue is priced over the same currency government bond yield curve. A liquid benchmark yield curve therefore is required to facilitate pricing. The extent of a corporate bond's yield spread over the government yield curve is a function of the market's view of the credit risk of the issuer (for which formal credit ratings are usually used) and the perception of the liquidity of the issue. The pricing of corporate bonds is sometimes expressed as a spread over the equivalent maturity government bond, rather than as an explicitly stated yield, or sometimes as a spread over another market reference index such as Libor. If there is no government bond of the same maturity as the corporate bond, the issuing bank will price the bond over an interpolated yield, obtained from the yields of two government bonds with maturities lying either side of the corporate issue. If there is no government bond that has a maturity beyond the corporate issue, the practice in developed economies is to take a spread over the longest dated government issue. In developing markets, however, the bond would probably not be issued.

Formal credit ratings are important in the corporate markets. Investors usually use both a domestic rating agency in conjunction with an established international agency such as Moody's or Standard & Poor's. As formal ratings are viewed as important by investors, it is in the interest of issuing companies to seek a rating from an established agency, especially if it is seeking to issue foreign currency debt and/or place its debt across national boundaries.

The secondary market

Corporate bonds virtually everywhere are traded on an over-the-counter (OTC) basis; that is, directly between counterparties over the telephone. Bonds are usually listed on an exchange though, as many institutional investors have limitations on the extent to which they may hold non-listed instruments. Eurobonds for example are usually listed on the London Stock Exchange or Luxembourg Stock Exchange, while those issued by Asian borrowers are frequently also listed on the Hong Kong or Singapore exchanges. In the United States there are more corporate bond issues listed on the New York Stock Exchange (NYSE) than there are equities, and the dollar value of daily bond trading is at least as high as that in equities. On the NYSE a low volume of trading in bonds does take place on the exchange itself, but this dwarfed by the volume of trading in the OTC market.

The level of liquidity varies greatly for corporate bonds, ranging from completely liquid (for example, a World Bank global bond issue) to completely illiquid, which is common when investors have bought the entire issue of a bond and held it to maturity. The number of market-makers in a particular issue will also determine its liquidity. In return for providing liquidity, market-makers also retain a major market privilege because they have exclusive access to inter-dealer broker price screens.

Another factor that is important to secondary market liquidity is the clearance and settlement system. In Japan, for example, the settlement system until very recently was a decentralised, paper-based system, which acted as a barrier to market liquidity. A computerised, de-materialised "book-entry" system for settling corporate bonds, as represented by Euroclear and Clearstream, contributes to liquidity because it assists market participants to trade without being exposed to delivery or payment risk.

Total issues	1985	1990	1991	1992	1993	1994	1995	1996	1997	1998
	165.7	299.9	389.8	471.1	646.6	498	573.2	n.a.	n.a.	n.a.
By type of offering:										
Public, domestic	119.6	189.3	286.9	379.1	486.9	365.2	408.8	386.3	397.2	374.1
Private placement, domestic	46.2	87	74.9	65.9	116.2	76.1	87.5	n.a.	n.a.	78.4
Foreign sales and other issues*	–	23.6	28.0	27.1	43.5	56.7	76.9	74.8	79.2	n.a.
By industry:										
Manufacturing	52.1	53.1	86.6	82.1	88.0	43.4	61.1	42.0	58.5	55.4
Commercial and miscellaneous	15.1	40.0	36.7	43.1	60.4	40.7	50.7	34.1	41.3	38.0
Transportation	5.7	12.7	13.6	9.8	10.8	6.9	8.4	5.1	6.9	5.5
Public utility	13.0	17.5	23.9	49.1	56.3	13.3	13.8	8.2	9.7	8.9
Communication	10.5	6.7	9.4	15.4	32.0	13.3	23.0	13.3	18.5	15.3
Real estate and financial	69.3	169.3	219.6	272.9	394.1	380.4	416.3	358.5	386.4	378.1

* Includes foreign sales only.

Note: Includes all debt security issues with a maturity greater than one year.

Table 5.2 Bond market financing by US Firms (in US$ billion)
Source: Federal Reserve Bulletin.

	1985	1992	1993	1994	1995	1996	1997	1998
Households	9.4	12.6	16.2	14.5	14.6	13.7	15.1	14.4
Foreign	14.3	12.8	12.5	12.3	11.8	12.7	13.3	13.7
Banks	11.7	11.3	10.7	10.4	9.6	9	8	7.7
Insurance	35.6	38.5	37.1	36.9	35.5	36.1	35.2	35.2
Private pensions	11.3	8.8	8.8	9.2	9.1	9.5	9.7	9.8
Public pensions	12.2	9.9	6.9	7.2	6.8	6.6	5.8	6
Mutual funds	2.9	4.5	5.7	6.9	8.7	8.2	8.3	8.6
Brokers dealers	2.6	1.7	2.2	2.5	3.2	2.6	2.8	2.7
Others	0	0	0	0	0.7	1.5	1.8	1.9

Table 5.3 Holders of US Corporate and Yankee bonds (in per cent of total)
Sources: Flow of Funds, Board of Governors of the Federal Reserve Board; IMF.

Fundamentals of corporate bonds

The market generally classifies corporate bonds by credit rating and by sector of issuer. In the United States, for example, issuers are classified as public utilities, transport companies, industrial companies, banking and financial institutions, and international (or *Yankee*) borrowers. Within these broad categories issuers are broken down further; for example, transportation companies are segmented into airlines, railway companies and road transport companies. In other respects, corporate bonds have similar characteristics to those described in Chapter 1, although it is often in the corporate market that exotic or engineered instruments are encountered, compared to the generally plain vanilla government market.

Term to maturity

In the corporate markets, bond issues usually have a stated term to maturity, although the term is often not fixed because of the addition of call or put features. The convention is for most corporate issues to be medium- or long-dated, and rarely to have a term greater than 20 years. In the US market prior to the Second World War it was once common for companies to issue bonds with maturities of 100 years or more, but this is now quite rare. Only the highest rated companies find it possible to issue bonds with terms to maturity greater than 30 years; during the 1990s such companies included Coca-Cola, Disney and British Gas.

Investors prefer to hold bonds with relatively short maturities because of the greater price volatility experienced in the markets since the 1970s, when high inflation and high interest rates were common. A shorter dated bond has lower interest rate risk and price volatility compared to a longer dated bond. There is thus a conflict between investors, whose wish is to hold bonds of shorter maturities, and borrowers, who would like to fix their borrowing for as long a period as possible. Although certain institutional investors such as pension fund managers have an interest in holding 30-year bonds, it would be difficult for all but the largest, best rated companies, to issue debt with a maturity greater than this.

Bond interest payment

Corporate bonds pay a fixed or floating-rate coupon. Floating-rate bonds were reviewed in Chapter 3. Zero-coupon bonds are also popular in the corporate market; indeed, corporate zero-coupon bonds differ from zero-coupon bonds in government markets in that they are actually issued by the borrower, rather than simply being the result of a market-maker stripping a conventional coupon bond.

The fixed interest rate payable by a conventional bond is called the bond *coupon*, and we used this term when describing bonds in Chapter 1. The term originates from the time when bonds were *bearer* instruments, and were issued with coupons attached to them. The bondholder would tear off each coupon and post it to the issuer as each interest payment became due. These days bonds are *registered* instruments, and the investor receives the interest payment automatically from the issuer's registrar or paying agent. Therefore it is technically incorrect to refer to a bond's "coupon" but the convention persists from earlier market infrastructure. Many bond issues including Eurobonds and US Treasuries are held in "de-materialised" form, which means only one "global" certificate is issued, which is held with the clearing or custody agent, and investors receive a computer print-out detailing their bond holding.

Zero-coupon bonds are issued in their own right in the corporate markets, but are otherwise similar to zero-coupon bonds in government markets. Note that the term "strip" for a zero-coupon bond is usually used only in the context of a government bond strip. In the US market zero-coupon bonds or "zeros" were first issued in 1981 and initially offered tax advantages for investors, who avoided the income tax charge associated with coupon bonds.[6] However, the tax authorities in the United States

[6] The first offer of zero-coupon bonds was by J.C. Penney Co. Inc. in the domestic US market in 1981.

implemented legislation that treated the capital gain on zeros as income, thus wiping out the tax advantage. The tax treatment for zeros is similar in most jurisdictions. Zeros are still popular with investors, however, because they carry no reinvestment risk. The lack of reinvestment risk is appreciated more by investors in a declining interest rate environment, whereas in a rising interest rate environment investors may prefer to have coupons to reinvest. Zeros are also preferred during a period of relatively high interest rates, as the compounding effect is greater.

As a zero-coupon bond is issued at a discount to its face value, and then repaid at par, there is a significant liability for the borrower on maturity. For a long-dated bond this liability can be very large. This may be a concern for bondholders, so it is usually only highly rated borrowers that are able to place zero-coupon bonds. Lower rated borrowers in the US domestic market have issued *deferred-interest bonds*, also known as *zero-coupon bonds*. With a deferred-interest bond the investor receives no interest payments for a set period after issue, say the first five years of the bond's life. At the end of the deferred interest period, the accumulated interest is paid out. The rate payable is usually considerably higher than the market level. This feature makes the bond attractive for lower rated companies or start-up companies who might be expected to suffer from cashflow problems in their early years. The thinking behind deferred-interest bonds is that, after the no-coupon period, the issuer will be in a financially stable state and able to pay off the accumulated interest, and indeed redeem the bond and refinance at a lower rate of interest.

In the case of default, bankruptcy laws in the United States, for example, allow the bondholder to claim back the value of the purchase price plus "accrued" interest up to the time the issuer went into liquidation. This value is essentially the value of the bond at the time. The face value of the bond, of course, cannot be claimed.

Bond security

International bonds and bonds sold in the Euro markets are unsecured. It is sometimes said that the best type of security is a company in sound financial shape that is able to service its debt out of its general cash flow, or a company with a high credit rating. While this is undoubtedly true, a secured bond is sometimes preferred by investors. In domestic markets, corporate bonds are often issued with a form of security attached in order to make them more palatable to investors. The type of security that is offered varies and can be either *fixed* or *floating*; that is, a specific or general charge on the assets of the borrowing company. The type of security sometimes defines the market that the bond trades in; for example, a mortgage-backed bond or a debenture. We consider the main types of security below.

Mortgage bonds

A bond that is secured with a *lien* over some or all of the issuer's mortgaged properties is known as a *mortgage bond.* A lien is the legal right to sell mortgaged property in the event that the borrower is unable to meet obligations arising from its bond issue. The coupon payable is lower than would otherwise be payable if the bond were issued without a first charge on the issuer's properties. In the US market such an unsecured bond is called a *debenture*, although confusingly a debenture in the UK domestic market is a bond that *is* secured, although on a floating rather than fixed asset.

An example of a bond with collateral in the form of a charge over property is the Annington Finance No. 4 plc issue (AF4), which dates from December 1997. This is a sterling bond and is described in Example 5.1 below.

EXAMPLE 5.1 Annington Finance No. 4 plc

Annington Finance is a public limited company incorporated in England, whose share capital is owned by Annington Homes Limited, a subsidiary of Annington Holdings plc. The holding company was established in 1996 to purchase housing stock from the United Kingdom's Ministry of Defence (MoD), who had previously run the housing for the benefit of members of the country's armed forces and their families. This housing was known as the Married Quarters Estate (MQE). Annington Holdings plc purchased the housing stock from the MoD and then leased it back to it.

As part of the purchase proceeds, Annington Holdings plc issued bonds secured on the assets themselves. The bonds consisted of:

- £1.24 billion Class A zero-coupon notes due December 2022
- £1 billion Class B zero-coupon notes due January 2023
- £900 million secured floating-rate notes due January 2023

The floating rate notes pay interest at Libor plus 10 basis points up to 2008, after which the interest steps up to Libor plus 100 basis points. The issuer has an option to redeem the floating-rate notes after 2008. The collateral for the issue consists of a first fixed security on the housing stock of the MQE, which is made up of 760 sites throughout the United Kingdom and approximately 55,000 housing units. The MQE was leased back to the MoD who pay rental fees on it. The cash flows for the bond issue are financed by these rental proceeds, as well as the proceeds from the occasional disposal of individual residential properties. On the basis of this security the bonds were rated "A2" by Moody's and "A" by Fitch IBCA. Duff & Phelps rated the class A notes as "AAA" and the other notes as "A". The class A notes rank ahead of the class B notes. On maturity the issuer is required to repay the interest and principal outstanding on all the notes.

Mortgage bonds may be issued as part of a *series*. This often happens when companies wish to finance their operations continuously through the issue of long-dated debt. This means that as one bond issue matures, another series is issued under the same mortgage.

There are restrictions on the amount of debt that may be issued with a charge over the same property. Generally, the terms of a mortgage bond issue state that property purchased by the borrower after the issue of the bonds is still covered by the lien attached to those bonds. This is known as an *after-acquired clause*. Additional borrowing secured by the properties is usually set as a percentage of the value of the after-acquired assets.

Other collateral

Debt is often issued by firms that do not possess fixed assets such as property or factories. These companies may offer security for bonds they issue in the form of other collateral that they own, such as government bonds and bonds and equity of other companies. In the US market, bonds that have been secured with collateral of this form are known as *collateral trust bonds*. Assuming the bonds are issued at par, the nominal value of an issue is always lower than the market value of the collateral pledged, to provide an element of safety for investors. Under the terms of the issue the borrower delivers the collateral that has been pledged into the safe custody of the bond's trustee or paying agent, which will hold them for the term of the bond's life. In the event of default, bondholders are entitled to ownership of the collateral; if part of this is equity, the voting rights of the equity are transferred to the bondholders at the same time.

Terms of issue of a collateral trust bond include certain provisions to protect investors. The main one is that the value of the collateral must remain at a specified level above the nominal value of the bonds, and if there is decline in value of the collateral the issuer must provide additional collateral to make up the shortfall. This is similar to a margin call in a repo transaction.

Debentures

In the US market a debenture bond is one that is not secured by a pledge on a specific fixed asset or property. Bondholders have only a claim on the assets of the issuer in the event of default in line with general creditors. In the UK market a *debenture* is a secured bond, one that is secured on the general assets of the issuing company rather than a specified fixed asset.

US market debentures generally are of two types: those that are issued by highly rated borrowers who do not need necessarily to provide security for investors, and those issued by borrowers who have already issued bonds secured on their assets, such as mortgage bonds. This second type of debenture pays a higher coupon than both the other debenture as well as the secured bonds of its issuer. A company that has debenture bonds outstanding but no secured bonds may provide a *negative pledge clause*, which states that the debenture issue will rank equally with any secured bonds that may be issued subsequently. This protects existing bondholders. Other terms under which the bonds are issued include a limitation on the amount of dividends that the company can pay, or the proportion of current earnings that can be used to pay a dividend. With share dividends themselves becoming increasingly unfashionable in the United States, these restrictions are seen less in the domestic bond market.

Subordinated bonds

Debt issued by companies that ranks behind both secured debt and debentures is known as *subordinated* debt. A subordinated bond therefore has the highest credit risk of any domestic bond issue, because it is not backed with security of any kind. As well as ranking behind secured bonds and debentures, subordinated bonds may also in some cases rank after other creditors such as trade creditors. For this reason subordinated bonds pay among the highest yields in a domestic market. They are often issued with other features that are designed to make them more attractive. Such features may include an option to convert the bond into the ordinary shares of the issuing company at a specified date or dates. A bond with such a feature is then a *convertible*. Convertible bonds are reviewed in Chapters 8–9. Another common feature is a *step-up* feature, which states that the bond will pay a higher coupon after a set period of time, say ten years if it is not redeemed at that point. The higher coupon is often set at a punitive rate, say 100 basis points higher than the initial coupon, which acts as an incentive to the issuer to redeem the bond after the initial period. Step up subordinated bonds are common in the sterling market, in both fixed-date and perpetual form, and have been issued by smaller borrowers such as independent merchant banks.[7]

The US market has also been tapped by borrowers issuing subordinated bonds that are convertible into the ordinary shares of another company. These are known as *exchangeable bonds*.

Redemption provisions

Highly rated corporate borrowers often are able to issue bonds without indicating specifically how they will be redeemed (by implication, maturity proceeds will be financed out of the company's general cash flows or by the issue of another bond). This luxury is not always available to borrowers with low ratings. To make their debt issue more palatable to investors, they may make specific provisions for paying off a bond issue on its maturity date. We consider the most common provisions in this section.

Sinking funds

The term *sinking fund* originally referred to a ring-fenced sum of cash that was put aside to form the proceeds used in the repayment of a fixed-term bond. Although the operation of sinking funds has since changed, the term is still used. Essentially, a sinking fund facility is where a set proportion of a bond issue is redeemed every year, say 5% of the nominal value, until the final year when the remaining outstanding amount is repaid. This outstanding amount is known as a *balloon maturity*. Although it is still possible to encounter the original type of sinking fund, the majority of them are those that pay off a small part of an issue each year during its life.

7 For example, in 1994 perpetual step-up sterling notes were issued by banks such as NM Rothschild, Barings and Robert Fleming.

Sinking funds that are set up for and apply to a specific issue are known as *specific* sinking funds. There are also sinking funds that are set up by issuers and apply to their entire range of bonds. These are known as *blanket* or *aggregate* sinking funds.

In most cases the issuer will pass the correct cash proceeds to the bond's trustee, who will use a lottery method to recall bonds representing the proportion of the total nominal value outstanding that is being repaid. The trustee usually publishes the serial numbers of bonds that are being recalled in a newspaper such as *The Wall Street Journal* or the *Financial Times*. Another method by which bonds are repaid is that the issuer will purchase the required nominal value of the bonds in the open market; these are then delivered to the trustee, who cancels them. There are two types of sinking funds, those that pay off the same amount of the issue each year, say 5% of the outstanding nominal value, or those that pay a progressively greater amount each year, say 5% in the first year and then 1% more each year until maturity, when the entire amount is redeemed. It is common to find utility and energy companies in the United States that have bond sinking funds that incorporate this variable provision. A *doubling option* in a sinking fund entitles the issuer to repay double the amount that was originally specified as going to be repaid, while a provision that allows the issuer to repay an amount larger than the specified value is known as an *accelerated provision*.

The price at which bonds are redeemed by a sinking fund is usually par. If a bond has been issued above par, the sinking fund may retire the bonds at the issue price and gradually decrease this each year until it reaches par. Sinking funds reduce the credit risk applying to a bond issue, because they indicate to investors that provision has been made to repay the debt. However, there is a risk associated with holding them, in that at the time bonds are paid off they may be trading above par due to a decline in market interest rates. In this case investors will suffer a loss if it is their holding that is redeemed.

Redemption and asset sales

Bonds that are secured through a charge on fixed assets such as property or plant often have certain clauses in their offer documents that state that the issuer cannot dispose of the assets without making provision for redemption of the bonds, as this would weaken the collateral backing for the bond. These clauses are known as *release-of-property* and *substitution-of-property* clauses. Under these clauses, if property or plant is disposed, the issuer must use the proceeds (or part of the proceeds) to redeem bonds that are secured by the disposed assets. The price at which the bonds are retired under this provision is usually par, although a special redemption price other than par may be specified in the repayment clause.

Call and refund provisions

A large number of corporate bonds, especially in the US market, have a call provision on dates ahead of the stated maturity date. Borrowers prefer to have this provision attached to their bonds as it enables them to refinance debt at cheaper levels when market interest rates have fallen significantly below the level they were at, at the time of the bond issue. A call provision is a negative feature for investors, as bonds are only paid off if their price has risen above par. Although a call feature indicates an issuer's interest in paying off the bond, because they are not attractive for investors callable bonds pay a higher yield than non-callable bonds of the same credit quality and maturity.

In general, callable bonds are not callable for the first five or ten years of their lives, a feature that grants an element of protection for investors. Thereafter a bond is usually callable on set dates up to the final maturity date. In the US market another restriction is the *refunding redemption*. This prohibits repayment of bonds within a set period after issue with funds obtained at a lower interest rate or through issue of bonds that rank with or ahead of the bond being redeemed. A bond with refunding protection during the first five or ten years of its life is not as attractive to a borrower as a bond with absolute call protection. Bonds that are called are usually called at par, although it is common also for bonds to have a call schedule that states that they are redeemable at specified prices above par during the call period.

There are also bonds that are callable in part rather than in whole. In this case the issuer or trustee will select the bonds to be repaid on a random basis, with the serial numbers of the bonds being called published in major news publications.

Corporate bond risks

The market risks associated with holding corporate bonds are identical to those reviewed in Chapter 1. Corporate bonds, however, hold additional risk for investors, unlike the developed market government bonds that were (implicitly) the subject of the earlier chapters. Although we cover this topic in greater detail in the chapter on risk management (Choudhry 2001), in this section we introduce the additional risks to investors of holding corporate debt.

Credit risk

Unlike a (developed economy) government bond, holding a corporate bond exposes investors to *credit risk*, also known as *default risk*. This is the risk that the issuing company will default on its bond's coupon payments or principal repayment, resulting in a loss to the bondholders. Default may occur due to general financial difficulties, which may turn out to be short-term in nature, or it may be a prelude to bankruptcy and liquidation. In the most extreme case it may be many years, if ever, before investors receive some of their money back.

The price of a corporate bond reflects the market's view of the credit risk associated with holding it. If the credit risk is perceived to be low, the *spread* of the issuer's bonds over the equivalent-maturity government bond will be low, while if the credit risk is deemed to be high, the yield spread will be correspondingly higher. This yield spread is sometimes referred to as the *credit spread* or *quality spread*. A 10-year bond issued by a highly rated corporate borrower will have a lower spread than a 10-year bond issued by a borrower with a lower credit rating. The higher yield on the bond issued by the lower rated borrower is the compensation required by investors for holding the paper. Bond issuers are rated for their credit risk by both investment houses' internal credit analysts and by formal rating agencies such as Standard & Poor's, Moody's, and Fitch. This topic is reviewed in Chapter 15.

Figure 5.4 illustrates an hypothetical "credit structure of interest rates". The credit structure is dynamic and will fluctuate with changes in market conditions and the general health of the economy.

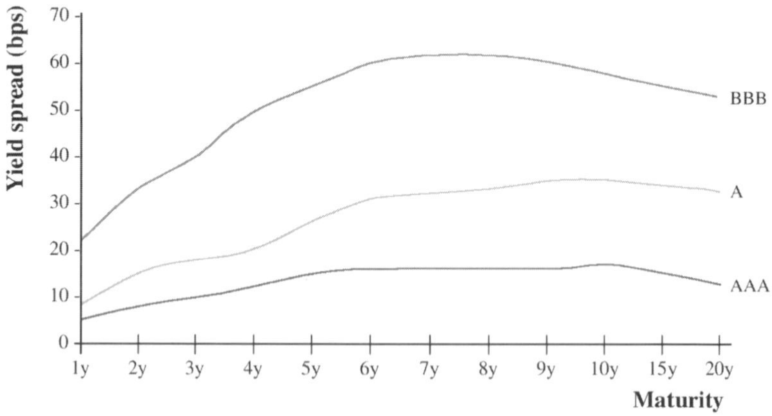

Figure 5.4 Credit structure of interest rates

Credit spreads over government yields and between corporate borrowers of different credit quality fluctuate with market conditions and in line with the business cycle. Spreads are highest when an economy is in a recession and corporate health is relatively weak. A significant downward market correction also tends to widen credit spreads as investors embark on a "flight to quality" that depresses government bond yields. At the height of an economic boom, spreads tend to be at their narrowest, not only because corporate balance sheets are in healthy shape but also because investors become less risk averse in times of a strong economy. This affects low-rated borrowers as well as highly rated ones, so that spreads fall generally during an economic boom. In Figure 5.5 note how the credit spread for the hypothetical BBB-rated bonds falls as maturity increases; this is because analysts view the credit spread as being more liable to improve over time, as a company is upgraded, while a bond issued by a company that is already well-rated can only stay where it is or suffer a downgrade.

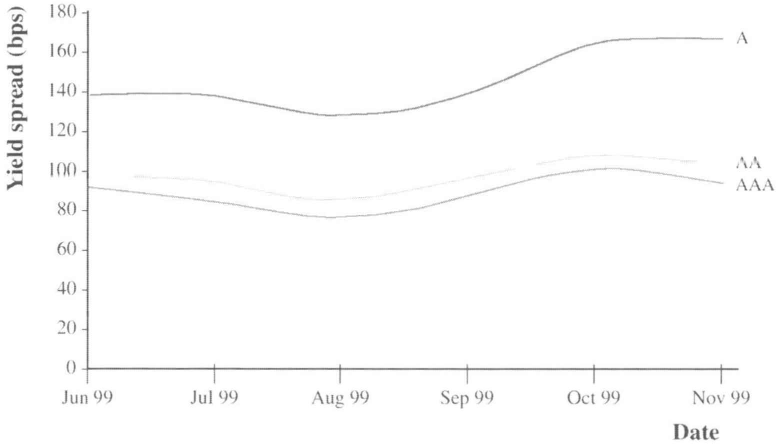

Figure 5.5 Sterling bonds 10-year yield spreads over gilts
Source: Halifax plc.

Liquidity risk

A bond with a ready market of buyers and sellers is always more attractive to investors than one that is difficult to trade. Such a bond is called a *liquid* bond. Liquidity is a function of the ease with which market participants may buy or sell a particular bond, the number of market-makers that are prepared to quote prices for the bond, and the spread between the buying and selling price (the bid–offer spread). Illiquid bonds will have wide spreads and perhaps a lack of market-makers willing to quote a bid price for them. Although some government bonds can sometimes be illiquid, liquidity risk, which is the risk that a bond held by an investor becomes illiquid, is primarily a corporate bond market risk. The yield on a bond that is, or about to become, illiquid, will be marked up by the market in compensation for the added risk of holding it. The best gauge of an issue's liquidity is the size of its bid–offer spread. Government bonds frequently have a spread of 0.03% or less, which is considered very liquid. Corporate spreads are wider but a spread of 0.10 to 0.25, up to 0.50 of 1% is considered liquid. A bid–offer spread wider than this is considered illiquid, while a spread of, say, 1% or more is virtually non-tradeable. Some bonds are not quoted with a bid price or an offer price, indicating they are completely illiquid.

Call risk

In the previous section we stated that many domestic bond issues in the US market have call or refunding features attached to them. Such callable bonds have an added risk associated with holding them, known as *call risk*. This is the risk that the bond will be called at a time and price that is disadvantageous to bondholders or exposes them to loss. For example, consider a 10-year bond with a call provision that states that the bond may be called at any time after the first five years, at par. For the last five years of the bond's life, if market interest rates fall below the bond's coupon rate, the price of the bond will not rise above par by as much as that of a similar maturity (and similar credit quality) bond that has no call feature. The price/yield relationship of a bond callable at par differs from a conventional bond, as the price will be less responsive to downward moves in yield once the price is at par.

Event risk

Event risk is peculiar to corporate bonds. This is the risk that, as a result of an unexpected corporate event, the credit risk of a bond increases greatly, so that the yield of the bond rises very quickly to much higher levels. The events can be external to the company, such as a natural disaster or regulatory change, or internal, such as a merger or acquisition. A natural disaster may be an earthquake or flood, while regulatory change might be a change in the accounting or tax treatment of certain types of corporate debt. Event risk can effect companies across an industry. An example of this was the fall of Barings Bank in 1995. The owners of Barings subordinated perpetual bonds suffered a loss as a result of the bankruptcy of the company; however, holders of bonds issued by similar companies also suffered losses as the market marked the yields on these bonds up as well. Figure 5.6 shows the change in average yield spread for bonds issued by N.M. Rothschild and Robert Fleming at the time of the Barings crash.

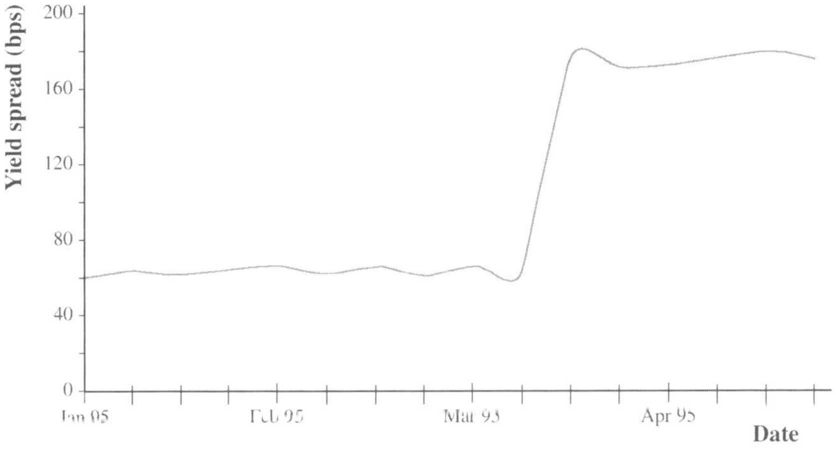

Figure 5.6 Impact of Barings Bank crisis on yield spread of bonds issued by similar companies
Source: ABN Amro Hoare Govett Sterling Bonds Limited.

A takeover is another example of an event that may result in loss for bondholders. For example, if, as a result of a merger or takeover, the debt of the amalgamated company is downgraded, bondholders will suffer a loss in capital value. To protect against event risk, bonds may have provisions in them that require an acquiring company to repurchase them, under specified conditions. Such provisions are known as *poison puts*. Other features that may be included in the terms of corporate bonds are *maintenance of net worth* and *offer to redeem* clauses. The former provision states that if an issue falls below a certain level of net worth, the borrower must redeem the bond at par. The latter clause is similar except that it does not apply to an entire issue, but only to those bonds whose holders wish to redeem.

Spens clause

In corporate markets a *Spens clause* is sometimes included in a bond's issue terms. This relates to the redemption proceeds of the bond. Under the terms of the clause, if there is a change in control of the issuing company, the company is required to redeem the notes within 45 days of the change of ownership. If the bonds are not redeemed in this time, bondholders may give notice to the issuer that the bond must be retired. The redemption amount is determined in accordance with (5.1) below, which essentially states that the yield at which the bond is redeemed is a spread over the benchmark government bond against which the corporate bond is priced. This spread is negotiable between the issuer and the bondholders, unless it is specified in the Spens clause itself.

$$P_{red} = \sum_{t=N_{red}}^{t=N_{mat}} \frac{C + M}{(1 + ry)[(t - N_{red})/B]} \tag{5.1}$$

where

P_{red} is the redemption proceeds
N_{mat} is the maturity date of the bond
N_{red} is the redemption date
C is the coupon
M is the principal repayment
ry is $\left(1 + \frac{rm}{2}\right)^2 - 1$
rm is the YTM of the benchmark bond over which the bond is priced
t is each coupon date and the number of days between N_{red} and N_{mat}
$t - N_{red}$ is the number of days between t and N_{red}
B is the day-count base (360 or 265).

High-yield corporate bonds

High-yield bonds were developed in the US corporate bond market, and have not as yet emerged as a significant investment outside the dollar market, except perhaps in the United Kingdom. The bonds were previously known as *junk bonds,* and this term is still used occasionally. They refer to bond issues with very low credit ratings, typically below BBB (S&P rating). Bonds in this category may not necessarily have started life as high-yield debt; they may have been rated as investment grade when originally issued and then suffered successive rating downgrades until rated as non-investment grade. The majority of high-yield bonds however were rated as below investment grade at the time of issue. Some of the bond structures are quite sophisticated examples of financial engineering, as when they have been issued as part of a "leveraged buy-out" finance package or as part of a re-capitalisation that results in higher levels of debt. For example, a high-yield bond structure may include deferred coupons, with no coupon payments for a number of years after issue. This recognises the fact that the debt burden of the issuer may result in severe cashflow problems in the early years, so that coupons are deferred. Where there is a deferred coupon structure, the bond may include a *step-up* feature, so that after a period of time the coupon rate is increased, to compensate for the low (or zero) coupon rate at the start of the bond's life.

Corporate bond offering circular

The following is an example of a typical bond issue offering circular, relating to a plain vanilla US dollar bond issued by a hypothetical company in the Euro markets. The bond has been underwritten by a hypothetical syndicate of banks, with two hypothetical banks involved as joint lead-managers, Jones Brothers International (Europe) and John Paul George Corporation. The content of the circular is fairly representative of a bond issue in the international markets, and there will be differences where, for example, the bond structure is not plain vanilla. These will only be detail differences however; the following can be taken to be a standard and fairly representative document.

OFFERING CIRCULAR

JACKFRUIT CORPORATION

(INCORPORATED IN SURREY, ENGLAND)

U.S. $500,000,000

$6^{3}/_{4}\%$ Senior Notes due 7 June 2009

Issued pursuant to its

EURO MEDIUM-TERM NOTE PROGRAM

The U.S. $500,000,000 $6\,^{7}/_{8}\,\%$ Senior Notes due on 7 June 2009 (the "Notes") of Jackfruit Corporation (the "Issuer") will be issued pursuant to the Issuer's Euro Medium-Term Note Program (the "Program"). Interest on the Notes will be payable annually on 7 June of each year, commencing on 7 June 1999, and at maturity. The Notes will not be redeemable prior to maturity except in certain circumstances affecting taxation, as more fully described in the Information Memorandum referred to below under the heading "Terms and Conditions of the Notes."

Applications have been made for the listing of and permission to deal in the Notes on The Stock Exchange of Singapore Limited and The Stock Exchange of Hong Kong Limited, which are expected to be effective on or about 23 June 1998 and 24 June 1997, respectively. Application will be made to The London Stock Exchange Limited (the "London Stock Exchange") for the Notes to be issued under the Issuer's Program, which will be amended in order to, among other things, increase the maximum principal amount of medium-term notes outstanding at any one time. An Information Memorandum and Information Memorandum Addendum, each expected to be dated 26 June 1998, together with the Issuer's Annual Report for the year ended 31 December 1997 and its Quarterly Report for the quarter ended 31 March 1998, will comprise the listing particulars expected to be approved by the London Stock Exchange (the "London Listing Particulars"). Draft copies of such documents expected to comprise the London Listing Particulars may be inspected during normal business hours on any weekday (excluding Saturdays) at the principal place of business of the Issuer and at the offices of the Fiscal Agent in London. It is expected that the Notes will be admitted to the Official List of the London Stock

Exchange, subject to the satisfaction of certain conditions, with effect on or about 2 July 1998.

The Notes will initially be represented by a temporary global Note without coupons which will be deposited with a common depositary acting on behalf of Cedel Bank and Euroclear on or about 20 June 1998, and will be exchangeable for definitive Notes in bearer form with coupons not earlier than 30 July 1998, upon certification of non-U.S. beneficial ownership.

This Offering Circular (including the Pricing Supplement relating to the Notes set forth herein) is supplemental to, and should be read in conjunction with, the Information Memorandum and Information Memorandum Addendum, each dated 19 June 1997, as may be amended or superseded from time to time (collectively, the "Information Memorandum"), which are annexed hereto. Terms defined in the Information Memorandum shall have the same meaning when used in this Offering Circular. References herein to "Dollars," "$" and "U.S.$" are to the lawful currency of the United States of America.

JONES BROTHERS INTL (EUROPE)	JOHN PAUL GEORGE CORPORATION
NATIONAL CREDIT BANK	SANBIN INTERNATIONAL
AKERS MARKETS	HENRY MARSHALL SECURITIES LIMITED
STEGAS SECURITIES LIMITED	CAPE LIMITED
THE ABC BANK plc	CLAXTON CAPITAL MARKETS (EUROPE) LTD

The date of this document is 18 June 1998.

TERMS OF THE NOTES

The Terms and Conditions of the Notes will include the information set forth in the Information Memorandum under the heading "Terms and Conditions of the Notes," as supplemented and modified by the Pricing Supplement set forth below.

Pricing Supplement Dated 18 June, 1998

Jackfruit Corporation
U.S. $500,000,000
6 $^{3}/_{4}$% Senior Notes due 7 June 2009 (the "Notes")
Issued pursuant to its
Euro Medium-Term Note Program

Terms used herein shall be deemed to be defined as such for the purposes of the Conditions; items in the form of pricing supplement included in the Information Memorandum that are not applicable to the Notes are omitted. The terms for the issue of the Notes are as follows:

TYPE OF NOTE

Form of Notes to be initially issued:	Temporary global Note in bearer form. Temporary Globe Note is exchangeable for a Permanent Global Note on 30 days' notice
Ranking:	The Notes are Senior Notes and will constitute direct unconditional and unsecured obligations of the Issuer and will rank pari passu in right of payment with all outstanding unsecured senior debt of the Issuer
Fixed Rate/Floating Rate/ Zero Coupon/Original Issue Discount/Indexed Redemption Amount/Indexed Interest/Dual Currency/Partly Paid/ Installment/Extendible/ Renewable/combination/other:	Fixed Rate
Convertible automatically or at the option of the Issuer and/or Noteholders into Note(s) of another Interest Basis:	No

DESCRIPTION OF THE NOTES

Provisions for exchange of Notes:	Interests in the temporary global Note in bearer form are exchangeable for definitive Notes in bearer form on or after the Exchange Date following certification as to the non-U.S. beneficial ownership thereof.

Talons for future Coupons to be attached to definitive Notes in bearer form:	No
Series Number:	10
Nominal Amount (Face Amount) of Notes to be issued:	U.S. $500,000,000
Specified Currency:	United States Dollars
Specified Denomination (s):	U.S. $1,000, U.S. $10,000 and U.S. $100,00.
Issue Price:	99.264%
Issue Date:	20 June 1998
Proceeds to Issuer:	U.S. $488,254,800

PROVISIONS RELATING TO INTEREST PAYABLE

Interest Basis:	Fixed Rate
Fixed Rate of Interest:	6 $^3/_4$%
Fixed Interest Dates:	7 June of each year, beginning 7 June 1999

PROVISIONS REGARDING REDEMPTION/MATURITY

Maturity Date:	7 June 2009
Redemption at Issuer's option:	No, except in certain circumstances affecting taxation, as set forth in Condition 10(b)
Redemption at Noteholder's option:	No

Final Redemption Amount for each Note:	100%

GENERAL PROVISIONS APPLICABLE TO THIS ISSUE OF NOTES

Additional sales restrictions:	In addition to the sales restrictions set forth in the Information Memorandum under the heading "Subscription and Sale," the following restrictions apply:

United Kingdom: With regard to the United Kingdom, references to Article 11 (3) of the Financial Services Act 1986 (Investment Advertisements) (Exemptions) Order 1995 in the Information Memorandum shall be deemed to refer to Article 11 (3) of the Financial Services Act 1986 (Investment Advertisements) (Exemptions) Order 1996 (as amended).

Hong Kong: Each Manager has represented and agreed that it has not offered or sold and will not offer or sell in Hong Kong by means of any document, any Notes other than to persons whose ordinary business it is to buy or sell shares or debentures (whether as principal or agent) or in circumstances which do not constitute an offer to the public within the meaning of the Companies Ordinance of Hong Kong. Each Manager has represented and agreed that until such time as the listing of the Notes on The Stock Exchange of Hong Kong Limited has been formally approved or unless it is a person permitted to do so under the securities laws of Hong Kong, it has not issued or had in its possession for the purpose of issue, and will not issue or have in its possession for the purpose of issue, in Hong Kong any advertisement, invitation or document relating to the Notes, other than with respect to Notes intended to be disposed of to persons outside Hong Kong or to be disposed of in Hong Kong only to persons whose business involves the acquisition, disposal or holding of securities, whether as principal or agent

Singapore: No prospectus in connection with the offer of the Notes will be registered with the Registrar of Companies in Singapore and the Notes will be offered in Singapore pursuant to an exemption invoked under Section 106C of the Companies Act, Chapter 50 of Singapore (the "Singapore Companies Act"). Accordingly each Manager has represented and agreed that documents or material prepared in connection with the offer of the Notes may not be, and have not been, circulated, and the Notes may not be, and have not been, offered or sold, directly or indirectly to the public or any member of the public in Singapore other than (i) to an institutional investor or other person specified in Section 106C of the Singapore Companies Act, (ii) to a sophisticated investor, and in accordance with the conditions, specified in Section 106D of the Singapore Companies Act, or (iii) otherwise pursuant to, and in accordance with the conditions of, any other applicable provision of the Singapore Companies Act.

Method of Distribution:	*Syndicated* Lead Managers: Jones Brothers International (Europe) John Paul George Corporation Co-Lead Managers: National Credit Bank Sanbin International Akers Securities Henry Marshall Securities Limited Stegas Securities The ABC Bank plc Claxton Capital Markets (Europe) Ltd
Commissions:	0.275% Management and Underwriting 1.35% Selling
Stabilizing Dealer/Manager:	In connection with the issue of the Notes, Jones Brothers International (Europe) may over-allot or effect transactions which stabilize or maintain the market price of the Notes at a level which might not otherwise prevail. Such stabilizing, if commenced, may be discontinued at any time. Such stabilizing shall be in compliance with all relevant laws and regulations.
Notes to be Listed:	Yes
Stock Exchange(s):	The London Stock Exchange Limited The Stock Exchange of Singapore Limited The Stock Exchange of Hong Kong Limited With regard to the London Stock Exchange listing of this issue of Notes, see "Other terms or special conditions" below.
Common Code for Euroclear and Cedel and ISIN:	Common Code: 001234554321Bank ISIN: XS001234554321

Selected bibliography and references

Alworth, J.S. and Borio, C.E.V. 1993, "Commercial paper markets: A survey," BIS Economic Papers No. 37, Bank for International Settlements.

Bank of England 1999, *Quarterly Bulletin*, August.

Choudhry, M. 2001, *The Bond and Money Markets: Strategy, Trading, Analysis*, Butterworth-Heinemann, Oxford, Chapters 2–10 and 39.

Economist 1999, "Much indebted to EU", 18 September.

Fabozzi, F.J. 1993, *Bond Markets, Analysis and Strategies*, 2nd edition, Prentice Hall, New Jersey.

Schinasi, G.J. and Todd Smith, R. 1998, "Fixed income markets in the United States, Europe, and Japan: Some lessons for emerging markets," a Working Paper of the International Monetary Fund, No. 98/173, December.

Wilson, R.S. and Fabozzi, F.J. 1996, *Corporate Bonds; Structures and Analysis*, FJF Associates, New Hope, PA.

This leads me to reflect on our youth of today; they are regarded by many as badly behaved, inconsiderate and selfish, and many deserve such criticism. But does this not stem from a lack of challenge, a lack of opportunity to take responsibility? ... What a waste of potential talent if it can only be released in a war situation.

– Alan "Kit" Kitley
Take Mary to the Pictures: A Fighter Pilot in Burma 1941–1945, Coston Publishing, 2003

CHAPTER

6

Corporate Issuers and Commercial Paper

Commercial paper (CP) is a money market product; however, CP is an important corporate finance instrument and it is worthwhile to review the subject here. Many large- and medium-sized corporations raise their short-term working capital in the CP market; the larger organstions such as GE Capital and Ford raise these funds directly in the market, while other companies use a network of CP dealers (large banks) to act as placing agent for them, for which the banks charge a fixed fee.

Companies fund part of their medium- and long-term capital requirements in the debt capital markets, through the issue of bonds. Short-term capital and *working* capital is usually sourced directly from banks, in the form of bank loans. An alternative short-term funding instrument however is commercial paper (CP), which is available to corporates that have a sufficiently strong credit rating. Commercial paper is a short-term unsecured promissory note. The issuer of the note promises to pay its holder a specified amount on a specified maturity date. In the United States, CP has a zero coupon and trades at a *discount* to its face value, whereas in the EuroCP (ECP) market CP trades on a yield basis. The discount represents interest to the investor in the period to maturity. CP is typically issued in bearer form, although some issues are in registered form.

Outside of the United States CP markets were not introduced until the mid-1980s, and in 1986 the US market accounted for over 90% of outstanding commercial paper globally.[1] In the United States, the market was developed in the late nineteenth century, and as early as 1922 there were 2200 issuers of CP with $700 million outstanding. In 1998 there was over $1 trillion outstanding, as shown in Table 6.1. CP was first issued in the United Kingdom in 1986, and subsequently in other European countries. Table 6.2 shows EuroCP volume outstanding.

1995	677,470
1996	779,365
1997	958,524
1998	1,161,022
1999	1,393,846
2000	1,602,064
2001	1,440,866
2002	1,342,862
2003	1,288,700
2004	1,402,600

Table 6.1 US Commercial paper market year-end outstandings ($ million), includes asset-backed CP outstanding
Source: Federal Reserve.

1998	128
1999	175
2000	226
2001	247
2002	305
2003	413
2004	482

Table 6.2 EuroCP year-end volume outstanding $ billion (all currencies)
Source: Euroclear.

1 OECD (1989).

Originally the CP market was restricted to borrowers with high credit rating, and although lower rated borrowers do now issue CP, sometimes by obtaining credit enhancements or setting up collateral arrangements, issuance in the market is still dominated by highly rated companies. The majority of issues are very short-term, from 30 to 90 days in maturity; it is extremely rare to observe paper with a maturity of more than 270 days or nine months. This is because of regulatory requirements in the United States,[2] which outlines that debt instruments with a maturity of less than 270 days need not be registered. Companies therefore issue CP with a maturity lower than nine months and so avoid the administration costs associated with registering issues with the SEC. Although in theory ECP can be issued up to 364-day maturity, in practice it is rare as there is very little liquidity and investor demand at this maturity.

	US CP	Eurocommercial CP
Currency	US dollar	Any Euro currency
Maturity	1–270 days	2–365 days
Common maturity	30–60, 90, 180 days	30–90 days
Interest	Zero-coupon, issued at discount	On CD yield
Quotation	On a discount rate basis	On a yield basis
Settlement	T + 0	T + 2
Registration	Bearer form	Bearer form
Negotiable	Yes	Yes
Dealer fee	5 bps	3 bps

Table 6.3 Comparison of US CP and EuroCP markets

As with medium-term notes (MTNs) there are two major markets, the US dollar market with an outstanding amount in 2004 of $1.4 trillion as noted above, and the Eurocommercial paper market with outstanding value of $482 billion at the end of 2004.[3] Commercial paper markets are wholesale markets, and transactions are typically very large size. In the United States over a third of all CP is purchased by money market unit trusts, known as mutual funds; other investors include pension fund managers, retail or commercial banks, local authorities and corporate treasurers. The main features of each market are summarised in Table 6.3.

2 This is the Securities Act of 1933. Registration is with the Securities and Exchange Commission (SEC).

3 *Source*: Federal Reserve and Euroclear.

Although there is a secondary market in CP, very little trading activity takes place since investors generally hold CP until maturity. This is to be expected because investors purchase CP that matches their specific maturity requirement. When an investor does wish to sell paper, it can be sold back to the dealer or, where the issuer has placed the paper directly in the market (and not via an investment bank), it can be sold back to the issuer.

Commercial Paper programs

The issuers of CP are often divided into two categories of company: banking and financial institutions and non-financial companies. The majority of CP issues are by financial companies. Those companies include not only banks but the financing arms of corporates such as General Motors, Ford Motor Credit, British Airways plc and Chrysler Financial. Most of the issuers have strong credit ratings, but lower rated borrowers have tapped the market, often after arranging credit support from a higher rated company, such as a *letter of credit* from a bank, or by arranging collateral for the issue in the form of high-quality assets such as Treasury bonds. CP issued with credit support is known as *credit-supported commercial paper*, while paper backed with assets is known naturally enough, as *asset-backed commercial paper*. Paper that is backed by a bank letter of credit is termed *LOC paper*. Although banks charge a fee for issuing letters of credit, borrowers are often happy to arrange for this, since by so doing they are able to tap the CP market. The yield paid on an issue of CP will be lower than a commercial bank loan.

Although CP is a short-dated security, typically of three- to six-month maturity, it is issued within a longer term program, usually for three to five years for euro paper; US CP programs are often open-ended. For example, a company might arrange a five-year CP program with a limit of $500 million. Once the program is established the company can issue CP up to this amount, say for maturities of 30 or 60 days. The program is continuous and new CP can be issue at any time, daily if required. The total amount in issue cannot exceed the limit set for the program. A CP program can be used by a company to manage its short-term liquidity, that is its working capital requirements. New paper can be issued whenever a need for cash arises, and for an appropriate maturity.

Issuers often roll over their funding and use funds from a new issue of CP to redeem a maturing issue. There is a risk that an issuer might be unable to roll over the paper where there is a lack of investor interest in the new issue. To provide protection against this risk, issuers often arrange a stand-by line of credit from a bank, normally for all of the CP program, to draw against in the event that it cannot place a new issue.

There are two methods by which CP is issued, known as *direct-issued* or *direct paper,* and *dealer-issued* or *dealer paper*. Direct paper is sold by the issuing firm directly to investors, and no agent bank or securities house is involved. It is common for financial companies to issue CP directly to their customers, often because they have continuous programs and constantly roll-over their paper. It is therefore cost-effective for them to have their own sales arm and sell their CP direct. The treasury arms of certain non-financial companies also issue direct paper; this includes for example British Airways plc corporate treasury, which runs a continuous direct CP program, used to provide short-term working capital for the company. Dealer paper is paper that is sold using a banking or securities house intermediary. In the United States, dealer CP is effectively dominated by investment banks, as retail (commercial) banks were until recently forbidden from underwriting commercial paper. This restriction has since been removed and now both investment banks and commercial paper underwrite dealer paper.

Although CP is issued within a program, like MTNs, there are of course key differences between the two types of paper, reflecting CP's status as a money market instrument. The CP market is issuer-driven, with daily offerings to the market. MTNs in contrast are more investor-driven; issuers will offer them when demand appears. In this respect MTNs issues are often "opportunistic", taking advantage of favourable conditions in the market.

Commercial paper yields

In the United States commercial paper is a discount instrument. There have been issues of coupon CP and floating-rate, but this is very unusual. Thus, CP is sold at a discount to its maturity value, and the difference between this maturity value and the purchase price is the interest earned by the investor. The CP day-count base is 360 days in the United States and Euro markets, and 365 days in the United Kingdom. The paper is quoted on a discount yield basis, in the same manner as Treasury bills. In the ECP market the paper is quoted as a yield, but the proceeds raised are at a discount to face value. So in other words, assume that an issuer is quoted an all-in yield of 2.50% in the ECP market. This will include the dealer fee of 3 bps (meaning the end-investor will be receiving a yield of 2.47%). This yield is then converted to a discount rate to calculate how much actual cash proceeds are raised and passed on to the issuer.

The yield on CP follows that of other money market instruments and is a function of the short-dated yield curve. The yield on CP is higher than the Treasury bill (T-bill) rate; this is due to the credit risk that the investor is exposed to when holding CP, for tax reasons (in certain jurisdictions interest earned on T-bills is exempt from income tax) and because of the lower level of liquidity available in the CP market. CP also pays a higher yield than Certificates of Deposit (CD), due to the lower liquidity of the CP market.

Although CP is a discount instrument and trades as such in the United States and United Kingdom, as we noted just now, Eurocommercial paper trades on a yield basis, similar to a CD. The discount rate for an instrument is discussed in Chapter 2 of the author's book *The Bond and Money Markets*. The expressions below are a reminder of the relationship between true yield and discount rate. Issuers who deal in both the USCP and ECP markets will use these formulas to convert between discount rate and true yield.

$$P = \frac{M}{1 + r \times \frac{\text{days}}{\text{year}}} \tag{6.1}$$

$$rd = \frac{r}{1 + r \times \frac{\text{days}}{\text{year}}} \tag{6.2}$$

$$r = \frac{rd}{1 - rd \times \frac{\text{days}}{\text{year}}} \tag{6.3}$$

where M is the face value of the instrument, rd is the discount rate and r the true yield (true interest rate).

EXAMPLE 6.1

A 60-day CP note has a nominal value of \$100,000. It is issued at a discount of $7\frac{1}{2}\%$ per annum. The discount is calculated as:

$$Dis = \frac{\$100{,}000\ (0.075 \times 60)}{360}$$

$$= \$1{,}250.$$

The issue price for the CP is therefore \$100,000 – \$1,250, or \$98,750.

The money market yield on this note at the time of issue is:

$$\left(\frac{360 \times 0.075}{360 - (0.075 \times 60)}\right) \times 100\% = 7.59\%.$$

Another way to calculate this yield is to measure the capital gain (the discount) as a percentage of the CP's cost, and convert this from a 60-day yield to a one-year (360-day) yield, as shown below.

$$r = \frac{1.250}{98.750} \times \frac{360}{60} \times 100\%$$

$$= 7.59\%$$

Note that these are US dollar CP and therefore have a 360-day base.

ABC plc wishes to issue CP with 90 days to maturity. The investment bank managing the issue advises that the discount rate should be 9.5%. What should the issue price be, and what is the money market yield for investors?

$$Dis = \frac{100\ (0.095 \times 90)}{360}$$

$$= 2.375.$$

The issue price will be 97.625.

The yield to investors will be:

$$\frac{2.375}{97.625} \times \frac{360}{90} \times 100\% = 9.73\%.$$

Asset-backed commercial paper

Introduction

The rise in securitisation has led to the growth of short-term instruments backed by the cash flows from other assets, known as *asset-backed commercial paper* (ABCP). Securitisation is the practice of using the cash flows from a specified asset, such as residential mortgages, car loans or commercial bank loans, as backing for an issue of bonds. The assets themselves are transferred from the original owner (the *originator*) to a specially created legal entity known as a *special purpose vehicle* (SPV), so as to make them separate and bankruptcy-remote from the originator. In the meantime, the originator is able to benefit from capital market financing, often charged at a lower rate of interest than that earned by the originator on its assets. Securitised products are not money market instruments, and although ABCP is, most textbooks treat ABCP as part of the structured products market rather than as a money market product. It is nevertheless a money market product, because of the maturity of the instrument.

Generally, securitisation is used as a funding instrument by companies for three main reasons: it offers lower cost funding compared with traditional bank loan or bond financing; it is a mechanism by which assets such as corporate loans or mortgages can be removed from the balance sheet, thus improving the lender's return on assets or return on equity ratios; and it increases a borrower's funding options. When entering into a securitisation, an entity may issue term securities against assets into the public or private market, or it may issue commercial paper via a special vehicle known as a *conduit*. These conduits are usually sponsored by commercial banks.[4]

Entities usually access the commercial paper market in order to secure permanent financing, rolling over individual issues as part of a longer term *program* and using interest rate swaps to arrange a fixed rate if required. Conventional CP issues are typically supported by a line of credit from a commercial bank, and so this form of financing is in effect a form of bank funding. Issuing ABCP enables an originator to benefit from money market financing that it might otherwise not have access to because its credit rating is not sufficiently strong. A bank may also issue ABCP for balance sheet or funding reasons. ABCP trades, however, exactly as conventional CP. The administration and legal treatment is more onerous because of the need to establish the CP trust structure and issuing SPV. The servicing of an ABCP program follows that of conventional CP and is carried out by the same entities, such as the "Trust" arms of banks; for example, JPMorgan Chase, Deutsche Bank and Bank of New York.

Example 6.2 below details a hypothetical ABCP issue and typical structure.

Basic characteristics

Asset-backed CP programs are issued out of specially incorporated legal entities, which in the money markets are known as conduits. They are typically established by commerical banks and finance companies to enable

[4] An SPV in the capital markets is usually called an SPV, whereas for some reason in the asset-backed money markets it is called a conduit.

them to access Libor-based funding, at close to Libor, and to obtain regulatory capital relief. This can be done for the bank or a customer.

An ABCP conduit has the following features:

- it is a bankruptcy-remote legal entity that issues commercial paper to finance a purchase of assets from a seller of assets;
- the interest on the CP issued by the conduit, and its principal on maturity, will be paid out of the receipts on the assets purchased by the conduit;
- they are sometimes set up to exploit credit arbitrage opportunities, such as raising finance at Libor to invest in high-quality assets such as investment-grade-rated structured finance securities that pay above Libor.

The assets that can be funded via a conduit program are many and varied; to date they have included:

- trade receivables and equipment lease receivables;
- credit card receivables;
- auto loans and leases;
- corporate loans, franchise loans and mortgage loans;
- real-estate leases;
- investment-grade-rated structured finance bonds such as ABS, MBS and CDO notes;
- future (expected) cash flows.

Conduits are classified into a "program type", which refers to the make-up of the underlying asset portfolio. This can be *single-seller* or *multi-seller*, which indicates how many institutions or entities are selling assets to the conduit. They are also designated as *funding* or securities *credit arbitrage* vehicles. A special class of conduit known as a structured investment vehicle (SIV, sometimes called a special investment vehicle) exists that issue, both CP and MTNs. These are usually credit arbitrage vehicles set up with their own equity capital.

Credit enhancement and liquidity support

To make the issue of liabilities from a conduit more appealing to investors (or to secure a particular credit rating), a program sponsor will usually arrange some form of credit enhancement and/or back-up borrowing facility.

Generally, two types of credit enhancement are used, either "pool-specific" enhancement or "program-wide". The first arrangement will cover only losses on a specific named part of the asset pool, and cannot be used to cover losses in any other parrt of the asset pool. Program-wide credit enhancement is a fungible layer of credit protection that can be drawn on to cover losses from the start or if any pool-specific facility has been used up.

Pool-specific credit enhancment instruments include the following:

- over-collateralisation, where the nominal value of the underlying assets exceeds that of the issued paper;
- surety bond: a guarantee of repayment from a sponsor or other bank;
- letter of credit: a stand-by facility that the issuer can use to draw funds from;
- irrevocable loan facility;
- excess cash, invested in eligible instruments such as T-bills.

The size of a pool-specific credit enhancement facility is quoted as a fixed percentage of the asset pool. Program-wide credit enhancement is in the same form as pool-specific enhancement, and acts as a second layer of credit protection. It may be provided by a third party such as a commercial bank as well as by the sponsor.

Liquidity support is separate from credit enhancement. While credit enhancement facilities cover losses due to asset default, liquidity providers undertake to make available funds should these be required for reasons other than asset default. A liquidity line is drawn on, if required, to ensure timely repayment of maturing CP. This might occur because of market disruption (such that the issuer could not place new CP in the market), an inability of the issuer to roll maturing CP, or because of asset and liability mismatches. This last item is the least serious situation, and reflects that in many cases long-dated assets are used to back short-dated liabilities, and cash flow dates often do not match. The availability of a liquidity arrangement provides comfort to investors that CP will be repaid in full and on time, and is usually arranged with a commercial bank. It is usually provided as a loan agreement, of an amount equal to 100% of the face amount of CP issued, under which the liquidity provider agrees to lend funds to the conduit as required. The security for the liquidity line comes from the underlying assets.

Figure 6.1 illustrates a typical ABC structure issuing to the USCP and ECP markets. Figure 6.2 shows a multi-seller conduit set up to issue in the ECP market.

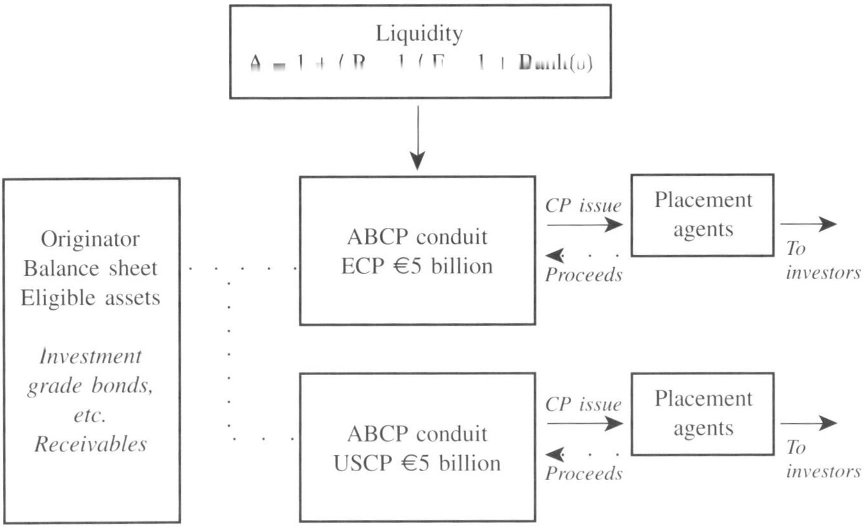

Figure 6.1 Single-seller conduit

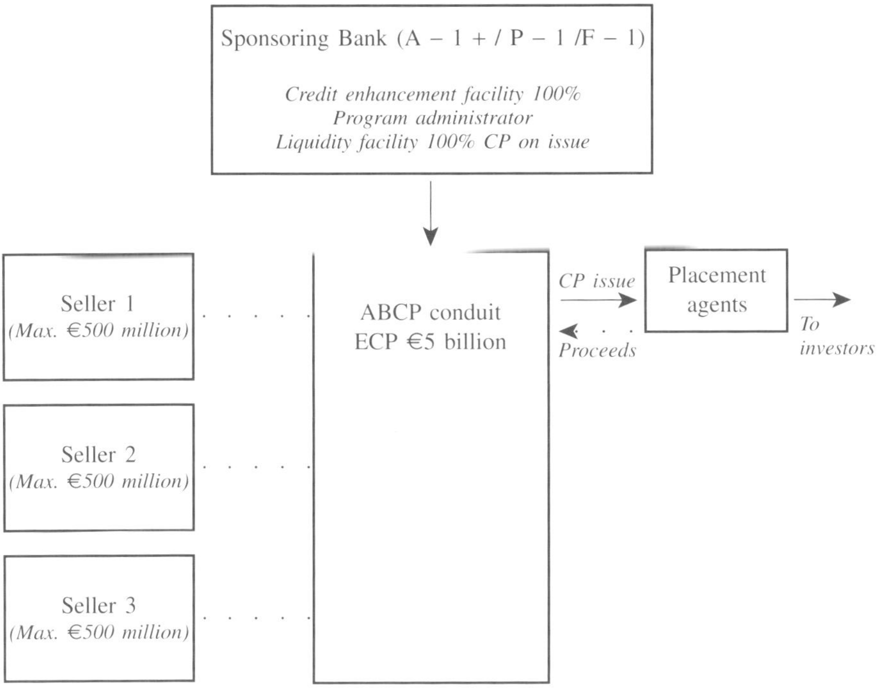

Figure 6.2 Multi-seller EuroABCP conduit

Market volumes

The CP market is a large and liquid market in which capital is raised efficiently. The ABCP markets have also grown such that they represent considerable depth and liquidity. For instance, as at 31 March 2004, the US CP market had $1.28 trillion of outstanding paper, of which $650 billion was ABCP. Figure 6.3 shows the trend in volume, with the increasing share of ABCP apparent.

The Euro CP (or ECP) market has also been experiencing this growth. Figure 6.4 shows the ECP market oustandings at end of Quarter 1, 2004, while Figure 6.5 shows the Euro ABCP (or EABCP) market as a percentage of the total ECP market.

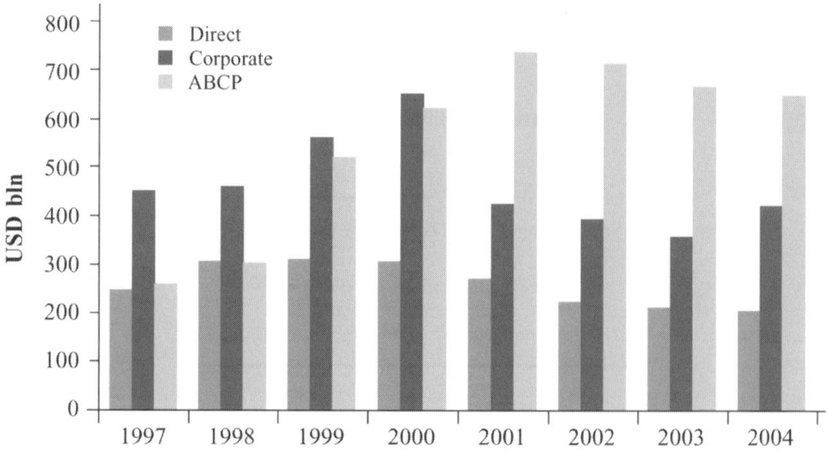

Figure 6.3 Total US CP market volumes, 2004
Source: Merrill Lynch.

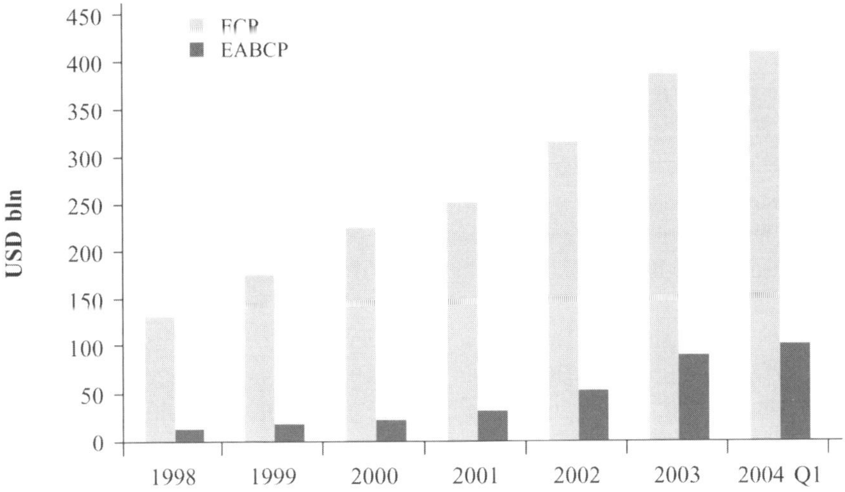

Figure 6.4 ECP market outstanding, 2004
Source: Merrill Lynch.

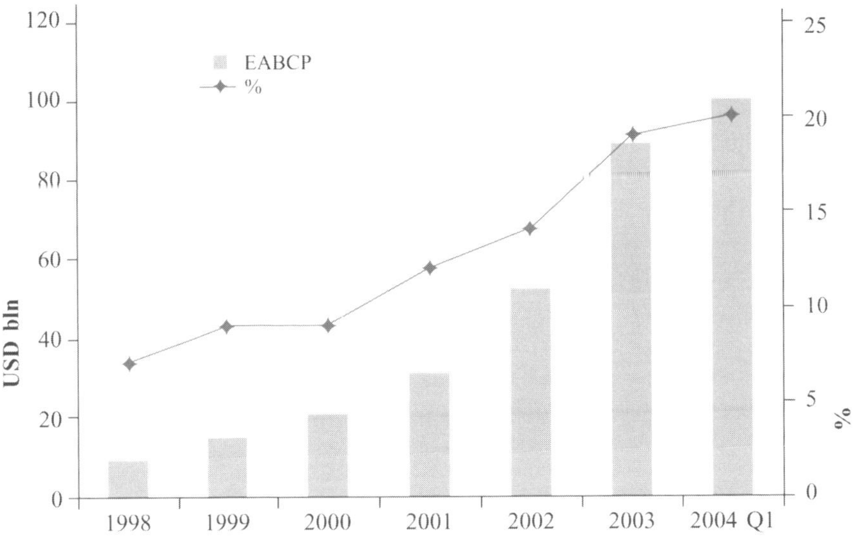

Figure 6.5 EABCP market as share of total ECP market, 2004
Source: Merrill Lynch.

EXAMPLE 6.2 Illustration of ABCP structure

In Figure 6.6 below we illustrate a hypothetical example of a securitisation of bank loans in an ABCP structure. The loans have been made by ABC Bank plc and are secured on borrowers' specified assets. They are denominated in sterling. These might be a lien on property, cash flows of the borrowers' business or other assets. The bank makes a "true sale" of the loans to an SPV, named Claremont Finance. This has the effect of removing the loans from its balance sheet and also protecting them in the event of bankruptcy or liquidation of ABC Bank. The SPV raises finance by issuing commercial paper, via its appointed CP dealer(s), which is the Treasury desk of MC investment bank. The paper is rated A-1/P-1 by the rating agencies Standard & Poor's and Moody's, and is issued in US dollars. The liability of the CP is met by the cash flow from the original ABC Bank loans.

ABC Manager is the SPV manager for Claremont Finance, a subsidiary of ABC Bank. Liquidity for Claremont Finance is provided by ABC Bank, which also acts as the hedge provider. The hedge is effected by means of a swap agreement between Claremont and ABC Bank; in fact, ABC will fix a currency swap with a swap bank counterparty, who is most likely to be the swap desk of MC investment bank. The trustee for the transaction is Trust Bank Limited, who acts as security trustee and represents the investors in the event of default.

The other terms of the structure are as follows:

Program facility limit:	US$500 million
Facility term:	The facility is available on an uncommitted basis renewable annually by the agreement of the SPV manager and the security trustee. It has a final termination date five years from first issue.
Tenor of paper:	Seven days to 270 days

Prepayment guarantee:	In the event of prepayment of a loan, the seller will provide Claremont Finance with a guaranteed rate of interest for the relevant interest period.
Hedge agreement:	Claremont Finance will enter into currency and interest-rate swaps with the hedge provider to hedge any interest rate or currency risk that arises.
Events of default:	Under event of default the issuance program will cease and in certain events will lead to Claremont Finance to pay loan collections into a segregated specific collection account. Events of default can include non-payment by Claremont Finance under the transaction documentation, insolvency or ranking of charge (where the charge ceases to be a first ranking charge over the assets of Claremont Finance).
Loans guarantee:	Loans purchased by Claremont Finance will meet a range of eligibility criteria, specified in the transaction offering circular. These criteria will include requirements on currency of the loans, their term to maturity, confirmation that they can be assigned, that they are not in arrears, and so on.

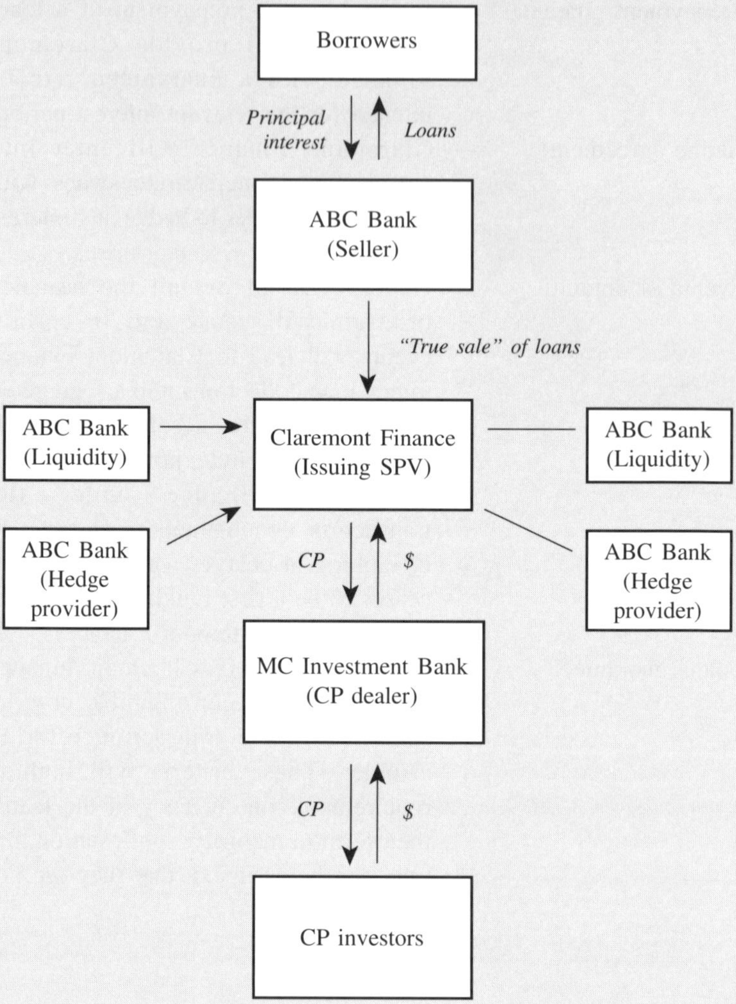

Figure 6.6 "Claremont Finance" ABCP structure

EXAMPLE 6.3 CP calculations

1. This is the same as Example 6.1 but as a 365-day basis. A 60-day CP note has a nominal value of £100,000. It is issued at a discount of $7^1/_2\%$ per annum. The discount is calculated as:

$$Dis = \frac{\pounds 100{,}000\ (0.075 \times 60)}{365}$$

$$= \pounds 1{,}232.88.$$

The issue price for the CP is therefore £100,000 – £1,232, or £98,768. The money market yield on this note at the time of issue is:

$$\left(\frac{365 \times 0.075}{365 - (0.075 \times 60)}\right) \times 100\% = 7.594\%.$$

Another way to calculate this yield is to measure the capital gain (the discount) as a percentage of the CP's cost, and convert this from a 60-day yield to a one-year (365-day) yield, as shown below.

$$r = (1{,}232/98{,}768) \times (365/60) \times 100\%$$
$$= 7.588\%$$

2. ABC plc wishes to issue CP with 90 days to maturity. The investment bank managing the issue advises that the discount rate should be 9.5%. What should the issue price be, and what is the money market yield for investors?

$$Dis = \frac{100(0.095 \times 90)}{365}$$

$$= 2.342$$

The issue price will be 97.658.

The yield to investors will be;

$$(2.342/97.658) \times (365/90) \times 100\% = 9.725\%.$$

Extendable note commercial paper

Extendable CP is a recent development in the asset-backed CP market and a number of conduits have been set up, or restructured, to enable them to issue it.[5] In many cases extendable CP acts as a back-up or substitute to the conventional bank liquidity line on a conduit. In this section we describe a generic extendable ABCP vehicle.

Extendable notes

Before we describe an extendable note ABCP structure, we should consider the form that the notes themselves take. Extendable notes are short-term liabilities issued by CP conduits in the normal way, but with certain structural features that enable them to act more as liquidity reserve facilities than a typical CP liability.

Extendable notes are issued in the following form:

- secured liquidity notes (SLNs);
- collateralised callable notes (CCNs).

SLNs are also referred to variously as *liquidity notes, structured liquidity notes* and *extendable commercial paper notes*. An SLN issued by a conduit is a secured note issued with a formal maturity date of up to 397 days from original issuance. (As such, its maturity exceeds the 270 or 364 days maximum maturity of US dollar or euro paper respectively). The key aspect of the SLN, however, is that its *expected* maturity date is shorter than the formal maturity date. The last expected maturity date of the note will be a function of the underlying assets in the vehicle, and the nature of the cash flows associated with these assets. Generally, the issuer is free to set the expected maturity date in line with its requirements, up to a maximum term in line with the formal maturity date.

On the expected maturity date of the SLN, the issuer will repay the note principal and interest, usually through a roll-over issue of new SLNs. At that point, the note is no different from a normal issue of ABCP. However, if for any reason a new issue of SLNs cannot be placed, then the SLN will not be repaid and instead it will be extended until its final maturity date. This is in effect similar to a liquidity facility; if the SLN cannot be rolled over, underlying assets must be sold to cover repayment on the formal maturity

[5] The first extendable ABCP issue was in 2002, from a number of vehicles including ABN Amro "Tulip" conduit and AIG's Orchard Park and Bluegrass conduits.

date. So, for instance, if an SLN is issued with expected maturity of 90 days, and on the 90th day new SLNs cannot be issued, the SLN remains outstanding from the 91st to the 397th day. During the 307-day period after the expected repay date, underlying assets are sold, or amortise, and the proceeds are used to repay the SLNs on or before the 397th day.

The advantage of the SLN facility over a traditional bank liquidity line is that the credit rating agencies assess the cash flow from the underlying assets (needed to repay the SLNs) for the end of the extension period. Hence, no bank liquidity would be required until this period, which would reduce the liquidity fee. Investors also view the extension of SLNs to be an unexpected occurrence, and would treat the initial issue to be normal ABCP in terms of required return.

Therefore, an SLN is essentially an ABCP issue with an extension feature at the option of the issuer. The most common occurrence is for SLNs to be issued with 90- or 180-day maturities, with a legal final maturity date of 397 days.

A CCN is a collateralised callable note issued with a final maturity date again of a maximum 397 days. The CCN has a call option that can be exercised by the issuer on a date prior to the final maturity date. The expected call date will depend on the nature of the cash flows of the underlying assets, but will be for a period inside the 397-day maximum. On the call date, the CCN will be called by the issuance of new CCNs. Again, this is similar to conventional ABCP. If new CCNs cannot be issued, then the CCN will not be called and it remains outstanding to its final maturity date. Unlike with an SLN, there is a yield penalty: if the issue is not called when expected, its yield is increased (by anything from 10 to 25 basis points) for the remaining term. If the CCN is not called, underlying assets must be realised to repay the proceeds on final maturity.

Investor perspective

In economic terms CCNs are identical to SLNs, although investors may view CCNs as more favourable because there is no extension risk associated with them. Also, from the point of view of a credit rating agency, a callable note that is not called can be considered a not abnormal occurrence, while the extension of a SLN could be construed to be a serious negative occurrence.

Where the market has a reasonable idea of the likelihood of an extended note facility actually being used, it is better able to determine how much of a return premium should be demanded by investors. For instance, the view among investors is that the ABN Amro "Tulip" and the Citibank "Dakota" vehicles are highly unlikely to exercise their extension facilities, hence this paper is treated more or less as conventional ABCP.[6]

Issuer benefits

By structuring, or restructuring, a conduit with an extendable note facility, issuers can reduce their overall cost of funding. It also gives issuers more flexibility with managing their liquidity requirements and to allow for unexpected occurrences.

The main advantages of an extendable note facility are:

- the freedom of having a one-year liquidity facility at lower cost than a normal liquidity line;
- the flexibility to issue to any term within the 397-day period;
- favourable credit rating agency treatment, who view the extendable notes as 397-day liabilities, thus any liquidity back-up need not kick in until then;
- if backed with a traditional liquidity facility, or (in synthetic ABCP programs) a guaranteed total-return swap contract (TRS), the extended note facility is viewed very favourably by investors and traded as conventional ABCP.

The credit rating agencies consider their liquidity management capabilities as an essential component when making their rating assessment of a bank. Typically, a rating agency will analyse the following factors in assigning a bank's rating:

- diversity of funding sources;
- structure and maturity of liabilities;
- balance sheet flexibility;
- ability to access the markets for funding in time of correction or illiquidity.

The addition of an extendable note facility to a bank's ABCP funding vehicles should strengthen the above points from the perspective of the

[6] In addition, the Dakota program stipulates a number of triggers under which the extended note facility will kick in, connected with cash flows on a Citibank credit card ABS program called Master Trust I. If these triggers, which relate to excess interest spread and an underlying asset principal repayment rate, are breached, the Dakota Notes will be extended. By measuring the likelihood of these triggers kicking in, investors can gauge the possibility of the SLNs being extended.

ratings agencies. In fact, a number of banks have set up extendable note ABCP vehicles, or restructured existing vehicles to issue both straight and extendable ABCP. These banks include Citibank, Sumitomo, Banco Santander, CDC Ixis, Bear Stearns and State Street.

Conduit structuring

It is possible to structure a CP vehicle to issue straight and extendable CP from inception or modify an existing vehicle for subsequent extendable note issuance. In the case of existing conduits that are set up to issue extendable paper, the restructuring can be effected by allowing extendable notes to be issued that are backed with:

- a facility to liquidate or amortise underlying assets within the extension period; market value risk of assets not being able to cover liabilities can be hedged through over-collateralisation, or a swap arrangement that pays out on any underperformance;
- setting up a total return swap (TRS) with a highly rated counterparty, or guaranteed by another bank, that supports the extendable notes on final maturity;
- a traditional bank liquidity facility that is drawn on to repay notes on final maturity.

A traditional bank liquidity facility is the most expensive option, as it carries with it a standing fee that is payable irrespective of whether the line is ever drawn on.

For existing vehicles, legal documentation describing the conduit structure (the Issue and Paying Agency agreement and the Placement agreement or "Private Placement Memorandum") would need to be re-drafted and executed. The redrafted documents would describe the new facility to issue both extendable and straight ABCP.

Figure 6.7 illustrates the structure diagram for a multi-seller, multi-SPV combined ABCP and extendable note program.

Commercial paper dealing sheet

The Treasury or money markets desk will keep a note of all liabilities of the vehicle so that they are aware of the roll-over schedule on each CP maturity. In Table 6.4 we show a typical dealing sheet for an ABCP program, as at 10 August 2004.

ABC Funding plc
CP dealing sheet

			1,558,180,000	1.435		38.69	23,055	0.089		1.576
10-Aug-04 10-Aug-04	**Value date**	**Maturity date**	**Nominal funds**	**Coupon**	**Term**	**Days to re-fix**	**bpv**	**Modified duration**	**p&l**	**Libor**
Dealer 1	29-Jul-04	8-Sep-04	15,828,000	1.500	41	29	99.63	0.0629	679	1.568
Dealer 2	8-Jul-04	8-Sep-04	75,000,000	1.480	62	29	472.18	0.0630	4,161	1.568
Dealer 1	10-Mar-04	8-Sep-04	21,123,000	1.150	182	29	133.42	0.0632	5,579	1.568
Dealer 1	14-Jul-04	9-Sep-04	94,223,000	1.490	57	30	618.93	0.0657	4,874	1.569
Dealer 3	11-Mar-04	9-Sep-04	61,351,000	1.130	182	30	404.44	0.0659	17,745	1.569
Dealer 2	15-Mar-04	10-Sep-04	81,462,000	1.140	179	31	559.33	0.0687	24,061	1.570
Dealer 3	17-Mar-04	13-Sep-04	40,230,000	1.140	180	34	309.37	0.0769	13,440	1.574
Dealer 2	12-Jul-04	14-Sep-04	50,133,000	1.490	64	35	397.92	0.079	3,415	1.576
Dealer 3	16-Mar-04	14-Sep-04	4,000,000	1.150	182	35	31.86	0.0796	1,357	1.576
Dealer 1	18-Jun-04	15-Sep-04	92,500,000	1.550	89	36	759.07	0.0821	2,068	1.577
Dealer 1	16-Mar-04	17-Sep-04	113,696,000	1.150	185	38	999.14	0.0879	42,971	1.580
Dealer 1	24-Jun-04	20-Sep-04	71,278,000	1.590	88	41	682.13	0.096	-387	1.584
Dealer 1	22-Jun-04	20-Sep-04	50,000,000	1.550	90	41	478.69	0.096	1,644	1.584
Dealer 2	20-Jul-04	21-Sep-04	45,121,000	1.530	63	42	444.41	0.0985	2,478	1.586
Dealer 2	8-Jul-04	5-Oct-04	77,159,000	1.600	89	56	1054.78	0.1367	589	1.606
Dealer 2	6-Jul-04	5-Oct-04	41,164,000	1.570	91	56	562.88	0.1367	2,003	1.606
Dealer 2	1-Jul-04	5-Oct-04	50,000,000	1.620	96	56	683.37	0.137	-985	1.606
Dealer 1	9-Aug-04	7-Oct-04	87,733,000	1.620	59	58	1247.05	0.142	-1,445	1.608

Dealer 2	5-Aug-04	7-Oct-04	226,655,000	1.650	63	58	3220.76	0.1421	-13,393	1.608
Dealer 3	15-Jul-04	14-Oct-04	59,240,000	1.600	91	65	955.59	0.1613	2,011	1.621
Dealer 3	12-Jul-04	15-Oct-04	40,168,000	1.580	95	66	659.05	0.164	2,834	1.623
Dealer 2	20-Apr-04	19-Oct-04	46,429,000	1.260	182	70	815.13	0.1756	30,228	1.631
Dealer 2	23-Jun-04	21-Dec-04	35,195,000	1.660	120	72	634.71	0.180	-1,603	1.635
Dealer 3	28-Jun-04	25-Dec-04	10,056,000	1.670	119	76	192.32	0.191	-527	1.643
Dealer 3	25-Jun-04	25-Dec-04	48,274,000	1.670	122	76	923.24	0.191	-2,531	1.643
Dealer 3	5-Aug-04	7-Jan-05	20,162,000	1.860	155	150	791.75	0.3927	-4,652	1.801
			1,558,180,000	1.435					$152,355	1.576
Liquidity maturity									-$55,001	

Next	8-Sep-04	15,828,000
Rollover schedule	8-Sep-04	75,000,000
	8-Sep-04	21,123,000

	Value date	Maturity date	CP rate	Issue price	CP nominal	Actual cash	Real interest	Term	Days to maturity
Nominal value									
Calculator	28 Aug 04	1 Jan 05	2.100%	99.253333%	251,880,709.30	250,000,000.00	2.1157980%	128	114

Table 6.4 Hypothetical ABCP program dealing sheet, for data as at 10 August 2004

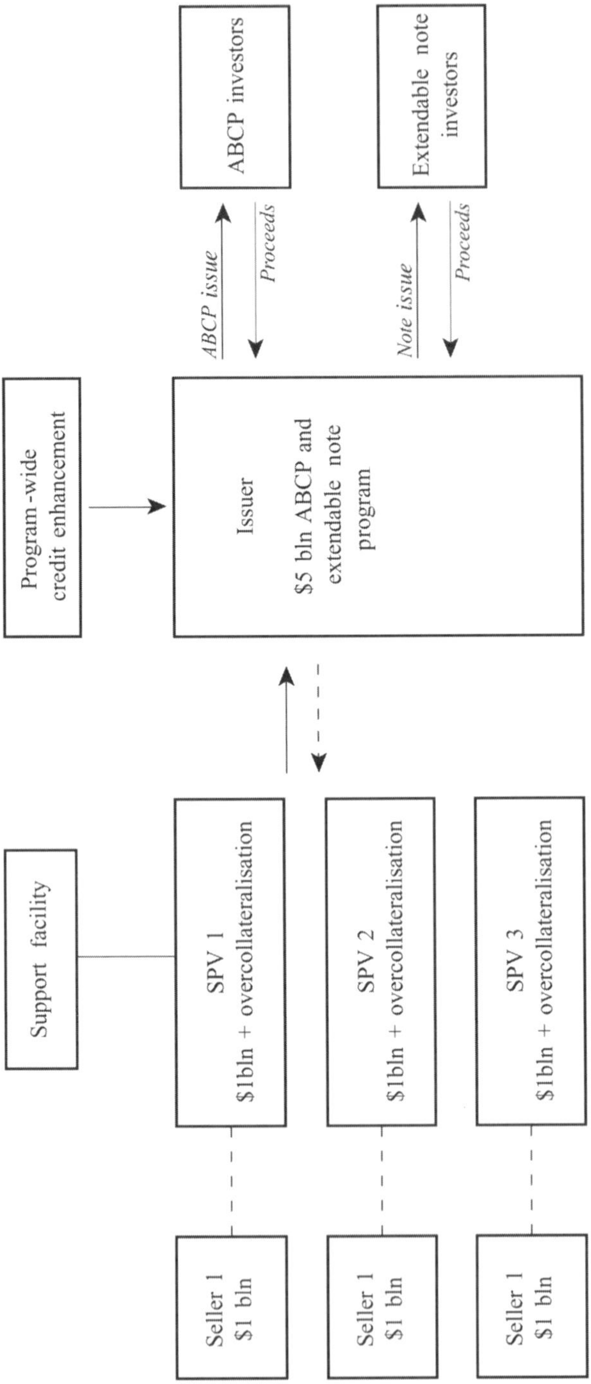

Figure 6.7 Combined ABCP/extendable note program

The dealing sheet shows data on each issue, with the name of the dealer, the term, discount rate, term to maturity, remaining term, and so on. We see that there is a timetable of continuous issuance, with the next roll-over of paper due on 8 September 2004.

Selected bibliography and references

Alworth, J. and Borio, C. 1993, "Commercial paper markets: A survey", *BIS Economic Papers No. 37*, Bank for International Settlements, Basle.

Choudhry, M. 2001, The Money Markets Handbook, John Wiley & Sons, Singapore.

Corporate Finance 1991, *A Guide to Commercial Paper in Europe 1991*, Euromoney Publications, September, London.

Corporate Finance 1993, *Guide to International Commercial Paper*, Euromoney Publications, January, London.

OECD 1989, *Competition in Banking*, OECD, Paris.

Stigum, M. 1990, *The Money Market*, Dow-Jones Irwin, New York.

You have to be in the business for a while before you realise that it's not that easy to make money off models. Unique and profitable trading strategies are rare.

— Professor Emanuel Derman
"For our eyes only?", *RISK*, August 2004

CHAPTER 7

Callable Bonds

In Chapter 1 we reviewed the yield to maturity (YTM) calculation, the main measure of bond return used in the fixed income markets. For conventional bonds the yield calculation is relatively straightforward because the issue's redemption date is known and fixed. This means that that the future cash flows that make up the total cash flows of the bond are known with certainty. As such the cash flows that are required to calculate the YTM are easily ascertained. Callable, putable and sinking fund bonds, generally termed bonds with *embedded options*, are not as straightforward to analyse. This is because some aspect of their cash flows, such as the timing or the value of their future payments, are not certain. The term *embedded* is used because the option element cannot be separated from the bond itself. Since callable bonds have more than one possible redemption date, the collection of future cash flows contributing to their overall return is not clearly defined. If we wish to calculate the YTM for such bonds, we must assume a particular redemption date and calculate the yield to this date. The market convention is to assume the first possible maturity date as the one to be used for yield calculation if the bond is priced above par, and the last possible date if the bond is priced below par. The term *yield-to-worst* is sometimes used to refer to a redemption yield calculation made under this assumption; this is the Bloomberg term. If the actual redemption date of a bond is different to the assumed redemption date, the measurement of return will be meaningless and irrelevant.

The market therefore prefers to use other measures of bond return for callable bonds. The most common method of return calculation is something known as *option-adjusted spread analysis* or OAS analysis; a very good account of OAS analysis is contained in Windas (1994). In this chapter we present one of the main methods by which callable bonds are priced. Although the discussion centres on callable bonds, the principles apply to all bonds with embedded option elements in their structure.

Understanding embedded option elements in a bond

Consider a hypothetical sterling corporate bond issued by ABC plc with a 6% coupon on 1 December 1999 and maturing on 1 December 2019. The bond is callable after five years, under the schedule shown in Table 7.1. We see that the bond is first callable at a price of 103.00, after which the call price falls progressively until December 2014, after which the bond is callable at par.

Date	Call price	Date	Call price
01-Dec-2004	103.00	01-Dec-2009	101.75
01-Dec-2005	102.85	01-Dec-2010	101.25
01-Dec-2006	102.65	01-Dec-2011	100.85
01-Dec-2007	102.50	01-Dec-2012	100.45
01-Dec-2008	102.00	01-Dec-2013	100.25
		01-Dec-2014	100.00

Table 7.1 Call schedule for "ABC plc" 6% bond due December 2019

Although our example is hypothetical, this form of call provision is quite common in the corporate debt market. The basic case can be stated quite easily; in our example the ABC plc bond pays a fixed semi-annual coupon of 6%. If the market level of interest rates rises after the bonds are issued, ABC plc effectively gains because it is paying below-market financing costs on its debt. If rates decline, however, investors gain from a rise in the capital value of their investment, but in this instance their upside is capped by the call provisions attached to the bond.

The difference between the value of a callable bond and that of an (otherwise identical) non-callable bond of similar credit quality is the value attached to the option element of the callable bond. This is an important relationship and one that we will consider, but first a word on the basics of option instruments.

Basic features of options

An option is a contract between two parties. The buyer of an option has the right, but not the obligation, to buy or sell an underlying asset at a specified price during a specified period or at a specified time (usually the expiry date of the option contract). The price of an option is known as the *premium*, which is paid by the buyer to the seller or *writer* of the option. An option that grants the holder the right to buy the underlying asset is known as a *call* option; one that grants the right to sell the underlying asset is a *put* option. The option writer is short the contract; the buyer is long. If the owner of the option elects to *exercise* her option and enter into the underlying trade, the option writer is obliged to execute under the terms of the option contract. The price at which an option specifies that the underlying asset may be bought or sold is known as the exercise or *strike* price. The expiry date of an option is the last day on which it may be exercised. Options that can be exercised anytime from the time they are struck up to and including the expiry date are called *American* options. Those that can be exercised only on the expiry date are known as *European* options.

The profit/loss profiles for option buyers and sellers are quite different. The buyer of an option has her loss limited to the price of that option, while her profit can in theory be unlimited. The seller of an option has her profit limited to the option price, while her loss can in theory be unlimited, or at least potentially very substantial.

The value or price of an option is comprised of two elements, its *intrinsic value* and its *time value*. The intrinsic value of an option is the value to the holder of an option if it were exercised immediately. That is, it is the difference between the strike price and the current price of the underlying asset. The holder of an option will only exercise it if there is underlying intrinsic value. For this reason, the intrinsic value is never less than zero. To illustrate, if a call option on a bond has a strike price of £100 and the underlying bond is currently trading at £103, the option has an intrinsic value of £3. An option with intrinsic value greater than zero is said to be *in-the-money*. An option where the strike price is equal to the price of the underlying is said to be *at-the-money*, while one whose strike price is above (call) or below (put) the underlying is said to be *out-of-the-money*.

The time value of an option is the difference between the intrinsic value of an option and its total value. An option with zero intrinsic value has value comprised solely of time value. That is,

Time value of an option = Option price − Intrinsic value.

The time value reflects the potential for an option to move into the money during its life, or move a higher level of being in-the-money, before expiry. Time value diminishes steadily for an option up to its expiry date, when it will be zero. The price of an option on expiry is comprised solely of intrinsic value.

Later in this chapter we will illustrate how the price of a bond with an embedded option is calculated by assessing the value of the "underlying" bond and the value of its associated option. The basic issues behind the price of the associated option are considered here.[1] The main factors influencing the price of an option on an interest rate instrument such as a bond are the:

- strike price of the option;
- current price of the underlying bond, and its coupon rate;
- time to expiry;
- short-term risk-free rate of interest during the life of the option;
- expected volatility of interest rates during the life of the option.

The effect of each of these factors will differ for call and put options, and American and European options. There are a number of option pricing models used in the market, the most well-known of which is probably the Black–Scholes model. Market participants often use their own variations of models or in-house developed varieties. The fundamental principle behind the Black–Scholes model is that a synthetic option can be created and valued by taking a position in the underlying asset and borrowing or lending funds in the market at the risk-free rate of interest. Although it is the basis for certain subsequent option models and is still used widely in the market, it is not necessarily appropriate for certain interest rate instruments. For instance, Fabozzi (1997) points out the unsuitability of the Black–Scholes model for certain bond options, based on its underlying assumptions. As a result, a number of other methods have been developed for callable bonds analysis.

[1] For a technical review of option pricing, see Chapters 43–46 in the author's book *The Bond and Money Markets* (Butterworth-Heinemann 2001).

The call provision

A bond with early redemption provisions essentially is a portfolio containing an underlying conventional bond, with the coupon and maturity date of the actual bond, and a put or call option on this underlying issue. Analysis therefore is interest rate dependent, it must consider the possibility of the option being exercised when valuing the bond. The value of a bond with an option feature is the sum of the values of the individual elements; that is, the underlying bond and the option component. This is expressed at (7.1):

$$P_{bond} = P_{underlying} + P_{option}. \tag{7.1}$$

Equation (7.1) states simply that the value of the actual bond is composed of the value of the underlying conventional bond together with the value of the embedded option(s). The relationship would hold for a true conventional bond, as the option component value would be zero. For a put-able bond, an embedded put option is an attractive feature for investors as the put feature contributes to its value by acting as a floor on the bond's price. Thus the greater the value of the put, the greater the value of the actual bond. We can express this by rewriting (7.1) as (7.2):

$$P_{bond} = P_{underlying} + P_{put}. \tag{7.2}$$

Expression (7.2) states that the value of a put-able bond is equal to the sum of the values of the underlying conventional bond and the embedded put option. If any of the components of the total price were to increase in value, then so would the value of the putable bond itself.

A callable bond is viewed as a conventional bond together with a short position in a call option, which acts as a cap on the actual bond's price. This "short" position in a call option reduces the total value of the actual bond, so we present the bond price in the form (7.3):

$$P_{bond} = P_{underlying} - P_{put}. \tag{7.3}$$

Equation (7.3) states that the price of a callable bond is equal to the price of the underlying conventional bond less the price of the embedded call option. Therefore if the value of the call option were to increase, the value of the callable bond would decrease. That is, when a bondholder of such a bond sells a call option, she receives the option price; the difference between the price of the option-free bond and the callable bond at any time is the price of the embedded call option. The precise nature of the behaviour of the attached option element will depend on the terms of the callable bond issue. If the issuer of a callable bond is entitled to call the issue at any time after the first call date, the bondholder has effectively sold the issuer an American call option. However, the call option price may vary with the date the option is exercised; this occurs when the call schedule for a bond has different call prices according to which date the bond is called. The underlying bond at the time the call is exercised is comprised of the remaining coupon payments that would have been received by the bondholder had the issue not been called. However, for ease of explanation the market generally analyses a callable bond in terms of a long position in a conventional bond and a short position in a call option, as stated by (7.3) above. Note of course that the option is embedded; it does not trade in its own right. Nevertheless it is clear that embedded options are important elements not only in the behaviour of a bond but in its valuation as well.

The binomial tree of short-term interest rates

In Chapter 2 we illustrated how a coupon bond yield curve could be used to derive spot (zero-coupon) and implied forward rates. A forward rate is defined as the one-period interest rate for a term beginning at a forward date and maturing one period later. Forward rates form the basis upon which a *binomial* interest rate tree is built. For an introduction to a binomial process, see Appendix 7.1.

An option model that used implied forward rates to generate a price for an option's underlying bond on a future date would implicitly assume that interest rates implied by the yield curve today for a date in the future would occur with certainty. Such an assumption would essentially repeat the errors associated with yield-to-worst analysis, which would be inaccurate because interest rates do not remain unchanged from a future today to a future pricing date. To avoid this inaccuracy, a binomial tree model assumes that interest rates do not remain fixed but fluctuate over time. This is done by treating implied forward rates, sometimes referred to as *short rates*,[2] as outcomes of a binomial process. In a binomial interest rate process we construct a binomial tree of possible short rates for each future time period. In the binomial tree we model two interest rates as the possible outcomes of a previous time period, when the interest rate was known.

[2] Although it is not strictly correct to refer to forward rates in this way.

EXAMPLE 7.1 An introduction to arbitrage-free pricing

Consider a hypothetical situation. Assume that the short-term yield curve describes the following environment:

Six-month rate: 5.00%
One-year rate: 5.15%

Assume further that in six months' time the then six-month rate will be either 5.01% or 5.50%, and that the probability of either new rate is equal at 50% each. Our capital market is a semi-annual one, that is convention is for bonds to pay a semi-annual coupon, as in the US and UK domestic markets. We can illustrate this state in the following way:

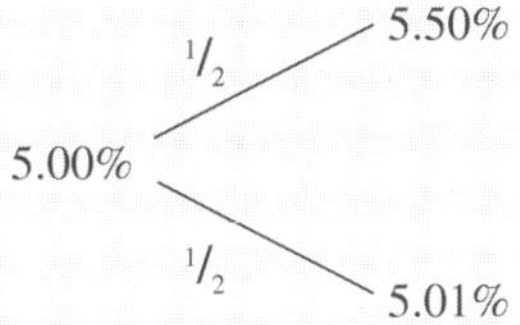

Figure 7.1 Binomial interest rate tree

Figure 7.1 is a *binomial interest rate tree* or *lattice* for the six-month interest rate. The tree is called "binomial" because there are precisely two possibilities for the future level of the interest rate. Using this lattice, we can calculate the tree for the prices of six month and one-year zero-coupon bonds. The six-month zero-coupon bond price today is given by 100/(1 + (0.05/2)) or 97.56098. The price tree is given at Figure 7.2.

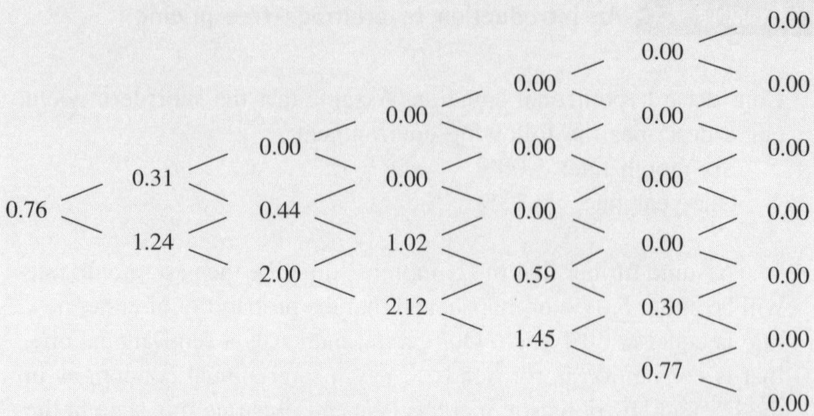

Figure 7.2 Price tree

Period 0 is today; period 1 is the point precisely six months from today. Given that we are dealing with a six-month zero-coupon bond, it is apparent that there is only one *state of the world* whatever the interest rate is in period 1; the maturity value of the bond, which is 100. The binomial lattice for the one-year zero-coupon bond is given in Figure 7.3.

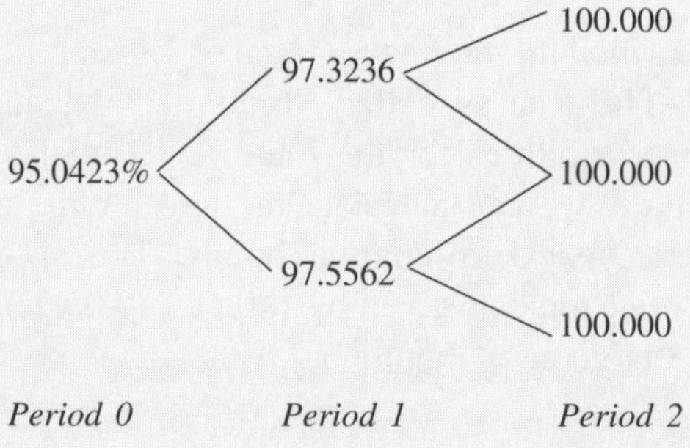

Figure 7.3 Binomial lattice for one-year bond

At period 0 the price of the one-year zero-coupon bond is $100/(1 + (0.0515/2)^2)$ or 95.0423. The price of the bond at period 1, at which point it is now a six-month piece of paper, is dependent on the six-month rate at the time, shown in the diagram. At period 2 the bond matures and its price is 100. The model at Figure 7.3 demonstrates that the average or *expected* value of the price of the one year bond at period 1 is ((0.5 × 97.3236) + (0.5 × 97.5562)) or 97.4399. This is the expected price at period 1; therefore, using this the price at period 0 is 97.4399/(1 + 0.05/2)) or 95.06332. However, we know that the market price is 95.0423. This demonstrates a very important principle in financial economics: that markets do not price derivative instruments on the basis of their expected future value. At period 0 the one-year zero-coupon bond is a more risky investment compared to the shorter dated bond; in the last six months of its life it will be worth either 97.32 or 97.55, depending on the direction of six-month rates. Investors' preference is for a bond that has a price of 97.4399 at period 1 with certainty. The price of such a bond at period 0 would be 97.4399/(1 + (0.05/2)) or 95.0633. In fact, the actual price of the one-year bond at that date, 95.0423, indicates the *risk premium* that the market places on the bond. We can now consider the pricing of an option. What value should be given to a six-month call option maturing in six months' time (period 1) written on 100 nominal of the six-month zero at a strike price of 97.40? The binomial tree for this option is given at Figure 7.4. This shows that at period 1 if the six-month rate is 5.50% the call option has no value, because the price of the bond is below the strike price. If on the other hand the six-month rate is at the lower level, the option has a value of 97.5562-94.40 or 0.1562.

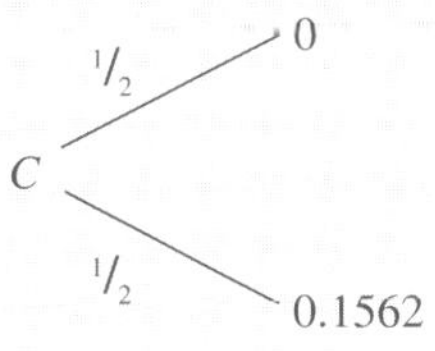

Figure 7.4 Option due binomial path

How do we calculate the price of the option? Option pricing theory states that to do this one must construct a *replicating portfolio* and find the value of this portfolio. In our example we must set up a portfolio of six-month and one-year zero-coupon bonds today that will have no value at period 1 if the six month rate rises to 5.50%, but will have a value of 0.1562 if the rate at that time is 5.01%. If we let the value of the six-month and one-year bonds in the replicating portfolio be C_1 and C_2 respectively at period 1, we may set the following equations:

$$C_1 + 0.973236C_2 = 0 \quad (7.4)$$

$$C_1 + 0.975562C_2 = 0.1562. \quad (7.5)$$

The value of the six-month zero-coupon bond in the replicating portfolio at period 1 is 100 as it matures. In the case of an interest-rate rise the value of the one-year bond (now a six-month bond) at period 1 is 97.3236. The total value of the portfolio is given by the first expression above, which states that this value must also be equal to the value of the option. The second expression gives the value of the replicating portfolio in the event that rates decrease, when the option value is 0.1562.

Solving the expressions above gives us $C_1 = -65.3566$ and $C_2 = 67.1539$. What does this mean? Basically to construct the replicating portfolio we purchase 67.15 of one-year zero-coupon bonds and sell short 65.36 of the six-month zero-coupon bond. However, the original intention behind the replicating portfolio was because we wished to price the option: the portfolio and the option have equal values. The value of the portfolio is a known quantity, as it is equal to the price of the six-month bond at period 0 multiplied by C_1 together with the price of the one-year bond multiplied by C_2. This is given by:

$$(0.9756 \times -65.3566) + (0.950423 \times 67.1539) = 0.0627$$

that is, the price of the six-month call option is 0.06. This is the *arbitrage-free* price of the option; below this price a market participant could buy the option and simultaneously sell short the replicating or portfolio and would be guaranteed a profit. If the option was quoted at a price above this, a trader could write the option and buy the portfolio. Note how the probability of the six-month rate increasing or decreasing was not part of the analysis. This reflects the arbitrage pricing logic. That is, the replicating portfolio must be equal in value to the option whatever direction interest rates move in. This means probabilities do not have an impact in the construction of the portfolio. This is not to say that probabilities do not have an impact on the option price, far from it. For example, if there is a very high probability that rates will increase (in our example), intuitively we can see that the value of an option to an investor will fall. However, this is accounted for by the market in the value of the option or callable bond at any one time. If probabilities change, the market price will change to reflect this.

Let us now turn to the concept of *risk neutral* pricing. Notwithstanding what we have just noted about how the market does not price instruments using expected values, there exist risk-neutral probabilities for which the discounted expected value does give the actual price at period 0. If we let p be the risk-neutral probability of an interest rate increase and $(1 - p)$ be the probability of a rate decrease, we may set p such that:

$$\frac{97.3236p + 97.5562(1 - p)}{1 + {}^{1}/_{2}\,0.05} = 95.0423.$$

We can calculate a value for p such that the discounted expected value, using the probability p rather than the actual probability of $^{1}/_{2}$, provides the true market price. The above expression solves to give $p = 0.5926$.

In our example from the option price tree in Figure 7.5 below, given the risk-neutral probability of 0.5926 we can calculate the option price to be:

$$\frac{(0.5926 \times 0) + (0.4074 \times 0.1562)}{1 + {}^{1}/_{2}\,0.05} = 0.0621.$$

This is virtually identical to the 0.062 option price calculated above. Put very simply, risk-neutral pricing works by first finding the probabilities that produce prices of the replicating or *underlying* security equal to the discounted expected value. An option on the security is valued by discounting this expected value under the risk-neutral probability.

We can now turn to binomial trees. In the description above we had a two-period tree, moving to period 2 we might have Figure 7.6.

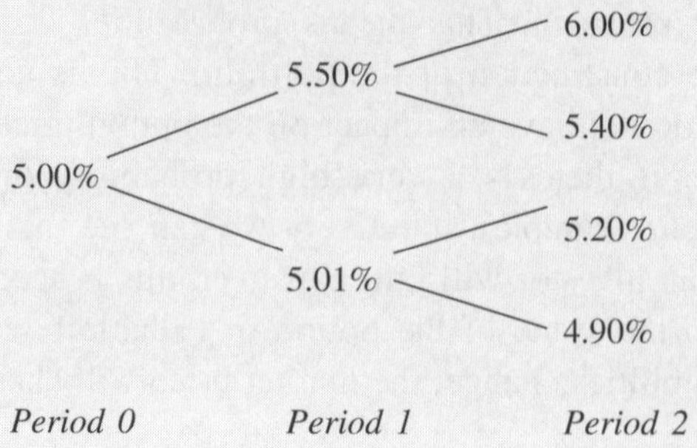

Figure 7.5 Option price tree

This binomial tree is known as a *non-recombining tree*, because each node branches out to two further nodes. This might seem more logical, and such trees are used in practice in the market. However, implementing it requires a considerable amount of computer processing power, and it is easy to see why. In period 1 there are two possible levels for the interest rate, and in period 2 there are four possible levels. After N interest periods there will be 2^N possible values for the interest rate. If we wished to calculate the current price, a 10-year callable bond that paid semi-annual coupons, we would have over one million possible values for the last period set of nodes. For a 20-year bond we would have over one trillion possible values. (Note also that binomial models are not used with a six-month time step between nodes in practice, but have much smaller time steps, further increasing the number of nodes).

For this reason certain market practitioners prefer to use a *recombining* binomial tree, where the upward–downward state has the same value as the downward–upward state. This is shown below.

The number of nodes and possible values at the latest time step is much reduced in a recombining tree. For example, the number of nodes used to price a 20-year bond that was being priced with one-week time steps would be $(52 \times 20) + 1$ or 1,041. Implementation is therefore more straightforward with a recombining tree.

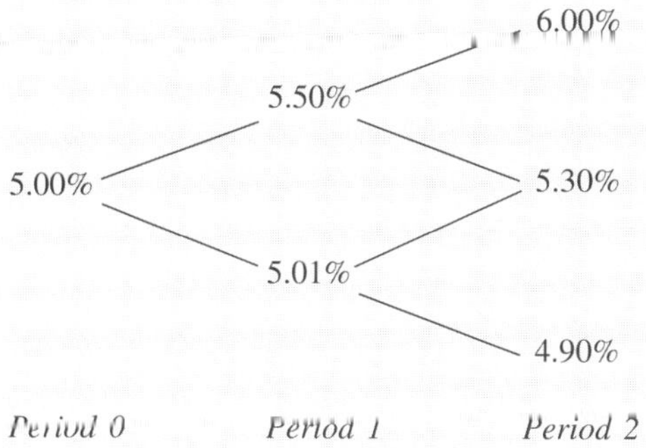

Figure 7.6 Recombining tree

Pricing callable bonds

We can now consider a simple pricing method for callable bonds. We will assume a binomial term structure model. The background to this is given in the example above, *An introduction to arbitrage-free pricing*. It is well worth reading this box, especially if one is not familiar with binomial models or the principle of the arbitrage-free pricing of financial instruments. For a background on the binomial process itself see Appendix 7.1. Using the binomial model we can derive a *risk-neutral* binomial lattice, where each lattice carries an equal probability of upward or downward moves, for the evolution of the six-month interest rate. The time step in the lattice is six months. This model is then used to price a hypothetical semi-annual coupon bond with the following terms:

Coupon	6%
Maturity	Three years
Call schedule:	
Year 1	103.00
Year 1.5	102.00
Year 2	101.50
Year 2.5	101.00
Year 3	100.00

Table 7.2 Call schedule

The tree is shown in Figure 7.7.

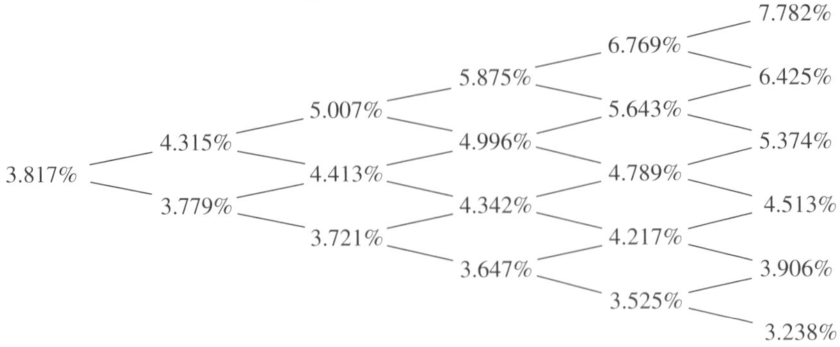

Figure 7.7

In the first instance we construct the binomial tree that describes the price process followed by the bond itself, if we ignore its call feature. This is shown at Figure 7.8. Note that the maturity value of the bond on the redemption date is given as 100.00; that is, we perform the analysis on the basis of the bond's ex-coupon value. The final cash flow would of course be 103.00.

We construct the tree from the final date backwards. At each of the nodes at year three, the price of the bond will be 100.00, the (ex-coupon) par value. At year 2.5 the price of the bond at the highest yield will be that at which the yield of the bond is 7.782%. At this point, the price of the bond after six months will be 103.00 in both the "up" state and the "down" state. Following risk-neutral pricing therefore the price of the bond at this node is:

$$P_{bond} = \frac{0.5 \times 103 + 0.5 \times 103}{1 + \dfrac{0.07782}{2}} = 99.14237.$$

The same process is used to obtain the prices for every node at year 2.5. Once all these prices have been calculated, we repeat the process for the prices at each node in year two. At the highest yield, 6.769%, the two possible future values are:

$$99.14237 + 3.0 = 102.14237 \text{ and } 99.79411 + 3.0 = 102.79411.$$

Therefore the price of the bond in this state is given by:

$$P_{bond} = \frac{0.5 \times 102.14237 + 0.5 \times 102.79411}{1 + \dfrac{0.06769}{2}} = 99.14237.$$

The same procedure is repeated until we have populated every node in the lattice. At each node the ex-coupon bond price is equal to the sum of the expected value and coupon, discounted at the appropriate six-month interest rate. The completed lattice is shown at Figure 7.8.

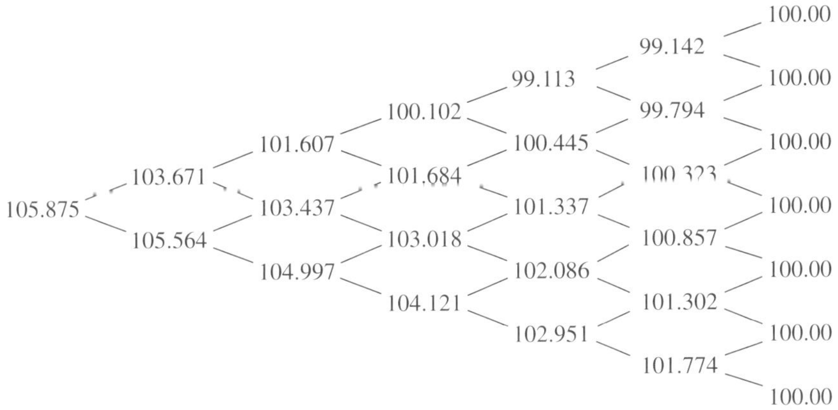

Figure 7.8

Once we have calculated the prices for the conventional element of the bond, we can calculate the value of the option element on the callable bond. This is shown in Figure 7.9. On the bond's maturity date the option is worthless, because it is an option to call at 100, which is the price the bond is redeemed at in any case. At all other node points a valuation analysis is called for.

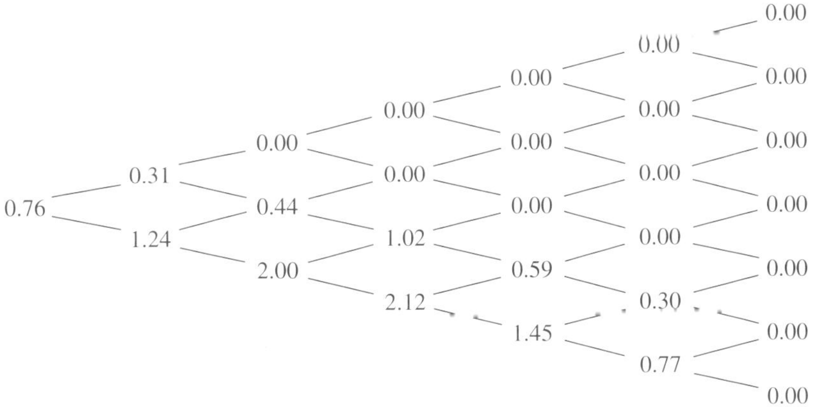

Figure 7.9

The holder of the option in the case of a callable bond is the issuing company. At any time during the life of the bond, the holder will either exercise the option on the call date or elect to hold it to the next date. The option holder must consider:

- the value of holding the option for an extra period, denoted by P_{Ct};
- the value of exercising the option straight away, denoted P_C.

If the value of the former exceeds that of the latter, the holder will elect to not exercise, and if the value at the exercise date is higher the holder will exercise immediately. At year 2.5 call date, for example, there is no value in holding the option because it will be worthless at year three. Therefore at any point where the option is in-the-money the holder will exercise.

We can express the general valuation as follows. The value of the option for immediate exercise is V_t; the value if one is holding on to the option for a further period is V_T. Additionally, let P be the value of the bond at any particular node, S the call option price, and V_h and V_l the values of the option in the up-state and down-state respectively. The value of the option at any specified node is V. The six-month interest rate at any specified node point is r. We have:

$$V_T = \frac{0.5V_h + 0.5V_l}{1 + \frac{1}{2}r} \tag{7.6}$$

$$V_t = \max.\ (0, P - S)$$

while the expression for V is $V = \max.\ (V_T.\ V_t)$.

The rule is as demonstrated above, to work backwards in time and apply the expression at each node, which produces the option value binomial lattice tree.

The general rule with an option is that they have more value "alive than dead". This means that it is sometimes optimal to run an in-the-money option rather than exercising straight away. The same is true for callable bonds. There are a number of factors that dictate whether an option should be exercised or not. The first is the asymmetric profile resulting when the price of the "underlying" asset rises; option holders gain if the price rises, but will only lose the value of their initial investment if the price falls. Therefore it is optimal to run with the option position. There is also time value, which is lost if the option is exercised early. In the case of callable bonds, it is often the case that the call price decreases as the bond approaches maturity. This is an incentive to delay exercise until a lower exercise price is available. The issue that may influence the decision to exercise sooner is coupon payments, as interest is earned sooner.

To return to our hypothetical example, we can now complete the price tree for the callable bond. Remember that the option in the case of a callable bond is held by the issuer, so the value of the option is subtracted from the price of the bond to obtain the actual value. We see from Figure 7.10 that the price of the callable bond today is 105.875 – 0.76 or 105.115. The price of the bond at each node in the lattice is also shown. By building a tree in this way, which can be programmed into a spreadsheet or as a front-end application, we are able to price a callable or putable bond.

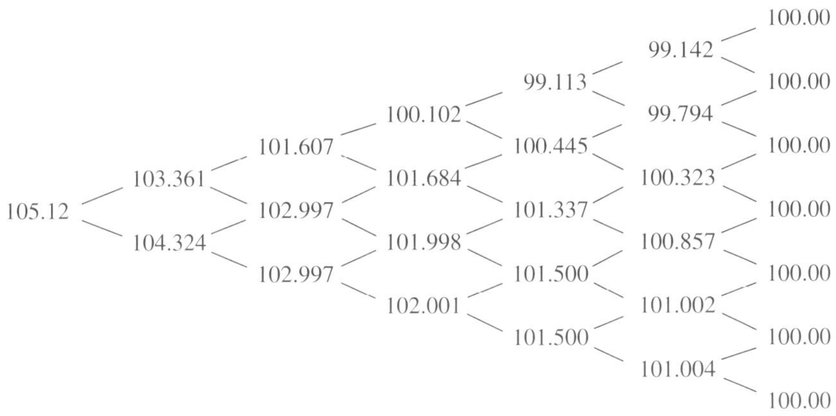

Figure 7.10 Final price tree

Price and yield sensitivity

As we saw in Chapter 2, the price/yield relationship for a conventional vanilla bond is essentially convex in shape, while for a bond with an option feature attached this relationship changes as the price of the bond approaches par, at which the bond is said to exhibit *negative convexity*. This means that the rise in price will be lower than the fall in price for a large change in yield of a given number of basis points. We summarise the price/yield relationship for both conventional and option-feature bonds in Table 7.3 below.

	Value of price change for:	
Change in yield	**Positive convexity**	**Negative convexity**
Fall of 100 bps	X%	Lower than Y%
Rise of 100 bps	Lower than X%	Y%

Table 7.3 Price/yield relationship

The price/yield relationship for a callable bond exhibits negative convexity as interest rates fall. Option-adjusted spread analysis is used to highlight this relationship for changes in rates. This is done by effecting a parallel shift in the benchmark yield curve, holding the spread level constant and then calculating the theoretical price along the nodes of the binomial price tree. The average present value then becomes the projected price for the bond. General results for a hypothetical callable bond, compared to a conventional bond, are shown at Figure 7.11. In our example, once the market rate falls below the 10% level, the bond exhibits negative convexity. This is because it then becomes callable at that point, which acts as an effective cap on the price of the bond.

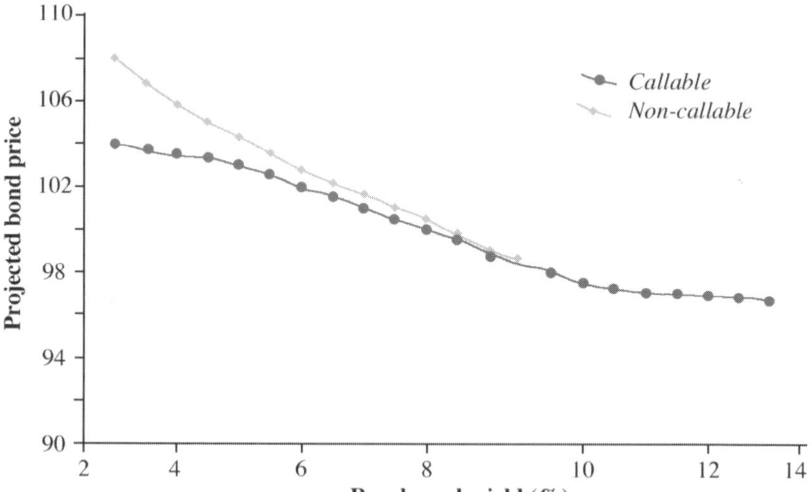

Figure 7.11 Projected prices for callable and conventional bonds with identical coupon and final maturity dates

The market analyses bonds with embedded options in terms of a yield spread, with a "cheap" bond trading at a higher yield spread and a "dear" bond trading at a lower yield spread. The usual convention is to quote yield spreads as the difference between the redemption yield of the bond being analysed and the equivalent maturity government bond. This is not accurate because the redemption yield is in effect a meaningless number – there is not a single rate at which all the cash flows comprising either bond should be discounted, but a set of spot or forward rates that are used for each successive interest period. The correct procedure for discounting therefore is to determine the yield spread over the spot or forward rate curve. With regard to the binomial tree, what we require is the constant spread that, when added to all the short-rates on the binomial tree, makes the theoretical (model-derived) price equal to the observed market price. The constant spread that satisfies this requirement is known as the *option-adjusted spread* (OAS). The spread is referred to as an "option-adjusted" spread because it reflects the option feature attached to the bond. The OAS will depend on the volatility level assumed in running the model. For any given bond price, the higher the volatility level specified, the lower will be the OAS for a callable bond, and the higher for a put-able bond. Since the OAS is calculated usually relative to a government spot or forward rate curve, it reflects the credit risk and any liquidity premium between the corporate bond and the government bond. Note that OAS analysis reflects the valuation model being used, and its accuracy is a reflection of the accuracy of the model itself.

Measuring bond yield spreads

The binomial model evaluates the return of a bond by measuring the extent to which its return exceeds the returns determined by the risk-free short-rates in the tree. The difference between these returns is expressed as a spread and may be considered the *incremental return* of a bond at a specified price. Determining the spread involves the following steps:

- the binomial tree is used to derive a theoretical price for the specified bond;
- the theoretical price is compared with the bond's observed market price;
- if the two prices differ, the rates in the binomial model are adjusted by a user-specified amount, which is the estimate of the spread;
- using the adjusted rates a new theoretical price is derived and compared with the observed price;
- the last two steps are repeated until the theoretical price matches the observed price.

The process can be carried out in a straightforward fashion using a software application.

Price volatility of bonds with embedded options

In Chapter 2 we reviewed traditional duration and modified duration measures for bond interest rate risk. Modified duration is essentially a predictive measure, used to describe the expected percentage change in bond price for a 1% change in yield. The measure is a snap-shot in time, based on the current yield of the bond and the structure of its expected cash flows. In analysing a bond with an embedded option, the bondholder must assume a fixed maturity date, based on the current price of the bond, and calculate modified duration based on this assumed redemption date. However, under circumstances where it is not exactly certain what the final maturity is, modified duration may be calculated to the first call date and to the final maturity date. This would be of little use to bondholders in these circumstances, since it may be unclear which measure is appropriate. The problem is more acute for bonds that are continuously callable (or put-able) from the first call date up to maturity.

Effective duration

To recap from Chapter 2, the duration for any bond is calculated using equation (7.7), which assumes annualised yields.

$$D = \frac{\sum_{t=1}^{n} \frac{tC_t}{(1 + rm)^t}}{P} \tag{7.7}$$

Fabozzi (1997) describes how the measure can be approximated using (7.8):

$$D_{\text{approx}} = \frac{P_{-} - P_{+}}{2P_0(\Delta rm)} \tag{7.8}$$

where

P_0 is the initial price of the bond
P_{-} is the estimated price of the bond if the yield falls by Δrm
P_{+} is the estimated price of the bond if the yield rises by Δrm
Δrm is the change in the yield of the bond.

The drawbacks of the traditional measure are overcome to a certain extent when OAS analysis is used to measure the *effective duration* of a bond. Whereas traditional duration seeks to predict a bond's price changes based on a given price and assumed redemption date, effective duration is solved from actual price changes that result from specified shifts in interest rates. Applying the analysis to a bond with an embedded option means that the new prices resulting from yield changes reflect changes in the cash flow. Effective duration may be thought of as a duration measure which recognises that yield changes may change the future cash flow of the bond. For bonds with embedded options the difference between traditional duration and effective duration can be significant; for example, for a callable bond the effective duration is sometimes half that of its traditional duration measure. For mortgage-backed securities the difference is sometimes greater still.

To calculate effective duration using the binomial model and (7.8) we employ the following procedure:

- calculate the OAS spread for the bond;
- change the benchmark yield through a downward parallel shift;
- construct an adjusted binomial tree using the new yield curve;
- add the OAS adjustment to the short-rates at each of the node points in the tree;
- use the modified binomial tree constructed above to calculate the new value of the bond, which then becomes P_+ for use in equation (7.8).

To determine the lower price resulting from a rise in yields we follow the same procedure but effect an upward parallel shift in the yield curve.

Effective duration for bonds that contain an embedded option is often referred to as *option-adjusted spread duration*. There are two advantages associated with using this measure. These are that, by incorporating the binomial tree into the analysis, the interest rate dependent nature of the cash flows is taken into account. This is done by holding the bond's OAS constant over the specified interest rate shifts, in effect maintaining the credit spread demanded by the market at a constant level. This takes into account the behaviour of the embedded option as interest rates change. The second, and possibly more significant advantage, is that OAS duration is calculated based on a parallel shift in the benchmark yield curve, which gives us an indication of the change in bond price with respect to changes in market interest rates rather than with respect to changes in its own yield.

The derivation of the expression for option-adjusted modified duration is given in Appendix 7.2.

Effective convexity

In the same way that we calculate an effective duration measure for bonds with embedded options, the standard measure of bond convexity we reviewed in Chapter 2 may well be inappropriate for such bonds, for the same reason that the measure does not take into account the impact of a change in market interest rates on a bond's future cash flows. The convexity measure for any bond may be approximated using (7.9), described in Fabozzi (1997).

$$CV = \frac{P_+ + P_- - 2P_0}{P_0(\Delta rm)^2} \tag{7.9}$$

If prices input to (7.9) are those assuming that remaining cash flows for the bond do not change when market rates change, the convexity value is that for an option-free bond. To calculate a more meaningful value for bonds with embedded options, the prices used in the equation are derived by changing the cash flows when interest rates change, based on the results obtained from the binomial model. This measure is called *effective convexity* or *option-adjusted convexity*. The derivation of this measure is given in Appendix 7.3.

Sinking funds

In some markets corporate bond issuers set up *sinking fund* provisions. They are more widely used in the US corporate market. For example, consider the following hypothetical bond issue:

Issuer	ABC plc
Issue date	1-Dec-99
Maturity date	1-Dec-19
Nominal	£100 million
Coupon	8%
Sinking fund provision	£5 million 1 December, 2009 to 2018

Table 7.4 Hypothetical bond issue

In the example of the ABC plc 8% 2019 bond, a proportion of the principal is paid out over a period of time. This is the formal provision. In practice the actual payments made may differ from the formal requirements.

A sinking fund allows the bond issuer to redeem the nominal amount using one of two methods. The issuer may purchase the stipulated amount in the open market, and then deliver these bonds to the trustee[3] for cancellation. Alternatively, the issuer may call the required amount of the bonds at par. This is in effect a *partial call*, similar to a callable bond for which only a fraction of the issue may be called. Generally, the actual bonds called are selected randomly by certificate serial numbers. Readers will have noticed however that the second method by which a portion of the issue is redeemed is actually a call option, which carries value for the issuer. Therefore the method by which the issuer chooses to fulfil its sinking fund requirement is a function of the level of interest rates. If interest rates have risen since the bond was issued, so that the price of the bond has fallen, the issuer will meet its sinking fund obligation by direct purchase in the open market. However, if interest rates have fallen, the issuing company will call the specified amount of bonds at par. In the hypothetical example given in Table 7.4, in effect ABC plc has ten options embedded in the bond, each relating to £5 million nominal of the bonds. Each option has a different maturity, so the first expires on 1 December 2009 and subsequent options mature on 1 December each following year until 2018.[4] The decision to exercise the options as they fall due is made using the same binomial tree method that we discussed earlier.

[3] Bond issuers appoint a trustee that is responsible for looking after the interests of bondholders during the life of the issue. In some cases the trustee is appointed by the underwriting investment bank or the issuer's solicitors. Specialised arms of commercial and investment banks carry out the trustee function; for example, JPMorgan Chase Bank, Deutsche Bank, Bank of New York, Citibank and others.

[4] The "options" are European options, in that they can only be exercised on the expiry date.

Appendices

APPENDIX 7.1 An illustration of the binomial process

In general we observe that bonds which contain embedded options trade in the market with the option element possessing little or no *intrinsic* value. If a callable bond is not immediately exercisable, by definition the option has no intrinsic value. This will hold regardless of the difference between the option exercise price and the price of the underlying bond. Since the embedded options in most callable and put-able bonds have no intrinsic value, the value that is attached to them is composed entirely of *time* value. It is important to measure this time value when analysing option-embedded bonds. There are several valuation methodologies that are used in the market to facilitate this. Whatever the model that is used, the objective is to derive a price distribution of the underlying security at a future date. This enables the analyst to measure the future intrinsic value and then calculate its present value today, which enables her to determine if the option will be exercised at that future date.

The binomial model is a commonly encountered valuation model. This is best illustrated using the example of tossing a coin, where the probabilities of the two expected outcome is from tossing it are precisely equal. To illustrate the principles involved, assume a coin-toss process whereby an outcome of "heads" results in a payout of £20, while an outcome of "tails" results in a payout of £0. There is an equal probability of achieving heads or tails for every coin toss. On a single toss of the coin, the only possible outcome is a payout of £20 or £0. Over a large number of coin tosses we would expect the outcome to be heads 50% of the time and tails 50% of the time. In general, the expected payoff of one toss is calculated by weighting the payoff associated with each possible outcome by the probability that the outcome will occur. This is expressed as (7.10):

$$E(w) = \sum_{i=1}^{n}(w_i \times p(i)) \tag{7.10}$$

where

$E(w)$ is the expected payoff from one coin toss
w_i is the payout received from an outcome i
p_i is the probability that an outcome i will occur
n is the number of possible different outcomes
i is 1, 2, 3, ... m.

In our case of a £20 gain from achieving a "heads" the expected payoff from one toss of a coin would therefore be calculated as follows:

$$= (w1 \times p(1)) + (w_2 \times p(2)) = ((20) \times (50\%)) + ((0) \times (50\%))$$
$$= £10.$$

Note that the expected outcome is £10, despite the fact that the only outcome from a single toss of the coin is £20 or £0. The way to interpret the result is that the payoff from a large number of tosses is an average of £10 per toss. In other words, the payoff from n coin tosses is n multiplied by the expected payoff from one coin toss. This is expressed formally as (7.11):

$$E(nw) = nE(w). \tag{7.11}$$

From (7.11) we would calculate that the expected payoff from 10 coin tosses would be £100.

As our hypothetical process has an expected payoff of £10 per coin toss, it is described as having value. To quantify the extent of this value, consider the following situation, where we are given the following choice:

- paying today for 10 tosses of the coin, to take place one year from today;
- buying today a *risk-free* one-year T-bill with a nominal value of £100, at a price of £95.18.

The payoff from 10 tosses of the coin is not certain. Although the highest probability outcome is a payoff of £100, it is of course possible to receive considerably more or less than this. This is because there is a probability that the outcome is more or less than five "heads". The outcome in the second case is certain: the T-bill will pay out £100 on maturity. The difference between these two choices is that the coin toss outcome has an element of risk, whereas there is no risk associated with the T-bill.

The gain achieved from purchasing the T-bill is the difference between the redemption amount and the current price, which is £4.82. This gain is risk-free, in that if we pay £95.18 today we will receive £100 in one year's time, a gain of £4.82. This gain is 5.064%, or an approximate bond-equivalent return of 5.00%. This is referred to as the *risk-free rate of return*. Given that this is the risk-free rate of return available to anyone in the market, it is also the minimum return we would accept from investing in the coin-toss, which means that the maximum we would pay for that investment is £95.18. A rational investor would not pay more than this because at that price a risk-free return is available in the shape of the T-bill. Therefore £95.18 represents the maximum present value of the expected outcome of ten coin tosses, as determined by the 5% risk-free rate. A feature of the market is that the present value of an expected future payoff is determined by the risk-free rate of return during the intervening period.

The coin toss illustration is an example of a *binomial* process. In a binomial process each action has only two possible outcomes. A *trinomial* process would have precisely three possible outcomes.

The binomial distribution

If any process meets the following conditions:

- there is a specified discrete number of trials;
- there are only two possible outcomes possible from each trial (for example, heads, tails; or defective, not defective);
- the probability of the outcomes in each trial does not change;
- the trials are independent; that is, the outcome of the previous trial has no bearing on the outcome of the current trial;

then it said to be a binomial distribution. Under these conditions we may use the binomial formula to calculate directly the probabilities of any process. The formula is given in (7.12):

$$p(r) = {}^{n}C_{r}\, p(r) q^{(n-r)} \tag{7.12}$$

where

${}^{n}C_{r}$ is the term for determining the number of different ways an event can occur

p is the probability of the outcome from the trial under investigation

q is $(1 - p)$, the probability of the specified outcome from the trial not occurring

n is the number of trials

r is the specified number of outcomes.

The term ${}^{n}C_{r}$ is calculated as follows:

$${}^{n}C_{r} = \frac{n!}{r!(n-r)!}$$

where ! is a factorial.

It is not always necessary to make the calculation of the probability directly as binomial tables exist; however, the tables typically show only the probabilities for certain combinations of n and p. Binomial tables are contained in standard statistics textbooks and are not reproduced here.

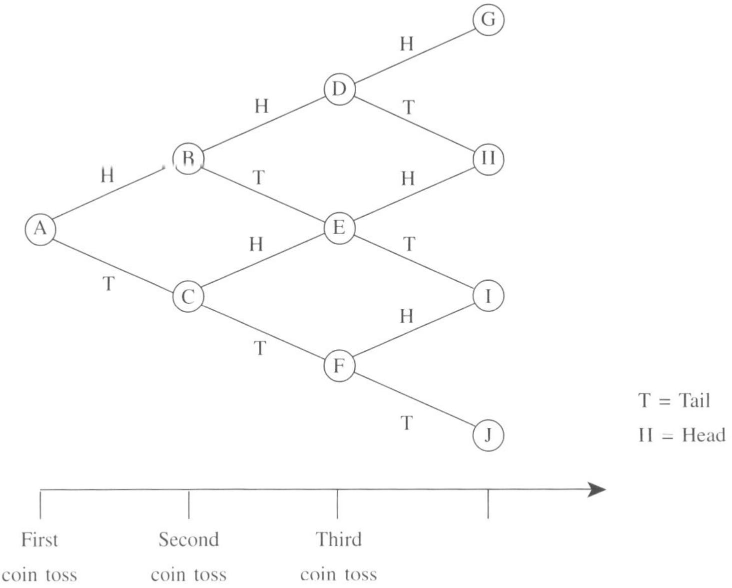

Figure A7.1 Binomial tree of outcome of tossing a coin three times

The binomial tree diagram illustrates the properties of a binomial process. These properties form the basis for the model used to evaluate options embedded in bonds. It is usually referred to as the *binomial tree of interest rates* and is demonstrated in this chapter.

APPENDIX 7.2 Deriving the modified duration expression for a bond with an embedded option

Consider a callable bond, the price of which may be expressed as (7.13):

$$P_{cbond} = P_{underlying} - P_{call}. \tag{7.13}$$

Differentiating (7.13) with respect to the bond yield *rm* we obtain (7.14):

$$\frac{dP_{cbond}}{drm} = \frac{dP_{underlying}}{drm} - \frac{dP_{call}}{drm}. \tag{7.14}$$

Dividing both sides of (7.14) by the price of the callable bond results in (7.15):

$$\frac{dP_{cbond}}{drm}\frac{1}{P_{cbond}} = \frac{dP_{underlying}}{drm}\frac{1}{P_{cbond}} - \frac{dP_{call}}{drm}\frac{1}{P_{cbond}}. \tag{7.15}$$

We then multiply the numerator and denominator of the right-hand side of (7.15) by the price of the underlying bond, shown as (7.16):

$$\frac{dP_{cbond}}{drm}\frac{1}{P_{cbond}} = \frac{dP_{underlying}}{drm}\frac{1}{P_{underlying}}\frac{P_{underlying}}{P_{cbond}} - \frac{dP_{call}}{drm}\frac{1}{P_{underlying}}\frac{P_{underlying}}{P_{cbond}}. \tag{7.16}$$

The components of (7.16) measure duration and modified duration of the underlying and callable bond, as shown by (7.17) and (7.18):

$$\frac{dP_{cbond}}{drm}\frac{1}{P_{cbond}} = -MD_{cbond} \tag{7.17}$$

$$\frac{dP_{underlying}}{drm}\frac{1}{P_{underlying}} = D_{underlying}. \tag{7.18}$$

This relationship is demonstrated in Chapter 7 of the author's book *The Bond and Money Markets*. We omit the negative sign in (7.17) as it does not have any impact on how the option-adjusted duration is derived.

Therefore we may state that:

$$MD_{cbond} = D_{underlying}\frac{P_{underlying}}{P_{cbond}} - \frac{dP_{call}}{drm}\frac{1}{P_{underlying}}\frac{P_{underlying}}{P_{cbond}}. \tag{7.19}$$

The change in the value of the embedded call for a change in yield is expressed by (7.20).

$$\frac{dP_{call}}{drm}. \tag{7.20}$$

Any change in the value of the embedded call is dependent on the change in the price of the underlying bond for a specified yield change. This may be expressed as (7.21):

$$P_{call} = fn\ (P_{underlying}) \tag{7.21}$$

$$P_{underlying} = g\ (rm).$$

By applying calculus, equation (7.20) may be expressed as (7.22):

$$\frac{dP_{call}}{drm} = \frac{dP_{call}}{dP_{underlying}} \frac{dP_{underlying}}{drm} \tag{7.22}$$

The change in the value of the embedded call resulting from a change in price of the underlying is contained in the first term of the right-hand side of (7.22). This is the definition of the *Delta* of an option. Therefore we may state the following:

$$\frac{dP_{call}}{drm} = \text{Delta} \times \frac{dP_{underlying}}{drm}. \tag{7.23}$$

Equation (7.23) may be used to obtain the expression for the call-adjusted duration of a callable bond; by substituting it into (7.19) and rearranging it we obtain (7.24), which is the duration of a callable bond, adjusted for the call feature.

$$MD_{cbond} = D_{underlying} \times \frac{P_{underlying}}{P_{cbond}} \times (1 - \text{Delta}). \tag{7.24}$$

APPENDIX 7.3 Option-adjusted convexity measure

This derivation is undertaken again for a callable bond, broken down as shown by (7.13). The convexity measure is the second derivative of the price/yield function, obtained by multiplying the second derivative by the reciprocal of the price of the bond at that point. Equation (7.14) above is the first derivative of the price of a callable bond. Applying calculus allows us to express (7.14) as (7.25):

$$\frac{dP_{cbond}}{drm} = \frac{dP_{underlying}}{drm} - \frac{dP_{call}}{dP_{underlying}} \frac{dP_{underlying}}{drm}. \tag{7.25}$$

The second derivative of this expression is (7.26):

$$\frac{d^2P_{cbond}}{drm^2} = \frac{d^2P_{underlying}}{drm^2} - \left[\frac{d^2P_{call}}{dP^2_{underlying}}\left(\frac{dP_{underlying}}{drm}\right) + \frac{dP_{call}}{dP_{underlying}} \frac{d^2P_{underlying}}{drm^2}\right] \tag{7.26}$$

The right-hand side of (7.26) contains the terms for establishing the value of the first and second derivatives. The first term on the right-hand side is the second derivative of the price of the underlying bond with respect to change in yield. Multiplying this term by the price of the underlying bond results in (7.27):

$$\frac{d^2P_{underlying}}{drm^2} \times \frac{P_{underlying}}{P_{underlying}}. \tag{7.27}$$

The expression at (7.27) is in fact simply the convexity of the underlying bond multiplied by its price, which we can express as (7.28):

$$CV_{underlying} \times P_{underlying}. \tag{7.28}$$

Consider next the term below:

$$\frac{d^2P_{underlying}}{dP^2_{underlying}}\left[\frac{dP_{underlying}}{drm}\right].$$

The first term is the expression for the rate of change of the delta of the call option component with respect to the change in the price of the underlying. This is in fact the definition of the *gamma* of an option, so that we may write:

$$\text{Gamma} \times \left[\frac{dP_{underlying}}{drm}\right]$$

which may also be expressed as:

$$\text{Gamma} \times \left[\frac{dP_{underlying}}{drm}\right] \times \frac{P^2_{underlying}}{P^2_{underlying}}.$$

This is equivalent to (7.29):

$$\text{Gamma} \times (D_{underlying})^2 \times P^2_{underlying}. \tag{7.29}$$

We may also set the second derivative of the price of the underlying bond in the following terms:

$$\text{Delta} \times CV_{underlying} \times P_{underlying}. \tag{7.30}$$

Substituting (7.28), (7.29) and (7.30) into (7.25) results in (7.31):

$$\frac{d^2P_{cbond}}{drm^2} = CV_{underlying} \times P_{underlying}$$
$$- (\text{Gamma} \times (D_{underlying})^2 \times \text{P}^2_{underlying} + \text{Delta} \times CV_{underlying} \times P_{underlying}). \tag{7.31}$$

If we multiply the right-hand side of (7.30) by the reciprocal of the price of the callable bond, and then rearrange the terms for the convexity, we obtain the expression for the option-adjusted convexity of a callable bond, shown as (7.32):

$$CV_{cbond}$$

$$= \frac{P_{underlying}}{P_{cbond}} [CV_{underlying} \times (1 - \text{Delta}) - \text{P}_{underlying} \times \text{Gamma } (D_{underlying})^2] \; . \tag{7.32}$$

Figure A7.2 below shows the Bloomberg page YAS for the France Telecom 1.6% 2009 bond, an EUR-denominated bond issued in 2005. We see that its convexity value is 0.14, compared to the OAS convexity of its nearest hedge bond, which is 0.15. The bond's conversion terms are shown at Figure A7.3, which is Bloomberg screen YA. Calculation date is 19 August 2005.

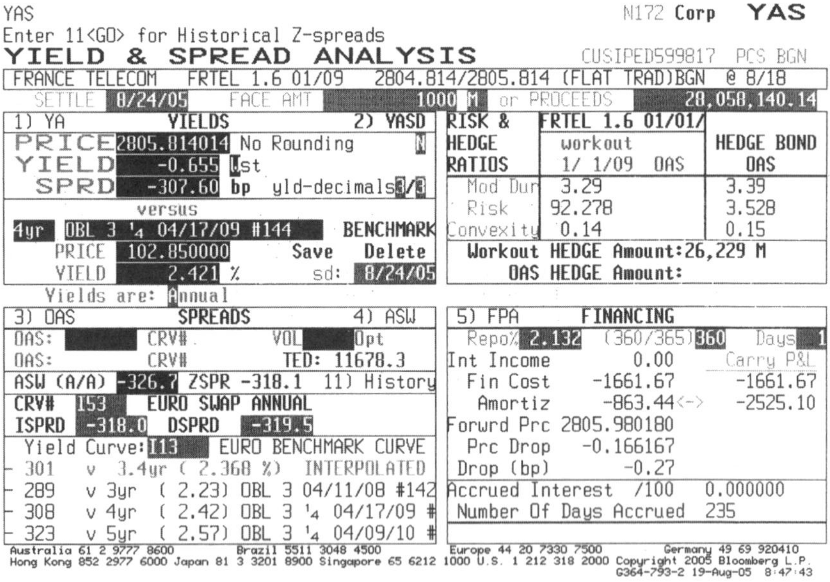

Figure A7.2 Bloomberg page YAS
© Bloomberg L.P. Used with permission.

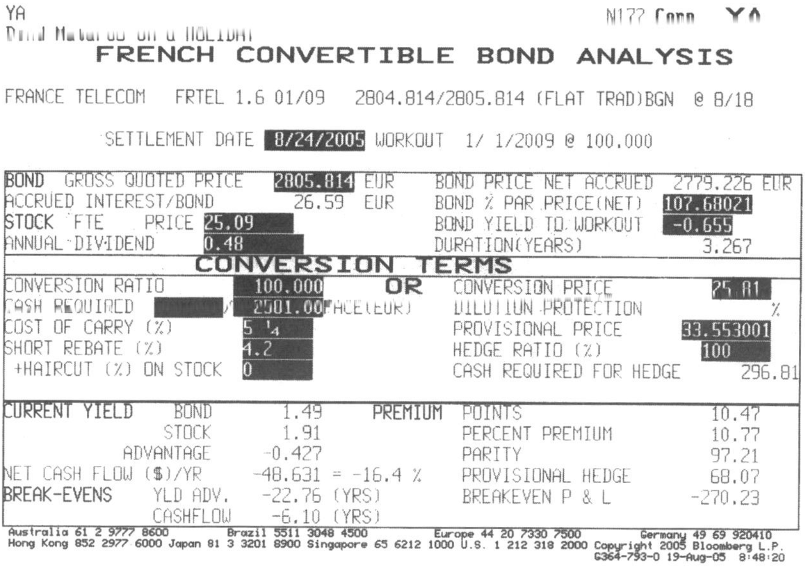

Figure A7.3 Bloomberg page YA

Selected bibliography and references

Bodie, Z. and Taggart, R. 1978, "Future investment opportunities and the value of the call provision on a bond", *Journal of Finance*, 33, pp. 1187–2000.

Fabozzi, F.J. 1997, *Fixed Income Mathematics: Analytical and Statistical Techniques*, 3rd edition, McGraw-Hill, New York, Chapter 16.

Kalotay, A., Williams, G.O. and Fabozzi, F.J. 1993, "A model for the valuation of bonds and embedded options", *Financial Analysts Journal*, May–June, pp. 35–46.

Kish, R. and Livingstone, M. 1992, "The determinants of the call feature on corporate bonds", *Journal of Banking and Finance*, 16, pp. 687–703.

Mitchell, K. 1991, "The call, sinking fund, and term-to-maturity features of corporate bonds: An empirical investigation", *Journal of Financial and Quantitative Analysis*, 26, June, pp. 201–22.

Narayanan, M.P. and Lim, S.P. 1989, "On the call provision on corporate zero-coupon bonds", *Journal of Financial and Quantitative Analysis*, 24, March, pp. 91–103.

Tuckman, B. 1996, *Fixed Income Securities*, John Wiley & Sons, New Jersey, Chapter 17.

Van Horne, J.C. 1986, *Financial Management and Policy*, Prentice Hall, New Jersey.

Windas, T. 1994, *An Introduction to Option-adjusted Spread Analysis*, Bloomberg Publications, Princeton.

This isn't the most original of industries. Hedge funds all go long the 10-year and short the two-year at the same time. Everyone buys and hedges theoretically cheap convertibles, and everyone will get out of them together, no doubt. And who isn't trying to hire someone who can do capital structure arbitrage?

– Professor Emanuel Derman
"For our eyes only?", *RISK*, August 2004

CHAPTER 8

Convertible Bonds I

A *convertible* bond is a corporate financing security that gives the bondholder the right, without imposing an obligation, to convert the bond into another security under specified conditions, usually the ordinary shares of the issuing company. The decision to convert is solely at the discretion of the bondholder.[1] Once converted into ordinary shares, the shares cannot be exchanged back into bonds. As a result of their structure and option feature, in the market convertibles display the characteristics of both debt and equity instruments, as such they are often referred to as *hybrid* instruments. In addition to convertible bonds, there are also *convertible preferred stock*, which are essentially preference shares that are convertible into ordinary shares, again under terms specified at the time of issue. Convertibles are an important element of corporate finance and have benefited from the development of complex valuation models as applied in the option markets. Due to their hybrid nature, convertibles have presented some issues in their analysis and valuation in the past, but modern techniques have essentially resolved this and issue volumes have been steadily increasing during the 1990s, with volumes usually highest during rising stock markets. The

[1] Although generally a corporate financing instrument, convertibles have also been issued by governments, where the bond is usually convertible into another debt instrument. Certain corporate issues are also convertible into the ordinary shares of another company, these are known as *exchangeable* bonds.

sustained bull-run in global equities markets during the second half of the 1990s, led by Wall Street but also observed in other markets, has also witnessed growth in convertibles volumes. This reflects the fact that issuing a right to share in future equity price growth is most attractive during times of rising markets, and this allows corporates to issue convertibles on favourable terms.

In this chapter we review the basic characteristics of convertible securities, and the advantages and disadvantages of the bonds for both issuers and investors. The following chapter reviews the valuation and analysis of convertible bonds.

Convertible bond issues in 2002 by currency	$bln
US dollars	106
Euros	66
Sterling	18
Other currencies	7

Table 8.1 Convertible bond issuance in 2002
Source: Strata Consulting.

Basic description

Convertible bonds are typically fixed coupon securities that are issued with an option to be converted, at the bondholder's discretion, into the equity of the issuing company under specified terms and conditions. They are usually subordinated securities, and may only be issued by companies with a strong enough credit rating to tap the markets. The view of the market on the performance of the issuing company's shares is also a key factor, because investors are buying into the right to subscribe for the shares at a later date and, if exercised, at a premium on the open market price. For this reason the price of a convertible bond at any time will reflect changes in the price of the underlying ordinary shares; it also reflects changes in interest rates. Convertibles are typically medium- to long-dated instruments, and are usually issued with maturities of ten to twenty years. The coupon on a convertible is always below the level payable on the same issuer's non-convertible bond of the same maturity. The bonds are usually convertible into ordinary shares of the issuing company under a set ration and a specified price.

In addition to the basic fixed coupon convertible there is a range of other instruments available to corporate borrowers. These include the *zero-coupon convertible*, which trades similarly to a zero-coupon vanilla bond and is issued at a deep discount. There is usually a low possibility of conversion with these bonds. A similar instrument to this is the *discount convertible*.

Some convertibles are also callable by the issuer, under pre-specified conditions. These are known as *convertible calls* and remove one of the advantages of the straight convertible – that conversion is at the discretion of the bondholder – because by calling a bond the issuer is able to force conversion, on potentially unfavourable terms. Put able convertible bonds are the opposite of this and allow bondholders to redeem the bond as well as effect conversion at their discretion. The *premium put convertible* may be converted on only one date during its life, compared to the *rolling put convertible*, which may be converted on a series of dates during its life; it is generally issued with a lower coupon than a conventional convertible. The addition of a put feature in a convertible is regarded as an extra inducement for investors, as they offer downside price protection. The *exchangeable* security is a bond that is issued by one company, but is convertible into the shares of another company, usually one in which the issuer holds a substantial interest. The *bond with warrant* is a convertible bond that is issued with an attached warrant, which may be detached and traded separately in the secondary market. Bonds with warrants are issued at a lower coupon than those issued as traditional convertibles. *Step-up convertible* bonds and preference shares are a more recent innovation. These pay a fixed coupon for a specified first part of their life, say the first five years, and then pay a higher coupon until they mature or are converted.

Convertible bonds have a long history in the capital markets, having been issued by utility companies in the United States in the nineteenth century. In 1997 the global convertibles market was estimated at over $360 billion. The United States is the largest issuer of convertibles, and historically the biggest issuers were utility and transport companies. Unlike domestic and international securities, the market is essentially an exchange-traded one, with bonds listed on an exchange such as the New York Stock Exchange or the London Stock Exchange. This provides an added advantage in that the instruments may be more liquid than OTC market domestic bonds, and are also more transparent. However, liquidity is also a function of the number of market-makers in the stock and the amount of an issue available for trading, so that some convertibles will be more illiquid than conventional bonds.

Terms and conditions

Consider a standard convertible bond issued by our hypothetical borrower ABC plc. In the example ABC plc has issued a bond that gives the right, but not the obligation, to the bondholder to convert into the underlying shares of ABC plc at a specified price during the next ten years (see Table 8.2).

Issuer	**ABC plc**
Coupon	10%
Maturity	December 2009
Issue size	£50,000,000
Face value	£1,000
Number of bonds	50,000
Issue price	£100
Current price	£103.50
Conversion price	£8.50
Dividend yield	3.50%

Table 8.2 ABC plc 10% convertible 2009

For our hypothetical issue the conversion right or *option* may or may not be taken up at any time during the life of the bond, known as an *American* option, as opposed to a *European* option convertible, which may only be converted on the maturity date of the bond. The majority of convertibles are American-style.

The ratio of exchange between the convertible bond and the ordinary shares can be stated either in terms of a *conversion price* or a *conversion ratio*. Bonds are always issued at a premium, which is the amount by which the conversion price, also known as the *exercise* or *strike* price, lies above the current share price.

The ABC plc bond has a face value of £1,000, and a conversion price of £8.50, which means that each bond is convertible into 117.64 ordinary shares. To obtain this figure we have simply divided the face value of the bond by the conversion price to obtain the conversion ratio, which is £1,000/£8.50 = 117.64 shares. This is also known as the *conversion ratio* and is given by (8.1):

$$\text{Conversion ratio} = \text{Bond denomination/Conversion price.} \qquad (8.1)$$

The terms and conditions under which a convertible is issued, and the terms under which it may be converted into the issuer's ordinary shares are listed in the offer particulars or *prospectus*. The legal obligations of issuers and the rights of bondholders are stated in the *indenture* of the bond.

The conversion privilege can be stated in terms of either the conversion price or the conversion ratio. Conversion terms for a convertible do not necessarily remain constant over time. In certain cases convertible issues will provide for increases or *step-ups* in the conversion price at periodic intervals. A £1,000 denomination face value bond may be issued with a conversion price of, say, £8.50 a share for the first three years, £10 a share for the next three years and £12 for the next five years, and so on. Under this arrangement the bond will convert to fewer ordinary shares over time which, given that the share price is expected to rise during this period, is a logical arrangement. The conversion price is also adjusted for any corporate actions that occur after the convertibles have been issued, such as rights issues or stock dividends. For example, if there was a two-for-one rights issue, the conversion price would be halved. This provision protects the convertible bondholders and is known as an *anti-dilution* clause.

The *parity* or *intrinsic value* of a convertible refers to the value of the underlying equity, expressed as a percentage of the nominal value of the bond. Parity is given by (8.2):

$$\text{Parity} = \text{Share price/Conversion price } \textit{or} \quad \text{Share price/Conversion ratio.} \tag{8.2}$$

The bond itself may be analysed – in the first instance – as a conventional fixed income security, so using its coupon and maturity date we may calculate a current yield (running yield) and YTM. The *yield advantage* is the difference between the current yield and the *dividend yield* of the underlying share, given by (8.3):

$$\text{Yield advantage} = \text{Current yield} - \text{Dividend yield.} \tag{8.3}$$

In this case the current yield of the bond is 9.66%, which results in a yield advantage of 6.16%. Equity investors also use another measure, the *break-even* value, which is given by (8.4):

$$\text{Break-even} = (\text{Bond price} - \text{Parity})/\text{Yield advantage.} \tag{8.4}$$

Investor analysis

The analytical requirements of the market investor are slightly different to those of the market-maker or trader. In this section we consider the former. When evaluating convertible securities the investor must consider the expected performance of the underlying shares, the future prospects of the company itself and the relative attraction of the bond as a pure fixed income instrument in the event that the conversion feature proves to be worthless. In addition, the assessment of the bond will take into account the credit quality of the issuer, the yield give-up suffered as a result of purchasing the convertible over a conventional bond, the conversion premium ratio, and the fixed income advantage gained over a purchase of the underlying shares in the first place.

We have already referred to the conversion ratio, which defines the number of shares of common stock that is received when the bond is converted. The conversion price is the actual price paid for the shares when conversion occurs.

$$\text{Conversion price} = \frac{\text{Par value of bond}}{\text{Conversion ratio}}. \tag{8.5}$$

The *conversion premium* is the percentage by which the conversion price exceeds the current share price. Using our previous illustration for ABC plc, the convertible has a conversion ratio of 117.64 (that is, 117.64 shares are received in return for the bond with a par value of £1,000) and therefore a conversion price of £8.50. If the current price of the share is £6.70, then we have:

$$\begin{aligned}\text{Percentage conversion premium} &= \frac{\text{Conversion price} - \text{Share price}}{\text{Share price}}\\ &= \frac{£\,8.50 - £6.70}{£\,6.70}\\ &= 26.87\%.\end{aligned}$$

The *conversion value* of the bond shows the current value of the shares received in exchange for the bond. It is given by:

$$\text{Conversion value} = \text{Share price} \times \text{Conversion ratio}. \tag{8.6}$$

As the current share price is £6.70, then the current conversion value would be:

Conversion value = £6.70 × £117.64 = £788.19.

Assume that the bond is trading at 103.50 (per 100), then the *percentage conversion price premium*, or the percentage by which the current bond price exceeds the current conversion value, is given by (8.7) below.

$$\text{Percentage conversion price premium} = \frac{\text{Price of bond} - \text{Conversion value}}{\text{Conversion value}} \tag{8.7}$$

In our example the premium value is $\frac{1035 - 788.19}{788.19} = 31.32\%$.

The premium value in a convertible may be illustrated as shown in Figure 8.1. Investors are concerned with the point at which the ratio of the parity of the bond to the investment value moves far above the bond floor. At this point the security trades more like equity than debt. The opposite to this is when the equity price falls to low levels, to the point at which it will need to appreciate by a very large amount before the conversion option has any value; at this point the convertible trades like a pure fixed income instrument. Investors sometimes view a convertible bond price in terms of where it is standing in terms of the premium line in Figure 8.1, and assess its chances of moving into the "hybrid" part of the chart. This analysis has no value however.

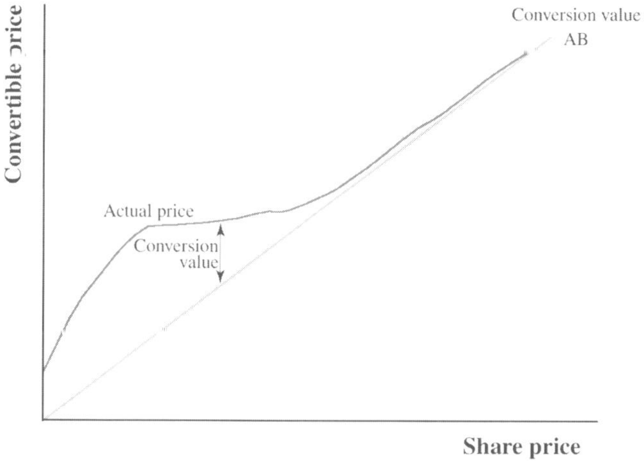

Figure 8.1 Convertible bond and conversion premium

The value of a convertible bond may be broken down and viewed as the sum of the value of two instruments, the straight bond of the issuer and a call option on the issuer's equity. Considering Figure 8.1, the value of the convertible bond minus the conversion feature is represented by the line AB. It is sometimes referred to as the *straight line* value and is the conventional redemption yield measure. As we noted above the value of a convertible if it is converted straight away is the conversion value. Therefore the minimum value of a convertible bond is the higher of its straight line value and conversion value.

As a convertible is viewed as a conventional bond with a warrant attached, its fair price is a combination of the price of a vanilla bond and the price of a call option, notwithstanding the dilution effect of the new shares that are issued and the coupon payments that are saved as a result of conversion.

The proportionate increase in the number of shares outstanding if all the bonds were to be converted, referred to as p, is given by (8.8):

$$p = \frac{\text{Number of convertible bonds} \times \text{Conversion ratio}}{\text{Number of shares outstanding before conversion}}. \tag{8.8}$$

The fair value of a convertible is given by (8.9):

$$\text{Price of convertible} = \text{Price of vanilla bond} + \frac{P_c}{1+p} \times \text{Conversion ratio} \tag{8.9}$$

where P_C is the value of an American call option with an exercise price equal to the conversion price and an expiry date equal to the maturity of the bond. The price of the vanilla bond is calculated in exactly the same way as a standard bond in the same risk class.

Equation (8.9) will give us the fair price of a convertible if the bond is not callable. However, some convertibles are callable at the issuer's option prior to the final maturity date. The issuer can therefore effect conversion when the share price has risen to the point where the value of the shares received on conversion equals the call price of the bond. As the firm has an incentive to call the bond when this occurs, the call price puts an effective ceiling on the price of the convertible given by (8.9).

We can calculate a realistic call date for a callable convertible by using the expression at (8.10):

$$\text{Call price} = \text{Current share price} \times (1+g)^t \times \text{Conversion ratio} \tag{8.10}$$

where g is the expected growth rate in the share price and t is the time in years. Let us then assume that the call price of the hypothetical ABC plc bond is £100 (that is, par per face value of £1,000), the conversion ratio is 117.64, and the current share price is £6.70 and is growing at 8.25% per year. Given that the right-hand side of expression (8.10) is the conversion value of the convertible in t years' time, we can calculate at what point the conversion value will equal the call price.

If we look again at (8.9) and using our assumed terms and values, we can see that the price of the convertible depends on the price of a vanilla bond with identical years to maturity (and a terminal value of £100) and a call option with the same years to expiry. The value of the option component is determined by using equity option models.

The attraction of a convertible for a bondholder lies in its structure being one of a combined vanilla bond and option. As we shall see in our introductory discussion of options, option pricing theory tells us that the value of an option increases with the price variance of the underlying asset. However, bond valuation theory implies that the value of a bond decreases with the price variance of the issuer's shares, because the probability of default is increased. Therefore attaching an option to a bond will act as a kind of hedge against excessive downside price movement, while simultaneously preserving the upside potential if the firm is successful, since the bondholder has the right to convert to equity. Due to this element of downside protection, convertible bonds frequently sell at a premium over both their bond value and conversion value, resulting in the premium over conversion value that we referred to earlier. The conversion feature also leads to convertibles generally trading at a premium over bond value as well; the higher the market price of the ordinary share relative to the conversion price, the greater the resulting premium.

EXAMPLE 8.1 Convertible bond analysis

Consider the following euroconvertible bond currently trading at 104.80.

Denomination:	£1,000
Coupon:	4.50%
Maturity:	15 years
Conversion price:	£25 per share

The issuer's shares are currently trading at £19.50.

- Number of shares into which the bond is convertible:
  Conversion ratio = £1,000/25 = 40

- Parity or conversion value:
  $$\frac{\text{Current share price}}{\text{Conversion price}} \times 100 = 78\%$$

- Effective conversion price:
  $$\frac{\text{Price of convertible}}{\text{Conversion ratio}} = 2.62 \text{ (that is, £26.20 per £1,000)}$$

- Conversion premium:
  $$\frac{\text{(Effective conversion price)} - \text{Current share price)}}{\text{Current share price}} \times 100 = 34.36\%$$

- Conversion premium – alternative formula:
  Convertible price/Parity = 34.36%

- What do the following represent in terms of intrinsic value and time value?
  Parity: parity value reflects the equity value of the bond.
  Premium: the ratio of the bond price divided by parity value; this includes a measure of time value.

Advantages of issuing and holding convertibles

Borrowers' advantages

The main advantage to a borrowing company in issuing convertible bonds is that the cost of the loan will be lower than a straight issue of debt. This is because, as a result of providing an equity option feature with the instrument, the coupon payable is lower than would be the case with a conventional bond. The bondholder accepts a lower coupon as the price for being able to share in the success of the company during the life of the bond, without having the direct exposure to the equity market that a holding in the ordinary shares would entail. The yield spread below which a convertible may be sold varies over time and with the quality of the issuer. Credit rating agencies generally rate convertible issues one grade below the straight debt of the issuer, although this would appear to reflect the price volatility of convertibles more than credit concerns. The second advantage to an issuer is that, under certain circumstances, it may be able to sell ordinary shares at a more favourable price via conversion than through a direct issue in the market. This may occur when, for example, the price of shares in a direct offer is lower because the shares represent investment in a project that is not expected to show returns until a period into the future. The company can issue callable convertibles with an exercise price above the direct market price, and then call the bond at a later date, forcing conversion at the higher price.

A disadvantage of issuing convertibles is where the company experiences a significant rise in its share price; in this case the interest cost may turn out to have been prohibitive and the company would have gained if it had issued shares directly. This however is only known in hindsight. The same occurs if there is a substantial drop in the share price after convertibles have been issued; here there is no incentive for bondholders to convert and the company is left with debt on its balance sheet until maturity, when it might have expected to have converted this to equity capital.

Investors' advantages

The advantages to an investor in holding convertible bonds centres on the ability to participate in the fortunes of the company without having to have a direct equity holding. The bondholder has a fixed coupon income stream, together with the advantages of senior debt (so it ranks above equity but below secured debt). If the underlying share price rises, the value of the convertible will rise as well, reflecting the increase in value of the embedded option, and if the conversion premium disappears the investor is able to realise an instant gain. This is the upside advantage. There is also a downside advantage, because if the price of the underlying share falls, the convertible price will fall only to the point at which it represents fair value for an equivalent conventional fixed interest security. Although the coupon available with a convertible is lower than that available on a conventional vanilla bond, it will be higher than the dividend yield available from holding the share directly. If there is a rise in interest rates, there is further downside protection available in the time value of the embedded option, which may also add a floor to the price. Therefore in theory convertibles offer the downside protection of a debt instrument as well as the upside potential of an equity instrument.

The disadvantages to an investor in holding convertibles mirror the effects of the advantages: the main one is that the investor must accept a lower yield compared to bonds of identical maturity and credit quality. If a convertible is also callable, then this is an additional disadvantage for the investor, as the issuer may force conversion of the bond at its choosing, under potentially unfavourable conditions for the investor. The other disadvantages of holding convertibles are only apparent in hindsight: if the issuer's share price does not appreciate, the investor will have accepted a below-market coupon level for the life of the bond, and possibly a drop in the price of the bond below its issue price.

There are a range of investor classes that may be interested in holding convertibles at one time or another. These include equity fund managers who are currently bearish of the market: purchasing convertibles allows them an element of downside market protection, while still enabling them to gain from upside movements. Equity managers who wish to enhance the income from their portfolios may also be interested in convertibles. For bond fund managers, convertibles provide an opportunity to obtain a limited exposure to the growth potential and upside potential associated with an option on equities.

Figure 8.2 is Bloomberg screen DES for a convertible bond issue in 2005, the France Telecom 1.6% 2009 bond; note that it is convertible until December 2008. The detailed conversion terms are shown at Figure 8.3.

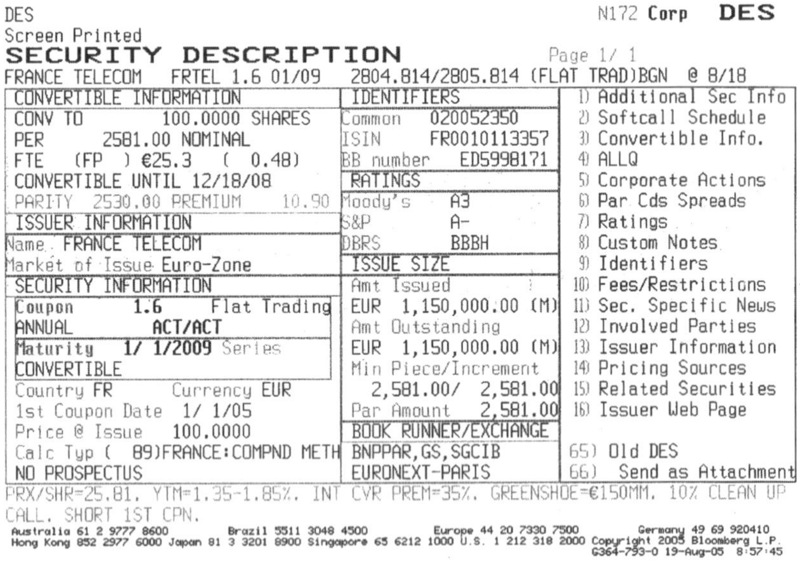
DES N172 Corp DES
Screen Printed
SECURITY DESCRIPTION Page 1/ 1
FRANCE TELECOM FRTEL 1.6 01/09 2804.814/2805.814 (FLAT TRAD)BGN @ 8/18
CONVERTIBLE INFORMATION
CONV TO 100.0000 SHARES
PER 2581.00 NOMINAL
FTE (FP) €25.3 (0.48)
CONVERTIBLE UNTIL 12/18/08
PARITY 2530.00 PREMIUM 10.90
ISSUER INFORMATION
Name FRANCE TELECOM
Market of Issue Euro-Zone
SECURITY INFORMATION
Coupon 1.6 Flat Trading
ANNUAL ACT/ACT
Maturity 1/ 1/2009 Series
CONVERTIBLE
Country FR Currency EUR
1st Coupon Date 1/ 1/05
Price @ Issue 100.0000
Calc Typ (89)FRANCE:COMPND METH
NO PROSPECTUS
IDENTIFIERS
Common 020052350
ISIN FR0010113357
BB number ED5998171
RATINGS
Moody's A3
S&P A-
DBRS BBBH
ISSUE SIZE
Amt Issued
EUR 1,150,000.00 (M)
Amt Outstanding
EUR 1,150,000.00 (M)
Min Piece/Increment
2,581.00/ 2,581.00
Par Amount 2,581.00
BOOK RUNNER/EXCHANGE
BNPPAR,GS,SGCIB
EURONEXT-PARIS
1) Additional Sec Info
2) Softcall Schedule
3) Convertible Info.
4) ALLQ
5) Corporate Actions
6) Par Cds Spreads
7) Ratings
8) Custom Notes
9) Identifiers
10) Fees/Restrictions
11) Sec. Specific News
12) Involved Parties
13) Issuer Information
14) Pricing Sources
15) Related Securities
16) Issuer Web Page
65) Old DES
66) Send as Attachment
PRX/SHR=25.81. YTM=1.35-1.85%. INT CVR PREM=35%. GREENSHOE=€150MM. 10% CLEAN UP CALL. SHORT 1ST CPN.
Australia 61 2 9777 8600 Brazil 5511 3048 4500 Europe 44 20 7330 7500 Germany 49 69 920410
Hong Kong 852 2977 6000 Japan 81 3 3201 8900 Singapore 65 6212 1000 U.S. 1 212 318 2000 Copyright 2005 Bloomberg L.P.
G364-793-0 19-Aug-05 8:57:45

Figure 8.2 Bloomberg Screen DES

© Bloomberg L.P. Used with permission.

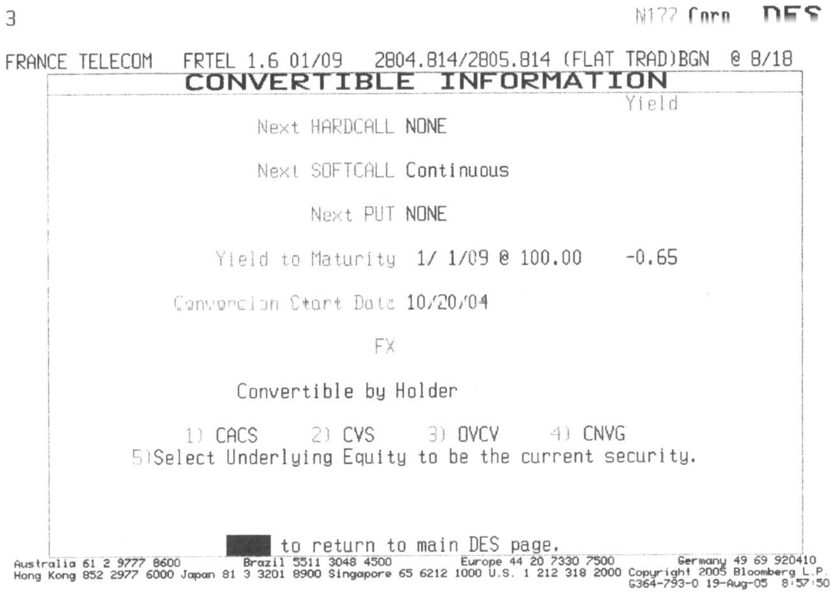

Figure 8.3 Bloomberg Screen conversion terms.
© Bloomberg L.P. Used with permission.

Selected Bibliography and References

Calamos, J. 1998, *Convertible Securities*, McGraw-Hill, New York.
Connolly, K. 1998, *Pricing Convertible Bonds*, John Wiley & Sons, Chichester.
Fabozzi, F. 1991, *Bond Markets, Analysis and Strategies*, Prentice Hall, New York.
Kitter, G. 1999, *Investment Mathematics for Finance and Treasury Professionals*, Chapter 6, John Wiley & Sons, Chichester.

This is the last time
That I will say these words
I remember the first time
The first of many lies
Sweep it into the corner
Or hide it under the bed
Say these things they go away
But they never do

The last time
You fall on me for anything you like

– Keane
"This Is the Last Time", from *Hopes and Fears,*
Universal Island Records, 2004

CHAPTER 9

Convertible Bonds II

In the previous chapter we reviewed convertible bond instruments and the features that differentiated them from conventional fixed interest bonds. In this chapter we consider the pricing and valuation of these securities.

Traditional valuation methodology

Let us consider another hypothetical security issued by ABC plc, a 20-year convertible bond with a coupon of 8%. "One" bond has a nominal amount of £100 and may be converted into 10 ordinary shares of ABC plc. In November 1999 the bond is trading at £102 and the underlying shares at £2.50. In 1999 the company paid a dividend of £0.08 per share, a dividend yield of 3.20%.

If an investor buys just £100 nominal of the convertible, the premium paid over a direct purchase of the ordinary shares is equal to (100 × 102%) – (2.50 × 10) or £77 per bond. The compensation for this premium is the cash flow differential between the convertible and the underlying shares, which is calculated as (£100 × 8%) – (25 × 3.20%) or £7.20. The number 25 above is the parity value for the convertible obtained by multiplying the current share price by the conversion ratio. The annual cash flow differential measure implies that the investor receives £7.20 per annum more income from holding the convertible than would be received in the form of dividends from a holding of ten ordinary shares in the company. This gives us a *payback period* measure of £77/7.20 or 10.694 years. Using the above analysis we may derive the formula at (9.1) as an expression for the payback period for a convertible bond.

$$\text{Payback} = \frac{\dfrac{Premium}{1 + Premium}}{rc - \dfrac{rd}{1 + Premium}} \tag{9.1}$$

where *rc* is the running yield on the convertible bond and *rd* is the dividend yield on the underlying ordinary shares. Note that (9.1) assumes a fixed coupon stream and therefore can only be used for bonds that pay a constant coupon. Bonds that have variable coupon payments, such as step-up convertibles, as well as bonds with no cash flow such as zero-coupon convertibles, cannot be analysed using (9.1). If we input the same parameters to (9.1) we will obtain the same value for the payback period of 10.694 years.

The concept of payback analysis for convertible securities is similar to payback or *break-even* analysis in corporate finance: the length of time after which the initial outlay in a capital project is recouped as a result of investment returns from the project. However, much corporate finance analysis now uses net present value and the concept of the internal rate of return for project appraisal. The assumptions behind the payback period are also restrictive; if we consider (9.1) we see that for the measure to be meaningful it requires a constant dividend yield and a flat yield curve. It also does not discount cash flows and ignores cash flows beyond the payback period. Although it is possible to introduce certain variations into the analysis, for example a (constant) dividend growth rate and the discounting of cash flows, the measurement does not take into account the option element of the convertible and the downside price floor available to investors. The value of a convertible must consider not only its premium over the underlying share price, but also the fact that investors have the right, but not the obligation, to convert their holding and conversion at their discretion. The decision to exercise is closely related to the future level of the issuer's share price, and therefore cannot be predicted. As well as holding a call option on the issuer's ordinary shares, bondholders are also holding in effect a put option, because if the share price falls and makes conversion uneconomic, they will elect to hold the bond to maturity and receive the redemption payment instead. Any fair valuation of a convertible should therefore ideally consider both option features of the bond.

The remainder of this chapter reviews a convertible valuation model that incorporates the likelihood of the option feature being exercised during the life of the bond.

Fair value of a convertible bond

The current analytical approach to convertible bond valuation is to consider the instrument as a conventional vanilla bond and an embedded option(s). That is, the value of a convertible is the sum of its bond value and the value of the embedded option. The bond element is valued using the standard redemption yield method described in Chapter 1. The option element is valued using a binomial option pricing model, which we review in this section. Readers should also be familiar with the capital asset pricing model (CAPM) for valuing equity stocks. This is introduced in Appendix 9.1.

The binomial model

The first option pricing model was developed by Fischer Black and Myron Scholes and was described in the *Journal of Political Economy* in 1973. Another approach, later termed the *binomial model,* was described by Cox, Ross and Rubinstein (1979). Convertible bond analysis, like callable and put-able bonds analysis, frequently uses the binomial model.

The fair price of a convertible bond is the one that provides no opportunity for arbitrage profit; that is, it precludes a trading strategy of running simultaneous but opposite positions in the convertible and the underlying equity in order to realise a profit. There is no need to take a view on the price expectations of the equity to arrive at such a fair price. In this section we consider an application of the binomial model to value a convertible security. Under the conditions of an option pricing model such as Black–Scholes or the binomial model, we assume no dividend payments, no transaction costs and a risk-free interest rate with no bid–offer spreads.

In similar fashion to the description in Chapter 7, application of the binomial model requires the binomial tree detailing the price outcomes from the start period. In the case of a convertible bond this will refer to the prices for the underlying asset, which is the ordinary share of the issuing company. This is shown in Figure 9.1 below.

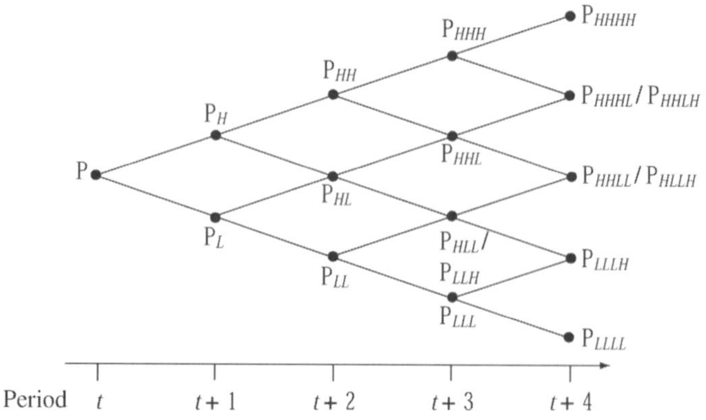

Figure 9.1 Underlying equity price binomial tree

If we accept that the price of the equity follows such a path, we assume that it follows a *multiplicative binomial process*. This is a geometric process which accelerates as the share price increases and decelerates as the share price falls. This assumption is key to the working of the model and has been the subject of some debate. Although it is not completely accurate, by assuming that market returns follow this pattern we are able to model a series of share price returns that in turn enable us to calculate the fair value of an instrument containing an embedded option.

In Figure 9.1 the current price of the underlying share is given as P, in period 1 at time t. In the next period, time $t + 1$, the share price can assume a price of P_H or P_L, with P_H higher than P and P_L lower than P. If the price is P_H in period 2, the price in period 3 can be P_{HH} or P_{HL}, and so on. The tree may be drawn for as many periods as required.

The value of a convertible bond is a function of a number of variables; for the purposes of this analysis we set the different parameters required as shown below.

P_{conv} is the price of the convertible bond
P_{share} is the price of the underlying equity
C is the bond coupon
r is the risk-free interest rate
N is the time to maturity
d is the risk of default
s is the annualised share price volatility

c is the call option feature
p is the put option feature
rd is the dividend yield on the underlying share.

In the first instance we wish to calculate the value of a call option on the underlying shares of a convertible bond. For Figure 9.1 if we state that the probability of a price increase is 50%, this leaves the probability of a price decrease as $1 - p$ or 50%. If we were to construct a portfolio of δ shares, funded by M pounds sterling, which mirrored the final payoff of the call option, we can state that the call option must be equal to the value of the portfolio, to remove any arbitrage possibilities. To solve this we set the following constraints:

$$\delta P_H + rM = P_H - X \tag{9.2}$$

$$\delta P_L + rM = 0 \tag{9.3}$$

where X is the strike price of the option. If we say that the exercise price is 100, then it will be higher than P_L and lower than P_H. This is illustrated by Figure 9.2.

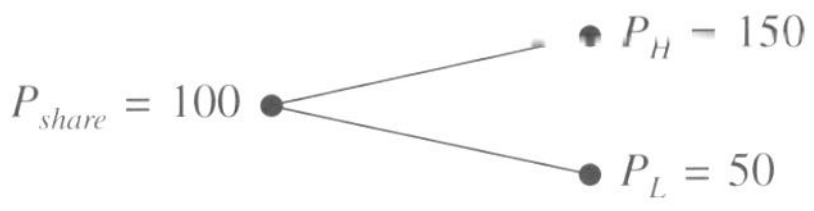

Figure 9.2 Binomial price outcome for a call option

From equation (9.3) we set:

$$rM = -\delta P_L \tag{9.4}$$

$$M = \frac{-(\delta P_L)}{r}. \tag{9.5}$$

Substituting (9.5) into (9.2) gives us:

$$\delta P_H - \delta P_L = P_H - X$$

$$\delta = \frac{P_H - X}{P(H - L)}. \tag{9.6}$$

The number of shares that would be held in the portfolio is δ, which is known as the *delta* or *hedge ratio*.

We use the relationships above to solve for the value of the borrowing component M, by substituting (9.6) into (9.3), giving us:

$\frac{P_H - X}{P(H - L)} \times PL + rM = 0$, and rearranging for M we obtain:

$$M = \frac{-L(P_H - X)}{r(H - L)} . \tag{9.7}$$

Given the relationships above, then we may set the fair value of a call option as (9.8):

$$c = \delta P + r. \tag{9.8}$$

Following Black–Scholes, an estimate of the extent of the increase and decrease in prices from period 1 is given by:

$$H = e^{r+s} \tag{9.9}$$

$$L = e^{r-s} \tag{9.10}$$

where r is the risk-free interest rate and s is the volatility of the share price at each time period.

We are now in a position to apply this analysis to a convertible security. Table 9.1 sets the terms and parameters for an hypothetical convertible bond and underlying share price.

Equity price	100
Conversion price	100
Coupon	5% s/a
Time to maturity	5 years
Volatility	10%
r	4%
"H"	1.095138
"L"	0.950716

Table 9.1 Convertible bond terms

Using the parameters above we may calculate the value of the underlying equity, which is priced at 100 in period 1. The volatility is assumed constant at 10%, and the maturity of the bond is five years or 1,825 days. The price is calculated over ten periods, with each period equal to a half-year or 180 days. The risk-free interest rate is 4%; however, this must be continuously compounded, which is calculated as follows:

$$r = ln(1.04) = 0.039220$$

and over one time period or 180 days this is 0.02017 or 2.017%. This is therefore the risk-free interest rate. The volatility level of 10% is an annualised figure, following market convention. This may be broken down per time period as well, and this is calculated by multiplying the annual figure by the square root of the time period required. This is shown below:

$$s \times \sqrt{t/N} = 0.10 \times \sqrt{0.5} = 0.07071.$$

This allows the calculation of H and L which are given below:

$$H = e^{0.012518+0.1424} = 1.095138$$
$$L = e^{0.012518-0.1424} = 0.950716.$$

Using these parameters the price tree for the underlying equity, from time periods t to $t + 10$ under the assumptions given, is shown at Table 9.2, with $t + 10$ representing the last period five years from now.

Period	0	1	2	3	4	5	6	7	8	9	10
0	100.00	114.89	124.51	144.08	179.06	205.12	235.69	269.07	294.45	341.25	398.74
1		89.02	100.05	115.94	125.86	155.86	174.60	189.98	245.49	276.48	315.68
2			79.32	88.05	101.04	118.59	136.98	154.87	181.46	207.63	237.87
3				70.14	81.13	90.89	103.74	120.46	138.37	168.74	192.58
4					57.43	67.63	79.03	90.65	103.58	128.41	142.35
5						49.06	56.90	69.05	84.14	94.18	106.41
6							40.14	50.05	61.29	74.85	83.34
7								35.89	45.20	55.04	67.32
8									31.24	42.03	51.26
9										27.67	33.49
10											22.07

Table 9.2 Underlying share price tree

The valuation now proceeds to the conventional bond element of the convertible. The bond has a coupon of 5.0% payable semi-annually and a maturity of five years. We assume a "credit spread" of 200 basis points above the risk-free interest rate, so a discount rate of 6.00% is used as the market rate required to value the bond. This credit spread is a subjective measure based on the perceived credit risk of the bond issuer. On maturity the bond must be priced at par or 100, while the final coupon is worth 2.50. Therefore the value of the bond on maturity in the final period (at $t + 10$) must be 102.50. This is shown in Table 9.3. The value of the bond at earlier nodes along the binomial tree is then calculated using straightforward discounting, using the 6% discount rate. For example, at $t + 9$ the valuation is obtained by taking the maturity value of 102.5 and discounting at the credit-adjusted interest rate, as shown below:

$$P = (102.5/1.03) + 2.5 = 102.01.$$

This process is continued all the way to time t.

Period	**0**	**1**	**2**	**3**	**4**	**5**	**6**	**7**	**8**	**9**	**10**
0	98.23	98.60	98.98	99.38	99.79	100.21	100.64	101.08	101.54	102.01	102.50
1		98.60	98.98	99.38	99.79	100.21	100.64	101.08	101.54	102.01	102.50
2			98.98	99.38	99.79	100.21	100.64	101.08	101.54	102.01	102.50
3				99.38	99.79	100.21	100.64	101.08	101.54	102.01	102.50
4					99.79	100.21	100.64	101.08	101.54	102.01	102.50
5						100.21	100.64	101.08	101.54	102.01	102.50
6							100.64	101.08	101.54	102.01	102.50
7								101.08	101.54	102.01	102.50
8									101.54	102.01	102.50
9										102.01	102.50
10											102.50

Table 9.3 Conventional bond price tree

We may take the analysis further for a conventional convertible bond plus embedded option. Table 9.4 shows the price tree for the conventional bond where the share price and conversion price is equal to 100 in the current time period. If we assume the share price in period $t + 9$ is 94.18, then in period $t + 10$ the share can assume only one of two possible values,

106.41 or 83.34 (see Table 9.2). In these cases the value of the call option c_H and c_l will be equal to the higher of the bond's conversion value or its redemption value, which is 106.41 if there is a rise in the price of the underlying or 102.50 if there is a fall in the price of the underlying. These are the range of possible final values for the bond; however, we require the current (present) value, which must be discounted at the appropriate rate. To determine the correct rate to use, consider the corresponding price of the conventional bond when the share price is 27.67 at period $t + 9$. The price of the bond is calculated on the basis that on maturity the bond will be redeemed irrespective of what happens to the share price. Therefore the appropriate interest rate to use when discounting a conventional bond is the credit-adjusted rate, as this is a corporate bond carrying credit risk. However, this does not apply at a different share price; consider the corresponding conventional bond price when the underlying share price is 341.25, in the same time period. The hedge ratio at this point on the binomial price tree is calculated using:

$$\delta = \frac{(c_H - c_L)}{P(H - L)} - 1.$$

The position of a bondholder at this point is essentially long of the underlying stock and also receiving a coupon. A position equivalent to a risk-free bond may be put on synthetically by holding the convertible bond and selling short one unit of the underlying equity. In the event of default the position is hedged, therefore in this case the correct discount rate to use is the risk-free interest rate. The correct rate to use is dependent on the price of the underlying share and how this affects the behaviour of the convertible, and will be either the risk-free rate or a credit-adjusted rate. The adjusted rate can be obtained using (9.11) and indeed all the convertible prices at period $t + 9$ are obtained using (9.11). The process is then carried out "backwards" to complete the entire price tree. At period t with the share price at 100, then the fair value of the convertible is seen to be 113.91.

$$r_{adjusted} = \delta \times r + (1 - \delta) \times \text{Credit adjustment} \qquad (9.11)$$

Period	0	1	2	3	4	5	6	7	8	9	10
0	113.91	120.21	134.70	158.87	188.08	207.34	237.69	270.61	295.12	341.25	398.74
1		106.32	108.73	126.95	135.73	159.09	178.05	190.65	246.67	276.48	315.68
2			104.50	107.12	118.40	125.40	142.28	155.87	182.43	207.63	237.87
3				102.47	105.39	112.58	118.79	122.86	138.98	168.74	192.58
4					101.05	103.41	106.08	108.43	112.79	128.41	142.35
5						100.21	102.76	103.36	103.08	106.07	106.41
6							100.64	101.98	101.75	102.01	102.50
7								101.08	101.54	102.01	102.50
8									101.54	102.01	102.50
9										102.01	102.50
10											102.50

Table 9.4 Convertible bond price tree

Analysis for call and put features

Convertible bonds are sometimes issued with call and/or put provisions embedded within them. Such features may be analysed using the same binomial tree as was used for valuing the straight convertible bond. Using the same hypothetical bond considered in the previous section, assume now that the bond additionally is callable at set dates, as specified below.

Call provision	
Year 2	115
Year 3	110
Year 4	105
Year 5	100

As specified above, the bond is not callable for the first two years after issue, after which it is callable at specified prices on each anniversary of issue until maturity. The call feature is academic after year 4 because the bond is redeemable at par on the maturity date in any case. As part of the analysis we assume that the issuer will act in its interests, and will call the bond if there is material advantage to be gained from so doing. This then enables us to introduce the call feature into the binomial tree.

The issuer will effect *forced conversion* at nodes on the binomial tree (that occur on bond issue anniversary dates from year 2) where the share price or parity value is greater than the exercise price. It is worthwhile for the issuer to call the bond in such cases because the option is worth more "alive" than "dead". We may consider forced conversion using the price tree in Table 9.5.

Period	0	1	2	3	4	5	6	7	8	9	10
0	109.34	118.69	130.46	158.87	187.98	206.34	236.89	268.56	294.45	341.25	398.74
1		102.35	110.60	125.95	134.63	158.67	177.27	190.07	245.49	276.48	315.68
2			102.80	105.68	117.64	123.85	141.08	155.28	181.46	207.63	237.87
3				100.76	105.56	108.55	115.75	121.05	138.37	168.74	192.58
4					102.57	101.21	103.45	105.43	103.58	128.41	142.35
5						100.21	100.91	102.06	103.08	106.07	106.41
6							100.64	101.98	101.75	102.01	102.50
7								101.08	101.54	102.01	102.50
8									101.54	102.01	102.50
9										102.01	102.50
10											102.50

Table 9.5 Convertible bond with call feature, binomial price tree

The callable bond price at $t + 8$ of 294.45 corresponds with the underlying share price at this time period. The holding period return of the convertible at this point may be calculated from the corresponding value at this point for the straight convertible bond, which is 295.12. It is worthwhile for the issuer to call the bond at this point (at a call price of 105) because this value is higher than the value of the bond if it is converted. Therefore we assume the issuer will call the bond at 105 and pay the accrued interest to date. Note that this is academic however because the bondholder will elect to convert and receive the higher of the parity value or 294.45, albeit at the cost of accrued interest.

If the underlying share price is lower than the conversion price, for example at 31.24 in period $t + 8$, the holding value of the convertible is of course the straight bond price of 101.54. There is no value to the company of calling the bond at this point.

Essentially, if the holding value of the bond plus accrued interest is higher than the call price, then the fair value of the bond will be equal to the higher of the call price plus accrued or parity value; otherwise the bond value will be equal to the higher of the holding value or the call price. In our illustration, the straight convertible bond had a value today of 113.91. The addition of a call feature has reduced the price of the bond (that is, increased the yield, as we would expect) to 109.34, so the call provision is worth 4.57.

Model parameters

The binomial model reviewed in the previous two sections will calculate the fair value for a convertible where certain parameters have been specified. It is immediately apparent that altering any of the inputs to the model will have an impact on the price calculation. In this section we consider the effect of changing one of these parameters.

Share price

The price of the underlying share is a key parameter of the model. A change in the value of the underlying share will result in a change in the value of the convertible; specifically, a rise in the underlying will result in a rise in the price of the convertible, and a fall in the price of the underlying will result in a fall in the price of the convertible. The *delta* of an option instrument measures the extent of this change. Figure 9.3 depicts a graph drawn from the values in Table 9.2. It shows that when the share price is at low levels relative to the conversion price, the sensitivity of the convertible to movements in the share price is low. However, when the share price is high, this sensitivity or *delta* approaches unity, so that a unit move in the price of the share is matched by a unit move in the price of the bond. In the former case the option is said to be "out-of-the-money", while in the latter case the option is "in-the-money". Where the delta approaches unity the option is said to be "deeply in-the-money".

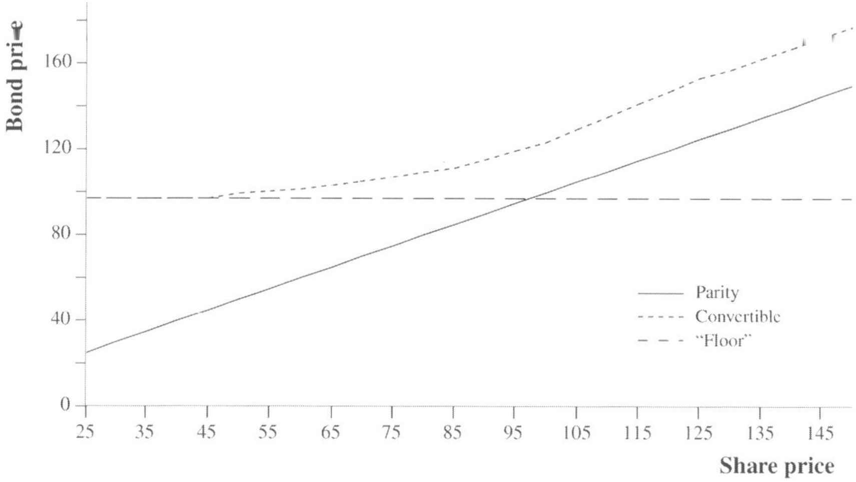

Figure 9.3 Convertible bond price sensitivity

The measure of the change in the price of the convertible with respect to a change in the price of the underlying equity is given by the delta of the convertible; that is,

$$\delta = \frac{\text{Change in convertible price}}{\text{Change in underlying price}}. \tag{9.12}$$

As we will note again in the introductory chapter on options, the delta is defined as the first derivative of the price of an instrument with respect to the price of the underlying asset. Here we are concerned with the delta being the measure of the change in the price of the convertible bond with respect to a change in the price of the underlying share. The value of delta in our illustration is given by the gradient of the convertible price line as shown in Figure 9.3. When the option feature of the convertible is deeply in-the-money, the convertible behaves more or less in the same way as the underlying share itself, but one that pays a coupon rather than a dividend.

The second derivative of the price change function, *gamma*, is the measure of the rate of change of delta with respect to the rate of change of the underlying share price, and is given by (9.13):

$$\gamma = \frac{\Delta\delta}{\Delta P_{share}}. \tag{9.13}$$

At low price levels for the underlying share, gamma is very low. This reflects the fact that at this price the delta is close to zero and the convertible behaves more like a conventional bullet bond, so that for small changes in the share price the delta will be unchanged. This pattern is repeated at high share price levels, where the delta is unity and gamma is close to zero: when a convertible is deep in-the-money and the delta is one, small increases in the share price will not affect the delta.

Volatility

A change in the volatility of the underlying share price will affect the price of the convertible, given that under the binomial model its value has been calculated based on a volatility level for the share. The measure of sensitivity of the convertible price to a change in the volatility of the underlying share is given by *vega*. Put simply, an increase in the volatility of the underlying has the effect that there is a greater probability of nodes on the binomial price tree being reached. This has the effect of increasing the value of the convertible.

Interest rate

A change in the risk-free interest rate will have an impact on the price of the convertible. The measure of sensitivity of a convertible bond's price to changes in the level of interest rates is given by *rho*. The key factor is that the price of deeply out-of-the-money convertibles is sensitive to changes in interest rates, because at this point the convertible behaves similarly to a conventional straight bond. Deep in-the-money convertibles behave more like the underlying equity and are hardly affected by changes in interest rates.

Further issues in valuing convertible bonds

Dilution

Up to now the discussion has focused on treating the convertibility feature of the convertible bond much as a call option on the underlying stock. There are practical reasons why a convertible is not precisely identical to a call option however. In the first instance, when a convertible bond is converted into the underlying shares, this results in the issue of new shares. This does not happen in the exercise of an equity call option, for which already existing shares are delivered. The effect on existing shareholders of a further issue of ordinary shares is termed *dilution*. In practice the effect of dilution is not often accounted for in the pricing of a convertible, although it is relevant.

The basic effect is given as (9.14) below, which we illustrate for an equity warrant. The exercise of a warrant results in the issue of new shares, upon which it may be shown that:

$$P_{warrant} = {}_{\max.}\,(P_{share} - E)/(1 + I),\ 0) \tag{9.14}$$

where E is the exercise price and I is the dilution factor resulting from the exercise of the warrant. This means that the holder of the warrant will receive the maximum of the diluted difference between the share price and exercise price, and zero. However, the share price will reflect the effect of the approaching exercise date; that is, it will incorporate the impact of the anticipated dilution. Logically this should have an impact on the price of the warrant or convertible, but is a function of how much in-the-money the convertible is. In a binomial model the probabilities can be adjusted to one and zero for the final price path, if the convertible is deeply in- or out-of-the-money. With certain probabilities entered, the analyst may work backwards along the tree to arrive at the probability of conversion at each node. The effect of dilution could then be ignored for deeply out-of-the-money convertibles.

A new issue of convertible bonds can be expected to have an effect on the volatility of the share price and its likely path along a binomial tree. As the bond approaches maturity a commonly observed phenomenon is of it being "pulled to the money". The share price is effectively capped as a significant rise would result in share selling as the hedge ratio approached 100%, with selling by market-makers who are long the convertible.

Volatility level

The pricing model reviewed in the previous section assumed a constant volatility level for the price returns of the underlying equity. This is clearly unrealistic over periods of time, although it is accepted by the market for short periods; this is because changes in volatility levels appear to occur quite slowly. Such changes also appear to be largely random rather than systematic; that is, volatility appears to be *stochastic*. There is a considerable literature on incorporating changing volatility levels into pricing models, although it is common for banks to use the static model described in this chapter. This is because the binomial model appears to perform well in practice. Instruments such as convertible bonds have relatively long maturities, and are less sensitive to jumps in short-term volatility levels. That is, the impact of a change in volatility is viewed as not material when pricing long-dated instruments.

There are a number of issues worth considering however. One of the most important is the concept of *mean reversion*. This is the term for a commonly observed behaviour pattern of volatility levels, whereby volatility levels return to a mean level after a period of corrections or market crashes. For example, after the 1987 stock market crash or "Black Monday" in the sterling market in 1992, individual volatility levels achieved very high figures (certain stock volatilities exceeded 100%), but it was only a matter of time before they reverted to a mean level. The same has been observed for commodity prices; for example, the crude oil price in the aftermath of the Gulf crisis of 1990/91.

The *implied volatility* levels of longer dated instruments such as convertible bonds reflect the fact that the market anticipates mean reversion. Observation of market behaviour also confirms that the volatility levels of individual shares tend to move in the same direction. This is logical, in the same way that share prices themselves reflect an element of specific company issues and an element that is attributed to the market in general. Another observation from the market is that share prices tend to be inversely related to changes in volatility levels. This is common for both individual shares as well as for market indices. The common explanation for this behaviour is that when share prices fall (rise), the debt/equity ratio rises (falls), which implies a higher (lower) risk level for equities. This indicates *skewed* distribution of returns. So far we have not discussed the distribution of stock price returns, which is generally assumed to follow a *normal* distribution, which is an assumption of the Black–Scholes and binomial models.[1] The market also accepts that this is not completely accurate, and that the distribution of returns tends to have fatter tails than a conventional normal distribution, a phenomenon known as *leptokurtosis*.[2] The existence of fatter tails will have an impact on pricing models, as deeply in- or out-of-the-money options will tend to be mispriced.

These issues are reviewed in Part V of the author's book *The Bond and Money Markets*.

---

1 Strictly speaking for the Black–Scholes model the assumption is that market returns follow a *geometric Brownian motion*.

2 This is discussed in Chapter 37 of the author's book *The Bond and Money Markets* (Butterworth-Heinemann 2001).

Convertible bond default risk

Virtually all convertible bonds are issued by corporates and therefore expose their holders to an element of *default* risk.[3] This is defined as the risk of a corporate failing to meet its contractual obligations regarding the payment of coupon or redemption proceeds. Although shareholders are at risk of the issuing company going bankrupt, strictly speaking this is not default risk because shares do not promise to pay a fixed interest cash flow for a set period of time in the future. The presence of default risk introduces further issues in the valuation of convertible bonds, which are considered in this section.

Credit ratings

The most commonly quoted ratings are those issued by Standard & Poor's and Moody's. Within domestic markets there are other local agencies that may be more influential or more frequently used. Rating agencies assign a formal credit rating to the individual issue of a corporate, although it is common for the market to refer to, say, a "double A-rated company". The ratings fall into two main categories: *investment grade* and *speculative grade*. There is also a third category, companies in default. The role of the formal rating agencies is reviewed in Chapter 15; the main areas that they assess include the debt/equity ratio, the asset base, volatility of earnings per share, and the level of subordination of debt. The agencies analyse published accounting data as well as qualitative data such as the credibility and strength of senior management, and publish forecasts on company performance.

The credit rating of a company is a major determinant of the yield that will be payable by that company's bonds. This is because, in an increasingly integrated and global capital market, *name recognition* (the traditional major determinant) plays a decreasing role. The yield spread of a corporate bond over the risk-free bond yield is known as the *default premium*. In practice, the default premium is composed of two elements, the compensation element specific to the company and the element related to market risk. This is because, in an environment where the default of one company was completely unrelated to the default of other companies, the return from a portfolio of corporate bonds would equal that of the risk-free bond, as the

[3] Certain developed country governments have issued convertible bonds, including the United Kingdom, but these are convertible into another debt issue.

gains from bonds of companies that did not default compensated for the loss from those that did default. The additional part of the default premium, the *risk premium* is the compensation for risk exposure that cannot be diversified away in a portfolio, known as *systematic* or *non-diversifiable* risk. Observation of the market tells us that in certain circumstances the default patterns of companies are related, for example in a recession there are more corporate defaults, and this fact is reflected in the risk premium.

The credit spread

Earlier in this chapter we reviewed a binomial pricing model for convertible bonds. One of the parameters of the model is the credit-risk adjusted discount rate. The appropriate rate to use for this parameter is not always clear cut, as it is a subjective matter as to what credit spread to apply to the risk-free rate. The analysis is less problematic if there is an equivalent-maturity conventional bond from the same issuer in existence. The yield spread between such a bond and the convertible bond can be said, simplistically, to reflect the market's appetite for the convertible over the straight bond. If this is not available, it may be appropriate to consider the conventional bond issued by a company that is in the same industry as the issuer, and has a similar capital structure. For deeply out-of-the money convertibles, the yield may be taken to be the equivalent of a conventional bond, and therefore it is possible to view the theoretical spread directly.

The sensitivity of the theoretical yield spread of a convertible bond to moves in the underlying equity price varies with credit rating. This is to be expected, since, in addition to their yields, lower rated bonds have higher price volatility levels. This sensitivity is at its highest during times of extreme volatility in the equity market and during times of recession, during which yield spreads widen most significantly. It is possible to plot this sensitivity, shown as Figure 9.4.

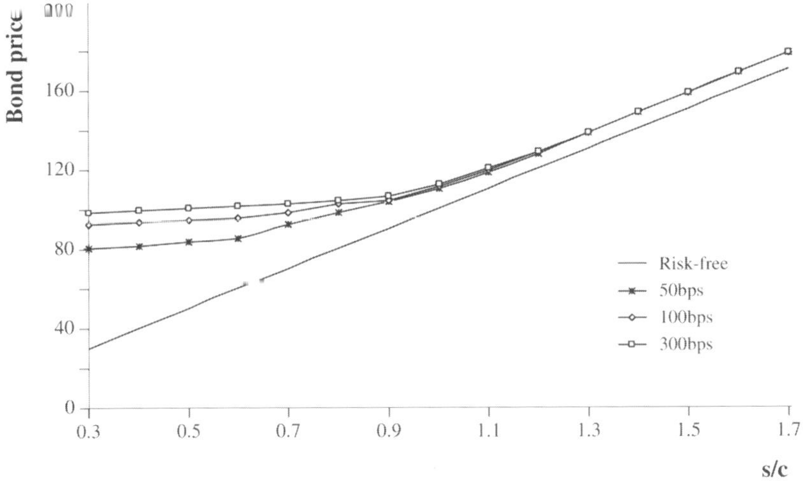

Figure 9.4 Price sensitivity of credit spread

The graph in Figure 9.4 shows the theoretical price profile of the hypothetical 1.50% coupon convertible bond introduced earlier, with different credit spreads selected. The risk-free interest rate is 1.50%, and the constant volatility level is 20% as before. The price profile is then plotted for credit-adjusted spreads of 50 basis points, 100 basis points and 300 basis points. When a convertible is deeply in-the-money, default risk is less significant, and at a delta value approaching unity, the risk-free rate becomes the relevant rate at which to value the bond; at this point, a change in the credit spread has little or no impact on the price of the convertible. The opposite is true when the convertible is deeply out-of-the-money and/or when the delta approaches zero.

Appendices

Appendix 9.1 Capital asset pricing model

We briefly discuss the capital asset pricing model because of the relevance of the underlying equity value in the valuation of convertibles. The capital asset pricing model (CAPM), attributable to Sharpe (1964), is a cornerstone of modern financial theory and originates from analysis on the cost of capital. The cost of capital of a company may be broken down as shown by Figure A9.1.

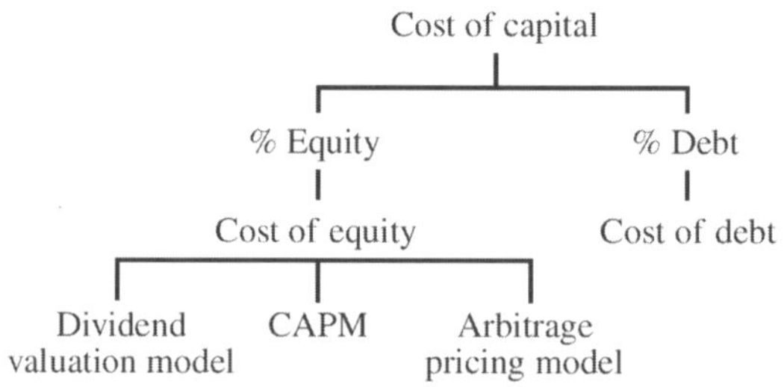

Figure A9.1 Components of the cost of capital

The three most common approaches used for estimating the cost of equity are the *dividend valuation model*, CAPM and the *arbitrage pricing theory*. CAPM is in a class of market models known as *risk premium* models which rely on the assumption that all individuals holding a risk-carrying security will demand a return in excess of the return they would receive from holding a risk-free security. This excess is the investor's compensation for her risk exposure. The risk premium in CAPM is measured by *beta*, it is known as *systematic*, *market* or *non-diversifiable* risk. This risk is caused by macroeconomic factors such as inflation or political events, which affect the returns of all companies. If a company is affected by these macroeconomic factors in the same way as the market (usually measured by a stock index), it will have a beta of 1.0, and will be expected to have returns equal to the market. Similarly, if a company's systematic risk is greater than the market, then its capital will be priced such that it is expected to have returns greater than the market. Essentially therefore beta is a measure of volatility, with a company's relative volatility being measured by comparing its returns to the market's returns. For example, if a share has a beta of 2.0, then on average for every 10% that the market index has returned above the risk-free rate, the share is expected to have returned 20%. Conversely, for every 10% the market has under-performed the risk-free rate, the share is expected to have returned 20% below. Beta is calculated for a share by measuring its variance relative to the variance of a market index such as the FTSE All Share or the S&P 500. The most common method of estimating beta is with standard regression techniques based on historical share price movements over, say, a five-year period.

To obtain the CAPM estimate of the cost of equity for a company, two other pieces of data are required: the risk-free interest rate and the equity risk premium. The risk-free rate represents the most secure return that can be achieved in the market. It is theoretically defined as an investment that has no variance and no covariance with the market; a perfect proxy for the risk-free rate therefore would be a security with a beta equal to zero, and no volatility. Such an instrument does not, to all intents and purposes, exist. Instead, the market uses the next best proxy available, which in a developed economy is the government-issued Treasury bill, a short-dated debt instrument guaranteed by the government.

The equity risk premium represents the excess return above the risk-free rate that investors demand for holding risk-carrying securities. The risk premium in the CAPM is the premium above the risk-free rate on a portfolio assumed to have a beta of 1.0. The premium itself may be estimated in a number of ways. A common approach is to use historical prices, on the basis that past prices are a satisfactory guide to the future[4] and use these returns over time to calculate an arithmetic or geometric average. Research has shown that the market risk premium for the United States and United Kingdom has varied between 5.5% and 11% historically (Mills 1994), depending on the time period chosen and the method used.

Once the beta has been determined, the cost of equity for a corporate is given by CAPM as (9.15):

$$k_e = r_f + (\beta \times r_e) \qquad (9.15)$$

[4] Not that any self-respecting independent financial advisor would say this!

where

k_e is the cost of equity
r_f is the risk-free interest rate
r_e is the equity risk premium
β is the share beta.

The primary assumption behind CAPM is that all the market-related risk of a share can be captured in a single indicator, the beta. This would appear to be refuted by evidence that fund managers sometimes demand a higher return from one portfolio than another when both apparently are equally a risk, having betas of 1.0. The difference in portfolio returns cannot be due to differences in specific risk, because diversification nearly eliminates such risk in large, well-balanced portfolios. If the systematic risk of the two portfolios were truly identical, then they would be priced to yield identical returns. Nevertheless, the CAPM is often used by analysts to calculate cost of equity and hence cost of capital.

If we consider the returns on an individual share and the market as positively sloping lines on a graph plotting return, beta is usually given by (9.16):

$$rs = \alpha_{sl} + \beta_{slrl} + \varepsilon_{sl} \tag{9.16}$$

where
rs is the return on security s
r_l is the return on the market (usually measured for a given index)
α_{sl} is the intercept between s and l, often termed the "alpha"
β_{sl} is the slope measurement or beta
ε is a random error term.

Selected bibliography and references

Bhattacharya, M. and Zhu, Y., "Valuation and analysis of convertible securities", in Fabozzi, F., *The Fixed Income Handbook*, 5th edition, McGraw-Hill, New York, pp. 791–817.

Bierman, H. 1973, "The cost of warrants", *Journal of Financial and Quantitative Analysis*, June, pp. 499–503.

Black, F. and Scholes, M. 1973, "The pricing of options and corporate liabilities", *Journal of Political Economy*, 81, pp. 637–59.

Brennan, M. and Schwartz, E. 1980, "Analysing convertible bonds", *Journal of Financial and Quantitative Analysis*, 15, November, pp. 907–29.

Calamos, J.P. 1988, *Investing in Convertible Securities*, Longman, Oxford.

Cooper, I. 1988, *The Relationship between Two Methods of Valuing Convertible Bonds*, London Business School, London.

Cowan, A.R., Nandkumar N. and Singh, A.K. 1993, "Calls and out of the money convertible bonds", *Financial Management*, 22, pp. 105–16.

Cox, J., Ross, S. and Rubinstein, M. 1979, "Option pricing: A simplified approach", *Journal of Financial Economics*, 7(3), September, pp. 229–63.

Dunn, K. and Eades, K. 1989, "Voluntary conversion of convertible securities and the option call strategy", *Journal of Financial Economics*, 23, pp. 273–301.

Gemmill, G. 1993, *Options Pricing*, McGraw-Hill International, New York.

Ho, T.S.Y. and Lee, S. 1986, "Term structure movements and pricing interest rate contingent claims", *Journal of Finance*, December, pp. 1–22.

Ingersoll, J. Jr 1977, "An examination of convertible call policies on convertible securities", *Journal of Finance*, 32, May, pp. 463–78.

Kim Yong-Cheol and Stultz, R. 1992, "Is there a global market for convertible bonds?", *Journal of Business*, 65, pp. 75–92.

King, R. 1984, "The effect of convertible bond equity values on dilution and leverage", *The Accounting Review*, 59, pp. 419–31.

Liebowitz, M. 1974, "Understanding convertible securities", *Financial Analysts Journal*, 30, pp. 57–67.

Lewis, C. 1991, "Convertible debt: Valuation and conversion in complex capital structures", *Journal of Banking and Finance*, 15, pp. 665–82.

McGuire, S. 1990, *Convertibles*, Woodhead-Faulkner, Oxford.

Mills. R. 1994, *Strategic Value Analysis*, Mars Business Associates, Oxford.

Sharpe, W. 1964, "Capital asset prices: A theory of market equilibrium under conditions of risk", *Journal of Finance*, September, pp. 213–245.

Walter, J. and Que, A. 1973, "The valuation of convertible bonds", *Journal of Finance*, 28, pp. 713–32.

Where you been? Ain't seen you for weeks …
Where were you, when I wanted to work …?
Oh yes, and I feel like giving in …

It's all my fault, yes I'm to blame,
Ain't got no money, ain't got no fame,
And that's why I feel like giving in.

– Felt,
Ballad of the Band (Creation Records) 1986

CHAPTER 10

The Eurobond Market

Virtually nowhere has the increasing integration and globalisation of the world's capital markets been more evident than in the Eurobond market. It is an important source of funds for many banks and corporates, not to mention central governments. The Eurobond market has benefited from much of the advances in financial engineering, and has undergone some innovative changes in the debt capital markets. It continues to develop new structures, in response to the varying demands and requirements of specific groups of investors. The range of innovations have customised the market to a certain extent and often the market is the only opening for certain types of government and corporate finance. Investors also often look to the Eurobond market due to constraints in their domestic market, and Euro securities have been designed to reproduce the features of instruments that certain investors may be prohibited from investing in, in their domestic arena. Other instruments are designed for investors in order to provide tax advantages. The traditional image of the Eurobond investor, the so-called "Belgian dentist", has changed and the investor base is both varied and geographically dispersed worldwide.

The key feature of Eurobonds is the way they are issued, internationally across borders and by an international underwriting syndicate. The method of issuing Eurobonds reflects the cross-border nature of the transaction, and unlike government markets where the auction is the primary issue method, Eurobonds are typically issued under a "fixed price re-offer" method or a "bought deal". There is also a regulatory distinction as no one central authority is responsible for regulating the market and overseeing its structure.

This chapter reviews the Eurobond market in terms of the structure of the market, the nature of the instruments themselves, the market players, the issuing process and technical aspects such as taxation and swap arrangements. A subsequent chapter reviews the secondary market.[1]

Eurobonds

A Eurobond is a debt capital market instrument issued in a "Eurocurrency" through a syndicate of issuing banks and securities houses, and distributed internationally when issued; that is, sold in more than one country of issue and subsequently traded by market participants in several international financial centres. The Eurobond market is divided into sectors depending on the currency in which the issue is denominated. For example, US dollar Eurobonds are often referred to as *Eurodollar* bonds, similar sterling issues are called *Eurosterling* bonds. The prefix "Euro" was first used to refer to deposits of US dollars in continental Europe in the 1960s. The Euro-deposit now refers to any deposit of a currency outside the country of issue of that currency, and is not limited to Europe. For historical reasons and also due to the importance of the US economy and investor base, the major currency in which Eurobonds are denominated has always been US dollars. The volume of non-sovereign Eurobond issues from 1996 to 1999 is shown in Figure 10.1.

The first Eurobond is generally considered to be the issue of $15 million nominal of 10-year $5^1/_2$% bonds by Autostrada, the Italian state highway authority, in July 1963.[2] The bonds were denominated in US dollars and paid an annual coupon in July each year. This coincides with the imposition in the United States of the Interest Equalisation Tax, a withholding tax on domestic corporate bonds, which is often quoted as being a prime reason behind the establishment of overseas deposits of US dollars.

---

1 Note that Eurobonds are also known as international securities. All Eurobonds settle or "clear" in the Euroclear and Clearstream settlement systems.

2 Decovny (1998) states that the first Eurobond issue was in 1957, but its identity is not apparent.

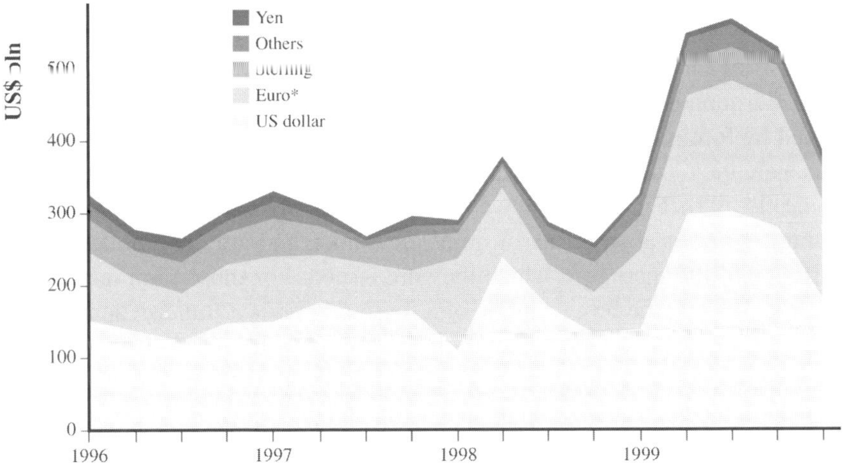

Figure 10.1 Non-government international bond issuance, 1996–1999
Source: Bank of England.
**Includes the 11 euro currencies before 1 Jan. 1999*

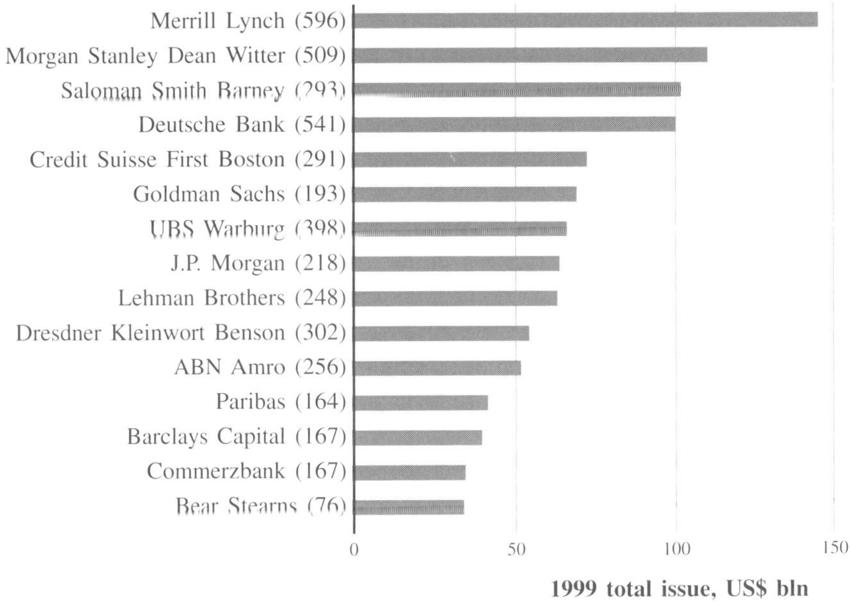

Figure 10.2 International bond issues in 1999, with leading book-runners (the number in brackets is the number of issues)
Source: *The Economist.*

Foreign bonds

At this stage it is important to identify "foreign bonds" and distinguish them from Eurobonds. Foreign bonds are debt capital market instruments that are issued by foreign borrowers in the domestic bond market of another country. As such they trade in a similar fashion to the bond instruments of the domestic market in which they are issued. They are usually underwritten by a single bank or a syndicate of domestic banks, and are denominated in the currency of the market in which they are issued. For those familiar with the sterling markets the best example of a foreign bond is a *Bulldog* bond, which is a sterling bond issued in the United Kingdom by a non-UK domiciled borrower. Other examples are *Yankee* bonds in the United States, *Samurai* bonds in Japan, *Rembrandt* bonds in the Netherlands, *Matador* bonds in Spain, and so on. Hence, a US company issuing a bond in the United Kingdom, denominated in sterling and underwritten by a domestic bank, would be issuing a Bulldog bond, which would trade as a gilt, except with an element of credit risk attached. In today's integrated global markets however the distinction is becoming more and more fine. Many foreign bonds pay gross coupons and are issued by a syndicate of international banks, so the difference between them and Eurobonds may be completely eroded in the near future.

The most important domestic market for foreign bond issues has been the US dollar market, followed by euros, Swiss francs and Japanese yen. There are also important markets in Canadian and Australian dollars, and minor markets in currencies such as Hong Kong dollars, Kuwaiti dinars and Saudi Arabian riyals.

Eurobond instruments

There is a wide range of instruments issued in the Eurobond market, designed to meet the needs of borrowers and investors. We review the main types in this section.

Conventional bonds

The most common type of instrument issued in the Euro markets is the conventional vanilla bond, with fixed coupon and maturity date. Coupon frequency is on an annual basis. The typical face value of such Eurobonds is \$1,000, €1,000, £1,000 or so on. The bond is unsecured, and therefore depends on the credit quality of its issuer in order to attract investors. Eurobonds have a typical maturity of five to ten years, although many high-

Issue	Moodys/ S&P rating	Coupon	Maturity	Issue size	Launch spread to benchmark (bps)
Daimler Chrysler NA	A3/BBB	4.875%	15 June 2010	USD 1,000 million	130
Development Bank of Japan	Aaa/AAA	4.25%	9 June 2015	USD 700 million	38.8
Federal Home Loan Bank	AAA	3.625%	20 June 2007	USD 4,000 million	17
GE Capital	Aaa/AAA	4.75%	15 June 2011	GBP 250 million	52
General Electric Capital Corp	Aaa/AAA	4.00%	15 June 2009	USD 500 million	48
If Skadeforsakring AB	Baa2/BBB	4.943%	Perpetual / callable	EUR 150 million	179.8; fixed coupon to June 2015, thereafter 3-mo Euribor + 265
ING Group N.V.	A2/A-	4.176%	Perpetual / callable	EUR 500 million	95.3; fixed coupon to June 2015, thereafter 3-mo Euribor + 80
Kingdom of Belgium	Aa1/AA+	3.000%	28 March 2010	EUR 6,145 million	9
Korea Exchange Bank	Baa3/BB+	5.00%	10 June 2015	USD 300 million	151
Lambay Capital Securities	Baa1	FRN	Perpetual	GBP 300 million	3-mo Libor + 166. Coupon step-up after 2015
LB Baden-Wuerttemberg	Aaa/AAA	6.50%	26 Nov. 2007	NZD 50 million	23
Legal & General Group	A2/A	4.00%	8 June 2025	EUR 600 million	85.1
Portugal Telecom	A3/A-	4.50%	16 Jun 2025	EUR 500 million	137
Republic of El Salvador	Baa3/BB+	7.65%	15 June 2035	USD 375 million	345
Republic of Turkey	B1/BB-	7.00%	5 June 2020	USD 1,250 million	332.4
Zurich Finance (USA) Inc.	Baa2/BBB+	4.50%	15 June 2025	EUR 500 million	135.00 to June 2015; thereafter 3-mo Euribor + 220

Table 10.1 Selected Eurobond issues in first half of June 2005
Source: Bloomberg L.P.

quality corporates have issued bonds with maturities of thirty years or even longer. The largest Eurobond market is in US dollars, followed by issues in euros, Japanese yen, sterling and a range of other currencies such as Australian, New Zealand and Canadian dollars, South African rand, and so on. Issuers will denominate bonds in a currency that is attractive to particular investors at the time, and it is common for bonds to be issued in more "exotic" currencies, such as East European, Latin American and Asian currencies.

Eurobonds are not regulated by the country in whose currency the bonds are issued. They are typically registered on a national stock exchange, usually London or Luxembourg. Listing of the bonds enables certain institutional investors, who are prohibited from holding assets that are not listed on an exchange, to purchase them. The volume of trading on a registered stock exchange is negligible however; virtually all trading is on an over-the-counter (OTC) basis directly between market participants.

Interest payments on Eurobonds are paid gross and are free of any withholding or other taxes. This is one of the main features of Eurobonds, as is the fact that they are "bearer" bonds; that is, there is no central register. Historically this meant that the bond certificates were bearer certificates with coupons attached; these days bonds are still designated "bearer" instruments but are held in a central depositary to facilitate electronic settlement.

Floating rate notes

An early innovation in the Eurobond market was the floating rate note (FRN). They are usually short- to medium-dated issues, with interest quoted as a spread to a reference rate. The reference rate is usually the London interbank offered rate (Libor), or the Singapore interbank offered rate for issues in Asia (Sibor). The euro interbank rate (Euribor) is also now commonly quoted. The spread over the reference rate is a function of the credit quality of the issuer, and can range from 10 to 150 basis points over the reference rate or even higher. Bonds typically pay a semi-annual coupon, although quarterly coupon bonds are also issued. The first FRN issue was by ENEL, an Italian utility company, in 1970. The majority of issuers are financial institutions such as banks and securities houses.

There are also perpetual, or undated, FRNs, the first issue of which was by National Westminster Bank plc in 1984. They are essentially similar to regular FRNs, except that they have no maturity date and are therefore "perpetual". Most perpetual FRNs are issued by banks, for whom they are attractive because they are a means of raising capital similar to equity but with the tax advantages associated with debt. They also match the payment characteristics of the banks' assets. Traditionally, the yield on perpetuals is higher than both conventional bonds and fixed-term FRNs.

Zero-coupon bonds

An innovation in the market from the late 1980s was the zero-coupon bond, or *pure discount* bond, which makes no interest payments. Like zero-coupon bonds initially in government markets, the main attraction of these bonds for investors was that, as no interest was payable, the return could be declared entirely as capital gain, thus allowing the bondholder to avoid income tax. Most jurisdictions, including the United States and United Kingdom, have adjusted their tax legislation so that the return on zero-coupon bonds now counts as income and not capital gain.

Convertible bonds[3]

Another instrument that is common in the Eurobond market is the convertible bond. A Eurobond is convertible if it may be exchanged at some point for another instrument, usually the ordinary shares (equity) of the issuing company. The decision to elect to convert is at the discretion of the bondholder. Convertibles are analysed as a structure comprised of a conventional bond and an embedded option.

The most common conversion feature is an *equity convertible*, which is a conventional bond that is convertible into the equity of the issuer. The conversion feature allows the bondholder to convert the Eurobond, on maturity or at specified times during the bond's life, into a specified number of shares of the issuing company at a set price. In some cases the bond is convertible into the shares of the company that is guaranteeing the bond. The issuing company must release new shares in the event of conversion. The price at which the bond is convertible into shares, known as the exercise price, is usually set at a premium above the market price of the ordinary shares in the market on the day the bond is issued. Investors will exercise their conversion rights only if the market price has risen sufficiently that a gain will be realised by converting. The incorporation of a conversion feature in a bond is designed to make the bond more attractive to investors, as it allows them to gain from a rise in the issuing company's share price. The conversion feature also acts as a floor for the bond price. The advantages of convertibles for borrowers include the following:

[3] Convertible bonds are reviewed in Chapters 8–9.

- as the bond incorporates an added attraction in the form of the conversion feature, the coupon payable on the bond is lower than it otherwise would be; this enables the borrower to save on interest costs;
- issuing convertibles is one method by which companies can broaden the geographical base of their equity holders;
- companies are usually able to raise a higher amount at one issue if the bond is convertible, compared to a conventional bond.

Against these factors must be weighed certain disadvantages associated with convertibles, which include the following:

- the investor's insurance against the volatility of share price movements, an attraction of the convertible, is gained at the cost of a lower coupon than would be obtained from a conventional bond;
- convertibles are often issued by companies that would have greater difficulty placing conventional paper. Convertibles are usually subordinated and are often viewed more as equity rather than debt. The credit and interest rate risk associated with them is consequently higher than for conventional bonds.

There have been variations on the straight convertible bond in the Eurobond market. This includes the *convertible preference share*. This is a combination of a perpetual debt instrument cash flow with an option to convert into ordinary shares. Sometimes these issues are convertible not into shares of the issuer, but rather into the equity of a company in which the issuer has a significant shareholding.

Another variation is the *equity note*, which is a bond that is redeemed in shares and not in cash. The equity note is not a true convertible, since the conversion feature is not an option for the bondholder but a condition of the bond issue, and is guaranteed to take place. A more accurate description of an equity note would be an "interest-bearing equity future" note.

Eurobonds have also been issued with a feature that allows conversion into other assets such as crude oil or gold, or into other bonds with different payment characteristics. These are known as *asset convertibles*. Examples of such bonds include FRNs that are convertible under specified circumstances into fixed-rate bonds. One version of this was the *drop-lock* bond, which was first introduced in the early 1980s during a period of high interest rates. Drop-lock bonds are initially issued as FRNs but convert to a fixed-rate bond at the point that the reference rate falls to a pre-set level. The bond then pays this fixed rate for the remainder of its life. During the 1990s, as interest rate volatility fell to relatively lower levels, drop-locks fell out of favour and it is now rare to see them issued.

Currency convertibles are bonds that are issued in one currency and are redeemed in another currency or currencies. Often this at the discretion of the bondholder; other currency convertibles pay their coupon in a different currency to the one they are denominated in. In certain respects currency convertibles possess similar characteristics to a conventional bond issued in conjunction with a forward contract. The conversion rate is specified at the time of issue, and may be either a fixed-rate option or a floating rate option. With a fixed-rate option the exchange rate between the currencies is fixed for the entire maturity of the bond at the time it is issued; with a floating-rate option the exchange rate is not fixed and is the rate prevailing in the market at the time the conversion is exercised. Initially, most currency convertibles offered a fixed-rate option, so that the foreign exchange risk resided entirely with the issuer. Floating-rate options were introduced in the 1970s when exchange rates began to experience greater volatility.

Eurowarrants

The Eurobond warrant or *Eurowarrant* is essentially a call option attached to a conventional bond. The call option is convertible into either ordinary shares or other bonds of the issuing company, or rarely, another company. A typical Eurobond warrant will be comprised of a conventional bond, issued in denominations of $1,000 or $10,000, paying a fixed coupon. The attached warrant will entitle the bondholder to purchase shares (or bonds) at a specified price at set dates, or a set time period, up until maturity of the warrant, whereupon the warrant expires worthless. Warrants are often detached from their host bond and traded separately.

The exercise price of a warrant is fixed at a premium over the market price of the equity at issue. This premium is separate to the premium associated with a warrant in the secondary market, which is the total premium cost connected with buying the warrant and immediately exercising it into the equity, and not the cost associated with a purchase of the equity in the open market.

There are several advantages that Eurobond warrants hold for investors. They are composed of two assets that are usually traded separately in the secondary market; indeed, warrants are often attached to bonds as a "sweetener" for investors. Investors have an interest in the performance of the shares of the issuer without having a direct exposure to them. Should the intrinsic value of the warrant fall to zero, there is still time value associated with the warrant up until the maturity of the bond. Warrants typically possess high *gearing*, which is defined as the ratio of the cost of the warrant to the cost of the shares that the warrant holder is entitled to purchase. Borrowers may also gain from attaching warrants to their bond issues. The advantages include being able to pay a lower coupon than might otherwise have been the case. The exercise of a warrant results in the issuer receiving cash for the shares that are purchased (albeit at a below-market rate), compared with a convertible bond where the issuer receives only bonds that are subsequently cancelled. This is a feature of the warrant's gearing, as the value of the warrant is always less than the price at which the company guarantees to issue new equity to the warrant holder. The disadvantage at the time the warrant is exercised is that the company is receiving a below-market price for its shares at a time when they are trading at a historically high level; however, there is a form of compensation for this since the company would have issued the bonds at a lower coupon rate than would have been the case had the warrants not been attached.

The issuing process: Market participants

When a company raises a bond issue its main concerns will be the success of the issue, and the interest rate that must be paid for the funds borrowed. An issue is handled by an international syndicate of banks. A company wishing to make a bond issue will invite a number of investment banks and securities houses to bid for the role of lead manager. The bidding banks will indicate the price at which they believe they can get the issue away to investors, and the size of their fees. The company's choice of lead manager will be based on the bids, but also the reputation and standing of the bank in the market. The lead manager, when appointed, will assemble a syndicate of other banks to help with the issue. This syndicate will often be made up of banks from several different countries. The lead manager has essentially agreed to underwrite the issue, which means that she guarantees to take the paper off the issuer's hands (in return for a fee). If there is an insufficient level of investor demand for the bonds the lead manager will be left holding ("wearing") the issue, which in addition to being costly will not help its name in the market. When we referred to an issuer assessing the reputation of potential lead managers, this included the company's view on the "placing power" of the bank, its perceived ability to get the entire issue away. The borrowing company would prefer the issue to be over-subscribed, which is when demand outstrips supply.

In many cases the primary issue involves a *fixed price re-offer* scheme. The lead manager will form the syndicate, which will agree on a fixed issue price, a fixed commission and the distribution among themselves of the quantity of bonds they agreed to take as part of the syndicate. The banks then re-offer the bonds that they have been allotted to the market, at the agreed price. This technique gives the lead manager greater control over a Eurobond issue. It sets the price at which other underwriters in the syndicate can initially sell the bonds to investors. The fixed price re-offer mechanism is designed to prevent underwriters from selling the bonds back to the lead manager at a discount to the original issue price, that is, "dumping" the bonds.

Before the bond issue is made, but after its basic details have been announced, it is traded for a time in the *grey market*. This is a term used to describe trading in the bonds before they officially come to the market, mainly market-makers selling the bond short to other market players or investors. Activity in the grey market serves as useful market intelligence to the lead manager, who can gauge the level of demand that exists in the market for the issue. A final decision on the offer price is often delayed until dealing in the grey market indicates the best price at which the issue can be got away.

Let us now consider the primary market participants in greater detail.

The borrowing parties

The range of borrowers in the Euromarkets is very diverse. From virtually the inception of the market, borrowers representing corporates, sovereign and local governments, nationalised corporations, supranational institutions, and financial institutions have raised finance in the international markets. The majority of borrowing has been by governments, regional governments and public agencies of developed countries, although the Eurobond market is increasingly a source of finance for developing country governments and corporates.

Governments and institutions access the Euromarkets for a number of reasons. Under certain circumstances it is more advantageous for a borrower to raise funds outside its domestic market, due to the effects of tax or regulatory rules. The international markets are very competitive in terms of using intermediaries, and a borrower may well be able to raise cheaper funds in the international markets. Other reasons why borrowers access Eurobond markets include:

- a desire to diversify sources of long-term funding. A bond issue is often placed with a wide range of institutional and private investors, rather than the more restricted investor base that may prevail in a domestic market. This gives the borrower access to a wider range of lenders, and for corporate borrowers this also enhances the international profile of the company;
- for both corporates and emerging country governments, the prestige associated with an issue of bonds in the international market;
- the flexibility of a Eurobond issue compared to a domestic bond issue or bank loan, illustrated by the different types of Eurobond instruments available.

Against this are balanced the potential downsides of a Eurobond issue, which include the following:

- for all but the largest and most creditworthy of borrowers, the rigid nature of the issue procedure becomes significant during times of interest and exchange rate volatility, reducing the funds available for borrowers;
- issuing debt in currencies other than those in which a company holds matching assets, or in which there are no prospects of earnings, exposes the issuer to foreign exchange risk.

Generally though, the Euromarket remains an efficient and attractive market in which a company can raise finance for a wide range of maturities.

The nature of the Eurobond market is such that the ability of governments and corporates to access it varies greatly. Access to the market for a first-time borrower has historically been difficult, and has been a function of global debt market conditions. There is a general set of criteria, first presented by van Agtmael (1983) that must be fulfilled initially, which for corporates include the following:

- the company should ideally be domiciled in a country that is familiar to Eurobond issuers, usually as a result of previous offerings by the country's government or a government agency. This suggests that it is difficult for a corporate to access the market ahead of a first issue by the country's government;
- the borrowing company must benefit from a level of name recognition or, failing this, a sufficient quality credit rating;
- the company ideally must have a track record of success, and needs

to have published financial statements over a sufficient period of time, audited by a recognised and respected firm, and the company's management must make sufficient financial data available at the time of the issue;
- the company's requirement for medium-term or long-term finance, represented by the bond issue, must be seen to fit into a formal strategic plan.

Generally, Eurobond issuers are investment-grade rated, and only a small number, less than 5%,[4] are not rated at all.

The underwriting lead manager

Issuers of debt in the Eurobond market select an investment bank to manage the bond issue for them. This bank is known as the underwriter because in return for a fee, it takes on the risk of placing the bond among investors. If the bond cannot be placed in total, the underwriting bank will take on the paper itself. The issuer will pick an investment bank with whom it already has an existing relationship, or it may invite a number of banks to bid for the mandate. In the event of a competitive bid, the bank will be selected on the basis of the prospective coupon that can be offered, the fees and other expenses that it will charge, the willingness of the bank to support the issue in the secondary market, the track record of the bank in placing similar issues, and the reach of the bank's client base. Often it is a combination of a bank's existing relationship with the issuer and its reputation in the market for placing paper that will determine whether or not it wins the mandate for the issue.

After the mandate has been granted, and the investment bank is satisfied that the issuer meets its own requirements on counterparty and reputational risk, both parties will prepare a detailed financing proposal for the bond issue. This will cover topics such as the specific type of financing, the size and timing of the issue, approximate pricing, fees, and so on. The responsibilities of the lead manager include the following:

- analysing the prospects of the bond issue being accepted by the market; this is a function of both the credit quality of the issuer and the market's capacity to absorb the issue;
- forming the *syndicate* of banks to share responsibility for placing the

4 *Source*: IMF report, 1998

issue. These banks are co-lead managers and syndicate banks;
- assisting the borrower with the prospectus, which details the bond issue and also holds financial and other information on the issuing company;
- assuming responsibility for the legal issues involved in the transaction, for which the bank's in-house legal team and/or external legal counsel will be employed;
- preparing the documentation associated with the issue;
- taking responsibility for the handling of the fiduciary services associated with the issue, which is usually handled by a specialised agent bank;
- if deemed necessary, establishing a pool of funds that can be used to stabilise the price of the issue in the *grey market*, used to buy (or sell) bonds if required.

These duties are usually undertaken jointly with other members of the syndicate. For first-time borrowers the prospectus is a very important document, as it is the main communication media used to advertise the borrower to investors. In a corporate issue, the prospectus may include the analysis of the company by the underwriters, financial indicators and balance sheet data, a detailed description of the issue specifications, the members of the underwriting syndicate, and details of placement strategies. In a sovereign issue, the prospectus may cover a general description of the economy of the country, including key economic indicators such as balance of payments figures and export and import levels, the state of the national accounts and budget, a description of the political situation (with an eye on the stability of the country), current economic activity, and a statement of the current external and public debt position.

The co-lead manager

The function of the co-lead manager in Eurobond issues developed as a consequence of the distribution of placing ability across geographic markets. For example, as the Eurobond market developed, underwriters who were mainly US or UK banks did not have significant client bases in, say, the continental European market, and so banking houses that had a customer base there would be invited to take on some of the issue. For a long time the ability to place $500,000 nominal of a new Eurobond issue was taken as the benchmark against a potential co-lead manager.

The decision by a lead manager to invite other banks to participate will depend on the type and size of the issue. Global issues such as those by the

World Bank, which have nominal sizes of $1 billion or more, have a fairly large syndicate. The lead manager will assess whether it can place all the paper, in order to achieve geographic spread (which may have been stipulated by the issuer), or if it needs to form a syndicate. It is common for small issues to be placed entirely by a single lead manager.

Investors

The structure of the Eurobond market, compared to domestic markets, lends a certain degree of anonymity, if such is desired, to end-investors. This is relevant essentially in the case of private investors. The institutional holders of investors are identical to those in the domestic bond markets. They include institutional investors such as insurance companies, pension funds, investment trusts, commercial banks and corporations. Other investors include central banks and government agencies; for example, the Kuwait Investment Office and the Saudi Arabian Monetary Agency both have large Eurobond holdings. In the United Kingdom, banks and securities houses are keen holders of FRN Eurobonds, usually issued by other financial institutions.

Fees, expenses and pricing

Fees

The fee structure for placing and underwriting a Eurobond issue is relatively identical for most issues. The general rule is that fees increase with maturity and decreasing credit quality of the issuer, and decrease with nominal size. Fees are not paid directly but are obtained by adjusting the final price paid to the issuer; that is, taken out of the sale proceeds of the issue. The allocation of fees within a syndicate can be slightly more complex, and in the form of an *underwriting allowance*. This is usually paid out by the lead manager.

Typical fees will vary according to the type of issue and issuer, and also whether the bond itself is plain vanilla or more exotic. Fees range from 0.25% to 0.75% of the nominal size of an issue. Higher fees may be charged for small issues

Expenses

The expenses associated with the launch of a Eurobond issue vary greatly. Table 10.2 illustrates the costs associated with a typical Eurobond transaction. Not every bond issue will incur every expense, however these elements are common.

Expenses
Printing (prospectus, certificates, and so on)
Legal counsel (issuer and investment bank)
Stock exchange listing fee
Promotion
Underwriters expenses
Clearing and bond issuance
Paying agent
Trustee
Custodian
Common depositary

Table 10.2 Expense elements, Eurobond issue

The expense items in Table 10.2 do not include the issuer's own expenses with regard to financial accounting and marketing. The reimbursement for underwriters is intended to cover such items as legal expenses, travel, delivery of bonds and other business expenses.

In general, Eurobonds are listed on either the London or Luxembourg stock exchanges. Certain issues in the Asian markets are listed on the Singapore exchange. To enable listing to take place an issuer will need to employ a listing agent, although this is usually arranged by the lead manager. The function of the listing agent is to (1) provide a professional opinion on the prospectus, (2) prepare the documentation for submission to the stock exchange and (3) make a formal application and conduct negotiations on behalf of the issuer.

Pricing

One of the primary tasks of the lead manager is the pricing of the new issue. The lead manager faces an inherent conflict of interest between its need to maximise returns from the syndication process and its obligation to secure the best possible deal for the issuer: its client. An inflated issue price invariably causes the yield spread on the bond to rise as soon as the bond trades in the secondary market. This would result in a negative impression being associated with the issuer, which would affect its next offering. On the other hand, too low a price can permanently damage a lead manager's relationship with the client.

For Eurobonds that are conventional vanilla fixed-income instruments, pricing does not present too many problems in theory. The determinants of the price of a new issue are the same as those for a domestic bond offering, and include the credit quality of the borrower, the maturity of the issue, the total nominal value, the presence of any option feature, and the prevailing level and volatility of market interest rates. Eurobonds are perhaps more heavily influenced by the target market's ability to absorb the issue, and this is gauged by the lead manager in its preliminary offering discussions with investors. The credit rating of a borrower is often similar to that granted to it for borrowings in its domestic market, although in many cases a corporate will have a different rating for its foreign currency debt compared to its domestic currency debt

In the grey market the lead manager will attempt to gauge the yield spread over the reference pricing bond at which investors will be happy to bid for the paper. The reference bond is the benchmark for the maturity that is equivalent to the maturity of the Eurobond. It is commonly observed that Eurobonds have the same maturity date as the benchmark bond that is used to price the issue. As lead managers often hedge their issue using the benchmark bond, an identical maturity date helps to reduce basis risk.

Issuing the bond

The three key dates in a new issue of Eurobonds are the announcement date, the offering day and the closing day. Prior to the announcement date the borrower and the lead manager (and co-lead managers if applicable) will have had preliminary discussions to confirm the issue specifications, such as its total nominal size, the target coupon and the offer price. These details are provisional and may well be different at the time of the closing date. At these preliminary meetings the lead manager will appoint a fiscal agent or trustee, and a principal paying agent. The lead manager will appoint other members of the syndicate group, and the legal documentation and prospectus will be prepared.

On the announcement date the new issue is formally announced, usually via a press release. The announcement includes the maturity of the issuer and a coupon rate or range in which the coupon is expected to fall. A telex is also sent by the lead manager to each prospective underwriter, which is a formal invitation to participate in the syndicate. These banks will also receive the preliminary offering circular, a timetable of relevant dates for the issue, and documentation that discloses the legal obligations that they are expected to follow should they decide to participate in the issue. The decision to join is mainly, but not wholly, a function of the bank's client's interest in the issue, which the bank needs to sound out.

The *pricing day* signals the end of the subscription period, the point at which the final terms and conditions of the issue are agreed between the borrower and the syndicate group. If there has been a significant change in market conditions, the specifications of the bond issue will change. Otherwise any required final adjustment of the price is usually undertaken by a change in the price of the bond relative to par. The ability of the lead manager to assess market conditions accurately at this time is vital to the successful pricing of the issue.

Once the final specifications have been determined, members of the syndicate have roughly 24 hours to accept or reject the negotiated terms; the bonds are then formally offered on the *offering day*, the day after the pricing day, when the issuer and the managing group sign the subscription or underwriting agreement containing the final specifications of the issue. The underwriting syndicate then enters into a legal commitment to purchase the bonds from the issuer at the price announced on the pricing day. A final offering circular is then produced, and the lead manager informs the syndicate of the amount of their allotments. The lead manager may wish to either over-allocate or under-allocate the number of available bonds, depending on its view on future levels and direction of interest rates. There then begins the *stabilisation period*, when the bonds begin to trade in the secondary period, where Eurobonds trade in an OTC market. About 14 days after the offering day, the *closing day* occurs. This is when syndicate members pay for bonds they have purchased, usually by depositing funds into a bank account opened and run by the lead manager on behalf of the issuer. The bond itself is usually represented by a *global note*, held in Euroclear or Clearstream, initially issued in temporary form. The temporary note is later changed to a *permanent* global note. Tranches of an issue targeted at US investors may be held in the Depositary Trust Corporation as a registered note.

The grey market

The subscription period of a new Eurobond issue is characterised by uncertainty about potential changes in market conditions. After the announcement of the issue, but before the bonds have been formally issued, the bonds trade in the *grey market*. This is where bonds are bought and sold, for settlement on the first settlement date after the offering day. Grey market trading enables the lead manager to gauge the extent of investor appetite for the issue, and make any adjustment to the coupon if required. A grey market that functions efficiently will at any time reflect the market's view on where the bond should trade, and at what yield the bond should be offered. It enables investors to trade in the primary market possessing information as to the likely price of the issue in the secondary market.

Another principal task of the lead manager is to stabilise the price of the bond issue for a short period after the bond has started trading in the secondary market. This is known as the stabilisation period, and the process is undertaken by the lead manager in concert with some or all of the syndicate members. A previously established pool of funds may be used for this purpose. The price at which stabilisation occurs is known as the *syndicate bid*.

Alternative issue procedures

In addition to the traditional issue procedure where a lead manager and syndicate offer bonds to investors based on a price set, on pricing day, based on a yield over the benchmark bond, there are a number of other issue procedures that are used. One of these methods include the *bought deal*, where a lead manager or a managing group approaches the issuer with a firm bid, specifying issue price, amount, coupon and yield. Only a few hours are allowed for the borrower to accept or reject the terms. If the bid is accepted, the lead manager purchases the entire bond issue from the borrower. The lead manager then has the option of selling part of the issue to other banks for distribution to investors, or doing so itself. In a volatile market the lead manager will probably parcel some of the issue to other banks for placement. However, it is at this time that the risk of banks dumping bonds on the secondary market is highest; in this respect lead managers will usually pre-place the bonds with institutional investors before the bid is made. The bought deal is focused primarily on institutional rather than private investors. As the syndicate process is not used, the bought deal requires a lead manager with sufficient capital and placement power to enable the entire issue to be placed.

In a *pre-priced offering* the lead manager's bid is contingent on its ability to form a selling group for the issue. Any alterations in the bid required for the formation of the group must be approved by the borrower. The period allocated for the formation of the group is usually 2–4 days, and after the group has been formed the process is identical to that for the bought deal.

Yet another approach is the *auction issue*, under which the issuer will announce the maturity and coupon of a prospective issue and invite interested investors to submit bids. The bids are submitted by banks, securities houses and brokers, and include both price and amount. The advantages of the auction process are that it avoids the management fees and costs associated with a syndicate issue. However, the issuer does not have the use of a lead manager's marketing and placement expertise, which means it is a method that can only be employed by very high quality, well-known borrowers.

Covenants

Eurobonds are unsecured and as such the yield demanded by the market for any particular bond will depend on the credit rating of the issuer. Until the early 1980s, Eurobonds were generally issued without covenants, due to the high quality of most issuers. Nowadays it is common for covenants to be given with Eurobond issues. Three covenants in particular are frequently demanded by investors:

- a negative pledge;
- an "event risk" clause;
- a gearing ratio covenant.

Negative pledge

A negative pledge is one that restricts the borrowings of the group which ranks in priority ahead of the debt represented by the Eurobond. In the case of an unsecured Eurobond issue this covenant restricts new secured borrowings by the issuer, as well as new unsecured borrowings by any of the issuer's subsidiaries, since these would rank ahead of the unsecured borrowings by the parent company in the event of the whole group going into receivership.

Disposal of assets covenant

This sets a limit on the amount of assets that can be disposed of by the borrower during the *tenor* (term to maturity) of the debt. The limit on disposals could be typically a cumulative total of 30% of the gross assets of the company. This covenant is intended to prevent a break-up of the company without reference to the Eurobond investors.

Gearing ratio covenant

This places a restriction on the total borrowings of the company during the tenor of the bond. The restriction is set as a maximum percentage of, say,

150–175% of the company's or group's net worth (share capital and reserves).

Trust services

A Eurobond issue requires an agent bank to service it during its life. The range of activities required are detailed below.

Depositary

The depositary for a Eurobond issue is responsible for the safekeeping of securities. In the Euromarkets well over 90% of investors are institutions, and so as a result issues are made in dematerialised form, and are represented by a global note. Trading and settlement is in computerised book-entry form via the two main international clearing systems, Euroclear and Clearstream. Both these institutions have appointed a group of banks to act on their behalf as depositaries for book-entry securities; this is known as *common depositaries*, because the appointment is common to both Euroclear and Clearstream. Both clearing firms have appointed separately a network of banks to act as specialised depositaries, which handled securities that have been issued in printed note or *definitive* form.

As at February 2004 there were 21 banks that acted as common depositaries on behalf of Euroclear and Clearstream, although the majority of the trading volume was handled by just three banks, Citibank NA, JPMorgan Chase and Deutsche Bank AG. The common depositary is responsible for:

- representing Euroclear and Clearstream, and facilitating delivery-versus-payment of the primary market issue by collecting funds from the investors, taking possession of the temporary global note (which allows securities to be released to investors), and making a single payment of funds to the issuer;
- holding the temporary global note in safe custody, until it is exchanged for definitive notes or a permanent global note;
- making adjustments to the nominal value of the global note that occur after the exercise of any options or after conversions, in line with instructions from Euroclear or Clearstream and the fiscal agent;
- surrendering the cancelled temporary global note to the fiscal agent after the exchange into definitive certificates or a permanent global note, or on maturity of the permanent global note.

A specialised depositary will hold definitive notes representing aggregate investor positions held in a particular issue; on coupon and maturity dates it presents the coupons or bond to the paying agent and passes the proceeds on to the clearing system.

Paying agent

Debt issuance in the Euromarkets requires a fiscal or principal paying agent, or in the case of a program of issuance (for example, a Euro-MTN program) an issuing and paying agent. The responsibility of the paying agent is to provide administrative support to the issuer throughout the lifetime of the issue. The duties of a paying agent include:

- issuing securities upon demand in the case of a debt program;
- authenticating definitive notes;
- collecting funds from the issuer and paying these out to investors as coupon and redemption payments;
- in the case of global notes, acting on behalf of the issuer to supervise payments of interest and principal to investors via the clearing systems, and in the case of definitive notes, paying out interest and coupon on presentation by the investor of the relevant coupon or bond to the paying agent;
- transferring funds to sub-paying agents, where these have been appointed. A security that has been listed in Luxembourg must have a local sub-paying agent appointed for it;
- maintaining an account of the cash flows paid out on the bond;
- arranging the cancellation and subsequent payment of coupons, matured bonds and global notes, and sending destroyed certificates to the issuer.

A paying agent will act solely on behalf of the issuer, unlike a trustee who has an obligation to look after the interests of investors. For larger bond issues there may be a number of paying agents appointed, of which the *principal paying agent* is the coordinator. A number of *sub-paying agents* may be appointed to ensure that bondholders in different country locations may receive their coupon and redemption payments without delay. The term *fiscal agent* is used to describe a paying agent for a bond issue for which no trustee has been appointed.

Registrar

The role of the registrar is essentially administrative and it is responsible for keeping accurate records of bond ownership for registered securities. As most Eurobonds are issued in bearer form, there is not a great deal of work for registrars in the Euromarket, and the number of holders of registered notes is normally quite low.

The responsibilities of the registrar include:

- maintaining a register of all bondholders, and records of all transfers of ownership;
- coordinating the registration, transfer or exchange of bonds;
- issuing and authenticating new bonds should any transfer or exchange take place;
- maintaining a record of the outstanding principal value of the bond;
- undertaking administrative functions relating to any special transfers.

Trustee

An issuer may appoint a trustee to represent the interests of investors. In the event of default, the trustee is required to discharge its duties on behalf of bondholders. In certain markets a trustee is obligatory by law; for instance, in the United States a trustee has been a legal requirement since 1939. In other markets an issuer may appoint a trustee in order to make the bond issue more attractive to investors, as it means that there is an independent body to help look after their interests. This is particularly important for a secured issue, where the trustee sometimes holds collateral for the benefit of investors. Assets that are held by the trustee can be protected from the creditors of the issuer in the event of bankruptcy. A trustee has a variety of powers and discretion, which are stated formally in the issue trust deed, and these include its duties in relation to the monitoring of covenants, and duties to bondholders.

Custodian

A custodian provides safekeeping services for securities belonging to a client. The client may be an institutional investor, such as a pension fund, that requires a portfolio of securities in many locations to be kept in secure custody on its behalf. As well as holding securities, the custodian usually manages corporate actions such as dividend payments.

Form of the bond

Eurobonds are issued in a temporary global form or in a permanent global form. If issued in temporary form, the note is subsequently changed into either permanent global form or *definitive* form, which may be either a bearer note or registered.

Temporary global form

On issue the majority of Eurobonds are in the form of a single document known as a temporary global bond. This document represents the entire issue, executed by an officer of the issuer and certified by the fiscal agent or principal paying agent. After a period of time the temporary global bond, as its name suggests, is exchanged for either a permanent global bond or bonds in definitive form, which are separate certificates representing each bond holding.

The main reason bonds are issued in temporary form is because of time constraints between the launch of issue, when the offer is announced to the market, and closing, when the bonds are actually issued. This period differs according to the type of issue and instrument; for example, for a plain vanilla issue it can be as little as two weeks, whereas for more exotic issues (such as a securitisation) it can be a matter of months. The borrower will be keen to have the periods as short as possible, as the financing is usually required quickly. As this results in there being insufficient time to complete the security printing and authentication of the certificates, which represent the final definitive form, a temporary bond is issued to enable the offering to be closed and to be placed in a clearing system, while the final certificates are produced. Bonds are also issued in temporary form to comply with certain domestic selling regulations and restrictions; for example, a US regulation that definitive bonds cannot be delivered for a 40-day period after issue. This is known as the *lock-up* period.

Permanent global bond

Like the temporary bond the permanent global bond is a word-processed document and not a security printed certificate, issued on the closing date. It represents the entire issue and is compiled by the underwriter's legal representatives. In most cases it is actually held for safe-keeping on behalf of Euroclear and Clearstream by the trust or clearing arm of a bank, known as the *common depositary*. Borrowers often prefer to issue notes in permanent global form because this carries lower costs compared to definitive notes, which are security printed.

Definitive form

Under any circumstances where it is required that investors have legal ownership of the debt obligation represented by a bond issue they have purchased, a borrower is obliged to issue the bond in definitive form. The situations under which this becomes necessary are listed on the permanent global bond document, and include the following:

- where an investor requires a definitive bond to prove legal entitlement to the bond (s)he has purchased, in the case of any legal proceedings undertaken concerning the bond issue;
- in the event of default, or if investors believe default to have occurred;
- where for any reason the bonds can no longer be cleared through a clearing system, in which case they must be physically delivered in the form of certificates.

Bonds issued in definitive form may be either *bearer* or *registered* securities. A bearer security has similar characteristics to cash money, in that the certificates are documents of value and the holder is considered to be the beneficiary and legal owner of the bond. The bond certificate is security printed and the nature of the debt obligation is detailed on the certificate. Transfer of a bearer security is by physical delivery. Some of the features of traditional bearer securities include:

- *coupons*, attached to the side of the certificate, and which represent each interest payment for the life of the bond. The holder is required to detach each coupon as it becomes due and send it to the issuer's paying agent;[5]
- a *promise to pay*, much like a bank note, which confirms that the issuer will pay the bearer the face value of the bond on the specified maturity date;
- in some cases, a *talon*; this is the right for the bondholder to claim a further set of coupons once the existing set has been used (this only applies to bonds that have more than 27 interest payments during

[5] This is the origin of the term "coupon" to refer to the periodic interest payments of a bond. There is a marvellous line in the film *Mission Impossible* when the character played by Tom Cruise, discussing terms in the back of a car with the character played by Vanessa Redgrave, demands payment in the form of US Treasury securities "with coupons attached". This is wonderfully out-of-date, but no less good fun for it!

their lifetime, as IPMA rules prohibit the attachment of more than 27 coupons to a bond on issue).

The administrative burdens associated with bearer securities is the main reason why the procedures associated with them are carried out via the clearing systems and paying agents, rather than individually by each investor.

Registered bonds

Bonds issued in registered from are transferred by an entry on a *register* held by the issuer or its agent; the promise to pay is made to those names that appear on the register. Most Eurobonds are issued in bearer form for ease in clearing. Issues that are placed wholly or partly in the United States do however include an option allowing investors to take the bonds in registered form. This is done as most issues in the United States are sold under *private placement*, in order to be exempt from SEC selling restrictions, and private placement in that country requires that the bonds are in registered form. In such cases the issuer will appoint a New York *registrar* for the issuer, usually the trust arm of a bank.

Fiscal agent

A Eurobond issuer will appoint either a fiscal agent or a trustee; both perform similar roles but under differing legal arrangements. The fiscal agent is appointed by and is the representative of the issuer, so unlike a trustee it does not represent the bondholders. The main responsibilities of the fiscal agent are to pay the principal and interest payments, and it performs a number of administrative roles as well, such as the publication of financial information and notices to investors.

Listing agent

Issuers must appoint a listing agent if they wish to list the bond on the London or Luxembourg stock exchanges, as this is a requirement of the rules of the exchange. The listing agent communicates with the exchange on behalf of the issuer, and lodges the required documentation with it. In the United Kingdom the listing agent must be authorised under financial regulatory legislation (at the time of writing, the *Financial Services Act 1986*, although this is in the process of being updated with new legislation covering the new Financial Services Authority regulatory body) and is usually the lead manager for the issue, although it is also common for a fiduciary service provider to be appointed to this role.

Clearing systems

The development of the international bond market has taken place alongside the introduction of specialised clearing systems, which are responsible (among other things) for the settlement and safekeeping of Eurobonds. The two main clearing systems are Euroclear and Clearstream.[6]

Euroclear was created by the Morgan Guaranty Trust Company of New York in 1968. Ultimately, ownership passed to a consortium of banks and it is now run by Euroclear Clearance Systems plc, and operated by a co-operative company in Brussels.

The original Cedel was created in 1970 in Luxembourg and is owned by a consortium of around 100 banks, no one of which may hold more than 5% of the company. The two clearing systems do not restrict their operations to the settlement and custody of Eurobonds.

Both clearing systems exist to avoid the physical handling of bearer instruments, both on issue and in the secondary market. This means that on issue the actual bond certificates, which may be in *definitive bearer* or *global* form, are passed on to a "trust" bank, known as the *depositary* for safekeeping. The clearing system will track holdings via a book entry. To participate in the clearing system set-up, an investor must have two accounts with it, which may be its own accounts or accounts held by her bank who will act as a nominee on her behalf; these are a *securities clearance* account, to which a security is credited, and a *cash* account, through which cash is received or paid out.

The clearing system will allocate a unique identification code, known as the International Securities Identification Number (ISIN) to each Eurobond issue, and a "Common Code" is derived from the ISIN. The Common Code is essentially the identification used for each bond issue whenever an instruction is sent to the clearing agent to deal in it. The ISIN will be in addition to any number issued by a domestic clearing agent; for example, the Stock Exchange number (SEDOL) for London-listed securities. Both clearing systems have specific roles in both the primary and secondary markets. In the primary market they accept a new issue of Eurobonds, and on *closing*, the required number of bonds are credited to the securities clearance account of the banks that are part of the issue syndicate. Securities

[6] Clearstream was previously known as Cedel Bank.

are then transferred (electronic book entry) to securities accounts of investors.

The clearance systems keep a record on the coupon payment and redemption dates for each bond, and "present" the bonds for payment on each appropriate date. Investors therefore do not need to present any coupons or certificates themselves, which is why the system is now paperless.

Market associations

International Securities Market Association

The International Securities Market Association (ISMA) is a self-regulatory body based in Zurich whose membership (from over 60 countries) consists of firms dealing in the international securities markets. It was originally known as the Association of International Bond Dealers. The body provides a regulatory framework for the international markets and has established uniform practices that govern nearly all transactions in Eurobonds between members. ISMA has also:

- introduced a standard method of calculating yields for Eurobonds;
- contributed towards the harmonisation of procedures for settling market transactions, and cooperation between the two main settlement institutions, Euroclear and Cedel;
- introduced TRAX, a computerised system for matching and reporting transactions in the market.

Dealers in the international markets must cooperate with national governments and ensure that market practice is consistent with national laws. ISMA provides a point of contact between the markets and government bodies. The ISMA centre at the University of Reading in England has also established itself as a leading research body, concentrating on the financial and securities markets, as well as offering Masters degrees in a range of capital markets subjects.[7]

International Primary Market Association

The International Primary Market Association (IPMA) is a trade association of the leading underwriters in the primary international capital markets. It is

[7] In October 2005 ISMA was due to change its name to the International Capital Markets Association (ICMA).

also a self-regulatory association that has issued practical guidelines it expects members to follow. Its specific interest is with new issues, the co-operation between underwriters in a syndicate and standardised documentation. Members of IPMA are required to belong to ISMA. The IPMA recommendations are applicable to new issues and relate to matters such as:

- early disclosure of the terms of an issue;
- underwriting commitments;
- allotments of securities with investors;
- payment of commissions;
- delivery of bond/share certificates;
- fixed price offerings and re-offer schemes.

IPMA has also issued statements of best practice concerned with topics on a range of issuance procedures; for example, in 1985 it published guidelines on the process of stabilisation. These guidelines emphasised the importance of correct pricing by lead managers.

Bloomberg screens

Eurobonds can be analysed using all the Bloomberg screens available for bonds generally. Figure 10.3 shows screen NIM on the Bloomberg which is the new issues monitor. It shows all new and recent issues in the market, in this case as at 13 August 2003. Issues that were placed on preceding days are also shown. We see that on the day in question seven bonds were placed in the market; another two were announced or were beginning to be placed by their underwriters.

Figure 10.4 shows a screen that can be obtained from the FMC menu page on Bloomberg, which stands for "Fair Market Curve". From this page a user can select the yield curve for a number of market sectors; our example shows AAA, A and BBB-rated euro-denominated Eurobond curves as at 13 August 2003. The curves are labelled "composite" because they take Eurobonds of the required rating from a number of different sectors, such as telecoms, utilities, industrials companies, and so on.

Figure 10.5 is the Bloomberg page BQ for a Eurobond issued by Citigroup in July 2005, analysed on 19 August 2005. This page is a combination of four pages of analysis. The first page shows asset swap spreads, and price quotes. The next three pages, shown as Figures 10.6, 10.7 and 10.8, shows (i) asset swap versus equity price performance, (ii) repo funding analysis and (iii) credit rating information.

GRAB | Pfd NIM
Enter # <GO> for DES. | Page 1 / 22
New Issues: Euro Market - All | Phone: 44-20-7330-7333

	Issuer	Cpn (%)	Mty (M/D/Y)	Sprd (BP)	Outstand Amt (Mil)	Book Mgr (*=group)	Note
	-------- WEDNESDAY, AUGUST 13 --------						
1)	VOLKSWAGEN FIN	$2\frac{7}{8}$	08/29/05		EUR 50	DZBK-sole	
2)	Standard Life Bank Begins Selling Floating-Rate Bonds in Euros						
3)	ABN AMRO BOUWFON	3.65	08/22/08		EUR 40	DRES	
4)	FREDDIE MAC	$2\frac{3}{4}$	08/15/06	+38	USD 5B	DB,ML,MS	PXD @ 99.923
5)	STANDARD LIFE	WI	08/26/05		EUR 250	DB,UBS	TO BE PRICED
6)	RABOBANK	$1\frac{1}{4}$	04/30/07		CHF 200	CSFB,DB	INC BY 50MM
7)	EUROHYPO SA LUX	$3\frac{1}{2}$	12/28/07	+116	USD 500	JOINT LEADS	
8)	ERSTE EUROPAEISC	FRN	09/19/05		CHF 200	UBS-sole	3ML FLAT
9)	Daimler to Sell $1.27 Bln in Asset-Backed Securities (Update2)						
	-------- TUESDAY, AUGUST 12 --------						
10)	FANNIE MAE	4	09/02/08	+75	USD 1B	C,LEH,ML	PXD @ 99.935
11)	BANCO BRADES CI	$6\frac{3}{4}$	08/20/10	+365	USD 200	ABN-sole	
12)	BANCO BRADES CI	FRN	08/20/10		USD 200	ABN-sole	3ML +68
13)	SPIRIT FUNDING	FRN	03/28/18		GBP 66	GS	FUNGIBLE
14)	SPIRIT FUNDING	FRN	12/28/31		GBP 41.5	GS	3ML +350
15)	SPIRIT FUNDING	FRN	09/28/29		GBP 25	GS	FUNGIBLE
16)	FHLMC Launches Sale of $5 Bln 3-Yr Reference Notes						
17)	GATX CORP	5	08/15/23		USD 115	C,DB,JPM	CVT-NC5
18)	AUSTRIAN T-BILL	ZERO	09/15/03		EUR 10		1MO

Australia 61 2 9777 8600 Brazil 5511 3048 4500 Europe 44 20 7330 7500 Germany 49 69 920410
Hong Kong 852 2977 6000 Japan 81 3 3201 8900 Singapore 65 6212 1000 U.S. 1 212 318 2000 Copyright 2003 Bloomberg L.P.
G657-802-3 13-Aug-03 15:21:51

Figure 10.3 Bloomberg new issues monitor
© Bloomberg L.P. Used with permission.

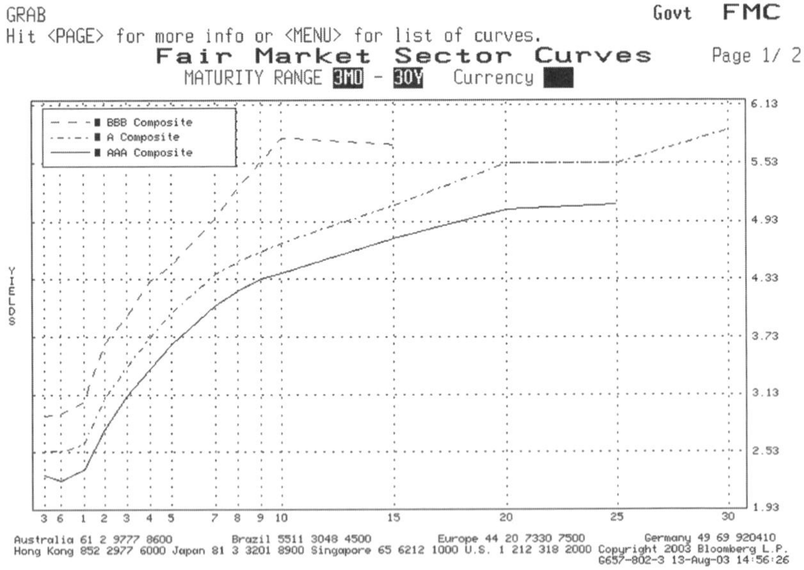

Figure 10.4 Fair market curves screen
© Bloomberg L.P. Used with permission.

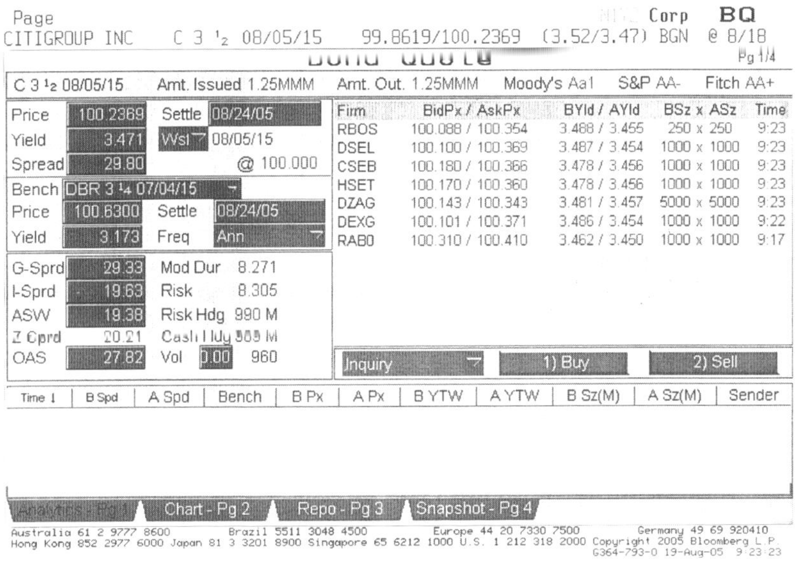

Figure 10.5 Bloomberg Screen BQ, Citigroup Eurobond issued in July 2005
© Bloomberg L.P. Used with permission.

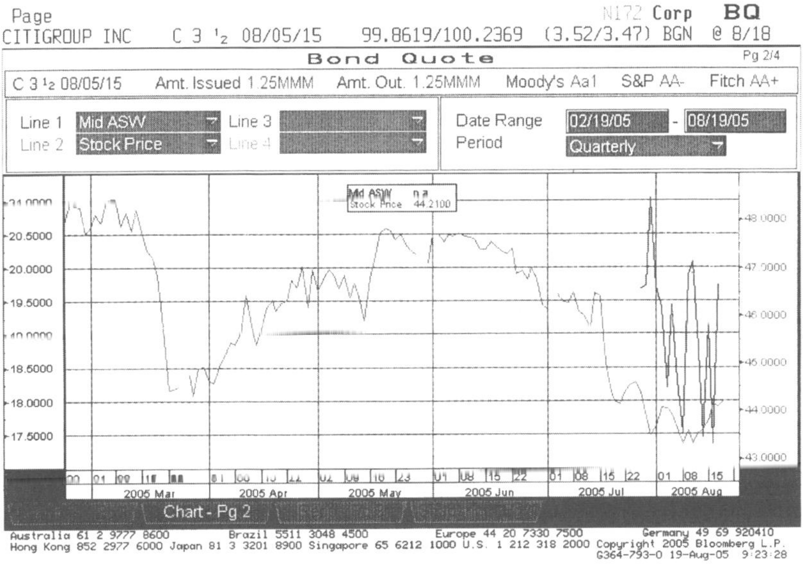

Figure 10.6 Asset swap versus equity price performance, Citigroup bond
© Bloomberg L.P. Used with permission.

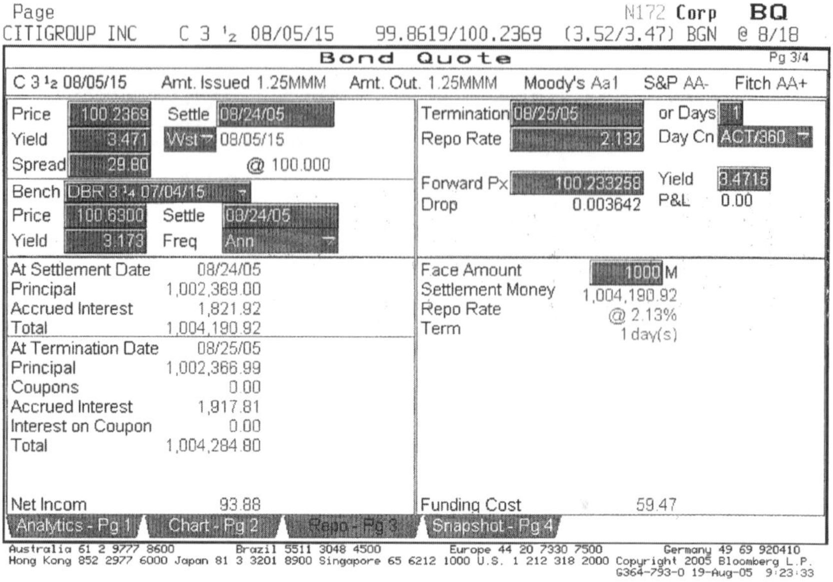

Page N172 Corp BQ
CITIGROUP INC C 3 ½ 08/05/15 99.8619/100.2369 (3.52/3.47) BGN @ 8/18

Bond Quote Pg 3/4

C 3 ½ 08/05/15 Amt. Issued 1.25MMM Amt. Out. 1.25MMM Moody's Aa1 S&P AA- Fitch AA+

Price 100.2369	Settle 08/24/05	Termination 08/25/05	or Days 1
Yield 3.471	Wst 08/05/15	Repo Rate 2.132	Day Cn ACT/360
Spread 29.80	@ 100.000	Forward Px 100.233258	Yield 3.4715
Bench DBR 3 ¼ 07/04/15		Drop 0.003642	P&L 0.00
Price 100.6300	Settle 08/24/05		
Yield 3.173	Freq Ann		

At Settlement Date	08/24/05	Face Amount	1000 M
Principal	1,002,369.00	Settlement Money	1,004,190.92
Accrued Interest	1,821.92	Repo Rate	@ 2.13%
Total	1,004,190.92	Term	1 day(s)
At Termination Date	08/25/05		
Principal	1,002,366.99		
Coupons	0.00		
Accrued Interest	1,917.81		
Interest on Coupon	0.00		
Total	1,004,284.80		
Net Incom	93.88	Funding Cost	59.47

Analytics - Pg 1 | Chart - Pg 2 | Repo - Pg 3 | Snapshot - Pg 4

Australia 61 2 9777 8600 Brazil 5511 3048 4500 Europe 44 20 7330 7500 Germany 49 69 920410
Hong Kong 852 2977 6000 Japan 81 3 3201 8900 Singapore 65 6212 1000 U.S. 1 212 318 2000 Copyright 2005 Bloomberg L.P.
G364-793-0 19-Aug-05 9:23:33

Figure 10.7 Repo funding analysis, Citigroup bond
© Bloomberg L.P. Used with permission.

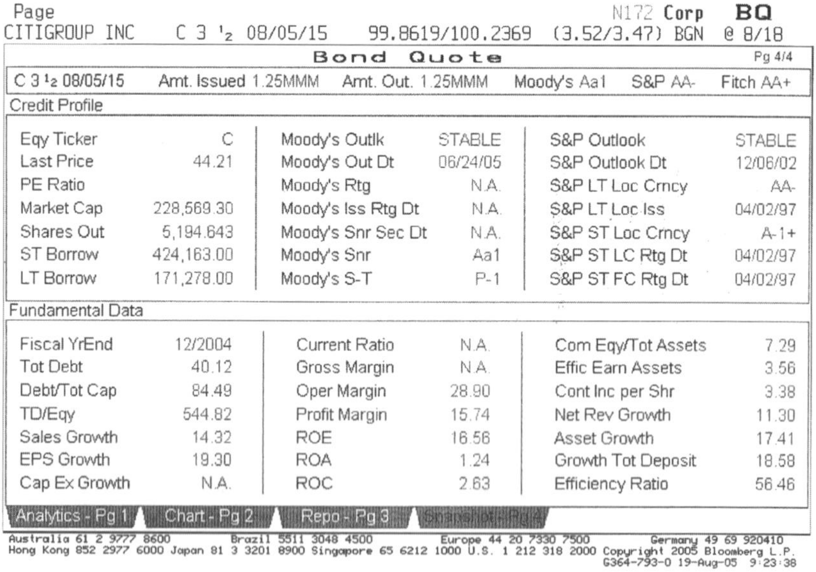

Page N172 Corp BQ
CITIGROUP INC C 3 ½ 08/05/15 99.8619/100.2369 (3.52/3.47) BGN @ 8/18

Bond Quote Pg 4/4

C 3 ½ 08/05/15 Amt. Issued 1.25MMM Amt. Out. 1.25MMM Moody's Aa1 S&P AA- Fitch AA+

Credit Profile

Eqy Ticker	C	Moody's Outlk	STABLE	S&P Outlook	STABLE
Last Price	44.21	Moody's Out Dt	06/24/05	S&P Outlook Dt	12/06/02
PE Ratio		Moody's Rtg	N.A.	S&P LT Loc Crncy	AA-
Market Cap	228,569.30	Moody's Iss Rtg Dt	N.A.	S&P LT Loc Iss	04/02/97
Shares Out	5,194.643	Moody's Snr Sec Dt	N.A.	S&P ST Loc Crncy	A-1+
ST Borrow	424,163.00	Moody's Snr	Aa1	S&P ST LC Rtg Dt	04/02/97
LT Borrow	171,278.00	Moody's S-T	P-1	S&P ST FC Rtg Dt	04/02/97

Fundamental Data

Fiscal YrEnd	12/2004	Current Ratio	N.A.	Com Eqy/Tot Assets	7.29
Tot Debt	40.12	Gross Margin	N.A.	Effic Earn Assets	3.56
Debt/Tot Cap	84.49	Oper Margin	28.90	Cont Inc per Shr	3.38
TD/Eqy	544.82	Profit Margin	15.74	Net Rev Growth	11.30
Sales Growth	14.32	ROE	16.56	Asset Growth	17.41
EPS Growth	19.30	ROA	1.24	Growth Tot Deposit	18.58
Cap Ex Growth	N.A.	ROC	2.63	Efficiency Ratio	56.46

Analytics - Pg 1 | Chart - Pg 2 | Repo - Pg 3 | Snapshot - Pg 4

Australia 61 2 9777 8600 Brazil 5511 3048 4500 Europe 44 20 7330 7500 Germany 49 69 920410
Hong Kong 852 2977 6000 Japan 81 3 3201 8900 Singapore 65 6212 1000 U.S. 1 212 318 2000 Copyright 2005 Bloomberg L.P.
G364-793-0 19-Aug-05 9:23:38

Figure 10.8 Credit rating information, Citigroup bond
© Bloomberg L.P. Used with permission.

Secondary market

Most Eurobonds are tradeable, although the liquidity of individual issues is variable. Although in theory transfer is by physical delivery because the bonds are bearer instruments, the great majority of bonds will settle by the Euroclear or Clearstream International ("Clearstream") settlement systems.[8] Liquidity in the market varies over time and for individual issues will be a function of:

- size of issue;
- level of investor demand for the paper;
- commitment of market-makers to support the issue.

A large number of Eurobonds are illiquid and market-makers will quote a bid price only. No offer price is made because the market-maker (unless she actually owns some of the issue) will be unable to find bonds to deliver to the buyer if it is illiquid. Many Eurobonds issued in the second-tier currencies, such as Greek drachma, will have been issued and then immediately asset-swapped, and hence there will be no paper available to trade (many large issuers will issue Eurobonds in a currency other than that which they require, in order to meet a specific customer demand for paper in that currency; after issue the proceeds are swapped into the desired currency. In the meantime the bonds will be held to maturity by the investors and usually not traded in the secondary market).

High-quality Eurobond issues will trade almost as government paper. For example, issues by the World Bank or the European Investment Bank (EIB) trade at very low spreads above the same currency government bonds and are highly liquid. For example, at times EIB sterling Eurobonds have traded at only 7–9 basis points above the same maturity gilt.

Settlement

Settlement of Eurobond transactions takes place within 28 days for primary market issues and T + 3 days for secondary market trades. Virtually all trades settle within the two main clearing systems, Euroclear and Clearstream. Euroclear was established in Brussels in 1968 by an international group of banks, the original entity known as Cedel was established in Luxembourg in 1970. Both clearing systems will settle in

8 In 1999 Cedel Bank and Deutsche Terminbourse merged their operations, and the resulting entity was named Clearstream International, or simply Clearstream. Cedel Bank had originally been known as Cedel.

T + 3 days; however, the facility exists to settle trades in T + 1 if both parties to a trade wish it.

In the Euroclear system bonds are placed in the custody of the clearing system, through a Europe-wide network of depositary banks. The transfer of bonds on settlement is undertaken by means of a computer book-entry. This was the basic concept behind the introduction of Euroclear, the substitution of book entries for the physical movement of bonds. The actual physical securities to which a trading party has title are not identified in the majority of transactions made through Euroclear. The clearing system is made possible because the terms and conditions of any Eurobond issue are objectively specified, so that all bonds of a particular issue are standardised, and so fungible for one another. There is no requirement to assign a specific bond serial number to an individual holder, which occurs with registered bonds. Clearstream operates on much the same basis. Participants in either system must be institutions with their own account (they may have an agent settle for them). Settlement takes place through the simultaneous exchange of bonds for cash on the books of the system. An "electronic bridge" connecting the two systems allows transfer of securities from one to the other.

Legal and tax issues

Investors and borrowers in the Eurobond market may at any one time fall under the auspicies of a number of countries' laws and regulations. These relate to the withholding tax on the bond coupons, income tax, disclosure and prospectus requirements, and restrictions on sales to certain classes of investor. The most important legal considerations for professional participants relate to (a) the possibility that the bonds are eventually distributed to residents in the United States, which is prohibited, and (b) London, as the principal financial centre where the sale and trading of bonds takes place. The first consideration means that the market is subject to legislation in the United States that dates from 1933[9] and Federal income tax regulations. The second consideration means that the market comes under certain aspects of English law. With regard to taxation, the key features of Eurobonds are that:

- the bonds are "bearer" rather than registered securities;
- interest and principal payments are not subject to withholding tax at source in the country where the issuer is resident for tax purposes.

[9] The US Securities Act of 1933.

The fact that payments of interest and principal on Eurobonds are not subject to any form of withholding tax at source in the country where the borrower is deemed to be resident for tax purposes is the primary feature of Eurobonds for investors, generally cited to be of key importance in making the market attractive for investors across a range of countries. Non-resident investors in Eurobonds are usually subject to the withholding tax requirements of the resident country of the bond issuer when that party repays interest or principal on bonds held by these non-residents. The tax advantages to an investor from the absence of withholding tax (combined with the fact that the bonds are issued in bearer form) are significant. A large proportion of Eurobonds are held by private investors, and much of this is made anonymously by means of external discretionary accounts, such as those run by Swiss banks. This is a source of some frustration to tax authorities in certain countries. The absence of withholding tax also confers a certain benefit to issuers of Eurobonds. Where a bond issue was subject to withholding tax, an issuer would need to make the terms of the issue more attractive, that is a higher coupon, in order to make the bond as attractive as the Eurobond issuer. This will carry higher associated costs for the issuer.

The secondary market

The market in trading Eurobonds is conducted on an OTC basis. In 1998 a number of automated electronic trading systems were also introduced. The pre-eminence of London as the main trading centre for the Eurobond market is well-established, although Brussels, Frankfurt, Zurich and Singapore are also important trading centres. The advantages of London as a trading centre are generally regarded as being:

- a low level of regulatory interference in the functioning of the market;
- the presence of well-established infrastructure and institutions, as well as experienced human resources;
- the use of the English language as the market's main language of communication.

There are over 40 different market-makers registered with ISMA, and although in theory they are all required to make two-way prices in their chosen markets, the level of commitment is very varied. The bid–offer spread can be as low as 0.10 for very liquid issues such as World Bank and EIB bonds, to no offer price quoted for illiquid issues. In between there are a range of spread sizes. The normal market size also varies, from £100,000 nominal to £500,000.

The valuation of Eurobonds is usually done on the basis of a yield spread over the relevant government bond yield curve. This yield spread is a function of the credit quality of the bond, its liquidity in the market and the level of supply and demand. The bonds also move in line with general moves in interest rates, so that if there is a change in the gilt yield curve, a sterling Eurobond will change in yield, irrespective of whether the bond's issuer was perceived as being a weaker or a stronger credit. A market-maker wishing to hedge a position in Eurobonds will usually use either the benchmark government bond against which the bond is priced or, if a non-cash option is preferred, will use bond futures contracts to hedge the position. These topics are all covered in chapters elsewhere.

Eurobonds and swap transactions

Readers who are unfamiliar with swap instruments may wish to consult a standard derivatives text first. The issue of new Eurobonds and the use of "asset swaps" in conjunction with issues is a vital part of the market, with investment banks keeping a close observation of the asset swap curve to spot any opportunities that may arise that makes a new issue of paper more attractive. New issues of Eurobonds are often launched to facilitate a swap which has been arranged in advance.

The existence of the currency swap and asset swap market is one of the key reasons for the growth and popularity of the Eurobond market. A borrower can issue bonds in virtually any liquid and convertible currency, according to where there is demand and what the yield curve looks like, and swap the proceeds into the currency that it requires. The cost of borrowing is usually significantly lower than if the borrower had issued bonds in the required currency. Swap-driven issues are very common in the Eurobond market, and the key motivator is that borrowing costs will be cheaper. If this cheap borrowing opportunity is not available, it is unlikely that the bond will be issued, because entering into a swap exposes the issuer to additional credit risk. Swap financing will require a borrower to obtain debt initially that has undesirable currency and/or coupon characteristics. If the counterparty to a swap defaults, the borrower will be left with a risk exposure on the original debt. However, swap financing remains attractive because of the opportunity to obtain cheaper borrowing costs, despite the additional exposure to credit risk entailed in the transaction.

The market in swaps is governed by the International Swap Dealers Association (ISDA). In the market the majority of transactions are plain vanilla in nature, and involve one of the following:

- cross-currency fixed-rate swaps, usually referred to as *currency swaps*;
- interest rate swaps;
- cross-currency hybrid swaps;
- basis swaps.

Currency swaps are very common in the market. Under the plain vanilla version, two counterparties issue fixed-rate debt denominated in different currencies. They then exchange the interest and (sometimes) the principal repayments on their respective debt obligations. Under the conventional pattern the amounts exchanged remain fixed at maturity. We will not cover the mechanics of a currency swap here as this is reviewed in any number of derivatives texts; likewise interest rate swaps and the concepts of comparative advantage and the fixed- versus floating-rate legs of an interest-rate swap. Swap agreements do not always involve the exchange of debt repayment streams. In certain cases one of the revenue streams exchanged in a swap can represent the income interest stream on an asset, or conventional security such as a corporate bond. Eurobond issues are frequently brought to the market primarily for the purpose of such "asset swapping". For the investment bank, swapping asset base interest payments is one means by which bond issues can be re-packaged.

Other instruments used include *basis swaps*, which involve the exchange of two floating-rate payments streams, each of which is based on a short-term interest rate. The most common of these instruments have the following reference rates:

- Libor versus the US commercial paper rate;
- Libor versus the prime rate.

Basis swaps are not the primary motivators of Eurobond issues, but are often included in more complex swap agreements which may involve Eurobond borrowing.

Selected bibliography and references

Andersen, T. 1982, "How the grey market became respectable", *Euromoney*, May.

Crawford, A. 1987, "Stabilization brings the jitters", *Euromoney*, April, p. 277.

Decovny, S. 1998, *Swaps*, FT Prentice Hall, London, p. 68.

Kerr, I. 1984, *A History of the Eurobond Market*, Euromoney Publications, Colchester.

van Agtmael, A. 1983, "Issuance of Eurobonds: Syndication and underwriting techniques and costs", in George, A. and Giddy, I. (eds), *International Financial Handbook*, Section 5.2, John Wiley & Sons, Chichester.

Cut the cackle and get me out of this before I go crazy!

– Captain Haddock
Prisoners of the Sun,
George Remi (1907–1982)

CHAPTER 11

Warrants

A warrant entitles its holder to purchase a specified asset at a set price at a specified date or dates. The terms defining a warrant usually remain unchanged during its entire life, and the asset may be bonds, equities, an index, commodities or other instruments. Hence a warrant is an option issued by a firm to purchase a given number of shares in that firm (*equity warrant*) or more of the firm's bonds (*bond warrant*), at a given exercise price at any time before the warrant expires. If the warrant is exercised, the firm issues new shares (or bonds) at the exercise price and so raises additional finance. Warrants generally have longer maturities than conventional options (five years or longer, although there is usually a liquid market in very long-dated OTC equity options), and some warrants are perpetual.

Warrants are usually attached to bonds (*host bond*) to start with, in most cases such warrants are detachable and can be traded separately. Equity warrants do not carry any shareholders' rights until they are exercised; for example, they pay no dividends and have no voting rights. Bond warrants can either be exercised into the same class of bonds as the host bond or into a different class of bond. In valuing a warrant it is important to recognise that exercising the warrant (unlike exercising an ordinary call option) will increase the number of shares outstanding. This will have the effect of diluting earnings per share and hence reducing the share price. Hence, although equity warrants are often valued in the same way as an American call option, the pricing must also take into account this dilution effect. Warrants are often used in conjunction with a new bond issue, to act as a "sweetener", and are common instruments in the Japanese bond and equity markets. If the issuing company performs well, the investor can eventually exercise the warrant and purchase the company's equity at the exercise price fixed at the time the warrant was issued. During this time, in the same way as for a convertible bondholder, the investor has the security of holding the company's fixed interest debt, which acts as a type of security in the event that the company's share price declines.

In the United Kingdom some companies use warrants to obtain a steady flow of new investment. For example, every year from 1988 the London-listed company BTR has issued bonus warrants free to its shareholders, with the exercise price set just out-of-the-money. From the investor's viewpoint warrants may be used as a means of having an exposure to a company's shares but with a relatively low capital outlay at the start. They also allow the investor already holding shares to sell them while still maintaining an equity stake. This is known as *cash extraction* and is a straightforward strategy. The investor sells the shares, uses some of the proceeds to buy warrants representing the same number of shares, and invests the remaining cash in interest-bearing instruments. The price of warrants, just like convertibles, do not move one-for-one with the underlying equity unless they are deep in-the-money however, so a rise in the share price will not be matched by the same rise in the warrant price. In the short term therefore an investor following a cash extraction strategy may miss out on share price performance, in addition to any dividend payments.

EXAMPLE 11.1 Tate & Lyle warrants

Tate & Lyle plc issued $5^3/_4$% 10-year bonds in March 1991, with 37,200 share warrants attached. The bond was issued with a face value of £5,000. Each share warrant entitles the holder to subscribe for 866 ordinary shares up to March 2001. The exercise price was £3,968.90 per warrant, or 458.3p per share until 20 March 1993, rising in annual increments to £5,143.75 per warrant (594p per share) from 20 March 2000. Alternatively, a warrant may be exercised by surrendering one bond for the same number of shares, rather than making a cash payment.

Analysis

As with ordinary options the value of a warrant has two components, an intrinsic value (which in the warrant market is known as *formula value*) and a time value (*premium* over formula value). Although the term *premium* is used in the options market to refer to the price paid for an option, in the warrant market the conventional term *price* is used. The *warrant premium* is usually used to refer to the amount by which the warrant price plus the exercise price exceeds the current underlying share price.

The formula value is determined by equation (11.1):

$$\text{Formula value} = (\text{Share price} - \text{Exercise price}) \times \text{Number of new shares issued on exercise.} \qquad (11.1)$$

If the exercise price exceeds the share price, the formula value is zero and the warrant is said to be "out-of-the-money". If the share price exceeds the exercise price the warrant is in-the-money and the formula value is positive. The time value is always positive up until expiry of the warrant. As with options the time value declines as the expiry date approaches and on the expiry date itself the time value is zero.

The fair price of a warrant is given by (11.2):

$$\text{Warrant value} = \frac{P_c}{1+p} \times \text{Number of new shares if warrant is exercised} \qquad (11.2)$$

where p is the proportionate increase in the number of shares outstanding if all the warrants were exercised, and P_c is the value of an American call option with the same exercise price and expiry date as the warrant.

If a company issues new shares in a rights issue at a price below the market price or issues convertible bonds or new warrants, the value of any existing warrants already in issue will be affected. It is usual therefore for companies to issue warrants with a provision that allows for the exercise price to be reduced in the event of any corporate action that adversely affects the current warrant price.

A warrant is attractive to investors because if the firm is successful and its share price rises accordingly, the warrant can be exercised and the holder can receive higher value shares at the lower exercise price. Virtually all warrants are issued by corporations and are equity warrants. In the late 1980s the Bank of England introduced *gilt warrants*, which could be exercised into gilts; however, none are in existence at present. Yet, it is of course possible to trade in OTC call options on gilts with a number of banks in the City of London.

Covered warrants are issued by a securities house or investment bank rather than the company itself. The aim of the securities house is to create an active and liquid market in the warrants, and to earn profit from making a market in them. When covered warrants are exercised there is no recourse to the company, and the company does not issue new shares. There is thus no dilution effect. The securities house must settle the warrant holder's application to subscribe for shares, either by providing shares already in issue or by the payment of sufficient cash to allow the warrant holder to buy shares in the market.

Bond warrants

Very occasionally bonds are issued with debt warrants attached. For example, an issue of bonds with a coupon of 5% could be made with warrants that give the holder the right to subscribe at a future date for more 5% bonds at a fixed price. The warrants would be attractive to investors who expect interest rates to fall in the future; a fall in rates could result in the warrants being exercised or sold on at a profit, as the lower rates would now make them more valuable.

Say that a bond warrant entitles its holder to purchase bonds with a face value of M at a price of E. The bonds issued on exercise of the warrants may be either a further tranche of an existing issue or a new issue. The exercise cost of purchasing the underlying bond via the warrant is given by (11.3):

$$Cost = \left(P_w + \frac{E \times M}{100} \right) \times \frac{100}{M} \tag{11.3}$$

where

P_w is the price of the warrant
E is the exercise price
M is the par value of the underlying bonds that may be purchased per warrant.

When a bond warrant is exercised, the cost to the purchaser includes the accrued interest up to the exercise date.

If the warrant entitles the holder to the right to purchase a bond that is already in existence, a premium or discount resulting from purchasing the bond via the warrant, as opposed to directly in the market, may be calculated using (11.4):

$$\text{Premium } \% = \left(\frac{\text{Exercise cost}}{P_{bond}} - 1 \right) \times 100 \qquad (11.4)$$

where P_{bond} is the clean price of the underlying bond.

EXAMPLE 11.2 ABC plc bond warrant

ABC plc has issued a bond warrant with the right to subscribe for 8% 2005 bonds. Each warrant gives the holder the right to subscribe for £1,000 nominal amount of the company's 8% bond due 2005, at the exercise price of 100% of the nominal amount plus accrued interest from the previous coupon date (payable 7 June and 7 December each year). The warrants are exercisable up to and including 7 June 2001. If the price of the warrant is £24, the exercise cost of purchasing the £1,000 nominal amount of the 8% bonds is:

$$(24 + (100 \times 1000) \,/\, 100) \times 100/1000$$

which is 102.4% in addition to any accrued interest.

If the bonds are trading in the market at 98.00, as the exercise cost of the bonds via the warrant is 102.4%, the premium is (102.4/98) − 1, which is 4.490%.

Comparison of warrants and convertibles

Warrants and convertibles are both hybrid instruments, both are issued by companies in the international markets. They are essentially similar in many respects, including:

- *valuation*: the theoretical value for a warrant is often calculated using the Black–Scholes or a similar model. In practice, however, investors are willing to pay only a fraction of the theoretical price of a warrant compared to convertibles, which trade near to or at fair value.

Investors often pay more for the conversion premium on an issue of convertibles than they will pay for warrants in an issue of bonds with warrants attached. It is often the case therefore that companies are able to raise more capital by issuing convertibles rather than by issuing bonds with warrants attached;

- *investor base*: although warrants can have a long term to maturity, often they are held by short-term investors who buy them in the expectation of re-selling them at a profit when the company's share price rises by a sufficient amount. Until the exercise date approaches, many investors do not intend to hold the warrants in order to subscribe for shares in the future. The opposite is usually true for convertible bonds, whose investors are more likely to hold convertibles until conversion or redemption;
- *call flexibility*: bonds with warrants attached are often non-callable. The company cannot therefore force warrant holders into an immediate decision whether or not to subscribe for shares. A call option is only rarely a feature of a warrant bond;
- *maturity:* the maturity of a bond with warrants attached is predictable (unless a call feature is also included), as the bond portion remains outstanding until maturity. In contrast, a convertible could remain outstanding for a proportionately much shorter time of its life, and be converted into equity. It is more common for convertibles to have call and/or put features attached. If a company required certainty of redemption dates for its financial planning, warrant bonds would be preferable to convertibles for this reason.

Generally, however, warrants are issued as a "sweetener" attached to a main issue, whereas convertibles are important corporate finance instruments in their own right. In certain markets though, for example in Japan, warrants are an important financing instrument.

Selected bibliography and references

Bird, A. 1971, "Evaluating warrants", *The Investment Analyst*, December.

Chen, A.H.Y. 1970, "A model of warrant pricing in a dynamic market", *Journal of Finance*, 25, December, pp. 1041–60.

Connolly, K.B. and Phillips, G.A. 1992, *Japanese Warrant Markets*, Macmillan, Oxford.

Crouhy, M. and Galai, D. 1988, *Warrant Valuation and Equity Volatility*, HEC.

Emmanuel, D. 1983, "Warrant valuation and exercise strategy", *Journal of Financial Economics,* 12, August, pp. 211–36.

Galai, D. and Schneller, M. 1978, "Pricing warrants and the value of the firm", *Journal of Finance*, 33, December, pp. 1333–42.

Giguere, G. 1958, "Warrants: A mathematical model of evaluation", *Analysts Journal,* 14, November.

Green, R. 1984, "Investment incentives, debt and warrants", *Journal of Financial Economics*, 13, pp. 115–36.

Lauterbach, B. and Schultz, P. 1990, "Pricing warrants: An empirical study of the Black–Scholes model and its alternatives", *Journal of Finance*, 45(4), pp. 1181–209.

Noreen, E. and Wolfson, M. 1981, "Equilibrium warrant pricing models and accounting for executive stock options", *Journal of Accounting Research*, 19, Autumn, pp. 384–98.

Schulz, G. and Trautman, S. 1990, "Valuation of warrants: Theory and empirical tests for warrants written on German stocks", unpublished paper, University of Stuttgart.

Schwartz, E. 1977, "The valuation of warrants: Implementing a new approach", *Journal of Financial Economics*, 4, January, pp. 79–93.

Shelton, J. 1967, "The relation of the pricing of a warrant to the price of its associated common stock", *Financial Analysts Journal*, 23, pp. 88–99.

Spatt, C. and Sterbenz, F. 1988, "Warrant exercise, dividends and re-investment policy", *Journal of Finance,* 43, pp. 493–506.

And when I'm lying in my bed
I think about life and I think about death …
And neither one particularly appeals to me.

– The Smiths
Nowhere Fast, Rough Trade Records, 1985

CHAPTER

12

Medium-term Notes

Medium-term notes (MTNs) are corporate bonds that have evolved into an important source of corporate funding. They are not exclusively corporate instruments however and have been issued by sovereigns, supra-nationals, and federal and local authorities. The first MTN was issued by the General Motors corporation in 1972, and was sold directly to investors rather than via an agent bank. During the 1970s the MTN market was largely illiquid, and in 1981 the volume of outstanding issues was less than $1 billion. In that year Merrill Lynch issued an MTN for Ford Motor Credit and also undertook to make a secondary market in the paper. Since then the MTN market has grown into a major corporate finance instrument, traded both domestically and internationally, and at the end of 2003 the outstanding volume of MTN issues around the world was over $1 trillion (see Table 12.1).

A medium-term note is essentially a plain vanilla debt security with a fixed coupon and maturity date. The term "medium-term" is something of a misnomer, as the bonds range in maturity from nine months to 30 years or more; however, the first MTNs generally had maturities of five years or less. They were originally designed to bridge the gap between *commercial paper* and long-dated bonds. An MTN is an unsecured debt, therefore the majority of MTNs are investment grade quality. In terms of the way they trade in the market, MTNs are virtually identical to conventional corporate bonds, and the main difference between an MTN and a corporate bond is the manner in which it is issued in the primary market. The unique characteristic of MTNs is that they are offered to investors continuously over a period of time by an agent of the issuer, as part of an MTN *program*. MTNs are usually offered in the market by investment banks acting as agents, and sold on a "best efforts" basis. The issuing bank does not act as an underwriter of the bonds, unlike with a conventional bond issue, and therefore the borrowing company is not guaranteed to place all its paper. As MTNs are usually offered as part of a continuous program, they are issued in smaller amounts than conventional bonds, which are generally sold in larger amounts at one time. Notes can be issued either as *bearer* securities or *registered* securities. A Euromarket in MTNs developed in the mid-1980s. Euro MTNs (EMTNs) trade in a similar fashion to Eurobonds; they are debt securities issued for distribution across markets internationally.

Market	Nominal outstanding ($ bln)
United States	
Domestic corporate issues	275
Federal agency	174
Other	46
Sub-total	495
International markets	
Euro-MTNs	489
Domestic markets	26
Sub-total	501
Total*	1012

Table 12.1 Size of the global MTN market, year-ending 2004
Source: Strata Consulting.
*(*Total includes some other markets that are not mentioned.)*

The majority of MTNs are conventional bonds with a fixed coupon rate and single maturity date. There is a wide range of structures available however, and MTNs have been issued with floating-rate coupons, call and put features, amortising nominal amounts, multi-currency structures or as part of more exotic structures such as asset swaps. Certain MTN issues are underwritten by investment banks as well, making them indistinguishable from conventional corporate bonds.

Introduction

The first MTN issue was made by General Motors Acceptance Corporation (GMAC) in the United States in 1972. At that time the instrument was seen as a longer dated version of commercial paper, which for regulatory reasons in the United States may not have a longer maturity than nine months or 270 days. GMAC and (shortly after) other motor car manufacturers were interested in sources of finance that matched the maturity of their car loans to consumers, which were cheaper to issue than conventional bond offerings. For this reason the first MTNs were issued to investors directly, thus avoiding underwriting fees. However, this resulted in a lack of liquidity in the secondary market. A requirement of the Securities and Exchange Commission (SEC) that regulatory approval be obtained for any change to a registered public offering also resulted in higher transaction costs for borrowers, some of whom issued MTNs via private placement. In the 1980s the market began to grow in volume after investment banks issued MTNs as agent and acted as market-makers in the secondary market.[1]

A new regulation instituted by the SEC, Rule 415, also assisted market development as it allowed for *shelf registration* of an MTN program. Under regulations in the United States, any corporate debt issued with a maturity of more than 270 days must be registered with the SEC. In 1982 the SEC adopted Rule 415 which permitted shelf registration of new corporate debt issues. A continuous MTN program can be registered in this way. The issuer must file with the SEC details on (a) historical and current financial information and (b) the type and amount of securities it plans to issue under the program. This is known as "filing a shelf". The adoption of Rule 415 made the administration of continuously offered notes relatively straightforward for the issuer. Under shelf registration, bonds may be sold for up to two years after the registration date without requiring another registration statement every time there is a new offer. Borrowers are able to

[1] Initially the banks would only quote prices for their own issues.

issue paper at short notice in response to favourable market conditions, such as a drop in market interest rates or investor demand for their paper, without having to register each new offering, as long as it is within the two-year period. For issues outside a shelf registration there is a delay between the filing with the SEC and the actual date of public offering, which may be up to five days and potentially prevent the borrower from taking advantage of market conditions.

The adoption of financial engineering techniques has also contributed to the growth of the market. Companies are able to publish a single prospectus that encompasses the entire MTN program, and within the program issue bonds with a variety of structures and in different currencies, to suit specific conditions and requirements. Individual issues within a single program may have a range of coupons, maturity dates and other structures. For example, MTNs have been issued as zero-coupon bonds, floating-rate bonds, with step-up or step-down coupons, denominated in a foreign currency or indexed to an exchange rate or commodity; they are frequently issued in conjunction with a swap structure. Floating-rate MTNs pay coupons linked to a reference rate such as Libor, but have been linked to the commercial paper rate, the Treasury bill rate, Federal funds rate and the *prime* rate. Floating-rate MTNs often pay monthly or quarterly coupons, compared to conventional FRNs which usually pay a semi-annual coupon. The larger borrowers issue debt as part of global MTN programs, which enable them to place debt in their domestic market and internationally in the Euro market, in any liquid currency they wish. The MTN market is flexible and individual programs may be adapted to suit the requirements of borrowers and investors alike; some of the most innovative structures have been observed in the MTN market before their introduction in the conventional corporate bond market.[2]

The primary market

MTN issues are arranged within a program. A continuous MTN program is established with a specified issue limit, and sizes can vary from $100 million to $5,000 million or more. Within the program MTNs can be issued at any time, daily if required. The program is similar to a revolving loan facility; as maturing notes are redeemed, new notes can be issued. The issuer usually

---

2 In July 1993 Walt Disney issued an MTN with a 100-year maturity as part of its rolling global Euro-MTN program. This is equal to the longest dated maturity conventional debt instrument issued in recent years.

specifies the maturity of each note issue within a program, but cannot exceed the total limit of the program.

EXAMPLE 12.1 ABC plc

ABC plc establishes a five-year $200 million MTN program and immediately issues the following notes:

$50 million of notes with a one-year maturity
$70 million of notes with a five-year maturity.

ABC plc can still issue a further $80 million of notes; however, in one year's time when $50 million of notes mature, it will be able to issue a further $50 million if required. The total amount in issue at any one time never rises above $200 million.

The first step for the borrower is to arrange shelf registration with the SEC. This ensures the widest possible market for the program; there are also no re-sale or transfer restrictions on the bonds themselves. The shelf registration identifies the investment bank or banks that will be acting as agents for the program and who will distribute the paper to the market. A domestic program may have only one agent bank, although two to four banks are typical. Global and Euro-MTN programs usually have more agent banks. Once registration is complete the borrower issues a prospectus supplement detailing the terms and conditions of the program. Often a draft prospectus is issued first, and only issued in final once the issuing bank has gauged market reaction. A draft prospectus is known as a *red herring*. Within a program a borrower may also issue conventional corporate bonds, underwritten by an investment bank, but there is none of the flexibility available compared to an MTN issue, which can be arranged at very short notice, so conventional bond offerings within a program are rare.

The agent banks sometimes publicise the maturities and yield spreads that are to be offered as part of the program; a typical example for a hypothetical program in the sterling market is given in Table 12.2.

Maturity	Yield spread (bps)	Benchmark bond	Current yield
9 months	20	13% 2000	5.80
12–24 months	25	7% 2001	6.25
2–3 years	35	7% 2002	6.37
3–4 years	45	6.5% 2003	6.38
4–5 years	50	6.75% 2004	6.34
5–6 years	55	8.5% 2005	6.36
9–11 years	50	5.75% 2009	5.77
15–20 years	30	8% 2021	5.02

Table 12.2 MTN program offer, October 1999

The exact date of a particular maturity issue is not always known at the time the program is announced, so yields are often given as a spread over the equivalent maturity government bond. If the borrower has a particular interest to tap the market at specific points of the yield curve, the spread offered at that point is increased in order to attract investors. Once the required funds have been raised, offer spreads are usually reduced. If the full amount stated in the registration details is raised, US domestic market borrowers need to file a new registration with the SEC. The size of individual issues within a program varies with the funding strategy of the borrower. Certain companies have a preference to raise large amounts at once, say $100 to $200 million, and raise funds using fewer issues. This also maintains a "scarcity value" for their paper compared to borrowers who tap the market more frequently. Other companies adopt the opposite approach, with small size issues of between $5 to $10 million spread over more dates.

Domestic market MTNs are primarily offered on an agency basis, although issues within a program are sometimes sold using other methods. Agent banks sometimes acquire the paper for their own book, trading it later in the secondary market. Specific issues may be underwritten by an agent bank, or sold directly to investors by the corporate treasury arm of the borrowing company.

The main issuers of MTNs in the US market are:

- general finance companies, including automobile finance companies, business credit institutions and securities houses;
- banks, both domestic and foreign;
- governments and government agencies;
- supranational bodies such as the World Bank;

- domestic industrial and commercial companies, primarily motor car and other industrial manufacturing companies, telecommunications companies and other utilities;
- savings and loan institutions.

During the 1980s the MTN market was dominated by financial institutions, accounting for over 90% of issue volume. This share was reduced to approximately 70% by 1992 (Crabbe 1992), the remainder of the issues being accounted for by other categories of borrower.

There is a large investor demand in the United States for high-quality corporate paper, much more so than in Europe where the majority of bonds are issued by financial companies. This demand is particularly great at the short- to medium-term maturity end. As the market has a large number of issuers, investors are able to select issues that meet precisely their requirements for maturity and credit rating. The main investors are:

- investment companies;
- insurance companies;
- banks;
- savings and loan institutions;
- corporate treasury departments;
- state institutions.

It can be seen that the investor base is very similar to the issuer base!

All the main US investment banks make markets in MTNs, including Merrill Lynch, Goldman Sachs, Morgan Stanley, CSFB and Salomon Smith Barney. In the United Kingdom active market-makers in MTNs include RBS Financial Markets and Barclays Capital.

MTNs and corporate bonds

A company wishing to raise a quantity of medium-term or long-term capital over a period of time has the choice of issuing MTNs or long-dated bonds. An MTN program is a series of issues over time, matching the issuer's funding requirement, and therefore should be preferred over a bond by companies that do not need all the funding at once, nor for the full duration of the program. Corporate bonds are preferred where funds are required immediately. They are also a better choice for issuers that expect interest rates to rise in the near future and wish to lock in a fixed borrowing rate for all the funds required. The decision on whether to raise finance using MTNs or corporate bonds will be taken after consideration of the interest cost and flexibility offered by each instrument. That MTNs offer financing advantages over conventional bonds under certain circumstances is reflected in the growth and current size of the market; however, the same borrowers are evident in both markets, which implies that both instruments possess advantages over the other under specific conditions.

The main difference between MTNs and corporate bonds is the process by which they are sold and distributed. There are other differentiating features however. MTNs are almost invariably sold at par on issue, whereas conventional bonds are usually offered at a slight discount to par. The proceeds on the day of issue are settled on the same day for MTNs (making them similar to money market instruments in this respect), while the settlement for new issue traditional bonds is the following day, or T + 3 for international issues. In the US market, corporate bonds pay semi-annual coupon on either the 1st or the 15th of the month; the latter is identical to Treasury securities. MTNs however have coupon dates payable on a fixed cycle basis, irrespective of their issue or maturity date. This payment convention means that MTNs have a long or short first coupon, and a short final coupon, whereas conventional bonds would always have a regular final coupon. MTNs pay interest on a 30/360 day-count basis, similar to Eurobonds and US domestic corporate bonds.

EXAMPLE 12.2 MTN program

An MTN program pays semi-annual interest on 1 June and 1 December each year and on maturity of the individual note. An issue within the program of £10 million 6.75% bonds with a two-year maturity on 1 July would pay a short first coupon of £281,250 on the first coupon date in December, regular coupons of £337,500 on the next three coupon dates and a short final coupon of £56,250 on the maturity date.

Issue size and liquidity

The size of an issue has the most significant impact on the relative cost of an MTN issue versus a straight bond. For large issues, which are regarded as nominal amounts of over $400 million borrowed over a medium or long term, the all-in cost of a straight bond issue is generally lower than the all-in cost of an MTN program. This reflects the economies of scale that may be achieved when issuing such an amount on one date, as well as the greater secondary market liquidity of larger sized issues. For this reason borrowers who have a heavy funding requirement for a specific period in time will usually prefer to raise the funds with a straight bond issue. The liquidity premium associated with large volume issues is not known with certainty, but is estimated at around 5 to 10 basis points (Kitter 1999); for large amounts this saving would be substantial. However, this premium is indicative of the improved liquidity in the MTN market.

Another factor that borrowers consider is the cost saving associated with the distribution process for MTNs. To fully place a large bond issue, perhaps because the whole issue has not been taken up by customers, the bond may need to be offered at a higher yield, which raises the coupon for the borrower. If an individual bond within an MTN program is not fully placed,[3] borrowers have the option of raising the remaining sum by offering another bond at a different maturity, or as part of a different structure to another group of investors. Since all the funding from an MTN issue need not be priced at the coupon required by the marginal buyers, and may be raised at slightly different times, the financing costs for MTNs are often below those of a straight bond issue.[4]

MTN issue options

The flexibility afforded by an MTN program is often behind the corporate treasurer's decision to employ them as funding instruments, irrespective of the interest cost advantage of straight bonds. A major flexibility of MTNs is their term to maturity. It is common for MTNs to be issued with non-standard terms to maturity, such as fifteen months, 3.5 years and so on. This contrasts with straight bonds, which are usually issued with maturities of two, five, seven, ten and thirty years in the US market and often just five or 10 years in the Euro market. This makes MTNs the preferred instrument when exact maturity terms are required; for example, when a borrower wishes to precisely match assets with liabilities. The cost of a bond underwriting makes small issues prohibitively expensive, and it is rare to see

[3] For example, the lead manager may have client orders for $460 million of a $500 million issue; in order to attract customer interest for the remaining paper, the coupon may need to be raised by 10–25 basis points.

[4] Another consideration is the commission to the agent bank, generally around 0.125% to 0.75% of the nominal value. Underwriting fees in a conventional bond offering range from 0.25% to 1.50%, and may be higher for international issues.

a bond offered with total nominal value outstanding of less than $100–150 million. If a corporate has a requirement for a smaller amount, it is more practical to issue an MTN. Some individual issues within MTN programs have been for as little as $5 million; again, this flexibility allows companies to meet their funding requirements more precisely.

A continuous program of MTN issues has the potential benefit of a lower average interest cost, compared to a single straight bond issue. For example, over a six-month period, five MTN issues of $20 million each may have a lower average interest cost than a single issue of $100 million in the same period. This may compensate for the lower interest cost of straight bonds, mentioned earlier, and is more likely during periods of relatively high interest rate volatility.

Once a program has secured shelf registration, the process of issuing an MTN can be very quick, often less than half a day. This enables agent banks to issue debt on behalf of a borrower in response to specific investor requirements, or to changes in the yield or swap curves. In fact, a substantial amount of MTN issues originate as a result of *reverse enquiry*. This is when investors have a requirement for debt products of a certain maturity and credit quality. For example, a bond fund manager may be interested in 10-year paper with an A-rating, paying at least 50 basis points above the government yield. This is detailed to the manager's investment bank, who is also an MTN agent bank, and if the requirements suit the borrower, there will be an issue of bonds from within the borrower's MTN program. Bonds issued in response to reverse enquiry are often the most exotic instruments in the MTN market, due to investor requirements. This includes some of the example bonds described later in this chapter. This flexibility again makes MTNs an attractive option for borrowers.

Finally, a significant volume of MTNs are placed privately with investors, directly or via an agent bank. An advantage of this distribution method is that it avoids publicity, as the transaction details may be known only to the investor and borrower (and agent). Companies may wish to avoid raising funds in the bond market, and the publicity associated with this, during times of market correction or volatility, or if they are in a state of financial distress. This makes the MTN market particularly attractive during recessions and market downturns. The private placement market is also used by overseas borrowers that seek to place paper in the US market, as SEC approval is only required for a public offering. However, generally the financing costs are lower in the public market than the private placement market, with its lower liquidity, so the majority of domestic borrowers use the public offering method.

Issue mechanism

The issue process

Issuers of MTNs usually specify an issuing and paying agent (IPA) responsible for providing investors with the ability to present interest coupons and notes in various locations around the world. The IPA function required for medium-term note programs is usually viewed as a processing and administration function, and is therefore normally of most interest to the settlements and processing areas of an issuing organisation.

Once an agent has been selected as the IPA for a new program, and draft legal documentation is available, it will allocate the transaction to a documentation department. This department will review the documentation from a legal perspective, and often calls in external legal firms to assist in the review. However the primary functions that the IPA performs is to receive an issuer's instructions, arrange for the issuance of the security to the relevant dealer via the international clearing systems, and then to service the security throughout it's term. Generally, Euro-MTN transactions are represented by a single security, known as the *global note*. When an issuer and underwriting bank agree to a new transaction, both parties will advise the IPA of the transaction details, such as the currency, amount, issue date, interest basis, maturity, issue price and so on. Although the dealer is not obligated to advise the IPA of the trade details, market practices are such that this has now become the norm. The IPA issues the security after receiving the instructions of the issuer together with an authorised pricing supplement, which is the term sheet listing the issue details.

Once trade details have been received, the IPA will contact Euroclear and Clearstream and advise them of the trade information. The clearing systems will then advise the IPA of the unique security codes, known as the International Securities Identification Number (ISIN) and the Common Code, which are used to identify the security during its term. The IPA will then input the trade and settlement information into a "new issuance account", while the dealer will input its instructions into the relevant clearing system. The IPA's instruction will be a securities delivery versus payment instruction, while the dealer's will be a securities receipt versus payment instruction. Processing the transaction on this basis means that all parties are protected and that the securities will never be issued unless the correct issue proceeds are paid. On the actual issuance date, the IPA will receive the cash proceeds from the dealer and will make onward payment to the issuer; it also creates the global note that represents the issue and delivers this to the *common depositary* for Euroclear and Clearstream. The common depositary is usually called the *custodian*.

Servicing the issue

The IPA is responsible for servicing the MTN during its life. Approximately ten business days before an interest payment date, or before the maturity date of an issue, it will advise the issuers of the forthcoming interest payment and provide them with payment details for the repayment amount due. On the instalment due date, the IPA will pay the clearing system(s) the amount due to the investors holding via their computer systems, and will also credit the proceeds to the relevant investor's account. Investors holding securities outside of a clearing system have to physically present their Euro-MTNs (and Eurobonds as well; see Footnote 5 below for a definition of Euro-MTN) for payment at one of the designated paying agents for the issue.

The activities described above summarise the core function that is performed by an IPA; in addition, throughout the life of a program the IPA also performs numerous other activities on behalf of the issuer. Such activities include:

- being responsible for the safekeeping of the master global notes;
- the submission of any reports required by regulatory entities, such as the Bank of England, Japanese Ministry of Finance and the Bundesbank;
- acting as the calculation agent service for cash flows paid by floating rate, indexed-linked, and dual-currency note issues;
- arranging for the listing of the note issues at a relevant stock exchange;
- arranging for the publication of notices in the financial press;
- maintaining comprehensive details of all transactions on its computer systems;
- responding to external enquiries, such as requests made by auditors.

The process followed by IPAs is very similar to that used in the Eurobond market (see Chapter 10).

The secondary market

A liquid secondary market in MTNs was first established in the US market by Merrill Lynch, which undertook to quote bid prices to any investor wishing to sell MTNs before maturity, provided that the investor had originally bought the notes through them. In other words, Merrill Lynch was guaranteeing a secondary market to borrowers that issued notes through it. This undertaking was repeated by other banks, resulting in a market that is now both large and liquid. That said, MTNs are not actively traded and market-makers do not quote real-time prices on dealing screens. The relatively low volume of secondary market trading stems from a disinclination of investors to sell notes they have bought, rather than a lack of market liquidity.

There is a wide range of maturities available for MTNs in the secondary market. The maturity of individual issues reflects the funding requirements of their issuers; for example, bonds issued by motor car finance companies usually match the duration of loans to their customers, so they tend to have three-year to five-year maturities. Bonds issued by industrial and manufacturing companies have longer maturities. The maturity profile of MTNs in the US market is shown in Figure 12.1.

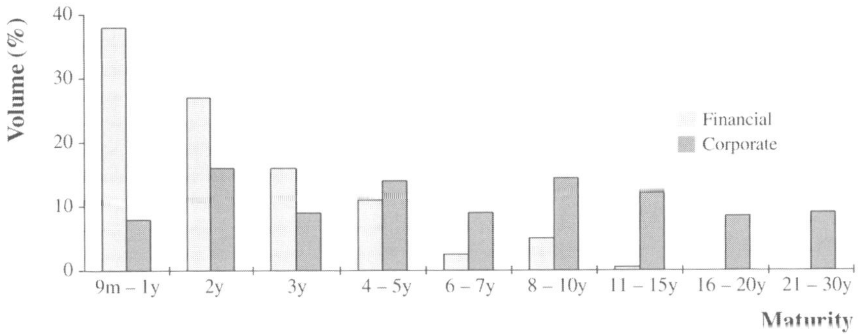

Figure 12.1 Maturity profile of US MTN market, 2004
Source: JPMorgan.

The yield on MTNs is a function of the credit quality of the issuer, as well as the liquidity of the paper in the secondary market and market-maker's support. In the US domestic market, MTNs are quoted on a yield basis, often as a spread over the equivalent maturity Treasury security. The highest yield spread is observed on the lowest rated bonds. Spreads vary according to market conditions and the business cycle (for example, they are at their widest during times of recession and after a market correction), as illustrated by Figure 12.2.

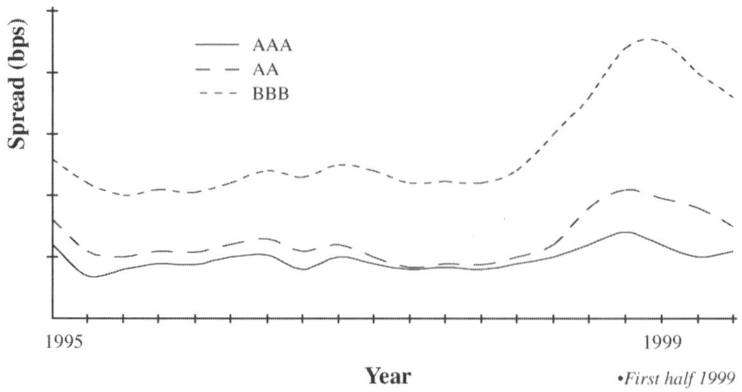

Figure 12.2 Credit structure of yield spreads, 10-year sterling MTNs, 1995–1999
Source: Greenwich NatWest.

The MTN market is a major instrument of corporate finance in the US market, and is growing in importance in the Euro market. An indication of its significance is given by its growing share of total investment-grade debt issuance. For instance in the US debt market, MTNs accounted for 47% of total investment grade debt issued in 1995, where total debt comprised MTNs and straight bond issues. This is an increase from around 12% in the early 1980s (Roland 2001).

Credit rating

MTNs are unsecured debt. A would-be issuer of MTNs will usually seek a credit rating for its issue from one or more of the main rating agencies such as Moody's or Standard & Poor's. The rating is given by the agency for a specific amount of possible new debt; should the issuer decide to increase the total amount of MTNs in issue it will need to seek a review of its credit rating. As MTNs are unsecured paper only the higher rated issuers, with an "investment grade" rating for their debt, are usually able to embark on a revolving facility. Although there are "junk"-rated MTNs, there is no liquid market in them, and they account for less than 1% of outstanding volume.

Companies issuing MTNs generally have high ratings within the "investment grade" category. During 1995, $65 billion of the $99 billion of MTNs issued in the US domestic market represented debt with a rating of "A" or higher, while at the end of that year approximately 98% of the outstanding debt in the US market was rated at investment grade level.

EXAMPLE 12.3 Reverse FRN with swap

A subsidiary of a global integrated banking house that engages in investment activity requires US dollar funding. A proportion of its funds are raised as part of a $5 billion Euro-MTN program. Due to demand for sterling assets they issue a 5-year pounds sterling reverse floating rate medium-term note as part of the MTN program, with the following details.

Issue size	£15 million
Issue date	20 January 1998
Maturity	21 January 2003
Rate payable	9% from 20/1/98 to 20/7/98
	19% – (2 × Libor 6-mo) thereafter to maturity
Price at issue	99.92
Proceeds	£14,988,000

As the issuer requires US dollar funding, it swaps the proceeds into dollars in the market in a cross-currency swap, and pays US dollar three-month Libor for this funding. On termination the original currencies are swapped back and the note redeemed.

The Euro-MTN market

The development of a market in offshore or internationally traded MTNs was originally due to US companies seeking sources of finance overseas. The Euro-MTN market has since expanded dramatically and it is now an important source of corporate funding for US, European, Japanese and Asian domiciled companies. Euro-MTNs trade essentially as Eurobonds; that is, they are international bonds that can be bought and sold across international boundaries. There is also a domestic market in MTNs in the United Kingdom, France, Germany and several other European countries, as well as Japan.[5] The main trading centre is in London, where most of the major

[5] Note that there is a cross-over in terminology, and the terms "international" and "Euro" are frequently interchanged. A bond issued in a domestic market in Europe is not a Eurobond, equally there are domestic MTN programs in several European countries. In this chapter the term "Euro-MTN" is used to refer to MTNs that trade across international boundaries, and can be in any currency.

underwriters and market-making banks trade out of. The growth of the Euro market has been even more rapid than the US one, rising from approximately $10 billion in 1990 to just under $500 billion in 1998 (Roland 2001). The flexibility of an MTN program, which was behind much of the growth in the US domestic market, is the key reason behind the expansion of the Euro market.

Euro-MTNs are essentially identical to MTNs in the US domestic market, with the key exception that they are not subject to national regulations or national registration requirements. The issuer base in the Euro market is much more concentrated among financial institutions and banks, and there is a lower appetite for lower grade credit quality paper. In 1998 over 65% of Euro-MTNs were rated at AAA or AA, compared to just 13% of domestic US MTNs (Roland 2001). Another slight difference is in the maturity structure; most Euro-MTNs have maturities of five to ten years, and it is rare to encounter maturities of thirty years. However, there is a diverse range of structured Euro-MTNs in the market, according to Roland (2001) structured transactions account for up to 60% of Euro-MTN issues, compared to under half of that in the US market. As one might expect, currency swap structures such as those described in Example 12.3 are more common in the Euro market; note that the bonds in that example are part of the Euro-MTN program of a major integrated banking house.

Structured MTNs

The application of financial engineering techniques has resulted in the introduction of exotic MTN structures. As a result, both borrowers and investors have had their requirements met precisely through the use of tailor-made bond structures. Put simply, in a structured MTN, the borrowing company issues an MTN, which may or may not be a plain vanilla instrument itself, that is part of a swap agreement that changes the nature of the interest payments that the borrower makes. The first structured notes involved the issue of a conventional MTN in conjunction with an interest rate swap. If the MTN was a fixed-coupon bond, the issuer would enter into an interest rate swap whereby it received fixed interest and paid floating-rate interest; the end result would be that the issuer now had a floating-rate interest rate liability and not a fixed-rate one. The relevant swap terms are identical to the MTN ones; that is, the fixed-rate payments are on the same date as the MTN coupon dates, and on the same interest basis. The borrower might do this because such an arrangement saves it interest payments not available through the issue of a straight floating-rate MTN. For borrowers, the primary motivation for entering into structured note arrangements is because a reduction in interest costs can be achieved. The interest savings must be sufficient to offset the increased transaction costs of structured deals, because these frequently require additional tax, accounting and legal advice, which may be supplied by the agent bank or by a separate advisory firm.

The flexibility of the MTN market has resulted in many structured transactions being created as a result of a reverse enquiry. An investor who has an interest in acquiring an instrument with specific terms – such as a link to an exotic exchange rate, equity index or commodity – may not be able to meet her requirements in the conventional market. If, via an agent bank, a borrower is able to issue an instrument that meets the specific needs of the enquiry, the investor will be able to purchase an instrument that fulfils its requirements precisely. The establishment of the inverse-floater MTN market in the United States in the early 1990s was in response to investor needs; the issuer's of inverse floaters usually hedged their interest rate risk exposure in the swap market.

The other drivers of structured deals are the investment banks themselves, who may present an idea for a particular deal to their investor clients. Often this occurs when the structured finance team at the bank has spotted an area of the market where value may be obtained for the client, or a price anomaly may be exploited. According to Crabbe (1993), structured deals in the US market accounted for between 20% to 30% of MTN issue volume in the first six months of 1993, from a figure of under 5% ten years previously. The growth of structured deals is further evidence of the flexibility of the MTN market, although of course many of the structures have also been observed in the conventional bond market. In the remainder of this section we present examples of structured MTNs that have been issued as part of a global US dollar Euro-MTN program by an investment banking group. They illustrate the wide range of features available to investors; in fact, it is probably accurate to say that the range of arrangements available is limited only by market participants' imaginations.

In Example 12.4 we present a description of some of the structured MTN deals that have taken place during 1998 and 1999. The issuer and counterparty banks are all large investment banking groups.

EXAMPLE 12.4 Medium-term notes issued as part of a global $5 billion Euro-MTN program

The issuer is an integrated banking house, a subsidiary of which is an investment vehicle in the United States. As such, the subsidiary's funding requirement is exclusively in US dollars; however, it issues paper wherever there is customer demand. Foreign currency issues are swapped into dollars, on which the issuer pays floating-rate interest. The subsidiary has a AAA-rating.

Japanese yen MTN

Issue size	JPY500 million
Maturity	5 years
Rate payable	0.1%
Issue price	100%
Proceeds	JPY500 million

This bond was swapped into US dollars, the equivalent amount of which was $3.56 million. During the life of the bond the issuer pays floating-rate interest on the US dollars, while the yen interest payments are made by the swap bank; on maturity the exact start proceeds are swapped back, enabling the issuer to redeem the bond. The structure is illustrated in Figure 12.3.

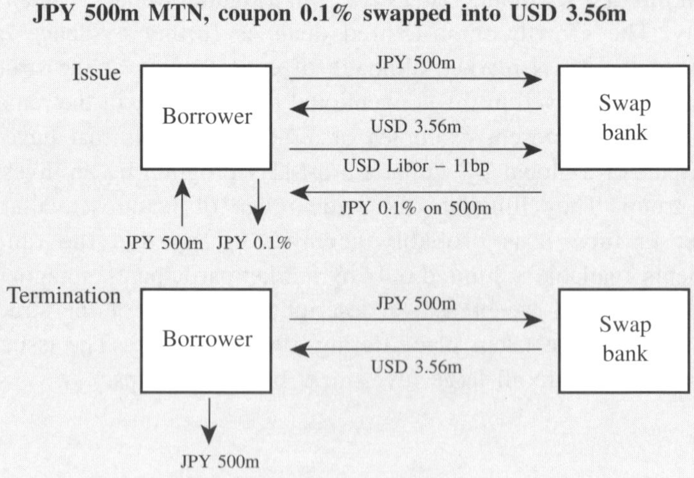

Figure 12.3 A structured MTN issue (1)

Swiss franc step-up notes

Issue date	25/3/1997		
Maturity	25/3/2002		
Issue size	CHF 15 million		
Issue price	100%		
Coupon	2.40% to 25/3/1999	Callable	25/3/1999
	2.80% to 25/3/2000		25/3/2000
	3.80% to 25/3/2001		25/3/2001
	4.80% to 25/3/2002		

This bond was issued in conjunction with a currency swap; that is, the CHF 15 million was swapped into $10.304 million, on which the issuer pays floating-rate interest. These amounts were to be swapped back on termination, although the bond was in fact called at the first call date and the swap cancelled. The structure is illustrated in Figure 12.4.

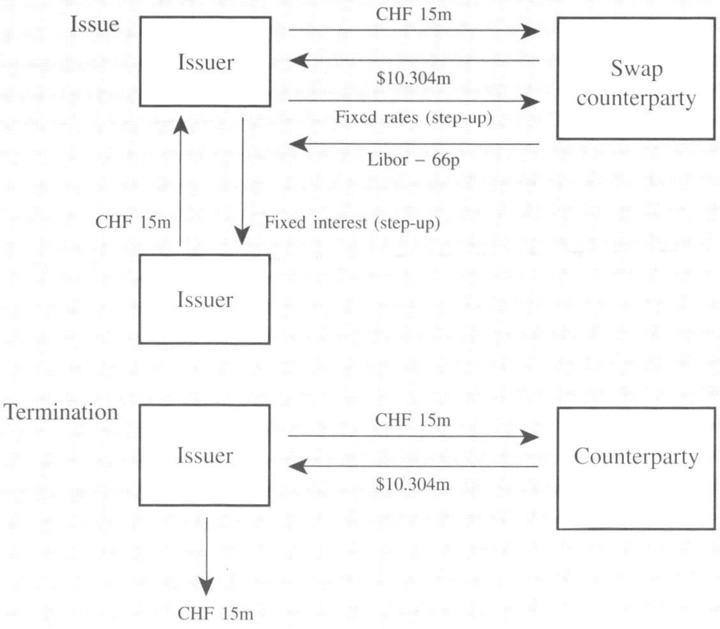

Figure 12.4 A structured MTN issue (2)

€6.15 million zero-coupon equity basket notes due January 2004

Issue date 22/1/1999
Maturity 22/1/2004
Issue price 100%
Interest basis Zero coupon
Final redemption amount:
The greater of (a) 100%, or
(b) 100% + (50% × (X_m – 2704/2704)),

subject to a maximum of 133%, where X_m is the level of the FTSE Eurotop 100 stock index.

The proceeds are swapped into dollars, an equivalent amount of \$7.178 million, on which the issuer pays floating-rate interest of three-month Libor minus 3 basis points, during the life of the bond. This is illustrated in Figure 12.5.

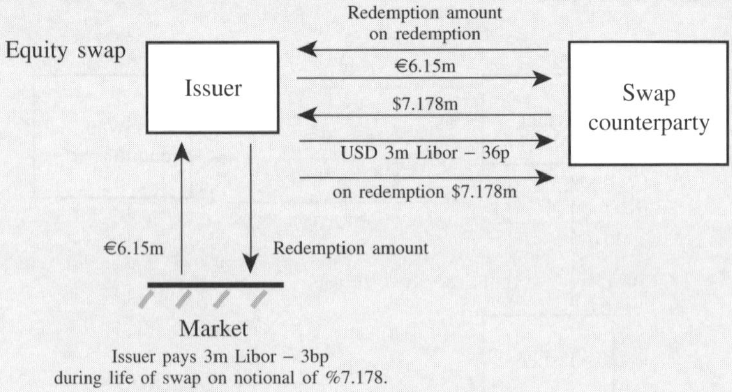

Figure 12.5 A structured MTN equity swap issue

Belgian franc "DEM Libor Accrual" note

Issue date 13/7/1998
Maturity 17/7/1999
Issue size BEF300 million
Coupon (3-month BEF-Libor + 0.90)% × (Accrual factor), where the coupon rate will accrue for each day on which the DEM-Libor rate is within a range of 3.42%–4.03%

The terms of this issue included an unusual feature, a collar within which interest can accrue. The collar was the Deutschmark Libor rate; if the rate moved outside this stated range, no interest was payable on the note. In return for this the investor received a relatively high interest rate from what was in effect a triple-A risk. The structure is illustrated in Figure 12.6.

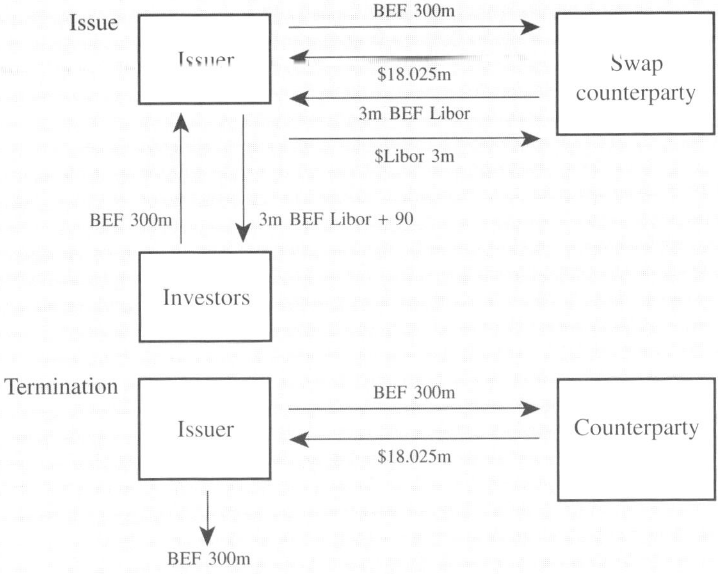

Figure 12.6 A structured MTN issue (3)

USD Brazil credit-linked notes

Issue date	11/3/1998
Maturity	11/9/2000
Issue size	$30 million
Issue price	100%
Interest basis	Six-month USD-Libor + 430 basis points, not payable if a "Brazilian Credit Event" has occurred

The redemption amount for this note is contingent on there being any relevant credit events occurring during the bond's life. A "credit event" is defined in the MTN issue terms and conditions, and is related to Brazilian corporate credit quality.

Japanese yen step-down notes due 2000

Issue date	4/1/1995
Maturity	29/3/2000
Issue size	JPY2.5 billion
Coupon	31% to 29/3/1995; thereafter 2.2% to redemption
Swap proceeds	$14 million

This is a straightforward MTN issue with yen proceeds swapped into dollars. Note, however, the very high initial coupon. This structure is illustrated in Figure 12.7.

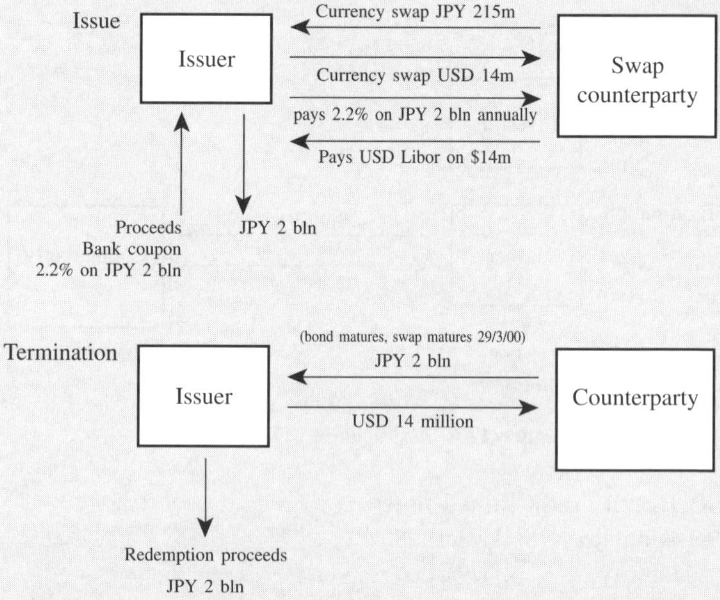

Figure 12.7 A structured MTN issue (4)

ECU 12 million Korea Development Bank credit-linked zero-coupon notes due June 2000

Issue date	16/06/1998
Maturity	16/06/2000
Issue price	83.40%
Interest basis	Zero-coupon

The bonds are redeemable at par, or in the event of a "credit event" (defined in the issue prospectus) prior to maturity they are redeemable at a "revised redemption amount". This is the greater of (a) zero and (b) a product of the future value percentage, recovery percentage and accreted notional, subject to a maximum of 100% (that is, redemption will be a maximum of ECU 12 million). The terms quoted here are defined in the issue prospectus.

US dollar zero-coupon basket-linked notes due 2001

Issue	1/07/98
Maturity	1/07/2000
Issue price	100%

Redemption amount:

The bond maturity value is 95% + (82% × (X_m − 100/100)), where X_m is the arithmetic mean of the values of a basket of global equities (the securities that constitute the equity basket are specified in the issue term sheet).

Selected bibliography and references

BPP Financial Publishing 1993, *Corporate Debt Markets*, BPP Holdings plc, London.

Crabbe, L. 1992, "Corporate medium-term notes", *The Continental Bank Journal of Applied Corporate Finance*, Winter, pp. 90–102.

Crabbe, L. 1993, "Anatomy of the medium-term note market", *Federal Reserve Bulletin*, August, pp. 751–68.

Fabozzi, F. 1993, *Bond Markets, Analysis and Strategies*, 2nd edition, Prentice Hall, New York, pp. 135–7.

Kitter, N. "Liquidity premium and bid–offer spread", in Fabozzi, F. (ed) Handbook of Fixed Income Securities 4th edition 1999, McGraw-Hill.

Post, M. 1992, "The effect of SEC amendments to Rule 2a-7 on the commercial paper market", *Finance and Economics Discussion Series 1992* (Board of Governors of the Federal Reserve System, May).

Roland, M. 2001, "Sterling corporate debt and the MTN market", unpublished paper, Birkbeck, University of London.

Nothing lasts forever, son.

– Benton Fraser's father
Due South, 1997

CHAPTER

13

Preference Shares and Preferred Stocks

Preference shares, or *preferred stock* as they are known in the United States, are a class of shares that entitle the holder to preferences over those of the company's ordinary shares. The most usual preference concerns dividend rights, but other provisions may sometimes be included. They are non-equity shares, but are sometimes described as equity. They are not debt instruments, although they trade similarly to certain types of debt, and often the preference share market-making desk is located within the bond division of a bank. Preference shares rank below debt instruments in the event of a wind-up of a company, but above ordinary shares. They have a long history; the market in preference shares was well established in both the United Kingdom and United States in the nineteenth century. The main types of preference share are fixed-dividend, adjustable-rate and auction market preference shares. These main variations will be reviewed later in the chapter.

Preference shares may be defined as shares that provide their holders an entitlement to receive a dividend, but only up to a specific limit, which is usually a fixed amount every year. They may also give their holders a limited right to participate in any surplus in the event of a winding up, should there be a liquidation and sale of the company's assets. Preference shares may also be redeemable on fixed terms or on terms dictated by the issuing company. Despite their name, however, preference shares are similar to debt capital and this is why it is necessary to review their characteristics here. However, preference shares are not debt, but are a form of ownership in a company, despite the fact that most forms of preference stocks do not grant their holders a voting right. The instruments might be fairly described as a peculiar cross between shares and bonds, and share some but not all characteristics of both. For example, certain preference shares are unlike ordinary shares in that if a dividend is not paid in one year, it will *accumulate* and must be paid before ordinary share dividends. Unlike bonds, however, a failure to pay dividends is not a default, although there are several negative implications associated with such an action. They are similar to bonds in that they do not entitle holders a vote in the company (usually, as long as the dividend is paid), although voting rights are usually granted if a dividend is not paid. The preference share market-making desk in a bank is usually situated in the fixed interest division, rather than in the equity division. This reflects that the valuation of preference shares fluctuates with the yield curve.

In this chapter we introduce the different types of preference shares, and see how they differ from conventional fixed income securities. In the United States and United Kingdom there is wide variety of preference shares in the market and we are only able to review them here; interested readers may wish to consult the references listed in the bibliography at the end of this chapter.

The size of the market

The majority of borrowers in the US domestic market are financial institutions. In the UK domestic market the instrument has been more popular with non-financial corporates, although banks have also been large-volume issuers. During the period 1983–1993, over $81 billion was raised in the US preferred market, of which around 62% was by financial companies.[1] Table 13.1 shows the level of issuance in the US market during this period.

Preference shares are purely a corporate financing instrument and credit ratings for individual share issues are as important as they are for corporate bonds. In the US domestic market, ratings are issued by four ratings firms, known as "nationally recognised statistical rating organisations" or NRSROs, which are Standard & Poor's, Moody's, Duff and Phelps, and Fitch Investors Service. The ratings issued by the NRSROs, although outwardly similar to

1 Wilson (1997).

the ratings for corporate bonds in some cases, need to be assessed differently however; this is because preferred stock should be analysed within the range of other preference shares, distinct from debt issues.

US preferred stock market	1983	1984	1985	1986	1987	1988	1989	1990	1991	1992	1993
Volumes ($ million)											
Fixed dividend	2,300	1,600	463	1,060	2,260	2,900	1,120	3,720	3,415	3,295	11,430
Variable dividend	2,800	4,375	3,180	5,480	6,290	5,325	5,980	2,480	1,370	6,740	3,990
Number of issues by industry sector											
Banks	19	32	26	54	73	62	49	21	14	28	31
Investment companies	–	–	–	–	–	–	20	7	12	25	24
Utility companies	49	42	21	13	32	42	16	11	16	23	54
Industrial/ transportation companies	6	7	4	18	14	8	15	8	5	3	15

Table 13.1 US preferred stock market, 1983–1993
Source: IFC.

Description and definition of preference shares

Introduction

An annual preference dividend is payable, usually on a semi-annual basis, as a fixed percentage amount of the nominal value of the share. Unlike the interest payable on a conventional bond though, which is paid out of the pre-tax profits of the issuing company, preference share dividends are paid out post-tax profits. The dividend on a preference share must be paid before any dividend can be paid to ordinary equity shareholders. The primary differentiating feature of preference shares compared to ordinary shares is the treatment of the dividend that is payable by them, which are at a fixed rate or variable rate. The dividend paid by a conventional preference share is at a fixed rate of the face value, or a fixed cash value per share. The dividend must be paid before any can be paid on ordinary shares; for the majority of preference shares the dividend is in cash. During the bull market of the mid-1980s up to the crash of October 1987, some preference shares in the US market paid dividends in the form of more shares. These were known as *PIKs* (payment-in-kind) preferred stock.

There are also preference shares that pay a variable rate dividend in the US market. Generally, these pay a dividend that is adjusted or re-set quarterly at a fixed spread to the Treasury yield curve. The spread, known as the dividend re-set spread, will lie above or at the level of one of three points on the yield curve, which are the three-month maturity point, the 10-year point and the 30-year point. Instead of using the redemption yield at these points, the adjusted dividend is based on the Treasury Constant Maturity (TCM) yield, which is calculated by the Federal Reserve. This means that the adjusted dividend is not a pure short- or long-term yield, but a composite of the two. Variable rate preferred stock in the United States is known as adjustable-rate preferred stocks or ARPS. They are singular instruments in that they are neither money market paper nor long-dated bonds. They possess some of the attributes of ordinary shares, in that they do not exhibit the "pull to par" effect of bonds with a fixed maturity. However, they are related to the debt market yield curve and their value will fluctuate with this.

In the United Kingdom the coupon rate of preference dividends is shown net of tax, as the amount of dividend that shareholders will receive in cash. The gross pre-tax dividend is this net amount plus a *tax credit* for the amount of income tax deducted. If the tax credit is 25%, the gross dividend is multiplied by 100/75 of the net dividend.

EXAMPLE 13.1 Preference shares

A company issues 6% preference shares of £1 and the tax credit is 25%. The gross dividend received by shareholders is £0.08, given by the net amount of £0.06 and the tax credit of 0.06 × 25/75. The gross dividend is therefore £0.06 × (£1.00 × 100/75), which is £0.08.

The tax credit on UK dividends was reduced from 25% to 20% in 1993. In the first budget of the Labour government (elected in May 1997) the right to re-claim this tax credit was removed. This has had profound effects on the preference share market in the United Kingdom, described in an extract from the *Financial Times*, which is reproduced with permission at the end of this chapter.

Rights in a liquidation

In the event of a liquidation of the company, the order of entitlement to payment from the proceeds of selling off the company's assets is that preference shareholders rank behind trade creditors, but ahead of ordinary shareholders. The amount receivable in a winding-up, however, is limited to the nominal value of the shares, and possibly also any unpaid dividend. Certain preference shares have issue terms that allow them to participate with the ordinary shares in the event of liquidation, which may seem to some to be a somewhat dubious advantage. For example, the preference share may entitle a holder to receive upon the company's liquidation twice the amount per share distributed on each ordinary share. This is more common in the US market.

Voting rights

Preference shares do not, as a rule, entitle holders to a vote in the running of the company. This is perhaps the chief difference between preference shares and ordinary shares. The general understanding is that, because preference shareholders receive a regular and fixed dividend, they do not require voting rights. This is not always the case, and certain issues do entitle holders to a vote. For example, the preferred stock of Southern California Edison, a US utility company, carries with it varying levels of voting rights. The cumulative preferred stockholders each has six votes per share, while the $100 cumulative preferred stock entitles its holders to two votes per share. The votes may be used cumulatively in the case of the election of company directors.

The general exception is when preference shares are in arrears after the non-payment of a dividend. In the US market if more than four dividends have not been paid, which in most cases would be over a two-year period, preference shares are allotted voting rights, sometimes just to be used in the election or re-election of directors. Where this provision is included in the terms of the share issue, they are known as *contingent voting stock*, because the right to vote is contingent on the preference shareholders not receiving the dividends to which they are entitled. When a dividend arrear(s) has been paid off, the voting rights will cease. Such provisions are common, sometimes because of regulatory requirements. The New York Stock Exchange, for example, states that non-voting preferred stock must be contingent voting stock, otherwise it cannot be listed on the exchange.

The other type of voting power that is often carried by preference shares relates to specific corporate actions that may affect the standing or value of the shares themselves. For instance, preference shareholders may be entitled to vote on proposals to increase the authorised amount of any class of stock that would rank ahead of the preference shares, in terms of dividends or rights to assets in the event of a liquidation. The shareholders may also be entitled to give their approval on a merger or consolidation, the results of which might adversely affect the rights and preferences of the preference shares. Shares that have this privilege written into their terms are known as *vetoing stock*. However, this veto power is usually available only if the preference shares are in dividend arrears, and will be removed if the arrears are paid off.

Types of preference shares

A "straight" or conventional preference share has the following characteristics:

- interest is paid at a fixed annual rate, but only if profits are sufficiently high for the company to afford the dividend;
- when any due dividend is unpaid, the shareholders do not have the right to payment in arrears at a later date;
- the share is *perpetual*; that is, it is irredeemable or "permanent".

In fact the majority of preference shares both in the United States and the United Kingdom are not conventional, rather they incorporate one or more of the following features: they may be *cumulative*, *participating*, *redeemable* or *convertible*. Preference shares may have one or more, or all, of these features.

- *Cumulative preference shares* entitle their holder to a fixed rate of dividend, and if any dividend is not paid on the due date, the arrears remain payable and will accumulate. The preference shareholders must receive their arrears of dividend before any ordinary share dividend can be paid to equity shareholders. This provision is a significant restriction to the management of a company and would result in the ordinary shares being marked down; it is rare for such shares not to receive a dividend unless the company is in serious financial difficulty. Certain cumulative preference shares impose other restrictions in the event that a dividend is not paid. For example, the issuer may not be able to redeem any stock that ranks below the preference shares. Shares that have a sinking fund attached to them may have their sinking payments suspended, with no funds being allowed to redeem preferred or ordinary shares.

- *Participating preference shares* have additional dividend rights. The holders of participating preference shares, in addition to receiving their fixed dividend, are also entitled to a share of the company's surplus profits. This extra *participating* dividend is usually set at a specified percentage of the dividend paid on the ordinary shares. In the US market virtually all the preferred stock in the market is non-participating. Holders of such shares will not benefit from the company posting ever-increasing after-tax profits after every year, except indirectly in that the rating of their preference shares will receive a boost.
- *Redeemable preference shares* are shares that either will be redeemed at a specified future date, or could be redeemed at a specified future date at the option of the company or the preference shareholders. The shares are redeemed at par or at a premium to par value. In the US market, preferred stock with no redemption provisions are rare, and are true perpetual securities. Most issues are callable during a time period after their initial issue, in whole or in part, at the option of the issuer and at pre-specified prices. The redemption value must include accrued dividend interest at the time of the call. The point at which the preferred stock is callable is often a medium- to long-term after issue, and may not be for ten or twenty years after the issue date. Callable issues are often protected from being called for a set period after the issue of debt or equity that ranks with or ahead of the preferred shares. This is to protect shareholders from capital loss arising from a new issue of stock, when the price would be expected to fall and the company could then cash in by redeeming the stock.
- *Convertible preference shares* entitle their holder to a right to convert the preference shares into ordinary shares of the company at a specified future date or between specified future dates, and at a specified rate of conversion. Convertible preference shares are usually redeemable; if they are not converted into equity they will eventually be redeemed. They are similar in many respects to convertible bonds, although the method of quoting prices differs according to which market they are traded in. In domestic markets the convention is to quote them in the same manner as ordinary shares; in international markets (Euro markets) they are quoted in a similar way to bonds; that is, as a percentage of nominal or par value.

EXAMPLE 13.2 Cumulative preference shares

A company with £10 million 6% cumulative preference shares of £1 nominal in issue was unable to pay the dividend on the last payment date, to both preference and ordinary shareholders. It would now like to resume dividend payments in the current year, beginning with an interim dividend. The company in fact is not able to pay an interim dividend to ordinary shareholders until the preference shareholders have been paid their dividend. This is £900,000, comprised of the arrears of the last dividend (6% of £10 million) and the interim dividend of half this amount (£300,000). If the preference shares had been non-cumulative, their holders would not be entitled to the arrears of the dividend and in the current year they would receive only the interim dividend of £300,000.

Another instrument that is an example of the close similarities between convertible bonds and convertible preference shares are *convertible capital bonds*. These were first issued in the euroconvertibles market in 1989 by J. Sainsbury plc, a UK supermarket group. The bonds can be converted into redeemable convertible preference shares at the option of the company.

It is common for companies to have many classes of preference share in issue at any one time. The terms of each class will have been determined separately at the time of their respective issuance.

EXAMPLE 13.3 (I) Convertible preference shares

The Rank Organisation plc, a UK leisure group, has an issue of 8% convertible redeemable preference shares of 20p each, convertible in any year from 1993–2003 into ordinary shares of 25p nominal value. The conversion rate is 10.6383 ordinary shares for every 100 of the preference shares. The company also has a call option and can redeem the shares at £1 per share at any time after 30 April 2003, and the shares will be redeemed in any event at £1 per share on 31 July 2007. The shares are listed on the London Stock Exchange and are priced in the same way as ordinary shares; that is, in pence per share.

13.3 (ii) Cumulative preference shares

Tate & Lyle plc has convertible cumulative preference shares in issue. They are convertible in any year up to 2008 into ordinary shares at a conversion ratio of 11.299 ordinary shares for every 25 of the preference shares. The preference shares have a nominal value of 12.5p each and are redeemable at £1 per share on the maturity date of 28 February 2013, but at the issuer's option at any time from 1 September 2008.

13.3 (iii) Redeemable preference shares

Thorn EMI (another UK leisure group) issued redeemable convertible preference shares in the Euro market in 1989. The shares are convertible into the company's ordinary shares and had a maturity of ten years. Although the bonds were described as preference shares they had most of the characteristics of convertible bonds, and in fact were referred to as "bonds" by most market analysts. The price of the shares was quoted as an amount per cent; for example, 129 per 100 nominal. The bonds offered a put option that entitled holders to redeem them at 130.22% on 2 February 1994 and 180.64% on 2 February 1999, when they matured. The bonds were also callable.

Sinking funds

A *sinking fund* provision in a preference share issue will operate in a similar fashion to a sinking fund with a bond. It will provide for the periodic redemption of a proportion of the issue, most commonly on an annual basis. For example, the sinking fund may pay off 5% of the original number of shares each year. Preference shares that are callable and also have sinking funds may set different dates when the two features are applicable, so that the sinking fund may come into operation after the stock ceases to be callable. Sinking fund payments may be made in shares of stock purchased in the open market or by the call of the required number of shares at the sinking fund call price, which is normally par or another stated value. As with the payment of dividends, the failure to make a sinking fund payment is not considered a default, unlike with a bond, and the company cannot be placed in bankruptcy.

Certain preferred issues have *purchase funds*. These are essentially optional on the part of the issuer because it will have to use its best efforts to retire a portion of the shares at periodic intervals if they can be purchased in the open market, or otherwise through a tender, at below the redemption price. If the shares are trading above the purchase price, the purchase fund cannot operate. A purchase fund can act as a floor for the price of the shares, at a time of high dividend yields, but will not operate in a low-yield environment.

Cost of preference share capital

The gross yield that investors expected from preference shares and bonds of the same issuing company was historically the same, although liquidity considerations meant that the yield on preference shares would be slightly higher. The yield on preference shares in the UK market is now considerably higher than in the bond market, as a result of tax changes introduced by the Labour government in 1997.[2] This has resulted in there being no real advantage to a UK company in raising capital in the preference share market, which may well become illiquid in the near future. For the purposes of analysis, let us consider a historical example that illustrates the considerations involved, which would apply in other markets.

EXAMPLE 13.4 Cost of capital

In March 1993 General Accident plc, a UK insurance group that subsequently merged with another insurer (Commercial Union) and is now known as CGU plc,[3] issued 110 million 7.875% cumulative irredeemable preference shares of £1 each at an issue price of 100.749p per share. The tax credit on UK dividends at that time was 25%, or 25/75 of the net cash dividend. The rate of interest payable on long-dated corporate bonds was then approximately 10.50%. What is the cost of the capital?

[2] The legislation did not take effect until the following year.
[3] It subsequently purchased Norwich Union plc and is now CGNU plc.

> The dividend of 7.875% is net of tax (at that time). The gross dividend is treated as an advance payment of corporation tax by the company, and the annual profit that the company needs to cover the dividend payments is £8,662,500, obtained by multiplying the nominal value of the shares and multiplying this by the coupon. If the company pays corporation tax at a rate of, say, 33%, a bond issuing paying a gross yield of 10.50% would have an after-tax cost of approximately 7%, obtained by multiplying the coupon rate of 10.50% by (100–33)%. The higher cost of the preference shares therefore might be attributable to the premium required for holding them because they are irredeemable.

Companies that are regarded as higher risk will pay a higher yield on their preference shares compared to their bonds. The yield on preference shares is usually shown as a current yield or, in the case of redeemable shares, a redemption yield. Preference shares that have an embedded option feature may be analysed using a yield-to-call or yield-to-put. The yield calculation uses an actual/360 or 30/360 basis in the US market and an actual/365 basis in the UK market. It is important to remember that the yield calculation is in effect a net yield, so that the value must be "grossed up" if returns are being compared to those of bond instruments. This is because the convention is to quote gross yields for bonds.

The preference share market

In the UK domestic market, preference shares are traded in the same way as ordinary shares; that is, they are listed on an exchange. Trading is on the exchange via its dealing system. Domestic issues of preference shares can be relatively small size, and they are often issued as part of a company financial restructuring or through a private placement to a small group of investors. In 1996 the Bank of Ireland issued conventional preference shares to raise part of the financing required in its take-over of the Bristol & West building society. The preference shares were also used to pay some of the membership of the building society, who were entitled to a share of the society's reserves in return for giving up ownership of it. In the United States, under half of all publicly issued preference shares are listed on the NYSE or the American Stock Exchange, with the remainder trading in the OTC market. The normal unit of trading is 100 shares, but this is not universal and some issues trade in lots of 10 shares. It is possible to deal in odd-lots of shares. Listing an issue may lead to a lower dividend yield for an issuer if it improves its marketability. This is more significant if the issue itself is of a relatively large size. Dealing via an exchange system also makes an issue more transparent in the market.

In international markets, companies usually issue redeemable convertible preference shares, which are regarded as part of the euroconvertibles market, together with convertible bonds and equity warrant bonds.

Auction market preferred stock (Amps)

Auction market preferred stock (Amps) is a particular type of preference share. Its main distinguishing feature is that the dividend payable on the shares is determined by auction at regular intervals. The Amps market was developed in the United States and the instrument has been issued by a number of foreign borrowers in the domestic US market.

Amps are placed through an investment bank or securities house that acts as lead manager for the issue. They are sold to investors through the auction process. They cannot be offered for sale to the general public, nor can they be traded on a stock exchange. A panel of investors is invited to participate in the auction, and they submit bids for the dividend rate that they will accept in return for purchasing a quantity of the stock. The stock is sold at a fixed price to the investors bidding at the lowest dividend level.

EXAMPLE 13.5 Amps

A US company is issuing Amps and a group of investment institutions is invited to bid for the stock. The size of the issue is \$100 million. Bids are received for \$60 million at a dividend yield of 6%, \$90 million at a yield of $6^1/_4$% and \$150 million at a yield of $6^1/_2$%. The shares will be sold to the investors bidding the lowest dividend yield, which is paid on the entire issue. Given the ratio of the bidding amount, the yield payable in our simple example is $6^1/_4$%. The investors who bid 6% will receive the full quantity of stock they bid for, on a yield of 6%, while the remaining \$40 million will be allotted to investors bidding at this level on a pro-rate basis. The stock is issued at par.

Auctions occur at regular intervals, sometimes as frequently as every four weeks. Investors wishing to buy Amps at an auction may submit a bid to receive a dividend yield of their choice; at subsequent auctions existing holders may sell part or all of their holding to bidders. After the primary issues existing holders can opt to hold their stock, bid for more of the shares or sell to another bidder. When all orders have been submitted an "auction agent" is responsible for deciding the allocation.

The number of Amps for which bid orders have been received is compared with the volume of Amps available. If the volume of orders exceeds the quantity of stock available the dividend rate is set at the lowest rate at which all the Amps will be taken up, and holders will subsequently receive this dividend level. At this point, Amps must be sold by existing holders who bid at a higher rate to successful new purchasers who bid at a lower rate. At each auction there is a maximum rate of dividend that will be paid on the stock. This level is a function of the credit rating of the stock at the time of the auction and is determined by a pre-set formula. If the credit rating is downgraded, the maximum rate payable will be raised, and this new rate of dividend is used as a default rate. The dividend rate payable until the next auction, which must not be held for a minimum of 28 days, is the default rate. There may be an insufficient number of bidders in an auction for the quantity of Amps that are available below the maximum (default) rate. When this happens, existing holders who wish to sell will be unable to do so.

EXAMPLE 13.6 Amps (ii)

ABC Inc, a US company, has an issue of $500 million of Amps. In an auction, bids are submitted for $300 million of stock at yields ranging from 6½% to 7%, and there are also hold orders for $150 million. The maximum rate is 7%. Therefore there are insufficient bids for the stock. Bidders for $300 million will be able to buy the stock, and existing holders of $150 million of stock will retain their holding. Holders of a further $50 million who wished to sell their stock will be unable to do so. They must hold their paper until at least the next auction. The dividend rate payable to the next auction is the default rate of 7%.

Dividends on Amps are paid at predetermined fixed intervals and sometimes match the auction cycle. For example, British Aerospace (now known as BAE Holdings) Amps pay a dividend every 49 days. Although they are known as "preferred stock" Amps are similar in many respects to bonds. The dividend on Amps is usually around 100 basis points above the yield on straight short-term fixed debt, but the advantages are that there are no covenants of any kind attached to Amps issues and they are redeemable only at the issuer's option. The cost of Amps to the issuer will increase however if its credit rating is downgraded. The default rate of a dividend that applies if an auction is unsuccessful could be raised at the next auction.

Issues of Amps vary in size, although in the mid-1990s the UK company issues in the US domestic market ranged in size from $100 million to $700 million.

Amps are only redeemable at the option of the issuer and in theory therefore are perpetual. They are issued without any form of covenant and a failure to pay a dividend on an Amps does not constitute a default (as is the case for all preference shares). Holders of Amps are not able to demand redemption in the event of non-payment of a dividend. The inability of shareholders to demand redemption was used at one point to argue that Amps should be regarded as equity finance. This was not accepted by the UK authorities. Amps may not be "perpetual" finance, as a company, having issued Amps, could find that its credit rating was downgraded. The dividend that would be payable would then rise at subsequent auctions, and if the downgrade were sufficiently great, the cost of paying dividends on the Amps might then become so high as to cause the issuer to redeem them. In the United Kingdom in the early 1990s, rising dividend costs on Amps made redemption an attractive option. For example, BET plc announced a £200 million rights issue in July 1992 in order to finance a redemption of most of its outstanding Amps. The cost of the dividend payment on the Amps had risen from a level just below the US commercial paper rate in 1991 to a premium of over 21% above CP rates in mid-1992. The extract below from the *Financial Times* for 15 July 1992 suggested that domestic US investors were not sufficiently familiar with the name to believe it was worthwhile holding the paper without a substantial rise in the dividend yield to compensate for whatever trouble they thought the company was getting into.

> The history of suspicion and misunderstanding of these instruments in the UK may seem odd to a US observer. But the market for Amps consists wholly of US investors who are interested primarily in big, familiar, triple-A US corporations like Coca-Cola and Exxon, rather than unknown foreign minnows.
>
> (*FT*, 15 July 1992, ©Pearson Group)

During this period other UK companies also redeemed their Amps issues. For example, Rank Organisation plc redeemed its $200 million Amps issue in April 1991 after its credit rating was downgraded from A- to BBB- by Standard & Poors.

Bloomberg screens

Preference shares can be analysed on Bloomberg using the same screens that are used for both fixed income and equities, depending on their particular terms and conditions. The specific preference share calculator is screen BC28, the preferred stock calculator. This is shown in Figure 13.1.

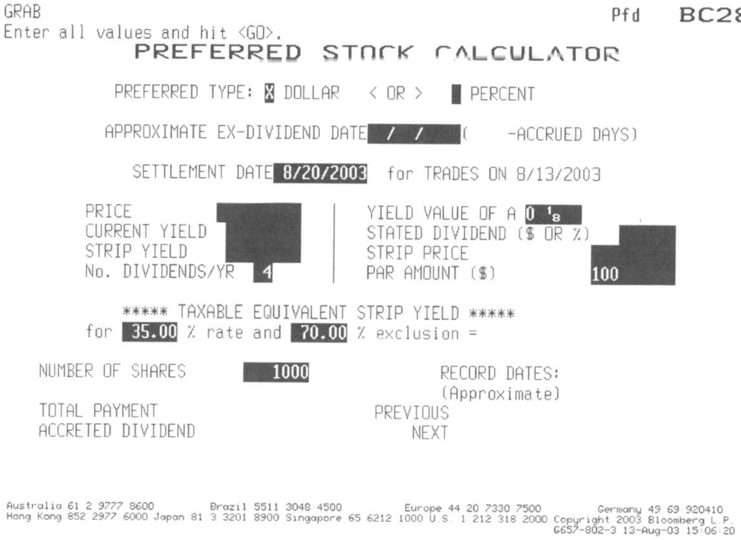

Figure 13.1 Bloomberg preferred stock calculator screen
© Bloomberg L.P. Used with permission.

Selected bibliography and references

Brealey, R. and Myers, S. 1996, *Principles of Corporate Finance*, McGraw-Hill, New York.

Finnerty, J.D. 1988, "Financial engineering in corporate finance: An overview", *Financial Management*, 17, Winter, pp. 14–31.

Ross, S., Westerfield, R. and Jaffe, J. 1998, *Corporate Finance*, Irwin/McGraw-Hill, New York.

Wilson, R. 1997, "Nonconvertible preferred stock", in Fabozzi, F., *The Handbook of Fixed Income Securities*, 5th edition, McGraw-Hill, New York, Chapter 14, pp. 263–86.

"Raisul, what shall we do? We have lost everything …"
"Sharif, was there never anything in your life for which it was worth losing everything for?"

– *The Wind and The Lion*
MGM Films, 1974

CHAPTER 14

High-yield Bonds

The high-yield corporate bond market developed in the United States during the 1980s, and was a symbol of market growth in that decade. The subsequent collapse of the "junk bond" market in 1990 signalled a downturn in the market, but in recent years it has been re-developed into a liquid and relatively stable market, regarded as a viable source of capital for non-rated companies and companies that are rated below investment grade. It is now referred to as the *high-yield* bond market and an equivalent market has also developed in the United Kingdom and Europe. Economic performance through the second half of the 1990s, which has seen low inflation and steady growth in the United States, and relatively low inflation and convergence of yields in Europe, as a result of the introduction of the euro currency, has depressed bond yields to historically low levels across the developed countries. Investors who require higher yielding debt assets must look to "emerging" markets or, increasingly, the high-yield market. In this chapter we provide a brief review of the US high-yield market, including the different types of securities that have been issued and the returns that were generated through the last decade.

Growth of the market

The US domestic high-yield market stood at approximately $200 billion nominal outstanding in 1990, and had grown to over $335 billion at the end of 1998.[1] The largest amount issued in one year was in 1993, when just under $70 billion was issued. Prior to 1990 around half of all issuance in the high-yield market was used to fund acquisitions and "leveraged buy-outs" (LBOs), but by 1995 over half of the new issues was used for the purposes of refinancing existing debt and as growth capital. The proportion used for LBOs had fallen to 4% in that year. The overall credit quality of the market improved steadily during the second half of the 1990s, which was explained by analysts as reflecting the performance and health of the US economy as a whole. Figure 14.1 shows the change of composition of the credit ratings in the market as a whole. The proportion of issuers rated at BB-grade had increased from 17% in 1987 to 48% in 1997. Figure 14.2 shows the growth in US high-yield bond market issuance.

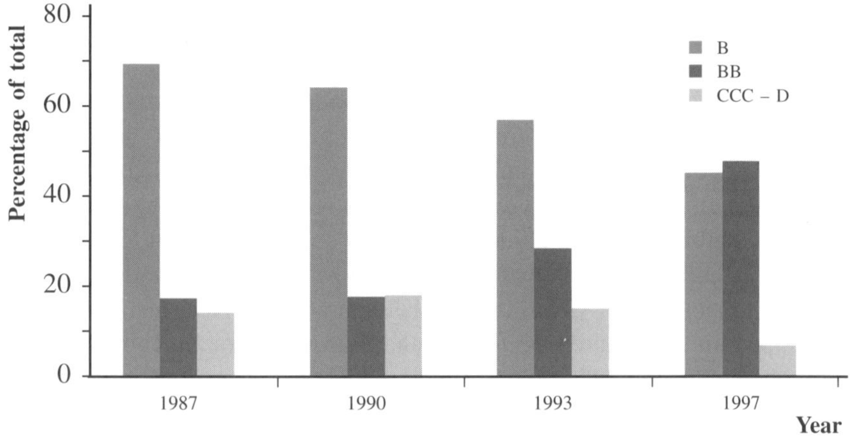

Figure 14.1 US high-yield bond market credit ratings, 1987–1997
Source: Standard & Poor's.

Bonds have been issued by representatives of a number of industry sectors. The highest growth has been observed in the media, telecommunications and cable sectors, which represented over 15% of total debt outstanding in 1997. Outside the industrial sectors, high-yield bonds

[1] The statistical data in this chapter is sourced from Bloomberg and Reuters, except where indicated.

have been issued by energy, utility and finance companies, as well as by Canadian companies, whose bonds are officially designated as Yankee bonds. Figure 14.3 below shows the breakdown of the US market by type of instrument.

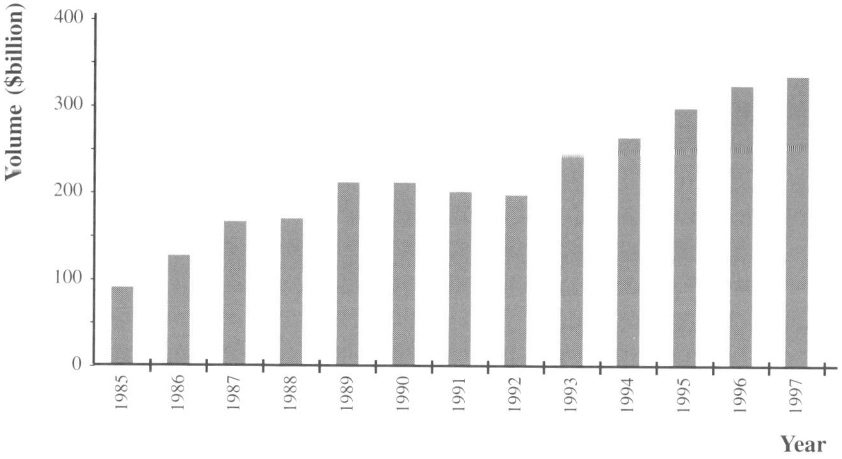

Figure 14.2 Growth of US high-yield bond market
Source: Lehman Brothers.

High-yield securities

The high-yield market contains a range of securities, which have developed as investor interest in the market has grown. The majority of issues have been conventional plain vanilla issues, however, although the market has also seen deferred-pay securities, which recognises that issuing companies will in all probability encounter cash-flow difficulties in their early years, as well as increasing-rate bonds. We present here a summary of the types of instruments traded in the market.

Conventional securities

The majority of bond issues are plain vanilla securities, with a fixed coupon; this type of security comprised over 90% of all domestic high-yield debt in 1997. The maturity of these bonds is between 7–12 years, although most bonds incorporate a call provision that is effective after the first three or five years. A call feature is important to issuers in the high-yield market, as it gives them an opportunity to refinance their debt at a lower interest rate when, as is hoped, their credit rating will have improved.

Split-coupon securities

A *split-coupon* security is one that pays no coupon for the first few years of its life, and then transforms into a fixed-coupon bond for its remaining years. They therefore begin life as zero-coupon bonds, typically for the first five years, although the no-interest period has been as low as two years and as high as seven years, before turning into conventional bonds. The bonds are issued at a discount, using the stated coupon as the discount rate. A split-coupon bond allows its issuer to build up its financial health before it has to service its debt. The most frequent issuers of split-coupon bonds have been operating in high-growth industry such as technology companies, or companies in the process of restructuring their operations.

Another approach adopted by new companies has been to "over-fund" their required proceeds, and use the overfunding to pay the interest charges on the debt for the first few years of the bond's life. This mirrors the effect achieved using a split-capital issue. For example, a funding requirement of $60 million is met through the issue of $100 million of a 9% coupon bond; the extra capital raised is used to pay interest on the debt for the first four years.[2] An overfunded bond is designed to appeal to investors who have an appetite for high-yield debt but do not wish to purchase instruments that do not pay any interest.

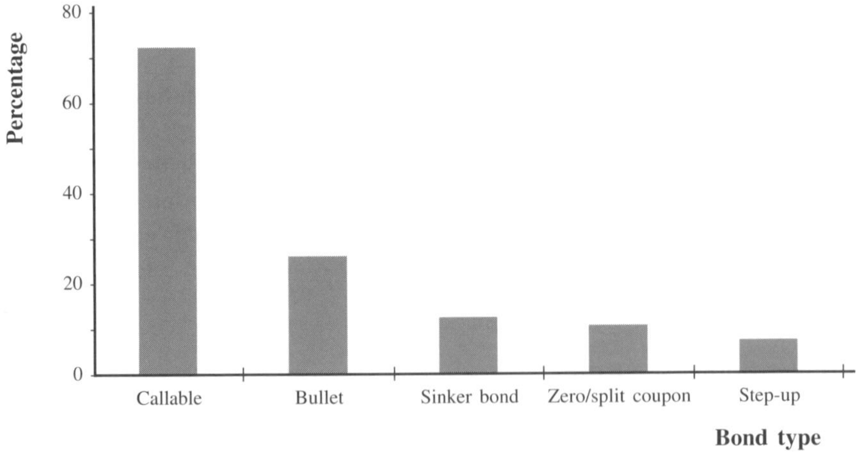

Figure 14.3 Types of high-yield securities, US domestic market, December 2001
Source: Lehman Brothers.

[2] There is "spare" $4 million left over at the end of the four years, but this is invested at the time of the issue in the same way as the required $60 million.

Payment-in-kind securities

A *payment-in-kind* (PIK) bond is one that allows the issuer the option of paying coupon interest either in cash or similar securities. The option is usually set only for a short, limited period of time, say three or five years. If the issuer chooses to pay in the form of in-kind securities, the principal amount of the debt will increase, raising the liability of the issuer after the in-kind option falls away. When the in-kind option is in effect, PIK bonds trade differently to other high-yield bonds, because no interest is payable in this period. Hence the bonds trade without accrued interest, and the coupon payment is reflected in the accreted price of the security. This is similar to the method for quoting cumulative preference shares whose preferred dividend has not been paid in one year.

Step-up coupon securities

These types of bonds are common in conventional corporate markets, issued by companies who wish to make their paper more attractive to investors, or to a wider group of investors. A step-up bond is similar to the split-coupon bond, and is issued for similar reasons, except during the initial period a coupon is payable, rising to a higher coupon at a specified date. The higher coupon is set at the time of issue, and remains in force until the bond is redeemed. The initial period is usually for around five years, but can be for a shorter period.

Exchangeable variable-rate notes

Exchangeable variable-rate notes (EVRNs) are subordinated, medium-term instruments that pay a floating, quarterly coupon. The interest is actually fixed for a short term, known as the "teaser" period, but after this initial period the rate changes to a floating one, linked to a reference rate such as the prime rate or the 90-day Treasury bill rate. In most cases the issuer has the option to exchange the notes for fixed-coupon notes with conventional features such as a fixed maturity date or call facility. The maximum maturity period of the bonds is usually five years.

Bond and stock units

Certain companies in high-growth and/or high-risk business sectors have issued combinations of bonds and equity. This is designed to appeal to investors who require an element of equity ownership in order to benefit from upside growth, to compensate them for the high risk incurred by debt holders. The resulting debt issue therefore has an element of equity attached, in the form of straight shares or warrants. Investors usually strip the equity or the warrants from the bonds on issue and may realise them immediately if they wish. Bonds issued with equity warrants are also known as *usable bonds*.

Springing issues

Start-up companies operating in a highly competitive, volatile environment sometimes issue securities that are specified to change one or more of their characteristics in response to a specific event occurring. For example, the market has seen a springing warrant issue, which is exercisable only if another party attempted to acquire the issuer. Another version of a springing security was one that was originally issued as a subordinated bond, but was converted to senior debt once an old outstanding debenture had been discharged. The analysis of a springing security must take into account the probability that the security will change its terms and conditions and what impact such an event will have on the security's price.

Extendible/re-set securities

An extendible or re-set security allows the issuer to re-set the coupon or extend the life of the bond on pre-specified dates. The general rule, stated on issue, is that the coupon must be re-set to a level that results in it trading at a certain yield, and which is determined by a third-party bank (usually the issuing investment bank). The alternative is for the bond to be issued with a cap or floor, or both. The ability to re-set the coupon can be a valuable asset if market rates have fallen since the time of issue, while it is also attractive to investors in a rising interest rate environment and as a form of protection against a decline in the issuer's credit quality. This will add to the overall debt burden of the issuer, however, so it may have negative effects.

Extendible bonds are issued with a final redemption date already stated. The issue may choose to have the bonds redeemed at one of a range of dates ahead of the final maturity date, and these dates are usually also associated with a *put* feature. If the issuer decides to extend the redemption date, a certain portion of the debt may have to be retired, or may be put back if investors so wish. This provision sometimes applies if the coupon is re-set as well.

Only a small number of such issues were still trading in the US market in 1997.

High-yield bank loans

The development of a market in tradeable bank loans has served to break down many of the distinctions between high-yield loans and bonds. There has been a steady increase in secondary loan trading during the 1990s; indeed, after the "junk" bond market collapsed in 1990, high-yield bank loans comprised virtually all of the debt issued to non-investment grade companies in that year. Over $40 billion of high-yield bank loans were issued in 1997. Another type of bank loan that trades in the secondary market is the "B loan", which is a long-dated loan that is serviced with interest payments only (that is, no repayment of principal) in the first few years after issue.

The main differences between high-yield bank loans and high-yield bonds are as follows:

- bank loans are typically floating-rate liabilities, while high-yield debt is almost invariably fixed-rate;
- bank loans are callable at any time;
- there is an element of security associated with most bank loans.

These differences ensure that the two markets remain distinct, if part of the overall "high-yield" market.

Notwithstanding that the large majority of high-yield bonds are plain vanilla securities, there has been a proliferation of the types of instrument traded in the high-yield market. Bonds have been issued that offer investors a share in the firm's profits, as well as a fixed coupon. Other issues have been backed by commodities.

A common method of issue of high-yield debt in the United States is via the SEC rule known as Rule 144A. Under this rule, securities sold initially through a private placement, which are then offered for re-sale to institutional investors, are not subject to review by the SEC. The borrower must register the securities within a short period of time, usually one to three months after issuance. By placing debt under this rule, the issue may be undertaken fairly quickly and at minimal cost. The type of bond issued is not relevant: any of the securities described here may be issued pursuant to Rule 144A.

High-yield bond performance

The performance of high-yield bonds in the US domestic market mirrors economic performance in the United States overall. The yield spread of high-yield debt over investment-grade corporate bonds is more of a function of the general outlook of the economy than of the health of the issuing companies themselves, although the latter is obviously important. Thus high-yield debt outperformed corporate bonds and other securities such as Treasury bonds and mortgage-backed securities in 1991 and 1992 as the US economy recovered from a recession, after having generated negative returns in 1990. During the period 1992–1995 the US economy was marked by a favourable combination of steady economic growth and low inflation and spreads moved to historical lows, before widening out considerably after the 1997 and 1998 bond market downturns, brought on (first) by the South-east Asian currency collapse and debt worries, and then by the Russian bond technical default. This triggered a "flight to quality" that affected both emerging market and high-yield debt alike.

Figure 14.4 illustrates how the yield spread on high-yield bonds of three different ratings compared during the late 1980s and 1990s.

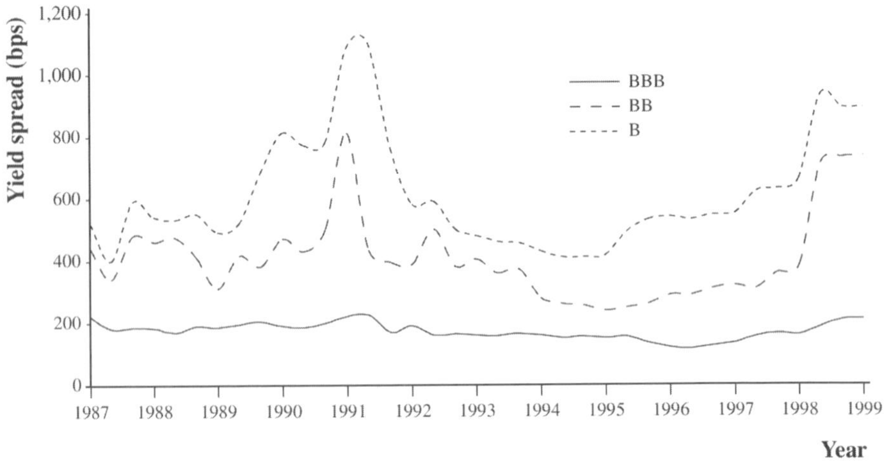

Figure 14.4 US high-yield bond spreads
Sources: Standard & Poor's, Bloomberg.

Another key indicator of high-yield bond performance is the level of default. The level of defaults has not unexpectedly been at the historically highest levels during times of recession. The default rate in 1990–1991 reflected the recession, as well as the hangover from the large-scale highly leveraged buy-outs of the late 1980s. The average default rate during the 1980s and 1990s has been approximately 3% to 3.5%. Figure 14.5 illustrates the actual default rates in the two decades. Table 14.1 shows that constituent bonds of a selected US high-yield index during 2000. Selected European high-yield bonds are shown in Table 14.2, while average spreads are shown in Figure 14.6. Figure 14.7 shows Bloomberg page HYI, which is the menu page for high-yield bond indices.

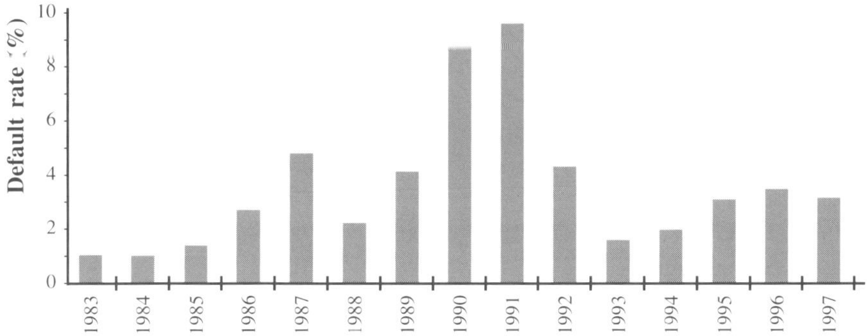

Figure 14.5 US high-yield market historical default rates, as a percentage of outstanding debt
Sources: Standard & Poor's, Lehman Brothers.

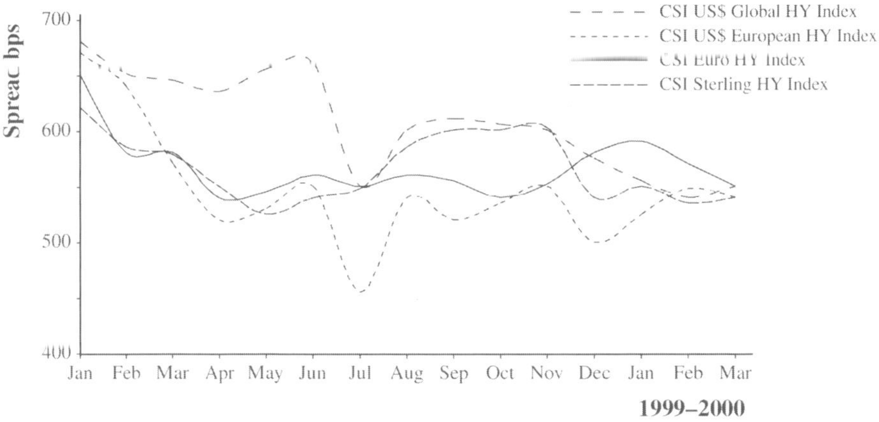

Figure 14.6 Average spreads in the European high-yield market, 1999–2000
Source: Chase Manhattan.

Issuer	Coupon (%)	Maturity	Nominal ($m)	Rating	Bid price	Spread (bp)
Adelphia Comms	Zero	Aug 2008	605	B1/BB-	42.000	464
Advanced Micro Devices	11.000	Aug 2003	400	B2/B	99.000	463
Advantica Rest Group	11.250	Jan 2008	550	B3/B	68.000	1,264
AK Stl	9.125	Dec 2006	546	Ba2/BB	98.250	279
Allied Waste North America	7.875	Jan 2009	875	Ba3/BB-	85.500	380
Amazon.Com	10.558	May 2008	530	Caa1/B	60.000	662
Budget Group	9.125	Apr 2006	400	B1/BB-	90.000	473
Caremark Rx	7.375	Oct 2006	450	B3/B	84.000	413
Chancellor Media Corp of LA	8.125	Dec 2007	500	B1/B	99.250	160
Charter Communication Holdings	8.625	Apr 2009	1,500	B2/B+	91.500	346
Crown Paper	11.000	Sep 2005	250	Caa1/CCC+	40.000	3,069
CSC Holdings	7.625	Jul 2018	500	Ba1/BB+	92.050	205
DR Horton	8.000	Feb 2009	385	Ba1/BB	87.000	364
Emmis Commun	8.125	Mar 2009	300	B2/B-	93.750	254
Exide	10.000	Apr 2005	300	B1/B+	95.250	449
Fairchild	10.750	Apr 2005	225	B3/B-	73.000	997
Flening Co.	10.625	Dec 2001	300	B1/B+	100.000	397
Formica	10.875	Mar 2009	215	B3/B-	88.000	657
Fox Family Worldwide	10.250	Nov 2007	605	B1/B	64.000	640
Friendly Ice Cream	10.500	Dec 2007	200	B2/B	80.000	827
Gaylord Container	9.375	Jun 2007	200	Caa1/B-	90.500	464
Globalstar	11.375	Feb 2004	499	Caa1/B	59.000	2,283
HMH Pptys	7.875	Aug 2008	1,200	Ba2/BB	87.500	348
Intermedia Comms	11.250	Jul 2007	648	B2/B	78.750	403
Level 3 Comms	9.125	May 2008	1,999	B3/B	91.500	406
Lyondell Comms	10.875	May 2009	500	B2/B+	95.500	507
Mandalay Resort Group	9.250	Dec 2005	275	Ba2/BB+	99.000	275
Nextel Communications	9.963	Feb 2008	1,627	B1/B	70.000	432

Ocean Energy	8.875	Jul 2007	200	Ba3/BB-	98.750	244
Playtex Products	[illegible]	[illegible]	[illegible]	B2/B	99.500	242
Pride International	9.375	May 2007	325	Ba3/BB	97.500	319
RBF Finance	11.000	Mar 2006	400	Ba3/BB-	105.750	301
REV Holdings	Zero	Mar 2001	770	Caa3/CCC+	23.000	19,344
Riverwood International	10.875	Apr 2008	400	Caa1/CCC+	95.000	520
Sterling Chemical	11.750	Aug 2006	275	Caa3/B	84.000	908
Tenet Healthcare	8.000	Jan 2005	900	Ba1/BB+	96.000	227
Time Warner Telecom	9.750	Jul 2008	400	B2/B	100.000	304
Trump Atlantic City Association	11.250	May 2006	1,200	B2/B-	70.000	1,316
WCI STL	10.000	Dec 04	300	B2/B+	99.500	337
Westpoint Stevens	7.875	Jun 05	525	Ba3/BB	88.000	417

Table 14.1 "Focus 40" US high-yield bond index, February 2000
Sources: IFR, Thompson Financial Bank Watch.

Issuer	Coupon (%)	Maturity	Currency	Nominal (mn)	Rating	Bid price	Spread (bp)
Atlantic Telecom	12.875	Feb 2010	EUR	200	B3/B-	113.00	510
Colt	7.625	Dec 2009	EUR	307	B1/B	96.00	290
Huntsman ICI	10.250	Jun 2009	EUR	200	B2/B+	105.00	375
IPC Magazines	9.625	Mar 2008	GBP	120	B3/B-	75.00	915
Jazztel	13.250	Dec 2009	EUR	400	Caa1/CCC+	105.00	680
Kappa	10.625	Jul 2009	EUR	370	B2/B	105.50	420
KPNQwest	7.125	Jun 2009	EUR	340	Ba1/BB	95.75	235
Luxfer	10.125	Mar 2009	GBP	160	B2/B	94.50	540
NTL	9.875	Nov 2009	EUR	350	B3/B-	100.50	435
NTL	9.500	Apr 2008	GBP	125	B3/B-	95.50	435
Telewest	9.875	Jan 2010	GBP	180	B1/B+	99.00	440
UPC	10.875	Aug 2009	EUR	300	B2/B-	98.00	570
UPC	13.375	Nov 2009	EUR	191	B2/B-	55.50	780
Versatel	11.875	Jul 2009	EUR	120	Caa1	107.00	510
William Hill	10.625	Apr 2008	GBP	150	B3/B-	101.00	440

Table 14.2 European high-yield bond pricing, February 2000
Sources: IFR, Euroweek.

GRAB Corp HYI
Screen Printed

HIGH YIELD Page 1 of [illegible]

SECTOR ID/NAME			SECTOR ID/NAME		
1)	BSAP	Asia/ Pacific Index	17)	CDYW	JPMorgan European HY YTW
2)	BSCM	C. Asia/ Middle East/ Africa	18)	CESW	JPM Euro High Yield STW
3)	BSEC	Bear Stearns ECU Index	19)	CEUR	JPMorgan Euro High Yield
4)	BSEM	Bear Stearns Emerging Market	20)	CEYW	JPMorgan Euro High Yield YTW
5)	BSER	Bear Stearns E.Eur/ Russia	21)	CSHY	CSFB High Yield Index
6)	BSGC	Bear Stearns Global HY Corp	22)	CSIY	JPMorgan US$ Global High Yld
7)	BSGS	Bear Stearns High Yield Indx	23)	CSSW	CHASE HIGH YIELD:SPD TO WRST
8)	BSGX	Bear Stearns High Yield	24)	CSYW	CHASE HIGH YIELD:YLD TO WRST
9)	BSIX	Bear Stearns High Yield	25)	DLJH	CSFB High Yield Index II
10)	BSLA	Bear Stearns Latin America	26)	DLJL	CSFB Leveraged Loan Index
11)	BSWU	Bear Stearns Western Europe	27)	DLJN	CSFB W. Euro HY Non USD Indx
12)	CBPD	JPMorgan Sterling High Yield	28)	DLJW	CSFB W. Euro HY Idx All Curr
13)	CBSW	JPMorgan Sterling HY STW	29)	EMTC	Clearing House Euro Turnover
14)	CBYW	JPMorgan Sterling HY YTW	30)	EMTP	PRIMARY EURO MARKET TURNOVER
15)	CDDE	JPMorgan European High Yield	31)	GLLI	GS/LPC LIQ LVRGD LOAN
16)	CDSW	JPMorgan European HY STW	32)	JPAS	JPMorgan High Sprd to Worst

Australia 61 2 9777 8600 Brazil 5511 3048 4500 Europe 44 20 7330 7500 Germany 49 69 920410
Hong Kong 852 2977 6000 Japan 81 3 3201 8900 Singapore 65 6212 1000 U.S. 1 212 318 2000 Copyright 2005 Bloomberg L.P.
0 16-Sep-05 7:32:33

Figure 14.7 Bloomberg screen HYI, high-yield bond index screen.
©Bloomberg L.P. Used with permission

Selected bibliography and references

Barnhill, T. (ed.) 1999, *High-yield Bonds: Market Structure, Valuation and Portfolio Strategies*, McGraw-Hill, New York.

Hickman, W. 1958, *Corporate Bond Quality and Investor Experience*, Princeton University Press and National Bureau of Economic Research.

Howe, J.T. 1987, *Junk Bonds*, Probus Publishing, Oxford.

Moody's Investors Service, Inc. 1993, "Corporate bond defaults and default rates 1970–1992", *Moody's Special Report*, January.

Rubin, 1990, *Junk Bonds*, Prentice-Hall, New York.

Yago, G. 1990, *Junk Bonds: How High-yield Securities Restructured Corporate America*, OUP.

The dreamers of the day are dangerous men, for they may act out their dream with open eyes, to make it possible.
This I did.

– T.E. Lawrence (1888–1935)
Seven Pillars of Wisdom

CHAPTER 15

Credit Analysis and Relative Value

The risks associated with holding a fixed interest debt instrument are closely connected with the ability of the issuer to maintain the regular coupon payments, as well as redeem the debt on maturity. Essentially, the *credit risk* is the main risk of holding a bond. Only the highest quality government debt, and a small number of supra-national issues, may be considered to be entirely free of credit risk. Therefore at any time the yield on a bond reflects investors' views on the ability of the issuer to meet its liabilities as set out in the bond's terms and conditions. A delay in paying a cash liability as it becomes due is known as technical default and is a cause for extreme concern for investors; failure to pay will result in the matter being placed in the hands of the legal court as investors seek to recover their funds. To judge the ability of an issue to meet its obligations for a particular debt issue, for the entire life of the issue, requires judgemental analysis of the issuer's financial strength and business prospects. There are a number of factors that must be considered, and larger banks, fund managers and corporates carry out their own *credit analysis* of individual borrowers' bond issues. The market also makes a considerable use of formal *credit ratings* that are assigned to individual bond issues by a formal credit rating agency. In the international markets arguably the two most influential ratings agencies are Standard & Poor's Corporation (S&P) and Moody's Investors Service, Inc.

(Moody's), based in the United States. In the US domestic market, Duff & Phelps Credit Rating Co. (D&P) and Fitch Investors Service, Inc. (Fitch) also have a high profile, as do IBCA and Dun & Bradstreet in the United Kingdom. The four US agencies all have similar ratings.[1]

The specific factors that are considered by a ratings agency, and the methodology used in conducting the analysis, differ slightly among the individual ratings agencies. Although in many cases the ratings assigned to a particular issue by different agencies are the same, they occasionally differ and in these instances investors usually seek to determine what aspect of an issuer is given more weight in an analysis by which individual agency. Note that a credit rating is not a recommendation to buy (or equally, sell) a particular bond, nor is it a comment on market expectations. Credit analysis does take into account general market and economic conditions; the overall purpose of credit analysis is to consider the financial health of the issuer and its ability to meet the obligations of the specific issue being rated. Credit ratings play a large part in the decision-making of investors, and also have a significant impact on the interest rates payable by borrowers.

In this chapter we review credit ratings and consider the main factors involved in corporate bond credit analysis.

We then discuss relative value analysis of the kind employed by institutions when making the trade decision.

Credit ratings

A credit rating is a formal opinion given by a rating agency of the *credit risk* for investors in a particular issue of debt securities. Ratings are given to public issues of debt securities by any type of entity, including governments, banks and corporates. They are also given to short-term debt such as commercial paper, as well as bonds and medium-term notes.

Purpose of credit ratings

Investors in securities accept the risk that the issuer will default on coupon payments or fail to repay the principal in full on the maturity date. Generally, credit risk is greater for securities with a long maturity, as there is a longer period for the issuer potentially to default. For example, if a company issues 10-year bonds, investors cannot be certain that the company will still exist in ten years' time. It may have failed and gone into liquidation some time before that. That said, there is also risk attached to short-dated debt

[1] Fitch and IBCA subsequently merged to become FitchIBCA and subsequetly Fitch Investors Service, usually referred to simply as "Fitch".

securities; indeed, there have been instances of default by issuers of commercial paper, which is a very short-term instrument.

The prospectus or offer document for an issue provides investors with some information about the issuer so that some credit analysis can be performed on the issuer before the bonds are placed. The information in the offer documents enables investors themselves to perform their own credit analysis by studying this information before deciding whether or not to invest. Credit assessments take up time however and also require the specialist skills of credit analysts. Large institutional investors do in fact employ such specialists to carry out credit analysis; however, often it is too costly and time-consuming to assess every issuer in every debt market. Therefore investors commonly employ two other methods when making a decision on the credit risk of debt securities:

- name recognition;
- formal credit ratings.

Name recognition is when the investor relies on the good name and reputation of the issuer and accepts that the issuer is of such good financial standing, or sufficient financial standing, that a default on interest and principal payments is highly unlikely. An investor may feel this way about, say, Microsoft or British Petroleum plc. However, the experience of Barings in 1995 suggested to many investors that it may not be wise to rely on name recognition alone in today's marketplace. The tradition and reputation behind the Barings name allowed the bank to borrow at Libor and occasionally at sub Libor interest rates in the money markets, which put it on a par with the highest quality clearing banks in terms of credit rating. However, name recognition needs to be augmented by other methods to reduce the risk against unforeseen events, as happened with Barings. Credit ratings are a formal assessment, for a given issue of debt securities, of the likelihood that the interest and principal will be paid in full and on schedule. They are increasingly used to make investment decisions about corporate or lesser developed government debt.

Formal credit ratings

Credit ratings are provided by the specialist agencies. The major credit rating agencies are Standard & Poor's, Fitch and Moody's, based in the United States, and the UK-based IBCA. There are other agencies both in the United States and other countries. On receipt of a formal request, the credit rating agencies will carry out a rating exercise on a specific issue of debt capital. The request for a rating comes from the organisation planning the issue of bonds. Although ratings are provided for the benefit of investors, the issuer must bear the cost. However, it is in the issuer's interest to request a rating as it raises the profile of the bonds, and investors may refuse to buy paper that is not accompanied with a recognised rating. Although the rating exercise involves a credit analysis of the issuer, the rating is applied to a specific debt issue. This means that in theory the credit rating is applied not to an organisation itself, but to specific debt securities that the organisation has issued or is planning to issue. In practice it is common for the market to refer to the creditworthiness of organisations themselves in terms of the rating of their debt. A highly rated company such as Commerzbank is therefore referred to as a "triple-A rated" company, although it is the bank's debt issues that are rated as triple-A.

The rating for an issue is kept constantly under review and if the credit quality of the issuer declines or improves, the rating will be changed accordingly. An agency may announce in advance that it is reviewing a particular credit rating, and may go further and state that the review is a precursor to a possible downgrade or upgrade. This announcement is referred to as putting the issue under *credit watch*. The outcome of a credit watch is in most cases likely to be a rating downgrade; however, the review may reaffirm the current rating or possibly upgrade it. During the credit watch phase the agency will advise investors to use the current rating with caution. When an agency announces that an issue is under credit watch, the price of the bonds will fall in the market as investors look to sell out of their holdings. This upward movement in yield will be more pronounced if an actual downgrade results. For example, in October 1992 the government of Canada was placed under credit watch and subsequently lost its AAA credit rating; as a result, there was an immediate and sharp sell-off in Canadian government Eurobonds, before the rating agencies had announced the actual results of their credit review.

Credit ratings vary between agencies. Separate categories are used by each agency for short-term debt (with original maturity of 12 months or less) and long-term debt of over one year original maturity. It is also usual to distinguish between higher "investment grade" ratings, where the credit risk is low, and lower quality "speculative grade" ratings, where the credit risk is greater. High-yield bonds are speculative-grade bonds and are generally rated no higher than double-B, although some issuers have been upgraded to triple-B in recent years, and a triple-B rating is still occasionally awarded to a high-yield bond. A summary of long-term ratings is shown at Table 15.1.

Ratings can be accessed on the Bloomberg system. A composite page is shown in Figure 15.1, the screen RATD.

Fitch	Moody's	Standard & Poors	Summary Description
Investment grade – High credit quality			
AAA	Aaa	AAA	Gilt edged, prime, lowest risk, risk-free
AA+	Aa1	AA+	
AA	Aa2	AA	High-grade, high credit quality
AA-	Aa3	AA-	
A+	A1	A+	
A	A2	A	Upper medium grade
A-	A3	A-	
BBB+	Baa1	BBB+	
BBB	Baa2	BBB	Lower medium grade
BBB-	Baa3	BBB-	
Speculative – Lower credit quality			
BB+	Ba1	BB+	
BB	Ba2	BB	Low grade; speculative
BB-	Ba3	BB-	
B1	B+		
B	B2	B	Highly speculative
B3	B-		
Highly speculative, substantial risk or in default			
		CCC+	
CCC	Caa	CCC	Considerable risk, in poor standing
		CCC-	
CC	Ca	CC	May already be in default, very speculative
C	C	C	Extremely speculative
		CI	Income bonds – no interest being paid
DDD			
DD			Default
D		D	

Table 15.1 Summary of credit rating agency bond ratings[2]
Source: Rating agencies.

[2] Following subsequent mergers, Fitch Inc. incorporates Fitch, IBCA and Duff & Phelps.

GRAB Govt RATD

LONG-TERM RATING SCALES COMPARISON Page 1/2

MOODY'S	Aaa	Aa1	Aa2	Aa3	A1	A2	A3	Baa1	Baa2	Baa3
S&P	AAA	AA+	AA	AA-	A+	A	A-	BBB+	BBB	BBB-
COMP	AAA	AA+	AA	AA-	A+	A	A-	BBB+	BBB	BBB-
TBW	AAA	AA+	AA	AA-	A+	A	A-	BBB+	BBB	BBB-
FITCH	AAA	AA+	AA	AA-	A+	A	A-	BBB+	BBB	BBB-
CBRS	AAA	AA+	AA	AA-	A+	A	A-	BBB+	BBB	BBB-
DOMINION	AAA	AAH	AA	AAL	AH	A	AL	BBBH	BBB	BBBL
R&I	AAA	AA+	AA	AA-	A+	A	A-	BBB+	BBB	BBB-
JCR	AAA	AA+	AA	AA-	A+	A	A-	BBB+	BBB	BBB-
MI	AAA		AA			A			BBB	

white = investment grade yellow = non-investment grade

GRAB Govt RATD

LONG-TERM RATING SCALES COMPARISON Page 2/2

MOODY'S	Ba1	Ba2	Ba3	B1	B2	B3	Caa1	Caa2	Caa3	Ca	C	
S&P	BB+	BB	BB-	B+	B	B-	CCC+	CCC	CCC-	CC	C	D
COMP	BB+	BB	BB-	B+	B	B-	CCC+	CCC	CCC-	CC	C	DDD
TBW	BB+	BB	BB-	CCC+	CCC	CCC-	CC+	CC	CC-			D
FITCH	BB+	BB	BB-	B+	B	B-	CCC+	CCC	CCC-	CC	C	D
CBRS	BB+	BB	BB-	B+	B	B-					C	D
DOMINION	BBH	BB	BBL	BH	B	BL	CCCH	CCC	CCCL	CC	C	D
R&I	BB+	BB	BB-	B+	B	B-	CCC+	CCC	CCC-	CC+	CC	CC-
JCR	BB+	BB	BB-	B+	B	B-		CCC		CC	C	D
MI		BB			B			CCC		CC		DDD

white = investment grade yellow = non-investment grade

Figure 15.1 Bloomberg credit rating screen RATD
© Bloomberg L.P. Used with permission.

Credit analysis

When ratings agencies were first set up the primary focus of credit analysis was on the default risk of the bond, or the probability that the investor would not receive the interest payments and the principal repayment as they fell due. Although this is still important, credit analysts these days also consider the overall economic conditions, as well as the chance that an issuer will have its rating changed during the life of the bond. There are differences in approach, depending on which industry or market sector the issuing company is part of.

In this section we review the main issues of concern to a credit analyst when rating bond issues. Analysts usually adopt a "top-down" approach, or a "big picture" approach, and concentrate on the macro-issues first before looking at the issuer-specific points in detail. The process therefore involves reviewing the issuer's industry, before looking at its financial and balance sheet strength, and finally the legal provisions concerning the bond issue. There are also detail differences in analysis depending on which industry the issuer is in.

The issuer industry

In the first instance the credit analysis process of a specific issue will review the issuer's industry. This is in order to place the subsequent company analysis in context. For example, a company that has recorded growth rates of 10% each year may appear to be a quality performer, but not if its industry has been experiencing average growth rates of 30%. Generally, the industry analysis will review the following issues:

- *Economic cycle*. The business cycle of the industry and its correlation with the overall business cycle are key indicators. That is, how closely does the industry follow the rate of growth of its country's GNP? Certain industries such as the electricity and food retail sectors are more resistant to recession than others. Other sectors are closely tied to changes in population and birth patterns, such as residential homes, while the financial services industry is influenced by the overall health of the economy as well as by the level of interest rates. As well as the correlation with macro-factors, credit analysts review traditional financial indicators in context; for example, the issuing company's *earnings per share* (EPS) against the growth rate of its industry.

- *Growth prospects.* This review is of the issuer industry's general prospects. A company operating within what is considered a high-growth industry is generally deemed to have better credit quality expectations than one operating in a low-growth environment. A scenario of anticipated growth in the industry has implications for the issuing company; for example, the extent to which the company will be able cope with capacity demands and the financing of excess capacity. A fast-growth industry also attracts new entrants, which will lead to over-supply, intensified competition and reduced margins. A slow-growth industry has implications for diversification, so that a company deemed to have plans for diversifying when operating in stagnant markets will be marked up.
- *Competition.* A review of the intensity of competitive forces within an industry, and the extent of pricing and over- or under-capacity, is an essential ingredient of credit analysis. Competition is now regarded as a global phenomenon and well-rated companies are judged able to compete successfully on a global basis while concentrating on the highest growth regions. Competition within a particular industry is related to that industry's structure and has implications for pricing flexibility. The type of market – for example, monopoly, oligopoly, and so on – also influences pricing policy and relative margins. Another issue arises if there is obvious over-capacity in an industry; this has been exemplified in the past in the airline industry and financial services (of some countries) when over-capacity often leads to intense price competition and price wars. This is frequently damaging for the industry as a whole, as all companies suffer losses and financial deterioration in the attempt to maintain or grow market share.
- *Supply sources.* The availability of suppliers in an industry influences a company's financial well-being. Monopoly sources of supply are considered a restrictive element and have negative implications. A vertically integrated company that is able to supply its own raw materials is less susceptible to economic conditions that might affect suppliers or leave it hostage to price rises. A company that is not self-sufficient in its factors of production, but is nevertheless in strong enough a position to pass on its costs, is in a good position.
- *Research and development.* A broad assessment of the growth prospects of a company must also include a review of its research and development (R&D) position. In certain industries, such as telecommunications, media and information technology, a heavy

investment in R&D is essential simply in order to maintain market share. In a high technology field it is common for products to obsolesce very quickly, therefore it is essential to maintain high R&D spending. In the short-term, however, a company with a low level of research expenditure may actually post above-average (relative to the industry) profits because it is operating at higher margins. This is not considered a healthy strategy for the long term, though.

Evaluating the R&D input of a company is not necessarily a straightforward issue of comparing ratios, however, as it is also important to assess correctly the direction of technology. That is, a successful company needs not only to invest a sufficient amount in R&D, it must also be correct in its assessment of the direction the industry is heading, technology-wise. A heavy investment in developing Betamax videos, for example, would not have assisted a company in the early 1980s.

- *Level of regulation.* The degree of regulation in an industry, its direction and its effect on the profitability of a company are relevant in a credit analysis. A highly regulated industry such as power generation, production of medicines or (in certain countries) telecommunications can have a restrictive influence on company profits. On the other hand, if the government has announced a policy of deregulating an industry, this is considered a positive development for companies in that industry.
- *Labour relations.* An industry with a highly unionised labour force or generally tense labour relations is viewed unfavourably compared to one with stable labour relations. Credit analysts will consider historic patterns of, say, strikes and production days lost to industrial action. The status of labour relations is also more influential in a highly labour-intensive industry than one that is more automated for example.
- *Political climate.* The investment industry adopts an increasingly global outlook and the emergence of sizeable tradeable debt markets in, for example, "emerging" countries means that ratings agencies frequently must analyse the general political and economic climate in which an industry is operating. Failure to foresee certain political developments can have far-reaching effects for investors, as recently occurred in Indonesia when that country experienced a change of government; foreign investors lost funds as several local banks went bankrupt.

Financial analysis

The traditional approach to credit analysis concentrated heavily on financial analysis. The more modern approach involves a review of the industry the company is operating in first, discussed above, before considering financial considerations. Generally, the financial analysis of the issuer is conducted in three phases, namely:

- the ratio analysis for the bonds;
- analysing the company's return on capital;
- non-financial factors such as management expertise and the extent of overseas operations.

Ratio analysis

There are a number of investor ratios that can be calculated. In themselves ratios do not present very much insight, although there are various norms that can be applied. Generally, ratio analysis is compared to the levels prevalent in the industry, as well as historical values, in an effort to place the analysis in context and compare the company with those in its peer group. The ratios that can be considered are:

- pre-tax interest cover, the level of cover for interest charges in current pre-tax income;
- fixed interest charge level;
- *leverage*, which is commonly defined as the ratio of long-term debt as a percentage of the total capitalisation;
- level of leverage compared to industry average;
- nature of debt, whether fixed- or floating-rate, short- or long-term;
- cash flow, which is the ratio of cash flow as a percentage of total debt. Cash flow itself is usually defined as net income from continuing operations, plus depreciation and taxes, while debt is taken to be long-term debt;
- net assets, as a percentage of total debt. The liquidity of the assets – meaning the ease with which they can be turned into cash – is taken into account when assessing the net asset ratio.

The ratings agencies maintain benchmarks that are used to assign ratings, and these are monitored and if necessary modified to allow for changes in the economic climate. For example, Standard & Poor's guidelines for pre-tax interest cover, leverage level and cash flow in 1997 are shown in Table 15.2. A pre-tax cover of above 9.00, for example, is consistent with a double-A rating.

Credit rating	Pre-tax interest cover	Leverage	Cash flow
AAA	17.99	13.2	97.5
AA	9.74	19.7	68.5
A	5.35	33.2	43.8
BBB	2.91	44.8	29.9

Table 15.2 S&P ratio benchmarks, 1997
Source: S&P.

Other ratios that are considered include:

- intangibles; that is, the portion of intangibles relative to the asset side of a balance sheet;
- unfunded pension liabilities; generally a fully funded pension is not seen as necessary; however, an unfunded liability that is over 10% of net assets would be viewed as a negative point;
- age and condition of plant;
- working capital.

Return on equity

There are a range of performance measures used in the market that are connected with return on equity (generally, the analysis concentrates on return on capital, or more recently return on risk-adjusted capital or RORAC). In analysing measures of return, analysts seek to determine trends in historical performance and comparisons with peer group companies. Different companies also emphasise different target returns in their objectives, usually an expression of their corporate philosophy, so it is common for companies in the same industry to have different return ratios. The range of ratios used by the credit ratings agencies is shown below. Note that "EBIT" is "earnings before interest and tax".

$$\text{Return on net assets} = \frac{\text{Profit}}{\text{Net assets}} \times 100$$

$$\text{Return on sales} = \frac{\text{Profit}}{\text{Sales turnover}} \times 100$$

$$\text{Return on equity} = (\text{Return on net assets} \times \text{Gearing}) \times 100$$

$$\text{Pre-tax interest cover} = \frac{\text{Pre-tax income from continuing operations}}{\text{Gross interest}}$$

$$\text{EBIT interest cover} = \frac{\text{Pre-tax income from continuing operations} + \text{Interest expense}}{\text{Gross interest}}$$

$$\text{Long-term debt as \% of capitalisation} = \frac{\text{Long-term debt}}{\text{Long-term debt} + \text{Equity}} \times 100$$

$$\text{Funds flow as \% of debt} = \frac{\text{Funds from operations}}{\text{Total debt}} \times 100$$

$$\text{Free cash flow as \% of debt} = \frac{\text{Free cash flow}}{\text{Total debt}} \times 100$$

The agencies make available data that may be consulted by the public; for example, Standard & Poor's has a facility known as "CreditStats", which was introduced in 1989. It contains the main financial ratios for a large number of companies, organised by their industry sectors.

Non-financial factors

The non-financial element of a company credit analysis has assumed a more important role in recent years, especially with regard to companies in exotic or emerging markets. Credit analysts review the non-financial factors relevant to the specific company after they have completed the financial and ratio analysis. These include the strength and competence of senior management, and the degree of exposure to overseas markets. The depth of overseas exposure is not always apparent from documents such as the annual report, and analysts sometimes need to conduct further research to determine this. Companies with considerable overseas exposure, such as petroleum companies, also need to be reviewed with respect to the political situation in their operating locations. A bank such as Standard Chartered, for example, has significant exposure to more exotic currencies in Asian, Middle-Eastern and African countries, and so is more at risk from additional market movements than a bank with almost exclusively domestic operations. The global, integrated nature of the bond markets also means that the foreign-exchange exposure of a company must be evaluated and assessed for risk.

The quality of management is a subjective, qualitative factor that can be reviewed in a number of ways. A personal familiarity with senior directors, acquired over a period of time, may help in the assessment. A broad breadth of experience, diversity of age, and strong internal competition for those aspiring to very senior roles, is considered positive. A company that had been founded by one individual, and in which there were no clear plans of "succession", might be marked down.

Industry-specific analysis

Specific industries will be subject to review that is more relevant to the particular nature of the operations of the companies within them. In this section we briefly consider two separate industries: power generation, water and certain other public service companies (or utilities); and financial companies.

Utility companies

The industry for power generation, water supply and until recently telecommunications has a tradition of being highly regulated. Until the mid-1980s, utility companies were public-sector companies, and the first privatisation of such a company was for British Telecom in 1984. In certain European countries, utility companies are still nationalised companies, and their debt trades virtually as government debt. Credit analysis for utility companies therefore emphasises non-financial factors such as the depth of regulation and the direction in which regulation is heading; for example, towards an easing or tightening. Even in a privatised industry, for example, new government regulation maybe targeted only at the utility sector; for example, the Labour government in the United Kingdom imposed a "windfall tax" on several privatised utility companies shortly after being elected in May 1997.

Another consideration concerns government direction on how the companies may operate, such as restrictions on where a power generation company may purchase coal from. In some countries such as Germany, coal must be bought from the country's own domestic coal industry only, which imposes costs on the generating company that it would escape if it were free to purchase coal from other, lower cost producers.

The financial analysis of a utility company essentially follows the pattern we described earlier.

Financial sector companies

The financial sector encompasses a large and diverse group of companies. They conduct an intermediary function in that they are a conduit for funds between borrowers and lenders of capital. At its simplest, financial service companies such as banks may earn profit by taking the spread between funds lent and borrowed. They also play an important role in managing the risk exposure for industrial companies, utilising option structures. In analysing a financial sector company the credit analyst will consider the type of customer base served by the company; for example, how much of a bank's lending is to the wholesale sector, how much is retail and so on. The financial strength and prospects of its customer base are important elements of a bank's credit rating.

Financial analysis of banks and securities houses is concerned (in addition to the factors discussed above) with the asset quality of the institution; for example, the extent of diversification of a bank's lending book. Diversification can be across customer base as well as geographically. A loan book that is heavily concentrated in one sector is considered to be a negative factor in the overall credit assessment of the bank. A credit analyst will be concerned with the level of loans compared with levels in peer companies and the risk involved with this type of lending. For example, the expected frequency of bad loans from direct unsecured retail customer loans is higher than for retail customer loans secured by a second mortgage on a property. The higher lending rate charged for the former is designed to compensate for this higher lending risk. There are a range of financial ratios that can be used to assess a bank's asset quality. These include:

- loss reserves/net charge-off level;
- net losses/average level of receivables;
- non-performing loans/average level of receivables.

However, unlike the more "concrete" financial ratios given earlier, there is a higher subjective element with these ratios as banks themselves will designate which loans are non-performing and those loans against which have been assigned charges. Nevertheless, these ratios are useful indicators and may be used to identify trends across the sector as well. The loss reserves/net charge-off ratio is perhaps the most useful as it indicates the level of "cushion" that a bank has; a falling ratio suggests that the bank may not be adding sufficient reserves to cover for future charge-offs. This trend, if continued, may then result in a future increase in the reserves and therefore a decrease in earnings levels as the expense of the reserves increase.

The leverage ratio is particularly important for financial sector companies as the industry and business itself are highly leveraged. Banks and securities companies are therefore permitted a significantly higher leverage level than other companies. For example, in a diversified banking group with a high level of asset quality, a leverage ratio of 5 : 1 or even higher is considered satisfactory by ratings agencies.

Another important measure for financial companies is *liquidity*. Due to the nature of the industry and the capital structure of banks, liquidity or, more accurately, the lack of liquidity is the primary reason behind banking failures. A bank that is unable to raise funds sufficiently quickly to meet demand will most probably fail, and certainly so if external support is not provided. An inability to raise funds may arise due to internal factors, such as a deterioration in earnings or a very poorly performing loan book, connected perhaps with a downgrade in credit rating, or from external factors such as a major structural fault in the money markets. For credit analysis purposes the traditional liquidity measures are:

- cash;
- cash equivalents;
- level of receivables under one year/level of short-term liabilities.

A higher ratio indicates a greater safety cushion. A further consideration is the extent of lines of credit from other banks in the market.

Other measures of strength for financial companies are *asset coverage*, the bank's earnings record including *earnings per share* (profit attributable to shareholders/number of shares in issue) and finally, the size of the institution. There is an element of thought which states that a very large institution, measured by asset size, cannot go bankrupt. This type of thinking can lead to complacency however and it did not prevent several large Japanese banks from getting into financial difficulty in the 1990s.[3]

[3] In fact, the Japanese government gave an implicit guarantee for the largest 20 "city" banks at one stage, shortly after the collapse of Yamaichi Securities in 1997.

Relative value analysis: bond spreads

Investors measure the perceived market value, or relative value, of a corporate bond by measuring its yield spread relative to a designated benchmark. This is the spread over the benchmark that gives the yield of the corporate bond. A key measure of relative value of a corporate bond is its swap spread. This is the basis point spread over the interest-rate swap curve, and is a measure of the credit risk of the bond. In its simplest form, the swap spread can be measured as the difference between the yield-to-maturity of the bond and the interest rate given by a straight-line interpolation of the swap curve. In practice traders use the asset-swap spread and the Z-spread as the main measures of relative value. The government bond spread is also used. In addition, now that the market in synthetic corporate credit is well established, using credit derivatives and credit default swaps (CDS), investors consider the Cash-CDS spread as well, which is known as the *basis*.

Credit derivatives are introduced in Appendix 20.1 of this book; readers also may wish to read the author's book on credit derivatives (Choudhry 2004b) as well as his paper on the CDS basis (Choudhry 2004a).

The spread that is selected is an indication of the relative value of the bond, and a measure of its credit risk. The greater the perceived risk, the greater the spread should be. This is best illustrated by the credit structure of interest rates, which will (generally) show AAA- and AA-rated bonds trading at the lowest spreads and BBB- , BB- and lower-bonds trading at the highest spreads. Bond spreads are the most commonly-used indication of the risk-return profile of a bond.

In this section we consider the Treasury spread, asset swap spread, Z-spread and basis.

Swap spread and Treasury spread

A bond's swap spread is a measure of the credit risk of that bond, relative to the interest-rate swaps market. Because the swaps market is traded by banks, this risk is effectively the interbank market, so the credit risk of the bond over-and-above bank risk is given by its spread over swaps. This is a simple calculation to make, and is simply the yield of the bond minus the swap rate for the appropriate maturity swap. Figure 15.2 shows Bloomberg page IRSB for Pounds sterling as at 10 August 2005. This shows the GBP swap curve on the left-hand side. The right-hand side of the screen shows the swap rates' spread over UK gilts. It is the spread over these swap rates that would provide the simplest relative value measure for corporate bonds denominated in GBP. If the bond has an odd maturity, say 5.5 years, we would interpolate between the five-year and six-year swap rates.

GRAB   Govt IRSB

British Pound

Ticker	TIME	Bid	Ask	Change	Open	High	Low	Prev Cls
GBP Swap Rates								
2) 1 YR	11:22	4.4940	4.5020	--	4.4980	4.5005	4.4870	4.4980
3) 18 MO	11:22	4.3925	4.4225	-.0037	4.4150	4.4175	4.3950	4.4163
4) 2 YR	11:18	4.4070	4.4150	-.0055	4.4150	4.4225	4.3975	4.4175
5) 3 YR	11:23	4.4110	4.4350	-.0008	4.4225	4.4275	4.4000	4.4238
6) 4 YR	11:23	4.4150	4.4150	-.0113	4.4250	4.4515	4.4085	4.4263
7) 5 YR	11:23	4.4230	4.4240	-.0127	4.4350	4.4370	4.4125	4.4363
8) 6 YR	11:23	4.4340	4.4625	-.0030	4.4500	4.4550	4.4233	4.4513
9) 7 YR	11:23	4.4440	4.4520	-.0157	4.4600	4.4690	4.4355	4.4638
10) 8 YR	11:23	4.4520	4.4590	-.0158	4.4675	4.4750	4.4422	4.4713
11) 9 YR	11:23	4.4580	4.4630	-.0157	4.4725	4.4800	4.4478	4.4763
12) 10 YR	11:23	4.4610	4.4640	-.0138	4.4750	4.4840	4.4550	4.4763
13) 12 YR	11:23	4.4610	4.4640	-.0138	4.4750	4.4750	4.4585	4.4763
14) 15 YR	11:23	4.4520	4.4550	-.0128	4.4650	4.4735	4.4335	4.4663
15) 20 YR	11:23	4.4210	4.4230	-.0118	4.4325	4.5250	4.3912	4.4338
16) 25 YR	11:21	4.3175	4.4475	-.0125	4.3975	4.4367	4.3763	4.3963
17) 30 YR	11:21	4.3430	4.3550	-.0078	4.3550	4.4500	4.3225	4.3588

Page 1

Ticker	TIME	Bid	Ask	Change	Open	High	Low	Prev Cls
GBP Swap Spread								
19) 1 YR	11:22	33.80	39.80	+2.10	31.40	33.80	29.90	31.7000
20) 2 YR	11:21	29.50	33.50	+1.00	29.00	[illegible]	[illegible]	[illegible]
21) 3 YR	11:21	31.00	35.00	+.75	30.75	33.25	30.00	32.2500
22) 4 YR	11:23	30.50	35.50	+.50	30.50	33.25	30.00	32.5000
23) 5 YR	11:14	26.50	36.00	-4.50	30.50	30.50	28.50	33.0000
24) 6 YR	11:23	32.75	37.75	+.50	32.50	35.50	32.50	34.7500
25) 7 YR	11:23	32.00	37.00	+.50	32.00	34.75	32.00	34.0000
26) 8 YR	11:21	31.00	36.00	+.50	30.75	33.75	30.75	33.0000
27) 9 YR	11:21	29.75	34.75	+.50	29.75	32.50	29.75	31.7500
28) 10 YR	8:05	29.75	34.75	+.25	32.25	32.50	32.25	32.0000
29) 15 YR	11:21	22.75	31.75	+.25	27.25	28.00	27.00	27.0000
30) 20 YR	11:21	19.00	32.00	+.13	25.50	26.00	25.25	25.3750
31) 30 YR	11:23	14.75	27.50	+.25	21.00	21.50	20.63	20.8750

For UK Govt Yield Curve, Click on any Tickers above & Select: IYC1 I22

For GBP Swap Curve, Click on any Tickers above & Select: IYC1 I55

Page 2

Australia 61 2 9777 8600 Brazil 5511 3048 4500 Europe 44 20 7330 7500 Germany 49 69 920410
Hong Kong 852 2977 6000 Japan 81 3 3201 8900 Singapore 65 6212 1000 U.S. 1 212 318 2000 Copyright 2005 Bloomberg L.P.
2 22-Sep-05 11:23:44

Figure 15.2 Bloomberg page IRSB for Pounds sterling, showing GBP swap rates and swap spread over UK gilts

The spread over swaps is sometimes called the *I-spread.* It has a simple relationship to swaps and Treasury yields, shown here in the equation for corporate bond yield,

$$Y = I + S + T$$

where

Y is the yield on the corporate bond
I is the I-spread or spread over swap
S is the swap spread
T is the yield on the Treasury security (or an interpolated yield).

In other words, the swap rate itself is given by $T + S$.

The *I*-spread is sometimes used to compare a cash bond with its equivalent CDS price, but for straightforward relative value analysis is usually dropped in favour of the asset-swap spread, which we look at later in this section.

Of course the basic relative value measure is the Treasury spread or government bond spread. This is simply the spread of the bond yield over the yield of the appropriate government bond. Again, an interpolated yield may need to be used to obtain the right Treasury rate to use. The bond spread is given by:

$$BS = Y - T.$$

Using an interpolated yield is not strictly accurate because yield curves are smooth in shape and so straight-line interpolation will produce slight errors. The method is still commonly used though.

Asset-swap spread

An asset swap is a package that combines an interest-rate swap with a cash bond, the effect of the combined package being to transform the interest-rate basis of the bond. Typically, a fixed-rate bond will be combined with an interest-rate swap in which the bond holder pays fixed coupon and receives floating coupon. The floating-coupon will be a spread over Libor (see Choudhry *et al* 2001). This spread is the asset-swap spread and is a function of the credit risk of the bond over and above interbank credit risk.[4] Asset swaps may be transacted at par or at the bond's market price, usually par. This means that the asset swap value is made up of the difference between the bond's market price and par, as well as the difference between the bond coupon and the swap fixed rate.

The zero-coupon curve is used in the asset swap valuation. This curve is derived from the swap curve, so it is the implied zero-coupon curve (see Chapter 2). The asset swap spread is the spread that equates the difference between the present value of the bond's cashflows, calculated using the swap zero rates, and the market price of the bond. This spread is a function of the

---

4 This is because in the interbank market, two banks transacting an interest-rate swap will be paying/receiving the fixed rate and receiving/paying Libor-flat. See also the author's "Learning Curve" article on asset swaps available on www.yieldcurve.com

bond's market price and yield, its cashflows and the implied zero-coupon interest rates.[5]

Figure 15.3 shows the Bloomberg screen ASW for a GBP-denominated bond, GKN Holdings 7% 2012, as at 10 August 2005. We see that the asset-swap spread is 121.5 basis points. This is the spread over Libor that will be received if the bond is purchased in an asset-swap package. In essence the asset swap spread measures a difference between the market-price of the bond and the value of the bond when cashflows have been valued using zero-coupon rates. The asset-swap spread can therefore be regarded as the coupon of an annuity in the swap market that equals this difference.

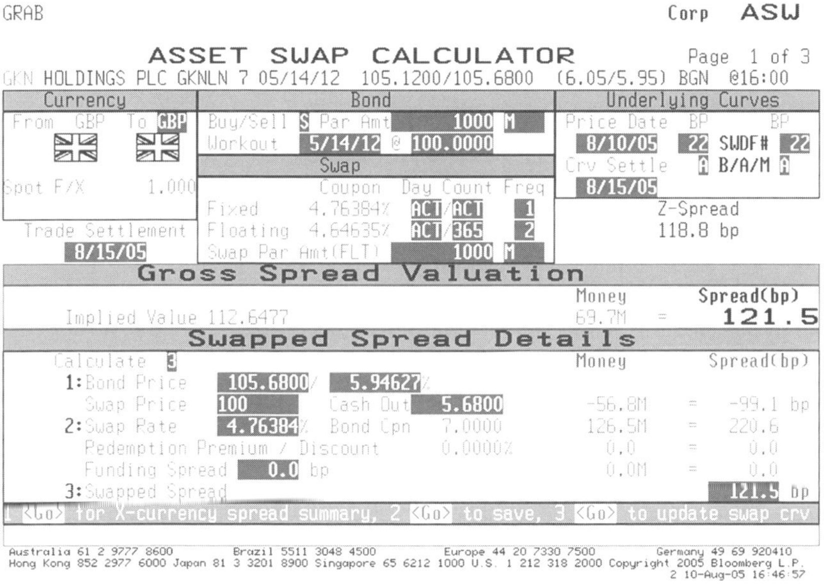

Figure 15.3 Bloomberg page ASW for GKN bond, 10 August 2005
© Bloomberg LP. Used with permission. Visit www.bloomberg.com

[5] Bloomberg refers to this spread as the Gross Spread.

Z-Spread

The conventional approach for analysing an asset swap uses the bond's yield-to-maturity (YTM) in calculating the spread. The assumptions implicit in the YTM calculation (see Chapter 2) make this spread problematic for relative analysis, so market practitioners use what is termed the Z-spread instead. The Z-spread uses the zero-coupon yield curve to calculate spread, so is a more realistic, and effective, spread to use. The zero-coupon curve used in the calculation is derived from the interest-rate swap curve.

Put simply, the Z-spread is the basis point spread that would need to be added to the implied spot yield curve such that the discounted cash flows of the a bond are equal to its present value (its current market price). Each bond cashflow is discounted by the relevant spot rate for its maturity term. How does this differ from the conventional asset-swap spread? Essentially, in its use of zero-coupon rates when assigning a value to a bond. Each cashflow is discounted using its own particular zero-coupon rate. The price of a bond's price at any time can be taken to be the market's value of the bond's cashflows. Using the Z-spread we can quantify what the swap market thinks of this value, that is, by how much the conventional spread differs from the Z-spread. Both spreads can be viewed as the coupon of a swap market annuity of equivalent credit risk of the bond being valued.

In practice the Z-spread, especially for shorter-dated bonds and for better credit-quality bonds, does not differ greatly from the conventional asset-swap spread. The Z-spread is usually the higher spread of the two, following the logic of spot rates, but not always. If it differs greatly, then the bond can be considered to be mis-priced.

Figure 15.4 is the Bloomberg screen YAS for the same bond shown in Figure 15.3, as at the same date. It shows a number of spreads for the bond. The main spread of 151.00 bps is the spread over the government yield curve. This is an interpolated spread, as can be seen lower down the screen, with the appropriate benchmark bind identified. We see that the asset-swap spread is 121.6 bps, while the Z-spread is 118.8 bps. When undertaking relative value analysis, for instance if making comparisons against cash funding rates or the same company name credit default swap (CDS), it is this lower spread that should be used.[6]

The same screen can be used to check spread history. This is shown at Figure 15.5, the Z-spread graph for the GKN bond for the six months prior to our calculation date.

---

6 On the date in question the 10-year CDS for this reference entity was quoted as 96.8 bps, which is a rare example of a negative basis, in this case of –22 basis points.

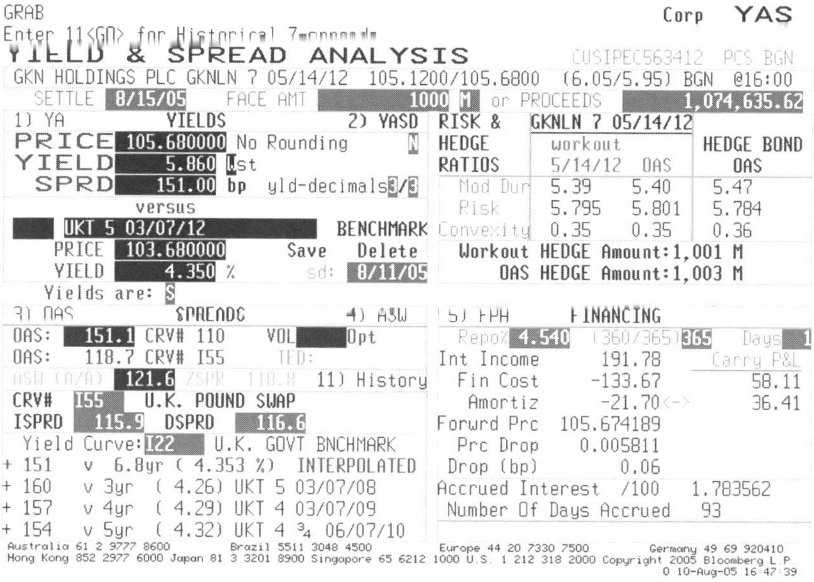

Figure 15.4 Bloomberg page YAS for GKN bond, 10 August 2005

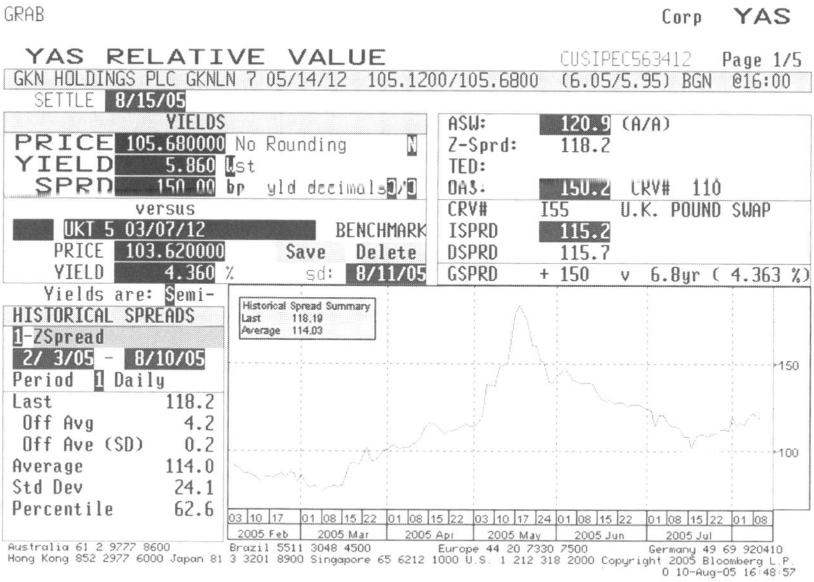

Figure 15.5 Bloomberg page YAS for GKN bond, 10 August 2005 showing Z-spread history

Z-spread is closely related to the bond price, as shown by equation (15.1),

$$P = \sum_{i=1}^{n}\left[\frac{C_i + M_i}{(1 + ((Z + S_i + T_i)/m))^i}\right] \tag{15.1}$$

where

- n is the number of interest periods until maturity
- P is the bond price
- C is the coupon
- M is the redemption payment (so bond cashflow is all C plus M)
- Z is the Z-spread
- m is the frequency of coupon payments.

In effect this is the standard bond price equation with the discount rate adjusted by whatever the Z-spread is; it is an iterative calculation. The appropriate maturity swap rate is used, which is the essential difference between the I-spread and the Z-spread. This is deemed to be more accurate, because the entire swap curve is taken into account rather than just one point on it. In practice though, as we have seen in the example above, there is often little difference between the two spreads.

To reiterate then, using the correct Z-spread, the sum of the bond's discounted cashflows will be equal to the current price of the bond.

We illustrate the Z-spread calculation at Figure 15.6. This is done using a hypothetical bond, the XYZ plc 5% of June 2008, a three-year bond at the time of the calculation. Market rates for swaps, Treasury and CDS are also shown. We require the spread over the swaps curve that equates the present values of the cashflows to the current market price. The cashflows are discounted using the appropriate swap rate for each cashflow maturity. With a bond yield of 5.635 %, we see that the I-spread is 43.5 basis points, while the Z-spread is 19.4 basis points. In practice the difference between these two spreads is rarely this large.

For readers benefit we also show the Excel formula in Figure 15.6. This shows how the Z-spread is calculated; for ease of illustration we have assumed that the calculation takes place for value on a coupon date, so that we have precisely an even period to maturity.

A1	B	C	D	E	F	G	H	I
2	**Issuer**		**XYZ plc**					
3	Settlement date		6/1/05					
4	Maturity date		6/1/08					
5	Coupon		5%	**YIELD**	**0.05635**			
6	Price		98.95	[Cell formula =YIELD(C4,C5,C6,C7,C8,C9,C10)]				
7	Par		100					
8	Semi-annual coupon		2	**PRICE**	**98.95000**			
9	act/act		1	[Cell formula =PRICE(C4,C5,C6,C6,C8,C9,C10)]				
10								
11	Bond yield		5.635%					
12	Sovereign bond yield		4.880%					
13	Swap rate (S)		5.200%					
14								
15	3-year CDS price		28 bps					
16								
17	**Treasury spread**							
18	5.635 - 4.88		55 bps					
19								
20	**I-spread**							
21	5.635 - 5.20		43.5 bps					
22								
23	**Z spread (Z)**		19.4 bps	0.00194				
24	The Z-spread is found using iteration							

Continued from pp. 455

25								
26								**Sum of PVs**
27	Cash flow date	12/1/05	6/1/06	12/1/06	6/1/07	12/1/07	6/1/08	
28	Cash flow maturity (years)	0.50	1.00	1.50	2.00	2.50	3.00	
29	0.5-year swap rate (S)	4.31%	4.84%	4.99%	5.09%	5.18%	5.20%	
30	Cash flow (CF)	2.50	2.50	2.50	2.50	2.50	102.50	
31	Discount factor	0.97797598	0.951498751	0.926103469	0.900947692	0.875835752	0.852419659	
32	(DF Calculation)	1/(1+(S+Z)/2)^1	1/(1+(S+Z)/2)^2	1/(1+(S+Z)/2)^3	1/(1+(S+Z)/2)^4	1/(1+(S+Z)/2)^5	1/(1+(S+Z)/2)^6	
33	CF present value (PV)	2.445	2.379	2.315	2.252	2.190	87.373	**98.95**
34								
35								
36								
37	A Z-spread of 19.4 basis points gives us the current bond price so is the correct one							
38	Using this value, the sum of all the discounted cashflows is equal to the market price							
39								
40	**CDS Basis**							
41	28 - 19.4	8.6 bps						
42	The basis is positive in this example							

Figure 15.6 Calculating the Z-spread, hypothetical 5% 2008 bond issued by XYZ plc (cont.)

Cash-CDS basis

The basis is the difference between a bond's asset swap spread, or alternatively its Z-spread, and the CDS price for the same bond issuer. So the basis is given by

$$B = D - I$$

where D is the CDS price. Where $D - I > 0$ it is a positive basis; the opposite is a negative basis.

Figure 15.7 shows page G <go> on Bloomberg, set up to show the Z-spread and CDS price history for the GKN 2012 bond, for the period March-Spetember 2005. We can select the "Table" option to obtain the actual values, which can then be used to plot the basis. This is shown at Figure 15.8, for the period 22 August to 22 September 2005. Notice how the basis was always negative during August-September; we see from Figure 6 that earlier in the year the basis had briefly been positive. Changes in the basis give rise to arbitrage opportunities between the cash and synthetic markets. This is discussed in greater detail in Choudhry (2004b).

Figure 15.7 Bloomberg graph using screen G <go>, plot of asset-swap spread and CDS price for GKN bond, April-September 2005

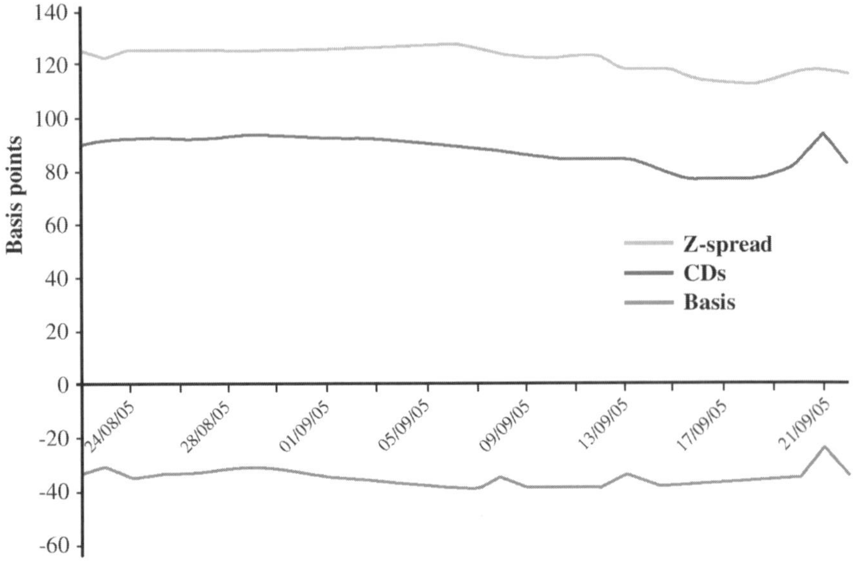

Figure 15.8 GKN bond, CDS basis during August-September 2005
Data source: Bloomberg L.P.

A wide range of factors drive the basis, which are described in detail in Choudhry (2004a). The existence of a non-zero basis has implications for investment strategy. For instance, when the basis is negative investors may prefer to hold the cash bond, whereas if for liquidity, supply or other reasons if the basis is positive the investor may wish to hold the asset synthetically, by selling protection using a credit default swap. Another approach is to arbitrage between the cash and synthetic markets, in the case of a negative basis by buying the cash bond and shorting it synthetically by buying protection in the CDS market.

Thus, we see that investors have a range of spreads to use when performing their relative value analysis.

Selected bibliography and references

Choudhry, M. 2004a, "The credit default swap basis: analysing the relationship between cash and synthetic credit markets", *Journal of Derivatives Use, Trading and Regulation*, Vol 10 No1, pp.8-26.

Choudhry, M. 2004b, *Structured Credit Products: Credit Derivatives and Synthetic Securitisation*, John Wiley & Sons (Asia).

Choudhry, M., Joannas, D., Pereira, R. and Pienaar, R. 2001, *Capital Market Instruments: Analysis and Valuation*, FT Prentice Hall.

Cohen, J., Zinbarg, E. and Zeikel, A. 1977, *Investment Analysis and Portfolio Management*, Richard D Irwin, New York.

S&P, *Credit Week*, 8 November 1993, Standard & Poor's.

S&P, *Credit Week*, 15 October 1999, Standard & Poor's.

Mills, R. 1994, *Strategic Value Analysis*, Mars Business Associates, Oxford.

Wilson, R. and Fabozzi F. 1996, *Corporate Bonds: Structures and Analysis*, FJF Associates, New Hope, PA.

The English cricketing ideal was well summed up in a message from Lord Harris to young cricketers in 1931.
"You do well to love it," he told them, "for it is more free from anything sordid, anything dishonourable, than any game in the world. To play it keenly, honourably, generously, self-sacrificingly is a moral lesson in itself, and the class is God's air and sunshine". It is as clear a statement of the value of the Game as you can get.

– Jeremy Paxman
The English: A Portrait of a People (Penguin) 1999, pp. 204

PART

III

Structured Financial Products

Structured products is the generic term used to refer to a wide variety of capital market instruments. They include bonds issued as part of a securitisation, such as asset-backed securities (ABS) and mortgage-backed securities (MBS), which are very well-established and were first introduced during the 1970s. A more recent product is the collateralised debt obligation (CDO), which is also well-established, the first such deal being introduced in 1988. Structured products also include various classes of instruments that are also called *hybrid products*, combinations of two or more basic products such as vanilla bonds and interest rate swaps, or vanilla bonds linked to external references or benchmarks. We considered these in Chapter 4.

In Part III of this book we concentrate on the products of securitisation, mainly ABS, MBS and CDO securities. These are now a very important element of corporate financing. Originally introduced by banks for balance sheet and regulatory capital management, they are now used by all manner of corporate entities to raise finance.

The other side of the market, the investors, has been behind the growth of the *synthetic* securitisation market, which we also look at in Part III. As we shall see, a lack of supply in the cash market has led to the rise in the synthetic market, where products arranged by the investment banks are purchased by investors who wish to gain an exposure to a particular segment of the corporate credit market. These so-called *structured credit products* are products that combine securitisation technology with credit derivative instruments. As such, they are also examples of *synthetic securitisation*: synthetic because they replicate the economic effects of securitisation without the actual "true sale" event, which is the building block of traditional securitisation.

It is interesting to note of course that investment in synthetic products, which may well provide an investor with an exposure to a specific named corporate entity, does not actually raise any cash for that entity. However, the existence of an active synthetic market contributes to the liquidity of the overall market, and so must be viewed as a positive development.

She said gently,
"Sometimes things don't turn out the way we plan. Don't feel hurt."
"The day I don't feel hurt, I hope they bury me … I am the type of person who, if he likes somebody, has to show it."

– Bernard Malamud (1914–1986)
The Assistant

CHAPTER

16

An Introduction to Securitisation[1]

In this chapter we introduce the basic concepts of securitisation and look at the motivation behind their use, as well as their economic impact. We illustrate the process with a brief hypothetical case study.

The concept of securitisation

Securitisation is a well-established practice in the global debt capital markets. It refers to the sale of assets, which generates cash flows, from the institution that owns them, to another company that has been specifically set up for the purpose, and the issuing of notes by this second company. These notes are backed by the cash flows from the original assets. The technique was introduced initially as a means of funding for US mortgage banks. Subsequently, the technique was applied to other assets such as credit card payments and leasing receivables. It has also been employed as part of asset/liability management, as a means of managing balance sheet risk.

Securitisation allows institutions such as banks and corporates to convert assets that are not readily marketable – such as residential mortgages or car loans – into rated securities that are tradeable in the secondary market. The investors that buy these securities gain an exposure to these types of original

[1] This chapter was co-authored with Anuk Teasdale of YieldCurve.com.

assets that they would not otherwise have access to. The technique is well established and was first introduced by mortgage banks in the United States during the 1970s. The later synthetic securitisation market is much more recent, dating from 1997. The key difference between cash and synthetic securitisation is that in the former, as we have noted, the assets in question are actually sold to a separate legal company known as a special purpose vehicle (SPV).[2] This does not occur in a synthetic transaction, as we shall see.

Sundaresan (1997, p. 359) defines securitisation as:

> … a framework in which some illiquid assets of a corporation or a financial institution are transformed into a package of securities backed by these assets, through careful packaging, credit enhancements, liquidity enhancements and structuring.

The process of securitisation creates *asset-backed bonds*. These are debt instruments that have been created from a package of loan assets on which interest is payable, usually on a floating basis. The asset-backed market was developed in the United States and is a large, diverse market containing a wide range of instruments. Techniques employed by investment banks today enable an entity to create a bond structure from any type of cash flow; assets that have been securitised include loans such as residential mortgages, car loans and credit card loans. The loans form assets on a bank or finance house balance sheet, which are packaged together and used as backing for an issue of bonds. The interest payments on the original loans form the cash flows used to service the new bond issue. Traditionally, mortgage-backed bonds are grouped in their own right as mortgage-backed securities (MBS) while all other securitisation issues are known as asset-backed bonds or ABS.

Figure 16.1 shows the growth in securitisation markets during the 1990s.

[2] An SPV is also referred to as a special purpose entity (SPE) or a special purpose company (SPC).

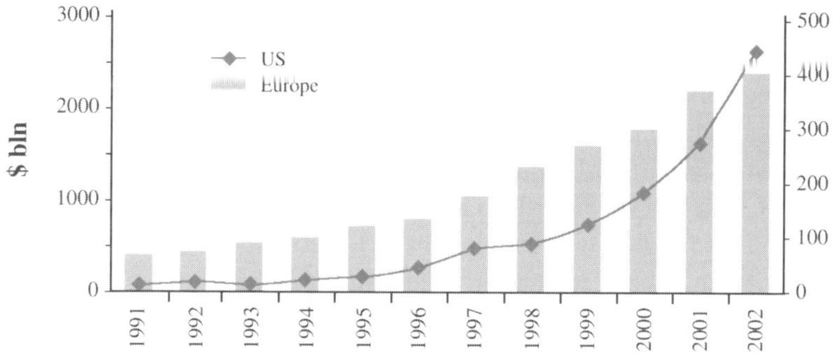

Figure 16.1 Asset-backed securities, notional amounts outstanding
Source: BBA, ISMA, Federal Reserve

Reasons for undertaking securitisation

The driving force behind securitisation has been the need for banks to realise value from the assets on their balance sheet. Typically, these assets are residential mortgages, corporate loans, and retail loans such as credit card debt. Let us consider the factors that might lead a financial institution to securitise a part of its balance sheet. These might be for the following reasons:

- if revenues received from assets remain roughly unchanged but the size of assets has decreased, this will lead to an increase in the return on equity ratio;
- the level of capital required to support the balance sheet will be reduced, which again can lead to cost savings or allows the institution to allocate the capital to other, perhaps more profitable, business;
- to obtain cheaper funding: frequently the interest payable on ABS securities is considerably below the level payable on the underlying loans. This creates a cash surplus for the originating entity.

In other words, the main reasons that a bank will securitise part of its balance sheet is for one or all of the following reasons:

- funding the assets it owns;
- balance sheet capital management;
- risk management and credit risk transfer.

We consider each of these in turn.

Funding

Banks can use securitisation to (a) support rapid asset growth, (b) diversify their funding mix, and reduce the cost of funding, and (c) reduce maturity mis-matches. The market for asset-backed securities is large, with an estimated size of US$1,000 billion invested in ABS issues worldwide annually, of which US$150 billion is in the European market alone.[3] Access to this source of funding will enable a bank to grow its loan books at a faster pace than if they were reliant on traditional funding sources alone. For example, in the United Kingdom a former building society turned bank, Northern Rock plc, has taken advantage of securitisation to back its growing share of the UK residential mortgage market. Securitising assets also allows a bank to diversify its funding mix. All banks will not wish to be reliant on only a single or a few sources of funding, as this can be high-risk in times of market difficulty. Banks aim to optimise their funding between a mix of retail, interbank and wholesale sources. Securitisation has a key role to play in this mix. It also enables a bank to reduce its funding costs. This is because the securitisation process de-links the credit rating of the originating institution from the credit rating of the issued notes. Typically, most of the notes issued by SPVs will be higher rated than the bonds issued direct by the originating bank itself. While the liquidity of the secondary market in ABS is frequently lower than that of the corporate bond market, and this adds to the yield payable by an ABS, it is frequently the case that the cost to the originating institution of issuing debt is still lower in the ABS market because of the latter's higher rating. Finally, there is the issue of maturity mismatches. The business of bank asset–liability management (ALM) is inherently one of maturity mismatch, since a bank often funds long-term assets such as residential mortgages, with short-asset liabilities such as bank account deposits or interbank funding. This can be removed via securitisation, as the originating bank receives funding from the sale of the assets, and the economic maturity of the issued notes frequently matches that of the assets.

Balance sheet capital management

Banks use securitisation to improve balance sheet capital management. This provides (a) regulatory capital relief, (b) economic capital relief and (c) diversified sources of capital. As stipulated in the Bank for International Settlements (BIS) capital rules,[4] also known as the Basel rules, banks must

---

3 *Source*: CSFB, *Credit Risk Transfer*, 2 May 2003.

4 For further information on this see Choudhry (2001).

maintain a minimum capital level for their assets, in relation to the risk of these assets. Under Basel I, for every $100 of risk-weighted assets a bank must hold at least $8 of capital; however, the designation of each asset's risk-weighting is restrictive. For example, with the exception of mortgages, customer loans are 100% risk-weighted regardless of the underlying rating of the borrower or the quality of the security held. The anomalies that this raises, which need not concern us here, is being addressed by the Basel II rules, which become effective from 2007. However, the Basel I rules, which have been in place since 1988 (and effective from 1992), are another driver of securitisation. As an SPV is not a bank, it is not subject to Basel rules and needs only such capital that is economically required by the nature of the assets contained. This is not a set amount, but is significantly below the 8% level required by banks in all cases. Although an originating bank does not obtain 100% regulatory capital relief when it sells assets off its balance sheet to an SPV, because it will have retained a "first-loss" piece out of the issued notes, its regulatory capital charge will be significantly reduced after the securitisation.[5]

To the extent that securitisation provides regulatory capital relief, it can be thought of as an alternative to capital raising, compared with the traditional sources of Tier 1 (equity), preferred shares, and perpetual loan notes with step-up coupon features. By reducing the amount of capital that has to be used to support the asset pool, a bank can also improve its return-on-equity (ROE) value. This will be received favourably by shareholders.

Risk management

Once assets have been securitised, the credit risk exposure on these assets for the originating bank is reduced considerably and, if the bank does not retain a first-loss capital piece (the most junior of the issued notes), it is removed entirely. This is because assets have been sold to the SPV. Securitisation can also be used to remove non-performing assets from banks' balance sheets. This has the dual advantage of removing credit risk and removing a potentially negative sentiment from the balance sheet, as well as freeing up regulatory capital as before. Further, there is a potential upside from securitising such assets: if any of them start performing again, or there is a recovery value obtained from defaulted assets, the originator will receive any surplus profit made by the SPV.

[5] We discuss first-loss in Chapter 20.

Benefits of securitisation to investors

Investor interest in the ABS market has been considerable from the market's inception. This is because investors perceive asset-backed securities as possessing a number of benefits. Investors can:

- diversify sectors of interest;
- access different (and sometimes superior) risk-reward profiles;
- access sectors that are otherwise not open to them.

A key benefit of securitisation notes is the ability to tailor risk-return profiles. For example, if there is a lack of assets of any specific credit rating, these can be created via securitisation. Securitised notes frequently offer better risk-reward performance than corporate bonds of the same rating and maturity. While this might seem peculiar (why should one AA-rated bond perform better in terms of credit performance than another just because it is asset-backed?), this often occurs because the originator holds the first-loss piece in the structure.

A holding in an ABS also diversifies the risk exposure. For example, rather than invest $100 million in an AA-rated corporate bond and be exposed to "event risk" associated with the issuer, investors can gain exposure to, for instance, 100 pooled assets. These pooled assets will clearly have a lower concentration risk.

The process of securitisation

We look now at the process of securitisation, the nature of the SPV structure, and issues such as credit enhancements and the cash flow waterfall.

Securitisation process

The securitisation process involves a number of participants. In the first instance is the *originator*, the firm whose assets are being securitised. The most common process involves an *issuer* acquiring the assets from the originator. The issuer is usually a company that has been specially set up for the purpose of the securitisation, which is the SPV and is usually domiciled offshore. The creation of an SPV ensures that the underlying asset pool is held separate from the other assets of the originator. This is done so that in the event that the originator is declared bankrupt or insolvent, the assets that have been transferred to the SPV will not be affected. This is known as being bankruptcy-remote. Conversely, if the underlying assets begin to deteriorate in quality and are subject to a ratings downgrade, investors have no recourse to the originator.

By holding the assets within an SPV framework, defined in formal legal terms, the financial status and credit rating of the originator becomes almost irrelevant to the bondholders. The process of securitisation often involves *credit enhancements*, in which a third-party guarantee of credit quality is obtained, so that notes issued under the securitisation are often rated at investment grade and up to AAA-grade.

The process of structuring a securitisation deal ensures that the liability side of the SPV – the issued notes – carries lower cost than the asset side of the SPV. This enables the originator to secure lower cost funding that it would not otherwise be able to obtain in the unsecured market. This is a tremendous benefit for institutions with lower credit ratings

Figure 16.2 illustrates the process of securitisation in simple fashion.

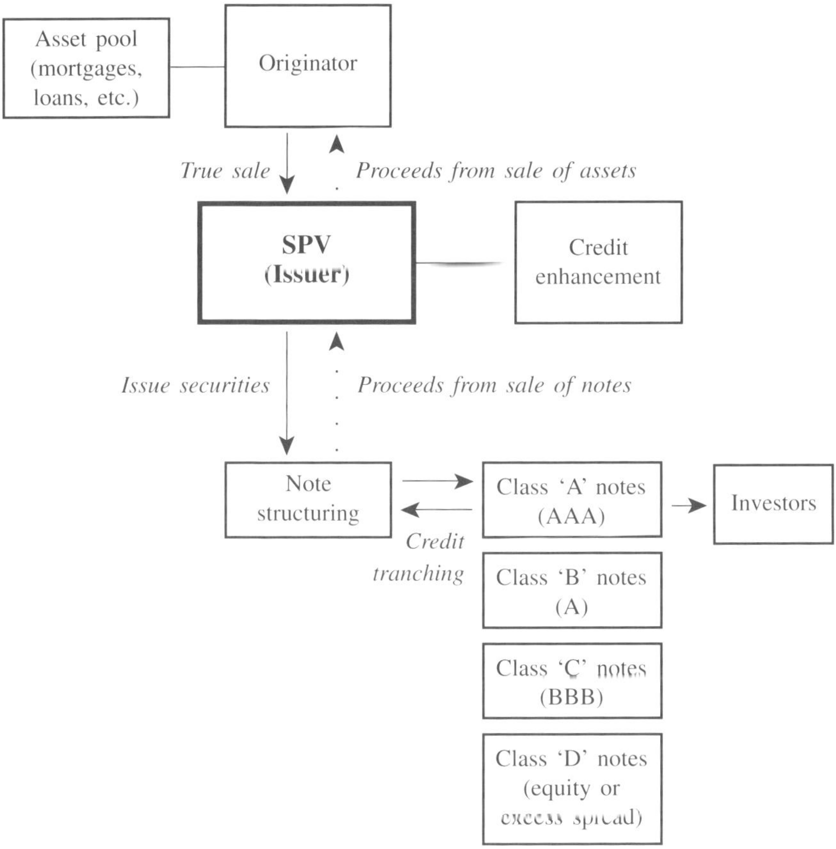

Figure 16.2 The securitisation process

Mechanics of securitisation

Securitisation involves a "true sale" of the underlying assets from the balance sheet of the originator. This is why a separate legal entity, the SPV, is created to act as the issuer of the notes. The assets being securitised are sold on to the balance sheet of the SPV. The process involves:

- undertaking "due diligence" on the quality and future prospects of the assets;
- setting up the SPV and then effecting the transfer of assets to it;
- underwriting of loans for credit quality and servicing;
- determining the structure of the notes, including how many tranches are to be issued, in accordance to originator and investor requirements;
- the notes being rated by one or more credit-rating agencies;
- placing notes in the capital markets.

The sale of assets to the SPV needs to be undertaken so that it is recognised as a true legal transfer. The originator will need to hire legal counsel to advise it in such matters. The credit-rating process will consider the character and quality of the assets, and also whether any enhancements have been made to the assets that will raise their credit quality. This can include *overcollateralisation,* which is when the principal value of notes issued is lower than the principal value of assets, and a liquidity facility provided by a bank.

A key consideration for the originator is the choice of the underwriting bank, which structures the deal and places the notes. The originator will award the mandate for its deal to an investment bank on the basis of fee levels, marketing ability and track record with assets being securitised.

SPV structures

There are essentially two main securitisation structures, amortising (pass-through) and revolving. A third type, the master trust, is used by frequent issuers.

Amortising structures

Amortising structures pay principal and interest to investors on a coupon-by-coupon basis throughout the life of the security, as illustrated in Figure 16.3. They are priced and traded based on expected maturity and weighted-average life (WAL), which is the time-weighted period during which principal is outstanding. A WAL approach incorporates various prepayment assumptions, and any change in this prepayment speed will increase or decrease the rate at which principal is repaid to investors. Pass-through structures are commonly used in residential and commercial mortgage-backed deals, and consumer loan ABS.

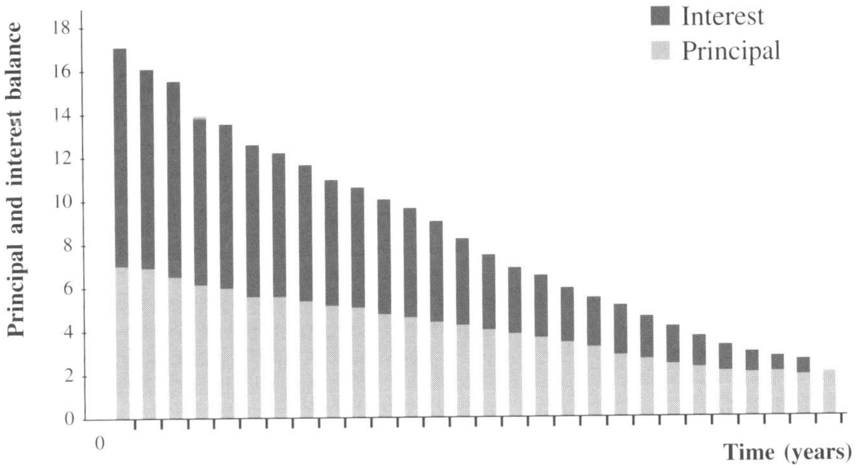

Figure 16.3 Amortising structure

Revolving structures

Revolving structures revolve the principal of the assets; that is, during the revolving period, principal collections are used to purchase new receivables that fulfil the necessary criteria. The structure is used for short-dated assets with a relatively high prepayment speed, such as credit card debt and auto-loans. During the amortisation period, principal payments are paid to investors either in a series of equal instalments (*controlled amortisation*) or the principal is "trapped" in a separate account until the expected maturity date and then paid in a single lump sum to investors (*soft bullet*).

Master trust

Frequent issuers under US and UK law use *master trust* structures, which allow multiple securitisations to be issued from the same SPV. Under such schemes, the originator transfers assets to the master trust SPV. Notes are then issued out of the asset pool based on investor demand. Master trusts have been used by MBS and credit card ABS originators.

Securitisation note tranching

As illustrated in Figure 16.2, in a securitisation the issued notes are structured to reflect specified risk areas of the asset pool, and thus are rated differently. The senior tranche is usually rated AAA. The lower rated notes usually have an element of *overcollateralisation* and are thus capable of absorbing losses. The most junior note is the lowest rated or non-rated. It is often referred to as the *first-loss piece*, because it is impacted by losses in the underlying asset pool first. The first-loss piece is sometimes called the *equity piece* or equity note (even though it is a bond) and is usually held by the originator.

Credit enhancement

Credit enhancement refers to the group of measures that can be instituted as part of the securitisation process for ABS and MBS issues so that the credit rating of the issued notes meets investor requirements. The lower the quality of the assets being securitised, the greater the need for credit enhancement. This is usually by either of the following methods:

- *Overcollateralisation*: where the nominal value of the assets in the pool are in excess of the nominal value of issued securities.
- *Pool insurance*: an insurance policy provided by a composite insurance company to cover the risk of principal loss in the collateral pool. The claims paying rating of the insurance company is important in determining the overall rating of the issue.
- *Senior/Junior note classes*: credit enhancement is provided by subordinating a class of notes ("class B" notes) to the senior class notes ("class A" notes). The class B note's right to its proportional share of cash flows is subordinated to the rights of the senior noteholders. Class B notes do not receive payments of principal until certain rating agency requirements have been met, specifically satisfactory performance of the collateral pool over a predetermined period, or in many cases until all of the senior note classes have been redeemed in full.
- *Margin step-up*: a number of ABS issues incorporate a step-up feature in the coupon structure, which typically coincides with a call date. Although the issuer is usually under no obligation to redeem the notes at this point, the step-up feature was introduced as an added incentive for investors, to convince them from the outset that the economic cost of paying a higher coupon would be unacceptable and that the issuer would seek to refinance by exercising its call option.

- *Excess spread*: this is the difference between the return on the underlying assets and the interest rate payable on the issued notes (liabilities). The monthly excess spread is used to cover expenses and any losses. If any surplus is left over, it is held in a reserve account to cover against future losses or (if not required for that) as a benefit to the originator. In the meantime the reserve account is a credit enhancement for investors.

All securitisation structures incorporate a *cash waterfall* process, whereby all the cash that is generated by the asset pool is paid in order of payment priority. Only when senior obligations have been met can more junior obligations be paid. An independent third-party agent is usually employed to run "tests" on the vehicle to confirm that there is sufficient cash available to pay all obligations. If a test is failed, then the vehicle will start to pay off the notes, starting from the senior notes. The waterfall process is illustrated in Figure 16.4.

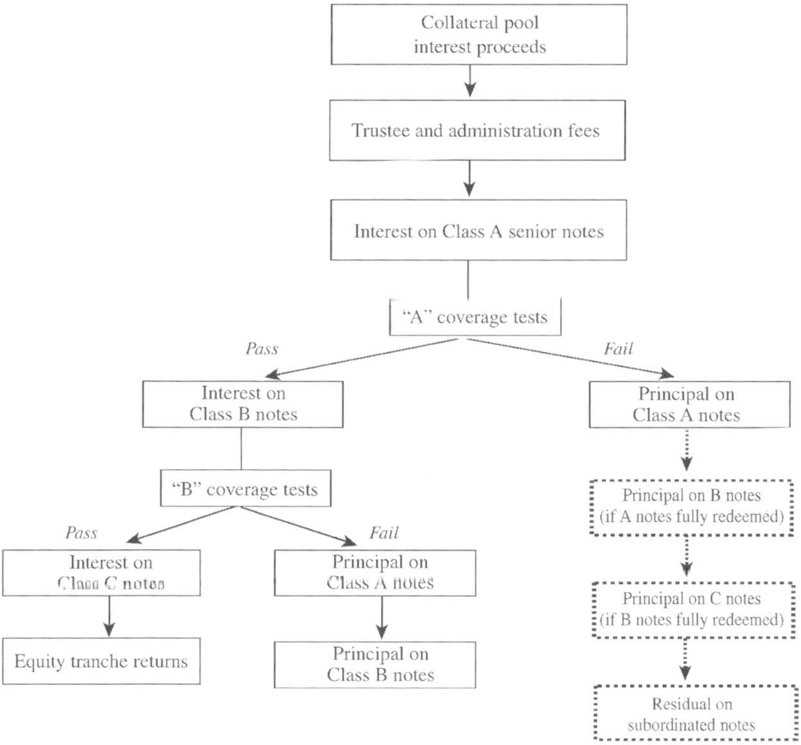

Figure 16.4 Cash flow waterfall (priority of payments)

Impact on balance sheet

Figure 16.5 illustrates through a hypothetical example the effect on the liability side of an originating bank's balance sheet from a securitisation transaction. Following the process, selected assets have been removed from the balance sheet, although the originating bank will usually have retained the first-loss piece. With regard to the regulatory capital impact, this first-loss amount is deducted from the bank's total capital position. For example, assume a bank has \$100 million of risk-weighted assets and a target Basel ratio of 12%,[6] and securitises all \$100 million of these assets. It retains the first-loss tranche that forms 1.5% of the total issue. The remaining 98.5% will be sold on to the market. The bank will still have to set aside 1.5% of capital as a buffer against future losses, but it has been able to free itself of the remaining 10.5% of capital.

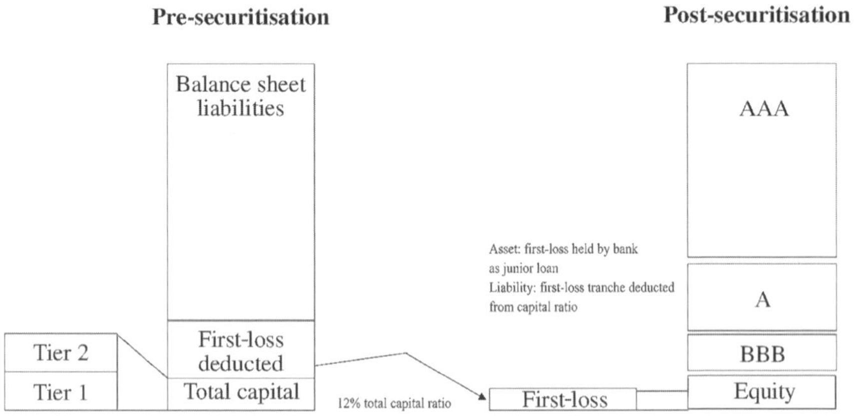

Figure 16.5 Regulatory capital impact of securitisation

Illustrating the process of securitisation

To illustrate the process of securitisation, we consider a hypothetical airline ticket receivables transaction, being originated by the fictitious ABC Airways plc and arranged by the equally fictitious XYZ Securities Limited. We show the kind of issues that will be considered by the investment bank that is structuring the deal.

6 The minimum is 8%, but many banks prefer to set aside an amount well in excess of this minimum required level.

Originator	ABC Airways plc
Issuer	"Airways No 1 Ltd"
Transaction	Ticket receivables airline future flow securitisation bonds €200m three-tranche floating rate notes, legal maturity 2010 Average life 4.1 years
Tranches	Class "A" note (AA), Libor plus [ ] bps Class "B" note (A), Libor plus [ ] bps Class "E" note (BBB), Libor plus [ ] bps
Arranger	XYZ Securities plc

Due diligence

XYZ Securities will undertake due diligence on the assets to be securitised. For this case, it will examine the airline performance figures over the last five years, as well as model future projected figures, including:

- total passenger sales;
- total ticket sales;
- total credit card receivables;
- geographical split of ticket sales.

It is the future flow of receivables, in this case credit card purchases of airline tickets, that is being securitised. This is a higher risk asset class than, say, residential mortgages, because the airline industry has a tradition of greater volatility of earnings than, say, mortgage banks.

Marketing approach

The present and all future credit card ticket receivables generated by the airline will be transferred to an SPV. The investment bank's syndication desk will seek to place the notes with institutional investors across Europe. The notes are first given an indicative pricing ahead of the issue, to gauge investor sentiment. Given the nature of the asset class, during November 2002 the notes would be marketed at around three-month Libor plus 70–80 basis points (AA note), 120–130 basis points (A note) and 260–270 basis points (BBB note). The notes are "benchmarked" against recent issues with similar asset classes, as well as the spread level in the unsecured market of comparable issuer names.

Deal structure

The deal structure is shown at Figure 16.6.

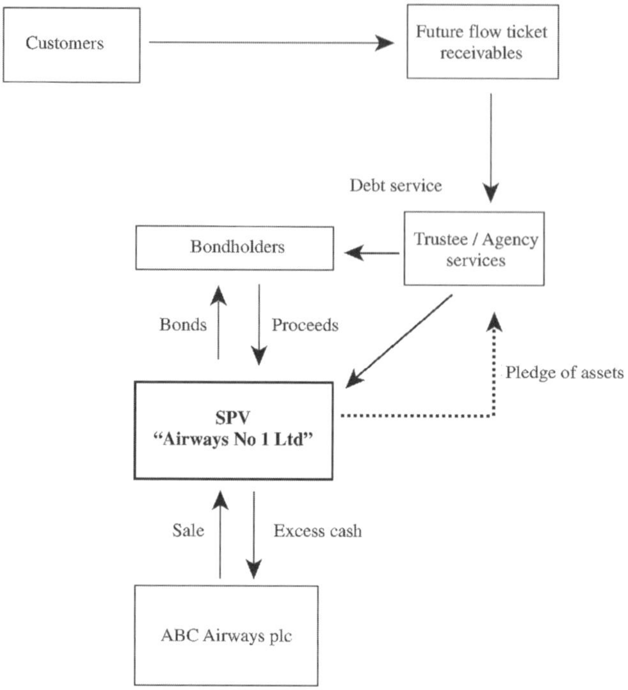

Figure 16.6 Airways No 1 deal structure

The process leading to the issue of notes is as follows:

- ABC Airways plc sells its future cash flow ticket receivables to an offshore SPV set up for this deal, incorporated as Airways No 1 Ltd;
- the SPV issues notes in order to fund its purchase of the receivables;
- the SPV pledges its right to the receivables to a fiduciary agent, the security trustee, for the benefit of the bondholders;
- the trustee accumulates funds as they are received by the SPV;
- the bondholders receive interest and principal payments, in the order of priority of the notes, on a quarterly basis.

In the event of default, the trustee will act on behalf of the bondholders to safeguard their interests.

Financial guarantors

The investment bank will consider if an insurance company, known as a monoline insurer, should be approached to "wrap" the deal by providing a guarantee of backing for the SPV in the event of default. This insurance is provided in return for a fee.

Financial modelling

XYZ Securities will construct a cash flow model to estimate the size of the issued notes. The model will consider historical sales values, any seasonal factors in sales, credit card cash flows, and so on. Certain assumptions will be made when constructing the model; for example, growth projections, inflation levels, tax levels, and so on. The model will consider a number of different scenarios, and also calculate the minimum asset coverage levels required to service the issued debt. A key indicator in the model will be the debt service coverage ratio (DSCR). The more conservative the DSCR, the more comfort there will be for investors in the notes. For a residential mortgage deal, this ratio might be approximately 2.5–3.0; however, for an airline ticket receivables deal, the DSCR would be unlikely to be lower than 4.0. The model will therefore calculate the amount of notes that can be issued against the assets, while maintaining the minimum DSCR.

Credit rating

It is common for securitisation deals to be rated by one or more of the formal credit ratings agencies such as Moody's, Fitch or Standard & Poor's. A formal credit rating will make it easier for XYZ Securities to place the notes with investors. The methodology employed by the ratings agencies takes into account both qualitative and quantitative factors, and will differ according to the asset class being securitised. The main issues in a deal such as our hypothetical Airway No 1 Ltd deal would be expected to include:

- corporate credit quality: these are risks associated with the originator, and are factors that affect its ability to continue operations, meet its financial obligations, and provide a stable foundation for generating future receivables. This might be analysed according to the following: (a) ABC Airways' historical financial performance, including its liquidity and debt structure; (b) its status within its domicile country; for example, whether it is state-owned; (c) the general economic conditions for industry and for airlines; and (d) the historical record and current state of the airline; for instance, its

safety record and age of its aeroplanes;
- the competition and industry trends: ABC Airways' market share, the competition on its network;
- regulatory issues, such as the need for ABC Airways to comply with forthcoming legislation that would impact on its cash flows;
- legal structure of the SPV and transfer of assets;
- cash flow analysis.

Based on the findings of the ratings agency, the arranger may redesign some aspect of the deal structure so that the issued notes are rated at the required level.

This is a selection of the key issues involved in the process of securitisation. Depending on investor sentiment, market conditions and legal issues, the process from inception to closure of the deal may take anything from three to twelve months or more. After the notes have been issued, the arranging bank will no longer have anything to do with the issue; however, the bonds themselves require a number of agency services for their remaining life until they mature or are paid off. These agency services include paying agent, cash manager and custodian.

Sample Transactions

CASE STUDY 1 Fosse Securities No 1 plc

This was the first securitisation undertaken by Alliance & Leicester plc, a former UK building society that converted into a commercial bank in 1997. The underlying portfolio was approximately 6,700 loans secured by first mortgages on property in the United Kingdom. The transaction was a £250 million securitisation via the SPV, named Fosse Securities No 1 plc. The underwriter was Morgan Stanley Dean Witter, which placed the notes in November 2000. The transaction structure was:

- a senior class "A" note with AAA/Aaa rating by Standard & Poor's and Moody's, which represented £235 million of the issue, with a legal maturity of November 2032;
- a class "B" note rated Aa/Aa3 of nominal £5 million;
- a class "C" note rated BBB/Baa2 of nominal £10 million.

The ratings agencies cited the strengths of the issue as:[7] the loans were *prime* quality; there was a high level of *seasoning* in the underlying asset pool, with an average age of 35 months; the average level of the loan-to-value ratio (LTV) was considered low, at 73.5%; and there were low average loan-to-income multiples among underlying borrowers.

CASE STUDY 2 SRM Investment No 1 Limited

Sveriges Bostadsfinansieringsaktiebolag (SBAB) is the Swedish state-owned national housing finance corporation. Its second-ever securitisation issue was the EUR 1 billion SRM Investment No 1 Limited, issued in October 2000. The underlying asset backing was Swedish residential mortgage loans, with properties being mainly detached and semi-detached single-family properties. The issue was structured and underwritten by Nomura International.

The underlying motives behind the deal were that it allowed SBAB to:

- reduce capital allocation, thereby releasing capital for further lending;
- remove part of its mortgage loan-book off the balance sheet;
- obtain a more diversified source for its funding.

The transaction was structured into the following notes:

- senior class "A1" floating-rate note rated AAA/Aaa by S&P and Moody's, issue size EUR 755 million, with a legal maturity date in 2057;
- senior class "A2" fixed coupon note, rated AAA/Aaa and denominated in Japanese yen, incorporating a step-up facility, legal maturity 2057; issue size JPY 20 billion;
- class "M" floating rate note rated A/A2, due 2057; issue size EUR 20 million;
- class "B" floating-rate note, rated BBB/Baa2, issue size EUR 10 million.

[7] *Source*: *International Securitisation Review*, London, November 2000.

The yen tranche reflects the targeting of a Japanese domestic investor base. On issue, the class A1 notes paid 26 basis points over euribor. The structure is illustrated in Figure 16.7.

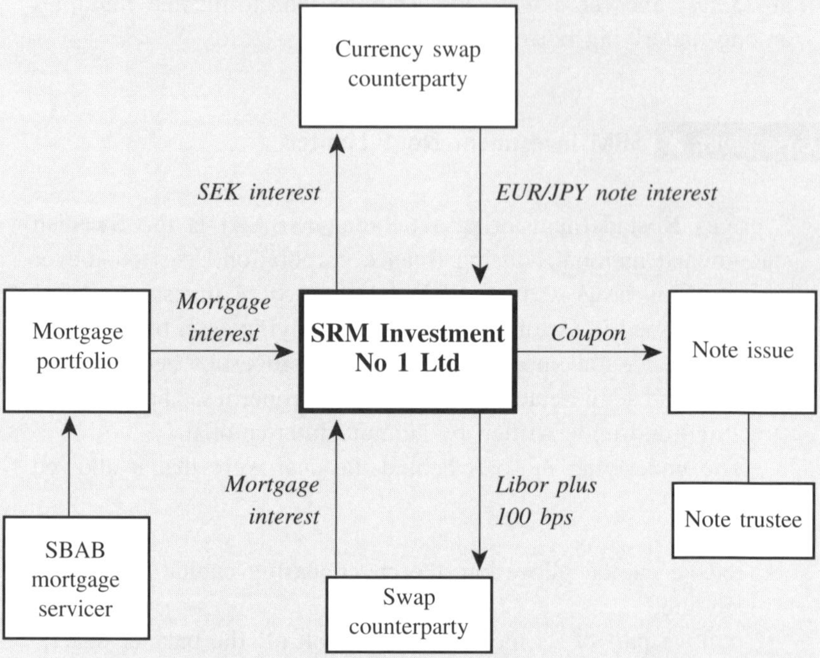

Figure 16.7 SRM Investment No 1 Limited

Structured finance securities such as RMBS issues have a different description page on the Bloomberg system compared to vanilla conventional bonds. This details additional information of use to investors, such as pool factors. Figure 16.8 shows Bloomberg page DES for an issue in May 2005, Granite Master Issuer plc 2005-2 A1. The originator is Northern Rock plc. As it is the very early stages of the bond issue, the pool factor is still 1.0000. This issue pays USD coupon on a monthly basis.

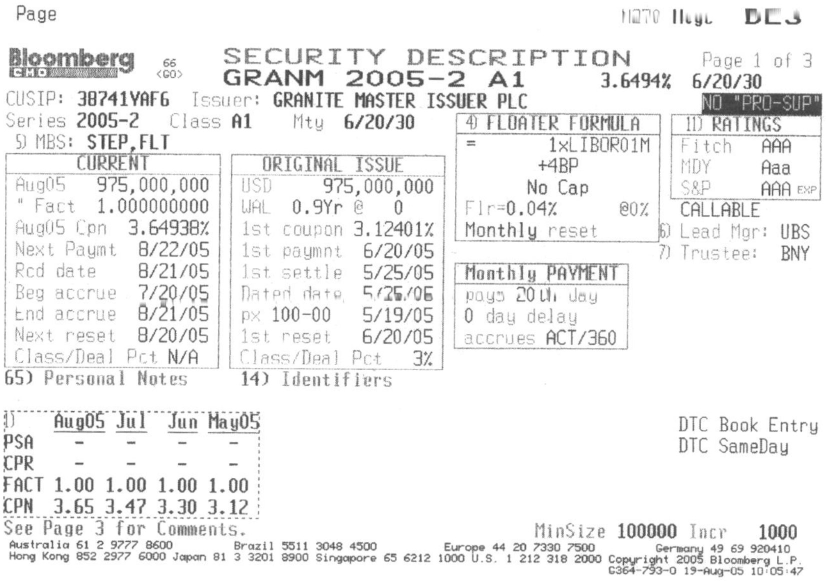

Figure 16.8 Bloomberg page DES for Northern Rock plc RMBS issue, May 2005

Selected bibliography and references

Bhattacharya, A. and Fabozzi, F. 1996, (eds), *Asset-backed Securities*, FJF Associates, New Hope, PA.

Choudhry, M. 2001, *The Bond and Money Markets: Strategy, Trading, Analysis*, Butterworth-Heinemann, Oxford.

Hayre, L. (ed) 2001, *The Salomon Smith Barney Guide to Mortgage-backed and Asset-backed Securities*, John Wiley & Sons, New Jersey.

Martellini, L., P., Priaulet, S. and Priaulet 2003, *Fixed Income Securities*, John Wiley & Sons, Chichester.

Morris, D. 1990, *Asset Securitisation: Principles and Practices*, Executive Enterprise, London.

Sundaresan, S. 1997, *Fixed Income Markets and Their Derivatives*, South-Western Publishing, Cincinatti, Chapter 9.

There are some days in the early spring when the weather is such that, no matter where you are, either in town or countryside, England is at her best and it's good to be alive.

– Geoffrey Wellum
First Light, Penguin Books 2002

CHAPTER

17

Mortgage-backed Securities

Earlier we introduced *asset-backed bonds*, debt instruments created from a package of loan assets on which interest is payable, usually on a floating basis. The asset-backed market was developed in the United States and it is a large, diverse market containing a wide variety of instruments. The characteristics of asset-backed securities (ABS) present additional features in their analysis, which are investigated in this and the next two chapters. Financial engineering techniques employed by investment banks today enable an entity to create a bond structure from any type of cash flow; the typical forms are high volume loans such as residential mortgages, car loans and credit card loans. The loans form assets on a bank or finance house balance sheet, which are packaged together and used as backing for an issue of bonds. The interest payments on the original loans form the cash flows used to service the new bond issue.

In this chapter we consider *mortgage-backed securities*, the largest of the asset-backed bond markets. The remaining chapters deal with the other asset-backed instruments available.[1]

---

[1] Many texts place mortgage-backed securities in a separate category, distinct from asset-backed bonds (for example, see the highly recommended Fabozzi, F., *Handbook of Structured Finance Products*, 1998). Market practitioners also tend to make this distinction. Generally, the market is viewed as being composed of mortgage-backed securities and asset-backed securities (which encompass all other asset types).

Mortgage-backed securities

A mortgage is a loan made for the purpose of purchasing property, which in turn is used as the security for the loan itself. It is defined as a debt instrument giving conditional ownership of an asset, and secured by the asset that is being financed. The borrower provides the lender a mortgage in exchange for the right to use the property during the term of the mortgage, and agrees to make regular payments of both principal and interest. The mortgage lien is the security for the lender, and is removed when the debt is paid off. A mortgage may involve residential property or commercial property and is a long-term debt, normally 25 to 30 years; however, it can be drawn up for shorter periods if required by the borrower. If the borrower or *mortgagor* defaults on the interest payments, the lender or *mortgagee* has the right to take over the property and recover the debt from the proceeds of selling the property. Mortgages can be either fixed-rate or floating-rate interest. Although in the United States mortgages are generally amortising loans, known as *repayment* mortgages, in the United Kingdom there are also *interest-only* mortgages where the borrower only pays the interest on the loan; on maturity the original loan amount is paid off by the proceeds of a maturing investment contract taken out at the same time as the mortgage. These are known as *endowment* mortgages and are popular in the UK market, although their popularity has been waning in recent years.

A lending institution may have many hundreds of thousands of individual residential and commercial mortgages on its book. If the total loan book is pooled together and used as collateral for the issue of a bond, the resulting instrument is a *mortgage-backed security.* This process is known as *securitisation*, which is the pooling of loan assets in order to use them as collateral for a bond issue. Sometimes a *special purpose vehicle* (SPV) is set up specifically to serve as the entity representing the pooled assets. This is done for administrative reasons and also sometimes to enhance the credit rating that may be assigned to the bonds. In the United Kingdom some SPVs have a triple-A credit rating, although the majority of SPVs are below this rating, while retaining investment grade status. In the US market, certain mortgage-backed securities are backed, either implicitly or explicitly, by the government, in which case they trade essentially as risk-free instruments and are not rated by the credit agencies. In the United States a government agency, the Government National Mortgage Association (GNMA, known as "Ginnie Mae") and two government-sponsored agencies, the Federal Home Loan Corporation and the Federal National Mortgage Association ("Freddie Mac" and "Fannie Mae" respectively), purchase mortgages for the purpose of pooling them and holding them in their portfolios; they may then be securitised. Bonds that are not issued by government agencies are rated in the same way as other corporate bonds. On the other hand, non-government agencies sometimes obtain mortgage insurance for their issue, in order to boost its credit quality. When this happens the credit rating of the mortgage insurer becomes an important factor in the credit standing of the bond issue.

Growth of the market

The mortgage-backed market in the United States is the largest in the world and witnessed phenomenal growth in the early 1990s. One estimate put the size of the total market at around $1.8 trillion at the end of 1995, with around $400 billion issued in that year alone.[2] The same study suggested the following advantages of mortgage-backed bonds:

- although many mortgage bonds represent comparatively high-quality assets and are collateralised instruments, the yields on them are usually higher than corporate bonds of the same credit quality. This is because of the complexity of the instruments and the uncertain nature of the mortgage cash flows. In the mid-1990s mortgage-backed bonds traded at yields of around 100–200 basis points above Treasury bonds;
- the wide range of products offers investors a choice of maturities, cash flows and security to suit individual requirements;
- agency mortgage-backed bonds are implicitly backed by the government and therefore represent a better credit risk than triple-A rated corporate bonds; the credit ratings for non-agency bonds is often triple-A or double-A rated;
- the size of the market means that it is very liquid, with agency mortgage-backed bonds having the same liquidity as Treasury bonds;
- the monthly coupon frequency of mortgage-backed bonds makes them an attractive instrument for investors who require frequent income payments; this feature is not available for most other bond market instruments.

In the United Kingdom the asset-backed market has also witnessed rapid growth, and many issues are triple-A rated because issuers create a *special*

[2] Hayre, L., Mohebbi, C. and Zimmermann, T. 1997, "Mortgage pass-through securities", in Fabozzi, F. (ed.), *The Handbook of Fixed Income Securities*, 5th edition, McGraw-Hill, New York,

purpose vehicle that is responsible for the issue. Various forms of credit insurance are also used. Unlike the US market, most bonds are floating-rate instruments, reflecting the variable-rate nature of the majority of mortgages in the United Kingdom.

The growth in selected markets in the United States is shown in Table 17.1 (approximate nominal value in $ billion).

	1986	**1987**	**1988**	**1989**	**1990**	**1991**	**1992**	**1993**	**1994**	**1995**	**1996**
GNMA	45	100	89	48	49	52	64	76	120	108	65
FHLMC	44	100.5	82	52	65	55	98	170	130	105	55
FNMA	25	65	55	52	75	80	115	175	240	130	120
Private	4.4	8	9	11	13	20	40	90	95	45	31

Table 17.1 Issue of mortgage pass-through securities 1986–1996
Source: Federal Reserve Board Bulletin.

Mortgages

In the US market, the terms of a conventional mortgage, known as a *level-payment fixed-rate mortgage*, will state the interest rate payable on the loan, the term of the loan and the frequency of payment. Most mortgages specify monthly payment of interest. These are in fact the characteristics of a level-payment mortgage, which has a fixed interest rate and fixed term to maturity. This means that the monthly interest payments are fixed, hence the term “level-pay”.

The singular feature of a mortgage is that, even if it charges interest at a fixed rate, its cash flows are not known with absolute certainty. This is because the borrower can elect to repay any or all of the principal before the final maturity date. This is a characteristic of all mortgages, and although some lending institutions impose a penalty on borrowers who retire the loan early, this is a risk for the lender, known as *prepayment risk*. The uncertainty of the cash flow patterns is similar to that of a callable bond, and as we shall see later this feature means that we may value mortgage-backed bonds using a pricing model similar to that employed for callable bonds.

The monthly interest payment on a conventional fixed-rate mortgage is given by (17.3), which is derived from the conventional present value analysis used for an annuity. Essentially, the primary relationship is:

$$M_{m0} = I\left(\frac{1 - [1/(1 + r)^n]}{r}\right) \tag{17.1}$$

from which we can derive:

$$I = \frac{M_{m0}}{\dfrac{1 - [\ 1/(1 + r)^n\ ]}{r}}. \tag{17.2}$$

This is simplified to:

$$I = M_{m0}\frac{r(1 + r)^n}{(1 + r)^n - 1} \tag{17.3}$$

where

M_{m0} is the original mortgage balance (the cash amount of loan)
I is the monthly cash mortgage payment
r is the simple monthly interest rate, given by (annual interest rate/12)
n is the term of the mortgage in months.

The monthly repayment includes both the interest servicing and a repayment of part of the principal. In Example 17.1, after the 264th interest payment, the balance will be zero and the mortgage will have been paid off. Since a portion of the original balance is paid off every month, the interest payment reduces by a small amount each month; that is, the proportion of the monthly payment dedicated to repaying the principal steadily increases. The remaining mortgage balance for any particular month during the term of the mortgage may be calculated using (17.4):

$$M_{mt} = M_{m0}\frac{(1 + r)^n - (1 + r)^t}{(1 + r)^n - 1} \tag{17.4}$$

where M_{mt} is the mortgage cash balance after t months and n remains the original maturity of the mortgage in months.

The level of interest payment and principal repayment in any one month during the mortgage term can be calculated using the equations below. If we wish to calculate the value of the principal repayment in a particular month during the mortgage term, we may use (17.5):

$$P_t = M_{m0}\frac{r(1 + r)^{t-1}}{(1 + r)^n - 1} \tag{17.5}$$

where p_t is the scheduled principal repayment amount for month t, while the level of interest payment in any month is given by (17.6):

$$i_t = M_{m0} \frac{r(1+r)^n - (1+r)^{t-1}}{(1+r)^n - 1} \tag{17.6}$$

where i_t is the interest payment only in month t.

EXAMPLE 17.1 Mortgage contract calculations

A mortgage borrower enters into a conventional mortgage contract, in which she borrows £72,200 for 22 years at a rate of 7.99%. What is the monthly mortgage payment?

This gives us n equal to 264 and r equal to (0.0799/12) or 0.0066583. Inserting the above terms into (17.3) we have:

$$I = 72{,}200 \left(\frac{0.0066583\ (1.0066583)^{264}}{(1.0066583)^{264} - 1} \right)$$

or I equal to £581.60.

The mortgage balance after ten years is given below, where t is 120:

$$M_{m120} = 72{,}200 \left(\frac{(1.0066583)^{264} - (1.0066583)^{120}}{(1.0066583)^{264} - 1} \right)$$

or a remaining balance of £53,756.93.

In the same month the scheduled principal repayment amount is:

$$P_{120} = 72{,}200 \frac{0.0066583\ (1.0066583)^{120-1}}{(1.0066583)^{264} - 1}$$

or £222.19.

The interest only payable in month 120 is shown below:

$$i_{120} = 72{,}200 \frac{0.0066583\ [(1.0066583)^{264} - (1.0066583)^{120-1}]}{(1.0066583)^{264} - 1}$$

and is equal to £359.41. The combined mortgage payment is £581.60, as calculated before.

Some mortgage contracts incorporate a *servicing fee*. This is payable to the mortgage provider to cover the administrative costs associated with collecting interest payments, sending regular statements and other information to borrowers, chasing overdue payments, maintaining the records and processing systems and other activities. Mortgage providers also incur costs when repossessing properties after mortgagors have fallen into default. Mortgages may be serviced by the original lender or another third-party institution that has acquired the right to service it, in return for collecting the fee. When a servicing charge is payable by a borrower, the monthly mortgage payment is comprised of the interest costs, the principal repayment and the servicing fee. The fee incorporated into the monthly payment is usually stated as a percentage, say 0.25%. This is added to the mortgage rate.

Another type of mortgage in the US market is the *adjustable-rate mortgage* or ARM, which is a loan in which the interest rate payable is set in line with an external reference rate. The re-sets are at periodic intervals depending on the terms of the loan, and can be on a monthly, six-monthly or annual basis, or even longer. The interest rate is usually fixed at a spread over the reference rate. The reference rate that is used can be a market-determined rate such as the prime rate, or a calculated rate based on the funding costs for US savings and loan institutions or *thrifts*. The cost of funds for thrifts is calculated using the monthly average funding cost on the thrifts' activities, and there are "thrift indexes" that are used to indicate the cost of funding. The two most common indices are the Eleventh Federal Home Loan Bank Board District Cost of Funds Index (COFI) and the National Cost of Funds Index. Generally, borrowers prefer to fix the rate they pay on their loans to reduce uncertainty, and this makes fixed-rate mortgages more popular than variable rate mortgages. A common incentive used to entice borrowers away from fixed-rate mortgages is to offer a below-market interest rate on an ARM mortgage, usually for an introductory period. This comfort period may be from two to five years or even longer.

Mortgages in the United Kingdom are predominantly *variable rate mortgages*, in which the interest rate is moved in line with the clearing bank base rate. It is rare to observe fixed-rate mortgages in the UK market, although short-term fixed-rate mortgages are more common (the rate reverts to a variable basis at the termination of the fixed-rate period).

A *balloon mortgage* entitles a borrower to long-term funding, but under its terms, at a specified future date the interest rate payable is renegotiated. This effectively transforms a long-dated loan into a short-term borrowing. The balloon payment is the original amount of the loan, minus the amount that is amortised. In a balloon mortgage therefore the actual maturity of the bonds is below that of the stated maturity.

A *graduated payment mortgage* (GPM) is aimed at lower earning borrowers, as the mortgage payments for a fixed initial period, say the first five years, are set at a lower level than would be applicable for a level-paying mortgage with an identical interest rate. The later mortgage payments are higher as a result. Hence, a GPM mortgage will have a fixed term and a mortgage rate, but the offer letter will also contain details on the number of years over which the monthly mortgage payments will increase and the point at which level payments will take over. There will also be information on the annual increase in the mortgage payments. As the initial payments in a GPM are below the market rate, there will be little or no repayment of principal at this time. This means that the outstanding balance may actually increase during the early stages, a process known as *negative amortisation.* The higher payments in the remainder of the mortgage term are designed to pay off the entire balance in maturity. The opposite to the GPM is the *growing equity mortgage* or GEM. This mortgage charges fixed-rate interest but the payments increase over time; this means that a greater proportion of the principal is paid off over time, so that the mortgage itself is repaid in a shorter time than the level-pay mortgage.

In the UK market it is more common to encounter hybrid mortgages, which charge a combination of fixed-rate and variable-rate interest. For example, the rate may be fixed for the first five years, after which it will vary with changes in the lender's base rate. Such a mortgage is known as a *fixed/adjustable hybrid mortgage*.

Mortgage risk

Although mortgage contracts are typically long-term loan contracts, running usually for twenty to thirty years or even longer, there is no limitation on the amount of the principal that may be repaid at any one time. In the US market there is no penalty for repaying the mortgage ahead of its term, known as a mortgage prepayment. In the United Kingdom some lenders impose a penalty if a mortgage is prepaid early, although this is more common for contracts that have been offered at special terms, such as a discounted loan rate for the start of the mortgage's life. The penalty is often set as extra interest; for example, six months' worth of mortgage payments at the time when the contract is paid off. As borrowers are free to prepay a mortgage at a time of their choosing, the lender is not certain of the cash flows that will be paid after the contract is taken out. This is known as *prepayment risk*.

A borrower may pay off the principal ahead of the final termination date for a number of reasons. The most common reason is when the property on which the mortgage is secured is subsequently sold by the borrower; this results in the entire mortgage being paid off at once. The average life of a mortgage in the UK market is eight years, and mortgages are most frequently prepaid because the property has been sold.[3] Other actions that result in the prepayment of a mortgage are when a property is repossessed after the borrower has fallen into default, if there is a change in interest rates making it attractive to refinance the mortgage (usually with another lender), or if the property is destroyed due to accident or natural disaster.

An investor acquiring a pool of mortgages from a lender will be concerned at the level of prepayment risk, which is usually measured by projecting the level of expected future payments using a financial model. Although it would not be possible to evaluate meaningfully the potential of an individual mortgage to be paid off early, it is tenable to conduct such analysis for a large number of loans pooled together. A similar activity is performed by actuaries when they assess the future liability of an insurance provider who has written personal pension contracts. Essentially, the level of prepayment risk for a pool of loans is lower than that of an individual mortgage. Prepayment risk has the same type of impact on a mortgage pool's performance and valuation as a call feature does on a callable bond. This is understandable because a mortgage is essentially a callable contract, with the "call" at the option of the borrower of funds.

The other significant risk of a mortgage book is the risk that the borrower will fall into arrears, or be unable to repay the loan on maturity (in the United Kingdom). This is known as *default risk*. Lenders take steps to minimise the level of default risk by assessing the credit quality of each borrower, as well as the quality of the property itself. A study has also found that the higher the deposit paid by the borrower, the lower the level of default.[4] Therefore lenders prefer to advance funds against a borrower's *equity* that is deemed sufficient to protect against falls in the value of the property. In the United Kingdom the typical deposit required is 25%, although certain lenders will advance funds against smaller deposits such as 10% or 5%.

Securities

Mortgage-backed securities are bonds created from a pool of mortgages. They are formed from mortgages that are for residential or commercial

---

3 *Source*: Halifax plc.

4 Brown, S. 1990, et al, *Analysis of Mortgage Servicing Portfolios*, Financial Strategies Group, Prudential-Bache Capital Funding.

property or a mixture of both. Bonds created from commercial mortgages are known as *commercial mortgage-backed securities*. There are a range of different securities in the market, known in the United States as *mortgage pass-though securities*. There also exist two related securities known as *collateralised mortgage securities* and *stripped mortgage-backed securities*. Bonds that are created from mortgage pools that have been purchased by government agencies are known as *agency mortgage-backed securities*, and are regarded as risk-free in the same way as Treasury securities.

A mortgage-backed bond is created by an entity out of its mortgage book or a book that it has purchased from the original lender (there is very often no connection between a mortgage-backed security and the firm that made the original loans). The mortgage book will have a total nominal value comprised of the total value of all the individual loans. The loans will generate cash flows, consisting of the interest and principal payments, and any prepayments. The regular cash flows are received on the same day each month, so the pool resembles a bond instrument. Therefore bonds may be issued against the mortgage pool. Example 17.2 is a simple illustration of a type of mortgage-backed bond known as a *mortgage pass-through security* in the US market.

EXAMPLE 17.2 Mortgage pass-through security

An investor purchases a book consisting of 5,000 individual mortgages, with a total repayable value of $500,000,000. The loans are used as collateral against the issue of a new bond, and the cash flows payable on the bond are the cash flows that are received from the mortgages. The issuer sells 1,000 bonds, with a face value of $500,000. Each bond is therefore entitled to 1/1,000 or 0.02% of the cash flows received from the mortgages.

The prepayment risk associated with the original mortgages is unchanged, but any investor can now purchase a bond with a much lower value than the mortgage pool, but with the same level of prepayment risk, which is lower than the risk of an individual loan. This would have been possible if an investor was buying all 100 mortgages, but by buying a bond that represents the pool of mortgages, a smaller cash value is needed to achieve the same performance. The bonds will also be more liquid than the loans, and the investor will be able to realise her investment ahead of the maturity date if she wishes. For these reasons the bonds will trade at higher prices than would an individual loan. A mortgage pass-through security therefore is a way for mortgage lenders to realise additional value from their loan book, and if it is sold to another investor (who issues the bonds), the loans will be taken off the original lender's balance sheet, thus freeing up lending lines for other activities.

A *collateralised mortgage obligation* (CMO) differs from a pass-through security in that the cash flows from the mortgage pool are distributed on a prioritised basis, based on the class of security held by the investor. In Example 17.2 this might mean that three different securities are formed, with a total nominal value of $100 million each entitled to a pro-rata amount of the interest payments, but with different priorities for the repayment of principal. For instance, $60 million of the issue might consist of a bond known as "class A", which may be entitled to receipt of all the principal repayment cash flows, after which the next class of bonds is entitled to all the repayment cash flow; this bond would be "class B" bonds, of which, say, $25 million was created, and so on. If 300 class A bonds are created, they would have a nominal value of $200,000 and each would receive 0.33% of the total cash flows received by the class A bonds. Note that all classes of bonds receive an equal share of the interest payments; it is the principal repayment cash flows received that differ. What is the main effect of this security structure? The most significant factor is that, in our illustration, the class A bonds will be repaid earlier than any other class of bond that is formed from the securitisation. It therefore has the shortest maturity. The last class of bonds will have the longest maturity. There is still a level of uncertainty associated with the maturity of each bond, but this is less than the uncertainty associated with a pass-through security.

Let us consider another type of mortgage bond, the *stripped mortgage-backed security*. As its name suggests, this is created by separating the interest and principal payments into individually distinct cash flows. This allows an issuer to create two very interesting securities: the IO-bond and the PO-bond. In a stripped mortgage-backed bond the interest and principal are divided into two classes, and two bonds are issued that are each entitled to receive one class of cash flow only. The bond class that receives the interest payment cash flows is known as an *interest-only* or IO class, while the bond receiving the principal repayments is known as a *principal-only* or PO class. The PO-bond is similar to a zero-coupon bond in that it is issued at a discount to par value. The return achieved by a PO-bondholder is a function of the rapidity at which prepayments are made; if prepayments are received in a relatively short time the investor will realise a higher return. This would be akin to the buyer of a zero-coupon bond receiving the maturity payment ahead of the redemption date, and the highest possible return that a PO-bond holder could receive would occur if all the mortgages were prepaid the instant after the PO-bond was bought! A low return will be achieved if all the mortgages are held until maturity, so that there are no prepayments. Stripped mortgage-backed bonds present potentially less advantage to an issuer compared to a pass-through security or a CMO; however, they are liquid instruments and are often traded to hedge a conventional mortgage bond book.

The price of a PO-bond fluctuates as mortgage interest rates change. As we noted earlier in the US market, the majority of mortgages are fixed-rate loans, so that if mortgage rates fall below the coupon rate on the bond, the holder will expect the volume of prepayments to increase as individuals refinance loans in order to gain from lower borrowing rates. This will result in a faster stream of payments to the PO-bondholder as cash flows are received earlier than expected. The price of the PO rises to reflect this, and also because cash flows in the mortgage will now be discounted at a lower rate. The opposite happens when mortgage rates rise and the rate of prepayment is expected to fall, which causes a PO-bond to fall in price. An IO-bond is essentially a stream of cash flows and has no par value. The cash flows represent interest on the mortgage principal outstanding, therefore a higher rate of prepayment leads to a fall in the IO price. This is because the cash flows cease once the principal is redeemed. The risk for the IO-bondholder is that prepayments occur so quickly that interest payments cease before the investor has recovered the amount originally paid for the IO-bond. The price of an IO is also a function of mortgage rates in the market, but exhibits more peculiar responses. If rates fall below the bond coupon, again the rate of prepayment is expected to increase. This would cause the cash flows for the IO to decline, as mortgages were paid off more quickly. This would cause the price of the IO to fall as well, even though the cash flows themselves would be discounted at a lower interest rate. If mortgage rates rise, the outlook for future cash flows will improve as the prepayment rate falls, however, there is also a higher discounting rate for the cash flows themselves, so the price of an IO may move in either direction.

Thus IO-bonds exhibit a curious characteristic for a bond instrument, in that their price moves in the same direction as market rates. Both versions of the stripped mortgage bond are interesting instruments, and they have high volatilities during times of market rate changes. Note that PO- and IO-bonds could be created from the hypothetical mortgage pool described above; therefore the combined modified duration of both instruments must equal the modified duration of the original pass-through security.

The securities described so far are essentially plain vanilla mortgage-backed bonds. Currently, there are more complicated instruments trading in the market.

Cash flow patterns

We stated that the exact term of mortgage-backed securities cannot be stated with accuracy at the time of issue, because of the uncertain frequency of mortgage prepayments. This uncertainty means that it is not possible to analyse the bonds using the conventional methods used for fixed-coupon bonds. The most common approach used by the market is to assume a fixed prepayment rate at the time of issue and use this to project the cash flows, and hence the life span, of the bond. The choice of prepayment selected therefore is significant, although it is recognised also that prepayment rates are not stable and will fluctuate with changes in mortgage rates and the economic cycle. In this section we consider some of the approaches used in evaluating the prepayment pattern of a mortgage-backed bond.

Prepayment analysis

Some market analysts assume a fixed life for a mortgage pass-through bond based on the average life of a mortgage. Traditionally, a "12-year prepaid life" has been used to evaluate the securities, as market data suggested that the average mortgage was paid off after the twelfth year. This is not generally favoured because it does not take into account the effect of mortgage rates and other factors. A more common approach is to use a *constant prepayment rate* (CPR). This measure is based on the expected number of mortgages in a pool that will be prepaid in a selected period, and is an annualised figure. The measure for the monthly level of prepayment is known as the *constant monthly repayment*, and measures the expected amount of the outstanding balance, minus the scheduled principal, that will be prepaid in each month. Another name for the constant monthly repayment is the *single monthly mortality rate* or SMM. In Fabozzi (1997) the SMM is given by (17.7) and is an expected value for the percentage of the remaining mortgage balance that will be prepaid in that month.

$$SMM = 1 - (1 - CPR)^{1/12}. \tag{17.7}$$

EXAMPLE 17.3 Constant prepayment rate

The constant prepayment rate for a pool of mortgages is 2% each month. The outstanding principal balance at the start of the month is £72,200, while the scheduled principal payment is £223. This means that 2% of £71,977, or £1,439, will be prepaid in that month. To approximate the amount of principal prepayment, the constant monthly prepayment is multiplied by the outstanding balance.

In the US market the convention is to use the prepayment standard developed by the Public Securities Association (PSA), which is the domestic bond market trade association.[5] The PSA benchmark, known as 100% PSA, assumes a steadily increasing constant prepayment rate each month until the thirtieth month, when a constant rate of 6% is assumed. The starting prepayment rate is 0.2%, increasing at 0.2% each month until the rate levels off at 6%.

For the 100% PSA benchmark we may set, if t is the number of months from the start of the mortgage, that if $t < 30$, the CPR = 6% × t/30 while if $t > 30$, then CPR is equal to 6%.

This benchmark can be altered if required to suit changing market conditions, so for example the 200% PSA has a starting prepayment rate and an increase that is double the 100% PSA model, so the initial rate is 0.4%, increasing by 0.4% each month until it reaches 12% in the thirtieth month, at which point the rate remains constant. The 50% PSA has a starting (and increases by a) rate of 0.1%, remaining constant after it reaches 3%.

The prepayment level of a mortgage pool will have an impact on its cash flows. As we saw in Example 17.1 if the amount of prepayment is nil, the cash flows will remain constant during the life of the mortgage. In a fixed-rate mortgage the proportion of principal and interest payment will change each month as more and more of the mortgage amortises. That is, as the principal amount falls each month, the amount of interest decreases. If we

[5] Since renamed the Bond Market Association.

assume that a pass-through security has been issued today, so that its coupon reflects the current market level, the payment pattern will resemble the bar chart shown in Figure 17.1 below.

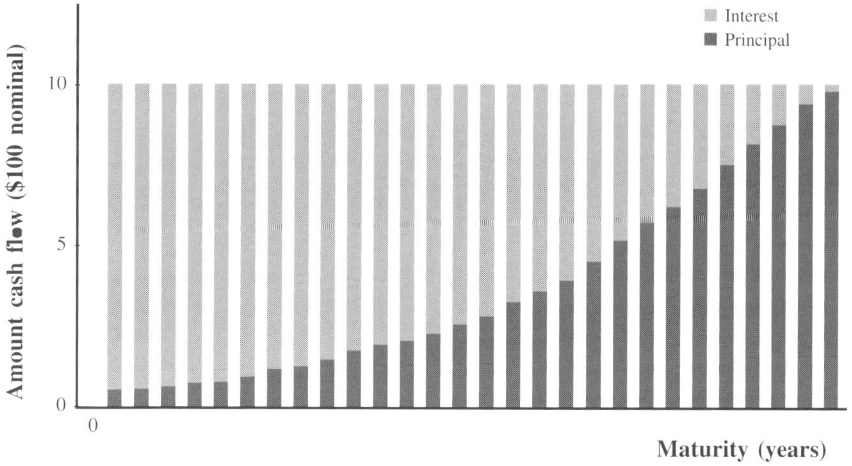

Figure 17.1 Mortgage pass-through security with 0% constant prepayment rate

When there is an element of prepayment in a mortgage pool, for example as in the 100% PSA or 200% PSA model, the amount of principal payment will increase during the early years of the mortgages and then becomes more steady, before declining for the remainder of the term. This is because the principal balance has declined to such an extent that the scheduled principal payments become less significant. The two examples are shown at Figures 17.2 and 17.3 below.

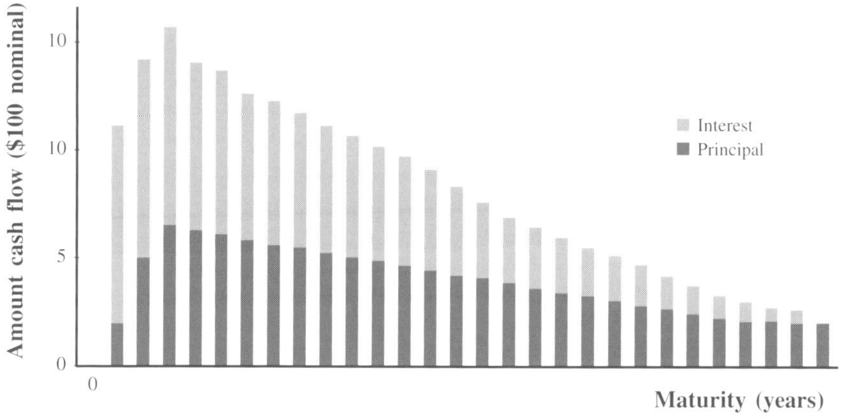

Figure 17.2 100% PSA model

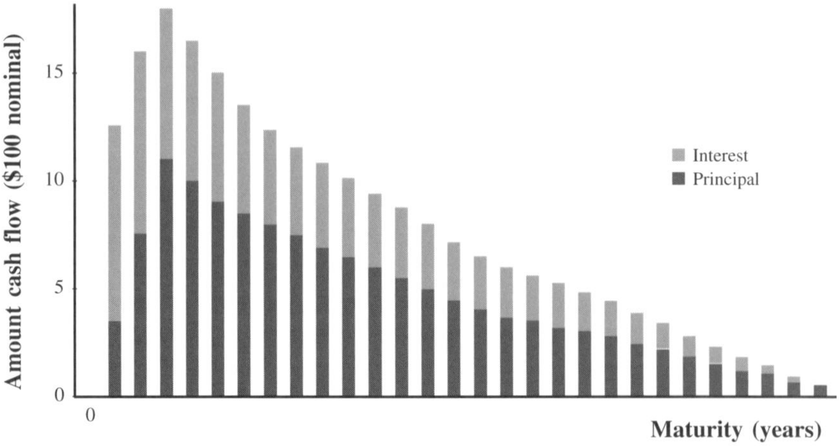

Figure 17.3 200% PSA model

The prepayment volatility of a mortgage-backed bond will vary according to the interest rate of the underlying mortgages. It has been observed that where the mortgages have interest rates of between 100 and 300 basis points above current mortgage rates, the prepayment volatility is the highest. At the bottom of the range, any fall in interest rates often leads to a sudden increase in the refinancing of mortgages, while at the top of the range, an increase in rates will lead to a decrease in the prepayment rate.

The actual cash flow of a mortgage pass-through of course is dependent on the cash flow patterns of the mortgages in the pool. The relationships described in Example 17.1 can be used to derive further expressions to construct a cash flow schedule for a pass-through security, using a constant or adjustable assumed prepayment rate. Fabozzi (1997) describes the projected monthly mortgage payment for a level-paying fixed rate mortgage in any month as:

$$\bar{I}_t = \bar{M}_{mt-1} \frac{r(1 + r)^{n-t+1}}{(1 + r)^{n-t+1} - 1} \qquad (17.8)$$

where

$\bar{I}_t$ is the projected monthly mortgage payment for month t

$\bar{M}_{mt-1}$ is the projected mortgage balance at the end of month t assuming that prepayments have occurred in the past.

To calculate the interest proportion of the projected monthly mortgage payment we use (17.9) where $\overline{i}_t$ is the projected monthly interest payment for month t.

$$\overline{i}_t = M_{mt-1} \times i \qquad (17.9)$$

Expression (17.9) states that the projected monthly interest payment can be obtained by multiplying the mortgage balance at the end of the previous month by the monthly interest rate. In the same way the expression for calculating the projected monthly scheduled principal payment for any month is given by (17.10), where $\overline{p}_t$ is the projected scheduled principal payment for the month t.

$$\overline{p}_t = \overline{I}_t - \overline{i}_t \qquad (17.10)$$

The projected monthly principal prepayment, which is an expected rate only and not a model forecast, is given by (17.11):

$$\overline{pp}_t = SMM_t\ (\overline{M}_{mt-1} - \overline{p}_t) \qquad (17.11)$$

where $\overline{pp}_t$ is the projected monthly principal prepayment for month t.

The above relationships enable us to calculate values for:
- the projected monthly interest payment;
- the projected monthly scheduled principal payment;
- and the projected monthly principal prepayment

These values may be used to calculate the total cash flow in any month that a holder of a mortgage-backed bond receives, which is given by (17.12) below, where cf_t is the cash flow receipt in month t.

$$cf_t = \overline{i}_t + \overline{p}_t + \overline{pp}_t \qquad (17.12)$$

The practice of using a prepayment rate is a market convention that enables analysts to evaluate mortgage-backed bonds. The original PSA prepayment rates were arbitrarily selected, based on the observation that prepayment rates tended to stabilise after the first thirty months of the life of a mortgage. A linear increase in the prepayment rate is also assumed. However, this is a market convention only, adopted by the market as a standard benchmark. The levels do not reflect seasonal variations in prepayment patterns, or the different behaviour patterns of different types of mortgages.

The PSA benchmarks can be (and are) applied to default assumptions to produce a default benchmark. This is used for non-agency mortgage-backed bonds only, as agency securities are guaranteed by one of the three government or government-sponsored agencies. Accordingly, the PSA *standard default assumption* (SDA) benchmark is used to assess the potential default rate for a mortgage pool. For example, the standard benchmark, 100SDA, assumes that the default rate in the first month is 0.02% and increases in a linear fashion by 0.02% each month until the 30th month, at which point the default rate remains at 0.60%. In month sixty the default rate begins to fall from 0.60% to 0.03% and continues to fall linearly until month 120. From that point the default rate remains constant at 0.03%. The other benchmarks have similar patterns.

Prepayment models

The PSA standard benchmark reviewed in the previous section uses an assumption of prepayment rates and can be used to calculate the prepayment proceeds of a mortgage. It is not, strictly speaking, a prepayment *model* because it cannot be used to estimate actual prepayments. A prepayment model on the other hand does attempt to predict the prepayment cash flows of a mortgage pool, by modelling the statistical relationships between the various factors that have an impact on the level of prepayment. These factors are the current mortgage rate, the characteristics of the mortgages in the pool, seasonal factors and the general business cycle. Let us consider them in turn.

The prevailing mortgage interest rate is probably the most important factor in the level of prepayment. The level of the current mortgage rate and its spread above or below the original contract rate will influence the decision to refinance a mortgage; if the rate is materially below the original rate, the borrower will prepay the mortgage. As the mortgage rate at any time reflects the general bank base rate, the level of market interest rates has the greatest effect on mortgage prepayment levels. The current mortgage rate also has an effect on housing prices, since if mortgages are seen as "cheap" the general perception will be that now is the right time to purchase: this affects housing market turnover. The pattern followed by mortgage rates since the original loan also has an impact, a phenomenon known as *refinancing burnout*.

Observation of the mortgage market has suggested that housing market and mortgage activity follows a strong seasonal pattern. The strongest period of activity is during the spring and summer, while the market is at its quietest in the winter. The various factors may be used to derive an expression that can be used to calculate expected prepayment levels. For example, a US investment bank uses the following model to calculate expected prepayments:[6]

Monthly prepayment rate = (Refinance incentive) × (Season multiplier) × (Month multiplier) × (Burnout).

Evaluation and analysis of mortgage-backed bonds

Term to maturity

The term to maturity cannot be given for certain for a mortgage pass-through security, since the cash flows and prepayment patterns cannot be predicted. To evaluate such a bond therefore it is necessary to estimate the term for the bond, and use this measure for any analysis. The maturity measure for any bond is important, as without it, it is not possible to assess over what period of time a return is being generated; also, it will not be possible to compare the asset to any other bond. The term to maturity of a bond also gives an indication of its sensitivity to changes in market interest rates. If comparisons with other securities such as government bonds are made, we cannot use the stated maturity of the mortgage-backed bond because prepayments will reduce this figure. The convention in the market is to use other estimated values, which are *average life* and the more traditional duration measure.

The *average life* of a mortgage pass-through security is the weighted-average time to return of a unit of principal payment, made up of projected scheduled principal payments and principal prepayments. It is also known as the *weighted-average life*. It is given by (17.13):

$$\text{Average life} = \frac{1}{12}\sum_{t=1}^{n}\frac{(\text{Principal received at } t)}{\text{Total principal received}} \tag{17.13}$$

where n is the number of months remaining. The time from the term measured by the average life to the final scheduled principal payment is the bond's *tail*.

[6] Fabozzi (1997).

In Chapter 2 we saw that, to calculate duration (or Macaulay's duration) for a bond we required the weighted present values of all its cash flows. To apply this for a mortgage-backed bond therefore it is necessary to project the bond's cash flows, using an assumed prepayment rate. The projected cash flows, together with the bond price and the periodic interest rate, may then be used to arrive at a duration value. The periodic interest rate is derived from the yield. This calculation for a mortgage-backed bond produces a periodic duration figure, which must be divided by 12 to arrive at a duration value in years (or by 4 in the case of a quarterly paying bond).

EXAMPLE 17.4 Macaulay duration

A 25-year mortgage security with a mortgage rate of 8.49% and monthly coupon is quoted at a price of $98.50, a bond-equivalent yield of 9.127%. To calculate the Macaulay duration we require the present value of the expected cash flows using the interest rate that will make this present value, assuming a constant prepayment rate, equate to the price of 98.50. Using the expression below,

$$rm = 2\ [(1 + r)^n - 1]$$

where rm is 9.127% and $n = 5$, this is shown to be 9.018%.

For the bond above this present value is 6,120.79. Therefore the mortgage security Macaulay duration is given by:

$$Dm = \frac{6{,}120.79}{98.50} = 62.14.$$

Therefore the bond-equivalent Macaulay duration in years is given by:

$$D = \frac{62.14}{12} = 5.178.$$

Calculating yield and price: static cash flow model

There are a number of ways that the yield on a mortgage-backed bond can be calculated. One of the most common methods employs the *static cash flow model.* This assumes a single prepayment rate to estimate the cash flows for the bond, and does not take into account how changes in market conditions might impact on the prepayment pattern.

The conventional yield measure for a bond is the discount rate at which the sum of the present values of all the bond's expected cash flows will be equal to the price of the bond. The convention is usually to compute the yield from the *clean* price; that is, excluding any accrued interest. This yield measure is known as the bond's *redemption yield* or *yield-to-maturity* (YTM). However, for mortgage-backed bonds it is known as a *cash flow yield* or *mortgage yield*. The cash flow for a mortgage-backed bond is not known with certainty, due to the effect of prepayments, and so must be derived using an assumed prepayment rate. Once the projected cash flows have been calculated, it is possible to calculate the cash flow yield. The formula is given by (17.14):

$$P = \sum_{n=1}^{N} \frac{C\ (t)}{(1 + ri/1200)^{t-1}}. \tag{17.14}$$

Note however that a yield so computed will be for a bond with monthly coupon payments,[7] so it is necessary to convert the yield to an annualised equivalent before any comparisons are made with conventional bond yields. In the US and UK markets, the bond-equivalent yield is calculated for mortgage-backed bonds and measured against the relevant government bond yield, which (in both cases) is a semi-annual yield. Although it is reasonably accurate to simply double the yield of a semi-annual coupon bond to arrive at the annualised equivalent,[8] to obtain the bond equivalent yield for a monthly paying mortgage-backed bond we use (17.15):

$$rm = 2[(1 + ri_M)^6 - 1] \tag{17.15}$$

where rm is the bond equivalent yield (we retain the designation that was used to denote YTM in Chapter 2) and ri_M is the interest rate that will equate the present value of the projected monthly cash flows for the mortgage-backed bond to its current price. The equivalent semi-annual yield is given by (17.16):

$$rm_{s/a} = (1 + ri_M)^6 - 1. \tag{17.16}$$

7 The majority of mortgage-backed bonds pay interest on a monthly basis, since individual mortgages usually do as well; certain mortgage-backed bonds pay on a quarterly basis.
8 See Chapter 4 for the formulas used to convert yields from one convention basis to another.

The cash flow yield calculated for a mortgage-backed bond in this way is essentially the redemption yield, using an assumption to derive the cash flows. As such, the measure suffers from the same drawbacks as it does when used to measure the return of a plain vanilla bond, which are that the calculation assumes a uniform reinvestment rate for all the bond's cash flows and that the bond will be held to maturity. The same weakness will apply to the cash flow yield measure for a mortgage-backed bond. In fact, the potential inaccuracy of the redemption yield measure is even greater with a mortgage-backed bond because the frequency of interest payments is higher, which makes the reinvestment risk greater. The final yield that is returned by a mortgage-backed bond will depend on the performance of the mortgages in the pool, specifically the prepayment pattern.

Given the nature of a mortgage-backed bond's cash flows, the exact yield cannot be calculated; however, it is common for market practitioners to use the cash flow yield measure and compare this to the redemption yield of the equivalent government bond. The usual convention is to quote the spread over the government bond as the main measure of value. When measuring the spread, the mortgage-backed bond is compared to the government security that has a similar duration, or a term to maturity similar to its average life.

It is possible to calculate the price of a mortgage-backed bond once its yield is known (or vice-versa). As with a plain vanilla bond, the price is the sum of the present values of all the projected cash flows. It is necessary to convert the bond-equivalent yield to a monthly yield, which is then used to calculate the present value of each cash flow. The cash flows of IO- and PO-bonds are dependent on the cash flows of the underlying pass-through security, which is itself dependent on the cash flows of the underlying mortgage pool. Again, to calculate the price of an IO- or PO-bond, a prepayment rate must be assumed. This enables us to determine the projected level of the monthly cash flows of the IO and the principal payments of the PO. The price of an IO is the present value of the projected interest payments, while the price of the PO is the present value of the projected principal payments, comprising the scheduled principal payments and the projected principal prepayments.

Bond price and option-adjusted spread

The concept of option-adjusted spread (OAS) and its use in the analysis and valuation of bonds with embedded options was first considered in Chapter 7, when OAS was discussed in the context of callable bonds. The behaviour of mortgage securities often resembles that of callable bonds, because effectively there is a call feature attached to them, in the shape of the prepayment option of the underlying mortgage holders. This option feature is the principal reason why it is necessary to use average life as the term to maturity for a mortgage security. It is frequently the case that the optionality of a mortgage-backed bond and the volatility of its yield have a negative impact on the bondholders. This is for two reasons: the actual yield realised during the holding period has a high probability of being lower than the anticipated yield, which was calculated on the basis of an assumed prepayment level, and mortgages are frequently prepaid at the time when the bondholder will suffer the most; that is, prepayments occur most often when rates have fallen, leaving the bondholder to reinvest repaid principal at a lower market interest rate.

These features combined represent the biggest risk to an investor of holding a mortgage security, and market analysts attempt to measure and quantify this risk. This is usually done using a form of OAS analysis. Under this approach the value of the mortgagor's prepayment option is calculated in terms of a basis point penalty that must be subtracted from the expected yield spread on the bond. This basis point value is calculated using a binomial model or a simulation model to generate a range of future interest rate paths, only some of which will cause a mortgagor to prepay her mortgage. The interest rate paths that would result in a prepayment are evaluated for their impact on the mortgage bond's expected yield spread over a government bond.[9] As OAS analysis takes account of the option feature of a mortgage-backed bond, it will be less affected by a yield change than the bond's yield spread. Assuming a flat yield curve environment, the relationship between the OAS and the yield spread is given by:

$$\text{OAS} = \text{Yield spread} - \text{Cost of option feature.}$$

This relationship can be observed occasionally when yield spreads on current coupon mortgages widen during upward moves in the market. As interest rates fall, the cost of the option feature on a current coupon mortgage will rise, as the possibility of prepayment increases. Put another

[9] The yield spread from OAS analysis is based on the discounted value of the expected cash flow using the government bond-derived forward rate. The yield spread of the cash flow yield to the government bond is based on YTM. For this reason, the two spreads are not strictly comparable. The OAS spread is added to the entire yield curve, whereas a yield spread is a spread over a single point on the government bond yield curve.

way, the option feature begins to approach being in-the-money. To adjust for the increased value of the option, traders will price in higher spreads on the bond, which will result in the OAS remaining more or less unchanged.

Effective duration and convexity

The modified duration of a bond measures its price sensitivity to a change in yield; the calculation is effectively a snapshot of one point in time. It also assumes that there is no change in expected cash flows as a result of the change in market interest rates. Therefore it is an inappropriate interest rate risk for a mortgage-backed bond, whose cash flows would be expected to change after a change in rates, due to the prepayment effect. Hence, mortgage-backed bonds react differently to interest rate changes compared to conventional bonds, because when rates fall, the level of prepayments is expected to rise (and vice-versa). Therefore when interest rates fall, the duration of the bond may also fall, which is opposite to the behaviour of a conventional bond. This feature is known as *negative convexity* and is similar to the effect displayed by a callable bond. The prices of both these types of security react to interest rate changes differently compared to the price of conventional bonds.

For this reason the more accurate measure of interest rate sensitivity to use is *effective duration* described by Fabozzi (1997). To recap from Chapter 7, effective duration is the approximate duration of a bond as given by (17.17):

$$\Delta_{app} = \frac{P_- - P_+}{2P_0\,(\Delta rm)} \tag{17.17}$$

where

P_0 is the initial price of the bond

P_- is the estimated price of the bond if the yield decreases by Δrm

P_+ is the estimated price of the bond if the yield increases by Δrm

Δrm is the change in the yield of the bond.

The approximate duration is the effective duration of a bond when the two values P_- and P_+ are obtained from a valuation model that incorporates the effect of a change in the expected cash flows (from prepayment effects) when there is a change in interest rates. The values are obtained from a pricing model such as the static cash flow model, binomial model or simulation model. The calculation of effective duration uses higher and lower prices that are dependent on the prepayment rate that is assumed.

Generally, analysts will assume a higher prepayment rate when the interest rate is at the lower level of the two.

Figure 17.4 illustrates the difference between modified duration and effective duration for a range of agency mortgage pass-through securities, where the effective duration for each bond is calculated using a 20 basis point change in rates. This indicates that the modified duration measure effectively overestimates the price sensitivity of lower coupon bonds. This factor is significant when hedging a mortgage-backed bond position, because using the modified duration figure to calculate the nominal value of the hedging instrument will not prove effective for anything other than very small changes in yield.

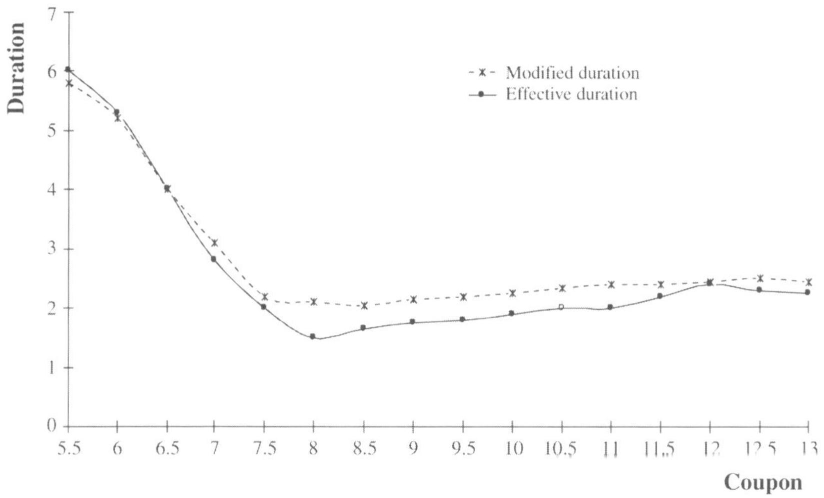

Figure 17.4: Modified duration and effective duration for agency mortgage-backed bonds

The formula to calculate approximate convexity (or *effective convexity*) is given below as (17.18); again if the values used in the formula allow for the cash flow to change, the convexity value may be taken to be the effective convexity. The effective convexity value of a mortgage pass-through security is invariably negative.

$$CV_{app} = \frac{P_+ + P_- - 2P_0}{P_0\,(\Delta rm)^2}. \tag{17.18}$$

Simulation modelling

The earlier section alluded to the main shortcomings of the static cash flow model when used for valuation and analysis, and usually to determine the spread between the cash flow yield of the mortgage-backed bond and the redemption yield of the equivalent government bond. In short, the main weaknesses of this model are that:

- neither yield measure takes sufficient account of the real government bond term structure (the spot yield curve);
- the cash flow yield ignores the cash flow effects of a change in yields.

To overcome these drawbacks certain analysts use simulation methodology to value mortgage-backed bonds. Put simply, this involves generating a set of cash flows based on simulated future mortgage refinancing rates, which themselves imply simulated prepayment rates. The simulation model used is usually a Monte Carlo simulation. Although running a simulation in order to generate future prices is straightforward enough to describe, it is in fact a complex procedure, and one that requires a considerable amount of computing power. In this section we describe only the concept behind the simulation model.

To run a simulation to generate future interest rates and hence future prices, a model requires the current government bond zero-coupon yield curve, and an assumption of interest rate volatility. The current zero-coupon curve, also known as the spot curve or the term structure of interest rates, is the starting point of the simulation, while the interest rate volatilities are used to generate a range of values for future interest rates. The average of this range of future spot rates for any maturity is equal to the current spot rate for that maturity. The simulation is run by generating scenarios of future interest rate paths. For each future month, a monthly interest rate and a mortgage rate is generated; this mortgage rate is in effect the refinancing rate for that month. The monthly mortgage rates are used to discount the projected cash flows in the scenario, and as a refinancing rate it is used to calculate the cash flow, as it represents the opportunity cost the mortgage borrower is facing at that point. Mortgage prepayments are determined by inputting the projected mortgage rate for that month and other parameters into a prepayment model. Using the projected prepayments it is possible to calculate the cash flow along an interest rate path. Once we have the interest rate path, it is possible to determine the present value of the cash flow on that path. The correct discount rate to use to calculate the present value is the simulated spot rate for each month on the interest rate path (there is also a spread to consider). The relationship between the simulated spot rate for month T on interest-rate path n, with the simulated future one-month rate is given by (17.19):

$$S_T(n) = ((1 + f_1(n))(1 + f_2(n)) \text{ L } (1 + f_T(n))^{1/T} - 1 \qquad (17.19)$$

where

$s_T(n)$ is the simulated spot rate for month T on price path n

$f_i(n)$ is the simulated future 1-month rate for month I on path n.

Hence we may set the present value of the cash flow for month T on interest rate path n discounted at the simulated spot rate for month T, together with an amount of spread as given by (17.20):

$$PV(C_T(n)) = \frac{C_T(n)}{(1 + S_T(n) + K)^{1/T}} \qquad (17.20)$$

where

$PV(C_T(n))$ is the present value of the cash flow for month T on path n

$C_T(n)$ is the cash flow for month T on path n

K is the spread.

The present value of path n is then the sum of all the present values of the cash flows for each month along path n, shown as (17.21):

$$PV(path(n)) = \sum_{t=1}^{T} PV(C_T(n)). \qquad (17.21)$$

We are now in a position to calculate a market fair value or theoretical value for the bond. If a particular interest rate path n is actually realised, the present value of that path, determined using (17.21), is the theoretical price of the mortgage-backed bond for that path. Therefore the theoretical price of the bond is the average of all the theoretical values for all the interest rate paths, shown as (17.22). This theoretical value is then compared to the actual observed price to determine if the bond is trading cheap or dear in the market.

$$P_{theo} = \frac{PV(\text{path}(1)) + PV(\text{path}(2)) + \text{L} + PV(\text{path}(N))}{N} \qquad (17.22)$$

where N is the number of interest rate paths.

Total return

To assess the value of a mortgage-backed bond over a given investment horizon it is necessary to measure the return generated during the holding period from the bond's cash flows. This is done using what is known as the *total return* framework. The cash flows from a mortgage-backed bond are comprised of (a) the projected cash flows of the bond (which are the projected interest payments and principal repayments and prepayments), (b) the interest earned on the reinvestment of all the payments, and (c) the projected price of the bond at the end of the holding period. The first sum can be estimated using an assumed prepayment rate during the period the bond is held, while the second cash flow requires an assumed reinvestment rate. To obtain (c) the bondholder must assume first, what the bond equivalent yield of the mortgage bond will be at the end of the holding period; and second, what prepayment rate the market will assume at this point. The second rate is a function of the projected yield at the time. The total return during the time the bond is held, on a monthly basis, is then given by (17.23),

$$\left[\frac{\text{Total future cash flow amount}}{P_m}\right]^{1/n} - 1 \qquad (17.23)$$

which can be converted to an annualised bond-equivalent yield using (17.15) or (17.16).

Note that the return calculated using (17.23) is based on a range of assumptions, which render it almost academic. The best approach to use is to calculate a yield for a range of different assumptions, which then give some idea of the likely yield that may be generated over the holding period, in the form of a range of yields (that is, an upper and lower limit).

EXAMPLE 17.5 Mortgage-backed bond issue

Bradford & Bingley Building Society £1 billion three-tranche MBS due 2031

Bradford & Bingley is a UK building society that planned to list on the London Stock Exchange (and convert to a bank) during 2000/2001. In August 2000 it issued a mortgage-backed security that was underwritten by UBS Warburg, via Aire Valley Finance (No. 2), a special purpose vehicle.

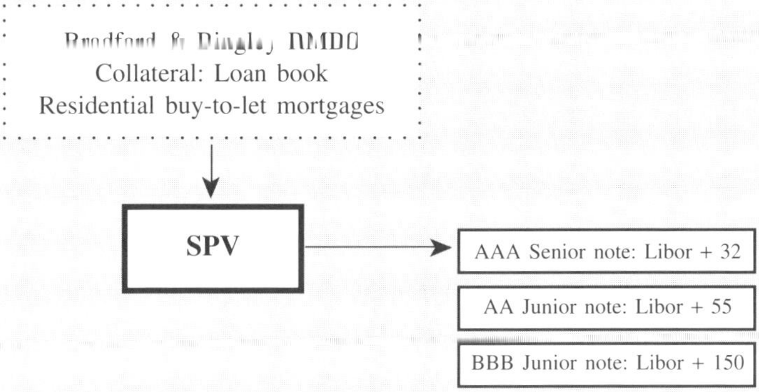

Figure 17.5 Bradford Bingley RMBS transaction

Loan portfolio

The underlying collateral consists of approximately 14,000 residential mortgages with an average loan balance of £74,000. Around two-thirds of the mortgages are on properties located in London and the south-east of England. An interesting feature of the mortgages is that they are *buy-to-let* loans; the issuer had previously undertaken a securitisation of its owner-occupier mortgage portfolio. These buy-to-let mortgages allow overpayment of the principal without penalty; consequently, early prepayment is more likely with this type of collateral.

Bond structure

The issue is callable, with the structure composed of the following notes:

- £892.5 million senior note with AAA-rating, offered at a yield of three-month Libor plus 32 bps;
- £57.5 million junior note with AA-rating, offered at three-month Libor plus 55 bps;
- £50 million junior note with BBB-rating, offered at Libor plus 150 bps.

Although the issue has a legal maturity to 2031, it is callable and the senior note has a feature that raises its coupon to Libor plus 80 bps if it is not called after September 2008. This makes it likely that the bond will be called at that time.

Investor profile

The issue was placed with around 50 institutional investors, with other UK banks and large building societies and European banks being the largest buyers of the senior notes; fund managers were purchasers of the junior notes.

Introduction to the evaluation and analysis of mortgage-backed bonds[10]

Term to maturity

The term to maturity cannot be given with any certainty for a mortgage pass-through security, since the cash flows and prepayment patterns cannot be predicted. To evaluate such a bond, therefore, it is necessary to estimate the term for the bond, and use this measure for any analysis. The maturity measure for any bond is important as, without it, it is not possible to assess over what period of time a return is being generated. Also, it will not be possible to compare the asset to any other bond. The term to maturity of a bond also gives an indication of its sensitivity to changes in market interest rates. If comparisons with other securities such as government bonds are made, we cannot use the stated maturity of the mortgage-backed bond because prepayments will reduce this figure. The convention in the market is to use other estimated values, which are average life and the more traditional duration measure.

The average life of a mortgage pass-through security is the weighted-average time to return of a unit of principal payment, made up of projected scheduled principal payments and principal prepayments. It is also known as the weighted-average life. It is given by (17.24).

$$\text{Average life} = \frac{1}{12} \sum_{t=1}^{n} \frac{t\,(\text{Principal received at } t)}{\text{Total principal received}} \qquad (17.24)$$

where n is the number of months remaining. The time from the term measured by the average life to the final scheduled principal payment is the bond's tail.

---

[10] The pricing and hedging of mortgage-backed securities is a complex one and space here does not allow a detailed treatment of it. Interested readers should consult Chapter 9 of Sundaresan (1997) or the other relevant references cited in the bibliography. Tuckman (1996) is also a good introduction to pricing models for mortgage securities; see his Chapter 18.

We've seen that to calculate duration (or Macaulay's duration) for a bond we required the weighted present values of all its cash flows. To apply this for a mortgage-backed bond, therefore, it is necessary to project the bond's cash flows, using an assumed prepayment rate. The projected cash flows, together with the bond price and the periodic interest rate, may then be used to arrive at a duration value. The periodic interest rate is derived from the yield. This calculation for a mortgage-backed bond produces a periodic duration figure, which must be divided by 12 to arrive at a duration value in years (or by four in the case of a quarterly paying bond).

Calculating yield and price: Static cash flow model

There are a number of ways that the yield on a mortgage-backed bond can be calculated. One of the most common methods employs the static cash flow model. This assumes a single prepayment rate to estimate the cash flows for the bond, and does not take into account how changes in market conditions might affect the prepayment pattern.

The conventional yield measure for a bond is the discount rate at which the sum of the present values of all the bond's expected cash flows will be equal to the price of the bond. The convention is usually to compute the yield from the clean price; that is, excluding any accrued interest. This yield measure is known as the bond's redemption yield or YTM. However, for mortgage-backed bonds it is known as a *cash flow yield* or mortgage yield. The cash flow for a mortgage-backed bond is not known with certainty, due to the effect of prepayments, and so must be derived using an assumed prepayment rate. Once the projected cash flows have been calculated, it is possible to calculate the cash flow yield. The formula is given as (17.25) below.

$$P = \sum_{n=1}^{N} \frac{C(t)}{(1 + ri / 1200)^{t-1}} \qquad (17.25)$$

Note, however, that a yield so computed will be for a bond with monthly coupon payments,[11] so it is necessary to convert the yield to an annualised equivalent before any comparisons are made with conventional bond yields. In the US and UK markets, the bond-equivalent yield is calculated for mortgage-backed bonds and measured against the relevant government bond

[11] The majority of mortgage-backed bonds pay interest on a monthly basis, since individual mortgages usually do as well; certain mortgage-backed bonds pay on a quarterly basis.

yield, which (in both cases) is a semi-annual yield. Although it is reasonably accurate to simply double the yield of a semi-annual coupon bond to arrive at the annualised equivalent, to obtain the bond equivalent yield for a monthly paying mortgage-backed bond we use (17.26), as shown below.

$$rm = 2[(1 + ri_M)^6 - 1] \tag{17.26}$$

where rm is the bond equivalent yield (we retain the designation that was used to denote YTM in Chapter 2) and ri_M is the interest rate that will equate the present value of the projected monthly cash flows for the mortgage-backed bond to its current price. The equivalent semi-annual yield is given by (17.27).

$$rm_{s/a} = (1 + ri_M)^6 - 1 \tag{17.27}$$

The cash flow yield calculated for a mortgage-backed bond in this way is essentially the redemption yield, using an assumption to derive the cash flows. In this, the measure suffers from the same drawbacks as when it is used to measure the return of a plain vanilla bond; that is, that the calculation assumes a uniform reinvestment rate for all the bond's cash flows and that the bond will be held to maturity. The same weakness will apply to the cash flow yield measure for a mortgage-backed bond. In fact, the potential inaccuracy of the redemption yield measure is even greater with a mortgage-backed bond because the frequency of interest payments is higher, which makes the reinvestment risk greater. The final yield that is returned by a mortgage-backed bond will depend on the performance of the mortgages in the pool, specifically the prepayment pattern.

Given the nature of a mortgage-backed bond's cash flows, the exact yield cannot be calculated. However, it is common for market practitioners to use the cash flow yield measure and compare this to the redemption yield of the equivalent government bond. The usual convention is to quote the spread over the government bond as the main measure of value. When measuring the spread, the mortgage-backed bond is compared to the government security that has a similar duration, or a term to maturity similar to its average life.

It is possible to calculate the price of a mortgage-backed bond once its yield is known (or vice-versa). As with a plain vanilla bond, the price is the sum of the present values of all the projected cash flows. It is necessary to convert the bond-equivalent yield to a monthly yield, which is then used to calculate the present value of each cash flow. The cash flows of IO- and PO-bonds are dependent on the cash flows of the underlying pass through security, which is itself dependent on the cash flows of the underlying mortgage pool. Again, to calculate the price of an IO- or PO-bond, a prepayment rate must be assumed. This enables us to determine the projected level of the monthly cash flows of the IO and the principal payments of the PO. The price of an IO is the present value of the projected interest payments, while the price of the PO is the present value of the projected principal payments, comprising the scheduled principal payments and the projected principal prepayments.

Bond price and option-adjusted spread

The concept of option-adjusted spread (OAS) and its use in the analysis and valuation of bonds with embedded options was considered briefly in Chapter 7, when OAS was discussed in the context of callable bonds. The behaviour of mortgage securities often resembles that of callable bonds, because effectively there is a call feature attached to them, in the shape of the prepayment option of the underlying mortgage holders. This option feature is the principal reason why it is necessary to use average life as the term to maturity for a mortgage security. It is frequently the case that the optional nature of a mortgage-backed bond, and the volatility of its yield, has a negative impact on the bondholders. This is for two reasons: the actual yield realised during the holding period has a high probability of being lower than the anticipated yield, which was calculated on the basis of an assumed prepayment level, and mortgages are frequently prepaid at the time when the bondholder will suffer the most. That is, prepayments occur most often when rates have fallen, leaving the bondholder to reinvest repaid principal at a lower market interest rate.

These features combined represent the biggest risk to an investor of holding a mortgage security, and market analysts attempt to measure and quantify this risk. This is usually done using a form of OAS analysis. Under this approach, the value of the mortgagor's prepayment option is calculated in terms of a basis-point penalty that must be subtracted from the expected yield spread on the bond. This basis-point value is calculated using a binomial model or a simulation model to generate a range of future interest rate paths, only some of which will cause a mortgagor to prepay her mortgage. The interest rate paths that would result in a prepayment are evaluated for their impact on the mortgage bond's expected yield spread over a government bond.[12] As OAS analysis takes account of the option feature of a mortgage-backed bond, it will be less affected by a yield change than the bond's yield spread. Assuming a flat yield-curve environment, the relationship between the OAS and the yield spread is given by:

$$\text{OAS} = \text{Yield spread} - \text{Cost of option feature.}$$

This relationship can be observed occasionally when yield spreads on current coupon mortgages widen during upward moves in the market. As interest rates fall, the cost of the option feature on a current coupon mortgage will rise, as the possibility of prepayment increases. Put another way, the option feature begins to approach being in-the-money. To adjust for the increased value of the option, traders will price in higher spreads on the bond, which will result in the OAS remaining more or less unchanged.

Effective duration and convexity

The modified duration of a bond measures its price sensitivity to a change in yield; the calculation is effectively a snapshot of one point in time. It also assumes that there is no change in expected cash flows as a result of the change in market interest rates. Therefore, it is an inappropriate measure of interest rate risk for a mortgage-backed bond, whose cash flows would be expected to change after a change in rates, due to the prepayment effect. Hence, mortgage-backed bonds react differently to interest rate changes compared to conventional bonds, because when rates fall, the level of prepayments is expected to rise (and vice-versa). Therefore, when interest rates fall, the duration of the bond may also fall, which is opposite to the behavior of a conventional bond. This feature is known as negative convexity and is similar to the effect displayed by a callable bond. The prices of both these types of security react to interest rate changes differently from the price of conventional bonds.

For this reason, the more accurate measure of interest rate sensitivity to use is effective duration. Effective duration is the approximate duration of a bond when, as given by (17.28) below,

[12] The yield spread from OAS analysis is based on the discounted value of the expected cash flow using the government bond-derived forward rate. The yield spread of the cash flow yield to the government bond is based on YTM. For this reason, the two spreads are not strictly comparable. The OAS spread is added to the entire yield curve, whereas a yield spread is a spread over a single point on the government-bond yield curve.

$$D_{app} = \frac{P_{-} - P_{+}}{2P_0(\Delta rm)} \tag{17.20}$$

where

P_0	is the initial price of the bond
P_{-}	is the estimated price of the bond if the yield decreases by Δrm
P_{+}	is the estimated price of the bond if the yield increases by Δrm
Δrm	is the change in the yield of the bond.

The approximate duration is the effective duration of a bond when the two values P_{-} and P_{+} are obtained from a valuation model that incorporates the effect of a change in the expected cash flows (from prepayment effects) when there is a change in interest rates. The values are obtained from a pricing model such as the static cash flow model, the binomial model or the simulation model. The calculation of effective duration uses higher and lower prices that are dependent on the prepayment rate that is assumed. Generally, analysts will assume a higher prepayment rate when the interest rate is at the lower level of the two.

Figure 17.6 illustrates the difference between modified duration and effective duration for a range of agency mortgage pass-through securities, where the effective duration for each bond is calculated using a 20 basis point change in rates. This indicates that the modified duration measure effectively overestimates the price sensitivity of lower coupon bonds. This factor is significant when hedging a mortgage-backed bond position, because using the modified-duration figure to calculate the nominal value of the hedging instrument will not prove effective for anything other than very small changes in yield.

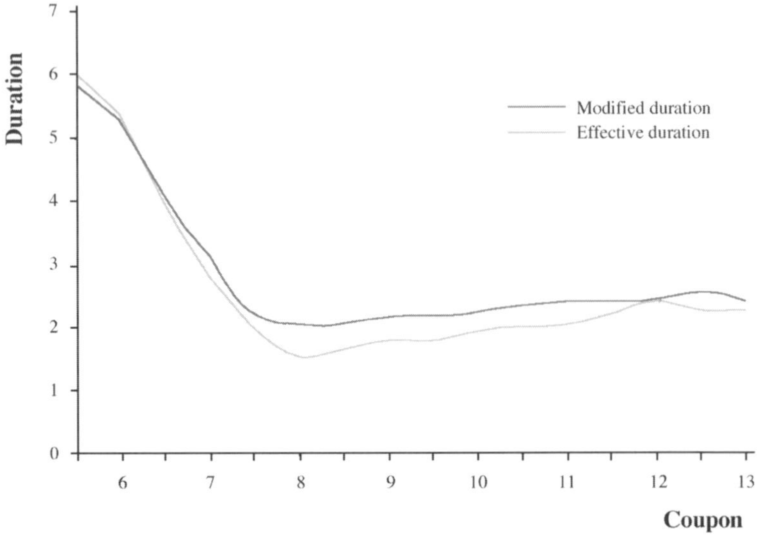

Figure 17.6 Modified duration and effective duration for agency mortgage-backed bonds

The formula to calculate approximate convexity (or effective convexity) is given below as (17.29). Again, if the values used in the formula allow for the cash flow to change, the convexity value may be taken to be the effective convexity. The effective convexity value of a mortgage pass-through security is invariably negative.

$$CV_{app} = \frac{P_+ + P_- - 2P_0}{P_0(\Delta rm)^2} \tag{17.29}$$

Total return

To assess the value of a mortgage-backed bond over a given investment horizon, it is necessary to measure the return generated during the holding period from the bond's cash flows. This is done using what is known as the total return framework. The cash flows from a mortgage-backed bond consist of (a) the projected cash flows of the bond (which are the projected interest payments and principal repayments and prepayments); (b) the interest earned on the reinvestment of all the payments; and (c) the projected price of the bond at the end of the holding period. The first sum can be estimated using an assumed prepayment rate during the period the bond is held, while the second cash flow requires an assumed reinvestment rate. To obtain (c) the bondholder must assume, first, what the bond-equivalent yield of the mortgage bond will be at the end of the holding period and, second, what prepayment rate the market will assume at this point. The second rate is a function of the projected yield at the time. The total return during the time the bond is held, on a monthly basis, is then given by (17.30).

$$\left[\frac{\text{Total future cash flow amount}}{P_m}\right]^{1/n} - 1 \qquad (17.30)$$

which can be converted to an annualised bond-equivalent yield using (17.26) or (17.27).

Note that the return calculated using (17.30) is based on a range of assumptions, which render it almost academic. The best approach is to calculate a yield for a range of different assumptions, which then give some idea of the likely yield that may be generated over the holding period, in the form of a range of yields (that is, an upper and lower limit).

Price-yield curves of mortgage pass-through, PO and IO securities

In this section, we present an introduction to the yield behaviour of selected mortgage-backed securities under conditions of changing interest rates. To recap, in an environment of high interest rates the holders of mortgage-backed bonds prefer prepayments to occur. This is because the mortgage will be paying at a low interest rate relative to market conditions, and the likelihood of mortgage prepayment at par results in a higher value for the bond. In the same way, when interest rates are low, noteholders would prefer that there not be any prepayment, as the bond will be paying interest at a relatively high rate and will therefore be price-valuable.

Figure 17.7 illustrates the price behaviour of pass-through securities, with nominal coupon of 7%.

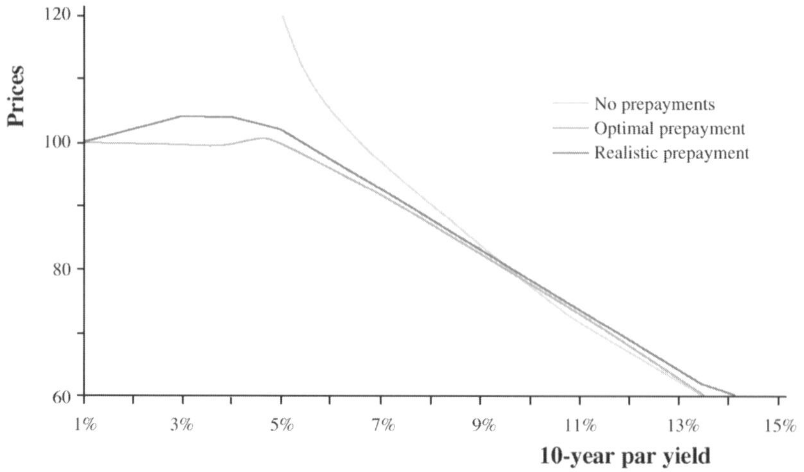

Figure 17.7 Price behaviour of pass-through security

Under conditions of no prepayments, the bond cash flows are certain and the price–yield behaviour resembles that of a conventional bond. Under optimal prepayment, the bond will behave similarly to a callable bond: in a high interest rate environment the bond behaves much like a vanilla bond, while under lower rates the price of the bond is capped at par. However, under what Tuckman (1996) calls "realistic payment" conditions the price behaviour is somewhat different, as illustrated in Figure 17.6. In an environment of very low rates, bond value is higher with the realistic payments assumption than the other two scenarios. This is because there are always a number of mortgage borrowers who will repay their loans irrespective of the level of interest rates, whether rates are low or high. Remember that noteholders desire prepayments when interest rates are high, and the bond value under the realistic payments model is higher than those of the other two, which predict no prepayments under high interest rate conditions.

As interest rates decline, certain mortgage borrowers will prepay their loans, but by no means all. As prepayment decreases the value of a mortgage under low interest rates, the fact that not all borrowers prepay under the "optimal" scenario results in an increase in value of a mortgage to a level greater than its optimal prepaid value. This non-prepayment behaviour can lead to an increase in bond value above par. This is something of an anomaly, as the bond is then priced above the level at which it can theoretically be called. The scenario concludes when eventually all borrowers redeem their mortgages as rates have fallen far enough. This is why the realistic prepayments curve moves down to par at very low levels of rates. The graph shows the existence of negative convexity as bond prices fall as interest rates decline, which reflects the behaviour of mortgage borrowers after a long enough period of very low rates. However, this does not mean that investors should not buy mortgage-backed bonds at that range of yields when negative convexity applies: as Tuckman notes, the mortgages will be earning rates at above-market levels. It is the total return of the bond over the holding period that is relevant, rather than its price behaviour.[13]

It is also worth commenting on the behavior of IO and PO securities, which we described earlier. To recap, an IO receives the interest payments of the underlying collateral while the PO receives principal payments. Figure 17.8 illustrates the price behavior of these instruments, based on a $100 nominal amount for both the underlying mortgage and the IO/PO.

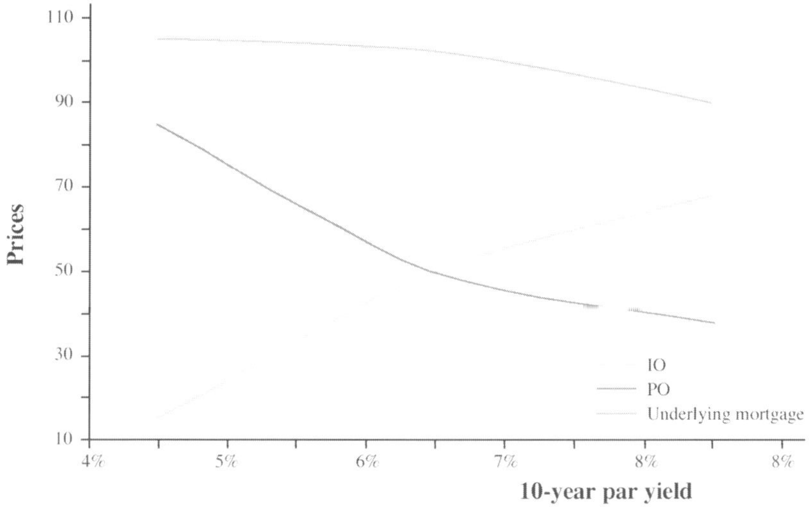

Figure 17.8 Price behaviour of IO and PO securities

[13] This is especially true when compared to the performance of other debt-market investments. Investment reasoning on price behaviour alone is "as bad as concluding that premium Treasuries should never be purchased because they will eventually decline in price to par"! (author's exclamation mark; Tuckman 1996, p 256).

Under very high interest rates and where prepayments are unlikely, a PO will act as is repayable at par on maturity, similar to a zero-coupon bond. As interest rates decline and the level of prepayments increases, the value of the PO will increase. However, other forces are at work that, as rates change further, make PO securities more interesting than vanilla strips. These are:

- the conventional price/yield effect, as lower interest rates cause higher prices;
- that the PO, again similarly to vanilla strips, is very sensitive to the price/yield effect;
- as the level of prepayments increases, with the expectation of higher levels still, the effective maturity of the PO declines. The effect of this lower maturity is to raise the price of the PO even higher.

The impact of these factors is that PO securities are highly volatile.

The price/yield relationship of the IO is a function of that for the PO, and is obtained by subtracting the value of the latter from that of the underlying mortgage. A significant feature is the high price volatility of the IO under conditions of lower and falling interest rates. This is explained as follows: in a high interest rate environment, with very low prepayment levels, IOs act as vanilla bonds, with cash flows known with certainty. This changes as interest rates start to fall, and the cash flows of the IO effectively disappear. This is because as more principal is repaid, the nominal amount of the mortgage on which interest is charged decreases in amount. However, unlike pass-through or other mortgage securities, which receive some principal payment when interest payments decline or cease, IOs receive no cash flow. The impact of a vanishing cash flow is that, as interest rates fall, the price of the IO declines dramatically.

As well as purchases by investors, this negative duration property of IOs makes them of use as interest rate hedging instruments by market-makers in mortgage-backed securities.

CASE STUDY 1 Shipshape Residential Mortgages No 1

Bristol & West plc is a former UK building society that is now part of the Bank of Ireland group. In October 2000 it issued £300 million of residential mortgage-backed securities through ING

Barings. It was the third time that Bristol & West had undertaken a securitisation of part of its mortgage book. The Shipshape Residential Mortgages No 1 was structured in the following way:

- a £285 million tranche senior note, rated Aaa by Moody's and Fitch IBCA, with an average life of 3.8 years and paying 25 basis points over three-month Libor;
- a class "B" note of £9 million, rated A1 by Moody's and paying a coupon on 80 basis points over three-month Libor. These notes had an average life of 6.1 years;
- a junior note of £6 million nominal, rated triple-B by Moody's and with an average life of 6.8 years. These notes paid a coupon of 140 basis points over Libor.

Covered bonds

Covered bonds are similar in most economic aspects to residential MBS instruments, but have detail differences in their structure and legal definition. The longest established covered bond market is that in German *Pfandbriefe*; there are also covered bond markets in other European markets such as the Netherlands, Ireland, Spain and the United Kingdom. In this section we describe UK covered bonds, which represent a new market for issuers and investors alike.

Covered bond markets and securitisation

The low profile of covered bonds in the financial literature is surprising, given that some of the earliest bond market instruments were in the form of covered bonds, including German *Pfandbriefe*, Danish *Realkreditobligationer* and French *Obligations Foncieres*. More recently, covered bonds have been introduced in Spain (*Cedulas Hipotecarias*) and Ireland. At the end of 2003 it was estimated that over €1.5 trillion of covered bonds was in issue in Europe.[14]

A covered bond may be defined as a full recourse debt issue secured against a pool of mortgages or public-sector assets. In certain countries, such

[14] *Source*: HBOS plc.

as Germany, the central authorities have enacted specific legislation that govern covered bonds. In countries where no specific legislation exists, such as the United Kingdom, originators have used traditional securitisation structuring techniques to create an identical instrument, the *structured covered bond*. With a covered bond, investors continue to have recourse to the originator, but it is only upon default that the assigned underlying collateral pool is used to repay the principal. Otherwise, the cash flows from the collateral are not used to service the debt. In a traditional securitisation, investors would have only the cash flows from the assigned collateral pool to repay their amount owed on the debt.

Hence, the key difference between a residential mortgage-backed security (RMBS) and a mortgage-backed covered bond is that an SPV is not created and assets are not transferred to an SPV. Instead, a wholly owned subsidiary is created within the originating bank or financial institution and assets are transferred to this legal entity. Hence, these assets are not taken off the originating entity's balance sheet, as they remain part of the group structure assets.

Issuer and investor factors

Covered bonds in the euro and sterling markets present new attractions for investors. For instance, they:

- offer a diversified alternative for investors' funds, away from traditional issuers;
- offer access to the residential mortgage market but outside of RMBS securities;
- present a structure that provides potentially a greater ability to repay liabilities on a stand-alone basis;
- are rated AAA/Aaa;
- are issued in large size and hence offer liquidity;
- are risk-weighted at 20% for Basel I capital purposes.

Covered bonds also present certain advantages for originators, these include:

- a potential new investor base that may not have been tapped previously;
- due to rating and collateral security, a lower cost of funds than a traditional (unsecured) MTN program, as well as more longer term

funding;[15] also a lower cost and longer term funding than securitised securities;
- potential ease of reissue under the program structure.

These points would suggest strong future growth potential in this market.

HBOS plc covered bond

As an example, consider the mortgage covered bond issued by Halifax plc (a former UK building society and part of the HBOS group). It is illustrated in Figure 17.9 below. This was created as follows:

- the arm of HBOS responsible for funding activity, HBOS Treasury, issued covered bonds to investors. It is legally obliged to pay the interest and principal on the bonds;
- funds raised by this issue were loaned to a new group company, Halifax LLP, a wholly owned subsidiary of HBOS group. The LLP guarantees the covered bonds;
- the group sold a pool of residential mortgages to Halifax LLP, at an overcollateralisation of 15%;
- Halifax LLP placed these assets under a security trust and guarantee which was placed in favour of the investors.

Unlike a traditional securitisation, the liabilities on the issues notes were held by HBOS Treasury, not the new legal entity. It funded the liabilities out of its normal activities, not out of the cash flows represented by the mortgages transferred to Halifax LLP. Only in the event of default on the issued notes would investors have recourse to the assets held by Halifax LLP. This structure presented certain advantages over traditional RMBS issues as it was operated as a program of rolling issues, and also appealed to a wider investor base.

The bonds were rated at AAA/Aaa/AAA. The initial pool was comprised entirely of Halifax plc, although there is freedom to include any mortgage (provided certain criteria are met) from within the HBOS group.

The covered bonds are part of a €14 billion MTN program set up by HBOS plc. For investor comfort, various tests are performed on the portfolio to ensure that it maintains minimum quality levels during the bonds' lives.

---

15 During Jan. 2004 the covered bond yield in the United Kingdom ranged around 5–10 basis points lower, compared to MTN yields from the same issuer.

This process is similar to the quality tests performed on CDO structures. The Halifax bond test is called the Asset Coverage Test; it is designed to protect investors and aims to ensure that the value of the underlying assets (mortgages, substitute assets and cash reserves) is equal to the outstanding principal. It includes:

- portfolio revaluation: the value of the portfolio is updated every quarter and is overcollateralised by 15% (that is, its value is calculated using 85% of the Halifax house price index);
- defaulted mortgages: any mortgage in the collateral pool that is over 90 days in arrears is designated a defaulted mortgage and for asset valuation purposes is assigned a zero value;
- repurchase and substitution: to satisfy the asset coverage test, Halifax must repurchase defaulted mortgages from the LLP company at principal value, and either assign replacement mortgages or supply cash collateral until the asset coverage test is passed.

The asset coverage test is:

$$AALA \geq \sum PAO$$

where
AALA is the adjusted aggregate loan amount; it is comprised as follows:

$$\begin{aligned} AALA = {} & \text{Outstanding loan value} + \text{Cash} + \text{Substitute assets} \\ & - (\text{Set-off risk} + \text{Redraws} + \text{Negative carry}) \end{aligned}$$

and where
PAO is the principal amount outstanding.

Other tests and triggers in the structure include the following:

- if the issuer's rating falls below a certain level, then Halifax must repurchase sufficient mortgages and/or inject cash into the LLP to cover the next maturing bond;
- if the issuer short-term rating falls below A–1+/P–1/F1+ then the LLP must establish a reserve fund, which will then accumulate interest to cover the coupon on the covered bond as it falls due;
- the LLP bank accounts must be maintained at an A–1+/P–1/F1+ rated bank.

The HBOS-covered bond was a ground breaking deal in the UK covered bond market. It established a precedent that subsequently attracted interest from other UK mortgage banks.

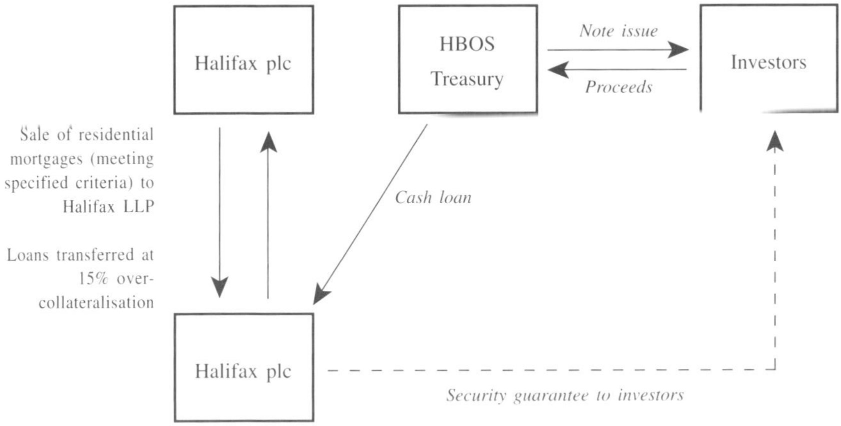

Figure 17.9 Halifax mortgage covered bond, July 2003
© HBOS. Reproduced with permission.

Selected bibliography and references

Fabozzi, F., Ramsey, C. and Ramirez, F. 1994, *Collateralized Mortgage Obligations: Structures and Analysis*, FJF Associates, New Hope, PA, Chapter 3.

Fabozzi, F. 1997, *Fixed Income Mathematics*, McGraw-Hill, New York.

Fabozzi, F. (ed.) 1989, *Handbook of Structured Financial Products*, FJF Associates, New Hope, PA.

Hayre, L. and Mohebbi, C. 1989, "Mortgage pass-through securities", in Fabozzi, F. (ed.), *Advances and Innovations in the Bond and Mortgage Markets*, Probus Publishing, New York, pp. 259–304.

Pinkus, S. and Chandoha, M. 1987, "The relative price volatility of mortgage securities", in Fabozzi, F. (ed.), *Mortgage-backed Securities: New Strategies, Applications and Research*, Probus Publishing, New York.

Life moves pretty fast.
If you don't stop to look around, you could miss it.

– Matthew Broderick
Ferris Bueller's Day Off, 1987

CHAPTER

18

Asset-backed Securities

The market in asset-backed securities contains instruments that have widely varying payment terms and conditions, and different collateral bases. The subject matter is a large one and so in this chapter we present only a summary of the main instruments. Interested readers may wish to consult the texts listed under the selected bibliography. Here we review the characteristics of the main asset-backed instruments, which were introduced in the US market, but are also now issued in other markets including those in the United Kingdom and Europe. The instruments we will consider are:

- collateralised mortgage obligations (in the US market), both agency and non-agency;
- commercial mortgage-backed securities;
- auto-loan-backed securities;
- credit card-backed securities.

We also present some further issues connected with the analysis of these securities.

Collateralised mortgage securities

Mortgage-backed bonds were introduced in Chapter 17. In this section we review some of the newer structures of these instruments. A large number of the instruments in the US market are collateralised mortgage obligations (CMOs), the majority of which are issued by government-sponsored agencies and so offer virtual Treasury bond credit quality, but at significantly higher yields. This makes the paper attractive to a range of institutional investors, as does the opportunity to tailor the characteristics of a particular issue to suit the needs of a specific investor. The CMO market in the United States experienced rapid growth during the 1990s, with a high of $324 billion issued in 1993; this figure had fallen to just under $100 billion during 1998.[1] The growth of the market has brought with it a range of new structures; for example, bondholders who wished to have a lower exposure to prepayment risk have invested in *planned amortisation classes* (PACs) and *targeted amortisation classes* (TACs). The uncertain term to maturity of mortgage-backed bonds has resulted in the creation of bonds that were guaranteed not to extend beyond a stated date, which are known as *very accurately defined maturity* (VDAM) bonds. In the United Kingdom and certain overseas markets, mortgage-backed bonds pay a floating-rate coupon, and the interest from foreign investors in the US domestic market led to the creation of bonds with coupons linked to the Libor rate. Other types of instruments in the market include interest-only (IO) and principal-only (PO) bonds, also sometimes called Strips, and inverse floating-rate bonds, which are usually created from an existing fixed-rate bond issue. Figure 18.1 illustrates the relative size of the different instruments in the US market at the beginning of 1997.

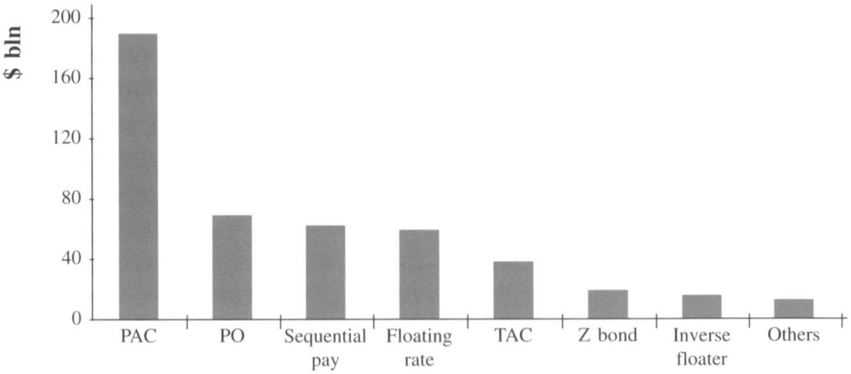

Figure 18.1 US market agency CMOs in issue 1997.
Source: Chase Manhattan.

[1] The source for statistical data in this section is *Inside Mortgage Securities*, Chase Manhattan, New York, February 1997 and *Asset-Backed Alert* (www.ABAlert.com).

The primary features of US-market CMOs are summarised as follows:

- *Credit quality.* CMOs issued by US government agencies have the same guarantee as agency pass-through securities, so may be considered risk-free. These bonds therefore do not require any form of credit insurance or credit enhancement. Whole-loan CMOs do not carry any form of government guarantee, and are rated by credit rating agencies. Most bonds carry a triple-A rating, either because of the quality of the mortgage pool or issuing vehicle, or because a form of credit enhancement as been used.
- *Interest frequency.* CMOs typically pay interest on a monthly basis, which is calculated on the current outstanding nominal value of the issue.
- *Cash flow profile.* The cash flow profile of CMOs is based on an assumed prepayment rate. This rate is based on the current market expectation of future prepayment levels and expected market interest rates, and is known as the *pricing speed.*
- *Maturity.* Most CMOs are long-dated instruments, and originally virtually all issues were created from underlying mortgage collateral with a 30-year stated maturity. During the 1990s issues were created from shorter dated collateral, including 5–7-year and 15–20-year mortgages.
- *Market convention.* CMOs trade on a yield, as opposed to a price, basis and are usually quoted as a spread over the yield of the nearest maturity Treasury security. The yields are calculated on the basis of an assumed prepayment rate. Agency CMOs are settled on a T+3 basis via an electronic book-entry system known as "Fedwire", the clearing system run by the Federal Reserve. Whole-loan CMOs also settle on a T+3 basis, and are cleared using either physical delivery or by electronic transfer. New issues CMOs settle from one to three months after the initial offer date.

Originally, mortgage-backed bonds were created from individual underlying mortgages. Agency CMOs are created from mortgages that have already been pooled and securitised, usually in the form of a pass-through security (see Chapter 17). Issuers of *whole loan* CMOs do not therefore need to create a pass-through security from a pool of individual mortgages, but a structure based on cash flows from the entire pool. In the same way as for agency pass-through securities, the underlying mortgages in a whole-loan pool are generally of the same risk type, maturity and interest rate. The other difference between whole-loan CMOs and agency pass-throughs is that the latter are comprised of mortgages of up to a stated maximum size, while larger loans are contained in CMOs. There are essentially two CMO structures, those issues that redirect the underlying pool interest payments and those issues that redirect both interest and principal. The main CMO instrument types pay out both interest and principal and are described below.

Whole-loan CMO structures also differ from other mortgage-backed securities in terms of what is known as *compensating interest*. Virtually all mortgage securities pay principal and interest on a monthly basis, on a fixed coupon date. The underlying mortgages however may be paid off on any day of the month. Agency mortgage securities guarantee their bondholders an interest payment for the complete month, even if the underlying mortgage has been paid off ahead of the coupon date (and so has not attracted any interest). Whole-loan CMOs do not offer this guarantee, and so any *payment interest shortfall* will be lost, meaning that a bondholder would receive less than one month's worth of interest on the coupon date. Some issuers, but not all, will pay a compensating interest payment to bondholders to make up this shortfall.

Planned amortisation class

The first issue of *planned amortisation classes* (PACs) was in 1986, after a period of sustained falls in the market interest rates led to a demand for less interest rate volatile mortgage-backed structures. PAC structures are designed to reduce prepayment risk and also the volatility of the weighted average life measure, which is related to the prepayment rate. The securities have a principal payment schedule that is maintained irrespective of any change in prepayment rates. The process is similar to a corporate bond sinking fund schedule, and is based on the minimum amount of principal cash flow that is produced by the underlying mortgage pool at two different prepayment rates, known as *PAC bands*. The PAC bands are set as a low and high PSA standard; for example, 50%PSA and 250%PSA. This has the effect of constraining the amount of principal repayment, so that in the early years of the issue the minimum of principal received is at the level of the lower of the two bands, while later in the bond's life the payment schedule is constrained by the upper PAC band. The total principal cash flow under the PAC schedule will determine the value of PACs in a structure.

A PAC schedule follows an arrangement whereby cash flow uncertainty of principal payment is directed to another class of security known as *companions*, or *support classes*. When prepayment rates are high, companion issues support the main PACs by absorbing any principal prepayments that are in excess of the PAC schedule. When the prepayment rate has fallen, the companion amortisation rates are delayed as the level of principal prepayment is not sufficient to reach the minimum level stipulated by the PAC bands. Essentially, the structure of PACs results in the companion issues carrying the prepayment uncertainty, since when prepayment rates are high the average life of the companions will be reduced as they are paid off, and when prepayment rates are low the companions will see their measure of average life increase as they remain outstanding for a longer period.

The principal cash flows of PACs and companions can be divided sequentially, similar to sequential-pay structures, which are reviewed in the next section. PACs have a lower price volatility than other mortgage securities, the level of which is relatively stable when the prepayment rates are within the PAC bands. When prepayment rates move outside the bands, the volatility increases by a lower amount than they otherwise would, because the prepayment risk is transferred to the companions. For this reason, PAC issues trade at lower spreads to the Treasury yield curve than other issues of similar average life. The companion bonds are always priced at a higher spread than the PACs, reflecting their higher prepayment risk.

PAC bonds that have a lower prepayment risk than standard PACs are known as *Type II* and *Type III PACs*. A Type II PAC is created from an existing PAC/companion structure, and has a narrower band than the original PAC. This reduces the prepayment risk. If prepayment rates remain within the bands, Type II PACs trade as PACs. If prepayment rates move outside the narrower band, the extra cash flow is redirected to the companion. Type II PACs are second in priority to the PACs and so carry a higher yield. If prepayment rates remain high over a period of time, such that all the companions are redeemed, the Type II PACs take over the function of companion, so that they then carry higher prepayment risk. A further PAC with yet narrower bands, created from the same structure, is known as a *Type III PAC*.

The upper and lower bands in a PAC may "drift" during the life of the CMO, irrespective of the level that actual prepayment rates are at. This drift arises because of the interaction between actual cash prepayments and the bands, and changes in collateral balance and the ratio between the PAC and companion nominal values. The impact of this drift differs according to where the prepayment rate is. The three possible scenarios are:

- *prepayment level lies within the current bands*: in this case the PAC will receive principal in line with the payment schedule, while any prepayments above the schedule amount will be redirected to the companion issue. The effect of this if it continues is that both the lower and upper bands will drift upwards; this is because any prepayment that occurs is within the bands. This causes the upper band to rise, the rationale being that as prepayments have been below it, they have been received at a slower rate than expected, leaving more companion issues to receive future prepayments. The lower band rises as well, the reasoning being that prepayments have been received faster than expected (as they have been above the minimum level) so that a lower amount of collateral is available to generate future principal payments. It has been observed that upper bands tend to rise at a higher rate than the lower rate, so that prepayment levels lying within the bands cause them to widen over time;
- *prepayment level lies above the upper band*: where prepayment rates are above the upper band, the PAC will receive principal in line with the payment schedule until it is paid off. If the prepayment rates stay above the upper band, the two bands will begin to narrow, because the number of companions available to receive faster prepayments will fall. The two bands will converge completely once all the companion bonds have been redeemed, and the PAC will trade as a conventional security from that point until it is paid off;
- *prepayment level lies below the lower band*: if prepayment rates lie below the lower PAC band, the upper band will drift upwards as more companion bonds are available to receive a greater level of prepayments in the future; the lower band may also rise by a small amount. This situation is relatively rare, however, as PACs have the highest priority of all classes in a CMO structure until the payment schedule is back on track.

The band drift process occurs over a long time period and is sometimes not noticeable. Significant changes to the band levels only takes place if the prepayment rate is outside the band for a long period. Prepayment rates that move outside the bands over a short time period do not have any effect on the bands.

Sequential-pay classes

One of the requirements that CMOs were designed to meet was the demand for mortgage-backed bonds with a wider range of maturities. Most CMO structures redirect principal payments *sequentially* to individual classes of bonds within the structure, in accordance with the stated maturity of each bond. That is, principal payments are first used to pay off the class of bond with the shortest stated maturity, until it is completely redeemed, before being reallocated to the next maturity band class of bond. This occurs until all the bonds in the structure are retired.

Sequential pay CMOs are attractive to a wide range of investors, particularly those with shorter term investment horizons, as they are able to purchase only the class of CMO whose maturity terms meets their requirements. In addition, investors with more traditional longer dated investment horizons are protected from prepayment risk in the early years of the issue, because principal payments are used to pay off the shorter dated bonds in the structure.

Targeted amortisation class

These bonds were created to cater for investors who require an element of prepayment protection but at a higher yield than would be available with a PAC. Targeted amortisation class bonds (TAC) offer a prepayment principal in line with a schedule, providing that the level of prepayment is within the stated range. If the level of principal prepayment moves outside of the range, the extra principal amounts are used to pay off TAC companion bonds, just as with PACs. The main difference between TACs and PACs is that TACs have extra prepayment risk if the level of prepayments falls below the amount required to maintain the payment schedule; this results in the average life of the TAC being extended. Essentially, a TAC is a PAC but with a lower "PAC band" setting. The preference to hold TACs over PACs is a function of the prevailing interest rate environment; if current rates are low and/or are expected to fall, there is a risk that increasing prepayments will reduce the average life of the bond. In this scenario, investors may be willing to do without the protection against an increase in the average life (deeming it unlikely to be required), and take the extra yield over PACs as a result. This makes TACs attractive compared to PACs under certain conditions, and because one element of the "PAC band" is removed, TACs trade at a higher yield

Z-class bonds

This type of bond is unique to the domestic US market, and has a very interesting structure. The Z-class bond (or *Z-bond*) is created from a CMO structure and is composed of a reallocation of both principal and interest payments. It is essentially a coupon-bearing bond that ranks below all other classes in the CMO's structure, and pays no cash flows for part of its life. When the CMO is issued, the Z-bond has a nominal value of relatively small size, and at the start of its life it pays out cash flows on a monthly basis as determined by its coupons. However, at any time that the Z-bond itself is receiving no principal payments, these cash flows are used to retire some of the principal of the other classes in the structure. This results in the nominal value of the bond being increased each month that the coupon payments are not received, so that the principal amount is higher at the end of the bond's life than at the start. This process is known as *accretion*. At the point when all classes of bond ahead of the Z-bond are retired, the Z-bond itself starts to pay out principal and interest cash flows.

The following example of a Z-bond cash flow structure is one described in Chapter 28 of *The Handbook of Fixed Income Securities*, edited by Frank Fabozzi (1997). The table is reproduced with the kind permission of McGraw-Hill.

EXAMPLE 18.1 Sample Z-bond cash flows

This is an example of a Z-bond created from a $7^1/_2$% 30-year mortgage pass-through bond. The nominal value of the bond on issue is \$118,000, but the initial coupon payments of \$737.50 (the bond pays a monthly coupon) are used as principal prepayments for other bonds in the CMO structure. These cash flows therefore accrete to the nominal value of the Z-bond. The accretion amounts increase as the principal amount increases. However, in month 133 the last sequential-pay bond in the structure is paid off, leaving the Z-class as the only bond left in the structure. At this point the bond has a principal value of \$270,203. From the next month the bond receives all the interest and principal payments and prepayments that are paid out by the underlying mortgage collateral.

Sequential Pay Z-Bond Structure
CMO created from 7.50% 30-year Mortgage Pass-Through Security
Cash flows $

Month	Starting balance	Coupon accretion	Coupon cash flow	Amortisation	Ending balance	Total cash flows
1	118,000.00	737.50	0.00	0.00	118,737.50	0.00
2	118,737.50	742.11	0.00	0.00	119,479.61	0.00
3	119,479.61	746.75	0.00	0.00	120,226.35	0.00
:	:	:	:	:	:	0.00
:	:	:	:	:	:	0.00
131	265,245.57	1,657.78	0.00	0.00	256,903.35	0.00
132	256,903.35	1,668.15	0.00	0.00	268,571.50	0.00
133	268,571.50	1,678.57	0.00	47.44	270,202.63	47.44
134	270,202.63	0.00	1,688.77	3,131.55	267,071.08	4,820.31
135	267,071.08	0.00	1,669.19	3,099.51	263,971.57	4,768.70

Table 18.1 Example of Z-bond cash flows in CMO structure
Source: Ames, C. 1997, "Collateralized mortgage obligation", in Fabozzi, F., *The Handbook of Fixed Income Securities*, 5th edition, McGraw-Hill. Reproduced with permission.

In the conventional sequential pay structure, the existence of a Z-bond will increase the principal prepayments in the CMO structure. The other classes in the structure receive some of their principal prepayments from the Z-bond, which lowers their average life volatility. Creating a Z-bond in a CMO structure reduces therefore the average life volatility of all the classes in the structure. Z-bonds are an alternative to investors who might otherwise purchase Treasury zero-coupon bonds, with a similar feature of no reinvestment risk. They also offer the added attraction of higher yields compared to those available on Treasury strips with a similar average life.

Interest-only and principal-only class

Stripped coupon mortgage securities were introduced in Chapter 17. They are created when the coupon cash flows payable by a pool of mortgages are split into interest-only (IO) and principal-only (PO) payments. The cash flows will be a function of the prepayment rate, since this determines the nominal value of the collateral pool. IO issues, also known as IO strips, gain whenever the prepayment rate falls, as interest payments are reduced as the principal amount falls. If there is a rise in the prepayment rate, PO bonds benefit because they are discount securities and a higher prepayment rate results in the redemption proceeds being received early. Early strip issues were created with an unequal amount of coupon and principal, resulting in a synthetic coupon rate that was different to the coupon on the underlying bond. These instruments were known as *synthetic coupon pass-throughs*. Nowadays it is more typical for all the interest to be allocated to one class, the IO issue, and all the principal to be allocated to the PO class. The most common CMO structures have a portion of their principal stripped into IO and PO bonds, but in some structures the entire issue is made up of IO and PO bonds. The amount of principal used to create stripped securities will reflect investor demand. In certain cases, IO issues created from a class of CMO known as *real estate mortgage investment conduits* (REMICs) have quite esoteric terms. For example, the IO classes might be issued with an amount of principal attached known as the nominal balance. The cash flows for bonds with this structure are paid through a process of amortising and prepaying the nominal balance. The balance itself is a small amount, resulting in a very high coupon, so that the IO has a multi-digit coupon and very high price (such as 1183% and 3626-12).[2]

Strips created from whole-loan CMOs trade differently from those issued out of agency CMOs. Agency CMOs pay a fixed coupon, whereas whole-loan CMOs pay a coupon based on a weighted average of all the individual mortgage coupons. During the life of the whole-loan issue this coupon value will alter as prepayments change the amount of principal. To preserve the coupon payments of all issues within a structure therefore, a portion of the principal and interest cash flows are stripped from the underlying mortgages, leaving collateral that has a more stable average life. This is another reason that IOs and POs may be created.

IO issue prices exhibit the singular tendency of moving in the same direction as interest rates under certain situations. This reflects the behaviour of mortgages and prepayment rates: when interest rates fall below the mortgage coupon rate, prepayment rates will increase. This causes the cash flow for an IO strip to fall, as the level of the underlying principal declines, which causes the price of the IO to fall as well. This is despite the fact that

---

2 Ames (1997).

the issue's cash flows are now discounted at a lower rate. Figure 18.2 shows the price of the sensitivity of a 7% pass-through security compared to the prices of an IO and a PO that have been created from it. Note that the price of the pass-through is not particularly sensitive to a fall in the mortgage rate below the coupon rate of 7%. This illustrates the *negative convexity* property of pass-through securities. The price sensitivity of the two strip issues is very different. The PO experiences a dramatic fall in price as the mortgage rate rises above the coupon rate. The IO on the other hand experiences a rise in price in the same situation, while its price falls significantly if mortgage rates fall below the coupon rate.

Both PO and IO issues are extremely price volatile at times of moves in mortgage rates, and have much greater interest rate sensitivity than the pass-through securities from which they are created.

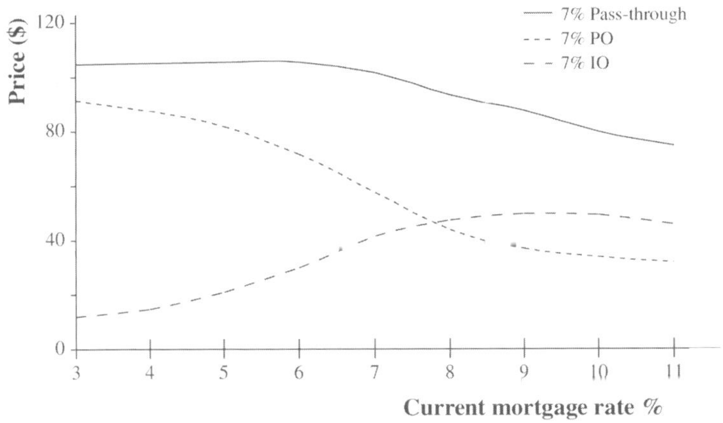

Figure 18.2 Price sensitivity of pass-through security, IO and PO to changes in mortgage rate
Price source and calculation: Bloomberg.

Structuring a CMO

The process of setting up a CMO structure can be quite involved, and is dependent on the level of customer demand for each of the different classes of instruments. Customer demand is a function of their individual requirements as well as the current market environment. Factors such as current mortgage rates and interest rate expectations also influence the demand for certain instruments. We can illustrate a CMO structure using a hypothetical example of an agency pass-through security. We have called this the "Agency 7% issue". The structuring bank then creates instruments to meet particular requirements. A series of sequential-pay CMOs are created first, which is typical but most frequent under expectations of stable interest and prepayment rates. The last of this series of issues is a Z-bond, aimed at investors who believe that interest rates will rise, and hence that prepayment rates will fall. Part of the cash flows from the Z-bond issue are used to provide principal payments to support a VADM issue. These are offered to investors who wish to purchase bonds that have the greatest protection against an extension in their average life. The structuring bank then creates an IO bond by stripping some of the interest cash flows. This may be done before or after the creation of any further issues. Assume that $^1/_2$% of the coupon is stripped, leaving the original bond now with a coupon of $6^1/_2$%. The different classes of instrument are shown in Figure 18.3.

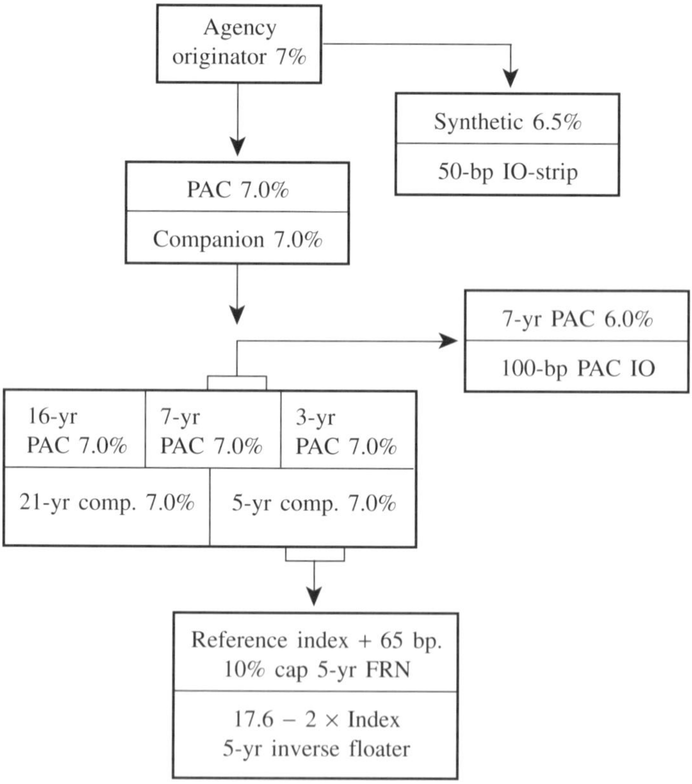

Figure 18.3 Hypothetical example of a CMO structure

In Figure 18.4 we show an alternative structure that might be set up in a different interest rate environment. If the market believes that interest rates and prepayment rates will experience high volatility levels, the structuring bank may create instead a series of PACs (or TACs) and companion bonds. A share of the collateral is used to create the PACs and their companions, with a range of maturities (measured as average lives). In addition, a floating-rate bond is created to meet demand from overseas investors, which is created from the five-year companion issue. The floating-rate bond is issued in conjunction with an inverse floater bond. The final element is an instrument created to meet the requirement of an investor who wishes to purchase a bond with lower coupon together with a strip. The seven-year PAC is used for this and split into the two new issues.

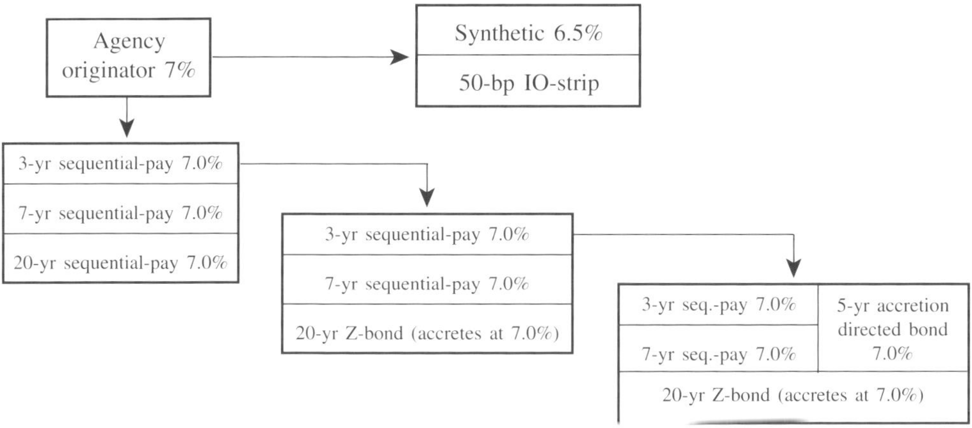

Figure 18.4 Alternative CMO structure

The examples illustrated in Figures 18.3 and 18.4 are an indication of how flexible CMO structures can be, and they are suitable for a wide range of investors with varying requirements.

Non-agency CMO bonds

There are no significant differences in the structure and terms of non-agency CMOs compared to agency CMOs. The key feature of non-agency CMOs, however, is that they are not guaranteed by government agencies, and so carry an element of credit risk, in the same way that corporate bonds expose investors to credit risk. To attract investors, therefore, most non-agency CMOs incorporate an element of *credit enhancement* designed to improve the credit standing of the issue. The use of credit enhancement usually results in a triple-A rating; indeed, a large majority of non-agency CMOs are triple-A rated, with very few falling below a double-A rating. All of the four main private credit rating agencies are involved in credit analysis and rating of non-agency CMOs. The rating granted to a particular issue of CMOs is dependent on a range of factors, which include:

- the term of the underlying loans;
- the size of the loans, whether *conforming* or *jumbo* (agency mortgages do not include mortgages above a certain stated size, whereas non-agency issues often are comprised of larger size loans known as *jumbo loans*);
- the interest basis for the loans, whether level-pay fixed-rate, variable or other type;
- the type of property;
- the geographical area within which the loans have been made;
- the purpose behind the loans, whether a first purchase or a refinancing.

In this section we discuss the credit enhancement facility that is used in non-agency CMOs.

Credit enhancements

CMOs are arranged with either an external or internal credit enhancement. An *external* credit enhancement is a guarantee made by a third party to cover losses on the issue. Usually, a set amount of the issue is guaranteed, such as 25%, rather than the entire issue. The guarantee can take the form of a letter of credit, bond insurance or *pool insurance*. A pool insurance policy would be written to insure against losses that arose as a result of default, usually for a cash amount of cover that would remain in place during the life of the pool. Certain policies are set up so that the cash coverage falls in value during the life of the bond. Pool insurance is provided by specialised agencies. Note that only defaults and foreclosures are included in the policy, which forces investors to arrange further cover if they wish to be protected for any other type of loss. A CMO issue that obtains credit enhancement from an external party still has an element of credit risk, but is now linked to the fortunes of the provider of insurance. That is, the issue is at risk from a deterioration in the credit quality of the provider of insurance. Investors who purchase non-agency CMOs must ensure that they are satisfied with the credit quality of the third-party guarantor, as well as the quality of the underlying mortgage pool. Note that an external credit enhancement has no impact on the cash flow structure of the CMO.

Internal credit enhancements generally have more complex arrangements and sometimes also affect the cash flow structures of the instruments themselves. The two most common types of internal credit enhancement are *reserve funds* and a senior/subordinated structure.

- *Reserve funds*. There are two types of reserve funds. A *cash reserve fund* is a deposit of cash that has been built up from payments arising from the issue of the bonds. A portion of the profits made when the bonds were initially issued are placed in a separate fund. The fund in turn places this cash in short-term bank deposits. The cash reserve fund is used in the event of default to compensate investors who have suffered capital loss. It is often set up in conjunction with another credit enhancement product, such as a letter of credit. An *excess servicing spread account* is also a separate fund, generated from excess spread after all the payments of the mortgage have been made; that is, the coupon, servicing fee and other expenses. For instance, if an issue has a gross weighted average coupon of 7.50%, and the service fee is 0.10% and the net weighted average coupon is 7.25%, then the excess servicing amount is 0.15%. This amount is paid into the spread account, and will grow steadily during the bond's life. The funds in the account can be used to pay off any losses arising from the bond that affect investors.
- *Senior/subordinated structure*. This is the most common type of internal credit enhancement method encountered in the market. Essentially, it involves a bond ranking below the CMO that absorbs all the losses arising from default, or other causes, leaving the main issue unaffected. The subordinated bond clearly has the higher risk attached to it, so it trades at a higher yield. Most senior/subordinated arrangements also incorporate a "shifting interest structure". This arranges for prepayments to be redirected from the subordinated class to the senior class. Hence, it alters the cash flow characteristics of the senior notes, irrespective of the presence of defaults or otherwise.

Commercial mortgage-backed securities

The mortgage-backed bond market includes a sector of securities that are backed by commercial, as opposed to residential, mortgages. These are known as *commercial mortgage-backed securities* (CMBS). They trade essentially as other mortgage securities, but there are detail differences in their structure, which are summarised in this section.

Issuing a CMBS

As with a residential mortgage security, a CMBS is created from a pool or "trust" of commercial mortgages, with the cash flows of the bond backed by the interest and principal payments of the underlying mortgages. A commercial mortgage is a loan made to finance or refinance the purchase of a commercial (business) property. There is a market in the direct purchase of a commercial loan book in addition to the more structured CMBS transaction. An issue of CMBS is rated in the same way as a residential mortgage security and usually has a credit enhancement arrangement to raise its credit rating. The credit rating of a CMBS takes into account the size of the issue as well as the level of credit enhancement support.

Classes of bonds in a CMBS structure are usually arranged in a sequential pay series, and bonds are retired in line with their rating in the structure; the highest rated bonds are paid off first.

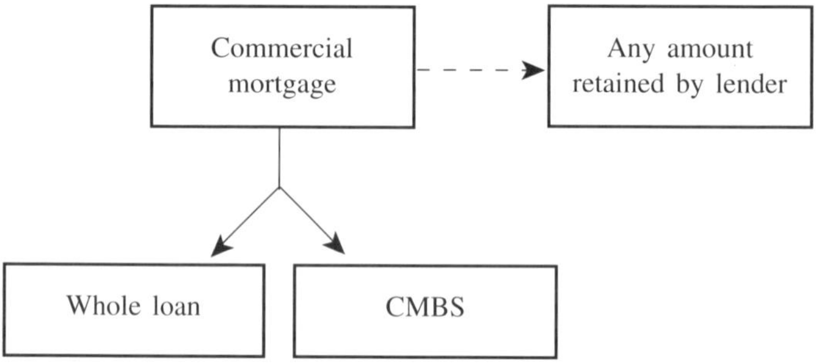

Figure 18.5 Commercial mortgage security issue

Commercial mortgages impose a penalty on borrowers if they are redeemed early, usually in the form of an interest charge on the final principal. There is no such penalty in the US residential mortgage market, although early retirement fees are still a feature of residential loans in the United Kingdom. The early payment protection in a commercial loan can have other forms as well, such as a prepayment "lockout", which is a contractual arrangement that prevents early retirement. This early prepayment protection is repeated in a CMBS structure, and may be in the form of call protection of the bonds themselves. There is already a form of protection in the ratings of individual issues in the structure, because the highest rated bonds are paid off first. That is, the triple-A rated bonds will be retired ahead of the double-A rated bonds, and so on. The highest rated bonds in a CMBS structure also have the highest protection from default of any of the underlying mortgages, which means that losses of principal arising from default will affect the lowest rated bond first.

As well as the early retirement protection, commercial mortgages differ from residential loans in that many of them are *balloon* mortgages. A balloon loan is one on which only the interest is paid, or only a small amount of the principal is paid as well as the interest, so that all or a large part of the loan remains to be paid off on the maturity date. This makes CMBSs potentially similar to conventional vanilla bonds (which are also sometimes called "bullet" bonds) and so attractive to investors who prefer less uncertainty on term to maturity of a bond.

Types of CMBS structures

In the US market there are currently five types of CMBS structures. They are:

- liquidating trusts;
- multi-property single borrower;
- multi-property conduit;
- multi-property non-conduit;
- single-property single-borrower.

We briefly describe the three most common structures here.

- *Liquidating trusts.* This sector of the market is relatively small by value and represents bonds issued against non-performing loans, hence the other name of *non-performing CMBS.* The market is structured in a slightly different way to regular commercial mortgage securities. The features include a *fast-pay structure*, which states that all cash flows from the mortgage pool be used to redeem the most senior bond first, and *overcollateralisation*, which is when the value of bonds created is significantly lower than the value of the underlying loans. This overcollateralisation results in bonds being paid off sooner. Due to the nature of the asset backing for liquidating CMBSs, bonds are usually issued with relatively short average lives, and will receive cash flows on only a portion of the loans. A target date for paying off is set and in the event that the target is not met, the bonds usually have a provision to raise the coupon rate. This acts as an incentive for the borrower to meet the retirement target.

- *Multi-property single borrower.* The single borrower/multi-property structure is an important and large-size part of the CMBS market. The special features of these bonds include *cross-collateralisation*, which is when properties that are used as collateral for individual loans are pledged against each loan. Another feature, known as *cross-default,* allows the lender to call each loan in the pool if any one of them defaults. Since cross-collateralisation and cross-default links all the properties together, sufficient cash flow is available to meet the collective debt on all of the loans. This influences the grade of credit rating that is received for the issue. A *property release provision* in the structure is set up to protect the investor against the lender removing or prepaying the stronger loans in the book. Another common protection against this risk is a clause in the structure terms that prevents the issuer from substituting one property for another.
- *Multi-borrower/conduit.* A *conduit* is a commercial lending entity that has been set up solely to generate collateral to be used in securitisation deals. The major investment banks have all established conduit arms. Conduits are responsible for originating collateral that meets requirements on loan type (whether amortising or balloon, and so on), loan term, geographic spread of the properties and the time that the loans were struck. Generally, a conduit will want to have a diversified range of underlying loans, known as *pool diversification*, with a wide spread of location and size. A diversified pool reduces the default risk for the investor. After it has generated the collateral, the conduit then structures the deal, on terms as similar to CMOs but with the additional features described in this section.

Auto-loan-backed securities

Description

Bonds issued against car loan finance are known as *auto-loan-backed securities* (auto-ABS) in the United States or simply as *car-loans* in the United Kingdom. The auto-loan-backed market in the United States is one of the largest in the asset-backed market. It is also one of the oldest sectors, with the first deal being issued in May 1985.[3] Auto-loans are amortising private loans in the manner of residential mortgages, but are typically of much shorter duration than mortgages and carry no prepayment risk. This makes bonds that are issued against them attractive instruments for investors who are seeking more stable, shorter dated paper of high credit quality but yielding more than Treasury bonds. As they are more straightforward, their analysis presents fewer problems than other asset-backed securities. Up to the middle of 1998 approximately $170 billion of auto-loan bonds had been issued in the United States, and the sector is a liquid and fairly transparent one.

Car loans in the United States are short-term amortising deals, ranging from three to six years in maturity. The average maturity is four years. Loans are made either direct at the dealership, in which case finance is supplied by an arm of the car manufacturer, or at a commercial (retail) bank. In the United Kingdom, car loans are of two types: the amortising loan from a bank, or a bullet loan usually taken from a finance house, known as leasing. Both types of loans are used as collateral in a car-loan bond issue. The US car loan market is dominated by the "Big Three" car manufacturers: General Motors, Ford Motor Corporation and Chrysler Corporation, who issued over 36% of all auto-ABS in 1998. The large commercial banks are also big issuers of auto-ABS bonds, and include Capital One, NationsBank and Chase Manhattan. Independent finance companies make up the third category of issuers, companies such as Western Financial and Union Acceptance Corporation. The independent houses are much more reliant on the auto-ABS market and can fund their books at lower rates directly as a result, since they create AAA securities out of securitised car loans that pay a lower yield than their individual credit standings would allow. To achieve a high credit rating most auto-ABS issues are structured with a form of credit enhancement. The most common form of enhancement is a senior/subordinated structure, similar to mortgage-backed bonds, although letters of credit and over-collateralisation are also used.

The underlying assets in an auto-ABS issue are bank or finance house car loans, which may be purchased or originated by a special purpose vehicle called a *special purpose corporation* (SPC). Interest payments from the original borrowers are passed to investors via the SPC. There are two main types of auto-ABS bonds: pass-through securities and *pay-through* securities. The majority of issues are pass-throughs.

---

[3] Statistics in this section are sourced from Zimmerman (1996) in Bhattacharya and Fabozzi (1996), Chapter 31 and *Asset-Backed News*, 2000 and 2001.

The prepayment risk on auto-ABS bonds is low. Car loans have a very low response to changes in market interest rates, and loans are rarely repaid ahead of the maturity date. Auto-ABS bonds therefore do not exhibit the negative convexity of mortgage-backed bonds. There are non-interest-rate reasons why prepayment might occur, however, such as customers "trading up" to another car, or theft or destruction of the vehicle.

Yield spreads

The structure of auto-ABS bonds is relatively straightforward compared to other asset-backed securities, and possibly simpler than credit card-backed securities. They are amortising bonds (in the United States) but because they have little prepayment risk they do not exhibit negative convexity. They are also shorter dated securities compared to other ABS issues; most auto pass-throughs have average lives of 1.8 to 2.2 years, which is considerably lower than mortgage bonds. The yield spread over Treasury securities for auto-ABS issues is tighter than mortgage securities, but slightly over that for credit card securities. During 1996 they typically yielded around 10–25 basis points over credit card securities, and on average 30–40 basis points below manufactured housing mortgage securities. The market places a premium on auto-ABS bonds issued by the independent finance companies, which trade at around 5–10 basis points above issues made by the Big Three manufacturers and the commercial banks.

Tranche issues	**Date**	**Amount ($m)**	**Average life (years)**	**Spread (bps)**
Premier 1996-1	21-Mar-96	1,250	2.0	34
Olympic 1996-A	07-Mar-96	600	2.0	40
Western Finance 1996-A	21-Mar-96	484	2.0	42
Pass-throughs				
Chase 1996-A	14-Feb-96	1,474	1.6	41
Banc One 1996-A	15-Feb-96	537	1.6	42
Fifth Third 1996-A	19-Mar-96	408	1.7	43
UAC 1996-A	09-Feb-96	203	1.9	49

Table 18.2 Auto-ABS issues during 1996
Source: Zimmerman, T. 1997, "Auto-loan-backed securities", in Fabozzi, F. (ed.), *The Handbook of Fixed Income Securities*, 5th edition, McGraw-Hill. Used with permission.

This is illustrated in Table 18.2. The Olympic 1996-A and Western Finance 1996-A were issued by independent finance houses, as was the UAC 1996-A. Note that each of these traded at a yield that was 6–8 basis points higher than the others, which were issued by commercial banks, although their relatively small issue will impact in their liquidity, for which there is a small yield premium.

Auto-ABS bonds have a wider range of payment windows than comparable securities and this makes their relative value more closely related to the shape of the yield curve. Securities such as credit card ABS bonds provide a higher return in an environment with a steeply positive short-date yield curve, due to their "roll down" effect, so that in a steepening yield curve scenario auto-ABS bonds will be outperformed by credit card securities. This reflects that in a stable yield curve environment auto-ABS bonds will achieve a higher total return, compared to their spread, than credit card securities.

Credit card-backed securities

Another large sector in the asset-backed market is the credit card market. It experienced steady growth during the 1990s, with over $369 billion nominal outstanding in June 1998.[4] The rise in credit card securitisation reflects the increasing use of credit cards by consumers, such that is now a significant national economic indicator. The public are now able to pay for a large number of goods and services using credit cards, and as a payment medium they are increasingly used for regular, "day-to-day" purchases as well as larger size one-off transactions. The first example of a credit card securitisation was in 1987 in the US domestic market, as banks sought to move credit card assets off their balance sheets, thus freeing up lending lines, and diversify their funding sources. The first banks to securitise their credit card books were Capital One, MBNA and Advanta, among others. They were able to benefit from funding at triple-A rates, due to the credit enhancement used on the bond structures and consequently low charges on their capital. The largest issuers of credit card-backed bonds in the US market are shown at Table 18.3 below.

[4] The source of the statistical data in this section is *Asset-Backed Alert*, *www.asset-backedalert.com*

Securitising banks	$ billion
Citibank	41.5
MBNA America	22.3
Discover	13.6
First USA	12.1
First Chicago	11.9
Household	10.2
Capital One	7.1
Chase Manhattan	6.0
Advanta	5.1

Table 18.3 Largest issuers of credit card-backed bonds, US domestic market, June 1998
Source: Chase Manhattan.

Credit card ABS bonds, along with auto-ABS issues, remain the most accessible instruments for investors who are interested in having an exposure to the asset-backed market. As they have maturities that are shorter than the average lives of mortgage-backed securities, as well as cash flow patterns that are more akin to conventional bonds, they are attractive investments to institutions such as banks and money market funds. In the United States, and increasingly in the United Kingdom and Europe, the combination of credit card, auto-loan and mortgage-backed securities means that there are highly rated asset-backed instruments, paying reasonable spreads over government securities, available along the entire yield curve.

Issuing structures

In the US market there are two different structures under which credit card debt is securitised. The *stand-alone trust* is a pool of credit card accounts that have been sold to a trust, and then used as collateral for a single security. As with CMOs there are usually several classes of bonds within a single issue. If a subsequent class of bonds is issued, the issuer must designate a new pool of *receivables* and sell these card accounts to a separate trust. This structure was used at the start of the market, but has been all but replaced by the *master trust*, which is a structure that allows the securitising bank to issue successive securities from the same trust, which are all backed by the same pool of credit card loan collateral. Under this arrangement the issuer retains greater flexibility for issuing securities, and without the cost associated with setting up a new trust each time a new issue is required.

EXAMPLE 18.2 Credit Card ABS master trust structure

An issuing bank transfers the cash flows represented by 100,000 credit card accounts, with a nominal value of $200 million, to a separate trust. It then issues different classes of securities, with different coupons, maturities and nominal values, all backed by the same collateral. At a later date the issuer requires further funding. It transfers the receivables from more card accounts to the same trust and issues more securities. The different tranches of receivables, transferred at two different times, are not differentiated from one another and are not segregated; that is, the combined receivables in the trust back all the bond issues made against the trust.

As a master trust will comprise receivables transferred to it over time, it will contain cash flows that have different payment terms and interest rates (or *annual payment rate* [APR], used in quoting credit card interest rates), reflecting the terms and conditions of cards issued at different times. For instance, a bank may issue cards under a special low interest rate as part of a special promotion designed to attract new customers. New cardholders will have accounts with different terms and cash flows to existing card holders. Investors in credit card ABS must be aware therefore that the composition of accounts in a master trust pool are liable to alter over time, sometimes significantly, as existing cardholder accounts are closed or fall dormant, and as new accounts are added, with or without different terms and conditions.

Issuers of credit card ABS in the US market are required to retain ownership, or a shared ownership, in the trust. This is so the issuer can ensure that fluctuations in the balance of the receivables due to seasonal factors, as well as factors such as returned goods and credit card fraud, can be handled. It is also an incentive for the issuer to maintain the credit quality of the pool. The participation level is set at the minimum level of the receivables balance in the trust, which is 7% in the US market. This minimum level is set at 10% in the UK market and for sterling credit card ABS. If the level of its participation falls below the minimum required, the issuer must add further credit card accounts to the trust.

The issuing structure for credit card ABS is similar irrespective of the type of trust that is used. Generally, there are three types of cash flow periods: *revolving, amortisation* (or otherwise *accumulation*) and *early amortisation*. Each period generates a different cash flow. This structure essentially replicates a conventional plain vanilla bond, with regular coupon payments and a single redemption amount on maturity, sometimes called the *bullet* payment. The main difference however is that credit card ABS pay monthly interest, instead of the traditional semi-annual interest basis. Credit card bonds also differ from other asset-backed securities because they do not have an amortising payment structure. Such an arrangement would not be appropriate for credit card bonds, since the average life of a receivable is shorter, ranging from between five to ten months. Under the amortising structure, which is used for mortgage-backed bonds and some auto-ABS bonds, payments of principal and interest are passed directly to investors each month. This would lead to an uncertain and volatile payment structure for credit card bonds. Therefore a revolving structure is used instead, with all cash flows being split into interest payments and principal payments. The monthly interest payment is used to cover the coupon on the bond. Also, cash flow that remains after this liability has been discharged, known as *excess spread*, is passed to the issuer or seller. The collection of principal differs according to the payment period, which is reviewed below.

- *Revolving period.* The revolving period in the structure is not fixed, and has ranged from two to eleven years. During the period, bondholders receive only interest payments, when monthly payments of principal are used to purchase new receivables in accounts held in the trust; if there are no new receivables, the cash flows are used to purchase a share of the issuer's participation. If there are insufficient receivables available, this effects an early amortisation, as the issuer's participation would have fallen to below the minimum level. This is an incentive to the issuer to maintain a participation above the minimum.
- *Amortisation/accumulation.* This period starts after the revolving period has ceased. An amortisation or *controlled amortisation*, principal payments are no longer used for reinvestment in more receivables, but instead are used to pay off bondholders in a series of amortisation payments. The size of these payments depends on how long the amortisation period runs for; the usual length is one year, so that investors receive twelve equal amortisation periods over the year. Excess principal payments received during this period are used to

purchase new receivables, similar to the process followed in the revolving period. Accumulation is similar to controlled amortisation, but for investors the results of the process are akin to a conventional bond. The monthly principal payments are deposited in a trust account or *principal funding account* over the twelve-month period, and then paid out to bondholders as one lump sum on the maturity date. During this time, interest payments are made each month on the balance of the total invested amount. Accumulation is therefore attractive to investors who wish the redemption payment to be a single bullet payment, and during the process they will not notice any change as the bond moves from the revolving period to the accumulation period.

- *Early amortisation.* An early amortisation is not a planned event, and is triggered if there is decline in asset quality, or the issuer is found to be in financial trouble. The bonds enter into an early amortisation so that investors start to receive their principal immediately, and not be subject to delays in repayment that might otherwise occur. The terms under which credit card ABS deals are issued specify a range of events that, if they occur, will cause the issue to enter early amortisation. These include failure to make required interest payments, failure to transfer receivables to the trust when required, and certain events of bankruptcy and default connected with the issuer. Other triggering events include if the excess spread falls to zero, and if the issuer's participation level falls below the minimum level. The occurrence of early amortisation is a rare event.

Credit enhancement

Bonds issued against credit card receivables are unsecured in that the receivables provide no collateral if cardholders default. Credit card bonds require therefore some form of credit enhancement if they are to receive investment-grade credit ratings, and the majority of them are highly rated once the enhancement has been set up. In this section we briefly describe the main types of credit enhancement that are arranged for credit card issues; many structures have two or more of these enhancements.

- *Excess spread.* The excess spread payment is the amount of cash flow over and above the amount required to discharge the bond's interest obligations. There is usually a significant excess spread due to the interest rate charged on credit cards being substantially higher than money market and bond market interest rates. For example, the average credit card APR in the United Kingdom market during 1998 was over 19%, and sometimes as high as 23%. This means that once the coupon on the bond has been issued and service and other charges paid, there is usually a substantial excess spread, often as high as 5%. The excess spread is used in one or more ways, including to pay the fees of credit enhancement institutions, being deposited in a trust reserve account or being released to the issuer.

- *Senior/subordinated notes.* Issues are often split into different classes of bonds, to suit investor taste. A common credit enhancement is the senior/subordinated structure, with bonds split into higher and lower rated issues. The subordinated notes absorb the losses in the structure ahead of the senior notes, if any other credit enhancement features have not proved sufficient. On maturity or early amortisation, the senior notes will be repaid ahead of the subordinated notes. The latter trade at a higher yield as a result.
- *Letter of credit.* As with other asset-backed markets, a bank letter of credit is a common form of credit enhancement used in the credit card market. This is a guarantee from a bank to provide payment in the event that the trust is unable to meet the commitments of the bond issue. The bank guarantee is up to an amount stipulated in the letter of credit. A fee is payable to the bank for providing the letter. This type of enhancement has proved less popular in recent years, after some issuers were themselves downgraded, leading to a downgrading of assets that they had provided letters of credit against.
- *Cash collateral account.* This is a segregated bank account for the benefit of the trust. It is set up and funded at the time of the issue, and funds in it may be used to cover occasions when there is insufficient payments received to cover required interest and principal payments. The funds in the account are borrowed from a third-party bank, and the terms of the issue usually provide for repayment of the cash collateral account only after all the bonds in the issue have been repaid. The excess spread may also be used to fund or top-up the account.
- *Collateral invested amount.* The collateral invested amount, also known as *collateral interest* or *enhancement invested amount*, is a share of ownership in the trust and works in the same way as the cash collateral account. It is usually placed with a third-party bank, and is also funded by part of the excess spread.

Credit analysis

Credit card ABS are rated by the four major credit ratings agencies, in the same way as other asset-backed bonds. The variables in the credit card market mean that there are a larger number of scenarios that the agencies must consider. For example, the quality of a pool of credit card receivables is a function of (among other issues) the:

- type of credit cards in the pool, whether standard, low-rate, affinity cards, store cards, and so on;
- credit scoring model used by the card issuer;
- interest rates charged on the cards, whether fixed or floating, and the frequency with which rates are changed or re-set;
- amount of dormant cards in the pool;
- behaviour of cardholders in the pool;
- yield on the portfolio;
- monthly payment rate, which will fluctuate as the number of accounts changes, or as cardholders pay a smaller amount of their balance each month or pay off balances entirely;
- coupon on the bonds: a floating coupon on the bond is more at risk if it is backed with card receivables that are fixed rate, and vice-versa.

The credit rating a bond issue receives will also consider the possibility that it will be forced into early amortisation. This is separate to the issue of credit enhancement, and unaffected by it. The rating of a credit card issue indicates the likelihood that the issue will be able to redeem in full all the bonds in the structure under any possible scenario. A triple-A rating indicates that investors should receive all their principal.

Static spread analysis of asset-backed bonds

It is apparent that the traditional gross redemption yield or YTM method for measuring the return available from a particular instrument, and its relative value compared to the government yield curve, is not appropriate in the case of asset-backed bonds. In order to calculate a meaningful redemption yield measure, the cash flows for a particular instrument must be known with a degree of certainty. This is not the case for many asset-backed securities. The inaccuracy of the redemption yield measure also must take into account the fact that, even for conventional bonds, it ignores the reinvestment and dispersion of coupon payments, discounting them all at the same rate. This is, to all and intents and purposes, glossed over for conventional bonds because the calculation treats all bonds the same, creating in effect a level-playing field.

Asset-backed bonds have subtle differences in cash flow profiles and prepayment rates, making it more difficult to analyse them all in the same way. The exception to this is most credit card–ABS issues, which have a single bullet payment on maturity and (usually, but not always) a fixed-coupon payment every month. It would be in order to compare the yield on such a bond with a conventional corporate bond. Other asset-backed issues such as mortgage and car loan securities do not have such a stable cash flow, mainly due to the amortising nature of the underlying loans. The simplest way to analyse these securities is to price them as a spread to the yield of the government bond whose maturity is closest to the weighted average life of the bonds being analysed. This is still an approximate measure and can be inaccurate under certain circumstances, and the convention now is to use the *static spread* measure.

Static spread analysis

Static spread analysis assumes that a particular bond itself represents a portfolio of individual securities, so that each cash flow is viewed as a zero-coupon bond. Under the static spread method each of these individual cash flows is discounted using a rate made up of the relevant government zero-coupon rate plus a spread. The spot rate used is the one whose duration matches that of the specific cash flow.[5] The spread at which the sum of the discounted cash flows equalled their nominal price is known as the static spread, *zero-volatility spread,* or *Z-spread.*

This is illustrated with the following example, which uses three hypothetical securities. The first bond (Bond A) has a maturity of one year (twelve months), while the remaining bonds B and C have average maturities of twelve months. Bond A has a single bullet redemption payment in exactly twelve months' time, exemplified by a conventional corporate bond or certain credit card-backed bonds. Bond B repays its principal over a twelve-month period beginning six months from now, similar to a credit card-backed bond that has a controlled amortisation process. Bond C has an

[5] In the United States, United Kingdom and certain European markets there is a market in zero-coupon government bonds, known as strips. Therefore it is straightforward to find the appropriate spot rate to use in discounting the asset-backed bond cash flows, although banks frequently use an implied spot-rate curve because of liquidity effects of the observed zero-coupon curve. In the absence of an actual strip market, the implied spot rate calculated from the benchmark government bond yield curve is used.

amortising principal repayment pattern, so that the amount of repayment declines gradually starting in the next month and finishing 21 months from now. This bond resembles an auto-ABS bond and certain mortgage pass-through securities. The principal payment cash flows are shown as Figures 18.6 (a), (b) and (c). Assume that all bonds are trading at a yield to maturity of 6.33%. The one-year government bond is trading at a yield of 5.98%, therefore the yield spread on the three bonds is 35 basis points.[6] This spread is also called the *nominal spread*.

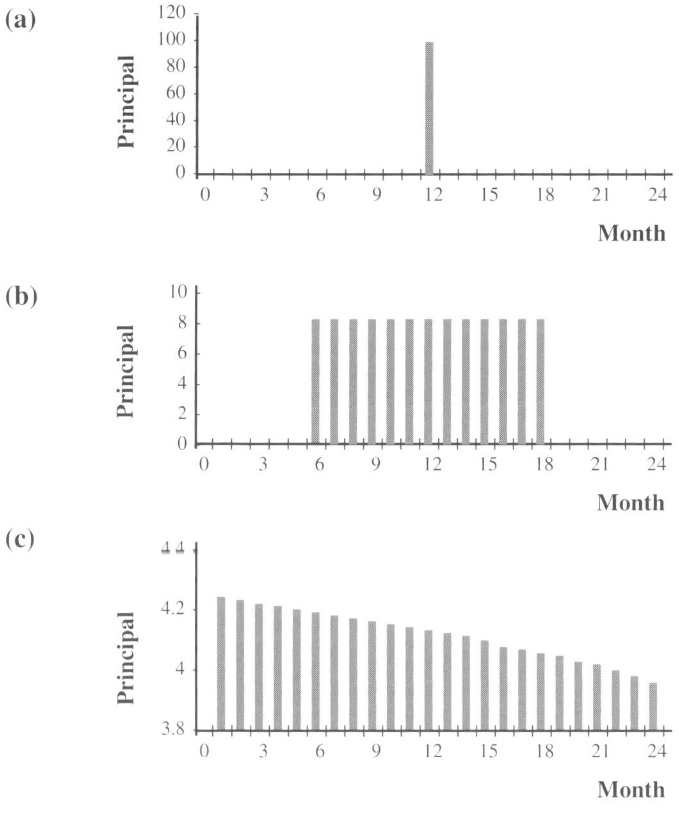

Figure 18.6 Cash flow profiles for bullet, controlled amortisation and amortised principal bonds (a), (b), (c).

[6] The yields are based on market conditions for sterling asset-backed bonds in October 1999, against the gilt yield curve at that time.

We know that the redemption yield calculation discounts each cash flow at the internal rate of return, here 6.33%, which has been based on the average maturity of twelve months for receipt of the principal. In a positively sloping short-term yield curve environment, cash flows received early on would be discounted at a rate that was above the actual rate for that term, while cash flows received later would be discounted at a rate that was below the actual rate. This is an accepted drawback of the redemption yield method, and is accepted on the belief that the two effects will cancel each other out.

The static spread gives a more accurate picture yield. Assume that the short-term zero-coupon yield curve is as follows, as shown in Figure 18.7:

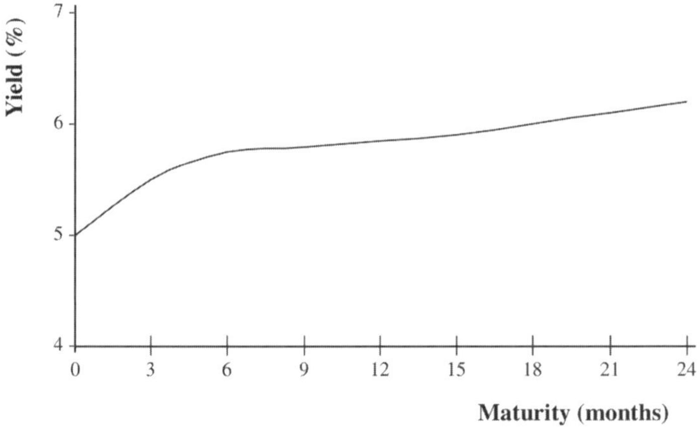

Figure 18.7 Short-term yield curve

This is obtained by observing the yield of government discount instruments in the market. If we use the relevant yields from this curve to discount each of the principal cash flows for bonds A, B and C, the static spreads that are obtained, in the case of bonds B and C, differ from the nominal spread. This is because using this method more accurately captures the value of each cash flow over the period that they are received. The static spreads are shown in Table 18.4.

	Bond A	Bond B	Bond C
Nominal spread	35	35	35
Static spread	35	30	28

Table 18.4 Static and nominal spreads of hypothetical bonds A, B and C

What is behind the difference in spreads for the two bonds with non-bullet principal repayment? Essentially, these bonds, when based on an average maturity yield level plus spread, are over-valued. This is because cash flows received after the average maturity date are more sensitive to the discount rate which, using the twelve-month yield, is below the actual rate in a positive yield curve environment. To allow for the lower present value of the individual cash flows to equate the higher price of the cash flows obtained using the single average maturity yield, the spread used to discount each cash flow must be lower. This is the static spread. Bond C has the greatest difference between the nominal spread and the static spread, because the cash flows are dispersed over a longer period, making each cash flow more sensitive to the discount rate used to obtain its present value. There is no difference in the two spreads for bond A, because the cash flow has been discounted at the correct rate.

In a positively sloped yield curve environment, the static spread on an amortising security will be lower than the nominal yield spread, while it will be higher than the nominal yield spread in a negative yield curve environment. The extent of the difference between the static spread and the nominal spread is a function of the slope of the yield curve and the dispersion of the bond's cash flows.

Yield analysis of asset-backed securities must take into account their uncertain cash flows. We have demonstrated that the traditional redemption yield measure, calculated using the security's average life maturity, is inappropriate, because it does not allow for the dispersed nature of the bond's cash. A mortgage or auto-loan-backed bond has a principal repayment structure that disperses the payments over a length of time, so the more accurate yield measure to use is static spread. As well as accounting for dispersion, this approach also overcomes the traditional drawback of YTM as it discounts each cash flow at the correct rate for that cash flow's maturity.

Synthetic ABS

The advent of a liquid and reasonably transparent market in credit derivatives has meant that investors are now looking at synthetic access to the ABS market. Credit derivatives are a separate topic in their own right,[1] we provide a basic introduction to them in Appendix 20.1 in this book. In Chapter 20 we also discuss CDS on MBS issues. To complete this chapter we also provide background on credit default swaps (CDS) written on ABS. This is a relatively recent market, with the first products being made available to investors in 2004. The demand for synthetic assets arose from a shortage of ABS paper in the cash market that year.

Credit derivatives and ABS markets

Credit derivatives markets have expanded rapidly since the first instruments were introduced in 1994. They have now been extended into the asset-backed and mortgage-backed markets, mainly due to the shortage of paper in the cash market. The standardisation of CDS contracts and trading terminology also facilitated the expansion of credit derivatives into structured finance markets.

There are a number of detail differences between ABS credit risk and corporate credit risk. A single-name corporate CDS transacted under the standard 2003 ISDA Credit Derivatives definitions[2] will be based on clearly defined trigger events ("credit events") and a transparent process of settlement, either physical or cash settlement. A CDS written on an ABS issue can present problematic issues with regard to both these items. Corporate CDS trigger events are, following some initial problems with definitions, straightforward to describe. They include bankruptcy, failure to pay, debt restructuring and in some cases ratings downgrade. Such occurrences can be identified easily in most cases. Also, the outstanding debt of a corporate entity can be expected to trade at roughly the same level in the event of issuer default, irrespective of coupon or maturity.

Structured finance securities such as ABS and MBS differ in both these respects. The key difference is that unlike corporate bonds, most ABS are issued by special purposes vehicles (SPVs), bankruptcy-remote legal entities

1 For instance see the author's book *Structured Credit Products: Credit Derivatives and Synthetic Securitisation* (John Wiley & Sons Asia) 2004

2 See www.isda.org

created solely for the purpose of facilitating the bond issue. Bankruptcy and restructuring rarely, if ever, apply to SPVs. Also it may be less clear in the case of an SPV that there has been a failure to pay. Unlike corporate entities, credit ratings of SPVs are based essentially on the quality of the underlying assets. The repayment of these assets is not known with certainty which is why ABS bonds are given long legal final maturities. Other issues that complicate the matter of CDS on ABS include the following:

- ABS structures with an element of uncertain cashflow patterns include the provision for the write-down of principal in the event of losses. This does not always constitute a "default" as the write-down can be reversed and made good later;
- many ABS structures allow for a delay in interest payment, for example during a time when the excess spread in the vehicle has been reduced. Again this may not constitute default and may not necessarily lead instantly to a ratings downgrade as the interest coverage may be expected to become sufficient again;
- the structure represents a distinct pool of assets, ring-fenced within the SPV. This contrasts with the general pool of assets represented in a corporate entity;
- it is quite possible for the more junior tranches of an ABS issue to be in default while the senior tranches are not, again representing the way the asset pool is performing.

The significant difference therefore, between an ABS CDS and a single-name corporate CDS is that the former is written against a specific security, while the latter is written at an entity level on a corporate name. However writing a contract on a specific security means that physical settlement on occurrence of a credit event is impractical. For this reason physical settlement is not used. Cash settlement may also be problematic because of the difficulty with ascertaining the market value of the ABS tranche. A new type of CDS, the pay-as-you-go CDS (PAUG CDS) has been developed for this market.

Pay-as-you-go CDS

PAUG credit default swaps have been developed to meet the distinct requirements of synthetic investment in ABS issues. A PAUG CDS acts like a standard CDS, with provision for termination on occurrence of specified credit events. The protection buyer pays a fixed basis point fee to the protection seller, which is also standard. However the PAUG contract also permits the following:

- payment of an additional floating payment from protection seller to protection buyer in event of principal write-down;
- payment of a fixed payment from protection buyer to protection seller in event of write-up;
- provision of altering cash flows in event of interest shortfall of ABS vehicle.

To illustrate, consider the case where the performance of the underlying asset pool in an ABS, due to underperformance or default, means that the principal amount of one or more of the overlying note tranches must be reduced.[3] The protection seller would make a floating payment to the protection buyer to cover this written-down amount. The CDS itself would not terminate. If at a later date the principal balance is reinstated, for example because the portfolio performance has improved, the protection buyer would then make a fixed payment to the seller.

Figure 18.8 illustrates the mechanics of a PAUG CDS in the event of write-down.

A standard CDS would generally cover the following credit events:

- failure to pay;
- credit rating downgrade to sub-investment grade;
- permanent write-down.

A PAUG CDS would also cover the following without being terminated:

- principal write-down;
- interest shortfall;
- failure to pay principal;

By incorporating this flexibility, investors are better able to gain a realistic exposure to the ABS market, albeit synthetically.

[3] This would normally be decided by the Trustee or the Servicer to the transaction.

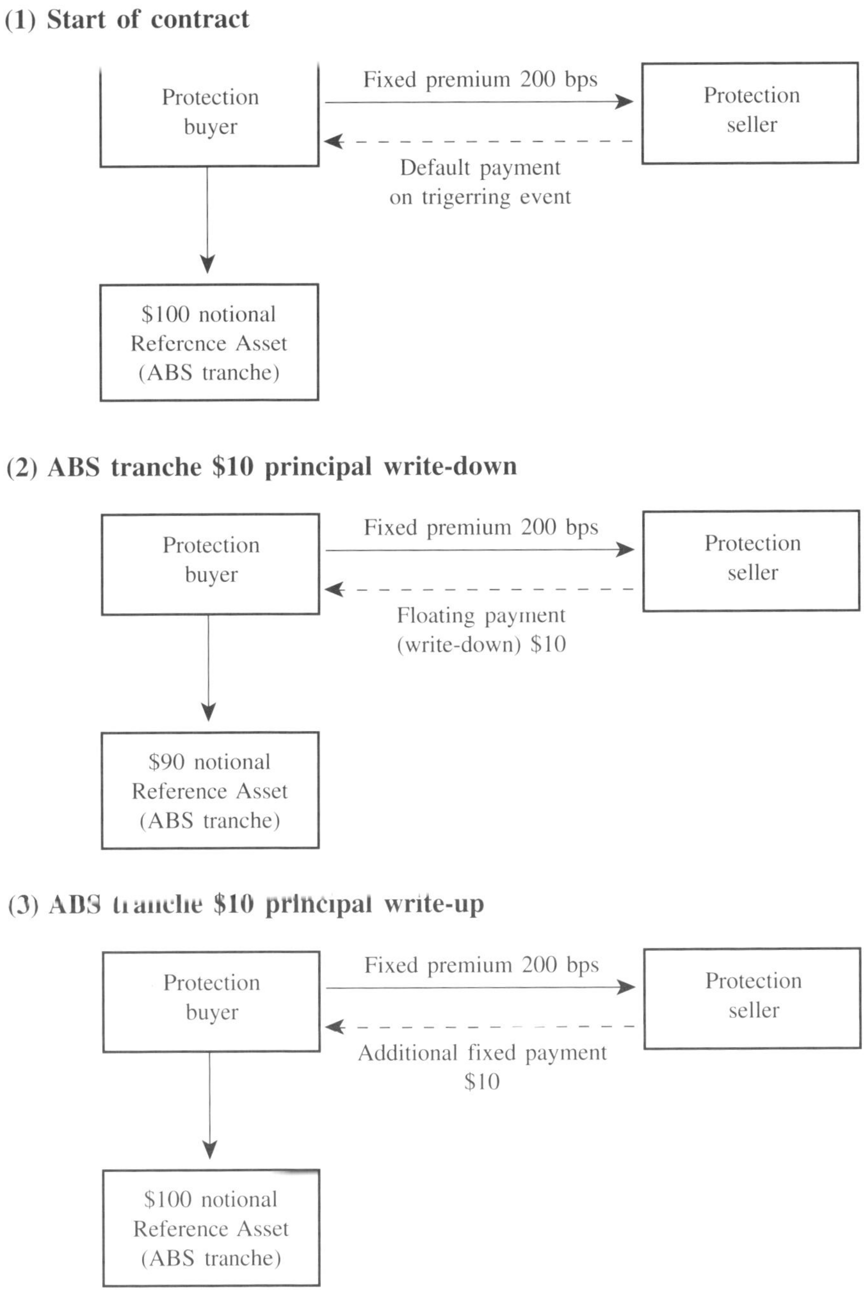

Figure 18.8 PAUG CDS cashflow mechanics in event of ABS note principal write-down

Market considerations

Generally the protection sellers in the ABS CDS market include investors who would normally hold cash ABS bonds. This is marked when there is a shortage of paper in the cash market. The ability to short ABS tranches means that investors can also take a view on ABS credit; previously this woult not necessarily have been straightforward because of the illiquid nature of the ABS repo market. The differences between the corporate and ABS markets are mirrored in the synthetic market. Investors will be aware that corporate entities are dynamic corporations that are proactively able to avoid credit events, which is not the case with SPVs. Synthetic ABS investors must therefore still be concerned primarily with the quality of the underlying collateral and the specific risk/return profile of the individual ABS tranche. Also, there is the issue of prepayment uncertainty. Most corporate bonds have a bullet maturity or fixed redemption date. Non-redemption would constitute a credit event. ABS securities however amortise over time, with the redemption date not known with certainty. (For analysis purposes the *average life* of the ABS note is used, this figure is an estimated repayment term based on an assumed level of prepayments). However, the non-redemption of a tranche in accordance with an average life estimate would not be deemed a credit event.

ABS tranches experience a declining notional balance over time as principal is repaid in stages in the underlying asset pool, due to prepayments and other factors. The outstanding notional value of ABS tranches therefore reduces over time; investors would observe this also occurring with ABS CDS contract notionals as they mirror the behaviour of the cash bond.

ABS CDS and cash bond valuation

In theory the basis between a PAUG CDS and its reference cash bond should be small because the contract mirrors the profile and behaviour of the cash bond closely.[4] In practice a number of market and structural factors cause the cash and synthetic markets to trade at a negative or positive basis. These include the following:

---

[4] See the author's paper, "The credit default swap basis: analysing the relationship between cash and synthetic markets", in the *Journal of Derivatives Use, Trading and Regulation*, Vol 10, Issue 1, June 2004, for more detail on the CDS basis.

- in the synthetic market, the investor is exposed additionally to counterparty risk, as it is the counterparty who is paying the coupon (CDS premium). The cash investor is exposed to the quality of the reference collateral only;
- the ABS CDS is an unfunded instrument and so carries no funding cost; this is an additional factor in relative value analysis;
- supply and demand factors may be more prevalent in the synthetic market, as the availability of protection buyers may be limited (unlike ABS transaction originators in the cash market, there is no natural market for protection buyers in the ABS CDS market outside market makers).

As a relatively new market, the depth and transparency of the ABS CDS market may be limited for certain sectors. This should not be a problem once the market develops.

Selected bibliography and references

Ames, C. 1997, "Collaterialised Mortgage Obligation", in Fabozzi, F. (ed.), *The Handbook of Fixed Income Securities*, 5th edition, McGraw-Hill.

Bear Stearns 1994, *Asset-backed Securities Special Report*, 5 December.

Bhattacharya, A. and Fabozzi, F. (eds) 1996, *Asset-backed Securities*, FJF Associates.

Fabozzi, F. 1998, *Handbook of Structured Financial Products*, FJF Associates.

Fabozzi, F. and Jacob, D. 1996, *The Handbook of Commercial Mortgage-backed Securities*, FJF Associates.

Fabozzi, F., Ramsey, C. and Ramirez, F. 1994, *Collateralized Mortgage Obligations*, FJF Associates.

Oppenheimer & Co. 1994, "Qualitatively assessing prepayments of current- and discount-coupon passthroughs", *Mortgage Research*, Oppenheimer & Co., Inc., 20 October.

When Lennon remarked in 1966 that The Beatles had become "more popular than Jesus", he put his finger on it. The Christian social values of the old culture were then giving way to a life dominated by consumer materialism, an impatient expectation of instant gratification, and a self-before-others ethic that has since fragmented Western society.

– Ian MacDonald
Revolution In The Head: The Beatles Records and the Sixties, Fourth Estate Limited, Revised edition, 1997, p. 336

CHAPTER 19

Collateralised Debt Obligations

Collateralised debt obligations (CDOs) are a form of securitised debt. The market in such bonds emerged in the United States in the late 1980s, first as a form of repackaged high-yield bond. The market experienced sharp growth in the second half of the 1990s, due to a combination of investor demand for higher yields allied to credit protection, and the varying requirements of originators, such as balance sheet management and lower cost funding. The term "CDO" is a generic one, used to cover what are known as *collateralised bond obligations* (CBOs) and *collateralised loan obligations* (CLOs). Put simply, a CBO is an issue of rated securities backed or "collateralised" by a pool of debt securities. A CLO on the other hand is an issue of paper that has been secured by a pool of bank loans. As the market has grown the distinction between the two types of structure has become blurred somewhat. Practitioners have taken to defining different issues in terms of the issuer's motivation, the type of asset backing and the type of market into which the paper is sold; for example, the commercial paper market. Different structures are now more often categorised as being *balance sheet* transactions, usually a securitisation of assets in order to reduce regulatory capital requirements and provide the originator with an alternative source of funding, or *arbitrage* transactions, in which the originator sets up a managed investment vehicle in order to benefit from a funding gap that exits between assets and liabilities. Balance sheet transactions are issuer driven, whereas arbitrage transactions are typically investor driven.

Over $107 billion of CDOs was issued during 1999.[1] This included over $51 billion of CBOs backed by high-yield bonds and just under $45 billion of CLOs. During 1999 the combined CBO/CLO market was thought to account for approximately 18–20% of the total US asset-backed bond market.[2] In this chapter we provide an introduction to the most common CDO structures, as well as an overview of the analysis of these instruments. We also discuss the use of credit derivatives in the CDO market.

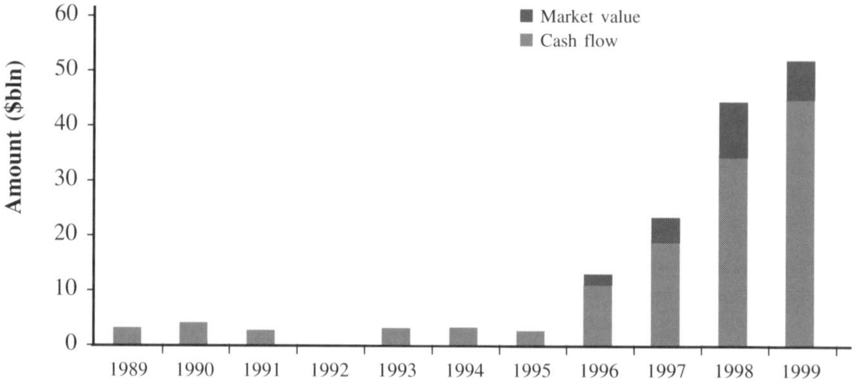

Figure 19.1 CDO issuance 1989–1999
Sources: Moodys, Fitch, Bloomberg.

An overview of CDOs

Introduction

Collateralised debt obligation or CDO is the generic term for two distinct products, so-called balance sheet transactions and arbitrage transactions. The common thread between these structures is that they are both backed by some form of commercial or corporate debt or loan receivable. The primary differences between the two types are the type of collateral backing the

[1] *Source*: *Risk*, 2000. This refers to CDO deals that had been rated by at least one of Moody's, S&P and Fitch rating agencies.

[2] *Risk*, 2000.

newly created securities in the CDO structure, and the motivations behind the transaction. The growth of the market has been in response to two key requirements: the desire of investors for higher yield investments in higher-risk markets, managed by portfolio managers skilled at extracting value out of poorly performing or distressed debt, and the need for banks to extract greater value out of assets on their balance sheet, almost invariably because they are generating a below-market rate of return. By securitising bond or loan portfolios, banks can lower their capital charge by removing them off their balance sheet and funding them at a lower rate. The market has its origins in investor-driven arbitrage transactions, with bank balance sheet transactions a natural progression after the banks applied securitisation techniques to their own asset base. Figure 19.2 is a summary of the key differences between balance sheet arbitrage and CDOs.

Collateralised debt obligations (CDOs)

Balance sheet CDOs	Arbitrage CDOs
Collateral: high-grade, bank-oriented commercial and corporate loans	**Collateral**: high-yield corporate bonds or corporate loans
Key motivations: reducing balance sheet to improve capital ratios; obtain off-balance sheet treatments; obtain lower funding rates	**Key motivations**: arbitrage opportunity; increase assets under management; assets purchased in secondary market
Typical issuers: domestic and international banks	**Typical issuers**: insurance companies; mutual funds; private equity funds
Market liquidity: generally lower than investor-driven trades	

Figure 19.2 Collateralised debt obligations

Balance sheet CDOs are structured securities that are usually backed with bank-originated, investment-grade commercial and corporate loans. Since this form of collateral is almost invariably loans, and very rarely bonds, these transactions are usually referred to as collateralised loan obligations or CLOs. Why would a bank wish to securitise part of its loan portfolio? In short, in order to improve its capital adequacy position. Securitising a bank's loans reduces the size of its balance sheet, thereby improving its capital ratio and lowering its capital charge. The first domestic balance sheet CLO in the US market was the NationsBank Commercial Loan Master Trust, series 1997–1 and 1997–2, issued in September 1997, which employed what is known as a Master Trust structure to target investors who had previously purchased asset-backed securities.[3]

As balance sheet CLOs are originated mainly by commercial banks, the underlying collateral is usually part of their own commercial loan portfolios, and can be fixed-term, revolving, secured and unsecured, syndicated and other loans. Although we note in Figure 19.6 that most CLOs have been issued by banks that are domiciled in the main developed economies, the geographical nature of the underlying collateral often has little connection with the home country of the originating bank. Most bank CLOs are floating-rate loans with average lives of five years or less. They are targeted mainly at bank sector Libor-based investors, and are structured with an amortising payoff schedule.

Arbitrage CDOs are backed with high-yield corporate bonds or loans. As the collateral can take either forms, arbitrage CDOs can be either CLOs or CBOs. Market practitioners often refer to all arbitrage deals as CDOs for simplicity, irrespective of the collateral backing them. The key motivation behind arbitrage CDOs is, unsurprisingly, the opportunity for arbitrage, or the difference between investment-grade funding rates and high-yield investment rates. In an arbitrage CDO, the income generated by the high-yield assets should exceed the cost of funding, as long as no credit event or market event takes place.

Although CDOs are not a recent innovation, the market only experienced high growth rates from 1995 onwards, and certain investors are still prone to regard it as an "emerging" asset class. However, in terms of volume in the US market, CDOs are comparable to credit card and automobile loan asset-backed securities, as illustrated in Figure 19.3 below.

---

[3] The Master Trust structure is a generic set-up that allows originators to issue subsequent asset-backed deals under the same legal arrangement, thus enabling such issues to be made quicker than they otherwise might be. Investors also welcome such a structure, as they indicate a commitment to liquidity by implying further issues into the market.

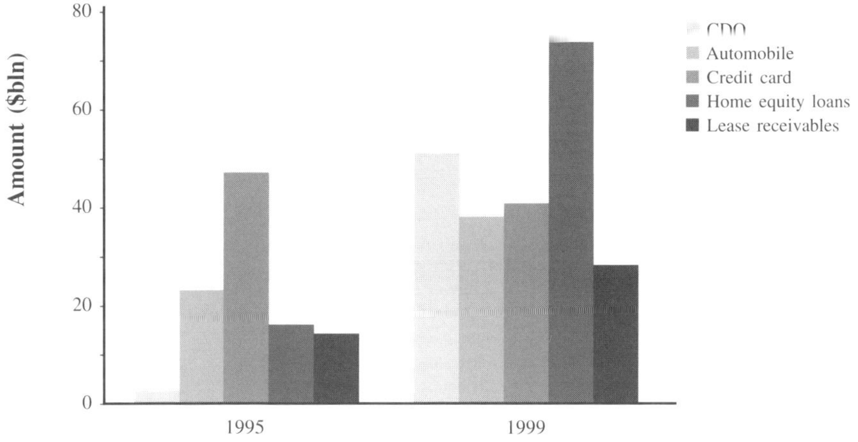

Figure 19.3 CDO supply versus other ABS products in US market, 1995 and 1999
Sources: Bloomberg, Bank of America.

Security structure

Arbitrage and balance sheet CDOs generally have similar structures. In essence, an SPV purchases loans or bonds directly from the originator or from the secondary market. SPVs have been set up in a number of ways: these include a *special purpose corporation*, a limited partnership or a limited liability corporation. An SPV will be bankruptcy-remote; that is, unconnected to any other entities that support it or are involved with it. The parties involved in a transaction, apart from the investors, are usually a portfolio manager, a bond trustee appointed to look after the interests of the investors, a credit enhancer and a back-up servicer. Some structures involve a swap arrangement where this is required to alter cash flows or set up a hedge, so in such cases a swap counterparty is also involved. A basic structure is shown in Figure 19.4, which is applicable to both CBOs and CLOs.

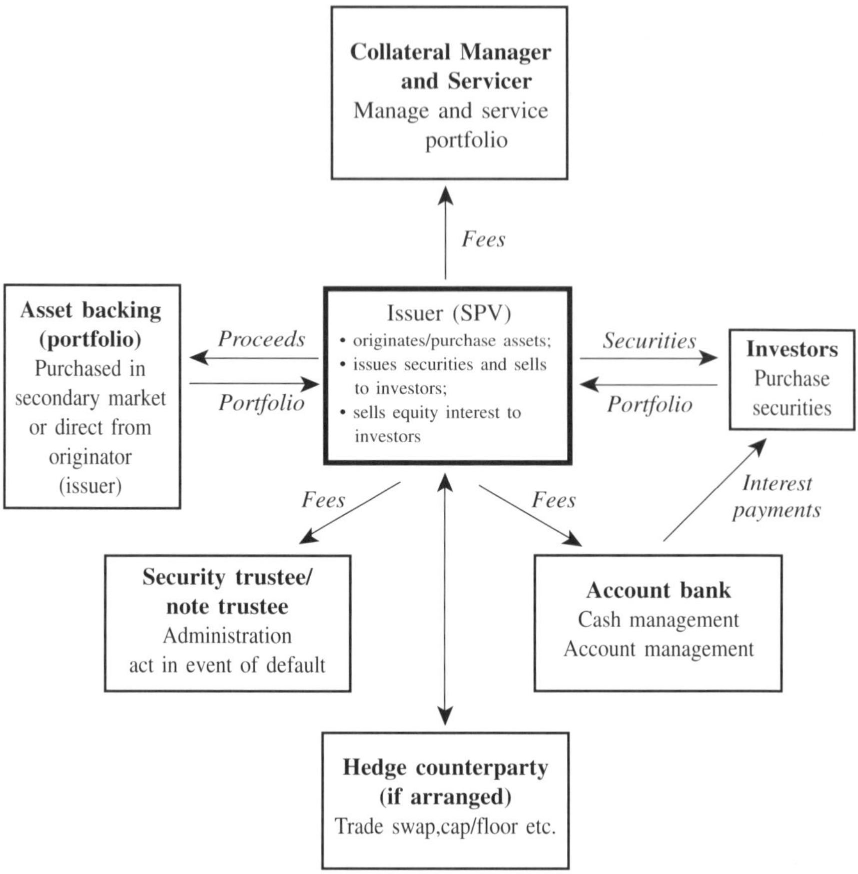

Figure 19.4 Basic CDO structure

Invariably the SPV will issue a number of classes of debt, with credit enhancements included in the structure such that different tranches of security can be issued, each with differing levels of credit quality. Other forms of protection may also be included, such as a cash reserve.

A further development has been the issue of *synthetic* CDOs. Synthetic CLO structures use credit derivatives that allow the originating bank to transfer the risk of the loan portfolio to the market. In a synthetic structure there is no actual transfer of the underlying reference assets; instead, the economic effect of a traditional CDO is synthesised by passing to the end investor(s) an identical economic risk associated with the underlying assets, the same that would have been transferred had the SPV actually purchased the assets. This effect is achieved by the provision by a counterparty of a *credit default swap*, or by the issue of *credit-linked notes* by the originating bank, or by a combination of these approaches. In a credit-linked CLO the loan portfolio remains on the sponsoring bank's balance sheet, and investors in the securities are exposed to the credit risk of the bank itself, in addition to the market risk of the collateralised portfolio. Therefore, the credit rating of the CLO can be no higher than that of the originating bank. We will look at these structures in more detail in Chapter 20. Figure 19.5 shows a simplified synthetic CDO structure.

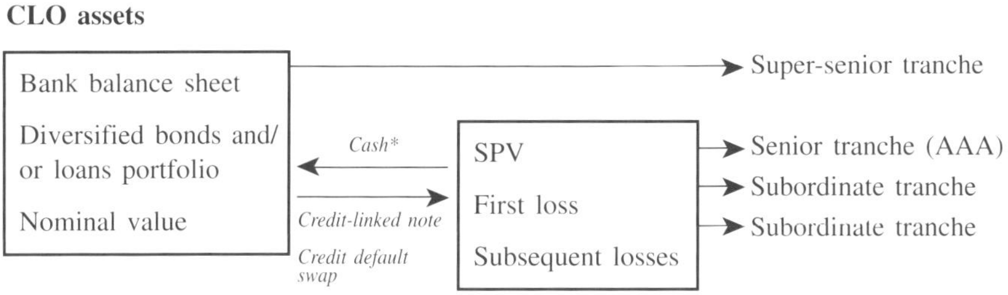

* Cash raised by the SPV goes to the originating bank in "linked" transactions or is invested in Treasury securities in "delinked" transactions.

Figure 19.5 Synthetic CDO structure

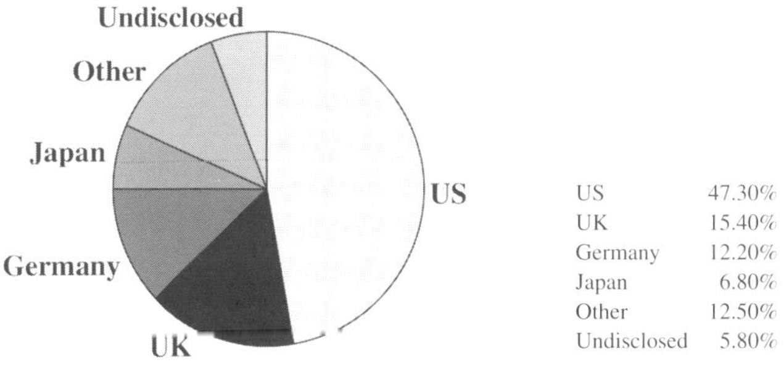

Figure 19.6 Outstanding bank CLOs by country of originating bank in 1999
Sources: Fitch, Bank of America.

Comparisons with other asset-backed securities

The CDO asset class has similarities in its fundamental structure with other securities in the ABS market. Like other asset-backed securities, a CDO is a debt obligation issued by an SPV, secured by a form of receivable. In this case though, the collateral concerned is high-yield loans or bonds, rather than, say, mortgage or credit card receivables. Again, similar to other ABS, CDO securities typically consist of different credit tranches within a single structure, and the credit ratings range from AAA to B or unrated. The rating of each CDO class is determined by the amount of credit enhancement in the structure, the ongoing performance of the collateral, and the priority of interest in the cash flows generated by the pool of assets. The credit enhancement in a structure is among items scrutinised by investors, who will determine the cash flow *waterfalls* for the interest and principal, the prepayment conditions, and the methods of allocation for default and recovery. Note that the term "waterfall" is used in the context of asset-backed securitisations that are structured with more than one tranche, to refer to the allocation of principal and interest to each tranche in a series. If there is excess cash and this can be shared with other series, the cash flows are allocated back through the waterfall, running over the successive tranches in the order of priority determined at issue.

A significant difference between CDOs and other ABS is the relationship to the servicer. In a traditional ABS the servicing function is usually performed by the same entity that sources and underwrites the original loans. These roles are different in a CDO transaction; for instance, there is no servicer that can collect on non-performing loans. Instead, the portfolio manager for the issuer must actively manage the portfolio. This might include sourcing higher quality credits, selling positions before they deteriorate and purchasing investments that are expected to appreciate. In essence, portfolio managers assume the responsibility of a servicer. Therefore investors in CDOs must focus their analysis on the portfolio manager as well as on the credit quality of the collateral pool. CDO structures also differ from other ABS in that they frequently hold non-investment grade collateral in the pool, which is not a common occurrence in traditional ABS structures. Finally, CDO transactions are (or rather, have been to date) private and not public securities.

CDO asset types

The arbitrage CDO market can be broken down into two main asset types: *cash flow* and *market value* CDOs. Balance sheet CDOs are all cash flow CDOs.

Cash flow CDOs share more similarities to traditional ABS than market value transactions. Collateral is usually a self-amortising pool of high-yield bonds and loans, expected to make principal and interest payments on a regular basis. Most cash flow CDO structures allow for a reinvestment period, and while this is common in other types of ABS, the period length tends to be longer in cash flow CDOs, typically with a minimum of four years. The cash flow structure relies upon the collateral's ability to generate sufficient cash to pay principal and interest on the rated classes of securities. This is similar to an automobile ABS, in which the auto-backed securities rely upon the cash flows from the fixed pool of automobile loans to make principal and interest payments on the liabilities. Trading of the CDO collateral is usually limited – for instance, in the event of a change in credit situation – and so the value of the portfolio is based on the par amount of the collateral securities.

Market value CDOs, which were first introduced in 1995, resemble hedge funds more than traditional ABS. The main difference between a cash flow CDO and a market value CDO is that the portfolio manager has the ability to freely trade the collateral. This means investors focus on expected appreciation in the portfolio, and the portfolio itself may be quite different in, say, three months' time compared to its composition today. This leads to the analogy with the hedge fund. Investors in market value CDOs are as concerned with the management and credit skills of the portfolio manager as they are with the credit quality of the collateral pool. Market value CDOs rely upon the portfolio manager's ability to generate total returns and to liquidate the collateral in a timely fashion, if necessary, in order to meet the cash flow obligations (principal and interest) of the CDO structure.

Different portfolio objectives result in distinct investment characteristics. Cash flow CDO assets consist mainly of rated, high-yield debt or loans that are *current* in their principal and interest payments; that is, they are not in default. In a market value CDO the asset composition is more diversified. The collateral pool might consist of, say, a 75 : 25 percentage split between assets to support liability payments and investments to produce increased equity returns. In this case, the first 75% of assets of a market value CDO asset will resemble those of a conventional cash flow CDO, with, say, 25% invested in high-yield bonds and 50% in high-yield loans. These assets should be sufficient to support payments on 100% of the liabilities. The remaining 25% of the portfolio might be invested in "special situations" such as distressed debt, foreign bank loans, hybrid capital instruments and other investments. The higher yielding investments are required to produce the higher yields that are marketed to equity investors in market value CDOs.

We have described in general terms the asset side of a CDO. The liability side of a CDO structure is similar to other ABS structures, and encompasses several investment-grade and non-investment-grade classes with an accompanying equity tranche that serves as the first loss position. In, say, a mortgage-backed transaction the equity class is not usually offered but instead held by the issuer. Typically, in the US market-rated CDO liabilities have a 10–12-year legal final maturity. The three main rating agencies[4] all actively rate cash flow CDOs, although commonly transactions carry ratings from only one or two of the agencies.

Liabilities for market value CDOs differ in some ways from cash flow CDOs. In most cases senior bank facilities provide more than half of the capital structure, with a 6–7-year final maturity. When a market value transaction is issued, cash generated by the issuance is usually not fully invested at the start. There is a *ramp-up* period to allow the portfolio manager time to make investment decisions and effect collateral purchases. Ramp-up periods result in a risk that cash flows on the portfolio's assets will not be sufficient to cover liability obligations at the start. Rating agencies consider this ramp-up risk when evaluating the transaction's credit enhancement. Ramp-up periods are in fact common to both cash flow and market value CDOs, but the period is longer with the latter transactions, resulting in more significant risk.

We noted that although CDOs were created at almost the same time as the first ABS issues, with the first structure appearing in 1988, it was only in the latter half of the 1990s that the product evolved sufficiently and in enough volume to be regarded as a distinct investment instrument. The US market has witnessed the most innovative structures, but interesting developments have also taken place in the United Kingdom and Germany. Table 19.1 summarises the evolution in the CDO product in the US market from its first appearance to present arrangements. In particular, collateral types backing the securities have grown considerably, with increasing sophistication in structure and cash flow mechanics. In 1999, CDOs covered

---

[4] That is, Standard & Poor's, Moody's and Fitch.

a wide spectrum of credit risk and investment returns, from a diverse pool of high yielding assets. Investors analyse CDOs as investment instruments in their own right and also with regard to the relative value offered by them vis-à-vis other ABS products.

Early CDO balance sheet

Assets	*Liabilities*
US domestic high-yield bonds	Fixed-rate private securities
	Equity

Present-day CDO balance sheet

Assets	*Liabilities*
US domestic high-yield bonds	AAA to BBB fixed-rate securities
US domestic high-yield loans	AAA to BBB floating-rate securities
Emerging market debt	BB mezzanine securities
Special situation/distressed debt	Contingent interest securities
Foreign bank loan	Credit-linked notes
	Equity

Table 19.1 CDO product evolution

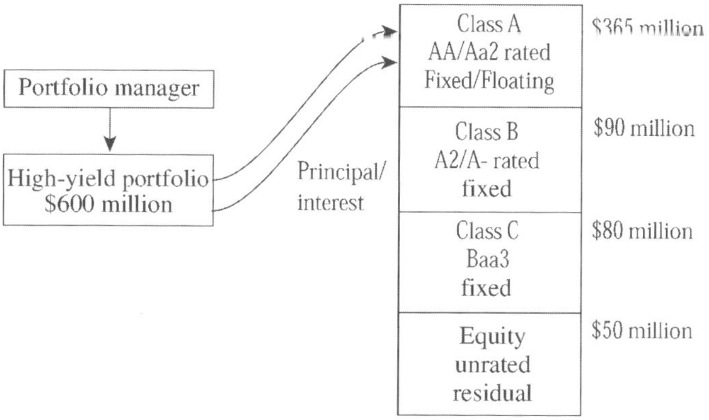

Figure 19.7 Hypothetical cash flow CBO structure

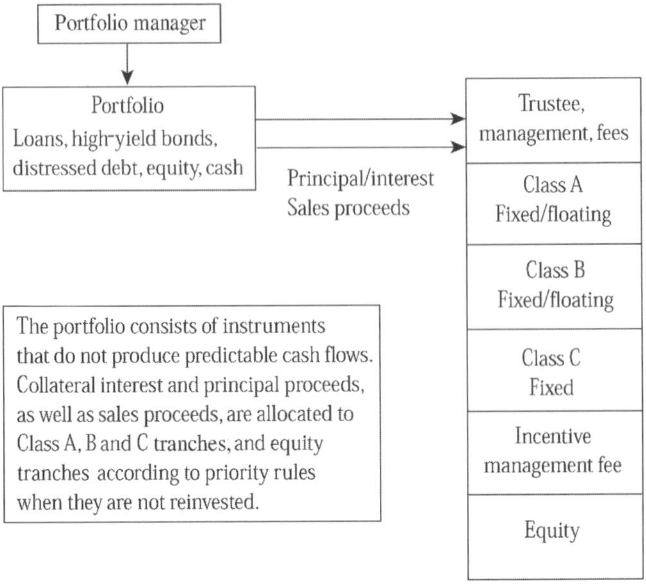

Figure 19.8 Hypothetical market value CBO structure

Investor Analysis

Investors have a number of motivations when considering the CDO market both in their domestic market and abroad. These include:

- the opportunity to gain exposure to a high-yield market on a diversified basis, without committing significant resources;
- the ability to choose from a number of portfolio managers that manage the CDO;
- CDOs acting as an initial entry point into the high-yield market;
- with respect to lower rated (BBB and below) tranches, achieving leveraged returns while gaining benefit from a diversified portfolio;
- the appeal of a wide investor base, with ratings ranging from AAA to B, and maturities from four years to as long as 20 years;
- a wide variety of collateral.

CDOs offer investors a variety of risk/return profiles, as well as market volatilities, and their appeal has widened as broader macroeconomic developments in the global capital markets have resulted in lower yields on more traditional investments.

Investors analysing CDO instruments will focus on particular aspects of the market. For instance, those with a low appetite for risk will concentrate in the higher rated classes of cash flow transactions. Investors that are satisfied with greater volatility of earnings, but who still wish to hold AA- or AAA-rated instruments, may consider market value deals. The "arbitrage" that exists in the transaction may be a result of:

- industry diversification;
- differences between investment grade and high-yield spreads;
- the difference between implied default rates in the high-yield market and expected default rates;
- the liquidity premium embedded in high-yield investments;
- the Libor rate versus the Treasury spread.

The CDO asset class cannot be compared in a straightforward fashion to other ABS classes, which makes relative value analysis difficult. Although a CDO is a structured finance product, it does not have sufficient common characteristics with other such products. The structure and cash flow of a CDO are perhaps most similar to a commercial mortgage-backed security; the collateral backing of the two types share comparable characteristics. Commercial mortgage pools and high-yield bonds and loans both have fewer obligors and larger balances than other ABS collateral, and each credit is rated. On the other hand, CDOs often pay floating-rate interest and are private securities,[5] whereas commercial MBS (in the US market) pay a fixed rate and are often public securities.

Historically, during 1998 and 1999 CDO spreads offered greater opportunity for spread tightening than traditional ABS, as CDO yields were observed to take a longer time to recover from the bond bear market that existed in the second half of 1998. This is illustrated in Figure 19.9 below, with a comparison to commercial mortgage-backed securities. Although these had returned to pre-bear market levels, CDO spreads remained at the higher levels; that is, they required a longer recovery period. From this picture at the start of the second quarter in 1999, CDP spreads had potentially a significant scope for tightening before reaching historically low

[5] In the US market, they are also filed under Rule 144A, as opposed to public securities which must be registered with the Securities and Exchange Commission. Rule 144A securities may only be sold to investors classified as professional investors under specified criteria. Rule 144A provides an exemption from the registration requirements of the Securities Act (1933) for resale of privately placed securities to qualified institutional buyers. Such buyers are deemed to be established and experienced institutions, and so the SEC does not regulate or approve disclosure requirements.

spreads. This was in fact confirmed in the second half of the year, when spreads came in to lower levels. In assessing relative value therefore an investor will assess the difference in spreads between CDOs and other ABS asset classes.

We have presented only an overview here; interested readers may wish to consult the references at the end of this chapter, principally Fabozzi (1998; Chapter 18) and the study by ING Barings (1999).

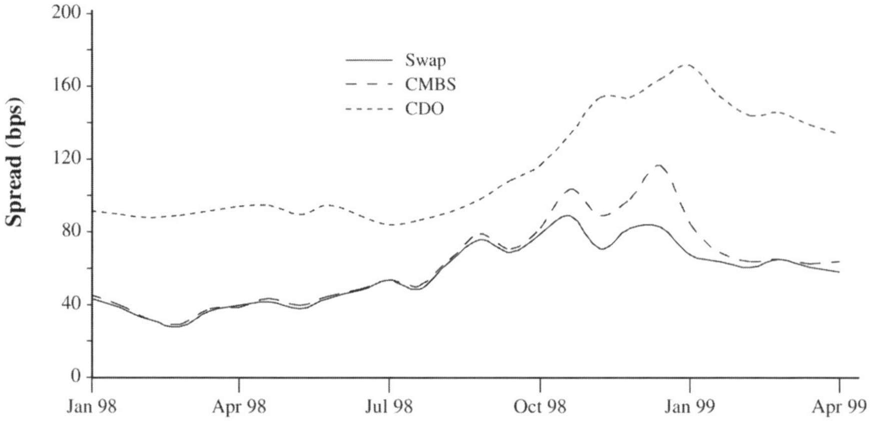

Figure 19.9 Historical spreads, January 1998–March 1999
Sources: Bloomberg, Bank of America.

Guaranteed investment contracts

A part of the cash raised from the liability side of a CDO is often invested in AAA bonds or other such high-quality assets, to act as a reserve for investors. The collateral reserve in a CDO can be invested in a number of ways. One option is a guaranteed investment contract or GIC. GICs are offered by certain insurance companies, and (less frequently) by banks.

A GIC can be interpreted in a number of ways. In trust banks, it is often no more than a bank account that pays a fixed spread below Libor for the term of the account. The payment frequency is tied in to match that of the coupon on the CDO note liabilities. Strictly speaking, this is not a GIC. Formally defined, a GIC is an obligation from the GIC provider to pay a guaranteed principal and interest rate on an invested premium. The investor places a lump-sum amount (the premium) in a GIC, and the GIC provider guarantees a specified cash amount that will be paid to the investor on the maturity date.

As an example, an investor places $10 million in a five-year GIC that pays an annual rate of 5.00%. The GIC maturity value is therefore:

$$10,000,000 \times (1.05)^5$$
$$= \$12,762,815.62$$

There are variations on GICs, but the standard version pays a fixed rate of interest so the investors know their final return with certainty. In some cases, a floating rate may apply, with a fixed spread to the floating-rate index. This is what is usually offered by banks, which do not usually offer the fixed-rate version. GIC maturities can range from one to 20 years. There can be a one-off lump-sum premium or regular premium payments by the investor. Also, some GICs pay interest on a periodic basis to the investor.

GICs therefore make suitable cash reserves for a CDO, but of course this is not risk-free like an investment in US Treasuries would be; rather, its risk is the credit quality of the insurance company; that is, the GIC provider. However, one advantage it has over of a bond is that its value is always postive, unlike that of a bond that suffers marked-to-market fluctuations, and compared to a bank account it offers a known return.

Selected bibliography and references

Braddock, J. 1997, *Derivatives Demystified: Using Structured Finance Products*, John Wiley & Sons, Chichester.

Fabozzi, F. 1998, *Handbook of Structured Financial Products*, FJF Associates, New Hope, PA.

ING Barings 1999, *International Asset Securitisation*, London.

Mattoo, M. 1996, *Structured Derivatives*, Pitman, Oxford.

Norton Rose 2000, *Collateralised Debt Obligations*.

Peng, S. and Dattatreya, R. 1994, *The Structured Note Market*, Pitman, Oxford.

But, me being me, I also worked hard at my cricket. I have always believed in giving my all to every task I have undertaken, and I was in the nets every day.

– Nasser Hussain
Playing With Fire (Penguin) 2004

CHAPTER

20

Synthetic Collateralised Debt Obligations and Mortgage-backed Securities

The previous chapter looked at cash CDOs, which have become an important part of the corporate debt markets and an additional asset class for investors in this market. This chapter looks at the *synthetic* CDO, a structure that uses credit derivatives in its construction. This is also popular as an investment vehicle, although it does not raise corporate finance in the traditional manner. However, it has become important as an asset class for investors, and is worth reviewing for this reason.

At the end of this chapter we consider another synthetic investment product, the synthetic MBS security, which is essentially a credit default swap that references an existing MBS security. It can be viewed as a separate asset class in its own right.

For readers unfamiliar with credit default swaps, which are the basic type of credit derivative, see Appendix 20.1.

Introduction

Cash flow CDO structures

Cash flow CDOs were introduced in Chapter 19 and are categorised as either balance sheet or arbitrage deals. Arbitrage CDOs are further categorised as cash flow or market-value deals. A later development, the *synthetic* CDO, now accounts for a growing number of transactions. We show a "family tree" of CDOs in Figure 20.1.

The total issuance of all cash flow deals in 2000 and 2001 is shown in Figure 20.2.

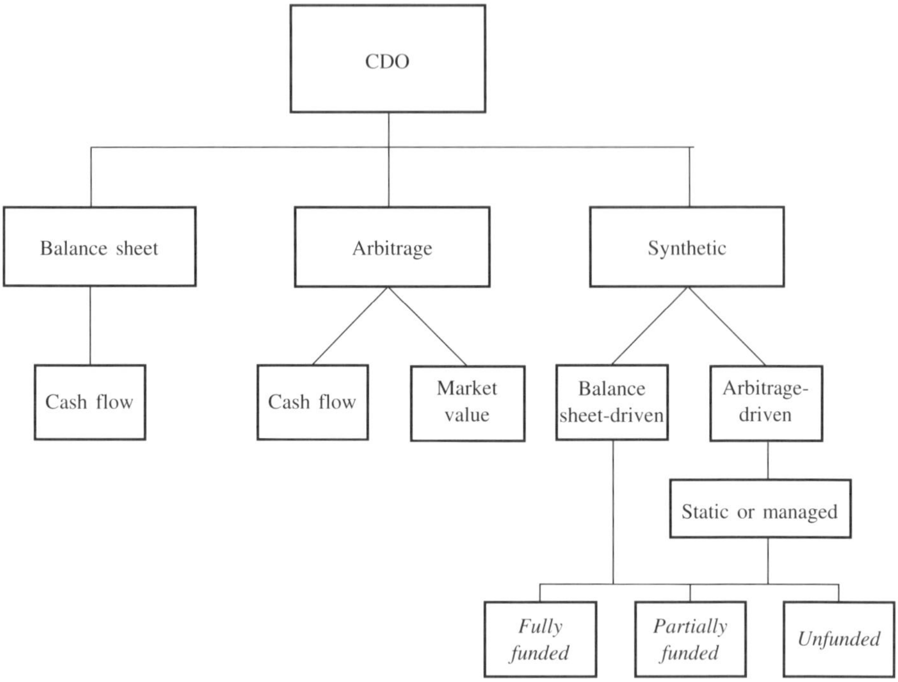

Figure 20.1 The CDO family

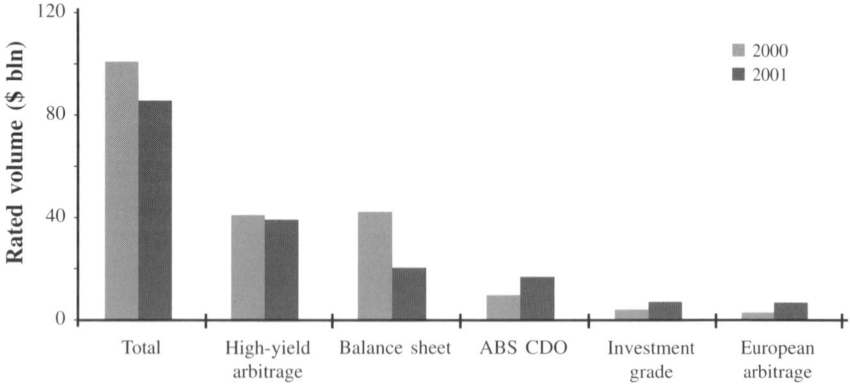

Figure 20.2 Global issuance of cash flow CDOs in 2000 and 2001

Cash flow CDO

These are similar to other asset-backed securitisations involving an SPV. Bonds or loans are pooled together and the cash flows from these assets used to back the liabilities of the notes issued by the SPV into the market. As the underlying assets are sold to the SPV, they are removed from the originator's balance sheet; hence, the credit risk associated with these assets is transferred to the holders of the issued notes. The originator also obtains funding by issuing the notes. The generic structure is illustrated in Figure 20.3.

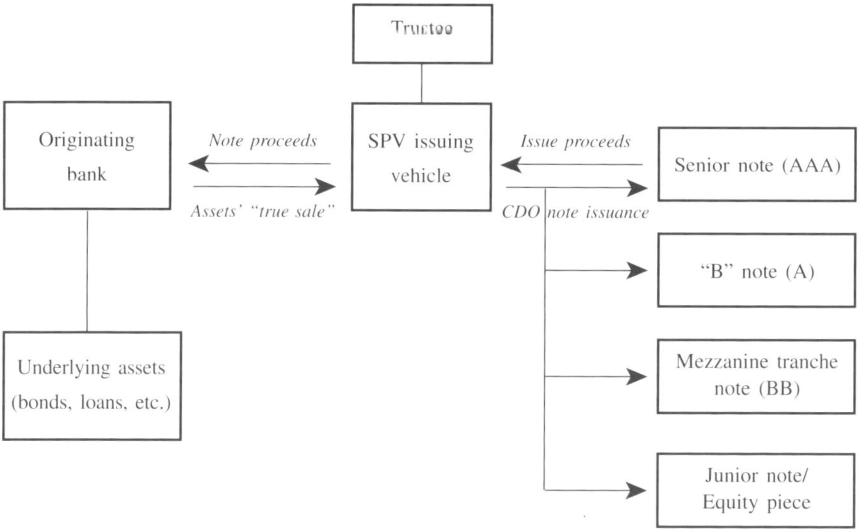

Figure 20.3 Generic cash flow CDO

Banks and other financial institutions are the primary originators of *balance sheet CDOs*. These are deals securitising banking assets such as commercial loans of an investment-grade or sub-investment-grade rating. The main motivations for entering into this arrangement are:

- to obtain regulatory relief;
- to increase return on capital via the removal of lower yielding assets from the balance sheet;
- to secure alternative and/or cheaper sources of funding.

Investors are often attracted to balance sheet CDOs because they are perceived as offering a higher return than, say, credit card ABS at a similar level of risk exposure. They also represent a diversification away from traditional structured finance investments. The asset pool in a balance sheet CDO is static; that is, it is not traded or actively managed by a portfolio manager; for this reason the structure is similar to more traditional ABS or repackaging vehicles. The typical note tranching is:

- senior note, AAA-rated, and 90%–95% of the issue;
- subordinated note, A-rated, 3%–5%;
- mezzanine note, BBB-rated, 1%–3%;
- equity note, non-rated, 1%–2%.

The cash flows of the underlying assets are used to fund the liabilities of the overlying notes. As the notes carry different ratings, there is a *priority of payment* that must be followed, which is the cash flow waterfall. The most senior payment must be paid in full before the next payment can be met, all the way until the most junior liability is discharged. If there are insufficient funds available, the most senior notes must be paid off before the junior liabilities can be addressed.

The waterfall process for interest payments is shown at Figure 20.4. Before paying the next priority of the waterfall, the vehicle must pass a number of compliance tests on the level of its underlying cash flows. These include interest coverage and principal (par) coverage tests.

During the life of the CDO transaction, a portfolio administrator will produce a periodic report detailing the quality of the collateral pool. This report is known as an investor or *Trustee* report and also shows the results of the compliance tests that are required to affirm that the notes of the CDO have maintained their credit rating.

Arbitrage CDOs are classified into either cash flow CDOs or market value CDOs. An arbitrage CDO will be designated as one of these two types, depending on the way the underlying asset pool is structured to provide value (cash proceeds) in the vehicle. The distinction is that:

- a cash flow CDO will have a collateral pool that is usually static, and which generates sufficient interest to cover fees, expenses and overlying liabilities, and sufficient principal to repay notes on maturity; whereas
- in a market value CDO the collateral pool is usually actively traded, and marked-to-market on a daily basis. The daily mark for all the assets indicates the total value of the collateral pool and this value must always be sufficient to cover the principal and interest liabilities.

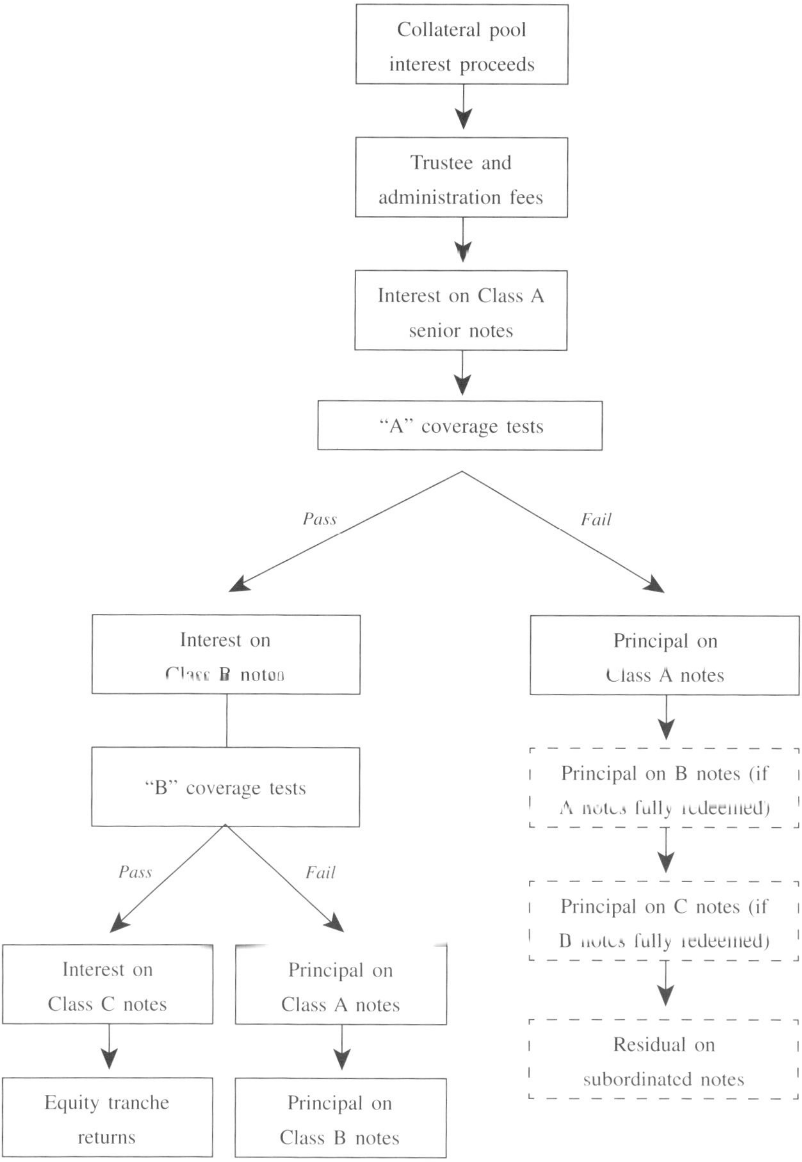

Figure 20.4 Interest cash flow waterfall for cash flow CDO

A cash flow arbitrage CDO has certain similarities with a balance sheet CDO, and if it is a static pool CDO it is also conceptually similar to an ABS deal.[1] The priority of payments is similar, starting from expenses, trustee and servicing fees, senior noteholders, and so on down to the most junior noteholder. Underlying assets on cash flow arbitrage deals are commonly lower rated bonds, commercial bank loans, high-yield debt and emerging market sovereign bonds. The basic structure is designed to split the aggregate credit risk of the collateral pool into various tranches, which are the overlying notes, each of which has a different credit exposure from the other. As a result, each note exhibits a different risk/reward profile, and so will attract itself to different classes of investor.

The different risk profiles of the issued notes result because they are subordinated; that is, the notes are structured in descending order of seniority. In addition, the structure makes use of *credit enhancements* to varying degrees, which include:

- overcollateralisation: the overlying notes are lower in value compared to the underlying pool; for example, $250 million nominal of assets are used as backing for $170 million nominal of issued bonds;
- cash reserve accounts: a reserve is maintained in a cash account and used to cover initial losses; the funds may be sourced from part of the proceeds;
- excess spread: cash inflows from assets that exceed the interest service requirements of liabilities;
- insurance wraps: insurance cover against losses suffered by the asset pool, for which an insurance premium is paid for as long as the cover is needed.

The quality of the collateral pool is monitored regularly and reported on by the portfolio administrator, who produces the investor report. This report details the results of various *compliance tests*, which are undertaken at the individual asset level as well as the aggregate level. Compliance tests include:

- weighted average spread and weighted average rating: the average interest spread and average credit rating of the assets, which must remain at a specified minimum;

[1] Except that in a typical ABS deal such as a consumer or trade receivables deal, or a residential MBS deal, there are a large number of individual underlying assets, whereas with a CBO or CLO there may be as few as twenty underlying loans or bonds.

- concentration: there will be a set maximum share of the assets that may be sourced from particular emerging markets, industrial sectors, and so on;
- diversity score: this is a statistical value that is calculated via a formula set by the rating agency analysing the transaction. It measures the level of diversity of the assets; in other words, how different they are – and hence how uncorrelated in their probability of default – from each other.

These tests are calculated on a regular basis and also each time the composition of the assets changes; for example, because certain assets have been sold, new assets purchased or because bonds have been paid off ahead of their legal maturity date. If the test results fall below the required minimum, trading activity is restricted to only those trades that will improve the test results. Certain other compliance tests are viewed as more important, since if any of them are "failed", the cash flows will be diverted from the normal waterfall and will be used to begin paying off the senior notes until the test results improve. These include:

- overcollateralisation: the overcollateralisation level vis-à-vis the issued notes must remain above a specified minimum; for instance, it must be at 120% of the nominal value of the senior note;
- interest coverage: the level of interest receivables on assets must be sufficient to cover interest liabilities but also to bear default and other losses.

Compliance tests are specified as part of the process leading up to the issue of notes, in discussion between the originator and the rating agency.[2] The ratings analysis is comprehensive and focuses on the quality of the collateral, individual asset default probabilities, the structure of the deal and the track record and reputation of the originator.

Market value CDOs

The originators of market value CDOs are predominantly fund managers. With these transactions, the originator has rather more freedom to actively trade assets in and out of the collateral pool, and sometimes a wider range of assets to choose from when trading. Assets are marked-to-market by the portfolio administrator on a regular basis, possibly as frequently as daily.

[2] Deals may be rated by more than one rating agency.

Investors are attracted by the perceived fund management credentials of the originator, and there are also the theoretical advantages that come from the flexibility of being better able to manage losses when the market is experiencing a correction.

Market value deals frequently experience a *ramp-up* period when assets are built up in the collateral pool. This can take several months. There is also a liquidity or *revolver* facility, essentially a funding line distinct from the issue of notes, which is in place prior to the closing of the transaction and which is used to fund the acquisition of assets. The principal repayment of liabilities is funded when underlying assets are sold or traded out of the pool, rather than when they mature.

Synthetic CDOs

The ongoing development of securitisation technology has resulted in more complex structures, illustrated perfectly by the synthetic CDO. These were introduced to meet differing needs of originators, where credit risk transfer is of more importance than funding considerations. Compared with conventional cash flow deals, which feature an actual transfer of ownership or *true sale* of the underlying assets to a separately incorporated legal entity, a synthetic securitisation structure is engineered so that the credit risk of the assets is transferred by the sponsor or originator of the transaction, from itself, to the investors by means of credit derivative instruments. The originator is therefore the credit protection buyer and investors are the credit protection sellers. This credit risk transfer may be undertaken either directly or via an SPV. Using this approach, underlying or *reference* assets are not necessarily moved off the originator's balance sheet, so it is adopted whenever the primary objective is to achieve risk transfer rather than balance sheet funding. The synthetic structure enables removal of credit exposure without asset transfer, so it may be preferred for risk management and regulatory capital relief purposes. For banking institutions it also enables loan risk to be transferred without selling the loans themselves, thereby allowing customer relationships to remain unaffected.

The first synthetic deals were observed in the US market, while the first deals in Europe were observed in 1998. Market growth in Europe has been rapid; the total value of cash and synthetic deals in Europe in 2001 approached $120 billion, and a growing share of this total has been of synthetic deals. Figure 20.5 illustrates market volume, while Figure 20.6 shows the breakdown of arbitrage CDOs, whether cash flow, market value or synthetic deals, in 2000 and 2001. Figure 20.6 appears to suggest that synthetic deals were a very small part of the market, but the total reflects the funded element of each transaction, which grew to 9% of all arbitrage deals in 2001. However, when the unfunded element of synthetic deals is included, we see that the synthetic deal share is substantially increased, as shown in Figure 20.7. Market share volumes reported by, say, the rating agencies generally include the note element; however, as a measure of actual risk transferred by a vehicle, it is logical to include the unfunded super-senior swap element as well. This suggests that in 2001 similar amounts of synthetic and cash business was transacted.

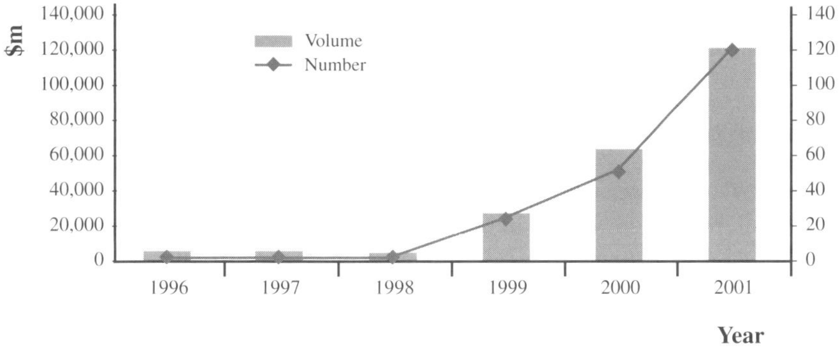

Figure 20.5 CDO market volume growth in Europe.
Values for volume include rated debt and credit default swap tranches and unrated super-senior tranches for synthetic CDOs, and exclude equity tranches

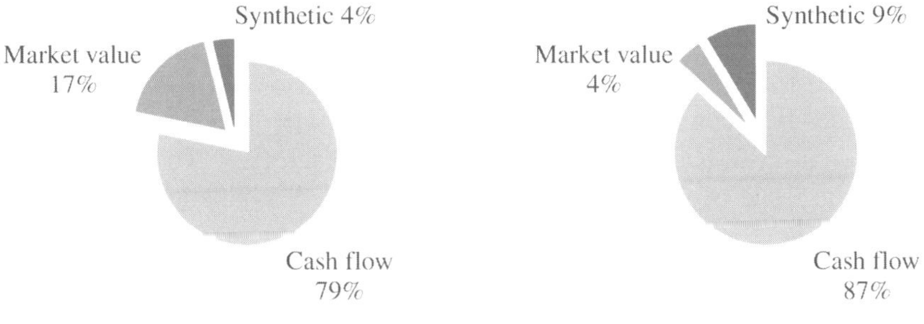

Figure 20.6 Market share of arbitrage CDOs in 2000 and 2001
Source: UBS Warburg

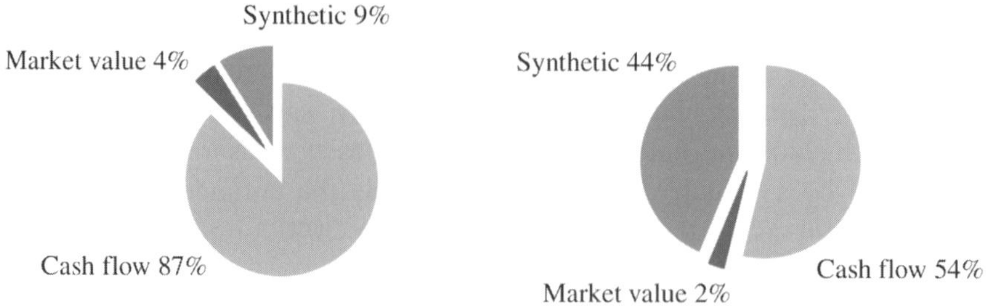

Figure 20.7 Market share of arbitrage CDOs in 2001, comparison when unfunded swap element of synthetic deals is included
Source: UBS Warburg.

The first European synthetic deals were balance sheet CLOs, with underlying reference assets being commercial loans on the originator's balance sheet. Originators were typically banking institutions. Arbitrage synthetic CDOs have also been introduced, typically by fund management institutions, and involve sourcing credit derivative contracts in the market and then selling these on to investors in the form of rated notes, at the arbitrage profit. Within the synthetic market, arbitrage deals were the most frequently issued during 2001, reflecting certain advantages they possess over cash CDOs. A key advantage has been that credit default swaps for single reference entities frequently trade at a lower spread than cash bonds of the same name and maturity, with consequent lower costs for the originator.

Motivations

Differences between synthetic and cash CDOs are perhaps best reflected in the different cost–benefit economics of issuing each type. The motivations behind the issue of each type usually also differ. A synthetic CDO can be seen as being constructed out of the following:

- a short position in a credit default swap (bought protection), by which the sponsor transfers its portfolio credit risk to the issuer;
- a long position in a portfolio of bonds or loans, the cash flow from which enables the sponsor to pay liabilities of overlying notes.

The originators of the first synthetic deals were banks who wished to manage the credit risk exposure of their loan books without having to resort to the administrative burden of true sale cash securitisation. They are a natural progression in the development of credit derivative structures, with single-name credit default swaps being replaced by portfolio default swaps. Synthetic CDOs can be "de-linked" from the sponsoring institution, so that investors do not have any credit exposure to the sponsor itself. The first deals were introduced (in 1998) at a time when widening credit spreads and the worsening of credit quality among originating firms meant that investors were sellers of cash CDOs that had retained a credit linkage to the sponsor. A synthetic arrangement also means that the credit risk of assets that are otherwise not suited to conventional securitisation may be transferred, while assets are retained on the balance sheet. Such assets include bank guarantees, letters of credit or cash loans that have some legal or other restriction on being securitised. For this reason synthetic deals are more appropriate for assets that are described under multiple legal jurisdictions.

The economic advantage of issuing a synthetic versus a cash CDO can be significant. Put simply, the net benefit to the originator is the gain in regulatory capital cost, minus the cost of paying for credit protection on the credit default swap side. In a partially funded structure, a sponsoring bank will obtain full capital relief when note proceeds are invested in 0% risk-weighted collateral such as Treasuries or gilts. The super senior swap portion will carry a 20% risk weighting.[3] In fact, a moment's thought should make clear to us that a synthetic deal would be cheaper: where credit default swaps are used, the sponsor pays a basis point fee, which for AAA security might be in the range 10–30 bps, depending on the stage of the credit cycle. In a cash structure where bonds are issued, the cost to the sponsor would be the benchmark yield plus the credit spread, which would be considerably higher compared to the default swap premium. This is illustrated in the example shown in Figure 20.8, where we assume certain spreads and premiums in comparing a partially funded synthetic deal with a cash deal. The assumptions are:

- that the super senior credit swap cost is 15 bps, and carries a 20% risk weight;
- the equity piece retains a 100% risk weighting;
- the synthetic CDO invests note proceeds in sovereign collateral that pays sub-Libor.

[3] This is as long as the counterparty is an OECD bank, which is invariably the case.

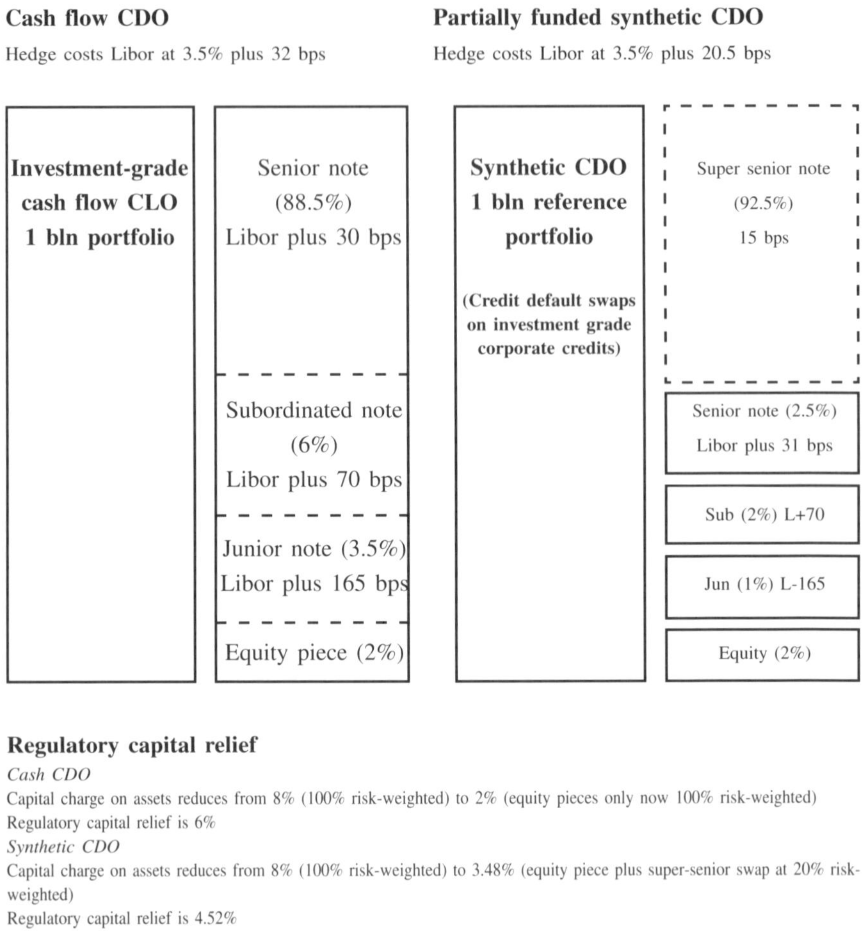

Figure 20.8 Cash flow economies; cash versus synthetic CDO

Synthetic deals can be unfunded, partially funded or fully funded. An unfunded CDO would be comprised wholly of credit default swaps, while fully funded structures would be arranged so that the entire credit risk of the reference portfolio was transferred through the issue of credit-linked notes. We discuss these shortly.

Mechanics

A synthetic CDO is so-called because the transfer of credit risk is achieved "synthetically" via a credit derivative, rather than by a "true sale" to an SPV.

Thus, in a synthetic CDO the credit risk of the underlying loans or bonds is transferred to the SPV using credit default swaps and/or total return swaps (TRS). However, the assets themselves are not legally transferred to the SPV, and they remain on the originator's balance sheet. Using a synthetic CDO, the originator can obtain regulatory capital relief[4] and manage the credit risk on its balance sheet, but will not be receiving any funding. In other words, a synthetic CDO structure enables originators to separate credit risk exposure and asset funding requirements. The credit risk of the asset portfolio, now known as the reference portfolio, is transferred, directly or to an SPV, through credit derivatives. The most common credit contracts used are credit default swaps. A portion of the credit risk may be sold on as credit-linked notes. Typically, a large majority of the credit risk is transferred via a "super-senior" credit default swap,[5] which is dealt with a swap counterparty but usually sold to monoline insurance companies at a significantly lower spread over Libor compared with the senior AAA-rated tranche of cash flow CDOs. This is a key attraction of synthetic deals for originators. Most deals are structured with mezzanine notes sold to a wider set of investors, the proceeds of which are invested in risk-free collateral such as Treasury bonds or *Pfandbriefe* securities. The most junior note, known as the "first-loss" piece, may be retained by the originator. On the occurrence of a credit event among the reference assets, the originating bank receives funds remaining from the collateral after they have been used to pay the principal on the issued notes, less the value of the junior note.

A generic synthetic CDO structure is shown in Figure 20.9. In this generic structure, the credit risk of the reference assets is transferred to the issuer SPV and ultimately to the investors, by means of the credit default swap and an issue of credit-linked notes. In the default swap arrangement, the risk transfer is undertaken in return for the swap premium, which is then paid to investors by the issuer. The note issue is invested in risk-free collateral rather than passed on to the originator, in order to de-link the credit ratings of the notes from the rating of the originator. If the collateral pool was not established, a downgrade of the sponsor could result in a downgrade of the issued notes. Investors in the notes expose themselves to the credit risk of the reference assets, and if there are no credit events they will earn returns at least the equal of the collateral assets and the default swap

4 This is because reference assets that are protected by credit derivative contracts, and which remain on the balance sheet, will, under Basel rules, attract a lower regulatory capital charge.

5 So called because the swap is ahead of the most senior of any funded (note) portion, the latter being "senior" means the swap must be "super-senior".

premium. If the notes are credit-linked, they will also earn excess returns based on the performance of the reference portfolio. If there are credit events, the issuer will deliver the assets to the swap counterparty and will pay the nominal value of the assets to the originator out of the collateral pool. Credit default swaps are unfunded credit derivatives, while CLNs are funded credit derivatives where the protection sellers (the investors) fund the value of the reference assets up-front, and will receive a reduced return on occurrence of a credit event.

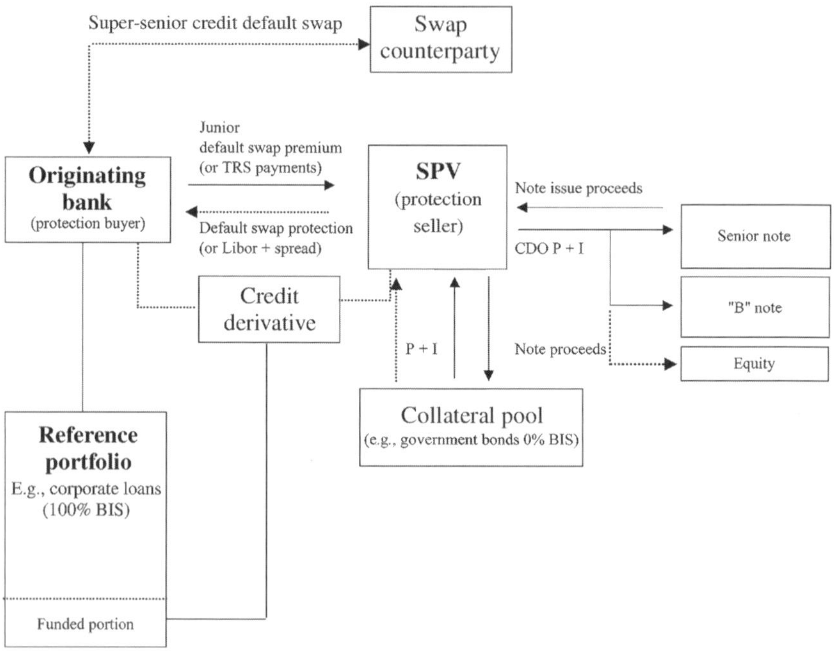

Figure 20.9 Synthetic CDO structure

Synthetic CDOs are popular in the European market due to less onerous legal documentation requirements. Across Europe the legal infrastructure is not uniform and in certain countries it has not been sufficiently developed to enable true sale securitisation to be undertaken. In addition, when the underlying asset pool is composed of bonds from different countries, a cash-funded CDO may present too many administrative difficulties. A synthetic CDO removes such issues by using credit derivatives, and in theory can be brought to market more quickly than a cash flow arrangement (although in practice this is not always the case). It is also able to benefit from a shorter ramp-up period prior to closing. Traditional cash CDOs suffer when only a portion of the portfolio is in place at the time of closing, especially holders of the equity piece who may receive no cash inflow during the ramp-up. This cost may be reduced if a *warehouse* facility is set up prior to closing the transaction. A warehouse, which is provided by the portfolio administrator in return for a fee, enables the CDO issuer to begin purchasing bonds before closing. Using a warehouse arrangement, issuers purchase target securities and hedge their interest rate risk using futures, interest rate swaps or by shorting government bonds. The credit risk on the bonds is not hedged of course, and equity holders bear losses if spreads widen due to credit deterioration (they will of course gain if spreads tighten). A shorter ramp-up period is a plus therefore, and although in a synthetic deal the manager will take some time while sourcing credit default swaps, this time is typically shorter than in a cash flow CDO.

EXAMPLE 20.1 BISTRO: the first synthetic securitisation

Generally viewed as the first synthetic securitisation, BISTRO is a JPMorgan vehicle brought to market in December 1997. The transaction was designed to remove the credit risk on a portfolio of corporate credits held on JPMorgan's books, with no funding or balance sheet impact. The overall portfolio was $9.7 billion, with $700 million of notes being issued, in two tranches, by the BISTRO SPV. The proceeds of the note issue were invested in US Treasury securities, which in turn were used as collateral for the credit default swap entered into between JPMorgan and the vehicle. This is a five-year swap written on the whole portfolio, with JPMorgan as the protection buyer. BISTRO, the protection seller, pays for the coupons on the issued notes from funds received from the collateral pool and the premiums on the credit default swap. Payments on occurrence of credit events are paid out from the collateral pool.

Under this structure, JPMorgan has transferred the credit risk on $700 million of its portfolio to investors, and retained the risk on a first-loss piece and the residual piece. The first loss piece is not a note issue, but a $32 million reserve cash account held for the five-year life of the deal. First losses are funded out of this cash reserve which is held by JPMorgan. This is shown in Figure 20.10.

The asset pool is static for the life of the deal. The attraction of the deal for investors included a higher return on the notes compared to bonds of the same credit rating and a bullet-maturity structure, compared to the amortising arrangement of other ABS asset classes.

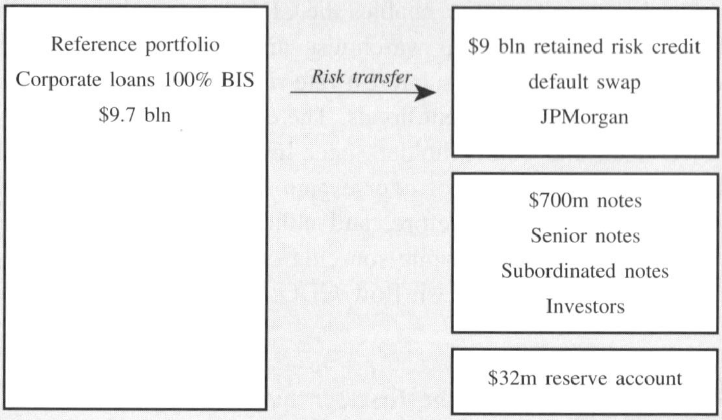

Figure 20.10 BISTRO

Summary: Advantages of synthetic structures

The introduction of synthetic securitisation vehicles was in response to specific demands of sponsoring institutions, and they present certain advantages over traditional cash flow structures. These include:

- speed of implementation: a synthetic transaction can, in theory, be placed in the market sooner than a cash deal, and the time from inception to closure can be as low as four weeks, with average execution time of 6–8 weeks compared to 3–4 months for the equivalent cash deal; this reflects the shorter ramp-up period noted above;
- no requirement to fund the super-senior element;
- for many reference names, the credit default swap is frequently cheaper than the same name underlying cash bond;
- transaction costs such as legal fees can be lower as there is no necessity to set up an SPV;

- banking relationships can be maintained with clients whose loans need not be actually sold off the sponsoring entity's balance sheet;
- the range of reference assets that can be covered is wider, and includes undrawn lines of credit, bank guarantees and derivative instruments that would give rise to legal and true sale issues in a cash transaction;
- the use of credit derivatives, which introduces greater flexibility to provide tailor-made solutions for credit risk requirements;
- the cost of buying protection is usually lower as there is little or no funding element and the credit protection price is below the equivalent-rate note liability.

This does not mean that the cash transaction is now an endangered species. It retains certain advantages of its own over synthetic deals, which include:

- no requirement for an OECD bank (the 20% BIS risk-weighted entity) to act as the swap counterparty to meet capital relief requirements;
- lower capital relief available compared to the 20% risk-weighting on the OECD bank counterparty;
- a larger potential investor base, as the number of counterparties is potentially greater (certain financial and investing institutions have limitations on the degree of usage of credit derivatives);
- a lower degree of counterparty exposure for the originating entity. In a synthetic deal the default of a swap counterparty would mean the cessation of premium payments or more critically a credit event protection payment, and termination of the credit default swap.

Investment banking advisors will structure the arrangement for their sponsoring client that best meets the latter's requirements. Depending on the nature of these, this can be either a synthetic or cash deal.

Variations in synthetic CDOs

Synthetic CDOs have been issued in a variety of forms, labelled in generic form as arbitrage CDOs or balance sheet CDOs. Structures can differ to a considerable degree from one another, having only the basics in common with each other. The latest development is the *managed synthetic* CDO.

A synthetic arbitrage CDO is originated generally by collateral managers who wish to exploit the difference in yield between that obtained on the underlying assets and that payable on the CDO, both in note interest and servicing fees. The generic structure is as follows: a specially created SPV enters into a total-return swap with the originating bank or financial institution, referencing the bank's underlying portfolio (the reference portfolio). The portfolio is actively managed and is funded on the balance sheet by the originating bank. The SPV receives the "total return" from the reference portfolio, and in return it pays Libor plus a spread to the originating bank. The SPV also issues notes that are sold into the market to CDO investors, and these notes can be rated as high as AAA as they are backed by high-quality collateral, which is purchased using the note proceeds. A typical structure is shown at Figure 20.11.

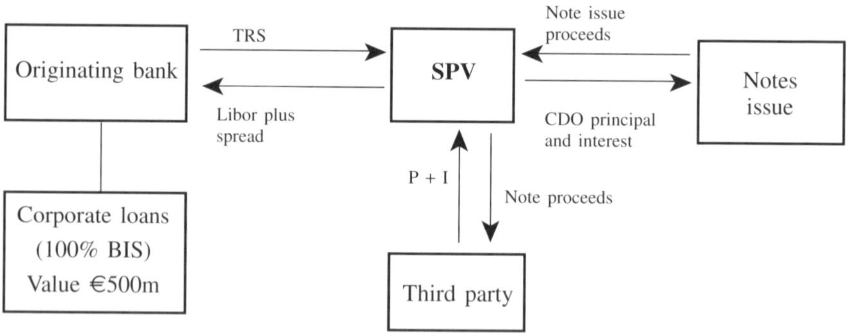

Figure 20.11 Synthetic arbitrage CDO structure

A balance sheet synthetic CDO is employed by banks that wish to manage regulatory capital. As before, the underlying assets are bonds, loans and credit facilities originated by the issuing bank. In a balance sheet CDO the SPV enters into a credit default swap agreement with the originator, with the specific collateral pool designated as the reference portfolio. The SPV receives the premium payable on the default swap, and thereby provides credit protection on the reference portfolio. There are three types of CDO within this structure. A fully synthetic CDO is a completely *unfunded* structure that uses credit default swaps to transfer the entire credit risk of the reference assets to investors who are protection sellers. In a *partially funded*

CDO, only the highest credit risk segment of the portfolio is transferred. The cash flow that would be needed to service the synthetic CDO overlying liability is received from the AAA-rated collateral that is purchased by the SPV with the proceeds of an overlying note issue. An originating bank obtains maximum regulatory capital relief by means of a partially funded structure, through a combination of the synthetic CDO and what is known as a *super-senior swap* arrangement with an OECD banking counterparty. A super-senior swap provides additional protection to that part of the portfolio, the senior segment, that is already protected by the funded portion of the transaction. The sponsor may retain the super-senior element or may sell it to a monoline insurance firm or credit default swap provider.

Some commentators have categorised synthetic deals using slightly different terms. For instance, Boggiano, Waterson and Stein (2002) define the following types:

- balance sheet static synthetic CDOs;
- managed static synthetic CDOs;
- balance sheet variable synthetic CDOs;
- managed variable synthetic CDOs.

As described by Boggiano et al., the basic structure is as we described earlier for a partially funded synthetic CDO. In fact, there is essentially little difference between the first two types of deal, in the latter an investment manager rather than the credit swap counterparty selects the portfolio. However, the reference assets remain static for the life of the deal in both cases. For the last two deal types, the main difference would appear to be that an investment manager, rather than the originator bank, trades the portfolio of credit swaps under specified guidelines. In the author's belief this is not a structural difference and so for this chapter we will consider them both as managed CDOs, which are described later.

A generic partially funded synthetic transaction is shown in Figure 20.12 below. It shows an arrangement whereby the issuer enters into two credit default swaps; the first with an SPV that provides protection for losses up to a specified amount of the reference pool,[6] while the second swap is set up with the OECD bank or, occasionally, an insurance company.[7]

---

6 In practice, to date this portion has been between 5% and 15% of the reference pool.

7 An "OECD" bank, thus guaranteeing a 20% risk-weighting for capital ratio purposes, under Basle I rules.

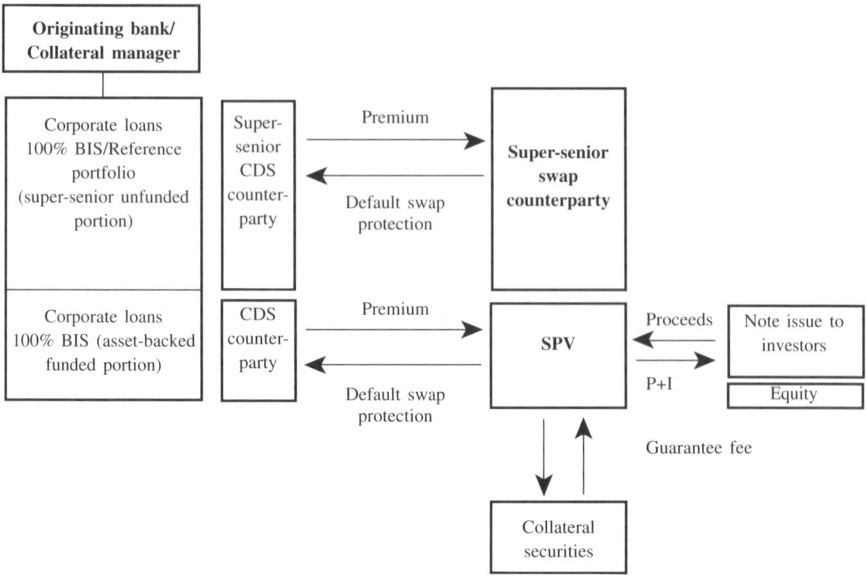

Figure 20.12 Partially funded synthetic CDO structure

A *fully funded* CDO is a structure where the credit risk of the entire portfolio is transferred to the SPV via a credit default swap. In a fully funded (or just "funded") synthetic CDO the issuer enters into the credit default swap with the SPV, which itself issues credit-linked notes (CLNs) to the entire value of the assets on which the risk has been transferred. The proceeds from the notes are invested in risk-free government or agency debt such as gilts, bunds or *Pfandbriefe*, or in senior unsecured bank debt. Should there be a default on one or more of the underlying assets, the required amount of the collateral is sold and the proceeds from the sale paid to the issuer to recompense for the losses. The premium paid on the credit default swap must be sufficiently high to ensure that it covers the difference in yield between that on the collateral and that on the notes issued by the SPV. The generic structure is illustrated in Figure 20.13.

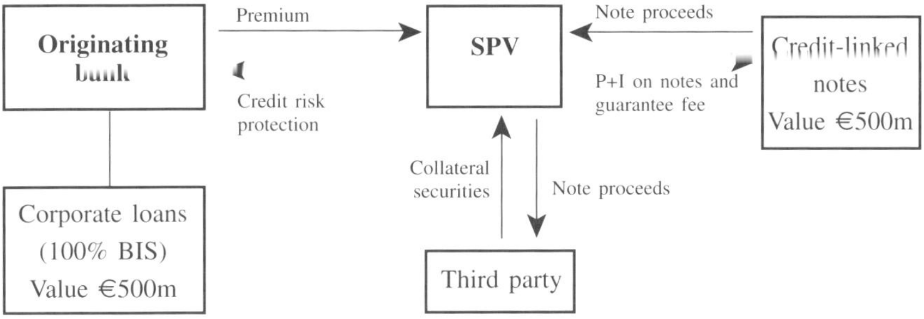

Figure 20.13 Fully funded synthetic balance sheet CDO structure

Fully funded CDOs are relatively uncommon. One of the advantages of the partially funded arrangement is that the issuer will pay a lower premium compared to a fully funded synthetic CDO, because it is not required to pay the difference between the yield on the collateral and the coupon on the note issue (the unfunded part of the transaction). The downside is that the issuer will receive a reduction in risk-weighting for capital purposes to 20% for the risk transferred via the super senior default swap.

The fully *unfunded* CDO uses only credit derivatives in its structure. It is illustrated in Figure 20.14 below. The swaps are rated in a similar fashion to notes, and there is usually an "equity" piece that is retained by the originator. The reference portfolio will again be commercial loans, usually 100% risk-weighted, or other assets. The credit rating of the swap tranches is based on the rating of the reference assets, as well as other factors such as the diversity of the assets and ratings performance correlation. The typical structure is illustrated in Figure 20.14. As well as the equity tranche, there will be one or more junior tranches, one or more senior tranches and a super-senior tranche. The senior tranches are sold on to AAA-rated banks as a portfolio credit default swap, while the junior tranche is usually sold to an OECD bank. The ratings of the tranches will typically be:

- super-senior: AAA
- senior: AA to AAA
- junior: BB to A
- equity: unrated.

The credit default swaps are not single-name swaps, but are written on a class of debt. The advantage for the originator is that it can name the reference asset class to investors without having to disclose the name of the specific loans. Default swaps are usually cash-settled and not physically settled, so that the reference assets can be replaced with other assets if desired by the sponsor.

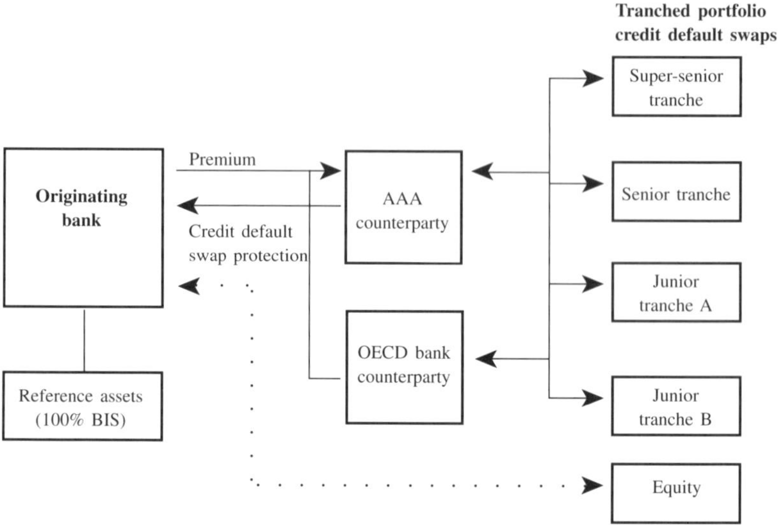

Figure 20.14 The fully synthetic or unfunded CDO

Within the European market, static synthetic balance sheet CDOs are the most common structure. The reasons that banks originate them are twofold:

- *capital relief*: banks can obtain regulatory capital relief by transferring lower yield corporate credit risk such as corporate bank loans off their balance sheet. Under Basle I rules all corporate debt carries an identical 100% risk-weighting; therefore, with banks having to assign 8% of capital for such loans, higher rated (and hence lower yielding) corporate assets will require the same amount of capital but will generate a lower return on that capital. A bank may wish to transfer such higher rated, lower yield assets from its balance sheet, and this can be achieved via a CDO transaction. The capital requirements for a synthetic CDO are lower than for corporate assets; for example, the funded segment of the deal will be supported by high-quality collateral such as government bonds, and via a repo arrangement with an OECD bank would carry a 20% risk-weighting, as does the super senior element;
- *transfer of credit risk*: the cost of servicing a fully funded CDO, and the premium payable on the associated credit default swap, can be prohibitive. With a partially funded structure, the issue amount is

typically a relatively small share of the asset portfolio. This lowers substantially the default swap premium. Also, as the CDO investors suffer the first loss element of the portfolio, the super-senior default swap can be entered into at a considerably lower cost than that on a fully funded CDO.

Synthetic deals may be either static or managed. Static deals hold the following advantages:

- there are no ongoing management fees to be borne by the vehicle;
- the investor can review and grant approval to credits that are to make up the reference portfolio.

The disadvantage is that if there is a deterioration in credit quality of one or more names, there is no ability to remove or offset this name from the pool and the vehicle continues to suffer from it. During 2001 a number of high-profile defaults in the market meant that static pool CDOs performed below expectation. This explains partly the rise in popularity of the managed synthetic deal, which we consider next.

The managed synthetic CDO

Managed synthetic CDOs are the latest variant of the synthetic CDO structure.[8] They are similar to the partially funded deals we described earlier, except that the reference asset pool of credit derivatives is actively traded by the sponsoring investment manager. It is the maturing market in credit default swaps, resulting in good liquidity in a large number of synthetic corporate credits, that has facilitated the introduction of the managed synthetic CDO. With this structure, originators can use credit derivatives to arbitrage cash and synthetic liabilities, as well as leverage off their expertise in credit trading to generate profit. The advantages for investors are the same as with earlier generations of CDOs, except that with active trading they are gaining a still larger exposure to the abilities of the investment manager. The underlying asset pool is again a portfolio of credit default swaps. However, these are now dynamically managed and actively traded, under specified guidelines. Thus, there is greater flexibility afforded to the sponsor, and the

[8] These are also commonly known as collateralised synthetic obligations or CSOs within the market. *RISK* magazine has called them collateralised swap obligations, which handily also shortens to CSOs. Boggiano et al. (2002) refer to these structures as managed variable synthetic CDOs, although the author has not come across this term in other literature.

vehicle will record trading gains or losses as a result of credit derivative trading. In most structures, the investment manager can only buy protection (short credit) in order to offset an existing sold protection default swap. For some deals, this restriction is removed and the investment manager can buy or sell credit derivatives to reflect its view.

Structure

The structure of the managed synthetic is similar to the partially funded synthetic CDO, with a separate legally incorporated SPV. On the liability side there is an issue of notes, whose note proceeds are invested in collateral or *eligible investments*, which is one or a combination of the following:

- a bank deposit account or guaranteed investment contract (GIC) which pays a pre-specified rate of interest;[9]
- risk-free bonds such as US Treasury securities, German *Pfandbriefe* or AAA-rated bonds such as credit-card ABS securities;
- a repo agreement with risk-free collateral;
- a liquidity facility with a AA-rated bank;
- a market-sensitive debt instrument, often enhanced with the repo or liquidity arrangement described above.

On the asset side, the SPV enters into credit default swaps and/or total return swaps, selling protection to the sponsor. The investment manager (or "collateral manager") can trade in and out of credit default swaps after the transaction has closed in the market.[10] The SPV enters into credit derivatives via a single basket credit default swap to one swap counterparty, written on a portfolio of reference assets, or via multiple single-name credit swaps with a number of swap counterparties. The latter arrangement is more common and is referred to as a *multiple dealer* CDO. A percentage of the reference portfolio will be identified at the start of work on the transaction, with the remainder of the entities being selected during the ramp-up period ahead of closing. The SPV enters into the other side of the credit default swaps by selling protection to one of the swap counterparties on specific reference

---

9 A GIC has been defined either as an account that pays a fixed rate of interest for its term, or more usually an account that pays a fixed spread below Libor or euribor, usually three-month floating rolled over each interest period.

10 This term is shared with other securitisation structures: when notes have been priced, and placed in the market, and all legal documentation signed by all named participants, the transaction has *closed*. In effect this is the start of the transaction, and all being well the noteholders will receive interest payments during the life of the deal and principal repayment on maturity.

entities. Thereafter the investment manager can trade out of this exposure in the following ways:

- buying credit protection from another swap counterparty on the same reference entity. This offsets the existing exposure, but there may be residual risk exposure unless premium dates are matched exactly or if there is a default in both the reference entity and the swap counterparty;
- unwinding or terminating the swap with the counterparty;
- buying credit protection on a reference asset that is outside the portfolio. This is uncommon as it will leave residual exposures and may affect premium spread gains.

The SPV actively manages the portfolio within specified guidelines, the decisions being made by the investment manager. Initially, the manager's opportunity to trade may be extensive, but this will be curtailed if there are losses. The trading guidelines will extend to both individual credit default swaps and at the portfolio level. They may include:

- parameters under which the investment manager (in the guise of the SPV) may actively close out, hedge or substitute reference assets using credit derivatives;
- guidelines under which the investment manager can trade credit derivatives to maximise gains or minimise losses on reference assets that have improved or worsened in credit quality or outlook.

Credit default swaps may be cash settled or physically settled, with physical settlement being more common in a managed synthetic deal. In a multiple dealer CDO the legal documentation must be in place with all names on the counterparty dealer list, which may add to legal costs as standardisation may be difficult.

Investors who are interested in this structure are seeking to benefit from the following advantages compared to vanilla synthetic deals:

- active management of the reference portfolio and the trading expertise of the investment manager in the corporate credit market;
- a multiple dealer arrangement, so that the investment manager can obtain the most competitive prices for default swaps;
- under physical settlement, the investment manager (via the SPV) has the ability to obtain the highest recovery value for the reference asset.

A generic managed synthetic CDO is illustrated in Figure 20.15.

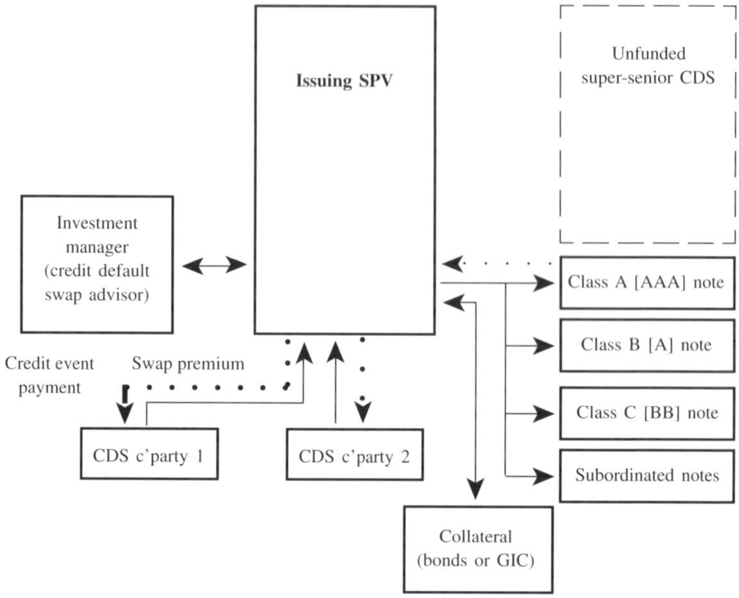

Figure 20.15 Generic managed synthetic CDO
Note: CDS = credit default swap.

Risk and return on CDOs

Risk-return analysis

The return analysis for CDOs performed by potential investors is necessarily different to that undertaken for other securitised asset classes. For CDOs the three key factors to consider are:

- default probabilities and cumulative default rates;
- default correlations;
- recovery rates.

Analysts make assumptions about each of these with regard to individual reference assets, usually with recourse to historical data. We consider each factor in turn.

Default probability rates

The level of default probability rates will vary with each deal. Analysts such as the rating agencies will use a number of methods to estimate default probabilities, such as individual reference credit ratings and historical probability rates. Since there may be as much as 150 or more reference names in the CDO, a common approach is to use the average rating of the reference portfolio. Rating agencies such as Moody's provide data on the default rates for different ratings as an "average" class, which can be used in the analysis.

Correlation

The correlation between assets in the reference portfolio of a CDO is an important factor in CDO returns analysis. A problem arises with what precise correlation value to use; these can be correlation between default probabilities, correlation between timing of default and correlation between spreads. The *diversity score* value of the CDO plays a part in this: it represents the number of uncorrelated bonds with identical par value and the same default probability.

Recovery rates

Recovery rates for individual obligors differ by issuer and industry classification. Rating agencies such as Moody's publish data on the average prices of all defaulted bonds, and generally analysts will construct a database of recovery rates by industry and credit rating for use in modelling the expected recovery rates of assets in the collateral pool. Note that for synthetic CDOs with credit default swaps as assets in the portfolio, this factor is not relevant.

Analysts undertake simulation modelling to generate scenarios of default and expected return. For instance, they may model the number of defaults up to maturity, the recovery rates of these defaults and the timing of defaults. All these variables are viewed as random variables, so they are modelled using a stochastic process.

CDO yield spreads

Fund managers consider investing in CDO-type products as they represent a diversification in the European bond markets, with yields that are comparable to credit-card or auto-loan ABS assets. A cash CDO also gives investors exposure to sectors in the market that may not otherwise be accessible to most investors; for example, credits such as small- or medium-sized corporate entities that rely entirely on bank financing. Also, the extent of credit enhancement and note tranching in a CDO means that they may show better risk/reward profiles than straight conventional debt, with a higher yield but incorporating asset backing and insurance backing. In cash and synthetic CDOs the issues notes are often bullet bonds, with fixed term to maturity, whereas other ABS and MBS products are amortising securities with only average (expected life) maturities. This may suit certain longer dated investors.

An incidentally perceived advantage of cash CDOs is that they are typically issued by financial institutions such as higher rated banks. This usually provides comfort on the credit side, but also on the underlying administration and servicing side with regard to underlying assets, compared to consumer receivables securitisations.

To illustrate yields, Figure 20.16 shows the spreads on a selected range of notes during January 2002 over the credit spectrum. Figure 20.17 shows a comparison of different asset classes in European structured products during February 2002. In Table 20.1 we show the note spread at issue for a selected number of synthetic CDOs closed during 2001–2002. The regression of these and selected other AAA-rated note spreads against maturity shows an adjusted R^2 of 0.82 in Figure 20.18, which suggests that for a set of AAA-rated securities, the term to maturity is not the only consideration.[11] Other factors that may explain the difference in yields include perception of the asset manager, secondary market liquidity and the placing power of the arranger of the transaction.

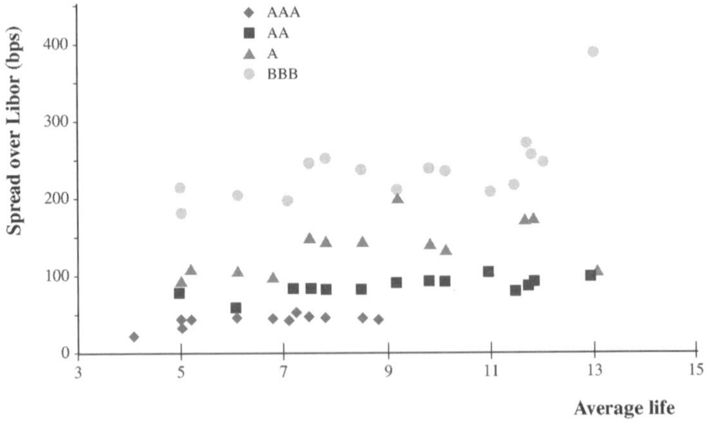

Figure 20.16 Rating spreads, February 2002.
Source: JPMorgan.

[11] Calculated from twelve synthetic CDO senior (AAA-rated) notes issued in Europe during Jan.–Jun. 2002; yields obtained from Bloomberg.

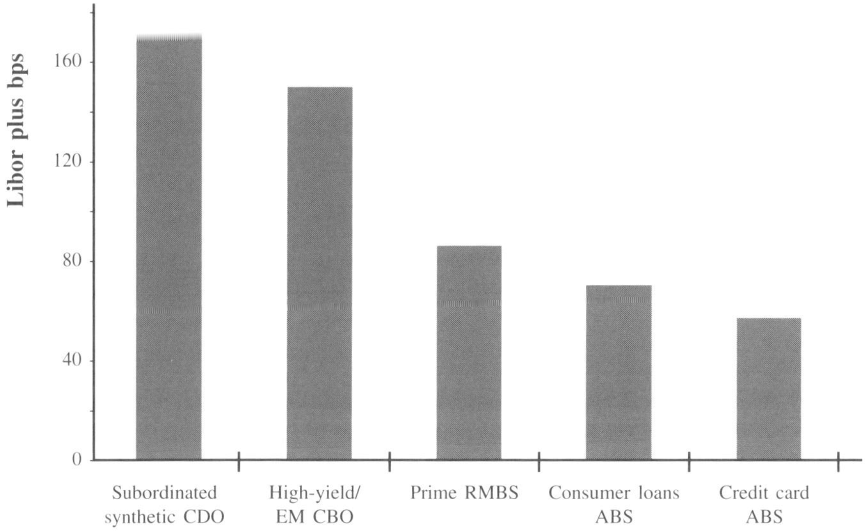

Figure 20.17 Comparing CDO yields to other securitisation asset classes

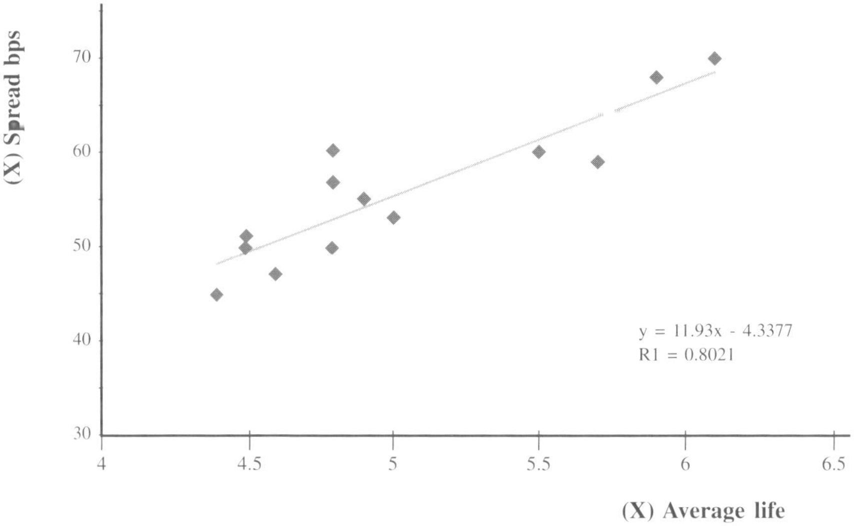

Figure 20.18 AAA spreads as at February 2002 (selected European CDO deals)

Deal name plus close date	Moodys	S&P	Fitch	Spread bps	Index
Jazz CDO Mar-02					
Class A	Aaa	AAA		47	6m Libor
Class B	Aa2	AAA		75	6m Libor
Class C-1		A-		135	6m Libor
Class D		BBB		240	6m Libor
Robeco III CSO Dec-01					
Class A	Aaa			55	3m Libor/euribor
Class B	Aa2			85	3m Libor
Class C	Baa1			275	3m Libor
Marylebone Road CBO III Oct-01					
Class A-1	Aaa	AAA		45	3m Libor
Class A-2	Aa1	AAA		65	3m Libor
Class A-3	A2	AAA		160	3m Libor
Brooklands € referenced linked notes Jul-01					
Class A	Aaa		AAA	50	3m Libor
Class B	Aa3		AA-	80	3m Libor
Class C	Baa2		BBB	250	3m Libor
Class D-1	n/a		BBB-	500	3m Libor
North Street Ref. Linked Notes 2000–2 Oct-00					
Class A			AAA	70	6m Libor
Class B			AA	105	6m Libor
Class C			A	175	6m Libor

Table 20.1 Selected synthetic deal spreads at issue
Source: Bloomberg.

CASE STUDIES

The latest manifestation of synthetic securitisation technology is the managed synthetic CDO or CSO. In Europe these have been originated by fund managers, with the first example being issued in 2000. Although they are, in effect, investment vehicles, the disciplines required to manage what is termed a "structured credit product" is not necessarily identical to those required for a corporate bond fund. Investment bank arrangers are apt to suggest that a track record in credit derivatives trading is an essential pre-requisite to being a successful CSO manager. There is an element of reputational risk at stake if a CDO suffers a downgrade; for example, during 2001 Moody's downgraded elements of 83 separate CDO deals, across 174 tranches, as underlying pools of investment-grade and high-yield corporate bonds experienced default.[12] Thus managing a CDO presents a high-profile record of a fund manager's performance.

In Europe, fund managers that have originated managed synthetic deals include Robeco, Cheyne Capital Management, BAREP Asset Management and Axa Investment Managers. In the second part of this case study we look at three specific deals as case studies, issued in the European market during 2001 and 2002.

The deals discussed are innovative structures and a creative combination of securitisation technology and credit derivatives. They show how a portfolio manager can utilise vehicles of this kind to exploit its expertise in credit trading, as well as provide attractive returns for investors. Managed synthetic CDOs also present fund managers with a vehicle to build on their credit derivatives experience. As the market in synthetic credit, in Europe at least, is frequently more liquid than the cash market for the same reference names, it is reasonable to expect more transactions of this type in the near future.

Blue Chip Funding 2001-1 plc

Blue Chip Funding is a managed synthetic CDO originated by Dolmen Securities, which closed in December 2001. The deal has a €1 billion reference portfolio, with the following terms:

[12] *Source*: CreditFlux, April 2002.

Name	Blue Chip Funding 2001-1 plc
Manager	Dolmen Securities Limited
Arranger	Dolmen Securities Limited
	Dresdner Kleinwort Wasserstein
Closing date	17 December 2001
Portfolio	1 billion of credit default swaps
Reference assets	80 investment-grade entities
Portfolio Administrator	Bank of New York

The structure is partially funded, with 80 million notes issued, or 8% of the nominal value. The share of the unfunded piece is comparatively high. The proceeds from the notes issue are invested in AAA securities, which are held in custody by the third-party agency service provider, which must be rated at AA- or higher. The diversity of the structure is reflected in there being eighty different credits, with a weighted average rating of A-, with no individual asset having a rating below BBB-.

The structure is illustrated at Figure 20.19.

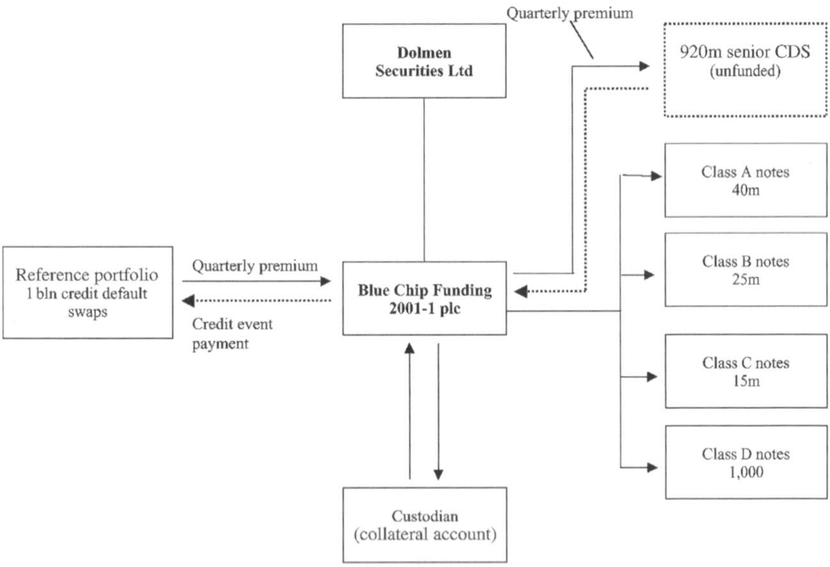

Figure 20.19 Blue Chip Funding managed synthetic CDO
Source: S&P. Reproduced with permission.

With this deal, the managers have the ability to trade the credit default swaps with a pre-specified panel of dealers. The default swap counterparties must have a short-term rating of A-1+ or better. Trading will result in trading gains or losses. This contrasts with a static synthetic deal, where investors have not been affected by trading gains or losses that arise from pool substitutions. The deal was rated by Standard & Poor's, which in its rating report described the management strategy as "defensive trading" to avoid acute credit deteriorations. There are a number of guidelines that the manager must adhere to, such as:

- the manager may both sell credit protection and purchase credit protection; however, the manager may only short credit (purchase credit protection) in order to close out or offset an existing previous sale of protection;
- there is a discretionary trading limit of 10% of portfolio value;
- a minimum weighted average premium of 60 bps for swaps must be maintained;
- a minimum reinvestment test must be passed at all times: this states that if the value of the collateral account falls below €80 million, interest generated by the collateral securities must be diverted from the equity (Class C and D notes) to the senior notes until the interest cover is restored.

The issuer has sold protection on the reference assets. On occurrence of a credit event, the issuer will make credit protection payments to the swap counterparty (see Figure 20.19). If the vehicle experiences losses as a result of credit events or credit default swap trading, these are made up from the collateral account.

Robeco CSO III B.V.

The Robeco III CDO is described as the first stand-alone, multiple dealer managed synthetic CDO in Europe. It is a €1 billion structure sponsored and managed by Robeco Asset Management in Rotterdam, the Netherlands. The manager can trade in credit default swaps but, as with Blue Chip Funding, is limited to purchasing swaps only in order to offset an existing sold protection swap. The motivation behind the structuring of the trade was partly the liquidity and depth of the credit derivatives market for European corporate credits, deemed to be greater than the equivalent cash market bonds for the same names.[13]

Name	Robeco CSO III B.V.
Manager	Robeco Institutional Asset Management B.V.
Arrangers	JPMorgan Chase Bank
	Robeco Alternative Investments
Closing date	15 December 2001
Maturity	September 2008
Portfolio	€1 billion of credit default swaps
Reference assets	80 investment-grade entities
Portfolio Administrator	JPMorgan Chase Bank Institutional Trust Services

Robeco CSO III BV tranching structure

Class	Amount €m	Per cent	Rating	Type	Coupon
Class A	213	21.30	AAA	Floating	3m euribor + 0.55%
Class B	15.5	1.55	Aa2	Floating	3m euribor + 0.85%
Class C	31.5	3.15	Baa1	Floating	3m euribor + 2.75%
Subordinated	40	4.00	NR	Variable	
Class P	7.5		Baa1	Variable	

Table 20.2 Robeco III structure and tranching
Source: Moodys.

[13] *Source*: *RISK*, March 2002.

The first managed synthetic deal in Europe, Robeco III-type structures have subsequently been adopted by other collateral managers. The principal innovation of the vehicle is the method by which the credit default swaps are managed, as part of a dynamically managed reference portfolio. The addition or offsetting of swaps at different spread levels creates trading gains or losses for the vehicle. The choice of reference credits on which swaps are written must, as expected with a CDO, follow a number of criteria set by the ratings agency, including diversity score, rating factor, weighted average spread, geographical and industry concentration, among others.

The reference portfolio is comprised of between 100 and 130 reference credits, of which at least 90% must be at investment grade rating. There is a minimum permitted weighted average credit rating of Baa2. On issue, the average rating factor was at around 250–260. The structure is 70% unfunded, as shown in Table 20.2 and Figure 20.20. The remaining 30% is funded through the issue of credit-linked notes, and after payment of the initial fees and expenses of the issuer, the proceeds of the note issue are invested in the following as collateral:

- €220 million invested in a unique ABS security, a credit card-backed bond issued by MBNA Bank and rated AAA, which has a scheduled maturity of September 2008;
- €80 million invested in a series of "guaranteed investment contracts" (GIC) paying an average rate of Libor minus 10 basis points.

The structure is of interest to investors who wish to exploit the liquidity of the credit derivative market for European credits that are not well represented in the cash markets. Investors who wish to diversify across the market can also leverage the expertise of the CDO manager in the synthetic credit market.

An introduction to credit default swaps (CDS) is given in Appendix 20.1 at the back of this chapter.

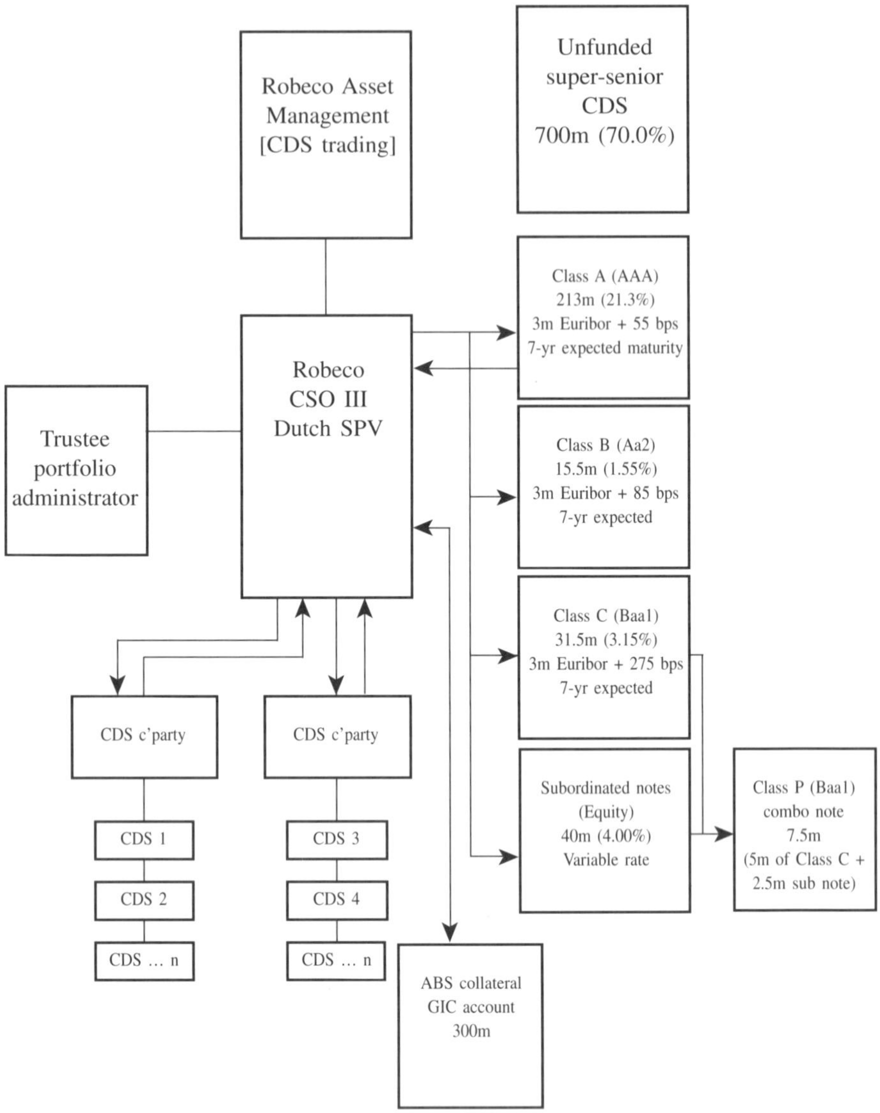

Figure 20.20 Robeco III structure and tranching
Source: Moodys.

Portfolio trading

Upon closure of the transaction, the issuer enters into credit default swaps with counterparties among a preselected list of seven swap dealers, building up over the ramp-up period to a maximum of €1 billion notional of swaps. At this point the portfolio of default swaps is dynamic, as the issuer may enter into additional default swaps, and unwind or offset existing swaps. The decisions on when and which swaps to trade is taken by the portfolio manager. The issuer sells credit protection through the network of established counterparties; it may buy protection but only to remove an existing reference entity exposure. The sale of a credit protection adds a new credit default swap to the portfolio, whereas buying a swap to offset an existing exposure adds a new swap but nets out the exposure. This trading leads to trading gains or losses. Trading gains are to the benefit of the vehicle and will increase the value of the collateral pool.

Each credit default swap is a vanilla single-name contract, under which the counterparty pays the regular credit protection premium to the issuer. On occurrence of a credit event for the reference entity, the counterparty will calculate a net loss amount that is paid by the issuer to the counterparty. The loss amount is defined as the difference between the nominal value of the reference entity and its market value at the time of the credit event. Payments required on occurrence of a credit event, and trading losses resulting from credit defauilt swap activity, are both paid out of the collateral account.

The portfolio manager must follow certain trading guidelines when adding or removing default swaps. As set out by Moody's,[14] the manager may add reference credits to the portfolio only if the total credit default swap notional amount is below €1 billion, and if the outstanding loss amount is below €25 million. For any single obligor name, the criteria are:

- a minimum rating of Ba3 or above;
- notional limits for a single name of €5 million, €10 million or €12.5 million, depending on credit rating.

Reference credits may be removed only if:

- there has been a fall in the reference credit default swap premium, so that trading it out creates a gain;
- the premium has increased by 25% (in other words, a kind of "stop loss");
- the reference entity has been subject to a credit rating downgrade.

Returns analysis

The structure of the vehicle, with 30% level of funding, adds to the attraction of the transaction for investors. In effect, the issuer represents a counterparty with 30% Tier 1 capital. This reduces the cost of capital of the vehicle and improves return for investors compared to a cash CDO. As reported by *RISK*,[15] a comparison with an equivalent cash vehicle resulted in returns of 20.1% compared to 11.9%, as shown in Figure 20.21. This reflected the significantly lower funding cost associated with the (lower) cost of the super-senior swap element, which was 70% of the structure.

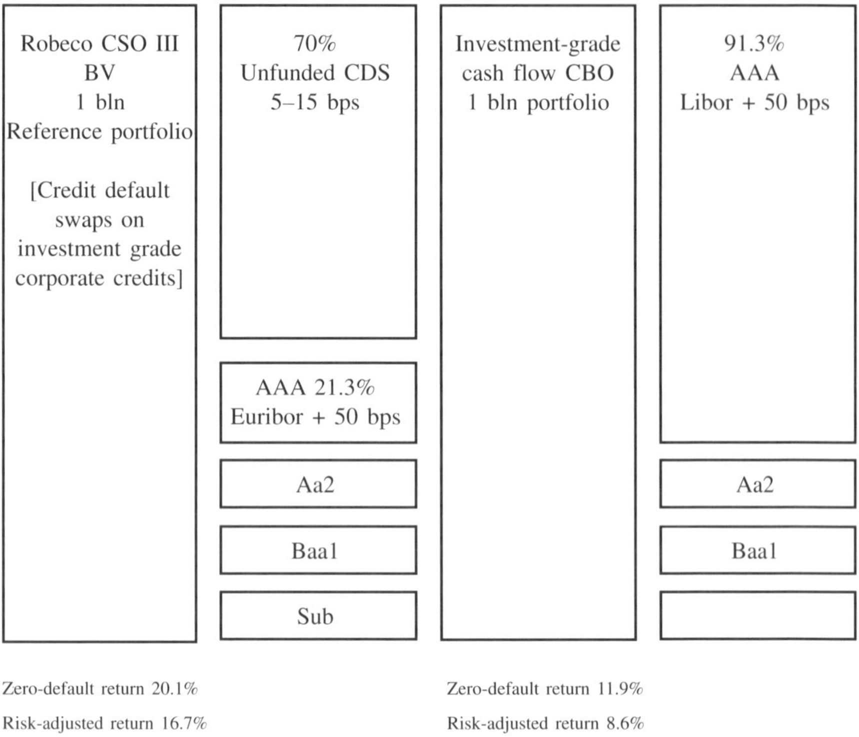

Figure 20.21 Reboco CSO returns analysis
Source: *RISK*. Used with permission.

---

[14] Robeco CSO III B.V., *Pre-sale report*, Moody's Investor Service, 7 December 2001.
[15] *RISK*, March 2002.

Priority of payments

The priority of payments followed by the vehicle follows a familiar pattern for CDOs. On each payment date, payments will be made in accordance with the waterfall shown in Table 20.3. These payments are funded by coupon from the collateral pool, including interest earned on the GIC account, and the credit default swap premiums. The principal payments waterfall is funded from the collateral security and funds held in the reserve account.

Interest proceeds waterfall	Principal proceeds waterfall
Trustee fees, costs, expenses	Fees, costs, expenses
Management fee	Credit default swaps payment
Class A interest	Management fee
(If pass Class B interest trigger test), Class B interest	Unpaid Class A interest
(If pass Class C interest trigger), Class C interest	Class A principal
Interest to subordinated Class	Unpaid Class B interest
Loss amount reserve payment	Class B principal
(If Class B trigger event), interest to Class B and deferred interest	Unpaid Class C interest
(If Class C trigger event), interest to Class C	Class C principal
Subordinated notes	Subordinated notes

Table 20.3 Robeco CSO waterfall
Source: Robeco offering circular.

Reporting

Investors track the performance of the vehicle from information in the periodic investor reports. These are prepared by the portfolio administrator, in consultation with the portfolio manager, and distributed on a monthly basis. A separate report is prepared on a quarterly basis and distributed on each payment date.

The monthly report includes the following information:

- the principal balance of the collateral pool security;
- the value of cash held in the collateral account and reserve accounts;

- any movements of securities in the collateral account; for instance, securities or eligible investments disposed of since the date of last report;
- detail of any default in collateral securities;
- the aggregate notional value of the synthetic portfolio, and details of each reference entity held in the synthetic portfolio (reference name, swap counterparty, trade date, maturity date, credit rating, fixed spread premium as percentage, notional amount);
- the diversity score;
- compliance test results, including weighted average rating, weighted average spread and weighted average recovery;
- the outstanding loss amount.

It is a requirement of the ratings agencies that the portfolio report be produced, or at least verified, by an independent third-party to the deal. The investor report is sent to the issuer, swap counterparties, rating agency and noteholders.

Synthetic mortgage-backed securities

In the author's book *Structured Credit Products: Credit Derivatives and Synthetic Securitisation*, synthetic MBS structures are defined as synthetic securitisations of pools of mortgage assets.

The term can also be used to refer to another product, which is essentially a credit default swap (CDS) that references an existing MBS tranche. This product is not an instrument of corporate finance, because it does not raise any funds for the original entity behind the MBS issue; rather, it has arisen due to the shortage of supply in the ABS and MBS cash markets.

Background on the basic CDS is given in Appendix 20.1 at the end of this chapter.

Product description

The concept we discuss can be applied to any structured finance product. That is, it is possible now for investors to access virtually any corporate entity or securitisation tranche (ABS, MBS or CDO) via the CDS market. So although we illustrate the concept with reference to one type of asset class, remember that the concept can be applied across any reference asset class and security provided a CDS market-maker is willing to quote a price for the specific security.

The bonds we will consider in this illustration are all examples of residential mortgage-backed securities (RMBS); in fact, a special class of RMBS known as Home Equity.[16] We show three of these bonds in Table 20.4.

Bond	Amount issued $m	CDS spread	Libor spread on Note	CUSIP number	Interest frequency
ACCR 2004-3 2M7	7.665	335	350	004375BX8	Monthly on 25th
CWL 2004-6 B	46.0	340	375	126673BL5	Monthly on 25th
NCHET 2004-2 M9	19.374	345	400	64352VGJ4	Monthly on 25th

Table 20.4 Securities used in illustration, showing CDS and cash market prices, 21 September 2004-09-26

Bond terms source: Bloomberg L.P.

CDS price source: KBC Financial Products.

All three bonds were part of new issues, for first settlement in September 2004. The mezzanine tranches were in high demand at the time of issue. Under conventional circumstances the CDS price for these securities would be expected to lie above the note yield. But in fact the opposite is true, as the market quotes shown in Table 20.4 indicate. This reflects the lack of supply of these bonds in the market, such that investors are forced to access them in the synthetic market.

The small size of these note tranches is a key reason behind the low availability of paper. We see that only $7.6 million of the ACCR bond is available, a very low figure in any securitisation. The entire securitisation itself is a large issue, as we see from Figure 20.22. This shows the Bloomberg DES page for the transaction, which is called Accredited Mortgage Loan Trust. From this we see that a total of $766.43 million of notes was issued as part of this deal, but the tranche in question – the Baa3/BBB-rated 2M7 piece – made up less than 1% of this total. Given this paucity of supply, the bond can be sourced more easily in the CDS market, but this carries with it a reduction in yield spread, associated with the greater demand over supply.[17]

[16] For further information on Home Equity securities see Fabozzi (2004).

[17] In effect the cash market note yield of 350 bps for this bond is a theoretical construct. As the bond in effect cannot be purchased, as no paper is available, the cash market yield for this name cannot actually be earned by any investor.

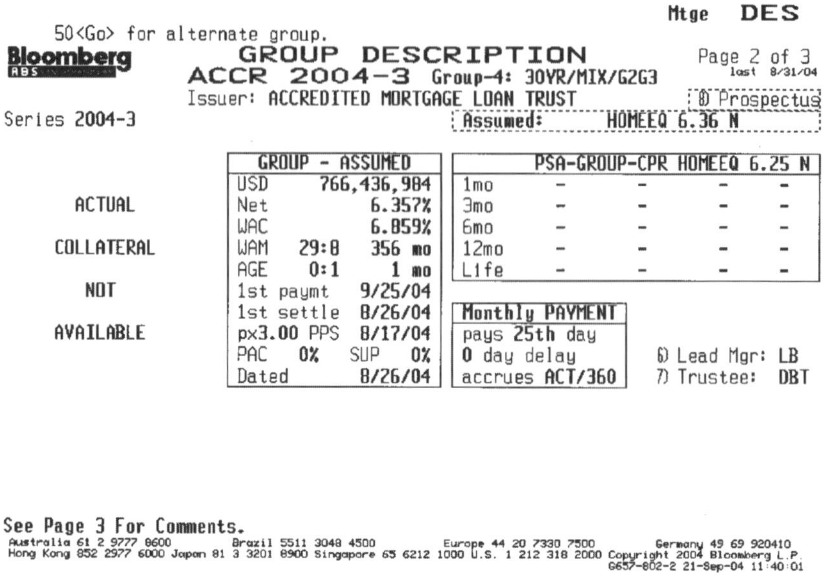

Figure 20.22 DES for ACCR Home Equity securitisation transaction
© Bloomberg L.P. Used with permission.

We observe similar characteristics for the two other bonds in our sample. The Countrywide Asset-Backed Certificates transaction is made up of a total of \$4.426 billion in 12 different tranches; the mezzanine tranche rated Baa3/BBB was issued in a size of only \$46 million. The total size of the New Century Home Equity Loan Trust deal was \$1.937 billion, while the particular mezzanine tranche we are interested in was issued in size of only 1% of this total. This bond exhibits the widest spread in our small group, with the CDS trading at a premium of 55 basis points to the theoretical cash price.

CDS mechanics

The CDS contracts written on these structured finance securities have minor differences in their terms compared to vanilla single-name CDS instruments. This includes the following:

- a premium payment set to match the payment date of the cash bond, in this case a monthly payment on the 25th of each month. The standard CDS payment terms are quarterly in arrears;

- in practice, an un-fixed maturity date. The CDS written on these bonds is set to match their maturity. From Figure 20.23, we see that the ACCR 2M7 tranche has a weighted-average life of 5.4 years. This is of course an estimate based on a specified prepayment rate, which is standard practice for all RMBS bonds. In reality, the bond may well pay off before or after 5.4 years. The CDS contract language specifies that the contract expires when the cash bond itself is fully paid off;
- the transaction undertaken by the investor for the CDS that references the ACCR 2M7 tranche was for a notional of $10 million. This is more than the actual amount in existence of the physical bond. Hence, it is standard practice for all structured finance CDS contracts to always be cash-settled instruments.

By setting the terms in this way, investors are able to access these types of names and asset classes where the cash market bond is no longer available to them, by selling protection on the bond tranches using a CDS.

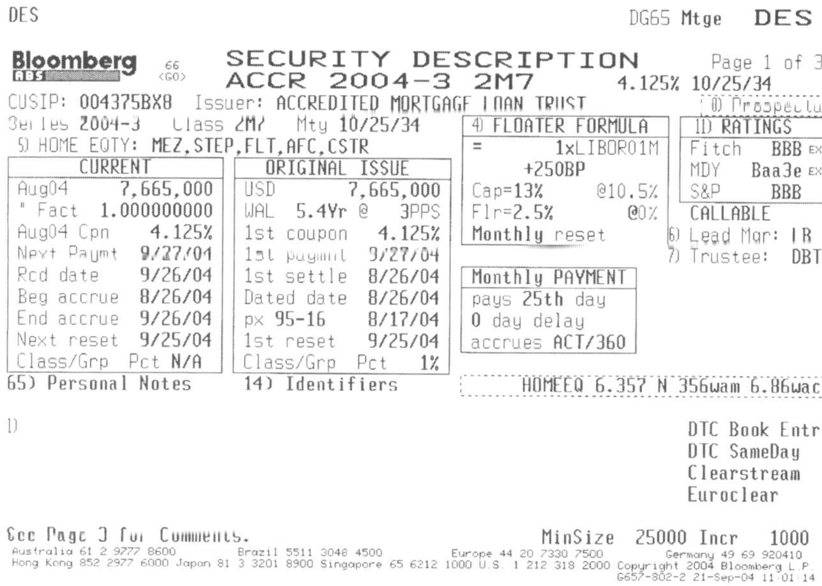

Figure 20.23 DES for 2M7 tranche of ACCR transaction, 21 September 2004

© Bloomberg L.P. Used with permission.

The CDS market-maker that is the counterparty to the CDS investor may gain from acting in this business in the following ways:

- buying protection on this class of assets releases economic capital that can be invested in higher yielding assets elsewhere;
- it may be able to find similar assets in the cash market that yield a higher spread than the CDS protection it is paying for;
- it can treat this business as trading activity – CDS market-making – and seek to gain a trading profit.

Irrespective of the motivation of the investor and the CDS counterparty to these trades, this business illustrates the contribution to market liquidity of credit derivatives, as well as the impact of supply and demand on reversing the market convention of a positive basis.

Example illustration

We assume a tranche of an existing MBS issue that pays Libor plus 50 basis points (L+50) and a CDS contract written on this tranche that pays L+50 to the protection seller. To illustrate the cash market investment against the synthetic investment, consider Figure 20.24 below, which compares and contrasts each type for a holding of $10 million nominal.

Note that for the cash investor, we assume that the bondholding can be funded at Libor-flat, so that the net return remains L+50. Although this is an unrealistic assumption (during 2004–2005 even a AAA-rated MBS bond would be funded no better than L+5 and possibly L+10, depending on the type of counterparty), we have done this for ease of illustration.

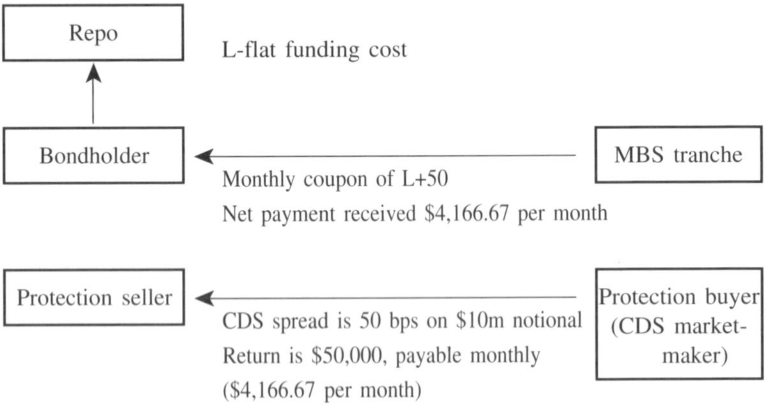

Figure 20.24 Illustrating cash and synthetic investment in an MBS note

Under the basic scenario, there are no credit events during the life of the CDS, and no interest shortfalls during this term for the cash bond. The return on both the CDS and bond are therefore identical.

Consider if the MBS tranche is written down by 20%. In this event, under the terms of the contract, the CDS suffers a nominal writedown of 20%. Both the MBS bond and the CDS pay coupon during the writedown period. For the cash bondholder, there is a loss of $1 million, while on the CDS a protection payment of $1 million is made by the protection seller (investor) to the protection buyer. In other words, the economic impact is identical for both types of investor. Following the writedown, cash flows for both the bond and the CDS are also identical; that is:

- on the bond there is a new face value of $9 million; hence, the coupon payment received is L+50 on notional of $9 million or $3,750.00 per month;
- on the CDS the new notional is $9 millon; hence, the contract now pays L+50 or $3,750.00 per month.

Now consider an event where on final maturity of the bond there is a failure to pay 50% of the principal balance. On CDS maturity, the reference bond pays only 50% of the scheduled principal. In this case, the protection seller pays $5 million to the protection buyer.[18] The bondholder will suffer this loss of $5 million, which actually needs to be paid to its repo counterparty, who is actually holding the bond.

Our final scenario concerns a non-payment of interest for a period of time, let us say six months. During this period no coupon is paid to the MBS bondholder, although the bondholder is still liable to pay the repo interest to the repo counterparty. For the CDS contract, the protection buyer will pay a reduced amount of premium because the reference security is not paying the full coupon, and so in this case premium payments will cease as well. However, because the CDS contract is an unfunded investment (see Choudhry 2004), the investor does not suffer the negative funding that the cash bondholder experiences. This is an advantage for the investor in the synthetic MBS. Assuming that the MBS starts to pay interest after the six-month no-interest period, the cash bondholder will recover all the unpaid interest to date, as does the CDS investor.

[18] This follows immediately after the protection buyer has paid the accrued last monthly CDS premium to the protection seller. This is standard for CDS contracts.

APPENDIX 20.1 An introduction to credit derivatives

Credit derivatives were introduced in significant volumes in the mid-1990s. They are financial instruments originally designed to protect banks and other institutions against losses arising from *credit events*. A succinct definition would be that they are instruments designed to lay off or take on credit risk. Since their inception, they have been used to trade credit for speculative purposes and as hedging instruments.

A payout under a credit derivative is triggered by a credit event. As banks may define default in different ways, the terms under which a credit derivative is executed usually include a specification of what constitutes a credit event. Typically, this can be:

- bankruptcy or insolvency of the reference asset obligor;
- a financial restructuring; for example, occasioned under administration or as required under US bankruptcy protection;
- technical default; for example, the non-payment of interest or coupon when it falls due;
- a change in credit spread payable by the obligor above a specified maximum level;
- a downgrade in credit rating below a specified minimum level.

A user of credit derivatives may be any institution that has an exposure to or desires an exposure to credit risk. This includes investment banks and commercial banks, insurance companies, corporates, fund managers, and hedge funds.

Credit default swaps

The most common credit derivative, and possibly the simplest, is the *credit default swap* (CDS), *default swap* or *credit swap*. This is a contract in which a periodic fixed fee or a one-off premium is paid to a *protection seller*, in return for which the seller will make a payment on the occurrence of a specified credit event. The fee is usually quoted as a basis point fee of the nominal value. The swap can refer to a single asset, known as the reference asset or underlying asset, or a basket of assets. The default payment can be paid in whatever way suits the protection buyer or both counterparties. For example, it may be linked to the change in price of the reference asset or another specified asset, it may be fixed at a predetermined recovery rate, or it may be in the form of actual delivery of the reference asset at a specified price. However it is structured, the credit default swap enables one party to transfer its credit exposure to another party, while retaining the asset on its balance sheet. Alternatively, banks may use default swaps to trade sovereign and corporate credit spreads without trading the actual assets themselves; for example, someone who has gone long on a default swap (the protection buyer) will gain if the reference asset obligor suffers a rating downgrade or defaults, and can sell the default swap at a profit if she can find a buyer counterparty. This is because the cost of protection on the reference asset will have increased as a result of the credit event. The original buyer of the default swap need never have owned a bond issued by the reference asset obligor.

The maturity does not have to match the maturity of the reference asset and in most cases does not. On default the swap is terminated and default payment by the protection seller or guarantor is calculated and handed over. The guarantor may have the asset delivered to her and pay the nominal value, or may cash settle the swap contract.

Figure A20.1 illustrates a standard CDS.

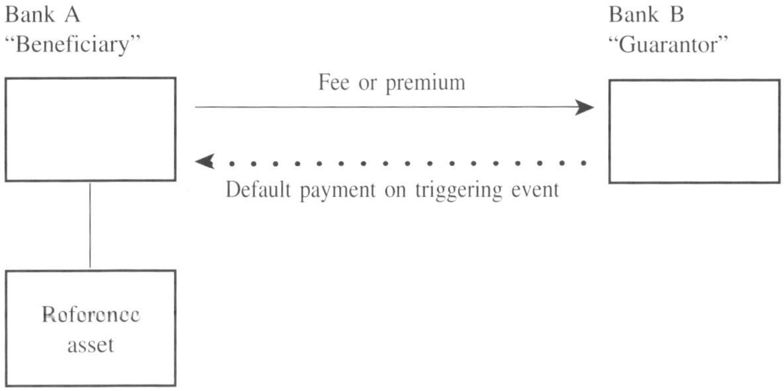

Figure A20.1 CDS

Total return swaps

Total return swaps (TRS)[19] are slightly different to credit default swaps. Anson (1999) makes the distinction that while default swaps are used to hedge credit risk exposure, a TRS is used to increase credit exposure. They are sometimes known as synthetic repos. A TRS is a bilateral contract in which the total return of an asset, such as a bond or bank loan, is exchanged

[19] Also known as *total rate of return swaps* or TRORs.

in return for a funding cash flow, which is usually Libor plus a spread. The return of a bond is defined as the coupon income plus any appreciation in price per nominal. For taking on an exposure to an asset's total return, the purchaser of the swap (the receiver of the total return) pays the Libor floating rate plus spread.

If the total return payer owns the underlying asset (reference asset), it has in effect transferred its economic exposure to the total return receiver. In other words, by entering into the TRS the owner has effected a credit derivative transaction and transferred its credit risk. The net effect is that the owner of the asset has a neutral position that is earning it Libor plus a spread. The asset is not transferred off the owner's balance sheet, only its interest rate and credit risk. This makes it similar to a repo, hence the name synthetic repo. The total return payer must continue to fund the underlying asset at its cost of funding capital.

On the other side of the swap, a TRS enables an investor to obtain an exposure to the economic benefits of an asset without having to own it. The investor is the total return receiver. On maturity of the swap the investor will pay the value of any decline in price of the asset to the TRS payer. If the asset has risen in price, the investor receives the difference in value between the higher current price and the original price at the time of the start of the trade. If the price of the asset has not changed, no final payment changes hands. In return for this exposure, the investor (TRS receiver) makes regular payments of Libor plus spread.

TRSs are attractive to investors who wish to gain a leveraged exposure to an asset such as a high-yield bond or bank loan without bearing the original cost, or who wish to diversify their portfolio credit exposure. The main difference compared to a credit default swap is that payments made to balance the change in value of the asset will take place irrespective of the occurrence of a credit event.

A TRS is illustrated in Figure A20.2. The total return receiver is long of both interest and credit risk of the reference asset, while the total return payer *may* be long of the asset itself.

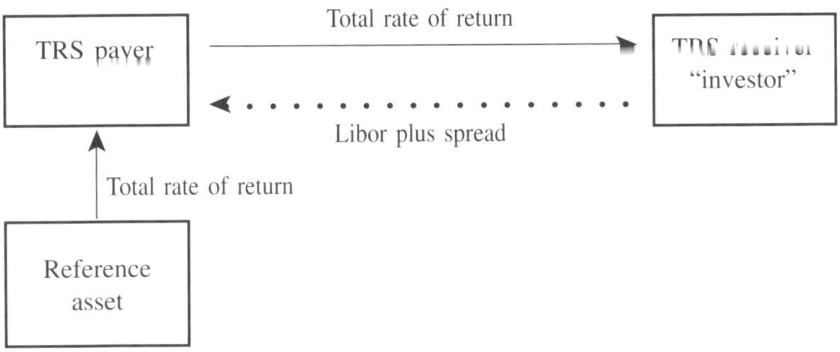

Example of TRS

Reference asset	ABC Bank plc bond
Notional amount	$100 million
Coupon	6.00%
Maturity	Five years
Term	One year
Initial price	100.00%
Investor pays	Libor + 80 bps + price depreciation
Investor receives	Coupon + price appreciation

Figure A20.2 Total return swap, with terms for a generic example

Credit-linked notes

Another type of credit derivative is the *credit-linked note* (CLN). These exist in a number of forms, but all contain a link between the return payable on them and the credit-related performance of the underlying asset. A standard credit-linked note is a loan or security, usually issued by an investment-graded entity, that has an interest payment and fixed maturity structure similar to a vanilla bond. The performance of the note, however, including the maturity value, is linked to the performance of specified underlying assets, as well as that of the issuing entity. CLNs are usually used to synthetically transfer credit risk of specified reference assets via the issuing SPV to the investor purchasing the note. The reference asset may be a pool of bonds or loans, or specified bonds or loans within a portfolio. On the occurrence of a credit event, losses in underlying loans will be transferred to noteholders according to the method specified in the deal documentation, usually as a percentage of the bond or loan value, or a market valuation based on competitive bids. The reference assets of CLNs issued as part of a synthetic CDO remain on the sponsor's balance sheet, so the rating of the overlying notes cannot be higher than that of the originator. By issuing CLNs against the notes, the originator will obtain regulatory capital relief on the referenced assets. In a synthetic CDO structure, the return on a CLN is increased by the premium received from the sale of a credit default swap.

Investors are attracted to CLNs because they offer a means to gain exposure to diversified markets that are frequently too expensive to enter.

An accessible introduction to credit-linked notes is given in Kasapi (1999).

Credit options

Credit options are another form of credit derivative. Like other options, a credit option is a contract designed to meet specific hedging or speculative requirements of an entity, which may purchase or sell the option to meet its objectives. A credit call option gives the buyer the right without the obligation to purchase the underlying credit-sensitive asset, or a credit spread, at a specified price and specified time (or period of time). A credit put option gives the buyer the right without the obligation to sell the underlying credit-sensitive asset or credit spread. By purchasing credit options, banks and other institutions can take a view on credit spread movements for the cost of the option premium only, without recourse to actual loans issued by an obligor. The writer of credit options seeks to earn fee income.

Settlement

Credit derivative settlement can follow one of two routes, specified at deal inception. With all credit derivatives, upon occurrence of a credit event, a credit event notice must be submitted. Typically, the notice must be supported by information posted on public news systems such as Bloomberg or Reuters. When used as part of a structured product, the terms of the deal may state that a credit event must be verified by a third-party verification agent. Upon verification, the contract will be settled in one of two ways, cash settlement or physical settlement.

A report from the BBA suggested that between 75%-85% of credit derivatives written in 2002 were physically-settled, while about 10%-20% were cash-settled. About 5% of contracts were settled under the fixed amount approach, under which the protection seller delivers a pre-specified amount to the protection buyer ahead of the determination of the reference asset's recovery value. However as the fixed amount approach is essentially cash settlement, we will consider it as such and prefer the more technical term for it noted below.

Contract settlement options

Credit derivatives have a given maturity, but will terminate early if a credit event occurs. On occurrence of a credit event, the swap contract is terminated and a settlement payment made by the protection seller or guarantor to the protection buyer. This termination value is calculated at the time of the credit event, and the procedure that is followed to calculate the termination value will depend on the settlement terms specified in the contract. Credit derivatives specify physical or cash settlement. In physical settlement, the protection buyer transfers to the protection seller the deliverable obligation (usually the reference asset or assets), with the total principal outstanding equal to the nominal specified in the default swap contract. The protection seller simultaneously pays to the buyer 100% of the nominal. In cash settlement, the protection seller hands to the buyer the difference between the nominal amount of the default swap and the final value for the same nominal amount of the reference asset. This final value is usually determined by means of a poll of dealer banks. This final value is in theory the recovery value of the asset; however as the recovery process can take some time, often the reference asset market value at time of default is taken and this amount used in calculating the final settlement amount paid to the protection buyer.

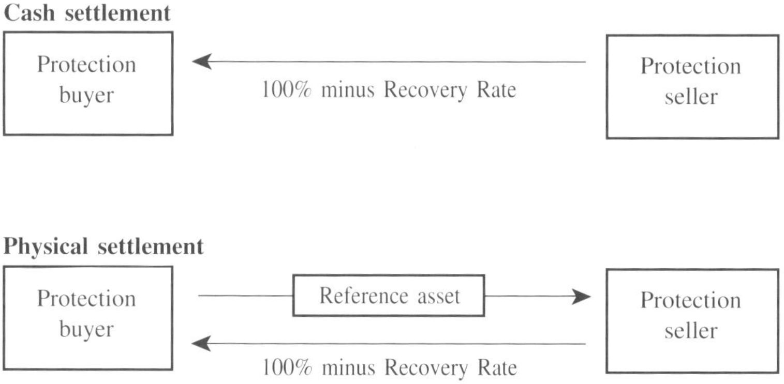

Figure A20.3 Settlement Physical and cash settlement

The settlement mechanisms are shown in Figure A20.3 and follow the following process:

- Cash settlement: the contract may specify a pre-determined pay-out value on occurrence of a credit event. This may be the nominal value of the swap contract. Such a swap is known as a fixed amount contract or in some markets as a digital credit derivative. Alternatively, the termination payment is calculated as the difference between the nominal value of the reference asset and either its market value at the time of the credit event or its recovery value. This arrangement is more common with cash-settled contracts.[20]
- Physical settlement: on occurrence of a credit event, the buyer delivers the reference asset to the seller, in return for which the seller pays the face value of the delivered asset to the buyer. The contract may specify a number of alternative assets that the buyer can deliver; these are known as deliverable obligations. This may apply when a swap has been entered into on a reference name rather than a specific obligation (such as a particular bond) issued by that name. Where more than one deliverable obligation is specified, the protection buyer will invariably deliver the asset that is the cheapest on the list of eligible assets. This gives rise to the concept of the cheapest-to-deliver, as encountered with government bond futures contracts, and is in effect an embedded option afforded the protection buyer.

In theory, the value of protection is identical irrespective of which settlement option is selected. However under physical settlement the protection seller can gain if there is a recovery value that can be extracted from the defaulted asset; or its value may rise as the fortunes of the issuer improve.

Use of credit derivatives

Banks use credit derivatives for a number of reasons. Some of these are summarised below.

[20] Determining the market value of the reference asset at the time of the credit event may be a little problematic: the issuer of the asset may well be in default or administration. An independent third-party Calculation Agent is usually employed to make the termination payment calculation.

Diversifying the credit portfolio

A bank may wish to take on credit exposure by providing credit protection on assets that it already owns, in return for a fee. This enhances income on their portfolio. They may sell credit derivatives to enable non-banking clients to gain credit exposures, if these clients do not wish to purchase the assets directly. In this respect the bank performs a credit intermediation role.

Reducing credit exposure

Another use of credit derivatives is to reduce credit exposure either for an individual asset or a sectoral concentration, by buying a CDS. This may be desirable for assets in their portfolio that cannot be sold for relationship or tax reasons.

Acting as a credit derivatives market-maker

A bank may wish to set itself up as a market-maker in credit derivatives; that is, become a credit trader. In this case the trader may or may not hold the reference assets directly, depending on appetite for risk and the liquidity of the market enabling her to offset derivative contracts as and when required.

Selected bibliography and references

Anson M. 1999, *Credit Derivatives*, FJF Associates, New Hope, PA, Chapter 3.

Boggiano, K., Waterson, and Stein, C. 2002, "Four forms of synthetic CDOs", *Derivatives Week*, Euromoney Publications, Vol. XI, No. 23, 10 June.

Choudhry, M. 2001, "Some issues in the asset-swap pricing of credit default swaps", *Derivatives Week*, Euromoney Publications, 2 December.

Choudhry, M. 2002, "Trading credit spreads: The case for a specialised exchange-traded credit futures contract", *Journal of Derivatives Use, Trading and Regulation*, Vol. 8, No. 1, June.

Choudhry, M. 2004, *Structured Credit Products*, John Wiley & Sons, Singapore.

Das, S. 2001, *Structured Products and Hybrid Securities*, John Wiley & Sons, Singapore, Chapter 12.

Fabozzi, F. and Goodman, L. (ed.) 2001, *Investing in Collateralised Debt Obligations*, FJF Associates, New Hope, PA.

Fabozzi, F. (ed.) 2004, *The Handbook of Fixed Income Securities*, 7th edition, McGraw Hill, New York.

Kasapi, A. 1999, *Mastering Credit Derivatives*, FT Prentice Hall, London.

He had a faint air of the First World War about him; just because there was a war on was no reason for lapses of courtesy, warmth and modest behaviour.

— Walter Thompson speaking about
Wing Commander Guy Gibson VC,
Lancaster to Berlin, Goodall Publications (1985)

CHAPTER 21

Credit-linked Notes

Credit-linked notes are a form of credit derivative, but are *funded* instruments and as such they are similar to cash bonds. Although they started out as elements of structured products such as CDOs, they are now increasingly used by corporate borrowers; for example, British Telecom has issued credit-linked notes directly to the market. The return of this bond (which we will look at later) is linked to movements in the company's credit rating. Used in this way, credit-linked notes are an important corporate finance instrument.

Irrespective of the particular instrument under consideration, all credit derivatives can be described under the following characteristics:

- the *reference entity*, which is the asset or name on which credit protection is being bought and sold;
- the credit event, or events, which indicate that the reference entity is experiencing or about to experience financial difficulty and which act as trigger events for payments under the credit derivative contract;
- the settlement mechanism for the credit derivative instrument, whether cash settled or physically settled;
- (under physical settlement) the deliverable obligation that the protection buyer delivers to the protection seller on the occurrence of a trigger event.

Credit derivatives are grouped into *funded* and *unfunded* variants. In an unfunded credit derivative, typified by a *credit default swap*, the protection seller does not make an upfront payment to the protection buyer. CDS have a number of applications and are used extensively for flow trading of single reference name credit risks or, in *portfolio swap* form, for trading a basket of reference credits.

In a funded credit derivative, typified by a credit-linked note (CLN), the investor in the note is the credit-protection seller and is making an upfront payment to the protection buyer when it buys the note. Thus, the protection buyer is the issuer of the note. If no credit event occurs during the life of the note, the redemption value of the note is paid to the investor on maturity. If a credit event does occur, then on maturity a value less than par will be paid out to the investor. This value will be reduced by the nominal value of the reference asset that the CLN is linked to. The exact process will differ according to whether *cash settlement* or *physical settlement* has been specified for the note. We will consider this later.

Credit default swaps and CLNs are used in structured products, in various combinations, and their flexibility has been behind the growth and wide application of the synthetic collateralised debt obligation and other credit hybrid products.

We now consider the credit-linked note.

Description of CLNs

CLNs exist in a number of forms, but all of them contain a link between the return they pay and the credit-related performance of the underlying asset. A standard CLN is a security, usually issued by an investment-graded entity, that has an interest payment and fixed maturity structure similar to a vanilla bond. The performance of the note, however, including the maturity value, is linked to the performance of a specified underlying asset or assets, as well as that of the issuing entity. Notes are usually issued at par. The notes are often used by borrowers to hedge against credit risk, and by investors to enhance the yield received on their holdings. Hence, the issuer of the note is the protection buyer and the buyer of the note is the protection seller.

Essentially, CLNs are hybrid instruments that combine a pure credit-risk exposure with a vanilla bond. The CLN pays regular coupons; however, the credit derivative element is usually set to allow the issuer to decrease the principal amount, and/or the coupon interest, if a specified credit event occurs.

Figure 21.1 shows Bloomberg screen SND and their definition of the CLN.

GRAB Mtge SND

Page 11/ 12

Credit Linked Notes (CLN): A hybrid debt security that offers investors a synthetic credit exposure to a specified Reference Entity or basket of Reference Entities. This credit exposure can be gained through a variety of methods including (but not limited to): a credit default swap, a credit spread swap, a total return swap, or as a repackaged note where the issuer passes through the risk of an underlying credit to the noteholder in exchange for an enhanced return. For example, a note might provide for its principal repayment to be reduced below par in the event that a reference obligation defaults.

20) Example: EC771465 <CORP> DES. A note that is linked to the credit of Sodexho Alliance SA. Following a credit event on the underlying reference obligation, this note will be redeemed early at less than par.

Repackaged Notes: A debt instrument secured by an underlying asset where the cashflows of that asset are reprofiled through a derivative contract while the credit risk is passed through to the investor of the Repackaged Note.

21) Example: EC785183 <CORP> DES. A note that is secured by Roche Holdings convertible notes and a swap agreement. Following an event of default on all or part of the underlying, this note will be redeemed early at an amount based on the underlying.

Page <FWD> for FFIEC 034 Structured Note Call Reporting Revision

Australia 61 2 9777 8600 Brazil 5511 3048 4500 Europe 44 20 7330 7500 Germany 49 69 920410
Hong Kong 852 2977 6000 Japan 81 3 3201 8900 Singapore 65 6212 1000 U.S. 1 212 318 2000 Copyright 2003 Bloomberg L.P.
H021-57-0 30-May-03 11:38:24

Figure 21.1 Bloomberg screen SND: definition of CLN
©Bloomberg L.P. Used with permission.

To illustrate a CLN, consider a bank issuer of credit cards that wants to fund its credit card loan portfolio via an issue of debt. The bank is rated AA–. In order to reduce the credit risk of the loans, it issues a two-year CLN. The principal amount of the bond is 100 (par) as usual, and it pays a coupon of 7.50%, which is 110 basis points above the two-year benchmark. At the time of issue, the equivalent spread for a vanilla bond issued by a bank of this rating would be of the order of 65 bps. With the CLN though, if the incidence of bad debt among credit card holders exceeds 10% then the terms state that noteholders will only receive back 85 per 100 par. The credit card issuer has in effect purchased a credit option that lowers its liability in the event that it suffers from a specified credit event, which in this case is an above-expected incidence of bad debts. The cost of this credit option is paid in the form of a higher coupon payment on the CLN. The credit card bank has issued the CLN to reduce its credit exposure, in the form of this particular type of credit insurance. If the incidence of bad debts is low, the

CLN is redeemed at par. However, if there is a high incidence of such debt, the bank will only have to repay a part of its loan liability.

Investors may wish to purchase the CLN because the coupon paid on it will be above what the credit card bank would pay on a vanilla bond it issued, and higher than other comparable investments in the market. In addition, such notes are usually priced below par on issue. Assuming the notes are eventually redeemed at par, investors will also have realised a substantial capital gain.

As with credit default swaps, CLNs may be specified under cash settlement or physical settlement. Specifically:

- under cash settlement, if a credit event has occurred, on maturity the protection seller receives the difference between the value of the initial purchase proceeds and the value of the reference asset at the time of the credit event;
- under physical settlement, on occurrence of a credit event, the note is terminated. At maturity the protection buyer delivers the reference asset or an asset among a list of deliverable assets, and the protection seller receives the value of the original purchase proceeds minus the value of the asset that has been delivered.

Figure 21.2 below illustrates a cash-settled credit-linked note.

CLNs may be issued directly by a financial or corporate entity or via an SPV. They have been issued with the form of credit-linking taking on one or more of a number of different guises. For instance, a CLN may have its return performance linked to the issuer's, or a specified reference entity's, credit rating, risk exposure, financial performance or circumstance of default. Figure 21.3 shows a Bloomberg screen CLN and a list of the various types of CLN issue that have been made. Figure 21.4 shows a page accessed from a Bloomberg screen "CLN", which is a list of CLNs that have had their coupon affected by a change in the reference entity's credit rating.

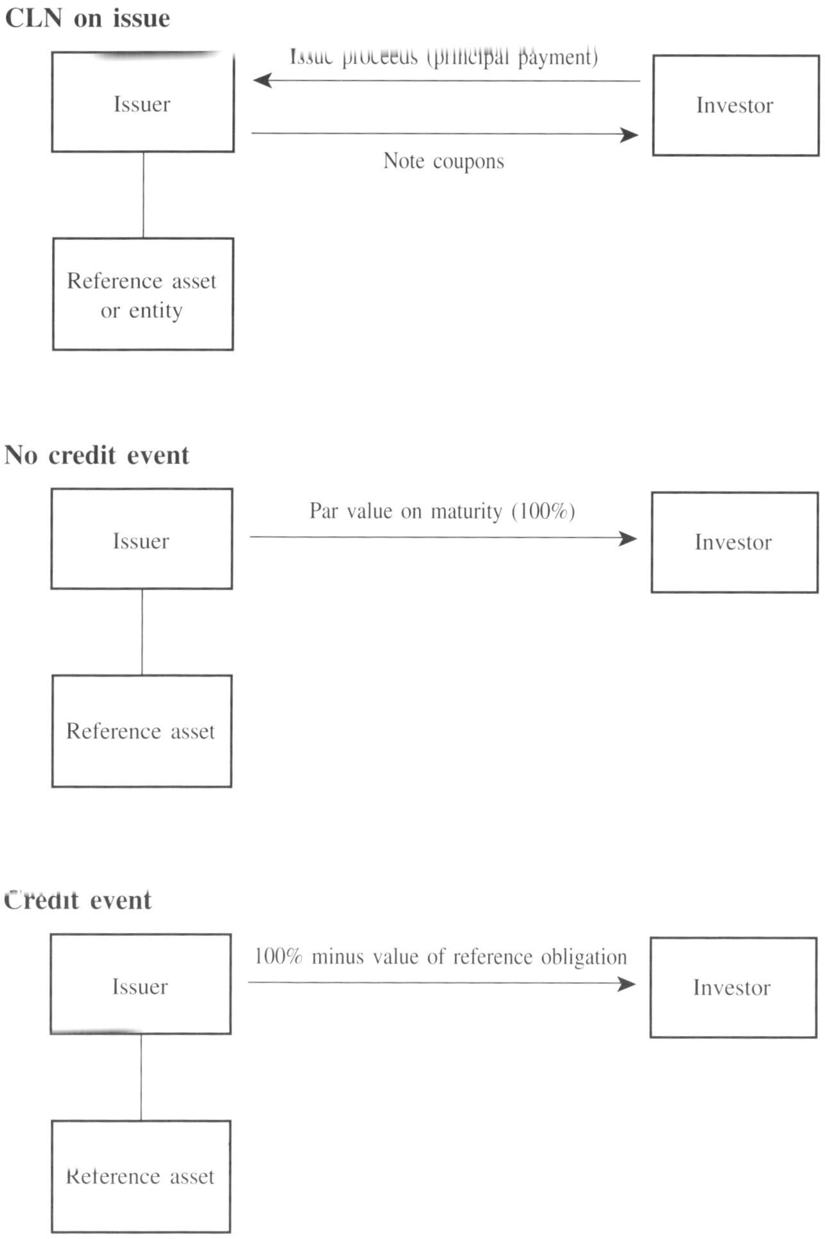

Figure 21.2 Credit-linked note

GRAB Corp CLN

CREDIT-LINKED NOTES
as of Oct 24, 2002

Issue Linked To	# Issues
1) Credit Event – Company Risk Exposure	957
2) Credit Event – Multiple Company Risk	406
3) Credit Event – North and South America Risk	175
4) Credit Event – Europe Risk	70
5) Credit Event – Asia/Middle East/Africa Risk	55
6) Credit Event – Multiple Countries Risk	32
7) Currency Constraint Event	27
8) Ratings Changes Event	17
9) 3rd-Party Tax Change Event	15
10) Miscellaneous Call Event	17

This page is no longer being updated. Please let us know if you would like to see more coverage of Credit Linked Notes made available on Bloomberg. To do this, hit your HELP key twice and let us know that you would like to see our "SRCH" function improved to include CLNs.

Figure 21.3 Bloomberg screen CLN
©Bloomberg L.P. Used with permission.

GRAB Corp CLN

Page 1/ 1

RATINGS CHANGES EVENT

	Issuer	Settle Date	Cpn	Crncy	Maturity Date	Rating Changes Exposure
1)	BHFBK	04/28/1998	6.25	DEM	04/28/2006	Govt of Ukraine
2)	BSPIR	03/21/2000	7.00	EUR	02/20/2010	B-Spires
3)	CATTLE	10/21/1999	8.63	GBP	12/07/2007	Cattle PLC
4)	CNTCNZ	09/14/2000	FRN	AUD	09/14/2007	Contact Energy
5)	CNTCNZ	09/14/2000	FRN	USD	09/14/2007	Contact Energy
6)	HI	11/13/1997	FRN	USD	11/13/2013	Household Fin Co
7)	IFCTF	08/04/1997	7.88	USD	08/04/2002	Indust Fin Corp
8)	IFCTF	08/04/1997	7.75	USD	08/04/2007	Indust Fin Corp
9)	KPN	06/13/2000	FRN	EUR	06/13/2002	KPN NV
10)	KPN	06/13/2000	FRN	EUR	06/13/2002	KPN NV
11)	KPN	06/13/2000	6.05	EUR	06/13/2003	KPN NV
12)	METALF	07/25/2000	6.75	EUR	07/25/2005	MetallGesell Fin
13)	METALF	07/25/2000	6.75	EUR	07/25/2005	MetallGesell Fin
14)	OSTDRA	02/16/2000	Var	EUR	02/16/2007	Oester Draukraft
15)	SIRSTR	06/25/1998	FRN	USD	10/06/2006	Bk Tokyo-Mitsub
16)	SOWLN	03/26/1998	6.89	GBP	03/26/2008	Southern Water
17)	SPIRES	01/26/1998	FRN	DEM	10/24/2007	Greece

Figure 21.4 Bloomberg screen showing a sample of CLNs impacted by change in reference entity credit rating, October 2002
©Bloomberg L.P. Used with permission.

The majority of CLNs are issued by issuers direct. An example of such a bond is shown in Figure 21.5. This shows Bloomberg screen DES for a CLN issued by British Telecom plc, the 8.125% note due in December 2010. The terms of this note state that the coupon will increase by 25 basis points for each one-notch rating downgrade below A–/A3 suffered by the issuer during the life of the note. The coupon will decrease by 25 basis points for each ratings upgrade, with a minimum coupon set at 8.125%. In other words, this note allows investors to take on a credit play on the fortunes of the issuer.

Figure 21.6 shows Bloomberg screen YA for this note, as at 29 May 2003. We see that a rating downgrade meant that the coupon on the note was now 8.375%.

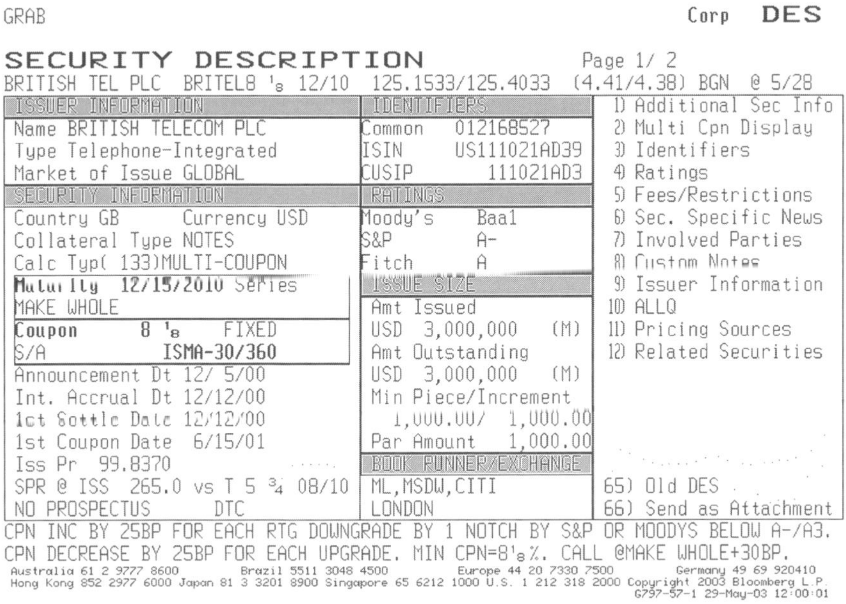
GRAB Corp DES
SECURITY DESCRIPTION Page 1/ 2
BRITISH TEL PLC BRITEL8 1/8 12/10 125.1533/125.4033 (4.41/4.38) BGN @ 5/28

ISSUER INFORMATION
Name BRITISH TELECOM PLC
Type Telephone-Integrated
Market of Issue GLOBAL
SECURITY INFORMATION
Country GB Currency USD
Collateral Type NOTES
Calc Typ(133)MULTI-COUPON
Maturity 12/15/2010 Series
MAKE WHOLE
Coupon 8 1/8 FIXED
S/A ISMA-30/360
Announcement Dt 12/ 5/00
Int. Accrual Dt 12/12/00
1st Settle Date 12/12/00
1st Coupon Date 6/15/01
Iss Pr 99.8370
SPR @ ISS 265.0 vs T 5 3/4 08/10
NO PROSPECTUS DTC

IDENTIFIERS
Common 012168527
ISIN US111021AD39
CUSIP 111021AD3
RATINGS
Moody's Baa1
S&P A-
Fitch A
ISSUE SIZE
Amt Issued
USD 3,000,000 (M)
Amt Outstanding
USD 3,000,000 (M)
Min Piece/Increment
1,000.00/ 1,000.00
Par Amount 1,000.00
BOOK RUNNER/EXCHANGE
ML,MSDW,CITI
LONDON

1) Additional Sec Info
2) Multi Cpn Display
3) Identifiers
4) Ratings
5) Fees/Restrictions
6) Sec. Specific News
7) Involved Parties
8) Custom Notes
9) Issuer Information
10) ALLQ
11) Pricing Sources
12) Related Securities
65) Old DES
66) Send as Attachment

CPN INC BY 25BP FOR EACH RTG DOWNGRADE BY 1 NOTCH BY S&P OR MOODYS BELOW A-/A3.
CPN DECREASE BY 25BP FOR EACH UPGRADE. MIN CPN=8 1/8%. CALL @MAKE WHOLE+30BP.
Australia 61 2 9777 8600 Brazil 5511 3048 4500 Europe 44 20 7330 7500 Germany 49 69 920410
Hong Kong 852 2977 6000 Japan 81 3 3201 8900 Singapore 65 6212 1000 U.S. 1 212 318 2000 Copyright 2003 Bloomberg L.P.
G797-57-1 29-May-03 12:00:01

Figure 21.5 Bloomberg screen DES for British Telecom plc 8.125% 2010 credit-linked note issued on 5 December 2000

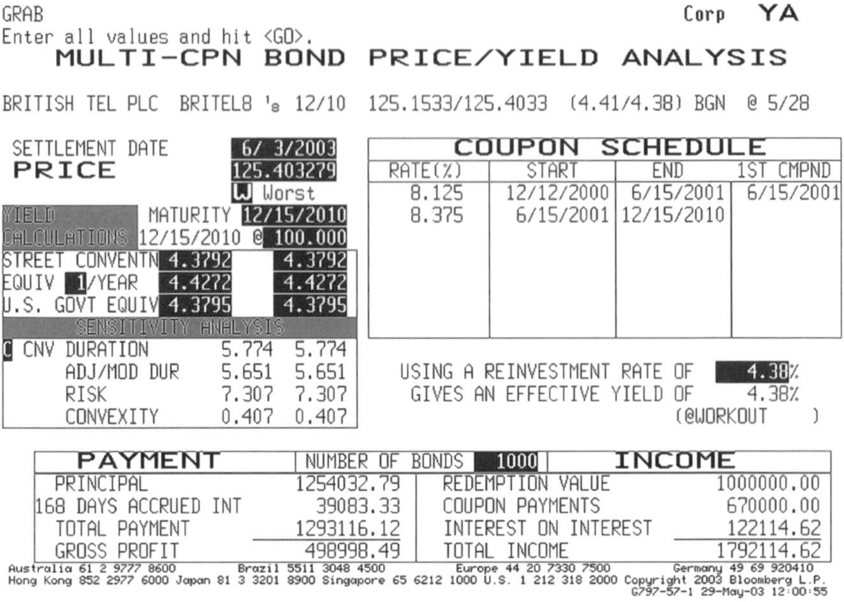

Figure 21.6 Bloomberg screen YA for British Telecom CLN, as at 29 May 2003 ©Bloomberg L.P. Used with permission.

CLNs have been issued with a number of different types of credit linking.

Figure 21.7 is the Bloomberg DES page for a USD-denominated CLN issued directly by the Household Finance Corporation (HFC).[1] Like the British Telecom bond, this is a CLN whose return is linked to the credit risk of the issuer, but in a different way. The coupon of the HFC bond was issued as floating USD-Libor, but in the event of the bond not being called from November 2001, the coupon would be the issuer's two-year "credit spread" over a fixed rate of 5.9%. In fact, the issuer called the bond with effect from the coupon change date. Figure 21.8 shows the Bloomberg screen YA for the bond and how its coupon remained as at first issue until the call date.

[1] HFC was subsequently acquired by HSBC.

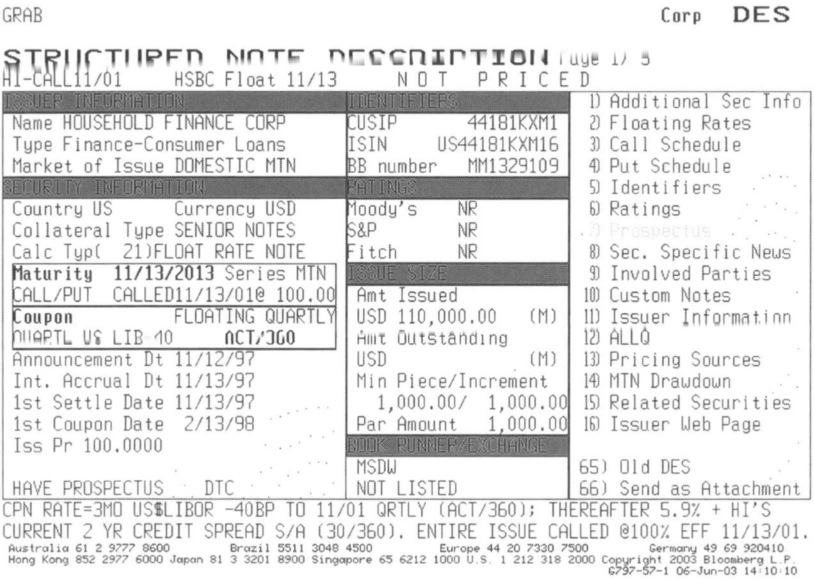

Figure 21.7 HFC bond, screen DES on Bloomberg
©Bloomberg L.P. Used with permission.

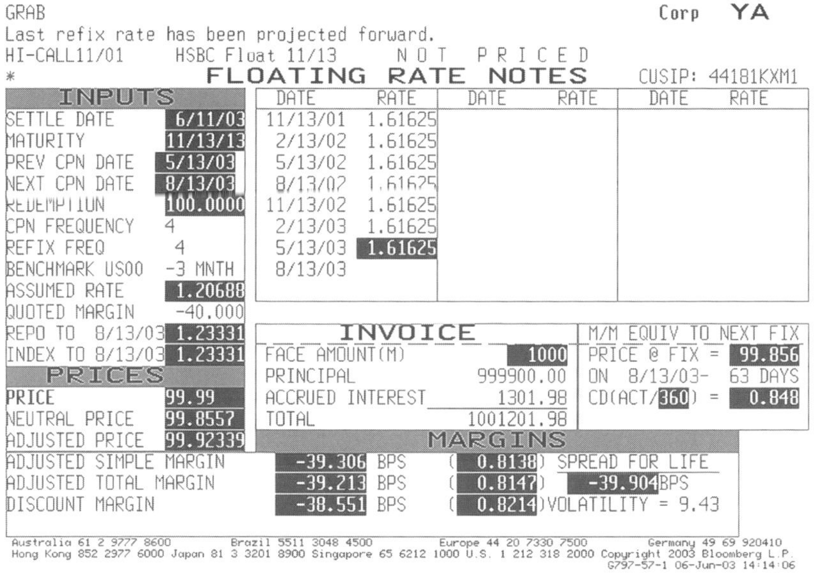

Figure 21.8 HFC bond YA screen
©Bloomberg L.P. Used with permission.

Another type of credit-linking is evidenced from the details shown in Figure 21.9. This is a JPY-denominated bond issued by Alpha-Spires, which is an MTN program vehicle set up by Merrill Lynch. The note itself is linked to the credit quality of Ford Motor Credit. In the event of a default of the reference name, the note will be called immediately. Figure 21.10 shows the rate fixing for this note as at the last coupon date. The screen snapshot was taken on 6 June 2003.

GRAB Corp **DES**

STRUCTURED NOTE DESCRIPTION Page 1/ 3

ALPHA-SIRES #121 ALSIRFloat 02/06 N O T P R I C E D

ISSUER INFORMATION	IDENTIFIERS	1) Additional Sec Info
Name ALPHA-SIRES LTD #121	Common 013499659	2) Floating Rates
Type Special Purpose Entity	ISIN XS0134996593	3) Identifiers
Market of Issue EURO MTN	BB number EC4441043	4) Ratings
SECURITY INFORMATION	RATINGS	5) Fees/Restrictions
Country KY Currency JPY	Moody's NA	6) Involved Parties
Collateral Type SECURED	S&P NA	7) Custom Notes
Calc Typ(21)FLOAT RATE NOTE	Fitch NA	8) ALLQ
Maturity 2/ 3/2006 Series MTN2	ISSUE SIZE	9) Pricing Sources
CALLABLE	Amt Issued	10) Related Securities
Coupon0.52875 FLOATING S/A	JPY 1,000,000 (M)	
S/A JY00 +45 **ACT/360**	Amt Outstanding	
Announcement Dt 8/24/01	JPY 1,000,000 (M)	
Int. Accrual Dt 9/18/01	Min Piece/Increment	
1st Settle Date 9/18/01	100000000/ 100000000	
1st Coupon Date 2/ 4/02	Par Amount 100000000	
Iss Pr 100.0000	BOOK RUNNER/EXCHANGE	
	ML-sole	65) Old DES
NO PROSPECTUS	NOT LISTED	66) Send as Attachment

CPN=6MO ¥LIBOR +45BP.SEC'D BY FORD MOTOR CREDIT CO BONDS & SWAP AGRMT. CALL/EXCH IF EVENT OF DEFAULT.SHORT 1ST CPN USES INTERPL LIBOR.

Australia 61 2 9777 8600 Brazil 5511 3048 4500 Europe 44 20 7330 7500 Germany 49 69 920410
Hong Kong 852 2977 6000 Japan 81 3 3201 8900 Singapore 65 6212 1000 U.S. 1 212 318 2000 Copyright 2003 Bloomberg L.P.
G797-57-1 06-Jun-03 14:37:26

Figure 21.9 Ford CLN DES page

©Bloomberg L.P. Used with permission.

Structured products such as synthetic collateralised debt obligations (CDOs) may combine both CLNs and credit default swaps, to meet issuer and investor requirements. For instance, Figure 21.11 shows a credit structure designed to provide a higher return for an investor on comparable risk to the cash market. An issuing entity is set up in the form of an SPV that issues CLNs to the market. The structure is engineered so that the SPV has a neutral position on a reference asset. It has bought protection on a single reference name by issuing a funded credit derivative, the CLN, and simultaneously sold protection on this name by selling a credit default swap on this name. The proceeds of the CLN are invested in risk-free collateral such as Treasury bills or a Treasury bank account. The coupon on the CLN will be a spread over Libor. It is backed by the collateral account and the fee generated by the SPV in selling protection with the credit default swap. Investors in the CLN will have exposure to the reference asset or entity, and the repayment of the note is linked to the performance of the reference entity. If a credit event occurs, the maturity date of the CLN is brought forward and the note is settled as par minus the value of the reference asset or entity.

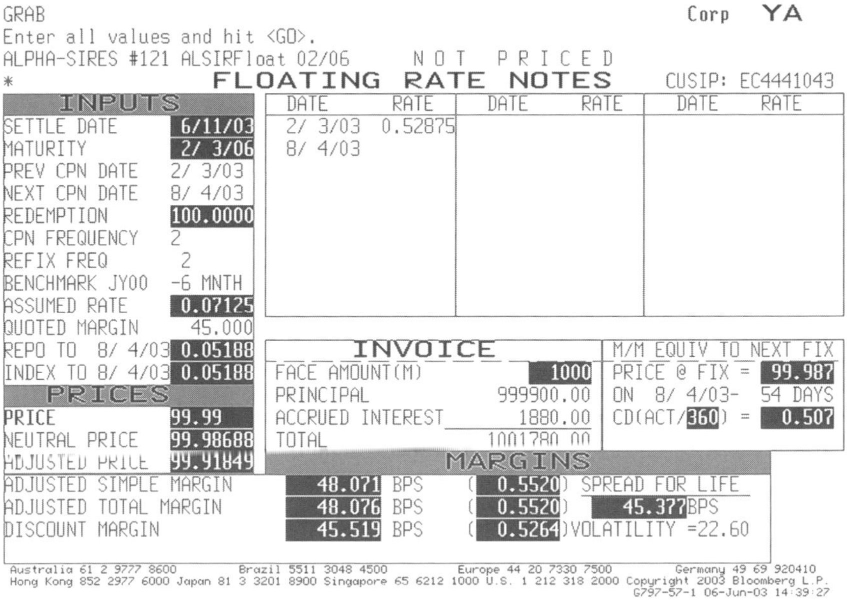

Figure 21.10 Ford CLN YA page
©Bloomberg L.P. Used with permission.

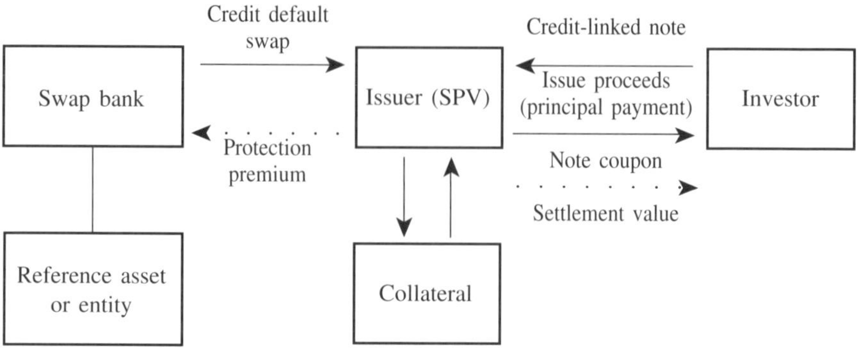

Figure 21.11 CLN and CDS structure on single reference name

The first-to-default CLN

A standard CLN is issued in reference to one specific bond or loan. An investor purchasing such a note is writing credit protection on a specific reference credit. A CLN that is linked to more than one reference credit is known as a *basket credit-linked note*. A development of the CLN as a structured product is the first-to-default CLN (FtD), which is a CLN that is linked to a basket of reference assets. The investor in the CLN is selling protection on the first credit to default.[2] Figure 21.12 shows this progression in the development of CLNs as structured products, with the *fully funded synthetic* collateralised debt obligation (CDO) being the vehicle that uses CLNs tied to a large basket of reference assets.

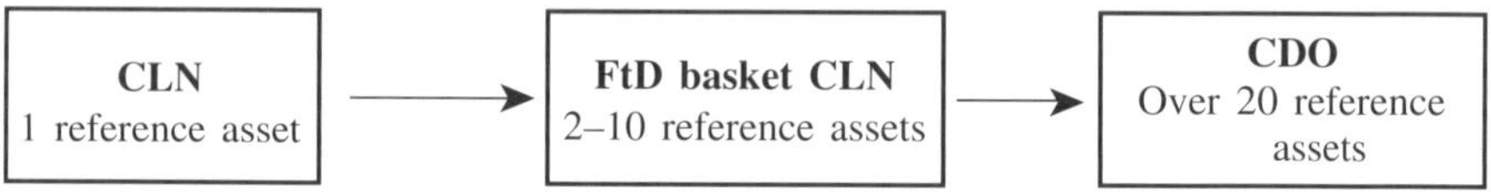

Figure 21.12 Progression of CLN development

[2] "Default" here meaning a credit event as defined in the ISDA definitions.

An FtD CLN is a funded credit derivative in which the investor sells protection on one reference in a basket of assets, whichever is the first to default. The return on the CLN is a multiple of the average spread of the basket. The CLN will mature early on occurrence of a credit event relating to any of the reference assets. Note settlement can be either of the following:

- physical settlement, with the defaulted asset(s) being delivered to the note holder;
- cash settlement, in which the CLN issuer pays redemption proceeds to the note holder calculated as (principal amount × reference asset recovery value).[3]

Figure 21.13 shows a generic FtD credit-linked note.

To illustrate, consider an FtD CLN issued at par with a term-to-maturity of five years and linked to a basket of five reference assets with a face value (issued nominal amount) of $10 million. An investor purchasing this note will pay $10 million to the issuer. If no credit event occurs during the life of the note, the investor will receive the face value of the note on maturity. If a credit event occurs on any of the assets in the basket, the note will redeem early and the issuer will deliver a deliverable obligation of the reference entity, or a portfolio of such obligations, for a $10 million nominal amount. An FtD CLN carries a similar amount of risk exposure on default to a standard CLN; namely, the recovery rate of the defaulted credit. However, its risk exposure prior to default is theoretically lower than a standard CLN, as it can reduce default probability through diversification. The investor can obtain exposure to a basket of reference entities that differ by industrial sector and by credit rating.

The matrix at Figure 21.14 illustrates how an investor can select a credit mix in the basket that diversifies risk exposure across a wide range – we show a hypothetical mix of reference assets to which an issued FtD could be linked. The precise selection of names will reflect investors' own risk/return profile requirements.

---

[3] In practice, it is not the "recovery value" that is used, but the market value of the reference asset at the time the credit event is verified. Recovery of a defaulted asset follows a legal process of administration and/or liquidation that can take some years, the final recovery value may not be known for certain for some time.

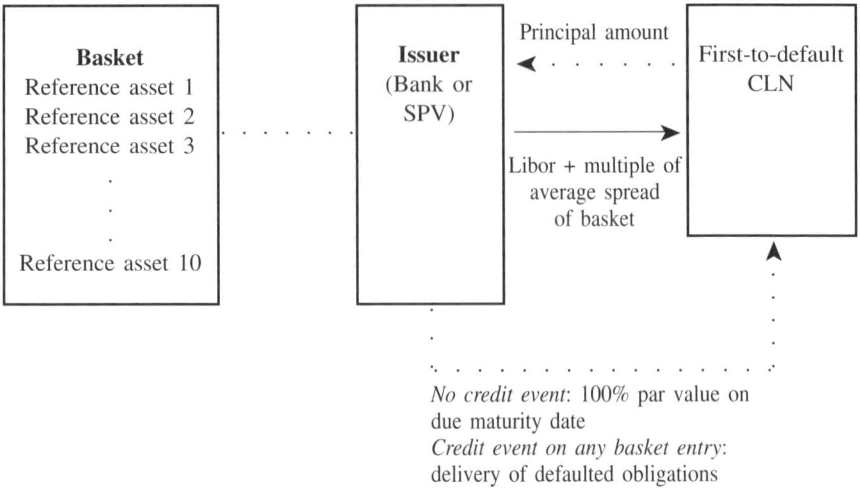

Figure 21.13 First-to-default CLN structure

	Automobiles	Banks	Electronics	Insurance	Media	Telecoms	Utilities
AAA							
Aa1							
Aa2				SunAlliance			
Aa3		RBoS					
A1							
A2							Powergen
A3						British Telecom	
Baa1			Philips		News Intl		
Baa2							
Baa3							

Figure 21.14 Diversified credit exposure to basket of reference assets: hypothetical reference asset mix

The FtD CLN creates a synthetic credit entity that features a note return with enhanced spread. Investors receive a spread over Libor that is the average return of all the reference assets in the basket. This structure serves to diversify credit risk exposure while benefiting from a higher average return. If the pool of reference assets is sufficiently large, the structure becomes similar to a *single-tranche CDO*. This is considered in Choudhry (2004).

Selected bibliography and references

Choudhry, M. 2004, *Structured Credit Products*, John Wiley & Sons, Singapore.

The crew of young sergeants, anxious to begin their tour, left the briefing room feeling very frustrated [at the cancellation of the mission], as did another new crew led by an officer who looked too young to drive a car, let alone fly an aeroplane.

– Miles Tripp, *The Eighth Passenger*
Wordsworth Editions Limited, 2002

APPENDIX

A

Financial Markets Arithmetic

Simple and compound interest

Simple interest

A loan that has one interest payment on maturity is accruing *simple interest.* On short-term instruments there is usually only the one interest payment on maturity, hence simple interest is received when the instrument expires. The terminal value of an investment with simple interest is given by (AA.1) below.

$$F = P\ (1 + r) \qquad \text{(AA.1)}$$

where
F is the terminal value or *future value*
P is the initial investment or *present value*
r is the interest rate.

So, for example, if P is £100, r is 5% and the investment is one year then:

$$\begin{aligned} F &= 100\ (1 + 0.1) \\ &= £105. \end{aligned}$$

The market convention is to quote interest rates as *annualised* interest rates, which is the interest that is earned if the investment term is one year. Consider a three-month deposit of £100 in a bank, placed at a rate of interest of 6%. In such an example the bank deposit will earn 6% interest for a period of 90 days. As the annual interest gain would be £6, the investor will expect to receive a proportion of this, which is calculated below:

$$£6.00 \times \frac{90}{365}.$$

Therefore the investor will receive £1.479 interest at the end of the term. The total proceeds after the three months is therefore £100 plus £1.479. If we wish to calculate the terminal value of a short-term investment that is accruing simple interest we use the following expression:

$$F = P\left(1 + r \times \frac{\text{Days}}{\text{Year}}\right). \tag{AA.2}$$

The fraction days/year refers to the numerator, which is the number of days the investment runs, divided by the denominator which is the number of days in the year. In the sterling markets, the number of days in the year is taken to be 365; however, certain other markets (including the euro currency markets) have a 360-day year convention. For this reason we simply quote the expression as "days" divided by "year" to allow for either convention.

Compound interest

Let us now consider an investment of £100 made for three years, again at a rate of 6%, but this time fixed for three years. At the end of the first year the investor will be credited with interest of £6. Therefore for the second year the interest rate of 6% will be accruing on a principal sum of £106, which means that at the end of year two the interest credited will be £6.36. This illustrates how *compounding* works, which is the principle of earning interest on interest. What will the terminal value of our £100 three-year investment be?

In compounding we are seeking to find a *future value* given a *present value,* a *time period* and an *interest rate*. If £100 is invested today (at time t_0) at 6%, then one year later (t_1) the investor will have £100 × (1 + 0.6) = £106. In our example the capital is left in for another two years, so at the end of year two (t_2) we will have:

$$\begin{aligned}\text{£}110 \times (1 + 0.6) \\ &= \text{£}100 \times (1 + 0.6) \times (1 + 0.6) \\ &= \text{£}100 \times (1 + 0.6)2 \\ &= \text{£}112.36.\end{aligned}$$

The outcome of the process of compounding is the *future value* of the initial amount. We don't have to calculate the terminal value long-hand as we can use the expression in (AA.3).

$$FV = PV\,(1 + r)^n \tag{AA.3}$$

where
FV is the future value
PV is initial outlay or *present value*
r is the periodic rate of interest (expressed as a decimal)
n is the number of periods for which the sum is invested.

In our example the initial £100 investment becomes $100 \times (1 + 0.06)^3$, which is equal to £119.10.

Compounding more than once a year

Now let us consider a deposit of £100 for one year, again at our rate of 6% but with quarterly interest payments. Such a deposit would accrue interest of £6 in the normal way but £1.50 would be credited to the account every quarter, and this would then benefit from compounding. Again, assuming that we can reinvest at the same rate of 6%, the total return at the end of the year will be:

$$\begin{aligned}&100 \times [(1 + 0.015) \times (1 + 0.015) \times (1 + 0.015) \times (1 + 0.015)] \\ &= 100 \times [(1 + 0.015)^4]\end{aligned}$$

which gives us 100×1.06136, a terminal value of £106.136. This is some 13 pence more than the terminal value using annual compounded interest.

In general, if compounding takes place m times per year, then at the end of n years mn interest payments will have been made and the future value of the principal is given by (AA.4) below:

$$FV = PV\left(1 + \frac{r}{m}\right)^{mn}. \tag{AA.4}$$

As we showed in our example the effect of more frequent compounding is to increase the value of the total return when compared to annual compounding. The effect of more frequent compounding is shown below, where we consider the annualised interest rate factors, for an annualised rate of 5%.

$$\text{Interest rate factor} = \left(1 + \frac{r}{m}\right)^m$$

Compounding frequency	**Interest rate factor**	
Annual	$(1 + r)$	= 1.050000
Semi-annual	$\left(1 + \frac{r}{2}\right)^2$	= 1.050625
Quarterly	$\left(1 + \frac{r}{4}\right)^4$	= 1.050945
Monthly	$\left(1 + \frac{r}{12}\right)^{12}$	= 1.051162
Daily	$\left(1 + \frac{r}{365}\right)^{365}$	= 1.051267

This shows us that the more frequent the compounding the higher the interest rate factor. The last case also illustrates how a limit occurs when interest is compounded continuously. Equation (AA.4) can be rewritten as follows:

$$\begin{aligned} FV &= PV\left[\left(1 + \frac{r}{m}\right)^{m/r}\right]^{rn} \\ &= PV\left[\left(1 + \frac{1}{m/r}\right)^{m/r}\right]^{rn} \\ &= PV\left[\left(1 + \frac{1}{n}\right)^{n}\right]^{rn} \end{aligned} \tag{AA.5}$$

where $n = m/r$. As compounding becomes continuous and m and hence n approach infinity, the expression in the square brackets in (AA.5) above approaches a value known as e, which is shown below.

$$e = \lim_{n\to\infty}\left(1 + \frac{1}{n}\right)^n = 2.718281$$

If we substitute this into (AA.5) this gives us:

$$FV = PVe^{rn} \tag{AA.6}$$

where we have continuous compounding. In (AA.6), *ern* is known as the *exponential function* of *rn* and it tells us the continuously compounded interest rate factor. If $r = 5\%$ and $n = 1$ year then:

$$e^r = (2.718281)0.05 = 1.051271.$$

This is the limit reached with continuous compounding. From our initial example, to illustrate continuous compounding, the future value of £100 at the end of three years, when the interest rate is 6%, is given by:

$$\begin{aligned} FV &= 100e^{(0.06) \times 3} \\ &= £119.72. \end{aligned}$$

Effective interest rates

The interest rate quoted on a deposit or loan is often the *flat* rate. However, we are often required to compare two interest rates that apply for a similar investment period but have different interest payment frequencies; for example, a two-year interest rate with interest paid quarterly compared to a two-year rate with semi-annual interest payments. This is normally done by comparing equivalent *annualised* rates. The annualised rate is the interest rate with annual compounding that results in the same return at the end of the period as the rate we are comparing.

The concept of the effective interest rate allows us to state that:

$$PV \times \left(1 + \frac{r}{n}\right)^n = PV \times (1 + aer) \qquad \text{(AA.7)}$$

where *aer* is the equivalent annual rate. Therefore if *r* is the interest rate quoted which pays *n* interest payments per year, the *aer* is given by (AA.8) below.

$$aer = \left[\left(1 + \frac{r}{n}\right)^n - 1\right] \qquad \text{(AA.8)}$$

The equivalent annual interest rate *aer* is known as the *effective* interest rate. We have already referred to the quoted interest rate as the "nominal" interest rate. We can rearrange equation (AA.8) above to give us (AA.9) which allows us to calculate nominal rates.

$$r = [(1 + aer)^{1/n} - 1] \times n \qquad \text{(AA.9)}$$

We can see then that the effective rate will be greater than the flat rate if compounding takes place more than once a year. The effective rate is sometimes referred to as the *annualised percentage rate* or APR.

Interest rate conventions

The convention in both wholesale and personal (retail) markets is to quote an annual interest rate. A lender who wishes to earn the interest at the rate quoted has to place her funds on deposit for one year. Annual rates are quoted irrespective of the maturity of a deposit, from overnight to ten years or longer. For example, if one opens a bank account that pays interest at a rate of 3.5%, but then closes it after six months, the actual interest earned will be equal to 1.75% of the sum deposited. The actual return on a three-year building society bond (fixed deposit) that pays 6.75% fixed for three years is 21.65% after three years. The quoted rate is the annual one-year equivalent. An overnight deposit in the wholesale or *interbank* market is still quoted as an annual rate, even though interest is earned for only one day.

The convention of quoting annualised rates is to allow deposits and loans of different maturities and different instruments to be compared on the basis of the interest rate applicable. We must also be careful when comparing interest rates for products that have different payment frequencies. As we have seen from the foregoing paragraphs the actual interest earned will be greater for a deposit earning 6% on a semi-annual basis compared to 6% on an annual basis. The convention in the money markets is to quote the equivalent interest rate applicable when taking into account an instrument's payment frequency.

Value date

In both the money markets and the bond markets, the *value date* of a transaction is the date on which the deal is effected, the date when money changes hands between buyer and seller. It is sometimes referred to as the "settlement date" but the two are not strictly synonymous. The date on which a buyer is expected to make payable good value of funds for the purchase, and the seller will expect to receive this cash and also deliver the securities, is always best referred to as the value date.

The standard money market value date is known as *spot* and refers to two business days after the trade date, also referred to as "T+2". Same-day settlement is also common in certificate of deposit (CD) and commercial paper (CP) markets, and is known as *cash* settlement or T+0. However, it is possible to deal T+0, T+1, T+2 and T+3 in many markets and instruments as long as both counterparties are agreeable.

For forward dealing and for setting maturity dates, the market convention is to move to the next relevant calendar date under a practice known as *modified following business day*. So a two-month transaction, or a two-month forward transaction, traded on 31 August 2004 would mature (or settle) on 31 October 2004. However, this is a non business day, ordinarily the maturity or settlement date would move to the next business day, but this changes the month (to November), so it would instead move back to 29 October 2004 as moving forward would change the month. But if both parties are agreeable, a maturity (or settlement) date of 1 November 2004 can be set.

The time value of money

Present values with single payments

Earlier we saw how a *future value* could be calculated given a known *present value* and rate of interest. For example, £100 invested today for one year at an interest rate of 6% will generate 100 × (1 + 0.06) = £106 at the end of the year. The future value of £100 in this case is £100. We can also say that £100 is the *present value* of £110 in our example.

In equation (AA.3) we established the following future value relationship:

$$FV = PV\ (1 + r)n.$$

By reversing this expression we arrive at the present value calculation given as (AA.10).

$$PV = \frac{FV}{(1 + r)^n} \tag{AA.10}$$

where the symbols represent the same terms as before. Equation (AA.10) applies in the case of annual interest payments and enables us to calculate the present value of a known future sum.

To calculate the present value for a short-term investment of less than one year we will need to adjust what would have been the interest earned for a whole year by the proportion of days of the investment period. Rearranging the basic equation, we can say that the present value of a known future value is:

$$PV = \frac{FV}{(1 + r \times {}^{\text{days}}/_{\text{year}})} \tag{AA.11}$$

Given a present value and a future value at the end of an investment period, what then is the interest rate earned? We can rearrange the basic equation again to solve for the *yield*.

$$yield = \left(\frac{FV}{PV} - 1\right) \times \frac{\text{Year}}{\text{Days}} \qquad \text{(AA.12)}$$

Using equation (AA.12) will give us the interest rate for the actual period. We can then convert this to an effective interest rate using (AA.13).

$$r = \left(1 + yield \times \frac{\text{Days}}{\text{Year}}\right)^{365/\text{days}} - 1 \qquad \text{(AA.13)}$$

When interest is compounded more than once a year, the formula for calculating present value is modified, as shown by (AA.14),

$$PV = \frac{FV}{\left(1 + \frac{r}{\text{m}}\right)^{mn}} \qquad \text{(AA.14)}$$

where as before FV is the cash flow at the end of year n, m is the number of times a year interest is compounded, and r is the rate of interest or discount rate. Illustrating this therefore, the present value of £100 that is received at the end of five years at a rate of interest of 5%, with quarterly compounding is:

$$PV = \frac{100}{\left(1 + \frac{0.05}{4}\right)^{(4)(5)}}$$

$$= £78.00.$$

Discount factors

The calculation of present values from future values is also known as *discounting*. The principles of present and future values demonstrate the concept of the *time value* of money, which is that in an environment of positive interest rates a sum of money has greater value today than it does at some point in the future because we are able to invest the sum today and earn interest. We will only consider a sum in the future compared to a sum today if we are compensated by being paid interest at a sufficient rate. Discounting future values allows us to compare the value of a future sum with a present sum.

Another way to write the expression in example (AA.14) is to say that we multiply £1,000 by the expression $1/(1.09)^5$, which is the *reciprocal* of $(1.09)^5$, and is denoted in this case as (1 + 0.09)–5. The rate of interest r that we use in equation (AA.2) is known as the *discount rate* and is the rate we use to *discount* a known future value in order to calculate a present value.

We can rearrange equation (AA.14) to give:

$$PV = FV(1 + r)^{-n}$$

and the term $(1 + r)^{-n}$ is known as the n-year *discount factor.*

$$Dn = (1 + r) - n \qquad \text{(AA.15)}$$

where Dn is the n-year discount factor.

The three-year discount factor when the discount rate is 9% is.

$$D_3 = (1 + 0.09) - 3$$
$$= 0.77218.$$

We can calculate discount factors for all possible interest rates and time periods to give us a *discount function.* Fortunately, we don't need to calculate discount factors ourselves as this has been done for us and discount tables for a range of rates are provided in Table AA.1 below.

EXAMPLE AA.1 Formula summary

Discount factor with simple interest:

$$D = \frac{1}{(1 + r \text{ days/year})}$$

Discount factor with compound interest:

$$D_n = \left(\frac{1}{1 + r}\right)^n$$

Earlier we established the continuously compounded interest rate factor as *ern*. Using a continuously compounded interest rate therefore we can establish the discount factor to be:

$$D = \frac{1}{1 + (e^{r \times \text{days/year}} - 1)} \qquad \text{(AA.16)}$$

$$= e^{-r \times \text{days/year}}$$

$$D_n = e^{-rn}$$

The continuously compounded discount factor is part of the formula that makes up certain option pricing models.

It is possible to calculate discount factors from the prices of government bonds. The traditional approach described in most textbooks requires that we first use the price of a bond that has only one remaining coupon, its last one, and calculate a discount factor from this bond's price. We then use this discount factor to calculate the discount factors of bonds with ever-increasing maturities, until we obtain the complete discount function. This method suffers from certain drawbacks and in practice more sophisticated techniques are used.

See Figure AA.3 below for an illustration of the discount function.

Present values with multiple discounting

Present values for short-term investments of under one year maturity often involve a single interest payment. If there is more than one interest payment, then any discounting needs to take this into account. If discounting takes place m times per year then we can use Equation (AA.4) to derive the present value formula as follows:

$$PV = FV\left(1 + \frac{r}{m}\right)^{-mn}. \tag{AA.17}$$

For example, what is the present value of the sum of £1000 that is to be received in five years where the discount rate is 5% and there is semi-annual discounting?

Using AA.17 above we see that:

$$\begin{aligned} PV &= 1{,}000\left(1 + \frac{0.05}{2}\right)^{-2\times 5} \\ &= £781.20. \end{aligned}$$

The effect of more frequent discounting is to lower the present value. As with continuous compounding, the limiting factor is reached with continuous discounting and we can use equation (AA.6) to derive the present value formula for continuous discounting.

$$PV = FVe^{-rn} \tag{AA.18}$$

Using this expression, if we consider the same example as before, but now with continuous discounting, we calculate the present value of £1,000 to be received in five years as:

$$PV = 1000e^{-(0.05)\times 5}$$
$$= £778.80.$$

Interpolation and extrapolation

Interest rates in the money markets are always quoted for standard maturities; for example, overnight, "tom next" (the overnight interest rate starting tomorrow, or "tomorrow to the next"), spot next (the overnight rate starting two days forward), one week, one month, two months, and so on up to one year. Figure AA.1 shows a typical broker's screen as seen on news services such as Reuters, Telerate or Bloomberg. We see that the rates quoted are for standard periods such as one week, one month, two months, and so on.

3 P1P300 Comdty TTDE
Screen Printed
14:43 TULLETT & TOKYO PAGE 1 / 2

	GBP Cash Deposits	Euro-Sterling Bid	Ask	Time		GBP Cash Deposits	Domestic Interbank Bid	Ask	Time
1)	T/N	4.2500	4.3500	8:57	18)	O/N	4.2500	4.3750	14:36
2)	S/N	4.2500	4.3500	8:57	19)	T/N	4.2500	4.3125	14:17
3)	1 Week	4.3500	4.3900	7:46	20)	1 Week	4.2500	4.3125	10:52
4)	2 Week	4.3300	4.3800	7:46	21)	2 Week	4.2813	4.3438	7:51
5)	3 Week	4.3200	4.3700	7:46	22)	1 Month	4.3125	4.3750	7:51
6)	1 Month	4.3200	4.3500	10:53	23)	2 Month	4.3438	4.4063	7:51
7)	2 Month	4.3500	4.3900	7:06	24)	3 Month	4.3750	4.4375	7:51
8)	3 Month	4.4100	4.4500	7:04	25)	4 Month	4.4375	4.5000	7:51
9)	4 Month	4.4500	4.4900	14:16	26)	5 Month	4.5000	4.5625	7:51
10)	5 Month	4.5200	4.5600	14:16	27)	6 Month	4.5625	4.6250	7:51
11)	6 Month	4.5800	4.6200	14:16	28)	9 Month	4.7188	4.7813	7:16
12)	7 Month	4.6200	4.6600	14:16	29)	12 Month	4.8750	4.9375	7:51
13)	8 Month	4.6800	4.7200	14:16					
14)	9 Month	4.7400	4.7800	14:16					
15)	10 Month	4.7900	4.8300	14:16					
16)	11 Month	4.8400	4.8800	8:49					
17)	12 Month	4.8900	4.9300	8:49					

Page forward for GBP CDs

Australia 61 2 9777 8600 Brazil 5511 3048 4500 Europe 44 20 7330 7500 Germany 49 69 920410
Hong Kong 852 2977 6000 Japan 81 3 3201 8900 Singapore 65 6212 1000 U.S. 1 212 318 2000 Copyright 2004 Bloomberg L.P.
0 10-May-04 14:43:01

Figure AA.1 Tullett brokers rates screen Tullett International
©Tullett International ©Bloomberg L.P. Used with permission.

If a bank or corporate customer wishes to deal for non-standard periods, an interbank desk will calculate the rate chargeable for such an "odd date" by *interpolating* between two standard period interest rates. If we assume that the rate for all dates in between two periods increases at the same steady state, we can calculate the required rate using the formula for *straight line* interpolation, shown at (AA.19).

$$r = r_1 + (r_2 - r_1) \times \frac{n - n_1}{n_2 - n_1} \qquad \text{(AA.19)}$$

where

r is the required odd-date rate for n days
r_1 is the quoted rate for n_1 days
r_2 is the quoted rate for n_2 days.

Let us imagine that the 1-month (30-day) offered interest rate is 5.25% and that the 2-month (60-date) offered rate is 5.75%. If a customer wishes to borrow money for a 40-day period, what rate should the bank charge? We can calculate the required 40-day rate using the straight line interpolation process. The increase in interest rates from 30 to 40 days is assumed to be 10/30 of the total increase in rates from 30 to 60 days. The 40-day offered rate would therefore be:

$$5.25\% + (5.75\% - 5.25\%) \times 10/30 = 5.4167\%.$$

EXAMPLE AA.2 Interpolation

An interbank desk is quoting the 7-day offered rate (the rate at which a bank will *offer* or lend money) at $5^{11}/_{16}\%$, while the 14-day rate is $5^{13}/_{16}\%$. What rate should it quote for the 10-day offered rate?

$$5.6875 + (5.8125 - 5.6875) \times 3/7 = 5.7411\%$$

What about the case of an interest rate for a period that lies just before or just after two known rates and not roughly in between them? When this happens we *extrapolate* between the two known rates, again assuming a straight line relationship between the two rates and for a period after (or before) the two rates.

EXAMPLE AA.3

The 1-month offered rate is 5.25% while the 2-month rate is 5.75% as before. What is the 64-day rate?

$$5.25 + (5.75 - 5.25) \times 34/30 = 5.8167\%$$

Figure AA.2 is a diagrammatic representation of interpolation and extrapolation.

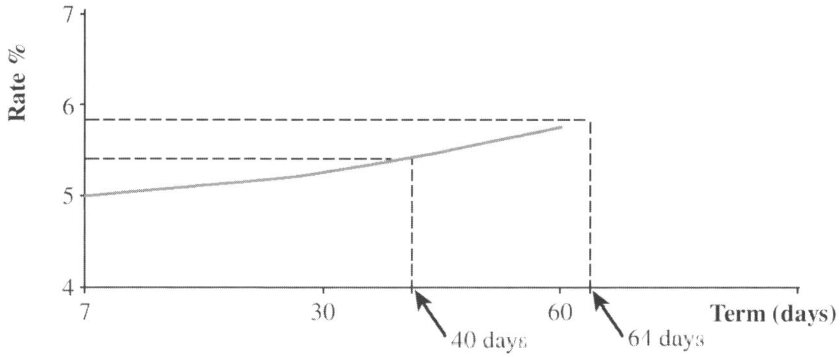

Figure AA.2 Interpolation and extrapolation

Note that the market uses a number of terms for term periods that are not standard. For instance, the term "broken date" is used to denote an odd date period, while FRA traders refer to non-standard term periods as "cockdates".

Measuring the rate of return

Rates of return are calculated in the market and by investors in order to measure the gain that has been achieved, as well as to compare the gains made by different investments. This is the market convention, presenting the profit made by an investment in percentage return figures rather than actual cash increments. In addition to comparing the performance of different investments, there are three other uses for rates of return.

- *Measuring historical performance*: a frequently used measure of investment performance is the historical rate of return, or the *realised rate of return* on an investment. This is the return that has already been realised as opposed to return anticipated in the future. In the US market this is also known as the *ex-post* rate of return.
- *Determining future investment*: investors often use historical rates of return to estimate future returns, and to gauge the level of risk associated with a particular security. Over a period of time, because of the higher associated risk, investors will expect a higher return from a higher risk stock compared to a less volatile one.
- *Estimating the cost of capital*: rates of return are also used to estimate a firm's cost of capital. Corporate decision-makers use their firm's cost of capital when making capital allocation and budget decisions, and one method for estimating the appropriate discount rate to apply in net present value (NPV) calculations uses the company's historical rate of return on equity.

The rate of return on an investment can be calculated in several ways and we will look at some of the methods in the rest of this section.

Simple rate of return

The simple rate of return measures the increase or decrease in the value of a given investment over a specified period of time. It is given by:

$$R = \frac{P_2 - P_1 + \mathrm{I}}{P_1} \qquad \text{(AA.20)}$$

where

P_1 is the initial value of the investment
P_2 is the investment value at the end of the period
I is the income earned during the investment.

For example, a bond is purchased at a price of £100 and held for a year, during which a coupon of £8 is paid. At the end of the period the bond price is £108. The rate of return is:

$$\frac{108 - 100 + 8}{100} = 0.16 \text{ or } 16\%.$$

The simple rate of return is effective when measuring investment performance that has only one dividend payment at the end of the period. If dividends are paid more frequently or during the period, the measurement loses accuracy.

The time-weighted rate of return

The simple rate of return can be adjusted to account for the timing of dividend or coupon payments and this is known as the *time weighted rate of return* or the *geometric mean rate of return*. If we take P as the initial value of an investment, FV as the final value, dn as the payment received by the investment in year n and MVn as the value of the investment when a dividend is received, the time-weighted rate of return is given by (AA.21).

$$(1 + r)^N = \left(\frac{MV_1}{P}\right)\left(\frac{MV_2}{MV_1 + d_1}\right)\left(\frac{MV_3}{MV_2 + d_2}\right)\cdots\left(\frac{FV}{MV_{N-1} + d_{N-1}}\right) \quad \text{(AA.21)}$$

Given that $(MV_1 / P) = (1 + r_1)$ or one plus the return on the investment in the first period, and that $(MV_2 / (\mathrm{MV}_1 + d_1) = (1 + r_2)$ and so on, the expression can be rewritten as shown in (AA.22).

$$(1 + r)^N = (1 + r_1)\,(1 + r_2)\,(1 + r_3)\,\ldots\,(1 + r_N) \quad \text{(AA.22)}$$

We can rearrange (AA.22) to solve for r and this gives us (AA.23) as shown.

$$r = [(1 + r_1)\,(1 + r_2)\,(1 + r_3)\,\ldots\,(1 + r_N)]^{1/T} - 1 \quad \text{(AA.23)}$$

Expression (AA.23) illustrates how the time-weighted return is in fact the *geometric* return of each individual period return.

Average rates of return

Where an investment is made up of a portfolio of assets the gain on the portfolio is calculated as an average return. An average is also used when measuring the return on a single asset over a period of years. The two main methods used are *arithmetic average* and *geometric average*.

The expression for calculating the average rate of return is given in (AA.24).

$$R_A = \frac{\sum_{t=1}^{m} R_t}{m} \quad \text{(AA.24)}$$

where

R_A is the average arithmetic rate of return
t is the length of the period
m is the number of observations.

The geometric method is an averaging method that compounds rates of return. That is, if £1 is invested in the first period, its future value will be $(1 + R_1)$ at the end of the period. We then assume that £$(1 + R_1)$ is invested in the second period, and at the end of period two the investment value will have risen to the value at the beginning of period two multiplied by the value of £1 invested in period two. We illustrate this by saying that the investment value at the end of the second period is $(1 + R_1)(1 + R_2)$. More formally we can express the geometric return as:

$$R_G = \left[\prod_{t=1}^{m}(1 + R_t)\right]^{1/m} - 1 \qquad \text{(AA.25)}$$

where R_G is the geometric rate of return and the symbol Π means "take the product of".[1]

The geometric average can be considered to be the actual growth rate of the assets. The arithmetic average should be used, on the other hand, when estimating the average performance across different securities for one period of time. The arithmetic average is also an unbiased estimate of future expected rates of return, and will exceed the geometric average whenever the rates of return are not constant.

$$I = I_{t-1}\left[\prod_{n=1}^{N}(1 + R_{i_t})\right]^{1/n} \qquad \text{(AA.26)}$$

In general, the arithmetic method produces higher values over time compared to the geometric method.

The internal rate of return

A common method of measuring the return on an investment, the internal rate of return (IRR) is also frequently used in corporate finance analysis and project analysis. It is also known as the *money-weighted rate of return.* If there is only a single cash flow to consider, the calculation involves the application of basic time value of money principles. Since $FV = PV(1 + r)^n$, the annual IRR on an investment that pays PV in n years' time can be obtained by solving the expression:

---

[1] For example, $y = \prod^{5} x_i$ means $y = (x_1)(x_2)(x_3)(x_4)(x_5)$.

$$(1 + r)^n = FV/PV$$

which we can rearrange to calculate the IRR, which would be:

$$r = (FV/PV)^{1/n} - 1. \tag{AA.27}$$

Consider an investment of £100 today that returns £131 in five years. The annual IRR is given by:

$$r = (131/100)1/5 \quad 1$$

which is 0.05549 or 5.55%.

The above example assumes annual compounding. If compounding occurs more than once a year, the expression for the annual IRR is modified as shown at (AA.28).

$$\left(1 + \frac{r}{m}\right)^{mN} = FV/PV \tag{AA.28}$$

which is then rearranged to solve for r:

$$r = m[(FV/PV)^{1/mN} - 1]. \tag{AA.29}$$

Let us consider our £100 investment example again but this time with semi-annual compounding. The annual IRR in such a case would then be:

$$r = 2[(131/100)^{1/(2\times5)} - 1]$$

which gives us 5.47%.

The limiting factor resulting from continuous compounding is given by (AA.30).

$$e^{rN} = FV/PV \tag{AA.30}$$

A general principle is that if $xb = y$, then b is known as the *logarithm* of y to base x. That is, we can say that $b = \log x\,(y)$. If we apply this to (AA.30) this results in:

$$rN = \log_e (FV/PV) \qquad \text{(AA.31)}$$

which means that rN is the logarithm of (FV/PV) to base e. Logarithms to base e are called natural logarithms and are shown as $b = \ln(y)$. This results in (AA.31) being changed to:

$$r = {}^1/_N \ln (FV/PV) \qquad \text{(AA.32)}$$

If we apply (AA.32) to our earlier example of the £100 investment over five years, but now assuming continuous compounding, the annual IRR is given by:

$$r = 1/5 \ln (131/100)$$

$$= 0.0540054$$

or 5.4%. As in earlier illustrations the continuous compounding effect has reduced the IRR.

If there is more than one payment in a future cash flow, for example multiple payments arising out of a continuous project or bond instrument, it will not be possible to solve for the IRR analytically. Where this happens the solution for r can be found by using either (AA.33) and (AA.34), which can be solved using a numerical process of trial and error.

$$FV = \sum_{n=1}^{N} d_n(1 + r)^{N-n} \qquad \text{(AA.33)}$$

$$PV = \sum_{n}^{N} d_n(1 + r)^{-n} \qquad \text{(AA.34)}$$

The process of solving for multiple payments is known as numerical iteration and involves using the formula for linear interpolation. In the case of an irredeemable bond with perpetual coupon payments the IRR is more straightforward to calculate and is given by (AA.35).

$$r = \frac{d}{PV} \qquad \text{(AA.35)}$$

Figure AA.4 illustrates the relationship between IRR and NPV.

Discount rate (%)

Years	1	2	3	4	5	6	7	8	9	10	12	15	20
1	0.990099	0.980392	0.970874	0.961538	0.952381	0.943396	0.934579	0.925926	0.917431	0.909091	0.892857	0.869565	0.833333
2	0.980296	0.961169	0.942596	0.924556	0.907029	0.889996	0.873439	0.857339	0.841680	0.826446	0.797194	0.756144	0.694444
3	0.970590	0.942322	0.915142	0.888996	0.863838	0.839619	0.816298	0.793832	0.772183	0.751315	0.711780	0.657516	0.578704
4	0.960980	0.923845	0.888487	0.854804	0.822702	0.792094	0.762895	0.735030	0.708425	0.683013	0.635518	0.571753	0.482253
5	0.951466	0.905731	0.862609	0.821927	0.783526	0.747258	0.712986	0.680583	0.649931	0.620921	0.567427	0.497177	0.401878
6	0.942045	0.887971	0.837484	0.790315	0.746215	0.704961	0.666342	0.630170	0.596267	0.564474	0.506631	0.432328	0.334898
7	0.932718	0.870560	0.813092	0.759918	0.710681	0.665057	0.622750	0.583490	0.547034	0.513158	0.452349	0.375937	0.279082
8	0.923483	0.853490	0.789409	0.730690	0.676839	0.627412	0.582009	0.540269	0.501866	0.466507	0.403883	0.326902	0.232568
9	0.914340	0.836755	0.766417	0.702587	0.644609	0.591898	0.543934	0.500249	0.460428	0.424098	0.360610	0.284262	0.193807
10	0.905287	0.820348	0.744094	0.675564	0.613913	0.558395	0.508349	0.463193	0.422411	0.385543	0.321973	0.247185	0.161506
11	0.896324	0.804263	0.722421	0.649581	0.584679	0.526788	0.475093	0.428883	0.387533	0.350494	0.287476	0.214943	0.134588
12	0.887449	0.788493	0.701380	0.624597	0.556837	0.496969	0.444012	0.397114	0.355535	0.318631	0.256675	0.186907	0.112157
13	0.878663	0.773033	0.680951	0.600574	0.530321	0.468839	0.414964	0.367698	0.326179	0.289664	0.229174	0.162528	0.093464
14	0.869963	0.757875	0.661118	0.577475	0.505068	0.442301	0.387817	0.340461	0.299246	0.263331	0.204620	0.141329	0.077887
15	0.861349	0.743015	0.641862	0.555265	0.481017	0.417265	0.362446	0.315242	0.274538	0.239392	0.182696	0.122894	0.064905
16	0.852821	0.728446	0.623167	0.533908	0.458112	0.393646	0.338735	0.291890	0.251870	0.217629	0.163122	0.106865	0.054088
17	0.844377	0.714163	0.605016	0.513373	0.436297	0.371364	0.316574	0.270269	0.231073	0.197845	0.145644	0.092926	0.045073
18	0.836017	0.700159	0.587395	0.493628	0.415521	0.350344	0.295864	0.250249	0.211994	0.179859	0.130040	0.080805	0.037561
19	0.827740	0.686431	0.570286	0.474642	0.395734	0.330513	0.276508	0.231712	0.194490	0.163508	0.116107	0.070265	0.031301
20	0.819544	0.672971	0.553676	0.456387	0.376889	0.311805	0.258419	0.214548	0.178431	0.148644	0.103667	0.061100	0.026084
21	0.811430	0.659776	0.537549	0.438834	0.358942	0.294155	0.241513	0.198656	0.163698	0.135131	0.092560	0.053131	0.021737
22	0.803396	0.646839	0.521893	0.421955	0.341850	0.277505	0.225713	0.183941	0.150182	0.122846	0.082643	0.046201	0.018114
23	0.795442	0.634156	0.506692	0.405726	0.325571	0.261797	0.210947	0.170315	0.137781	0.111678	0.073788	0.040174	0.015095
24	0.787566	0.621721	0.491934	0.390121	0.310068	0.246979	0.197147	0.157699	0.126405	0.101526	0.065882	0.034934	0.012579
25	0.779768	0.609531	0.477606	0.375117	0.295303	0.232999	0.184249	0.146018	0.115968	0.092296	0.058823	0.030378	0.010483
26	0.772048	0.597579	0.463695	0.360689	0.281241	0.219810	0.172195	0.135202	0.106393	0.083905	0.052521	0.026415	0.008735
27	0.764404	0.585862	0.450189	0.346817	0.267848	0.207368	0.160930	0.125187	0.097608	0.076278	0.046894	0.022970	0.007280
28	0.756836	0.574375	0.437077	0.333477	0.255094	0.195630	0.150402	0.115914	0.089548	0.069343	0.041869	0.019974	0.006066
29	0.749342	0.563112	0.424346	0.320651	0.242946	0.184557	0.140563	0.107328	0.082155	0.063039	0.037383	0.017369	0.005055
30	0.741923	0.552071	0.411987	0.308319	0.231377	0.174110	0.131367	0.099377	0.075371	0.057309	0.033378	0.015103	0.004213

Table AA.1 Discount factor table

$$D.F. = \frac{1}{(1 + r)^n}$$

$$r = \sqrt[n]{\frac{1}{D.F.}} - 1$$

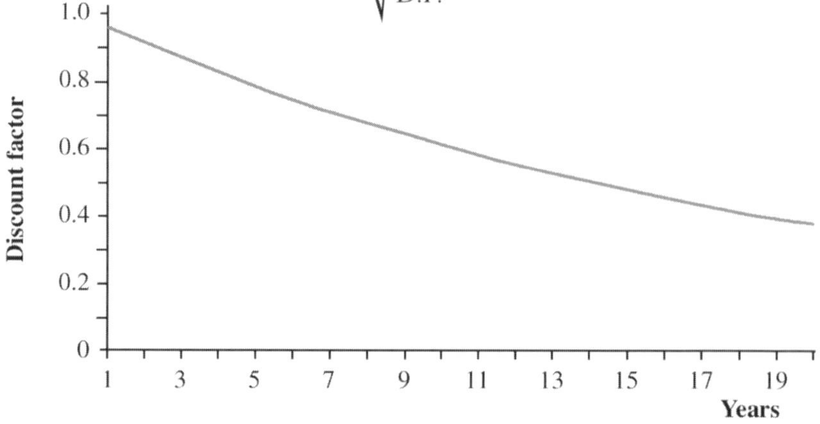

Figure AA.3 Discount function with the rate at 5%

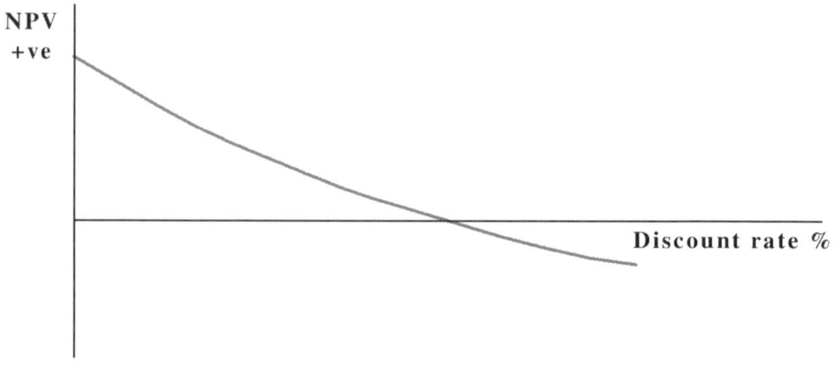

Figure AA.4 Relationship between IRR and NPV

Selected bibliography and references

Fabozzi, F. 1996, *Fixed Income Mathematics*, FJF Associates, New Hope, PA.

Higson, C. 1995, *Business Finance*, Butterworth, Oxford.

Tuckman, B. 1996, *Fixed Income Securities*, John Wiley & Sons, New York.

Van Horne, J. 1995, *Financial Management and Policy*, 10th edition, Prentice Hall International, New York, Chapters 16–20.

Weston, J.F. and Copeland, T.E. 1986, *Managerial Finance*, Dryden, Oxford.

… what is striking is how few companies have traded in derivatives. … Less than half of America's top 1,000 companies have ever used derivatives, and only the biggest 5% of the country's banks. The use of credit derivatives is restricted to a mere 0.2% of American banks.

– "Off target"
The Economist, 15 March 2003

APPENDIX

B

Interest Rate Derivatives

Bond futures

A widely used risk management instrument in the bond markets is the government bond futures contract. This is an exchange-traded standardised contract that fixes the price today at which a specified quantity and quality of a bond will be delivered at a date during the expiry month of the futures contract. Unlike short-term interest rate futures, which only require cash settlement, bond futures require the actual physical delivery of a bond when they are settled.

In this appendix we review bond futures contracts and their use for trading and hedging purposes.

Introduction

A *futures contract* is an agreement between two counterparties that fixes the terms of an exchange that will take place between them at some future date. They are standardised agreements as opposed to "over-the-counter" or OTC ones, as they are traded on an exchange, so they are also referred to as *exchange traded futures*. In the United Kingdom financial futures are traded on LIFFE, the London International Financial Futures Exchange, which opened in 1982. LIFFE is the biggest financial futures exchange in Europe in terms of volume of contracts traded. There are four classes of contract traded on LIFFE: short-term interest rate contracts, long-term interest rate contracts (bond futures), currency contracts and stock index contracts.

Bond futures contracts, which are an important part of the bond markets, are used for hedging and speculative purposes. Most futures contracts on exchanges around the world trade at three-month maturity intervals, with maturity dates fixed at March, June, September and December each year. This includes the contracts traded on LIFFE. Therefore at pre-set times during the year a contract for each of these months will *expire*, and a final *settlement* price is determined for it. The further out one goes the less liquid the trading is in that contract. It is normal to see liquid trading only in the *front month* contract (the current contract, so that if we are trading in April 2002 the front month is the June 2002 future), and possibly one or two of the next contracts, for most bond futures contracts. The liquidity of contracts diminishes the further one trades out in the maturity range.

When a party establishes a position in a futures contract, it can either run this position to maturity or close out the position between the trade date and maturity. If a position is closed out the party will have either a profit or loss to book. If a position is held until maturity, the party who is long futures will take delivery of the underlying asset (bond) at the settlement price; the party who is short futures will deliver the underlying asset. This is referred to as *physical settlement* or sometimes, confusingly, as *cash settlement.*

There is no counterparty risk associated with trading exchange-traded futures, because of the role of the *clearing house*, such as the London Clearing House (LCH). This is the body through which contracts are settled. A clearing house acts as the buyer to all contracts sold on the exchange, and the seller to all contracts that are bought. So in the London market the LCH acts as the counterparty to all transactions, so that settlement is effectively guaranteed. The LCH requires all exchange participants to deposit *margin* with it, a cash sum that is the cost of conducting business (plus brokers' commissions). The size of the margin depends on the size of a party's net *open* position in contracts (an open position is a position in a contract that is held overnight and not closed out). There are two types of margin, *maintenance margin* and *variation margin.* Maintenance margin is the minimum level required to be held at the clearing house; the level is set by the exchange. Variation margin is the additional amount that must be deposited to cover any trading losses and as the size of the net open positions increases. Note that this is not like margin in, say, a repo transaction. Margin in repo is a safeguard against a drop in value of collateral that has been supplied against a loan of cash. The margin deposited at a futures exchange clearing house acts essentially as "good faith" funds, required to provide comfort to the exchange that the futures trader is able to satisfy the obligations of the futures contract.

Contract specifications

We have noted that futures contracts traded on an exchange are standardised. This means that each contract represents exactly the same commodity, and it cannot be tailored to meet individual customer requirements. In this section we describe two very liquid and commonly traded contracts, starting with the US T-bond contract traded on the Chicago Board of Trade (CBOT). The details of this contract are given in Table AB.1.

Unit of trading	US Treasury bond with notional value of $100,000 and a coupon of 8%
Deliverable grades	US T-bonds with a minimum maturity of 15 years from first day of delivery month
Delivery months	March, June, September, December
Delivery date	Any business day during the delivery month
Last trading day	12:00 noon, seventh business day before last business day of delivery month
Quotation	Per cent of par expressed as points and thirty seconds of a point, e.g., 108–16 is 108 16/32 or 108.50
Minimum price movement	1/32
Tick value	$31.25
Trading hours	07:20–14:00 (trading pit) 17:20–20:05 22:30–06:00 hours (screen trading)

Table AB.1 CBOT US T-bond futures contract
Source: CBOT.

The terms of this contract relate to a US Treasury bond with a minimum maturity of fifteen years and a *notional* coupon of 8%. The concept of the notional bond is discussed in my book *The Repo Handbook* (Butterworth-Heinemann 2002). A futures contract specifies a notional coupon to prevent delivery and liquidity problems that would arise if there were a shortage of bonds with exactly the coupon required, or if one market participant purchased a large proportion of all the bonds in issue with the required coupon. For exchange-traded futures, a short future can deliver any bond that fits the maturity criteria specified in the contract terms. Of course, a long future would like to deliver a high-coupon bond with significant accrued interest, while the short future would want to deliver a low-coupon bond with low interest accrued. In fact, this issue does not arise because of the way the *invoice amount* (the amount paid by the long future to purchase the bond) is calculated. The invoice amount on the expiry date is given as equation (AB.1):

$$Inv_{amt} = P_{fut} \times CF + AI \tag{AB.1}$$

where

Inv_{amt} is the invoice amount
P_{fut} is the price of the futures contract
CF is the conversion factor
AI is the bond accrued interest.

Any bond that meets the maturity specifications of the futures contract is said to be in the *delivery basket*, the group of bonds that are eligible to be delivered into the futures contract. Every bond in the delivery basket will have its own *conversion factor*, which is used to equalise coupon and accrued interest differences of all the delivery bonds. The exchange will announce the conversion factor for each bond before trading in a contract begins; the conversion factor for a bond will change over time, but remains fixed for one individual contract. That is, if a bond has a conversion factor of 1.091252, this will remain fixed for the life of the contract. If a contract specifies a bond with a notional coupon of 7%, like the long gilt future on LIFFE, then the conversion factor will be less than 1.0 for bonds with a coupon lower than 7% and higher than 1.0 for bonds with a coupon higher than 7%. A formal definition of conversion factor is given below.

Conversion factor

The conversion factor (or price factor) gives the price of an individual cash bond such that its YTM on the delivery day of the futures contract is equal to the notional coupon of the contract. The product of the conversion factor and the futures price is the forward price available in the futures market for that cash bond (plus the cost of funding, referred to as the gross basis).

Although conversion factors equalise the yield on bonds, bonds in the delivery basket will trade at different yields, and for this reason they are not 'equal' at the time of delivery. Certain bonds will be cheaper than others, and one bond will be the *cheapest-to-deliver* bond. The cheapest-to-deliver bond is the one that gives the greatest return from a strategy of buying a bond and simultaneously selling the futures contract, and then closing out positions on the expiry of the contract. This so-called *cash-and-carry trading* is actively pursued by proprietary trading desks in banks. If a contract is purchased and then held to maturity the buyer will receive, via the exchange's clearing house, the cheapest-to-deliver gilt. Traders sometimes try to exploit arbitrage price differentials between the future and the cheapest-to-deliver gilt, known as *basis trading*.

The mathematical calculation of the conversion factor for the gilt future is given in Example AB.1 below.

We summarise the contract specification of the long gilt futures contract traded on LIFFE in Table AB.2. There is also a medium gilt contract on LIFFE, which was introduced in 1998 (having been discontinued in the early 1990s). This trades a notional five-year gilt, with eligible gilts being those of four to seven years' maturity.

Unit of trading	UK gilt bond having a face value of £100,000, a notional coupon of 7% and a notional maturity of 10 years (changed from contract value of £50,000 from the September 1998 contract)
Deliverable grades	UK gilts with a maturity ranging from $8^3/_4$ to 13 years from the first day of the delivery month (changed from 10–15 years from the December 1998 contract)
Delivery months	March, June, September, December
Delivery date	Any business day during the delivery month
Last trading day	11:00 hours, two business days before last business day of delivery month
Quotation	Per cent of par expressed as points and hundredths of a point; for example, 114.56 (changed from ticks and 1/32nds of a point, as in 117"17 meaning 114 17/32 or 114.53125, from the June 1998 contract)
Minimum price movement	0.01 of one point (one tick)
Tick value	£10
Trading hours	08:00–18:00 hours. All trading conducted electronically on LIFFE CONNECT™ platform

Table AB.2 LIFFE long gilt future contract specification
Source: LIFFE.

Futures pricing

Theoretical principle

Although it may not appear so on first trading, floor trading on a futures exchange is probably the closest one gets to an example of the economist's perfect and efficient market. The immediacy and liquidity of the market will ensure that at virtually all times the price of any futures contract reflects fair value. In essence, because a futures contract represents an underlying asset, albeit a synthetic one, its price cannot differ from the actual cash market price of the asset itself. This is because the market sets futures prices such that they are arbitrage-free. We can illustrate this with a hypothetical example.

Let us say that the benchmark 10-year bond, with a coupon of 8% is trading at par. This bond is the underlying asset represented by the long bond futures contract; the front month contract expires in precisely three months. If we also say that the three-month Libor rate (the repo rate) is 6%, what is fair value for the front month futures contract?

For the purpose of illustration let us start by assuming the futures price to be 105. We could carry out the following arbitrage-type trade:

- buy the bond for £100;
- simultaneously sell the future at £105;
- borrow £100 for three months at the repo rate of 6%.

As this is a leveraged trade we have borrowed the funds with which to buy the bond, and the loan is fixed at three months because we will hold the position to the futures contract expiry, which is in exactly three months' time. At expiry, as we are short of futures, we will deliver the underlying bond to the futures clearing house and close out the loan. This strategy will result in cash flows for us as shown below.

Futures settlement cash flows	
Price received for bond	= 105.00
Bond accrued	= 2.00 (8% coupon for three months)
Total proceeds	= 107.00
Loan cash flows	
Repayment of principal	= 100.00
Loan interest	= 1.500 (6% repo rate for three months)
Total outlay	= 101.50

The trade has resulted in a profit of £5.50, and this profit is guaranteed as we have traded the two positions simultaneously and held them both to maturity. We are not affected by subsequent market movements. The trade is an example of a pure arbitrage, which is risk-free. There is no cash outflow at the start of the trade because we borrowed the funds used to buy the bond. In essence, we have locked in the forward price of the bond by trading the future today, so that the final settlement price of the futures contract is irrelevant. If the situation described above were to occur in practice it would be very short-lived, precisely because arbitrageurs would buy the bond and sell the future to make this profit. This activity would force changes in the prices of both bond and future until the profit opportunity was removed.

So in our illustration the price of the future was too high (and possibly the price of the bond was too low as well) and not reflecting fair value because the price of the synthetic asset was out of line with the cash asset.

What if the price of the future was too low? Let us imagine that the futures contract is trading at 95.00. We could then carry out the following trade:

- sell the bond at £100;
- simultaneously buy the future for £95;
- lend the proceeds of the short sale (£100) for three months at 6%.

This trade has the same procedure as the first one with no initial cash outflow, except that we have to cover the short position in the repo market, through which we invest the sale proceeds at the repo rate of 6%. After three months we are delivered a bond as part of the futures settlement, and this is used to close out our short position. How has our strategy performed?

Futures settlement cash flows

Clean price of bond	= 95.00
Bond accrued	= 2.00
Total cash outflow	= 97.00

Loan cash flows

Principal on loan maturity	= 100.00
Interest from loan	= 1.500
Total cash inflow	= 101.500

The profit of £4.50 is again a risk-free arbitrage profit. Of course our hypothetical world has ignored considerations such as bid–offer spreads for the bond, future and repo rates, which would apply in the real world and impact on any trading strategy. Yet again, however, the futures price is out of line with the cash market and has provided opportunity for arbitrage profit.

Given the terms and conditions that apply in our example, there is one price for the futures contract at which no arbitrage profit opportunity is available. If we set the future price at 99.5, we would see that both trading strategies, buying the bond and selling the future, or selling the bond and buying the future, yield a net cash flow of zero. There is no profit to be made from either strategy. So at 99.5 the futures price is in line with the cash market, and it will only move as the cash market price moves; any other price will result in an arbitrage profit opportunity.

Arbitrage-free futures pricing

The previous section demonstrated how we can arrive at the fair value for a bond futures contract provided we have certain market information. The market mechanism and continuous trading will ensure that the fair price *is* achieved, as arbitrage profit opportunities are eliminated. We can determine the bond future's price given:

- the coupon of the underlying bond, and its price in the cash market;
- the interest rate for borrowing or lending funds, from the trade date to the maturity date of the futures contract. This is known as the *repo* rate.

For the purpose of deriving this pricing model we can ignore bid–offer spreads, and borrowing and lending spreads. We set the following:

r	is the repo rate
rc	is the bond's running yield
P_{bond}	is the price of the cash bond
P_{fut}	is the price of the futures contract
t	is the time to the expiry of the futures contract.

We can substitute these symbols into the cash flow profile for our earlier trade strategy, that of buying the bond and selling the future. This gives us:

Futures settlement cash flows

Clean price for bond	$= P_{fut}$
Bond accrued	$= rc \times t \times P_{bond}$
Total proceeds	$= P_{fut} + (rc \times t \times P_{bond})$

Loan cash flows

Repayment of loan principal $= P_{bond}$

Loan interest $= r \times t \times P_{bond}$

Total outlay $= P_{bond} + (r \times t \times P_{bond})$

The profit from the trade would be the difference between the proceeds and outlay, which we can set as follows:

$$\text{Profit} = P_{fut} + rc \times t \times P_{bond} - P_{bond} + r \times t \times P_{bond}. \qquad \text{(AB.2)}$$

We have seen how the futures price is at fair value when there is no profit to be gained from carrying out this trade, so if we set profit at zero, we obtain the following:

$$0 = P_{fut} + rc \times t \times P_{bond} - P_{bond} + r \times t \times P_{bond}.$$

Solving this expression for the futures price P_{fut} gives us:

$$P_{fut} = P_{bond} + P_{bond}\, t\,(r - rc).$$

Rearranging this we get:

$$P_{fut} = P_{bond}\,(1 + t\,(r - rc)). \qquad \text{(AB.3)}$$

If we repeat the procedure for the other strategy, that of selling the bond and simultaneously buying the future, and set the profit to zero, we will obtain the same equation for the futures price as given in equation (AB.3).

It is the level of the repo rate in the market, compared to the running yield on the underlying bond, that sets the price for the futures contract. From the examples used at the start of this section we can see that it is the cost of funding compared to the repo rate that determines if the trade strategy results in a profit. The equation $(r - rc)$ from (AB.3) is the net financing cost in the arbitrage trade, and is known as the *cost of carry*. If the running yield on the bond is higher than the funding cost (the repo rate) this is positive funding or *positive carry*. Negative funding (*negative carry*) is when the repo rate is higher than the running yield. The level of $(r - rc)$ will determine whether the futures price is trading above the cash market price or below it. If we have positive carry (when $rc > r$) then the futures price will trade below the cash market price, known as trading at a *discount*. Where $r > rc$ and we have negative carry, then the futures price will be at a premium over the cash market price. If the net funding cost was zero, such that we had neither positive nor negative carry, then the futures price would be equal to the underlying bond price.

The cost of carry related to a bond futures contract is a function of the yield curve. In a positive yield curve environment, the three-month repo rate is likely to be lower than the running yield on a bond so that the cost of carry is likely to be positive. As there is generally only a liquid market in long bond futures out to contracts that mature up to one year from the trade date, with a positive yield curve it would be unusual to have a short-term repo rate higher than the running yield on the long bond. So in such an environment we would have the future trading at a discount to the underlying cash bond. If there is a negative-sloping yield curve, the futures price will trade at a premium to the cash price. It is in circumstances of changes in the shape of the yield curve that opportunities for relative value and arbitrage trading arise, especially as the bond that is cheapest-to-deliver for the futures contract may change with large changes in the curve.

A trading strategy that involved simultaneous and opposite positions in the cheapest-to-deliver bond (CTD) and the futures contract is known as *cash-and-carry* trading or *basis trading*. However, by the law of no-arbitrage pricing, the payoff from such a trading strategy should be zero. If we set the profit from such a trading strategy as zero, we can obtain a pricing formula for the fair value of a futures contract, which summarises the discussion above, and states that the fair value futures price is a function of the cost of carry on the underlying bond. This is given as equation (AB.4):

$$P_{fut} = \frac{(P_{bond} + AI_0) \times (1 + rt) - \sum_{i=1}^{N} C_i(1 + rt_{i,del}) - AI_{del}}{CF} \tag{AB.4}$$

where

AI_0 is the accrued interest on the underlying bond today

AI_{del} is the accrued interest on the underlying bond on the expiry or delivery date (assuming the bond is delivered on the final day, which will be the case if the running yield on the bond is above the money market rate)

C_i is the ith coupon

N is the number of coupons paid from today to the expiry or delivery date

r is the repo rate

t is the time period (in years) over which the trade takes place

CF is the bond conversion factor

$t_{i,del}$ is the period from receipt of the ith coupon to delivery.

Hedging using bond futures

Introduction

Bond futures are used for a variety of purposes. Much of one day's trading in futures will be speculative; that is, a punt on the direction of the market. Another main use of futures is to hedge bond positions. In theory, if hedging a cash bond position with a bond futures contract, if cash and futures prices move together, then any loss from one position will be offset by a gain from the other. When prices move exactly in lock-step with each other, the hedge is considered perfect. In practice, the price of even the cheapest-to-deliver bond (which one can view as being the bond being traded – implicitly – when one is trading the bond future) and the bond future will not move exactly in line with each other over a period of time. The difference between the cash price and the futures price is called the *basis*. The risk that the basis will change in an unpredictable way is known as *basis risk*.

Futures are a liquid and straightforward way of hedging a bond position. By hedging a bond position the trader or fund manager is hoping to balance the loss on the cash position by the profit gained from the hedge. However, the hedge will not be exact for all bonds except the CTD bond, which we can assume is the futures contract underlying bond. The basis risk in a hedge position arises because the bond being hedged is not identical to the CTD bond. The basic principle is that if the trader is long (or net long, where the desk is running long and short positions in different bonds) in the cash market, an equivalent number of futures contracts will be sold to set up the hedge. If the cash position is short the trader will buy futures. The hedging requirement can arise for different reasons. A market-maker will wish to hedge positions arising out of client business, when they are unsure when the resulting bond positions will be unwound. Fund managers may, for example, know that they need to realise a cash sum at a specific time in the future to meet fund liabilities, and sell bonds at that time. The market-maker will want to hedge against a drop in value of positions during the time the bonds are held. The fund manager will want to hedge against a rise in interest rates between now and the bond sale date, to protect the value of the portfolio.

When putting on the hedge position the key is to trade the correct number of futures contracts. This is determined by using the *hedge ratio* of the bond and the future, which is a function of the volatilities of the two instruments. The amount of contracts to trade is calculated using the hedge ratio, which is given by:

$$\textit{Hedge ratio} = \frac{\textit{Volatility of bond to be hedged}}{\textit{Volatility of hedging instrument}}$$

Therefore one needs to use the volatility values of each instrument. We can see from the calculation that if the bond is more volatile than the hedging instrument, then a greater amount of the hedging instrument will be required. Let us now look in greater detail at the hedge ratio.

There are different methods available to calculate hedge ratios. The most common ones are the conversion factor method, which can be used for deliverable bonds (also known as the *price factor* method) and the modified duration method (also known as the basis point value method).

Where a hedge is put on against a bond that is in the futures delivery basket it is common for the conversion factor to be used to calculate the hedge ratio. A conversion factor hedge ratio is more useful as it is transparent and remains constant, irrespective of any changes in the price of the cash bond or the futures contract. The number of futures contracts required to hedge a deliverable bond using the conversion factor hedge ratio is determined using equation (AB.5):

$$\textit{Number of contracts} = \frac{M_{bond} \times CF}{M_{fut}} \tag{AB.5}$$

where M is the nominal value of the bond or futures contract.

The conversion factor method may only be used for bonds in the delivery basket. It is important to ensure that this method is only used for one bond. It is an erroneous procedure to use the ratio of conversion factors of two different bonds when calculating a hedge ratio, as detailed in Galitz (1995) and elsewhere.

Unlike the conversion factor method, the modified duration hedge ratio may be used for all bonds, both deliverable and non-deliverable. In calculating this hedge ratio the modified duration is multiplied by the dirty price of the cash bond to obtain the *basis point value* (BPV). The BPV represents the actual impact of a change in the yield on the price of a specific bond. The BPV allows the trader to calculate the hedge ratio to reflect the different price sensitivity of the chosen bond (compared to the CTD bond) to interest rate movements. The hedge ratio calculated using BPVs must be constantly updated, because it will change if the price of the bond and/or the futures contract changes. This may necessitate periodic adjustments to the number of lots used in the hedge.

The number of futures contracts required to hedge a bond using the BPV method is calculated using the following:

$$Number\ of\ contracts = \frac{M_{bond}}{M_{fut}} \times \frac{BPV_{bond}}{BPV_{fut}} \tag{AB.6}$$

where the BPV of a futures contract is defined with respect to the BPV of its CTD bond, as given by equation (AB.7):

$$BPV_{fut} = \frac{BPV_{CTDbond}}{CF_{CTDbond}} \tag{AB.7}$$

The simplest hedge procedure to undertake is one for a position consisting of only one bond, the CTD bond. The relationship between the futures price and the price of the CTD given by equation (AB.4) indicates that the price of the future will move for moves in the price of the CTD bond, so therefore we may set:

$$\Delta P_{fut} \cong \frac{\Delta P_{bond}}{CF} \tag{AB.8}$$

where CF is the CTD conversion factor.

The price of the futures contract, over time, does not move tick-for-tick with the CTD bond (although it may on an intra-day basis), but rather by the amount of the change divided by the conversion factor. It is apparent therefore that to hedge a position in the CTD bond we must hold the number of futures contracts equivalent to the value of bonds held multiplied by the conversion factor. Obviously, if a conversion factor is less than one, the number of futures contracts will be less than the equivalent nominal value of the cash position; the opposite is true for bonds that have a conversion factor greater than one. However, the hedge is not as simple as dividing the nominal value of the bond position by the nominal value represented by one futures contract.

To measure the effectiveness of the hedge position, it is necessary to compare the performance of the futures position with that of the cash bond position, and to see how much the hedge instrument mirrored the performance of the cash instrument. A simple calculation is made to measure the effectiveness of the hedge, given by equation (AB.9), which is the percentage value of the hedge effectiveness:

$$Hedge\ effectiveness = -\left(\frac{Fut\ p/l}{Bond\ p/l}\right) \times 100. \tag{AB.9}$$

Hedging a bond portfolio

The principles established above may be applied when hedging a portfolio containing a number of bonds. It is more realistic to consider a portfolio holding not just bonds that are outside the delivery basket, but that are also not government bonds. In this case we need to calculate the number of futures contracts to put on as a hedge based on the volatility of each bond in the portfolio compared to the volatility of the CTD bond. Note that in practice, there is usually more than one futures contract that may be used as the hedge instrument. For example, in the sterling market it would be more sensible to use LIFFE's medium gilt contract, whose underlying bond has a notional maturity of four to seven years, if hedging a portfolio of short- to medium-dated bonds. However, for the purposes of illustration we will assume that only one contract, the long bond, is available.

To calculate the number of futures contracts required to hold as a hedge against any specific bond, we use equation (AB.10).

$$Hedge = \frac{M_{bond}}{M_{fut}} \times Vol_{bond/CTD} \times Vol_{CTD/fut} \qquad \text{(AB.10)}$$

where

M is the nominal value of the bond or future

$Vol_{bond/CTD}$ is the relative volatility of the bond being hedged compared to that of the CTD bond

$Vol_{CTD/fut}$ is the relative volatility of the CTD bond compared to that of the future.

It is not necessarily straightforward to determine the relative volatility of a bond vis-à-vis the CTD bond. If the bond being hedged is a government bond, we can calculate the relative volatility using the two bonds' modified duration. This is because the yields of both may be safely assumed to be strongly positively correlated. If however the bond being hedged is a corporate bond and/or non-vanilla bond, we must obtain the relative volatility using regression analysis, as the yields between the two bonds may not be strongly positively correlated. This is apparent when one remembers that the yield spread of corporate bonds over government bonds is not constant, and will fluctuate with changes in government bond yields. To use regression analysis to determine relative volatilities, historical price data on the bond is required; the daily price moves in the target bond and the CTD bond are then analysed to assess the slope of the regression line. In this section we will restrict the discussion to a portfolio of government bonds.

If we are hedging a portfolio of government bonds we can use equation (AB.11) to determine relative volatility values based on the modified duration of each of the bonds in the portfolio,

$$Vol_{bond/CTD} = \frac{\Delta P_{bond}}{\Delta P_{CTD}} \approx \frac{MD_{bond} \times P_{bond}}{MD_{CTD} \times P_{CTD}} \qquad \text{(AB.11)}$$

where MD is the modified duration of the bond being hedged or the CTD bond, as appropriate.[1] Once we have calculated the relative volatility of the bond being hedged, equation (AB.12) (obtained from (AB.8) and (AB.11)) tells us that the relative volatility of the CTD bond to that of the futures contract is approximately the same as its conversion factor. We are then in a position to calculate the futures hedge for each bond in a portfolio.

$$Vol_{CTD/fut} = \frac{\Delta P_{CTD}}{\Delta P_{fut}} \approx CF_{CTD} \qquad \text{(AB.12)}$$

Table AB.3 below shows a portfolio of five UK gilts on 20 October 1999. The nominal value of the bonds in the portfolio is £200 million, and the bonds have a market value excluding accrued interest of £206.84 million. Only one of the bonds is a deliverable bond, the $5^3/_4\%$ 2009 gilt which is in fact the CTD bond. For the Dec '99 futures contract the bond had a conversion factor of 0.9124950. The fact that this bond is the CTD explains why it has a relative volatility of one. We calculate the number of futures contracts required to hedge each position, using the equations listed above. For example, the hedge requirement for the position in the 7% 2002 gilt was calculated as follows:

$$\frac{5{,}000{,}000}{100{,}000} \times \frac{2.245 \times 101.50}{7.235 \times 99.84} \times 0.9124950 = 14.39.$$

The volatility of all the bonds is calculated relative to the CTD bond, and the number of futures contracts determined using the conversion factor for the CTD bond. The bond with the highest volatility is not surprisingly

[1] In certain textbooks and practitioner research documents, it is suggested that the ratio of the conversion factors of the bond being hedged (if it is in the delivery basket) and the CTD bond can be used to determine the relative volatility of the target bond. This is a specious argument. The conversion factor of a deliverable bond is the price factor that will set the yield of the bond equal to the notional coupon of the futures contract on the delivery date, and it is a function mainly of the coupon of the deliverable bond. The price volatility of a bond on the other hand, is a measure of its modified duration, which is a function of the bond's duration (that is, the weighted average term to maturity). Therefore using conversion factors to measure volatility levels will produce erroneous results. It is important not to misuse conversion factors when arranging hedge ratios.

the 6% 2028, which has the longest maturity of all the bonds and hence the highest modified duration. We note from Table AB.3 that the portfolio requires a hedge position of 2091 futures contracts. This illustrates how a "rough-and-ready" estimate of the hedging requirement, based on nominal values, would be insufficient as that would suggest a hedge position of only 2000 contracts.

CTD	5.75% 2009
Modified duration	7.234565567
Conversion factor	0.9124950
Price	99.84

Bond	Nominal amount (£m)	Price	Yield %	Duration	Modified duration	Relative volatility	Number of contracts
UKT 8% 2000	12	102.17	5.972	1.072	1.011587967	0.143090242	15.67
UKT 7% 2002	5	101.50	6.367	2.388	2.245057208	0.315483336	14.39
UKT 5% 2004	38	94.74	6.327	4.104	3.859791022	0.50626761	175.55
UKT 5.75% 2009	100	99.84	5.770	7.652	7.234565567	1.00	912.50
UKT 6% 2028	45	119.25	4.770	15.031	14.34666412	2.368603078	972.60
Total	**200**						**2090.71**

Table AB.3 Bond futures hedge for hypothetical gilt portfolio, 20 October 1999

The effectiveness of the hedge must be monitored over time. No hedge will be completely perfect, however, and the calculation illustrated above, as it uses modified duration value, does not take into account the convexity effect of the bonds. The reason why a futures hedge will not be perfect is because in practice, the price of the futures contract will not move tick-for-tick with the CTD bond, at least not over a period of time. This is the basis risk that is inherent in hedging cash bonds with futures. In addition, the calculation of the hedge is only completely accurate for a parallel shift in yields, as it is based on modified duration, so as the yield curve changes around pivots, the hedge will move out of line. Finally, the long gilt future is not the appropriate contract to use to hedge three of the bonds in the portfolio, or over 25% of the portfolio by nominal value. This is because these bonds are short- or medium-dated, and so their price movements will not track the futures price as closely as longer dated bonds. In this case, the more appropriate futures contract to use would have been the medium gilt contract, or (for the first bond, the 8% 2000) a strip of short sterling contracts. Using shorter dated instruments would reduce some of the basis risk contained in the portfolio hedge.

The margin process

Institutions buying and selling futures on an exchange deal with only one counterparty at all times: the exchange clearing house. The clearing house is responsible for the settlement of all contracts, including managing the delivery process. A central clearing mechanism eliminates counterparty risk for anyone dealing on the exchange, because the clearing house guarantees the settlement of all transactions. The clearing house may be owned by the exchange itself, such as the one associated with the Chicago Mercantile Exchange (the CME Clearinghouse), or it may be a separate entity, such as the London Clearing House, which settles transactions on LIFFE. The LCH is also involved in running clearing systems for swaps and repo products in certain currencies.

One of the key benefits to the market of the clearing house mechanism is that counterparty risk, as it is transferred to the clearing house, is virtually eliminated. The mechanism that enables the clearing house to accept the counterparty risk is the *margining* process that is employed at all futures exchanges. A bank or local trader must deposit margin before commencing dealing on the exchange; each day a further amount must be deposited or will be returned, depending on the results of the day's trading activity.

The exchange will specify the level of margin that must be deposited for each type of futures contract that a bank wishes to deal in. The *initial margin* will be a fixed sum per lot, so for example if the margin were £1,000 per lot, an opening position of 100 lots would require margin of £100,000. Once the initial margin has been deposited, there is a mark-to-market of all positions at the close of business; exchange-traded instruments are the most transparent products in the market, and the closing price is not only known to everyone, it is also indisputable. The closing price is also known as the *settlement price*. Any losses suffered by a trading counterparty, whether closed out or run overnight, are entered as a debit on the party's account and must be paid the next day. Trading profits are credited and may be withdrawn from the margin account the next day. This daily process is known as *variation margining*. Thus the margin account is updated on a daily basis and the maximum loss that must be made up on any morning is the maximum price movement that occurred the previous day. It is a serious issue if a trading party is unable to meet a margin call. In such a case, the exchange will order it to cease trading, and will also liquidate all its open positions; any losses will be met out of the firm's margin account. If the level of funds in the margin account is insufficient, the losses will be made good from funds paid out of a general fund run by the clearing house, which is maintained by all members of the exchange.

Payment of a margin is made by electronic funds transfer between the trading party's bank account and the clearing house. Initial margin is usually paid in cash, although clearing houses will also accept high-quality securities such as Treasury bills or certain government bonds, to the value of the margin required. Variation margin is always cash. The advantage of depositing securities rather than cash is that the depositing firm earns interest on its margin. This is not available on a cash margin, and the interest foregone on a cash margin is effectively the cost of trading futures on the exchange. However, if securities are used, there is effectively no cost associated with trading on the exchange (we ignore of course infrastructure costs and staff salaries).

The daily settlement of exchange-traded futures contracts, as opposed to when the contract expires or the position is closed out, is the main reason why futures prices are not equal to forward prices for long-dated instruments.

EXAMPLE AB.1 The conversion factor for the long gilt future

Here we describe the process used for the calculation of the *conversion factor* or *price factor* for deliverable bonds of the long gilt contract. The contract specifies a bond of maturity $8^3/_4$ 13 years and a notional coupon of 7%. For each bond that is eligible to be in the delivery basket, the conversion factor is given by the following equation: $P(7)/100$ where the numerator $P(7)$ is equal to the price per £100 nominal of the deliverable gilt at which it has a gross redemption yield of 7%, calculated as at the first day of the delivery month, less the accrued interest on the bond on that day.

This calculation uses the formula given in equation (AB.13) and the equation used to calculate accrued interest.

The numerator $P(7)$ is given by equation (AB.13):

$$p(7) = \frac{1}{1.035^{t/s}}\left(c_1 + \frac{c_2}{1.035} + \frac{C}{0.07}\left(\frac{1}{1.035} - \frac{1}{1.035^n}\right) + \frac{100}{1.035^n}\right) - AI \qquad \text{(AB.13)}$$

where

- c_1 is the cash flow due on the following quasi-coupon date, per £100 nominal of the gilt. c_1 will be zero if the first day of the delivery month occurs in the ex-dividend period or if the gilt has a long first coupon period and the first day of the delivery month occurs in the first full coupon period. c_1 will be less than c_2 if the first day of the delivery month falls in a short first coupon period. c_1 will be greater than c_2 if the first day of the delivery month falls in a long first coupon period and the first day of the delivery month occurs in the second full coupon period
- c_2 is the cash flow due on the next but one quasi-coupon date, per £100 nominal of the gilt. c_1 will be greater than c_2 if the first day of the delivery month falls in a long first coupon period and in the first full coupon period. In all other cases, $c_2 = c_1$; C is the annual coupon of the gilt, per £100 nominal
- t is the number of calendar days from and including the first day of the delivery month up to but excluding the next quasi-coupon date
- s is the number of calendar days in the full coupon period in which the first day of the delivery month occurs
- n is the number of full coupon periods between the following quasi-coupon date and the redemption date
- AI is the accrued interest per £100 nominal of the gilt.

The accrued interest used in the formula above is given according to the following procedures.

If the first day of the delivery month occurs in a standard coupon period, and the first day of the delivery month occurs on or before the ex-dividend date, then:

$$AI = \frac{t}{s} \times \frac{C}{2}. \qquad \text{(AB.14)}$$

If the first day of the delivery month occurs in a standard coupon period, and the first day of the delivery month occurs after the ex-dividend date, then:

$$AI = \left(\frac{t}{s} - 1\right) \times \frac{C}{2} \qquad \text{(AB.15)}$$

where

t is the number of calendar days from and including the last coupon date up to but excluding the first day of the delivery month

s is the number of calendar days in the full coupon period in which the first day of the delivery month occurs.

If the first day of the delivery month occurs in a short first coupon period, and the first day of the delivery month occurs on or before the ex-dividend date, then:

$$AI = \frac{t^*}{s} \times \frac{C}{2}. \qquad \text{(AB.16)}$$

If the first day of the delivery month occurs in a short first coupon period, and the first day of the delivery month occurs after the ex-dividend date, then:

$$AI = \frac{t^* - n}{s} \times \frac{C}{2} \qquad \text{(AB.17)}$$

where

t^* is the number of calendar days from and including the issue date up to but excluding the first day of the delivery month

n is the number of calendar days from and including the issue date up to but excluding the next quasi-coupon date.

If the first day of the delivery month occurs in a long first coupon period, and during the first full coupon period, then:

$$AI = \frac{u}{s_1} \times \frac{C}{2}. \qquad \text{(AB.18)}$$

If the first day of the delivery month occurs in a long first coupon period, and during the second full coupon period and on or before the ex-dividend date, then:

$$AI = \left(\frac{p_1}{s_1} - \frac{p_2}{s_2}\right) \times \frac{C}{2}. \qquad \text{(AB.19)}$$

If the first day of the delivery month occurs in a long first coupon period, and during the second full coupon period and after the ex-dividend date, then:

$$AI = \left(\frac{p_2}{s} - 1\right) \times \frac{C}{2} \qquad \text{(AB.20)}$$

where

u is the number of calendar days from and including the issue date up to but excluding the first day of the delivery month

s_1 is the number of calendar days in the full coupon period in which the issue date occurs

s_2 is the number of days in the next full coupon period after the full coupon period in which the issue date occurs

p_1 is the number of calendar days from and including the issue date up to but excluding the next quasi-coupon date; p_2 is the number of calendar days from and including the quasi-coupon date after the issue date up to but excluding the first day of the delivery month which falls in the next full coupon period after the full coupon period in which the issue date occurs.

Interest rate swaps

Swaps are off-balance sheet instruments involving combinations of two or more basic building blocks. Most swaps currently traded in the market involve combinations of cash market securities; for example, a fixed interest rate security combined with a floating interest rate security, possibly also combined with a currency transaction. However, the market has also seen swaps that involve a futures or forward component, as well as swaps that involve an option component. The market in, say, dollar, euro and sterling interest rate swaps is very large and very liquid. The main types of swap are interest rate swaps, asset swaps, basis swaps, fixed-rate currency swaps and currency coupon swaps. The market for swaps is organised by the International Swap Dealers Association.

Swaps are now one of the most important and useful instruments in the debt capital markets. They are used by a wide range of institutions, including banks, mortgage banks and building societies, corporates, and local authorities. The demand for them has grown as the continuing uncertainty and volatility of interest rates and exchange rates has made it ever more important to hedge their exposures. As the market has matured the instrument has gained wider acceptance, and is regarded as a "plain vanilla" product in the debt capital markets. Virtually all commercial and investment banks will quote swap prices for their customers, and as they are OTC instruments, dealt over the telephone, it is possible for banks to tailor swaps to match the precise requirements of individual customers. There is also a close relationship between the bond market and the swap market, and corporate finance teams and underwriting banks keep a close eye on the government yield curve and the swap yield curve, looking out for possibilities regarding new issue of debt.

Description

Interest rate swaps are the most important type of swap in terms of volume of transactions. They are used to manage and hedge interest rate risk and exposure, while market-makers will also take positions in swaps that reflect their view on the direction of interest rates. An interest rate swap is an agreement between two counterparties to make periodic interest payments to one another during the life of the swap, on a predetermined set of dates, based on a *notional* principal amount. One party is the fixed-rate payer, and this rate is agreed at the time of trade of the swap; the other party is the floating-rate payer, the floating rate being determined during the life of the swap by reference to a specific market index. The principal or notional amount is never physically exchanged, hence the term "off-balance sheet", but is used merely to calculate the interest payments. The fixed-rate payer receives floating-rate interest and is said to be "long" or to have "bought" the swap. The long side has conceptually purchased a floating-rate note (because it receives floating-rate interest) and issued a fixed coupon bond (because it pays out fixed interest at intervals); that is, it has in principle borrowed funds. The floating-rate payer is said to be "short" or to have "sold" the swap. The short side has conceptually purchased a coupon bond (because it receives fixed-rate interest) and issued a floating-rate note (because it pays floating-rate interest). So an interest rate swap is:

- an agreement between two parties;
- it is used to exchange a stream of cash flows;
- calculated as a percentage of a *notional* sum;
- calculated on different interest bases.

For example, in a trade between Bank A and Bank B, Bank A may agree to pay fixed semi-annual coupons of 10% on a notional principal sum of £1 million, in return for receiving from Bank B the prevailing six-month sterling Libor rate on the same amount. The known cash flow is the fixed payment of £50,000 every six months by Bank A to Bank B.

Interest rate swaps trade in a secondary market so their value moves in line with market interest rates, in exactly the same way as bonds. If a five-year interest rate swap is transacted today at a rate of 5%, and five-year interest rates subsequently fall to 4.75%, the swap will have decreased in value to the fixed-rate payer, and correspondingly increased in value to the floating-rate payer, who has now seen the level of interest payments fall. The opposite would be true if five-year rates moved to 5.25%. Why is this? Consider the fixed-rate payer in an interest rate swap to be a borrower of funds; if she fixes the interest rate payable on a loan for five years, and then this interest rate decreases shortly afterwards, is she better off? No, because she is now paying above the market rate for the funds borrowed. For this reason a swap contract decreases in value to the fixed-rate payer if there is a fall in rates. Equally, a floating-rate payer gains if there is a fall in rates, as she can take advantage of the new rates and pay a lower level of interest; hence, the value of a swap increases to the floating-rate payer if there is a fall in rates.

A bank swaps desk will have an overall net interest rate position arising from all the swaps it has traded that are currently on the book. This position is an interest rate exposure at all points along the term structure, out to the maturity of the longest dated swap. At the close of business each day all the swaps on the book will be *marked-to-market* at the interest rate quoted for that day.

A swap can be viewed in two ways, either as a bundle of forward or futures contracts, or as a bundle of cash flows arising from the "sale" and "purchase" of cash market instruments. If we imagine a strip of futures contracts, maturing every three or six months out to three years, we can see how this is conceptually similar to a three-year interest rate swap. However, in the author's view it is better to visualise a swap as being a bundle of cash flows arising from cash instruments.

Let us imagine that we have only two positions on our book:

- a long position in £100 million of a three-year FRN that pays six-month Libor semi-annually, and is trading at par;
- a short position in £100 million of a three-year gilt with coupon of 6% that is also trading at par.

Being short a bond is the equivalent to being a borrower of funds. Assuming this position is kept to maturity, the resulting cash flows are shown in Table AB.4.

Cash flows resulting from a long position in FRN and short position in gilt

Period (6 mo)	FRN	Gilt	Net cash flow
0	–£100 m	+£100 m	£0
1	+(Libor × 100)/2	–3	+(Libor × 100)/2 – 3.0
2	+(Libor × 100)/2	–3	+(Libor × 100)/2 – 3.0
3	+(Libor × 100)/2	–3	+(Libor × 100)/2 – 3.0
4	+(Libor × 100)/2	–3	+(Libor × 100)/2 – 3.0
5	+(Libor × 100)/2	–3	+(Libor × 100)/2 – 3.0
6	+[(Libor × 100)/2] + 100	–103	+(Libor × 100)/2 – 3.0

Table AB.4 Three-year cash flows. The Libor rate is the six-month rate prevailing at the time of the setting; for instance, the Libor rate at period 4 will be the rate actually prevailing at period 4

There is no net outflow or inflow at the start of these trades, as the £100 million purchase of the FRN is netted with receipt of £100 million from the sale of the gilt. The resulting cash flows over the three-year period are shown in the last column of Table AB.4. This net position is exactly the same as that of a fixed-rate payer in an IR swap. As we had at the start of the trade, there is no cash inflow or outflow on maturity. For a floating-rate payer, the cash flow would mirror exactly a long position in a fixed-rate bond and a short position in an FRN. Therefore the fixed-rate payer in a swap is said to be short in the bond market, that is a borrower of funds; the floating-rate payer in a swap is said to be long in the bond market.

Market terminology

Virtually all swaps are traded under the legal terms and conditions stipulated in the International Swaps and Derivatives Association (ISDA) standard documentation. The trade date for a swap is, not surprisingly, the date on which the swap is transacted. The terms of the trade include the fixed interest rate, the maturity and notional amount of the swap, and the payment bases of both legs of the swap. The date from which floating interest payments are determined is the *setting date*, which may also be the trade date. Most swaps fix the floating-rate payments to Libor, although other reference rates that are used include the US prime rate, euribor, the Treasury bill rate and the commercial paper rate. In the same way as for FRA and eurocurrency deposits, the rate is fixed two business days before the interest period begins. The second (and subsequent) setting date will be two business days before the beginning of the second (and subsequent) swap periods. The *effective date* is the date from which interest on the swap is calculated, and this is typically two business days after the trade date. In a *forward*-start swap the effective date will be at some point in the future, specified in the swap terms. The floating interest rate for each period is fixed at the start of the period, so that the interest payment amount is known in advance by both parties (the fixed rate is known of course, throughout the swap by both parties).

Although for the purposes of explaining swap structures, both parties are said to pay interest payments (and receive them), in practice only the net difference between both payments changes hands at the end of each interest period. This eases the administration associated with swaps and reduces the number of cash flows for each swap. The counterparty that is the net payer at the end of each period will make a payment to the counterparty. The first payment date will occur at the end of the first interest period, and subsequent payment dates will fall at the end of successive interest periods. The final payment date falls on the maturity date of the swap. The calculation of interest is given by equation (AB.21).

$$I = M \times r \times \frac{n}{B} \tag{AB.21}$$

where

I is the interest amount

M is the nominal amount of the swap

B is the interest day-base for the swap.

Dollar and euro-denominated swaps use an actual/360 day-count, similar to other money market instruments in those currencies, while sterling swaps use an actual/365 day-count basis.

The cash flows resulting from a vanilla interest rate swap are illustrated in Figure AB.1, using the normal convention where cash inflows are shown as an arrow pointing up, while cash outflows are shown as an arrow pointing down. The counterparties in a swap transaction only pay across net cash flows, however, so at each interest payment date only one actual cash transfer will be made, by the net payer. This is shown as Figure AB.1(c).

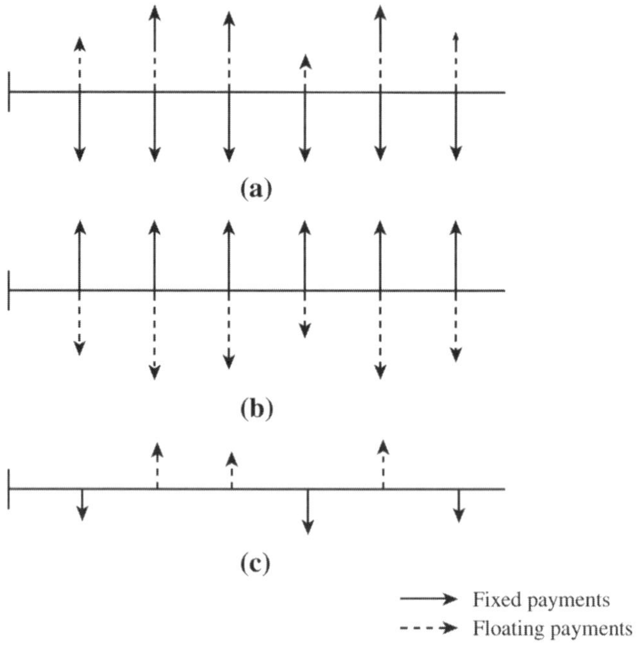

Figure AB.1 Cash flows for typical interest rate swap
(a) Cash flows for a fixed-rate payer
(b) Cash flows for a floating-rate payer
(c) Net cash flows

Swap spreads and the swap yield curve

In the market, banks will quote two-way swap rates, on screens and on the telephone or via a dealing system such as Reuters. Brokers will also be active in relaying prices in the market. The convention in the market is for the swap market-maker to set the floating leg at Libor and then quote the fixed rate that is payable for that maturity. So for a five-year swap, a bank's swap desk might be willing to quote the following:

Floating-rate payer:	pay 6-mo Libor receive fixed rate of 5.19%
Fixed-rate payer:	pay fixed rate of 5.25% receive 6-mo Libor

In this case the bank is quoting an offer rate of 5.25%, which the fixed-rate payer will pay, in return for receiving Libor flat. The bid price quote is 5.19%, which is what a floating-rate payer will receive fixed. The bid–offer spread in this case is therefore 6 basis points. The fixed-rate quotes are always at a spread above the government bond yield curve. Let us assume that the five-year gilt is yielding 4.88%; in this case then the five-year swap bid rate is 31 basis points above this yield. So the bank's swap trader could quote the swap rates as a spread above the benchmark bond yield curve, say 37 – 31, which is her swap spread quote. This means that the bank is happy to enter into a swap paying fixed 31 basis points above the benchmark yield and receiving Libor, and receiving fixed 37 basis points above the yield curve and paying Libor. The banks screen on, say, Bloomberg or Reuters might look something like Table AB.5, which quotes the swap rates as well as the current spread over the government bond benchmark.

1 year	4.50	4.45	+17
2 years	4.69	4.62	+25
3 years	4.88	4.80	+23
4 years	5.15	5.05	+29
5 years	5.25	5.19	+31
10 years	5.50	5.40	+35

Table AB.5 Swap quotes

The swap spread is a function of the same factors that influence the spread over government bonds for other instruments. For shorter duration swaps, say up to three years, there are other yield curves that can be used in comparison, such as the cash market curve or a curve derived from futures prices. For longer dated swaps the spread is determined mainly by the credit spreads that prevail in the corporate bond market. Because a swap is viewed as a package of long and short positions in fixed- and floating-rate bonds, it is the credit spreads in these two markets that will determine the swap spread. This is logical; essentially, it is the premium for greater credit risk involved in lending to corporates that dictates that a swap rate will be higher than the same maturity government bond yield. Technical factors will be responsible for day-to-day fluctuations in swap rates, such as the supply of corporate bonds and the level of demand for swaps, plus the cost to swap traders of hedging their swap positions.

We can summarise by saying that swap spreads over government bonds reflect the supply and demand conditions of both swaps and government bonds, as well as the market's view on the credit quality of swap counterparties. There is considerable information content in the swap yield curve, much like that in the government bond yield curve. During times of credit concerns in the market, such as the corrections in Asian and Latin American markets in the summer of 1998, and the possibility of default by the Russian government regarding its long-dated US dollar bonds, the swap spread will increase, more so at higher maturities. To illustrate this, let us consider the sterling swap spread in 1998/99. The UK swap spread widened from the second half of 1998 onwards, a reaction to bond market volatility around the world. At such times investors embark on a "flight to quality" that results in yield spreads widening. In the swap market, the spread between two-year and 10-year swaps also increased, reflecting market concern with credit and counterparty risk. The spreads narrowed in the first quarter of 1999, as credit concerns brought about by market corrections in 1998 declined. The change in swap spreads is shown in Figure AB.2.

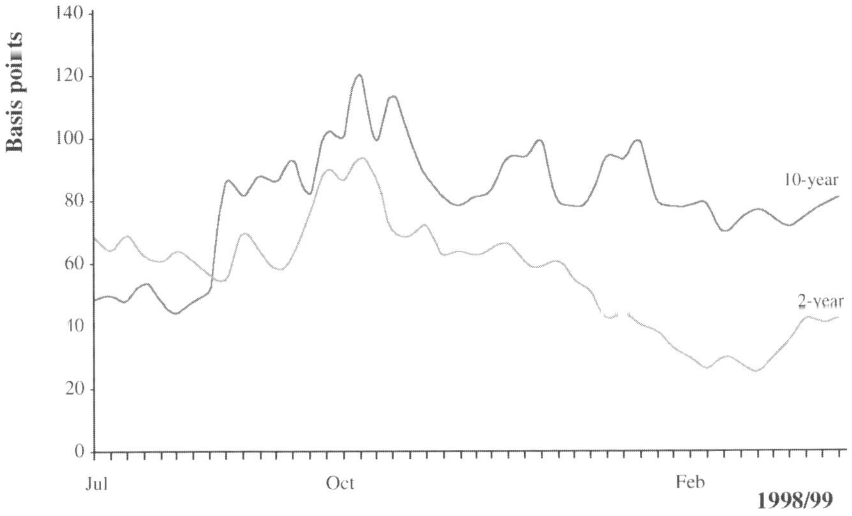

Figure AB.2 Sterling two-year and ten-year swap spreads 1998/99

Generic swap valuation

Banks generally use *par* swap or *zero-coupon* swap pricing. We will look at this method shortly; first, however, we will introduce an intuitive swap valuation method.

Generic swap pricing

Assume we have a vanilla interest rate swap with a notional principal of N that pays n payments during its life, to a maturity date of T. The date of each payment is on t_i with $i = 1, \ldots, n$. The present value today of a future payment is denoted by $PV(0, t)$. If the swap rate is r, the value of the fixed-leg payments is given by equation (AB.22) below:

$$PV_{fixed} = N \sum_{i=1}^{n} PV(0, t_i) \times \left[r \times \left(\frac{t_i - t_{i-1}}{B} \right) \right] \quad \text{(AB.22)}$$

where B is the money market day base. The term $t_i - t_{i-1}$ is simply the number of days between the ith and the i–1th payments.

The value of the floating-leg payments at the date t_1 for an existing swap is given by:

$$PV_{float} = N \times \left[rl \times \frac{t_i}{B} \right] + N - [N \times PV(t_1, t_n)] \quad \text{(AB.23)}$$

where rl is the Libor rate that has been set for the next interest payment. We set the present value of the floating-rate payment at time 0 as follows:

$$PV(0,t_1) = \frac{1}{1 + rl(t_1)\left(\frac{t_1}{B}\right)} . \qquad \text{(AB.24)}$$

For a new swap the value of the floating payments is given by:

$$PV_{float} = N \times \left[rl \times \frac{t_i}{B} + 1\right] \times PV(0, t_1) - PV(0, t_n) \qquad \text{(AB.25)}$$

The swap valuation is then given by $PV_{fixed} - PV_{float}$. The swap rate quoted by a market-making bank is that which sets $PV_{fixed} = PV_{float}$ and is known as the par or zero-coupon swap rate. We consider this next.

Zero-coupon swap pricing

So far we have discussed how vanilla swap prices are often quoted as a spread over the benchmark government bond yield in that currency, and how this swap spread is mainly a function of the credit spread required by the market over the government (risk-free) rate. This method is convenient and also logical because banks use government bonds as the main instrument when hedging their swap books. However, because much bank swap trading is now conducted in non-standard, tailor-made swaps, this method can sometimes be unwieldy as each swap needs to have its spread calculated to suit its particular characteristics. Therefore banks use a standard pricing method for all swaps known as *zero-coupon* swap pricing.

In Chapter 2 we referred to zero-coupon bonds and zero-coupon interest rates. Zero-coupon rates, or *spot rates,* are true interest rates for their particular term to maturity. In zero-coupon swap pricing, a bank will view all swaps, even the most complex, as a series of cash flows. The zero-coupon rates that apply now for each of the cash flows in a swap can be used to value these cash flows. Therefore to value and price a swap, each of the swap's cash flows are present valued using known spot rates; the sum of these present values is the value of the swap.

In a swap, the fixed-rate payments are known in advance and so it is straightforward to present value them. The present value of the floating-rate payments is usually estimated in two stages. First, the implied forward rates can be calculated using equation (AB.26). We are quite familiar with this relationship from our reading of the earlier chapter.

$$rf_i = \left(\frac{df_i}{df_{i+1}} - 1\right)N \qquad \text{(AB.26)}$$

where

rf_i is the one-period forward rate starting at time i
df_i is the discount factor for the maturity period I
df_{i+1} is the discount factor for the period $i+1$
N is the number of times per year that coupons are paid.

By definition the floating-payment interest rates are not known in advance, so the swap bank will predict what these will be, using the forward rates applicable to each payment date. The forward rates are those that are currently implied from spot rates. Once the size of the floating-rate payments has been estimated, these can also be valued by using the spot rates. The total value of the fixed and floating legs is the sum of all the present values, so the value of the total swap is the net of the present values of the fixed and floating legs.

While the term *zero-coupon* refers to an interest rate that applies to a discount instrument that pays no coupon and has one cash flow (at maturity), it is not necessary to have a functioning zero-coupon bond market in order to construct a zero-coupon yield curve. In practice, most financial pricing models use a combination of the following instruments to construct zero-coupon yield curves:

- money market deposits;
- interest rate futures;
- forward rate agreements (FRAs);
- government bonds.

Frequently, an overlap in the maturity period of all instruments is used; FRA rates are usually calculated from interest rate futures so it is necessary to use only one of either FRA or futures rates.

Once a zero-coupon yield curve (*term structure*) is derived, this may be used to value a future cash flow maturing at any time along the term structure. This includes swaps: to price an interest rate swap, we calculate the present value of each of the cash flows using the zero-coupon rates and then sum all the cash flows. As we noted above, while the fixed-rate payments are known in advance, the floating-rate payments must be estimated, using the forward rates implied by the zero-coupon yield curve. The net present value of the swap is the net difference between the present values of the fixed- and floating-rate legs.

Calculating the forward rate from the spot rate discount factors

Remember that one way to view a swap is as a long position in a fixed-coupon bond that was funded at Libor, or against a short position in a floating-rate bond. The cash flows from such an arrangement would be paying floating rate and receiving fixed rate. In the former arrangement, where a long position in a fixed-rate bond is funded with a floating-rate loan, the cash flows from the principals will cancel out, as they are equal and opposite (assuming the price of the bond on purchase was par), leaving a collection of cash flows that mirror an interest rate swap that pays floating and receives fixed. Therefore, as the fixed rate on an interest rate swap is the same as the coupon (and yield) on a bond priced at par, calculating the fixed rate on an interest rate swap is the same as calculating the coupon for a bond that we wish to issue at par.

The price of a bond paying semi-annual coupons is given by equation (AB.27), which may be rearranged for the coupon rate r to provide an equation that enables us to determine the par yield, and hence the swap rate r, given by equation (AB.28):

$$P = \frac{r_n}{2}df_1 + \frac{r_n}{2}df_2 + \ldots + \frac{r_n}{2}df_n + Mdf_2 \qquad \text{(AB.27)}$$

where r_n is the coupon on an n-period bond with n coupons and M is the maturity payment. It can be shown then that:

$$r_n = \frac{1 - df_n}{\frac{df_1}{2} + \frac{df_2}{2} + \cdots + \frac{df_n}{2}} = \frac{1 - df_n}{\sum_{i=1}^{n} \frac{df_i}{2}} \qquad \text{(AB.28)}$$

For annual coupon bonds there is no denominator for the discount factor, while for bonds paying coupons on a frequency of N we replace the denominator 2 with N.[2] Equation (AB.28) may be rearranged again, using F

[2] The equation also assumes an actual/365 day-count basis. If any other day-count convention is used, the $1/N$ factor must be replaced by a fraction made up of the actual number of days as the numerator and the appropriate year base as the denominator.

for the coupon frequency, to obtain an equation that may be used to calculate the nth discount factor for an n-period swap rate, given as equation (AB.29).

$$df_n = \frac{1 - r_n \sum_{i=1}^{n-1} \frac{df_i}{N}}{1 + \frac{r_n}{N}}. \tag{AB.29}$$

Equation (AB.29) is the general equation for the *boot-strapping* process of constructing a zero-coupon curve. Essentially, to calculate the n-year discount factor we use the discount factors for the years 1 to $n - 1$, and the n-year swap rate or zero-coupon rate. If we have the discount factor for any period, we may use equation (AB.29) to determine the same period zero-coupon rate, after rearranging it, shown as equation (AB.30):

$$rs_n = \sqrt[t_n]{\frac{1}{df_n}} - 1. \tag{AB.30}$$

Discount factors for spot rates may also be used to calculate forward rates. We know that:

$$df_1 = \frac{1}{\left(1 + \frac{rs_1}{N}\right)} \tag{AB.31}$$

where rs is the zero-coupon rate. If we know the *forward rate* we may use this to calculate a second discount rate, shown by equation (AB.32):

$$df_2 = \frac{df_1}{\left(1 + \frac{rf_1}{N}\right)} \tag{AB.32}$$

where rf_1 is the forward rate. This is no use in itself; however, we may derive from it an equation to enable us to calculate the discount factor at any point in time between the previous discount rate and the given forward rate for the period n to $n + 1$, shown as equation (AB.33), which may then be rearranged to give us the general equation to calculate a forward rate, given as equation (AB.34).

$$df_{n+1} = \frac{df_n}{\left(1 + \frac{rf_n}{N}\right)} \tag{AB.33}$$

$$rf_n = \left(\frac{df_n}{df_{n+1}} - 1\right) N \tag{AB.34}$$

The general equation for an n-period discount rate at time n from the previous period forward rates is given by equation (AB.35).

$$df_n = \frac{1}{\left(1 + \frac{rf_{n-1}}{N}\right)} \times \frac{1}{\left(1 + \frac{rf_{n-2}}{N}\right)} \times \ldots \times \frac{1}{\left(1 + \frac{rf_n}{N}\right)} \qquad \text{(AB.35)}$$

$$df_n = \prod_{n=1}^{n-1} \left[\frac{1}{\left(1 + \frac{rf_i}{N}\right)} \right].$$

From the above we may combine equations (AB.28) and (AB.34) to obtain the general expression for an n-period swap rate and zero-coupon rate, given by equations (AB.36) and (AB.37) respectively.

$$r_n = \frac{\sum_{i=1}^{n} \frac{rf_{i-1} df_i}{N}}{\sum_{i=1}^{n} \frac{df_i}{F}} \qquad \text{(AB.36)}$$

$$1 + rs_n = {}^{t_n}\sqrt{\prod_{i=0}^{n-1} \left(1 + \frac{rf_1}{N}\right)}\,. \qquad \text{(AB.37)}$$

The swap rate, which we have denoted as r_n is shown by equation (AB.36) to be the weighted average of the forward rates. Consider that a strip of FRAs would constitute an interest rate swap; that is, a swap rate for a continuous period could be covered by a strip of FRAs. Therefore an average of the FRA rates would be the correct swap rate. As FRA rates are forward rates, we may be comfortable with equation (AB.36), which states that the n-period swap rate is the average of the forward rates from rf_0 to rf_n. To be accurate we must weight the forward rates, and these are weighted by the discount factors for each period. Note that although swap rates are derived from forward rates, interest payments under a swap are paid in the normal way at the end of an interest period, while payments for an FRA are made at the beginning of the period and must be discounted.

Equation (AB.37) states that the zero-coupon rate is calculated from the geometric average of (one plus) the forward rates. The n-period forward rate is obtained using the discount factors for periods n and n – 1. The discount factor for the complete period is obtained by multiplying the individual discount factors together, and exactly the same result would be obtained by using the zero-coupon interest rate for the whole period to obtain the discount factor.[3]

Illustrating the principles for an interest rate swap

The rate charged on a newly transacted interest rate swap is the one that gives its net present value as zero. The term *valuation* of a swap is used to denote the process of calculating the net present value of an existing swap, when marking-to-market the swap against current market interest rates. Therefore when we price a swap, we set its net present value to zero, while when we value a swap we set its fixed rate at the market rate and calculate the net present value.

To illustrate the basic principle, we price a plain vanilla interest rate swap with the terms set out below; for simplicity we assume that the annual fixed-rate payments are the same amount each year, although in practice there would be slight differences. Also assume we already have our zero-coupon yields as shown in Table AB.6.

Period	Zero-coupon rate %	Discount factor	Forward rate %	Fixed payment	Floating payment	PV fixed payment	PV payment floating payment
1	5.5	0.947867298	5.5	689,625	550000	653672.9858	521327.0142
2	6	0.88999644	6.502369605	689,625	650236.9605	613763.7949	578708.58
3	6.25	0.833706493	6.751770257	689,625	675177.0257	574944.8402	562899.4702
4	6.5	0.777323091	7.253534951	689,625	725353.4951	536061.4366	563834.0208
5	7	0.712986179	9.023584719	689,625	902358.4719	491693.094	643369.1194
		4.161879501				2870137	2870137

Table AB.6 Generic interest rate swap

[3] Zero-coupon and forward rates are also related in another way. If we change the zero-coupon rate rs_n and the forward rate rf_i into their continuously compounded equivalent rates, given by $\ln(1 + rs_n)$ and the $\ln(1 + rf_i)$, we may obtain an equation for the continuously compounded zero-coupon rate as being the simple average of the continuously compounded forward rates, given by:

$$rs'_n = \frac{1}{t_n} \sum_{i=0}^{n-1} \frac{rf'_i}{F}.$$

We use the zero-coupon rates to calculate the discount factors, and then use the discount factors to calculate the forward rates. This is done using equation (AB.34). These forward rates are then used to predict what the floating-rate payments will be at each interest period. Both fixed-rate and floating-rate payments are then present valued at the appropriate zero-coupon rate, which enables us to calculate the net present value.

The fixed rate for the swap is calculated using equation (AB.28) to give us:

$$\frac{1 - 0.71298618}{4.16187950}$$

or 6.8963%.

Nominal principal	£10,000,000
Fixed rate	6.8963%
Day-count fixed	Actual/365
Day-count floating	Actual/365
Payment frequency fixed	Annual
Payment frequency floating	Annual
Trade date	31 January 2000
Effective date	2 February 2000
Maturity date	2 February 2005
Term	Five years

For reference, the Microsoft Excel® formulas are shown in Table AB.7. It is not surprising that the net present value is zero, because the zero-coupon curve is used to derive the discount factors, which are then used to derive the forward rates, which are used to value the swap. As with any financial instrument, the fair value is its break-even price or hedge cost, and in this case the bank that is pricing the five-year swap shown in Table AB.6 could hedge the swap with a series of FRAs transacted at the forward rates shown. If the bank is paying fixed and receiving floating, the value of the swap to it will rise if there is a rise in market rates, and fall if there is a fall in market rates. Conversely, if the bank was receiving fixed and paying floating, the swap value to it would fall if there was a rise in rates, and vice versa.

This method is used to price any interest rate swap, even exotic ones.

CELL	C	D	E	F	G	H	I	J
21			10000000					
22								
23	**Period**	**Zero-coupon rate %**	**Discount factor**	**Forward rate %**	**Fixed payment**	**Floating payment**	**PV fixed payment**	**PV floating fixed**
24	1	5.5	0.947867298	5.5	689,625	22(F24*10000000)/100	22G24/1.055	22H24/(1.055)
25	2	6	0.88999644	22((E24/E25)1)*100	689,625	22(F25*10000000)/100	22G24/(1.06)1^2	22H25/(1.06)1^2
26	3	6.25	0.833706493	(E25/E26 1)*100	689,625	22(F26*10000000)/100	22G24/(1.0625)1^3	22H26(1.0625)E1^3
27	4	6.5	0.777323091	22((E26/E27)1)*100	689,625	22(F27*10000000)/100	22G24/(1.065)1^4	22H27/(1.065)1-4
28	5	7	0.712986179	22((E27/E28)1)*100	689,625	22(F28*10000000)/100	22G2-/(1.07)1^5	22H28/(1.07)1^
			22SUM(E24:E28)				2,870,137	2,870,137

Table AB.7 Generic interest rate swap (Excel formulas)

Valuation using final maturity discount factor

A short-cut to valuing the floating-leg payments of an interest rate swap involves using the discount factor for the final maturity period. This is possible because, for the purposes of valuation, an exchange of principal at the beginning and end of the swap is conceptually the same as the floating-leg interest payments. This holds because, in an exchange of principal, the interest payments earned on investing the initial principal would be uncertain, as they are floating rate, while on maturity the original principal would be returned. The net result is a floating-rate level of receipts, exactly similar to the floating-leg payments in a swap. To value the principals then, we need only the final maturity discount rate.

To illustrate, consider Table AB.6, where the present value of both legs was found to be £2,870,137. The same result is obtained if we use the five-year discount factor, as shown below:

$$PV_{floating} = (10{,}000{,}000 \times 1) - (10{,}000{,}000 \times 0.71298618) = 2{,}870{,}137.$$

The first term is the principal multiplied by the discount factor 1; this is because the present value of an amount valued immediately is unchanged (or rather, it is multiplied by the immediate payment discount factor, which is 1.0000).

Therefore we may use the principal amount of a swap if we wish to value the swap. This is of course for valuation only, as there is no actual exchange of principal in a swap.

Summary of IR swap

Let us summarise the chief characteristics of swaps. A plain vanilla swap has the following characteristics:

- one leg of the swap is fixed-rate interest, while the other will be floating-rate, usually linked to a standard index such as Libor;
- the fixed rate is fixed through the entire life of the swap;
- the floating rate is set in advance of each period (quarterly, semi-annually or annually) and paid in arrears;
- both legs have the same payment frequency;
- the maturity can be standard whole years up to 30 years, or set to match customer requirements;
- the notional principal remains constant during the life of the swap.

Of course, to meet customer demand, banks can set up swaps that have variations on any or all of the above standard points. Some of the more common variations are discussed.

Non-vanilla interest rate swaps

The swap market is very flexible and instruments can be tailor-made to fit the requirements of individual customers. A wide variety of swap contracts have been traded in the market. Although the most common reference rate for the floating leg of a swap is six-month Libor, for a semi-annual paying floating leg, other reference rates that have been used include three-month Libor, the prime rate (for dollar swaps), the one-month commercial paper rate, the Treasury bill rate and the municipal bond rate (again, for dollar swaps). The term of a swap need not be fixed; swaps may be *extendable* or *putable*. In an extendable swap, one of the parties has the right but not the obligation to extend the life of the swap beyond the fixed maturity date, while in a putable swap one party has the right to terminate the swap ahead of the specified maturity date. It is also possible to transact options on swaps, known as *swaptions*. A swaption is the right to enter into a swap agreement at some point in the future, during the life of the option. Essentially, a swaption is an option to exchange a fixed-rate bond cash flow for a floating-rate bond cash flow structure. As a floating-rate bond is valued on its principal value at the start of a swap, a swaption may be viewed as the value on a fixed-rate bond, with a strike price that is equal to the face value of the floating-rate bond.

- A *constant maturity swap* is a swap in which the parties exchange a Libor rate for a fixed swap rate. For example, the terms of the swap might state that six-month Libor is exchanged for the five-year swap rate on a semi-annual basis for the next five years, or for the five-year government bond rate. In the US market the second type of constant maturity swap is known as a *constant maturity Treasury swap*.
- *Accreting and amortising swaps*: In a plain vanilla swap the notional principal remains unchanged during the life of the swap. However, it is possible to trade a swap where the notional principal varies during its life. An accreting (or *step-up*) swap is one in which the principal starts off at one level and then increases in amount over time. The opposite, an amortising swap, is one in which the notional reduces in size over time. An accreting swap would be useful where, for instance, a funding liability that is being hedged increases over time.

The amortising swap might be employed by a borrower hedging a bond issue that featured sinking fund payments, where a part of the notional amount outstanding is paid off at set points during the life of the bond. If the principal fluctuates in amount, for example increasing in one year and then reducing in another, the swap is known as a *roller-coaster swap*. Another application for an amortising swap is as a hedge for a loan that is itself an amortising one. Frequently, this is combined with a forward-starting swap, to tie in with the cash flows payable on the loan. The pricing and valuation of an amortising swap is no different in principle to a vanilla interest rate swap; a single swap rate is calculated using the relevant discount factors, and at this rate the net present value of the swap cash flows will equal zero at the start of the swap.

- *Libor-in-arrears swap*: In this type of swap (also known as a *back-set swap*) the setting date is just before the end of the accrual period for the floating rate setting and not just before the start. Such a swap would be attractive to a counterparty who had a different view on interest rates compared to the market consensus. For instance, in a rising yield curve environment, forward rates will be higher than current market rates, and this will be reflected in the pricing of a swap. A Libor-in-arrears swap would be priced higher than a conventional swap. If the floating-rate payer believed that interest rates would in fact rise more slowly than forward rates (and the market) were suggesting, she may wish to enter into an arrears swap as opposed to a conventional swap.
- *Basis swap*: In a conventional swap one leg comprises fixed-rate payments and the other floating-rate payments. In a basis swap both legs are floating rate, but linked to different money market indices. One leg is normally linked to Libor, while the other might be linked to the CD rate, say, or the commercial paper rate. This type of swap would be used by a bank in the United States that had made loans that paid at the prime rate, and financed its loans at Libor. A basis swap would eliminate the *basis risk* between the bank's income and expense cash flows. Other basis swaps have been traded where both legs are linked to Libor, but at different maturities; for instance, one leg might be at three-month Libor and the other at six-month Libor. In such a swap the basis is different and so is the payment frequency: one leg pays out semi-annually while the other would be paying on a quarterly basis. Note that where the payment frequencies differ, there is a higher level of counterparty risk for one of the parties. For

instance, if one party is paying out on a monthly basis but receiving semi-annual cash flows, it would have made five interest payments before receiving one in return.

- *Margin swap*: It is common to encounter swaps where there is a margin above or below Libor on the floating leg, as opposed to a floating leg of Libor flat. If a bank's borrowing is financed at Libor + 25 bps, it may wish to receive Libor + 25 bps in the swap so that its cash flows match exactly. The fixed-rate quote for a swap must be adjusted correspondingly to allow for the margin on the floating side, so in our example if the fixed-rate quote is, say, 6.00%, it would be adjusted to around 6.25%; differences in the margin quoted on the fixed leg might arise if the day-count convention or payment frequency were to differ between fixed and floating legs. Another reason why there may be a margin is if the credit quality of the counterparty demanded it, so that highly rated counterparties may pay slightly below Libor, for instance.
- *Off-market swap*: When a swap is transacted its fixed rate is quoted at the current market rate for that maturity. Where the fixed rate is different to the market rate, this is an off-market swap, and a compensating payment is made by one party to the other. An off-market rate may be used for particular hedging requirements, for example, or when a bond issuer wishes to use the swap to hedge the bond as well as to cover the bond's issue costs.
- *Differential swap*: A differential swap is a basis swap but with one of the legs calculated in a different currency. Typically, one leg is floating rate, while the other is floating rate but with the reference index rate for another currency, but denominated in the domestic currency. For example, a differential swap may have one party paying six-month sterling Libor, in sterling, on a notional principal of £10 million, and receiving euro-Libor, minus a margin, payable in sterling and on the same notional principal. Differential swaps are not very common and are the most difficult for a bank to hedge. The hedging is usually carried out using what is known as a *quanto* option.
- *Forward-start swap*: A forward-start swap is one where the *effective date* is not the usual one or two days after the trade date but a considerable time afterwards; for instance, say six months after the trade date. Such a swap might be entered into where one counterparty wanted to fix a hedge or cost of borrowing now, but for a point some time in the future. Typically, this would be because the party

considered that interest rates would rise or the cost of hedging would rise. The swap rate for a forward-starting swap is calculated in the same way as that for a vanilla swap.

An overview of interest rate swap applications

In this section we review some of the principal uses of swaps as a hedging tool for bond instruments and also how to hedge a swap book.

Corporate applications

Swaps are part of the over-the-counter (OTC) market and so they can be tailored to suit the particular requirements of the user. It is common for swaps to be structured so that they match particular payment dates, payment frequencies and Libor margins, which may characterise the underlying exposure of the customer. As the market in interest rate swaps is so large, liquid and competitive, banks are willing to quote rates and structure swaps for virtually all customers, although it may be difficult for smaller customers to obtain competitive price quotes as notional values below £10 million or £5 million.

Swap applications can be viewed as being one of two main types, asset-linked swaps and liability-linked swaps. Asset-linked swaps are created when the swap is linked to an asset such as a bond in order to change the characteristics of the income stream for investors. Liability-linked swaps are traded when borrowers of funds wish to change the pattern of their cash flows. Of course, just as with repo transactions, the designation of a swap in such terms depends on from whose point of view one is looking at the swap. An asset-linked swap hedge is a liability-linked hedge for the counterparty, except in the case of swap market-making banks who make two-way quotes in the instruments.

A straightforward application of an interest rate swap is when a borrower wishes to convert a floating-rate liability into a fixed-rate one, usually in order to remove the exposure to upward moves in interest rates. For instance, a company may wish to fix its financing costs. Let us assume a company currently borrowing money at a floating rate, say six-month Libor + 100 basis points, fears that interest rates may rise in the remaining three years of its loan. It enters into a three-year semi-annual interest rate swap with a bank, as the fixed-rate payer, paying, say, 6.75% against receiving six-month Libor. This fixes the company's borrowing costs for three years at 7.75% (7.99% effective annual rate). This is shown in Figure AB.3.

EXAMPLE AB.1 Liability-linked swap fixed- to floating- to fixed-rate exposure

A corporate borrows for five years at a rate of 6% and shortly after enters into a swap paying floating rate, so that its net borrowing cost is Libor + 40 bps. After one year, swap rates have fallen such that the company is quoted four-year swap rates as 4.90–84%. The company decides to switch back into fixed-rate liability in order to take advantage of the lower interest rate environment. It enters into a second swap paying fixed at 4.90% and receiving Libor. The net borrowing cost is now 5.30%. The arrangement is illustrated in Figure AB.4. The company has saved 95 basis points on its original borrowing cost, which is the difference between the two swap rates.

Figure AB.3 Changing liability from floating to fixed rate

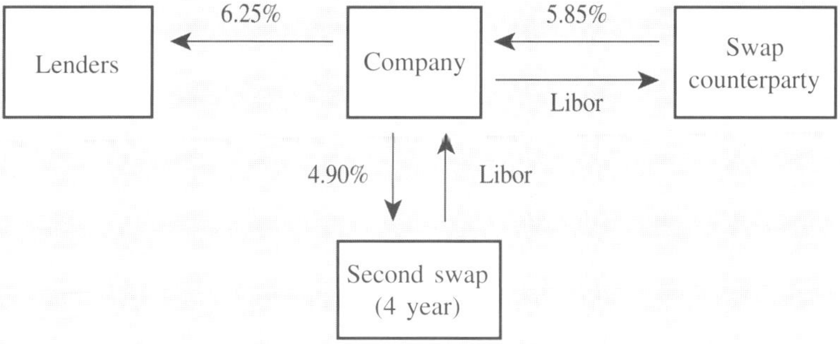

Figure AB.4

Asset-linked swap structures might be required when, for example, investors require a fixed interest security when floating-rate assets are available. Borrowers often issue FRNs, the holders of which may prefer to switch the income stream into fixed coupons.

As an example, consider a local authority pension fund holding two-year floating-rate gilts. This is an asset of the highest quality, paying Libid (the London interbank rate) minus 12.5 bps. The pension fund wishes to swap the cash flows to create a fixed-interest asset. It obtains a quote for a tailor-made swap where the floating leg pays Libid, the quote being 5.55–50%. By entering into this swap the pension fund has in place a structure that pays a fixed coupon of 5.375%. This is shown in Figure AB.5.

Figure AB.5 Transforming a floating-rate asset to fixed rate

Hedging bond instruments using interest rate swaps

We illustrate here a generic approach to the hedging of bond positions using interest rate swaps. The bond trader has the option of using other bonds, bond futures or bond options, as well as swaps, when hedging the interest rate risk exposure of a bond position. However, swaps are particularly efficient instruments to use because they display positive convexity characteristics; that is, the increase in value of a swap for a fall in interest rates exceeds the loss in value with a similar magnitude rise in rates. This is exactly the price/yield profile of vanilla bonds.

The primary risk measure we require when hedging using a swap is its present value of a basis point or PVBP.[4] This measures the price sensitivity of the swap for a basis point change in interest rates. The PVBP measure is used to calculate the hedge ratio when hedging a bond position. The PVBP can be given by:

$$PVBP = \frac{Change\ in\ swap\ value}{Rate\ change\ in\ basis\ points} \qquad \text{(AB.38)}$$

which can be written as:

$$PVBP = \frac{dS}{dr}. \qquad \text{(AB.39)}$$

[4] This is also known as DVBP or dollar value of a basis point in the US market.

Using the basic relationship for the value of a swap, which is viewed as the difference between the values of a fixed-coupon bond and an equivalent-maturity floating-rate bond (see Table AB.4) we can also write:

$$PVBP = \frac{dFixed\ bond}{dr} - \frac{dFloating\ bond}{dr} \tag{AB.40}$$

which essentially states that the basis point value of the swap is the difference in the basis point values of the fixed-coupon and floating-rate bonds. The value is usually calculated for a notional £1 million of swap. The calculation is based on the duration and modified duration calculations used for bonds[5] and assumes that there is a parallel shift in the yield curve.

Table AB.8 illustrates how equations (AB.39) and (AB.40) can be used to obtain the PVBP of a swap. Hypothetical five-year bonds are used in the example. The PVBP for a bond can be calculated using Bloomberg or the MDURATION function on Microsoft Excel. Using either of the two equations above we see that the PVBP of the swap is £425.00. This is shown below.

Interest rate swap

Term to maturity	5 years
Fixed leg	6.5%
Basis	Semi-annual, act/365
Floating leg	6-month Libor
Basis	Semi-annual, act/365
Nominal amount	£1,000,000

	Present value (£)		
	Rate change −10 bps	0 bps	Rate change +10 bps
Fixed-coupon bond	1,004,940	1,000,000	995,171
Floating-rate coupon	1,000,640	1,000,000	999,371
Swap	4,264	0	4,236

Table AB.8 PVBP for interest rate swap

[5] See Chapter 2.

Calculating the PVBP using equation (AB.39) we have:

$$PVBP_{swap} = \frac{dS}{dr} = \frac{4264 - (-4236)}{20} = 425 \qquad \text{(AB.41)}$$

while using equation (AB.40) we obtain the same result using the bond values:

$$\begin{aligned} PVBP_{swap} &= PVBP_{fixed} - PVBP_{floating} \qquad \text{(AB.42)} \\ &= \frac{1004940 - 995171}{20} - \frac{1000640 - 999371}{20} \\ &= 488.45 - 63.45 \\ &= 425.00 \end{aligned}$$

The swap basis point value is lower than that of the five-year fixed-coupon bond; that is, £425 compared to £488.45. This is because of the impact of the floating-rate bond risk measure, which reduces the risk exposure of the swap as a whole by £63.45. As a rough rule of thumb, the PVBP of a swap is approximately equal to that of a fixed-rate bond that has a maturity similar to the period from the next coupon re-set date of the swap through to the maturity date of the swap. This means that a 10-year semi-annual paying swap would have a PVBP close to that of a 9.5-year fixed-rate bond, and a 5.50-year swap would have a PVBP similar to that of a five-year bond.

When using swaps as hedge tools, we bear in mind that over time the PVBP of swaps behaves differently to that of bonds. Immediately preceding an interest re-set date the PVBP of a swap will be near-identical to that of the same-maturity fixed-rate bond, because the PVBP of a floating-rate bond at this time has essentially nil value. Immediately after the re-set date the swap PVBP will be near-identical to that of a bond that matures at the next re-set date. This means that at the point (and this point only) right after the re-set the swap PVBP will decrease by the amount of the floating-rate PVBP. In between re-set dates the swap PVBP is quite stable, as the effects of the fixed- and floating-rate PVBP changes cancel each other out. Contrast this with the fixed-rate PVBP, which decreases in value over time in stable fashion.[6] This feature is illustrated in Figure AB.6. A slight anomaly is that the PVBP of a swap actually increases by a small amount between re-set

[6] This assumes no large-scale sudden yield movements.

dates; this is because the PVBP of a floating-rate bond decreases at a slightly faster rate than that of the fixed-rate bond during this time.

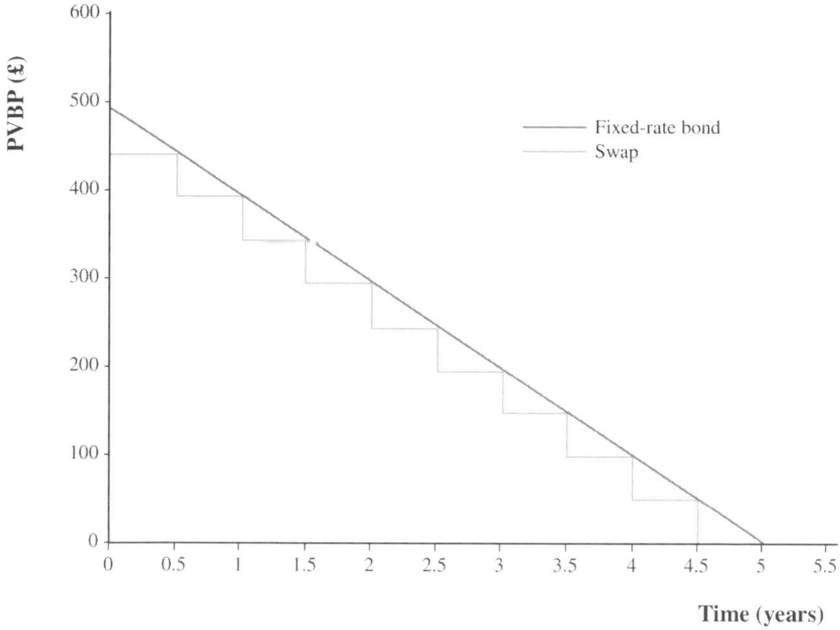

Figure AB.6 PVBP of 5-year swap

Hedging bond instruments with interest rate swaps is conceptually similar to hedging with another bond or with bond futures contracts. If one is holding a long position in a vanilla bond, the hedge requires a long position in the swap: remember that a long position in a swap is to be paying fixed (and receiving floating). This hedges the receipt of fixed from the bond position. The change in the value of the swap will match the change in value of the bond, only in the opposite direction.[7] The maturity of the swap should match as closely as possible that of the bond. As swaps are OTC contracts, it should be possible to match interest dates as well as maturity dates. If one is short the bond, the hedge is to be short the swap, so the receipt of fixed matches the pay-fixed liability of the short bond position.

[7] The change will not be an exact mirror. It is very difficult to establish a precise hedge for a number of reasons, which include differences in day-count bases, maturity mismatches and basis risk.

The correct nominal amount of the swap to put on is established using the PVBP hedge ratio. This is given as:

$$\text{Hedge ratio} = \frac{PVBP_{bond}}{PVBP_{swap}}. \qquad \text{(AB.43)}$$

This technique is still used in the market but suffers from the assumption of parallel yield curve shifts and can therefore lead to significant hedging error at times. More advanced techniques are used by banks when hedging books using swaps, which space does not permit any discussion of. Some of these techniques are discussed in Das (1994), Jarrow and Turnbull (2000) and Kolb (2000).

Bloomberg screens

Users can set up their own swap using screen SWPM. This is shown at Figure AB.7. This shows a USD swap with the following terms:

Trade date	19 August 2005
Effective date	23 August 2005
Maturity date	23 August 2010
Pay fixed	4.450% s/a
Receive	3-month Libor floating
Nominal	USD 10,000,000.00

Users can select the terms and parameters required to analyse any type of swap. If the user selects "page forward", Figure AB.8 shows the discount function for the swap, together with the interest-rate risk sensitivity of the swap. This is shown as DV01 of USD 4,438.49. Figure AB.9 is the payments schedule, and Figure AB.10 is the detailed risk analysis.

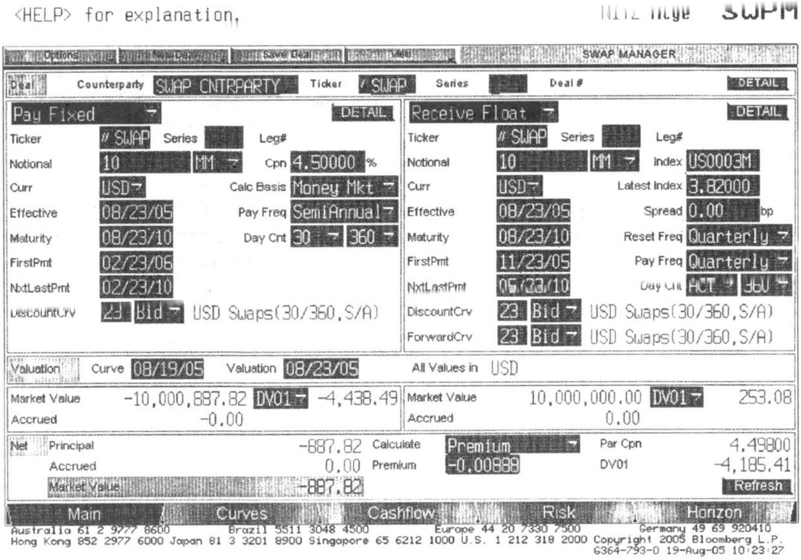

Figure AB.7

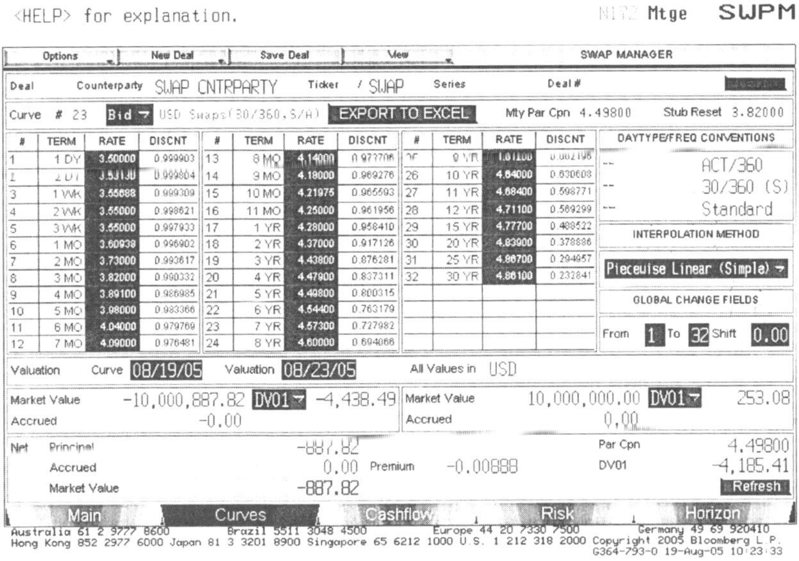

Figure AB.8

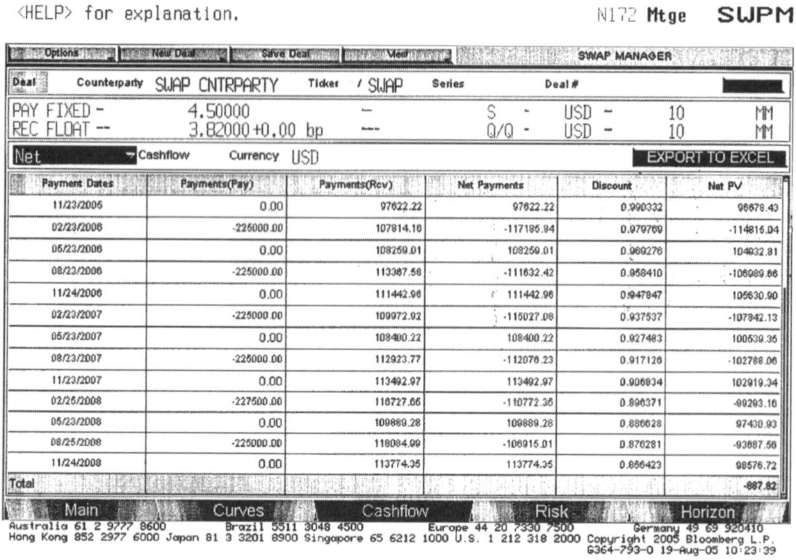

<HELP> for explanation. N172 Mtge SWPM

Options | New Deal | Save Deal | View | SWAP MANAGER

Deal Counterparty SWAP CNTRPARTY Ticker / SWAP Series Deal #

PAY FIXED - 4.50000 — S - USD - 10 MM
REC FLOAT -- 3.82000 +0.00 bp --- Q/Q - USD - 10 MM

Net Cashflow Currency USD EXPORT TO EXCEL

Payment Dates	Payments(Pay)	Payments(Rcv)	Net Payments	Discount	Net PV
11/23/2005	0.00	97622.22	97622.22	0.990332	96678.43
02/23/2006	-225000.00	107814.16	-117185.84	0.979769	-114816.04
05/23/2006	0.00	108259.01	108259.01	0.969276	104932.81
08/23/2006	-225000.00	113367.58	-111632.42	0.958410	-106989.86
11/24/2006	0.00	111442.96	111442.96	0.947847	105630.90
02/23/2007	-225000.00	109972.92	-115027.08	0.937537	-107842.13
05/23/2007	0.00	108400.22	108400.22	0.927483	100539.36
08/23/2007	-225000.00	112923.77	-112076.23	0.917126	-102788.06
11/23/2007	0.00	113492.97	113492.97	0.906834	102919.34
02/26/2008	-227500.00	116727.65	-110772.35	0.896371	-99293.16
05/23/2008	0.00	109889.28	109889.28	0.886628	97430.93
08/25/2008	-225000.00	118084.99	-106915.01	0.876281	-93687.56
11/24/2008	0.00	113774.35	113774.35	0.866423	98576.72
Total					-887.82

Main | Curves | Cashflow | Risk | Horizon

Australia 61 2 9777 8600 Brazil 5511 3048 4500 Europe 44 20 7330 7500 Germany 49 69 920410
Hong Kong 852 2977 6000 Japan 81 3 3201 8900 Singapore 65 6212 1000 U.S. 1 212 318 2000 Copyright 2005 Bloomberg L.P.
G364-793-0 19-Aug-05 10:23:39

Figure AB.9

© Bloomberg L.P. Used with permission.

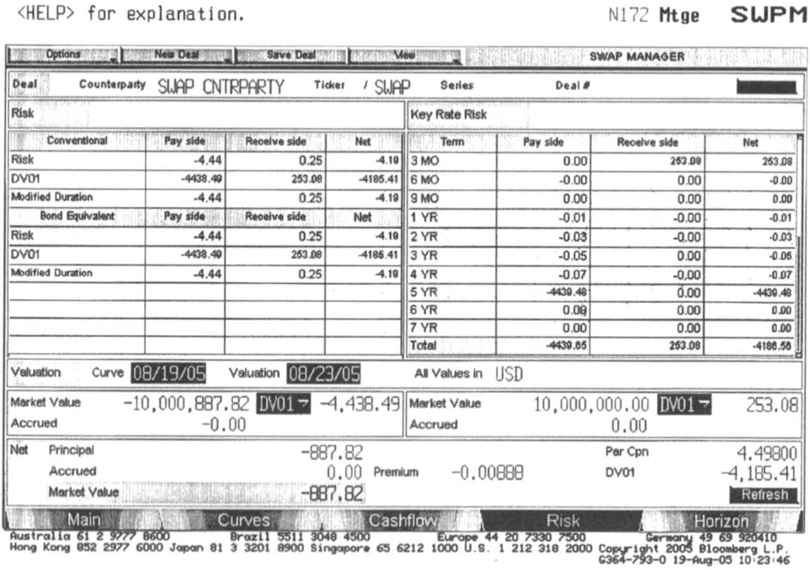

<HELP> for explanation. N172 Mtge SWPM

Options | New Deal | Save Deal | View | SWAP MANAGER

Deal Counterparty SWAP CNTRPARTY Ticker / SWAP Series Deal #

Risk

Conventional	Pay side	Receive side	Net
Risk	-4.44	0.25	-4.19
DV01	-4438.49	253.08	-4185.41
Modified Duration	-4.44	0.25	-4.19
Bond Equivalent	**Pay side**	**Receive side**	**Net**
Risk	-4.44	0.25	-4.19
DV01	-4438.49	253.08	-4185.41
Modified Duration	-4.44	0.25	-4.19

Key Rate Risk

Term	Pay side	Receive side	Net
3 MO	0.00	253.08	253.08
6 MO	-0.00	0.00	-0.00
9 MO	0.00	0.00	0.00
1 YR	-0.01	-0.00	-0.01
2 YR	-0.03	-0.00	-0.03
3 YR	-0.05	0.00	-0.06
4 YR	-0.07	-0.00	-0.07
5 YR	-4439.48	0.00	-4439.48
6 YR	0.00	0.00	0.00
7 YR	0.00	0.00	0.00
Total	-4439.65	253.08	-4186.56

Valuation Curve 08/19/05 Valuation 08/23/05 All Values in USD

Market Value -10,000,887.82 DV01 -4,438.49 Market Value 10,000,000.00 DV01 253.08
Accrued -0.00 Accrued 0.00

Net Principal -887.82 Par Cpn 4.49800
Accrued 0.00 Premium -0.00888 DV01 -4,185.41
Market Value -887.82 Refresh

Main | Curves | Cashflow | Risk | Horizon

Australia 61 2 9777 8600 Brazil 5511 3048 4500 Europe 44 20 7330 7500 Germany 49 69 920410
Hong Kong 852 2977 6000 Japan 81 3 3201 8900 Singapore 65 6212 1000 U.S. 1 212 318 2000 Copyright 2005 Bloomberg L.P.
G364-793-0 19-Aug-05 10:23:46

Figure AB.10

© Bloomberg L.P. Used with permission.

Selected bibliography and references

Bicksler, J. and Chen, A. 1986, "An economic analysis of interest rate swaps", *Journal of Finance*, 41(3), pp. 645–55.

Brotherton-Ratcliffe, R. and Iben, B. 1993, "Yield curve applications of swap products", in Schwartz, R. and Smith, C. (eds), *Advanced Strategies in Financial Risk Management*, New York Institute of Finance, New York.

Choudhry, M. 2001, *Bond Market Securities*, FT Prentice Hall, London.

Das, S. 1994, *Swaps and Financial Derivatives*, 2nd edition, IFR Publishing, London.

Decovny, S. 1998, *Swaps*, 2nd edition, FT Prentice Hall, London.

Dunbar, N. 2000, "Swaps volumes see euro wane", *Risk*, September.

Eales, B. 1995, *Financial Risk Management*, McGraw-Hill, New York, Chapter 3.

Fabozzi, F. 1993, *Fixed Income Mathematics*, Probus, New York.

Fabozzi, F. 1998 (ed.), *Perspectives on Interest Rate Risk Management for Money Managers and Traders*, FJF Associates, New Hope, PA.

Galitz, L. 1995, *Financial Engineering*, FT Pitman, Oxford.

Gup, B. and Brooks, R. 1993, *Interest Rate Risk Management*, Irwin, New York.

Henna, P. 1991, *Interest-rate Risk Management using Futures and Swaps*, Probus, Oxford.

International Swaps and Derivatives Association 1991, *Code of Standard Working, Assumptions and Provisions for Swaps*, New York.

Jarrow, R. and Turnbull, S. 2000, *Derivative Securities*, 2nd edition, South-Western, Cincinatti.

Khan, M. 2000, "Online platforms battle for business", *Risk*, September.

Kolb, R. 2000, *Futures, Options and Swaps*, 3rd edition, Blackwell, Oxford.

Li, A. and Raghavan, V. R. 1996, "Libor-in-arrears Swaps", *Journal of Derivatives*, 3, Spring, pp. 44–8.

Lindsay, R. 2000, "High wire act", *Risk*, August.

Marshall, J. and Kapner, K. 1990, *Understanding Swap Finance*, South-Western, Cincinatti.

Turnbull, S. 1987, "Swaps: A zero-sum game", *Financial Management*, 16, Spring, pp. 15–21.

I think the people that wrote the Bible, when they said 'The Garden of Eden', and they thought it was the Tigris-Euphrates river valley, 'cos that was all the writers of the document knew about, but I think, really, the whole of Earth is the Garden of Eden. We've been given paradise to live in...Think about this for a minute: we've been looking out of telescopes for three hundred years; we've been sending probes out into space, and we have never seen anything as beautiful as what we see when we walk out the front door.

— Alan Bean (Apollo 12 astronaut)
quoted in Smith, A., *Moondust: In Search of the Men Who Fell to Earth*,
Bloomsbury Press 2005, page 171

Glossary

Accreting: An accreting principal is one that increases during the life of the deal. See **amortising, bullet**.

Accreting swap: Swap whose notional amount increases during the life of the swap (opposite of **amortising** swap).

Accrued benefit obligation: Present value of pension benefits that have been earned by an employee to date, whether vested in the employee or not. It can be an important measure when managing the asset/liability ration of pension funds.

Accrued interest: The proportion of interest or coupon earned on an investment from the previous coupon payment date until the value date.

Accumulated value: The same as **future value**.

ACT/360: A day/year count convention taking the number of calendar days in a period and a "year" of 360 days.

ACT/365: A day/year convention taking the number of calendar days in a period and a "year" of 365 days. Under the ISDA definitions used for interest rate swap documentation, ACT/365 means the same as **ACT/ACT**.

ACT/ACT: A day/year count convention taking the number of calendar days in a period and a "year equal to the number of days in the current coupon period multiplied by the coupon frequency. For an interest rate swap, that part of the interest period falling in a leap year is divided by 366 and the remainder is divided by 365.

Add on factor: Simplified estimate of the potential future increase in the replacement cost, or market value, of a derivative transaction.

All-in price: See "**dirty price**".

All or nothing: Digital option. This option's **put** (call) pays out a pre-determined amount ("the all") if the index is below (above) the strike price at the option's expiration. The amount by which the **index** is below (above) the **strike** is irrelevant; the payout will be all or nothing.

American: An American option is one which may be exercised at any time during its life.

Amortising: An amortising principal is one that decreases during the life of a deal, or is repaid in stages during a loan. Amortising an amount over a period of time also means accruing for it pro rata over the period. See **accreting, bullet**.

Annuity: An investment providing a series of (generally equal) future cash flows.

Appreciation: An increase in the market value of a currency in terms of other currencies. See **depreciation, revaluation**.

Arbitrage: The process of buying securities in one country, currency or market, and selling identical securities in another to take advantage of price differences. When this is carried out simultaneously, it is in theory a risk-free transaction. There are many forms of arbitrage transactions. For instance, in the cash market a bank might issue a money market instrument in one money centre and invest the same amount in another centre at a higher rate, such as an issue of three-month US dollar CDs in the United States at 5.5% and a purchase of three-month Eurodollar CDs at 5.6%. In the futures market, arbitrage might involve buying three-month contracts and selling forward six-month contracts.

Arbitrageur: Someone who undertakes arbitrage trading.

Arch: (autoreggressive conditional heteroscedasticity) A discrete-time model for a random variable. It assumes that variance is stochastic and is a function of the variance of previous time steps and the level of the underlying.

Asian: An Asian option depends on the average value of the underlying over the option's life.

Ask: See **offer**.

Asset: Probable future economic benefit obtained or controlled as a result of past events or transactions. Generally classified as either current or long term.

Asset & Liability Management (ALM): The practice of matching the term structure and cash flows of an organisation's asset and liability portfolios to maximise returns and minimise risk.

Asset allocation: Distribution of investment funds within an asset class or across a range of asset classes for the purpose of diversifying risk or adding value to a portfolio.

Asset securitisation: The process whereby loans, receivables and other illiquid assets in the balance sheet are packaged into interest-bearing securities that offer attractive investment opportunities.

Asset-backed security: A security which is collaterised by specific assets – such as mortgages – rather than by the intangible creditworthiness of the issuer.

Asset swap: An interest rate swap or currency swap used in conjunction with an underlying asset such as a bond investment. See **liability swap**.

Asset-risk benchmark: Benchmark against which the riskiness of a corporation's assets may be measured. In sophisticated corporate risk management strategies the dollar risk of the liability portfolio may be managed against an asset-risk benchmark.

Asset-sensitivity estimates: Estimates of the effect of risk factors on the value of assets.

At-the-money (ATM): An option is at-the-money if the current value of the underlying is the same as the strike price. See **in-the-money, out-of-the-money**.

Auction: A method of issue where institutions submit bids to the issuer on a price or yield basis. Auction rules vary considerably across markets.

Average cap: Also known as an average rate cap, a cap on an average interest rate over a given period rather than on the rate prevailing at the end of the period. See also **average price (rate) option**.

Average price (rate) option: Option on a currency's average exchange rate or commodity's average spot price in which four variables have to be agreed to between buyer and seller: the premium, the **strike** price, the source of the exchange rate or commodity price data and the sampling interval (each day, for example). At the end of the life of the option the **average spot exchange rate** is calculated and compared with the strike price. A cash payment is then made to the buyer of the option that is equal to the face amount of the option times the difference between the two rates (assuming the option is **in-the-money**; otherwise it expires worthless).

Average worst case exposure: The expression of an exposure in terms of the average of the worst case exposure over a given period.

Back-testing: The validation of a model by feeding it historical data and comparing the results with historical reality.

Backwardation: The situation when a forward of futures price for something is lower than the spot price (the same as forward discount in foreign exchange). See **contango**.

Balance sheet: Statement of the financial position of an enterprise at a specific point in time, giving assets, liabilities and stockholders' equity.

Band: The Exchange Rate Mechanism (ERM II) of the European Union links the currencies of Denmark and Greece in a system that limits the degree of fluctuation of each currency against the euro within a band (of 15% for the drachma and 2 $^1/_4$% for the krone) either side of an agreed par value.

Banker's acceptance: See **Bill of exchange**.

Barrier option: A barrier option is one that ceases to exist, or starts to exist, if the underlying reaches a certain barrier level. See **knock out/in**.

Base currency: Exchange rates are quoted in terms of the number of units of one currency (the variable or counter currency) that corresponds to one unit of the other currency (the base currency).

Basis: The underlying cash market price minus the futures price. In the case of a bond futures contract, the futures price must be multiplied by the conversion factor for the cash bond in question.

Basis points: In interest rate quotations, 0.01%.

Basis risk: A form of market risk that arises whenever one kind of risk exposure is hedged with an instrument that behaves in a similar, but not necessarily identical way. For instance, a bank trading desk may use three-month interest rate futures to hedge it commercial paper or a euronote program. Although eurocurrency rates, to which futures prices respond, are well correlated with commercial paper rates they do not always move in lock step. If therefore commercial paper rates move by 10 basis points, but futures prices dropped by only 7 basis points, the 3-points gap would be the basis risk.

Basis swap: An interest rate swap where both legs are based on floating rate payments.

Basis trade: Buying the basis means selling a futures contract and buying the commodity or instrument underlying the futures contract. Selling the basis is the opposite.

Basket option: Option based on an underlying basket of bonds, currencies, equities or commodities.

Bearer bond: A bond for which physical possession of the certificate is proof of ownership. The issuer does not know the identity of the bondholder. Traditionally, the bond carries detachable coupons, one for each interest payment date, which are posted to the issuer when payment is due. At maturity the bond is redeemed by sending in the certificate for repayment. These days bearer bonds are usually settled electronically, and while no register of ownership is kept by the issuer, coupon payments may be made electronically.

Bear spread: A spread position taken with the expectation of a fall in value in the underlying.

Benchmark: A bond whose terms set a standard for the market. The benchmark usually has the greatest liquidity, the highest turnover and is usually the most frequently quoted. It also usually trades expensive to the yield curve, due to higher demand for it among institutional investors.

Beta: The sensitivity of a stock relative to swings in the overall market. The market has a beta of one, so a stock or portfolio with a beta greater than one will rise or fall more than the overall market, whereas a beta of less than one means that the stock is less volatile.

Bid: The price at which a market-maker will buy bonds. A tight bid–offer spread is indicative of a liquid and competitive market. The bid rate in a **repo** is the interest rate at which the dealer will borrow the **collateral** and lend the cash. See **offer**.

Bid figure: In a foreign exchange quotation, the exchange rate omitting the last two decimal places. For example, when EUR/USD is 1.1910/20, the big figure is 1.19. See **points**.

Bid–Offer: The two-way price at which a market will buy and sell stock.

Bilateral netting: The ability to offset amounts owed to a counterparty under one contract against amounts owed to the same counterparty under another contract; for example, where both transactions are governed by one master agreement. Also known as **"cherry-picking"**.

Bill: A **bill of exchange** is a payment order written by one person (the drawer) to another, directing the latter (drawee) to pay a certain amount of money at a future date to a third party. A bill of exchange is a bank draft when drawn on a bank. By accepting the draft, a bank agrees to pay the face value of the obligation if the drawer fails to pay, hence the term **bankers acceptance**. A **Treasury bill** is short-term government paper of up to one year's maturity, sold at a discount to principal value and redeemed at par.

Bill of exchange: A short-term, **zero-coupon** debt issued by a company to finance commercial trading. If it is guaranteed by a bank, it becomes a banker's acceptance.

Binomial tree: A mathematical model to value options, based on the assumption that the value of the underlying can move either up or down a given extent over a given short time. This process is repeated many times to give a large number of possible paths (the "tree") that the value could follow during the option's life.

Black–Scholes: A widely used option pricing formula devised by Fischer Black and Myron Scholes.

Blended interest rate swap: Result of adding a forward swap to an existing swap and blending the rates over the total life of the transaction.

Bloomberg: The trading, analytics and news service produced by Bloomberg LP; also used to refer to the terminal itself.

Bond basis: An interest rate is quoted on a bond basis if it is on an **ACT/365**, **ACT/ACT** or **30/360** basis. In the short term (for accrued interest, for example), these three are different. Over a whole (non-leap) year, however, they all equate to 1. In general, the expression "bond basis" does not distinguish between them and is calculated as ACT/365. See **money-market basis**.

Bond-equivalent yield: The yield that would be quoted on a US treasury bond which is trading at par and which has the same economic return and maturity as a given Treasury bill.

Bootstrapping: Building up successive zero-coupon yields from a combination of coupon-bearing yields.

Bpv: Basis point value. The price movement due to a one basis point change in yield.

Bräss/Fangmeyer: A method for calculating the yield of a bond similar to the **Moosmüller** method, but in the case of bonds that pay coupons more frequently than annually, using a mixture of annual and less than annual **compounding**.

Break forward: A product equivalent to a straightforward option, but structured as a forward deal at an off-market rate that can be reversed at a penalty rate.

Broken date: A maturity date other than the standard ones (such as one week; one, two, three, six and 12 months) normally quoted.

Broker-Dealers: Members of the London Stock Exchange who may intermediate between customers and market-makers; may also act as principals, transacting business with customers from their own holdings of stock.

Bulldog: Sterling domestic bonds issued by non-UK domiciled borrowers. These bonds trade under a similar arrangement to gilts and are settled via the Central Gilts Office (now CREST).

Bull spread: A spread position taken with the expectation of a rise in value in the **underlying**.

Bullet: A loan/deposit has a bullet maturity if the principal is all repaid at maturity. See **amortising**.

Business intelligence tools: Term used to describe the latest generation of access tools, which are expected to support both data extraction and subsequent analysis.

Buy/sell-back: Opposite of **sell/buy-back**.

Cable: The exchange rate for sterling against the US dollar.

CAD: The European Union's Capital Adequacy Directive.

Calendar spread: The simultaneous purchase/sale of a futures contract for one date and the sale/purchase of a similar futures contract for a different date. See **spread**.

Callable bond: A bond that provides the borrower with an option to redeem the issue before the original maturity date. In most cases certain terms are set before the issue, such as the date after which the bond is callable and the price at which the issuer may redeem the bond.

Call option: An option to purchase the commodity or instrument underlying the option. See **put**.

Call price: The price at which the issuer can call in a bond or preferred bond.

Cancelable swap: Swap in which the payer of the fixed rate has the option, usually exercisable on a specified date, to cancel the deal (see also **swaption**).

Cap: A series of borrower's **IRG**s, designed to protect a borrower against rising interest rates on each of a series of dates.

Capital market: Long-term market (generally longer than one year) for financial instruments. See **money market**.

Capped option: Option where the holder's ability to profit from a change in value of the underlying is subject to a specified limit.

Caption: Option on a **cap**.

Cash: See **cash market**.

Cash and carry: Term for an arbitrage trade involving simultaneous purchase (sale) of a cash bond against sale (purchase) of the government bond futures contract.

Cash market: The market in full cash instruments, as opposed to derivatives, for which the full nominal value is paid for up front on purchase.

CBOT: The Chicago Board of Trade, one of the two futures exchanges in Chicago, United States, and one of the largest in the world.

CD: See **certificate of deposit**

Cedel: Centrale de Livraison de Valeurs Mobilieres; a clearing system for Euro-currency and international bonds. Cedel is located in Luxembourg and is jointly owned by a number of European banks.

Ceiling: The same as **cap**.

Central Gilts Office: The office of the Bank of England that runs the computer-based settlement system for gilt-edged securities and certain other securities (mostly Bulldogs) for which the Bank acts as Registrar.

Central line theorem: The assertion that as sample size, *n*, increases, the distribution of the mean of a random sample taken from almost any population approaches to a normal distribution.

Certificate of deposit (CD): A money market instrument of up to one year's maturity (although CDs of up to five years have been issued) that pays a bullet interest payment on maturity. After issue, CDs can trade freely in the secondary market, the ease of which is a function of the credit quality of the issuer.

CGBR: Central Government Borrowing Requirment.

CGBCR: Central Government Net Cash Requirement.

CGO reference prices: Daily prices of gilt-edged and other securities held in CGO that are used by CGO in various processes, including revaluing stock loan transactions, calculating total consideration in a repo transaction, and DBV assembly.

Cheapest to deliver (CTD): In a bond futures contract, the one underlying bond among all those that are deliverable, which is the most price-efficient for the seller to deliver.

Cherry-picking: See **bilateral netting**.

Classic repo: Repo is short for "sale and repurchase agreement" – a simultaneous spot sale and forward purchase of a security, equivalent to borrowing money against a loan of collateral. A reverse repo is the opposite. The terminology is usually applied from the perspective of the repo dealer. For example, when a central bank does repos, it is lending cash (the repo dealer is borrowing cash from the central bank).

Clean deposit: The same as **time deposit**.

Clean price: The price of a bond excluding accrued coupon. The price quoted in the market for a bond is generally a clean price rather than a **dirty price**.

Close-out netting: The ability to net a portfolio of contracts with a given counterparty in the event of default. See also **bilateral netting**.

Closing leg: The maturity cash flows in a repo; the start cash flows are the "opening leg".

CMO: Central Moneymarkets Office which settles transactions in Treasury bills and other money markets instruments, and provides a depository.

CMTM: Current **mark-to-market** value. See **current exposure** and **replacement cost**.

Collar: The simultaneous sale of a **put (or call) option** and purchase of a call (or put) at different strikes – typically both **out-of-the-money**.

Collateral: Something of value, often of good creditworthiness such as a government bond, given temporarily to a counterparty to enhance a party's creditworthiness. In a **repo**, the collateral is actually sold temporarily by one party to the other rather than merely lodged with it.

Commercial paper: A short-term security issued by a company or bank, generally with a zero coupon.

Commodity swap: Swap where one of the cash flows is based on a fixed value for the underlying commodity and the other is based on a floating index value. The commodity is often oil or natural gas, although copper, gold, other metals and agricultural commodities are also commonly used. The end-users are consumers, who pay a fixed-rate, and the producer.

Competitive bid: A bid for the stock at a price stated by a bidder in an auction. A **non-competitive bid** is a bid where no price is specified; such bids are allotted at the weighted average price of successful competitive bid prices.

Compound interest: When some interest on an investment is paid before maturity and the investor can reinvest it to earn interest on interest, the interest is said to be compounded. Compounding generally assumes that the reinvestment rate is the same as the original rate. See **simple interest.**

Compound option: Option on an option, the first giving the buyer the right, but not the obligation to buy the second on a specific date at a predetermined price. There are two kinds. One, on currencies, is useful for companies tendering for overseas contracts in a foreign currency. The interest rate version comprises **captions** and **floortions**.

Consideration: The total price paid in a transaction, including taxes, commissions and (for bonds) accrued interest.

Contango: The situation when a forward or futures price for something is higher than the spot price (the same as forward premium in foreign exchange). See **backwardation**.

Contingent option: Option where the premium is higher than usual but is only payable if the value of the underlying reaches a specified level. Also known as a contingent premium option.

Continuous compounding: A mathematical, rather than practical, concept of compound interest where the period of compounding is infinitesimally small.

Contract date: The date on which a transaction is negotiated. See **value date**.

Contract for differences: A deal such as an **FRA** and some futures contracts, where the instrument or commodity effectively bought or sold cannot be delivered; instead, a cash gain or loss is taken by comparing the price dealt with the market price, or an index, at maturity.

Conventional gilts (included double-dated): Gilts on which interest payments and principal repayments are fixed.

Conversion factor: In a bond futures contract, a factor to make each deliverable bond comparable with the contract's notional bond specification. Defined as the price of one unit of the deliverable bond required to make its yield equal the notional coupon. The price paid for a bond on delivery is the futures settlement price times the conversion factor.

Convertible currency: A currency that may be freely exchanged for other currencies.

Convexity: A measure of the curvature of a bond's price/yield curve (mathematically, $\frac{d^2P}{dr^2}$ / dirty price).

Correlation matrices: Statistical constructs used in the value-at-risk methodology to measure the degree of relatedness of various market forces.

Corridor: The same as **collar**.

Cost of carry: The net running cost of holding a position (which may be negative); for example, the cost of borrowing cash to buy a bond less the coupon earned on the bond while holding it.

Cost volatility: Volatility relating to operational errors or the fines and losses a business unit may incur. Reflected in excess costs and penalty charges posted to the profit and losses. See also **revenue volatility**.

Counterparty risk weighting: See **risk-weighting**.

Country risk: The risks, when business is conducted in a particular country, of adverse economic or political conditions arising in that country. More specifically, the credit risk of a financial transaction or instrument arising from such conditions.

Coupon: The interest payment(s) made by the issuer of security to the holders, based on the coupon rate and the face value.

Coupon swap: An interest rate swap in which one leg is fixed-rate and the other floating-rate.

Cover: To cover an exposure is to deal in such a way as to remove the risk – either reversing the position, or hedging it by dealing in an instrument with a similar but opposite risk profile. Also the amount by how much a bond auction is subscribed.

Covered call/put: The sale of a covered call option is when the option writer also owns the underlying. If the underlying rises in value so that the option is exercised, the writer is protected by her position in the underlying. Covered puts are defined analogously. See **naked**.

Covered interest arbitrage: Creating a loan/deposit in one currency by combining a loan/deposit in another with a forward foreign exchange swap.

CP: See **commercial paper**.

Credit (or default) risk: The risk that a loss will be incurred if a counterparty to a derivatives transaction does not fulfil its financial obligations in a timely manner.

Credit derivatives: Financial contracts that involve a potential exchange of payments in which at least one of the cash flows is linked to the performance of a specified underlying credit-sensitive asset or liability.

Credit-equivalent amount: As part of the calculation of the risk-weighted amount of capital the Bank for International Settlements (BIS) advises each bank to set aside against derivative credit risk, banks must compute a credit equivalent amount for each derivative transaction. The amount is calculated by summing the **current replacement cost**, or market value, of the instrument and an **add-on factor**.

Credit risk (or default risk) exposure: The value of the contract exposed to default. If all transactions are marked-to-market each day, such positive market value is the amount of previously recorded profit that might have to be reversed and recorded as a loss in the event of counterparty default.

Credit spread: The interest rate spread between two debt issues of similar duration and maturity, reflecting the relative creditworthiness of the issuers.

Credit swaps: An agreement between two counterparties to exchange disparate cash flows, at least one of which must be tied to the performance of a credit-sensitive asset or to a portfolio or index of such assets. The other cash flow is usually tied to a **floating-rate index** (such as **Libor**) or a fixed rate, or is linked to another credit-sensitive asset.

Credit value-at-risk (CVAR): See **value-at-risk (VAR).**

CREST: The paperless share settlement system through which trades conducted on the London Stock Exchange can be settled. The system is operated by CRESTCo and was introduced in 1996.

CRND: Commissioners for the Reduction of the National Debt, formally responsible for investment of funds held within the public sector; for example, National Insurance Fund.

Cross: See **cross-rate**.

Cross-rate: Generally an exchange rate between two currencies, neither of which is the US dollar. In the US market, spot cross is the exchange rate for US dollars against Canadian dollars in its direct form.

CTD: See **cheapest to deliver**.

cum-dividend: literally "with dividend", stock that is traded with interest or dividend accrued included in the price.

Cumulative default rate: See **probability of default**.

Currency option: The option to buy or sell a specified amount of a given currency at a specified rate at or during a specified time in the future.

Currency swap: An agreement to exchange a series of cash flows determined in one currency, possibly with reference to a particular fixed or floating interest payment schedule, for a series of cash flows based in a different currency. See **interest rate swap**.

Current assets: Assets that are expected to be used or converted to cash within one year or one operating cycle.

Current exposure: A risk management term referring to current outstanding aggregate interest rate risk.

Current liabilities: Obligations that the firm is expected to settle within one year or one operating cycle.

Current yield: Bond coupon as a proportion of clean price per 100; does not take principal gain/loss or time value of money into account. See **yield to maturity**, **simple yield to maturity**.

Cylinder: The same as **collar**.

DAC-RAP: Delivery against collateral – receipt against payment. Same as **DVP**.

Daily range: The difference between the high and low points of a single trading day.

Day-count: The convention used to calculate accrued interest on bonds and interest on cash. For UK gilts the convention changed to actual/actual from actual/365 on 1 November 1998. For cash the convention in sterling markets is actual/365.

DBV (delivery by value): A mechanism whereby a CGO member may borrow from or lend money to another CGO member against overnight gilt collateral. The CGO system automatically selects and delivers securities to a specified aggregate value on the basis of the previous night's CGO reference prices; equivalent securities are returned the following day. The DBV functionality allows the giver and taker of collateral to specify the classes of security to included within the DBV. The options are: all classes of security held within CGO, including strips and bulldogs; coupon-bearing gilts and bulldogs; coupon-bearing gilts and strips; only coupon-bearing gilts.

DEaR: Daily earnings at risk.

Debenture: In the US market, an unsecured domestic bond, backed by the general credit quality of the issuer. Debentures are issued under a trust deed or indenture. In the UK market, a bond that is secured against the general assets of the issuer.

Debt management office (DMO): An executive arm of the UK Treasury, responsible for cash management of the government's borrowing requirement. This includes responsibility for issuing government bonds (gilts), a function previously carried out by the Bank of England. The DMO began operations in April 1998.

Default correlation: The degree of covariance between the probabilities of default of a given set of counterparties. For example, in a set of counterparties with positive default correlation, a default by one counterparty suggests an increased probability of a default by another counterparty.

Default probability: See **probability of default**.

Default risk: See **credit risk**.

Default risk exposure: See **credit risk exposure**.

Default start options: Options purchased before their "lives" actually commence. A corporation might, for example, decide to pay for a deferred start option to lock into what it perceives as current advantageous pricing for an option that it knows it will need in the future.

Deferred strike option: An option where the strike price is established at a future date on the basis of the spot foreign exchange price prevailing at that future date.

Delegation costs: Incentive costs incurred by banks in delegating monitoring activities.

Deliverable bond: One of the bonds that is eligible to be delivered by the seller of a bond futures contract at the contract's maturity, according to the specifications of that particular contract.

Delivery: Transfer of gilts (in settlements) from seller to buyer.

Delivery versus payment (DVP): The simultaneous exchange of securities and cash. The assured payment mechanism of the CGO achieves the same protection.

Delta (δ): The change in an option's value relative to a change in the underlying's value.

Depreciation: A decrease in the market value of a currency in terms of other currencies. See **appreciation, devaluation**.

Derivative: Strictly, any financial instrument whose value is derived from another, such as a forward foreign exchange rate, a futures contract, an option, an interest rate swap, and so on. Forward deals to be settled in full are not always called derivatives, however.

Devaluation: An official one-off decrease in the value of a currency in terms of other currencies. See **revaluation, depreciation**.

Diffusion effect: The potential for increase over time of the credit exposure generated by a derivative: as time progresses, there is more likelihood of larger changes in the underlying market variables. Depending on the type and structure of the instrument this effect may be moderated by the **amortisation effect**.

Digital option: Unlike simple European and American options, a digital option has fixed payouts and, rather like binary digital circuits, which are either on or off, pays out either this amount or nothing. Digital options can be added together to create assets that exactly mirror index price movements anticipated by investors. See **one touch all-or-nothing**.

Direct: An exchange rate quotation against the US dollar in which the dollar is the **variable currency** and the other currency is the **base currency**.

Dirty price: The price of a bond including accrued interest. Also known as the "all-in" price.

Discount: The amount by which a currency is cheaper, in terms of another currency, for future delivery than for spot, is the forward discount (in general, a reflection of interest rate differentials between two currencies). If an exchange rate is "at a discount" (without specifying to which of the two currencies this refers), this generally means that the **variable currency** is at a discount. See **premium**.

Discount house: In the UK money market, originally securities houses that dealt directly with the Bank of England in Treasury bills and bank bills, or discount instruments; hence, the name. Most discount houses were taken over by banking groups and the term is not generally used, as the Bank of England now also deals directly with clearing banks and securities houses.

Discount rate: The method of market quotation for certain securities (US and UK treasury bills, for example), expressing the return on the security as a proportion of the face value of the security received at maturity – as opposed to a **yield**, which expresses the yield as a proportion of the original investment.

Discount swap: Swap in which the fixed-rate payments are less than the internal rate of return on the swap, the difference being made up at maturity by a balloon payment.

Dividend discount model: Theoretical estimate of market value that computes the economic or the net present value of future cash flows due to an equity investor.

DMO: The UK Debt Management Office.

DMR: The *Debt Management Report*, published annually by HM Treasury.

Down-and-in option: Barrier option where the holder's ability to exercise is activated if the value of the underlying drops below a specified level. See also **up-and-in option**.

Down-and-out-option: Barrier option where the holder's ability to exercise expires if the value of the underlying drops below a specified level.

DRM: Debt and Reserves Management Team in HM Treasury.

Dual currency option: Option allowing the holder to buy either of two currencies.

Dual currency swap: Currency swap where both the interest rates are fixed rates.

Dual strike option: Interest rate option, usually a **cap** or a **floor**, with one floor or ceiling rate for part of the option's life and another for the rest.

Duration: A measure of the weighted average life of a bond or other series of cash flows, using the present values of the cash flows as the weights. See **modified duration**.

Duration gap: Measurement of the interest rate exposure of an institution.

Duration weighting: The process of using the modified duration value for bonds to calculate the exact nominal holdings in a spread position. This is necessary because £1 million nominal of a two-year bond is not equivalent to £1 million of, say, a five-year bond. The modified duration value of the five-year bond will be higher, indicating that its "basis point value" (bpv) will be greater, and that therefore £1 million worth of this bond represents greater sensitivity to a move in interest rates (risk). As another example, consider a fund manager holding £10 million of five-year bonds. The fund manager wishes to switch into a holding of two-year bonds with the same overall risk position. The basis point values of the bonds are 0.041583 and 0.022898 respectively. The ratio of the bpvs are 0.041583/0.022898 = 1.816. The fund manager therefore needs to switch into £10 million × 1.816 = £18.160 million of the two-year bond.

DVP: Delivery versus payment, in which the settlement mechanics of a sale or loan of securities against cash is such that the securities and cash are exchanged against each other simultaneously through the same clearing mechanism and neither can be transferred unless the other is.

Early exercise: The exercise or assignment of an option prior to expiration.

ECU: The European Currency Unit, a basket composed of European Union currencies, now defunct following the introduction of the euro currency.

Effective rate: An effective interest rate is the rate that, earned as simple interest over one year, gives the same return as interest paid more frequently than once per year and then compounded. See **nominal rate**.

Efficient frontier method: Technique used by fund managers to allocate assets.

Embedded option: Interest rate-sensitive option in a debt instrument that affects its redemption. Such instruments include **mortgage-backed securities** and **callable bonds.**

End-end: A money market deal commencing on the last working day of a month and lasting for a whole number of months, maturing on the last working day of the correlation.

Epsilon (ε): The same as **vega**.

Equity: The residual interest in the net assets of an entity that remains after deducting the liabilities.

Equity options: Options on shares of an individual common stock.

Equity warrant: Warranty, usually attached to a bond, entitling the holder purchase share(s).

Equity-linked swap: Swap where one of the cash flows is based on an equity instrument or index, when it is known as an equity index swap.

Equivalent life: The weighted average life of the principal of a bond where there are partial **redemptions**, using the **present values** of the partial redemptions as the weights.

ERA: See **exchange rate agreement**.

Eta (ε): The same as **vega**.

Euribor: The reference rate for the euro currency, set in Frankfurt.

Euro: The name for the domestic currency of the European Monetary Union. Not to be confused with **Eurocurrency**.

Euroclear: An international clearing system for Eurocurrency and international securities. Euroclear is based in Brussels and managed by Morgan Guaranty Trust Company.

Eurocurrency: A currency owned by a non-resident of the country in which the currency is legal tender. Not to be confused with **Euro.**

Euro-issuance: The issue of gilts (or other securities) denominated in Euro.

Euromarket: The international market in which **Eurocurrencies** are traded.

European: A European **option** is one that may be exercised only at **expiry**. See **American**.

Exchange controls: Regulations restricting the free convertibility of a currency into other currencies.

Exchange rate agreement: A **contract for differences** based on the movement in a **forward–forward** foreign exchange swap price. Does not take account of the effect of **spot** rate changes as an **FXA** does. See **SAFE**.

Exchange-traded: **Futures** contracts are traded on a futures exchange, as opposed to **forward** deals, which are **OTC**. **Option** contracts are similarly exchange traded rather than **OTC**.

Ex-dividend: The time period before a bond's coupon date when it is traded without its accrued interest payment. This period is usually one or two weeks.

Ex-dividend (xd) date: A bond's record date for the payment of coupons. The coupon payment will be made to the person who is the registered holder of the stock on the xd date. For UK gilts this is seven working days before the coupon date.

Exercise: To exercise an **option** (by the **holder**) is to require the other party (the **writer**) to fulfil the underlying transaction. Exercise price is the same as **strike** price.

Expected (credit) loss: Estimate of the amount a derivative's counterparty is likely to lose as a result of default from a derivative's contract, with a given level of probability. The expected loss of any derivative position can be derived by combining the distributions of credit exposures, rate of recovery and probabilities of default.

Expected default rate: Estimate of the most likely rate of default of a counterparty expressed as a level of probability.

Expected rate of recovery: See **rate of recovery**.

Expiry: An option's expiry is the time after which it can no longer be **exercised**.

Exposure: Risk to market movements.

Exposure profile: The path of worst case or expected exposures over time. Different instruments reveal quite differently shaped exposures profiles due to the interaction of the diffusion and amortisation effects.

Extinguishable option: Option in which the holder's right to exercise disappears if the value of the underlying passes a specified level. See also **barrier option**.

Extrapolation: The process of estimating a price or rate for a particular value date, from other known prices, when the value date required lies outside the period covered by the known prices. See **interpolation**.

Face value: The principal amount of a security generally repaid ("redeemed") all at maturity, but sometimes repaid in stages, on which the **coupon** amounts are calculated.

Fence: The same as **collar**.

Fixing: See **Libor fixing**.

Floating rate: An interest rate set with reference to an external index. Also an instrument paying a floating rate is one where the rate of interest is refixed in line with market conditions at regular intervals, such as every three or six months. In the current market, an exchange rate determined by market forces with no government intervention.

Floating rate CD: CD on which the rate of interest payable is refixed in line with market conditions at regular intervals (usually six months).

Floating rate gilt: Gilt issued with an interest rate adjusted periodically in line with market interbank rates

Floating rate note: **Capital market** instrument on which the rate of interest payable is refixed in line with market conditions at regular intervals (usually six months).

Floor: A series of lender's **IRGs**, designed to protect an investor against falling interest rates on each of a series of dates.

Floortion: Option on a **floor**.

Forward: In general, a deal for value later than the normal value date for that particular commodity or instrument. In the foreign exchange market, a forward price is the price quoted for the purchase or sale of one currency against another where the value date is at least one month after the **spot** date. See **short date**.

Forward band: Zero-cost collar that is one in which the premium payable as a result of buying the **cap** is offset exactly by that obtained from selling the **floor**.

Forward break: See **break forward**.

Forward exchange agreement: A **contract for differences** designed to create exactly the same economic result as a foreign exchange cash **forward–forward** deal. See **ERA**, **SAFE**.

Forward–forward: Short-term exchange of currency deposits. (See also **forward–forward deposit**).

Forward–forward deposit: Deposit of cash where the interest rate is effective from a future date (t_1 to a later date, t_2).

Forward rate agreement: Short-term interest rate **hedge**. Specifically, a contract between buyer and seller for an agreed interest rate on a notional deposit of a specified maturity on a predetermined future date. No principal is exchanged. At maturity the seller pays the buyer the difference if rates have risen above the agreed level, and vice versa.

Forward swap: **Swap** arranged at the current rate but entered into at some time in the future.

FRA: See **forward rate agreement**.

FRCD: See **floating rate CD**.

FRN: See **floating rate note**.

Framework document: Sets out the Direct Management Office's responsibilities, objectives and targets, its relationship with the rest of the Treasury and its accountability as an Executive Agency.

Fraption: Option on a forward rate agreement. Also known as an interest rate guarantee.

FSA: The Financial Services Authority, the body responsible for the regulation of investment business, and the supervision of banks and money market institutions in the United Kingdom. The FSA took over these duties from nine "self-regulatory organisations" that had previously carried out this function, including the Securities and Futures Authority (SFA), which had been responsible for regulation of professional investment business in the City of London. The FSA commenced its duties in 1998.

FTSE-100: Index comprising 100 major UK shares listed on The International Stock Exchange in London. Futures and options on the index are traded at the London International Financial Futures and Options Exchange (**LIFFE**).

Funds: The **USD/CAD** exchange rate for value on the next business day (standard practice for **USD/CAD** in preference to **spot**).

Fungible: A financial instrument that is equivalent in value to another, and easily exchanged or substituted. The best example is cash money, as a £10 note has the same value and is directly exchangeable with another £10 note. A bearer bond also has this quality.

Future: A futures contract is a contract to buy or sell securities or other goods at a future date at a predetermined price. Futures contracts are usually standardised and traded on an exchange.

Future exposure: See **potential exposure**.

Future value: The amount of money achieved in the future, including interest, by investing a given amount of money now. See **time value for money**, **present value**.

Futures contract: A deal to buy or sell some financial instrument or commodity for value on a future date. Unlike a **forward** deal, futures contracts are traded only on an exchange (rather than **OTC**), have standardised contract sizes and value dates, and are often only **contract for differences** rather than deliverable.

FXA: See **forward exchange agreement**.

G7: The "Group of Seven" countries, the United States, Canada, United Kingdom, Germany, France, Italy and Japan.

Gamma (γ): The change in an option's delta relative to a change in the underlying's value.

Gap ratio: Ratio of interest rate-sensitive assets to interest rate-sensitive liabilities; used to determine changes in the risk profile of an institution with changes in interest rate levels.

Gapping: Feature of commodity markets whereby there are large and very rapid price movements to new levels followed by relatively stable prices.

GDP: Gross domestic product, the value of total output produced within a country's borders.

GEMM: A gilt-edged market-maker, a bank or securities house registered with the Bank of England as a market-maker in gilts. A GEMM is required to meet certain obligations as part of its function as a registered market-maker, including making two-way price quotes at all times in all gilts and taking part in gilt auctions. The Debt Management Office now make a distinction between conventional gilt GEMMs and index-linked GEMMs, known as IG GEMMs.

General collateral (GC): Securities, which are not "special", used as collateral against cash borrowing. A repo buyer will accept GC at any time that a specific stock is not quoted as required in the transaction. In the gilts market GC includes DBVs.

GIC: Guaranteed investment contract.

Gilt: A UK government sterling denominated, listed security issued by HM Treasury with initial maturity of over 365 days when issued. The term "gilt" (or gilt-edged) is a reference to the primary characteristic of gilts as an investment: their security.

Gilt-edged market-maker: See **GEMM.**

GNP: Gross national product, the total monetary value of a country's output, as produced by citizens of that country.

Gold warrant: Naked or attached warrant exercisable into gold at a predetermined price.

Gross redemption yield: The same as **yield to maturity**; "gross" because it does not take tax effects into account.

GRY: See **gross redemption yield**.

Hedge ratio: The ratio of the size of the position it is necessary to take in a particular instrument as a hedge against another, to the size of the position being hedged.

Hedging: Protecting against the risks arising from potential market movements in exchange rates, interest rates or other variables. See **cover**, **arbitrage**, **speculation**.

Herstatt risk: See **settlement risk**.

High coupon swap: Off-market coupon swap where the coupon is higher than the market rate. The floating-rate payer pays a front-end fee as compensation. Opposite of **low coupon swap**.

Historic rate rollover: A **forward rate swap** in FX where the settlement exchange rate for the near date is based on a historic **off-market** rate rather than the current market rate. This is prohibited by many central banks.

Historic volatility: The actual **volatility** recorded in market prices over a particular period.

Historical simulation methodology: Method of calculating **value-at-risk (VAR)** using historical data to assess the likely effect of market moves on a portfolio.

Holder: The holder of an **option** is the party that has purchased it.

IDB: Inter-dealer broker, in this context a broker that provides facilities for dealing in bonds between market-makers.

IG: Index-linked gilt whose coupons and final redemption payment are related to the movements in the Retail Price Index (RPI).

Immunisation: This is the process by which a bond portfolio is created that has an assured return for a specific time horizon irrespective of changes in interest rates. The mechanism underlying immunisation is a portfolio structure that balances the change in the value of a portfolio at the end of the investment horizon (time period) with the return gained from the reinvestment of cash flows from the portfolio. As such, immunisation requires the portfolio manager to offset interest rate risk and reinvestment risk.

Implied repo rate: The break-even interest rate at which it is possible to sell a bond **futures contract**, buy a **deliverable bond**, and **repo** the bond out. See **cash and carry**.

Implied volatility: The **volatility** used by a dealer to calculate an **option** price; conversely, the volatility implied by the price actually quoted.

Index option: An **option** whose **underlying** security is an index. Index options enable a trader to bet on the direction of the index.

Indexed notes: Contract whereby the issuer usually assumes the risk of unfavourable price movements in the instrument, commodity or index to which the contract is linked, in exchange for which the issuer can reduce the cost of borrowing (compared with traditional instruments without the risk exposure).

Index swap: Sometimes the same as a **basis swap**. Otherwise a swap like an **interest rate swap** where payments on one or both of the legs are based on the value of an index – such as an equity index, for example.

Indirect: An exchange rate quotation against the US dollar in which the dollar is the **base currency** and the other currency is the **variable currency**.

Initial margin: The excess either of cash over the value of securities, or of the value of securities over cash in a repo transaction at the time it is executed and, subsequently, after margin calls.

Interbank: The market in unsecured lending and trading between banks of roughly similar credit quality.

Interest rate cap: See **cap.**

Interest rate floor: See **floor.**

Interest rate guarantee: An **option** on an **FRA**.

Interest rate option: Option to pay or receive a specified rate of interest on or from a predetermined future date.

Interest rate swap: An agreement to exchange a series of cash flows determined in one currency, based on fixed or **floating** interest payments on an agreed **notional** principal, for a series of cash flows based in the same currency but on a different interest rate. May be combined with a **currency swap**.

Intermarket spread: A spread involving futures contracts in one market spread against futures contracts in another market.

Internal rate of return: The yield necessary to discount a series of cash flows to an **NPV** of zero.

Interpolation: The process of estimating a price or rate for value on a particular date by comparing the prices actually quoted for value dates either side. See **extrapolation**.

Intervention: Purchases or sales of currencies in the market by central banks in an attempt to reduce exchange rate fluctuations or to maintain the value of a currency within a particular band, or at a particular level. Similarly, central bank operations in the money markets to maintain interest rates at a certain level.

In-the-money: A **call (put) option** is in-the-money if the underlying is currently more (less) valuable than the **strike** price. See **at-the-money**, **out-of-the-money**.

Intrinsic value: The amount by which an option is in-the-money.

IRG: See **interest rate guarantee**.

IRR: See **internal rate of return**.

IRS: See **interest rate swap**.

ISMA: The International Securities Market Association. This association drew up with the PSA (now renamed the Bond Market Association) the PSA/ISMA Global Master repurchase Agreement.

Issuer risk: Risk to an institution when it holds debt securities issued by another institution. (See also **credit risk exposure**).

Iteration: The repetitive mathematical process of estimating the answer to a problem, by trying how well this estimate fits the data, adjusting the estimate appropriately and trying against it, until the fit is acceptably close. Used, for example, in calculating a bond's **yield** from its price.

Junk bonds: The common term for high-yield bonds; higher risk, low-rated debt.

Kappa (κ): An alternative term to refer to volatility; see **vega**.

Knock out/in: A knock out (in) **option** ceases to exist (starts to exist) if the underlying reaches a certain trigger level. See **barrier option**.

Lambda (λ): The same as **vega**.

Lender option: Floor on a single-period forward rate agreement.

Leptokurtosis: The non-normal distribution of asset-price returns. Refers to a probability distribution that has a fatter tail and a sharper hump than a normal distribution.

Level payment swap: Evens out those fixed-rate payments that would otherwise vary, for example, because of the amortisation of the principal.

Leverage: The ability to control large amounts of an underlying variable for a small initial investment.

Liability: Probable future sacrifice of an economic benefit due to present obligations to transfer assets or provide services to other entities as a result of past events or transactions. Generally classed as either current or long term.

Liability swap: An interest rate swap or currency swap used in conjunction with an underlying liability such as a borrowing. See **asset swap**.

Libid: The London interbank bid rate, the rate at which banks will pay for funds in the interbank market. See **Libor**.

Libor: The London interbank offered rate, the lending rate for all major currencies up to one-year set at 11 a.m. each day by the British Bankers Association.

Libor fixing: The Libor rate "fixed" by the British Bankers Association (BBA) at 11 a.m. each day, for maturities up to one year.

LIFFE: The London International Financial Futures and Options Exchange, the largest futures exchange in Europe.

Limean: The arithmetic average of Libor and Libid rates.

Limit up/down: **Futures** prices are generally not allowed to change by more than a specified total amount in a specified time, in order to control risk in very volatile conditions. The maximum movements permitted are referred to as limit up and limit down.

Liquidation: Any transaction that closes out or offsets a futures or options position.

Liquidity: A word describing the ease with which one can undertake transactions in a particular market or instrument. A market where there are always ready buyers and sellers willing to transact at competitive prices is regarded as liquid. In banking, the term is also used to describe the requirement that a portion of a bank's assets be held in short-term risk-free instruments, such as government bonds, Treasury bills and high-quality Certificates of Deposit.

Loan-equivalent amount: Description of derivative exposure that is used to compare the credit risk of derivatives with that of traditional bonds or bank loans.

Lognormal: A variable's **probability distribution** is lognormal if the logarithm of the variable has a normal distribution.

Lognormal distribution: The assumption that the log of today's interest rate, for example, minus the log of yesterday's rate is normally distributed.

Long: A long position is a surplus of purchases over sales of a given currency or asset, or a situation that naturally gives rise to an organisation benefiting from a strengthening of that currency or asset. To a money market dealer, however, a long position is a surplus of borrowings taken in over money lent out (which gives rise to a benefit if that currency weakens rather than strengthens). See **short**.

Long-dated forward: Forward foreign exchange contract with a maturity of greater than one year. Some long-dated forwards have maturities as great as ten years.

Long-term assets: Assets that are expected to provide benefits and services over a period longer than one year.

Long-term liabilities: Obligations to be repaid by the firm more than one year later.

Lookback option: Option that allows the purchaser, at the end of a given period of time, to choose as the rate for exercise any rate that has existed during the option's life.

Low coupon swap: Tax-driven swap, in which the fixed-rate payments are significantly lower than current market interest rates. The floating-rate payer is compensated by a front-end fee.

LSE: London Stock Exchange.

Macaulay duration: See **duration**.

Mapping: The process whereby a treasury's derivative positions are related to a set of risk "buckets".

Margin: Initial margin is **collateral**, placed by one party with a counterparty at the time of the deal, against the possibility that the market price will move against the first party, thereby leaving the counterparty with a credit risk. Variation margin is a payment or extra collateral transferred subsequently from one party to the other because the market price has moved. Variation margin payment is either in effect a settlement of profit/loss (for example, in the case of a **futures** contract) or the reduction of credit exposure (for example, in the case of a **repo**). In gilt **repos**, variation margin refers to the fluctuation band or threshold within which the existing collateral's value may vary before further cash or **collateral** needs to be transferred. In a loan, margin is the extra interest above a **benchmark** (for example, a margin of 0.5% over **Libor**) required by a lender to compensate for the credit risk of that particular borrower.

Margin call: A request following mark-to-market of a repo transaction for the initial margin to be reinstated or, where no initial margin has been taken to restore the cash/securities ratio to parity.

Margin default rate: See **probability of default**.

Margin transfer: The payment of a **margin call**.

Market comparables: Technique for estimating the fair value of an instrument for which no price is quoted by comparing it with the quoted prices of similar instruments.

Market-maker: Market participant who is committed, explicitly or otherwise, to quoting two-way bid and offer prices at all times in a particular market.

Market risk: Risks related to changes in prices of tradable macroeconomic variables, such as exchange rate risks.

Mark-to-market: The act of revaluing securities to current market values. Such revaluations should include both coupon accrued on the securities outstanding and interest accrued on the cash.

Matched book: This refers to the matching by a repo trader of securities repoed in and out. It carries no implications that the trader's position is "matched" in terms of exposure; for example, to short-term interest rates.

Maturity date: Date on which stock is redeemed.

Mean: Average.

Minmax option: One of the strategies for reducing the cost of options by forgoing some of the potential for gain. The buyer of a currency option, for example, simultaneously sells an option on the same amount of currency but at a different strike price.

MLV: Maximum likely potential increase in value.

Modified duration: A measure of the proportional change in the price of a bond or other series of cash flows, relative to a change in yield. (Mathematically $-\frac{dP}{di}$ / dirty price.) See **duration**.

Modified following: The convention that if a value date in the future falls on a non-business day, the value date will be moved to the next following business day, unless this moves the value date to the next month, in which case the value date is moved back to the last previous business day.

Momentum: The strength behind an upward or downward movement in price.

Money market: Short-term market (generally up to one year) for financial instruments. See **capital market**.

Money-market basis: An interest rate quoted on an ACT/360 basis is said to be on a money-market basis. See **bond basis**.

Monte Carlo simulation: Technique used to determine the likely value of a derivative or other contract by simulating the evolution of the underlying variables many times. The discounted **average** outcome of the simulation gives an approximation of the derivative's value. Monte Carlo simulation can be used to estimate the **value-at-risk (VAR)** of a portfolio. Here it generates a simulation of many correlated market movements for the markets to which the portfolio is exposed, and the positions in the portfolio are revalued repeatedly in accordance with the simulated scenarios. This gives a probability distribution of portfolio gains and losses from which the **VAR** can be determined.

Moosmüller: A method for calculating the yield of a bond.

Mortgage-backed security (MBS): Security guaranteed by a pool of mortgages. MBS markets include the United States, United Kingdom, Japan and Denmark.

Moving average convergence/divergence (MACD): The crossing of two exponentially smoothed moving averages that oscillate above and below an equilibrium line.

Multi-index option: **Option** that gives the holder the right to buy the asset that performs best out of a number of assets (usually two). The investor would typically buy a call allowing him or her to buy the **equity**.

Naked: A naked **option** position is one not protected by an off-setting position in the **underlying**. See **covered call/put**.

NAO: National Audit Office.

Negative divergence: When at least two indicators, indexes or averages show conflicting or contradictory trends.

Negotiable: A security that can be bought and sold in a **secondary market** is negotiable.

Net present value: The net present value of a series of cash flows is the sum of the present values of each cash flow (some or all of which may be negative).

NLF: National Loans Fund, the account that brings together all UK government lending and borrowing.

Noise: Fluctuations in the market that can confuse or impede interpretation of market direction.

Nominal amount: Same as **face value** of a security.

Nominal rate: A rate of interest as quoted, rather than the **effective rate** to which it is equivalent.

Normal: A normal **probability distribution** is a particular distribution assumed to prevail in a wide variety of circumstances, including the financial markets. Mathematically, it corresponds to the probability density function:

$$\frac{1}{\sqrt{2\pi}}e^{-\frac{1}{2}\phi^2}.$$

Notional: In a bond futures contract, the bond bought or sold is a standardised non-existent notional bond, as opposed to the actual bonds which are **deliverable** at maturity**. Contracts for differences** also require a notional principal amount on which settlement can be calculated.

Novation: Replacement of a contract or, more usually, a series of contracts with one new contract.

NPV: See **net present value**.

O/N: See **overnight.**

Odd date: See **broken date**.

Offer: The price at which a market-maker will sell bonds. Also called "**ask**".

Off-market: A rate that is not the current market rate.

Off-market coupon swap: Tax-driven swap strategy in which the fixed-rate payments differ significantly from current market rates. There are high and low coupon swaps.

One touch all-or-nothing: Digital option. The option's put pays out a predetermined amount (the "all") if the index goes below (above) the strike price at any time during the option's life. How far below (above) the strike price the index moves is irrelevant; the payout will be the "all" or nothing.

Open interest: The quantity of **futures** contracts (of a particular specification) that have not yet been closed out by reversing. Either all **long** positions or all **short** positions are counted but not both.

Opening leg: The first half of a repo transaction (see "**closing leg**").

Operational Market Notice: Sets out the DMO's (previously the bank's) operations and procedures in the gilt market.

Operational risk: Risk of loss occurring due to inadequate systems and control, human error, or management failure.

Opportunity cost: Value of an action that could have been taken if the current action had not been chosen.

Option: The right (but not the obligation) to buy or sell securities at a fixed price within a specified period.

Option forward: See **time option**.

Ornstein-Uhlenbeck equation: A standard equation that describes mean reversion. It can be used to characterise and measure commodity price behaviour.

OTC (**over the counter**): Strictly speaking any transaction not conducted on a registered stock exchange. Trades conducted via the telephone between banks, and contracts such as FRAs and (non-exchange traded) options are said to be "over-the-counter" instruments. OTC also refers to non-standard instruments or contracts traded between two parties; for example, a client with a requirement for a specific risk to be hedged with a tailor-made instrument may enter into an OTC structured option trade with a bank that makes markets in such products.

Out-of-the-money: A **call (put) option** is out-of-the-money if the **underlying** is currently less (more) valuable than the strike price. See **at-the-money**, **in-the-money**.

Outright: An outright (or **forward** outright) is the sale or purchase of one foreign currency against another value on any date other than spot. See **spot, swap, forward, short date.**

Over the counter: An OTC transaction is one dealt privately between any two parties, with all details agreed between them, as opposed to one dealt on an exchange; for example, a **forward** deal as opposed to a **futures contract**.

Overborrowed: A position in which a dealer's liabilities (borrowings taken in) are of longer maturity than the assets (loans out).

Overlent: A position in which a dealer's assets (loans out) are of longer maturity than the liabilities (borrowings taken in).

Overnight: A deal from today until the next working day ("tomorrow").

Paper: Another term for a bond or debt issue.

Par: In foreign exchange, when the **outright** and **spot** exchange rates are equal, the **forward swap** is zero or par. When the price of a security is equal to the face value, usually expressed as 100, it is said to be trading at par. A par swap rate is the current market rate for a fixed **interest rate swap** against **Libor**.

Par yield curve: A curve plotting maturity against **yield** for bonds priced at par.

Parity: The official rate of exchange for one currency in terms of another which a government is obliged to maintain by means of intervention.

Participation forward: A product equivalent to a straightforward **option** plus a **forward** deal, but structured as a forward deal at an **off-market** rate plus the opportunity to benefit partially if the market rate improves.

Path-dependent: A path-dependent **option** is one that depends on what happens to the **underlying** throughout the option's life (such as the **American** or **barrier** option) rather than only at expiry (a **European** option).

Peak exposure: If the worst case or the expected credit risk exposures of an instrument is calculated over time, the resulting graph reveals a credit risk exposure profile. The highest exposure marked out by the profile is the peak exposure generated by the instrument.

Periodic resetting swap: Swap where the floating-rate payment is an average of floating rates that have prevailed since the last payment, rather than the interest rate prevailing at the end of the period. For example, the average of six one-month **Libor** rates rather than one six-month Libor rate.

Pips: See **points**.

Plain vanilla: See **vanilla.**

Points: The last two decimal places in an exchange rate. For example, when EUR/USD is 1.1910/1.1920, the points are 10/20. See **bid figure**.

Portfolio variance: The square of the **standard deviation** of a portfolio's return from the mean.

Positive cash flow collar: Collar other than a zero-cost collar.

Potential exposure: Estimate of the future replacement cost, or positive market value, of a derivative transaction. Potential exposure should be calculated using probability analysis based on broad confidence intervals (for example, two standard deviations) over the remaining term of the transaction.

Preference shares: These are a form of corporate financing. They are normally fixed interest shares whose holders have the right to receive dividends ahead of ordinary shareholders. If a company were to go into liquidation, preference shareholders would rank above ordinary shareholders for the repayment of their investment in the company. Preference shares ("prefs") are normally traded within the fixed interest division of a bank or securities house.

Premium: The amount by which a currency is more expensive, in terms of another currency, for future delivery than for spot, is the forward premium (in general, a reflection of interest rate differentials between two currencies). If an exchange rate is "at a premium" (without specifying to which of the two currencies this refers), this generally means that the **variable currency** is at a premium. See **discount**.

Present value: The amount of money that needs to be invested now to achieve a given amount in the future when interest is added. See **time value of money**, **future value**.

Pre-settlement risk: As distinct from credit risk arising from intra-day settlement risk, this term describes the risk of loss that might be suffered during the life of the contract if a counterparty to a trade defaulted and if, at the time of default, the instrument had a positive economic value.

Price–earnings ratio: A ratio giving the price of a stock relative to the earnings per share.

Price factor: See **conversion factor**.

Primary market: The market for new debt, into which new bonds are issued. The primary market is made up of borrowers, investors and the investment banks that place new debt into the market, usually with their clients. Bonds that trade after they have been issued are said to be part of the secondary market.

Probability distribution: The mathematical description of how probable it is that the value of something is less than or equal to a particular level.
Probability of default: The probability that an asset will suffer from issuer default over the next twelve months, calculated on historical rates of default among the same class of issuer.
Probit procedures: Methods for analysing qualitative dependent methods where the dependent variable is binary, taking the values zero or one.
Put: A put option is an option to sell the commodity or instrument **underlying** the option. See **call option**.

Quanto: An option that has its final payoff linked to two or more underlying assets or reference rates.
Quanto swap: A **swap** where the payments of one or both legs are based on a measurement (such as the interest rate) in one currency but payable in another currency.
Quasi-coupon date: The regular date for which a **coupon** payment would be scheduled if there were one. Used for price/yield calculations for **zero-coupon** instruments.

Range forward: A **zero-cost collar** where the customer is obliged to deal with the same bank at spot if neither limit of the collar is breached at **expiry**.
Rate of recovery: Estimate of the percentage of the amount exposed to default – that is, the credit risk exposure – that is likely to be recovered by an institution if a counterparty defaults.
Record date: A **coupon** or other payment due on a security is paid by the issuer to whoever is registered on the record date as being the owner. See **ex-dividend**, **cum-dividend**.
Redeem: A security is said to be redeemed when the principal is repaid.
Redemption yield: The rate of interest at which all future payments (coupons and redemption) on a bond are discounted so that their total equals the current price of the bond (inversely related to price).
Redenomination: A change in the currency unit in which the nominal value of a security is expressed (in context, from sterling to euro).
Reduced-cost option: Generic term for options for which there is a reduced premium, either because the buyer undertakes to forgo a percentage of any gain, or because she offsets the cost by writing other options (for example, minmax, range forward). See also **zero-cost option**.

Refer: The practice whereby a trader instructs a broker to put "under reference" any prices or rates she has quoted to her, meaning that they are no longer "firm" and the broker must refer to the trader before she can trade on the price initially quoted.

Register: Record of ownership of securities. For gilts, excluding bearer bonds, entry in an official register confers title.

Registered bond: A bond for which the issuer keeps a record (register) of its owners. Transfer of ownership must be notified and recorded in the register. Interest payments are posted (more usually electronically transferred) to the bondholder.

Registrar's Department: Department of the Bank of England that maintains the register of holdings of gilts.

Reinvestment rate: The rate at which interest paid during the life of an investment is reinvested to earn interest-on-interest, which in practice will generally not be the same as the original yield quoted on the investment.

Relative performance option: Option whose value varies in line with the relative value of two assets.

Replacement cost: The present value of the expected future net cash flows of a derivative instrument. Aside from various conventions dealing with the **bid/ask** spread, synonymous with the "market value" or "current exposure" of an instrument.

Repo: Usually refers in particular to **classic repo**. Also used as a term to include classic repos, **buy/sell-backs** and **securities lending**.

Repo rate: The return earned on a repo transaction expressed as an interest rate on the cash side of the transaction.

Repurchase agreement: See **repo**.

Return on assets: The net earnings of a company divided by its assets.

Return on equity: The net earning of a company divided by its equity.

Return on value-at-risk (ROVAR): An analysis conducted to determine the relative rates of return on different risks, allowing corporations to compare different risk capital allocations and capital structure decisions effectively.

Revaluation: An official one-off increase in the value of a currency in terms of other currencies. See **devaluation**.

Revenue volatility: Another term for value of income at risk from market fluctuations.

Reverse: See **reverse repo**.

Reverse repo: The opposite of a **repo**.

Rho (ρ): The change in an option's value relative to a change in interest rates.

Risk reversal: Changing a long (or short) position in a call option to the same position in a put option by selling (or buying) forward, and vice versa.

Risk-weighting: The level of risk assigned to a certain type of collateral or counterparts, as used in Basel I capital calculations.

Rollover: See **tom/next**. Also refers to a renewal of a loan.

Running yield: Same as **current yield**.

Rump: A gilt issue so designated because it is illiquid, generally because there is a very small nominal amount left in existence.

S/N: See **spot/next**.

S/W: See **spot-a-week**.

SAFE: See **synthetic agreement for forward exchange**.

Secondary market: The market in instruments after they have been issued. Bonds are bought and sold after their initial issue by the borrower, and the marketplace for this buying and selling is referred to as the secondary market. The new issues market is the *primary* market.

Securities and Exchange Commission: The central regulatory authority in the United States, responsible for policing the financial markets including the bond markets.

Securities lending: When a specific security is lent against some form of collateral. Also known as stock lending.

Security: A financial asset sold initially for cash by a borrowing organisation (the "issuer"). The security is often negotiable and usually has a maturity date when it is redeemed.

Sell/buy-back: Simultaneous spot sale and forward purchase of a security, with the forward price calculated to achieve an effect equivalent to a classic repo.

Settlement: The process of transferring stock from seller to buyer and arranging the corresponding movement of funds between the two parties.

Settlement bank: Bank which agrees to receive and make assured payments for gilts bought and sold by a CGO member.

Settlement date: Date on which the transfer of gilts and payments occur, usually the next working date after the trade is conducted.

Settlement risk: The risk that occurs when there is a non-simultaneous exchange of value. Also known as "delivery risk" and "Herstatt risk".

Sharpe ratio: A measure of the attractiveness of the return on an asset by comparing how much risk premium the investor can expect it to receive in return for the incremental risk (volatility) the investment carries. It is the ratio of the risk premium to the volatility of the asset.

Short: A short position is a surplus of sales over purchases of a given currency or asset, or a situation that naturally gives rise to an organisation benefiting from a weakening of that currency or asset. To a money market dealer, however, a short position is a surplus of money lent out over borrowings taken in (which give rise to a benefit if that currency strengthens rather than weakens). See **long**.

Short date: A deal for value on a date other than spot but less than one month after spot.

Simple interest: When interest on an investment is paid all at maturity or not reinvested to earn interest on interest, the interest is said to be simple. See **compound interest**.

Simple yield to maturity: Bond coupon plus principal gain/loss amortised over the time to maturity, as a proportion of the clean price per 100. Does not take time value of money into account. See **yield to maturity, current yield**.

SLA: Service Level Agreement, in this context between the DMO and service suppliers in the bank and HM Treasury.

Special: A security that for any reason is sought after in the repo market, thereby enabling any holder of the security to earn incremental income (in excess of the *General Collateral* rate) through lending them via a repo transaction. The repo rate for a special will be below the GC rate, as this is the rate the borrower of the cash is paying in returning for supplying the special bond as collateral. An individual security can be in high demand for a variety of reasons, for instance if there is sudden heavy investor demand for it, or (if it is a benchmark issue) it is required as a hedge against a new issue of similar maturity paper.

Speculation: A deal undertaken because the dealer expects prices to move in her favour, as opposed to **hedging** or **arbitrage**.

Spot: A deal to be settled on the customary value date for that particular market. In the foreign exchange market this is for value in two working days' time.

Spot-a-week: Money market deposit value spot (T + 2) for one week.

Spot/next: A transaction from **spot** until the next working day.

Spread: The difference between the bid and offer prices in a quotation. Also a strategy involving the purchase of an instrument and the simultaneous sale of a similar related instrument, such as the purchase of a **call option** at one **strike** and the sale of a call option at a different strike.

Square: A position in which sales exactly match purchases, or in which assets exactly match liabilities. See **long**, **short**.

Standard deviation (σ): A measure of how much the values of something fluctuate around its mean value. Defined as the square root of the **variance**.

Step-down swap: Swap in which the fixed-rate payment decreases over the life of the swap.

Step-up swap: Swap in which the fixed-rate payment increases over the life of the swap.

Stock lending: See **securities lending**.

Stock index future: Future on a stock index, allowing a hedge against, or bet on, a broad equity market movement.

Stock index option: Option on a stock index future.

Stock option: Option on an individual stock.

Straddle: A position combining the purchase of both a call and put at the same strike for the same date. See **strangle**.

Strangle: A position combining the purchase of both a call and a put at different strikes for the same date. See **straddle**.

Street: The "street" is a term for the market, originating as "Wall Street". A US term for market convention, so in the US market there is the convention for quoting the price or yield for a particular instrument.

Stress testing: An analysis that gives the value of a portfolio under a range of worst case scenarios.

Strike: The strike price or strike rate of an option is the price or rate at which the holder can insist on the underlying transaction being fulfilled.

Strip: A zero-coupon bond which is produced by separating a standard coupon-bearing bond into its constituent principal and interest components. To strip a bond is to separate its principal amount and its coupons and trade each individual cash flow as a separate instrument ("*s*eparately *t*raded and *r*egistered for *i*nterest and *p*rincipal"). Also, a strip of **futures** is a series of short-term futures contracts with consecutive delivery dates, which together create the effect of a longer term instrument (for example, four consecutive three-month futures contracts as a **hedge** against a one-year swap). A strip of **FRA**s is similar.

Swap: A foreign exchange swap is the purchase of one currency against another for delivery on one date, with a simultaneous sale to reverse the transaction on another value date. See also **interest rate swap, currency swap**.

Swaption: An **option** on an **interest rate swap, currency swap**.

Switch: Exchanges of one gilt holding for another, sometimes entered into between the DMO and a GEMM as part of the DMO's secondary market operations.

Synthetic: A package of transactions that is economically equivalent to a different transaction (for example, the purchase of a **call option** and simultaneous sale of a **put** option at the same **strike** is a synthetic **forward** purchase.)

Synthetic agreement for forward exchange: A generic term for **ERA**s and **FXA**s.

T/N: See **tom/next**.

Tail: The exposure to interest rates over a forward–forward period arising from a mismatched position (such as a two-month borrowing against a three-month loan). A forward foreign exchange dealer's exposure to **spot** movements.

Tap: The issue of a gilt for exceptional market management reasons and not on a pre-announced schedule.

Term: The time between the beginning and end of a deal or investment.

Theta (τ): The change in an option's value relative to a change in the time left to expiry.

Tick: The minimum change allowed in a futures price.

Time deposit: A non-**negotiable** deposit for a specific term.

Time option: A forward currency deal in which the value date is set to be within a period rather than on a particular day. The customer sets the exact date two working days before settlement.

Time value of money: The concept that a future cash flow can be valued as the amount of money which it is necessary to invest now in order to achieve that cash flow in the future. See **present value, future value**.

Today/tomorrow: See **overnight**.

Tom/next: A transaction from the next working day ("tomorrow") until the day after ("next day"; that is, **spot** in the foreign exchange market).

Total return swap: Swap agreement in which the total return of bank loans or credit-sensitive securities is exchanged for some other cash flow usually tied to **Libor**, or other loans, or credit-sensitive securities. It allows participants to effectively go **long** or **short** the credit risk of the **underlying** asset.

Traded option: Option that is listed on and cleared by an exchange, with standard terms and delivery months.

Tranche: One of a series of two or more issues with the same coupon rate and maturity date. The tranches become fungible at a future date, usually just after the first coupon date.

Transaction risk: Extent to which the value of transactions that have already been agreed is affected by market risk.

Transparent: A term used to refer to how clear asset prices are in a market. A transparent market is one in which a majority of market participants are aware of what level a particular bond or instrument is trading.

Trigger option: See **barrier option**

Treasury bill: A short-term security issued by a government, generally with a zero **coupon**.

Tunnel: The same as **collar**.

Tunnel options: Set of collars, typically zero-cost, covering a series of maturities from the current date. They might, for example, be for dates six, 12, 24 months ahead. The special feature of a tunnel is that strike price on both sets of options, not just on the options bought that is constant.

Uncovered option: When the writer of the option does not own the underlying security. Also known as a **naked option**.

Undated gilts: Gilts for which there is no final date by which the gilt must be redeemed.

Underlying: The underlying of a futures or option contract is the commodity of financial instrument on which the contract depends. Thus underlying for a bond option is the bond; the underlying for a short-term interest rate futures contract is typically a three-month deposit.

Underwriting: An arrangement by which a company is guaranteed that an issue of debt (bonds) will raise a given amount of cash. Underwriting is carried out by investment banks, who undertake to purchase any part of the debt issue not taken up by the public. A commission is charged for this service.

Unexpected default rate: The distribution of future default rates is often characterised in terms of an expected default rate (for example, 0.05%) and a worst case default rate (for example, 1.05%). The difference between the worst case default rate and the expected default rate is often termed the "unexpected default" (that is, 1% = 1.05 – 0.05%).

Unexpected loss: The distribution of credit losses associated with a derivative instrument is often characterised in terms of an **expected loss** or a **worst case loss**. The unexpected loss associated with an instrument is the difference between these two measures.

Up-and-away option: See **up-and-out option**.

Up-and-in option: Type of barrier option that is activated if the value of the underlying goes above a predetermined level. See also **down-and-in option**)

Up-and-out option: Type of barrier option that is extinguished if the value of the underlying goes above a predetermined level. See also **down-and-out option**.

Value-at-risk (VAR): Formally, the probabilistic bound of market losses over a given period of time (known as the holding period) expressed in terms of a specified degree of certainity (known as the confidence interval). Put more simply, the VAR is the worst case loss that would be expected over the holding period within the probability set out by the confidence interval. Larger losses are possible but with a low probability. For instance, a portfolio whose VAR is $20 million over a one-day holding period, with a 95% confidence interval, would have only a 5% chance of suffering an overnight loss greater than $20 million.

Value date: The date on which a deal is to be consummated. In some bond markets, the value date for coupon accruals can sometimes differ from the settlement date.

Vanilla: A vanilla transaction is a straightforward one.

VAR: See **value-at-risk**

Variable currency: Exchange rates are quoted in terms of the number of units of one currency (the variable or counter currency) that corresponds to one unit of the other currency (the **base currency**).

Variance (σ^2): A measure of how much the values of something fluctuate around its mean value. Defined as the average of (value – mean)≤. See **standard deviation**.

Variance-covariance methodology: Methodology for calculating the **value-at-risk** of a portfolio as a function of the **volatility** of each asset or liability position in the portfolio and the correlation between the positions.

Variation margin: The band agreed between the parties to a repo transaction at the outset within which the value of the collateral may fluctuate before triggering a right to call for cash or securities to reinstate the initial margin on the repo transaction.

Vega: The change in an option's value relative to a change in the **underlying's volatility**.

Volatility: The **standard deviation** of the continuously compounded return on the **underlying**. Volatility is generally annualised. See **historic volatility**, **implied volatility**.

Warrant: A security giving the holder a right to subscribe to a share or bond at a given price and from a certain date. If this right is not exercised before the maturity date, the warrant will expire worthless.

Warrant-driven swap: Swap with a warrant attached allowing the issuer of the fixed-rate bond to go on paying a floating rate in the event that she exercises another warrant allowing her to prolong the life of the bond.

When-issued trading: Trading a bond before the issue date; no interest is accrued during this period. Also known as the "grey market".

Worst case (credit risk) exposure: Estimate of the highest positive market value a derivative contract or portfolio is likely to attain at a given moment or period in the future, with a given level of confidence.

Worst case (credit risk) loss: Estimate of the largest amount a derivative counterparty is likely to lose, with a given level of probability, as a result of default from a derivatives contract or portfolio.

Worst case default rate: The highest rates of default that are likely to occur at a given moment or period in the future, with a given level of confidence.

Write: To sell an option is to write it. The person selling an option is known as the **writer**.

Writer: The same as "seller" of an **option**.

X: Used to denote the strike price of an option; sometimes this is denoted using the term *K*.

Yield: The interest rate that can be earned on an investment, currently quoted by the market or implied by the current market price for the investment – as opposed to the **coupon** paid by an issuer on a security, which is based on the coupon rate and the face value. For a bond, generally the same as yield to maturity unless otherwise specified.

Yield curve: Graphical representation of the maturity structure of interest rates, plotting yields of bonds that are all of the same class or credit quality against the maturity of the bonds.

Yield-curve option: Option that allows purchasers to take a view on a yield curve without having to take a view about a market's direction.

Yield-curve swap: Swap in which the index rates of the two interest streams are at different points on the yield curve. Both payments are refixed with the same frequency whatever the index rate.

Yield to equivalent life: The same as **yield to maturity** for a bond with partial redemptions.

Yield to maturity: The **internal rate of return** of a bond – the yield necessary to discount all the bond's cash flows to an **NPV** equal to its current price. See **simple yield to maturity**, **current yield**.

YTM: See **yield to maturity**.

Zero-cost collar: A **collar** where the premiums paid and received are equal, giving a net zero cost.

Zero-cost option: An option structure combining puts and calls, or buys and sells, that result in a zero net premium for the purchaser.

Zero-coupon: A zero-coupon security is one that does not pay a **coupon**. Its price is correspondingly less to compensate for this. A zero coupon **yield** is the yield which a zero-coupon investment for that term would have if it were consistent with the **par yield curve**.

Zero-coupon bond: Bond on which no coupon is paid. It is either issued at a discount or redeemed at a premium to face value.

Zero-coupon swap: Swap converting the payment pattern of a zero-coupon bond, either to that of a normal, coupon-paying **fixed-rate** bond or to a **floating rate**.

Zero-premium option: Generic term for options for which there is no premium, either because the buyer undertakes to forgo a percentage of any gain or because she offsets the cost by **writing** other options.

But we have to try. If we don't try, then we don't do. And if we don't do, then why are we here on this earth?

– James Stewart
Shenandoah (1965)

Index